Canadian Dance Visions and Stories

Edited by

Selma Landen Odom and Mary Jane Warner

Toronto, 2004

Canadian Dance: Visions and Stories
Copyright© 2004 individual authors
Co-Editors: Selma Landen Odom and Mary Jane Warner
Production Editor: Amy Bowring
Design and Layout: LAMA Labs

Published by:
Dance Collection Danse Press/es
145 George Street
Toronto, ON M5A 2M6 Canada
www.dcd.ca   talk@dcd.ca
(416) 365-3233

Library and Archives Canada Cataloguing in Publication

Canadian dance: visions and stories / editors, Selma Landen Odom
and Mary Jane Warner.

Includes bibliographical references.
ISBN 0-929003-46-2

1. Dance--Canada--History. I. Odom, Selma Landen II. Warner, Mary
Jane

GV1625.C34 2004 792.8'0971   C2004-905261-6

Dance Collection Danse gratefully acknowledges organizational support from the
Canada Council for the Arts, the Ontario Arts Council, the City of Toronto through the
Toronto Arts Council, and individual donors. Special thanks to Nick Laidlaw.

ISBN 0-929003-46-2   Manufactured in Canada

Table of Contents

Preface   7

Part I. Statements of Belief

Françoise Sullivan: An Introduction   10
Allana Lindgren

Dance and Hope   11
Françoise Sullivan

Grant Strate: An Introduction   20
Selma Landen Odom

Canadian Dance in Progress: A Personal View   21
Grant Strate

Part II. Pioneers

Anne Fairbrother Hill: Canada's Chaste and Elegant Dancer   35
Mary Jane Warner

Professor John Freeman Davis: Nineteenth-Century   49
Dancing Master
Kathryn Noxon

The Victorian Era Ball   59
Janet Wason

Maud Allan: Misunderstood?   75
Carol Bishop

Hector Charlesworth and E.R. Parkhurst: Looking at Dance   83
in Early Twentieth-Century Toronto
Norma Sue Fisher-Stitt

Music and Movement: The Overlapping Careers of   95
Madeleine Boss Lasserre and Saida Gerrard
Selma Landen Odom

Creating a Canadian Imaginative Background: Herman Voaden   107
and Symphonic Expressionism
Anton Wagner

Evelyn Geary: Versatility in Motion   131
Mary Jane Warner

Boris Volkoff: Father of Canadian Ballet   145
Clifford Collier

June Roper: Ballet Pioneer in Vancouver   153
Leland Windreich

Marion Stark Errington: From Kilts to Companies in   177
London, Ontario
Amy Bowring

Stories of Dancing Women in Alberta   185
Anne Flynn

Part III. Politics and Perseverance

Stepping Out: A New Look at Canada's Early Ballet   197
Companies, 1939 to 1960
    Cheryl Smith

The Ballet Problem: The Kirstein-Buckle Ballet Survey   225
for the Canada Council
    Katherine Cornell

The History of a Devolving Nationalism: Three Dance Films   239
of the National Film Board of Canada
    Jody Bruner

Nesta Toumine's Legacy: From the Ballets Russes to the   255
Ottawa Ballet
    Rosemary Jeanes Antze

Politics and Dance in Montreal, 1940s to 1980s: 271
The Imaginary Maginot Line between Anglophone
and Francophone Dancers
    Iro Valaskakis Tembeck

Three Intrepid Montreal Dancers of the 1940s and 1950s   287
    Pierre Lapointe

Dance and the Outsiders: Ballet and Modern Dance   297
Companies in Nova Scotia
    Pat Richards

Rachel Browne: Dancing Toward the Light   311
    Carol Anderson

Part IV. Visions and Revisions

Re-Placing Performance: The Inter-Media Practice of   329
Françoise Sullivan
    Karen Stanworth

From Post-Ballet to Post-Modern: The 1972 Debut of   339
Toronto's Ground-Breaking 15 Dance Collective
    Jennifer Fisher

Moving Forward Looking Back: Lawrence and Miriam Adams   345
and Dance Collection Danse
    Carol Anderson

Terrill Maguire: Choreographer and Instigator   353
    Susan Cash and Holly Small

A Conversation with Christopher House   365
    Francis Mason

Walking the Tightrope: Acrobatics and Athleticism on the   377
Montreal Stage
    Iro Valaskakis Tembeck

Impressions of a Reconstruction: The ENCORE! ENCORE!   389
Project
    Rhonda Ryman

Gweneth Lloyd and *The Wise Virgins*: Arguments for the   **405**
Reconstruction of a Canadian Ballet
    Anna Blewchamp

Dance Defined: An Examination of Canadian Cultural Policy   **415**
on Multicultural Dance
    Katherine Cornell

Learning Belly Dance in Toronto: Pyramids, Goddesses   **423**
and Other Weird Stuff
    Kathleen Wittick Fraser

***The Rebel Goddess*: An Investigation of the Shift in Narrative**   **435**
in Indian Classical Dance
    Sarala Dandekar

Contributors   **447**

Illustration Credits   **453**

Preface

This book offers new perspectives on Canadian dance and its history. Thirty contributors represent the growing force of scholars, journalists, librarians and curators who began to explore uncharted territory during the 1970s, when universities in Canada first recognized dance as a major field of study. Between 1975 and 1995, the magazines *Dance in Canada* and *Dance Connection* offered crucial outlets for writing on Canadian dance. The 1990s brought a surge of significant new books, spearheaded by Dance Collection Danse, the publishing arm of the Toronto-based theatrical dance archives, which was augmented by books from several trade and academic presses. Graduate programmes at York University and Université du Québec à Montréal created communities for dance research, and occasional conferences and symposia brought like-minded people together in cities across the country. In all of these venues, writers raised questions that had not been asked before about dancers and the contexts of their work. By investigating Canadians dancing in many different social, school and theatre settings, they identified a host of stories that needed to be told. This anthology aims to make a spectrum of writing from dance and theatre publications and from the world of academia more widely accessible.

Several themes emerge from this project. A rich dance heritage can be found from Vancouver to St. John's and centres in between. Immigrant and Canadian-born dancers have shared practices and knowledge from all corners of the globe to create a dance scene of striking diversity. This book celebrates the achievements of teachers whose contributions often have gone un-recognized. In many settings large and small, they taught countless young people to dance and coached the select few who showed exceptional promise, helping them to launch careers as dancers in Canada and abroad. The book also probes the ideas and productions of notable choreographers, telling of their struggles for artistic freedom, recognition and survival.

The involvement of communities in patronage and backstage volunteerism set other significant patterns of work and cooperation. As dance companies and schools were founded in cities across Canada, leaders emerged who took on the challenge of organizing regional and national events. From the time of the first Canadian Ballet Festival held in Winnipeg in 1948, dancers have banded together to assert the place of dance in Canadian culture. Public funding for dance increased gradually after the Canada Council first gave financial support to major ballet institutions in the late 1950s. Several years later, federal and provincial arts councils extended funding to a few modern dance companies, but it was only in the mid-1980s that grants became available to independent artists and, soon after, to multicultural and Aboriginal groups. Several essays examine the issues that underlie these shifting policies.

Others explain recent efforts to develop archives and to preserve Canadian dance through reconstructions of key works.

The anthology is divided into four parts. *Statements of Belief* (Part I) presents the views of Françoise Sullivan and Grant Strate, two larger-than-life figures whose active careers span over half a century. Artists and advocates, they have envisioned huge vistas that opened the way for many others. *Pioneers* (Part II) introduces a cross section of remarkable dancers, teachers and critics of the nineteenth and twentieth centuries. Their stories help us imagine the early dance scenes of Toronto, Vancouver, Calgary, Edmonton and London, Ontario. *Politics and Perseverance* (Part III) offers perspective on challenges dancers faced in establishing companies and schools, gaining media recognition and developing individual careers under adverse conditions. These stories take us to Winnipeg, Montreal, Ottawa, Halifax and, again, Toronto. Finally, *Visions and Revisions* (Part IV) focuses on many facets of contemporary dance in Canada, including experimental work, reconstructions, festivals, culturally diverse dance and arts policy.

Acknowledgements

This book would not have come into being without the dedication of the contributors, who have been responsive yet patient through a long production process. We are also grateful for the editorial assistance of Miriam Adams, Carol Bishop, Amy Bowring, Kathleen Fraser, Christina Halliday and Samara Thompson. Since 1994 the Graduate Programme in Dance of York University has published two volumes of *Canadian Dance Studies*, from which we have selected many essays for this anthology.

Grants from York University through the Faculty of Fine Arts and the Social Sciences and Humanities Research Council Small Grants Program provided initial funding for the project. The Herman Voaden Foundation and Professor Ray Ellenwood generously subsidized illustrations. Finally, we thank Dance Collection Danse for providing most of the illustrations as well as encouragement and steadfast interest in this publication. We wish to dedicate *Canadian Dance: Visions and Stories* to the memory of Lawrence Adams, in gratitude for his boundless inspiration.

Selma Landen Odom and Mary Jane Warner

Toronto

Part I

Statements of belief

Françoise Sullivan: An Introduction

Born June 10, 1925, Françoise Sullivan has devoted her life to dance and visual art. Sullivan studied ballet with Gérald Crevier in Montreal and later temporarily moved to New York to study modern dance with Franziska Boas and Mary Anthony, among others. From 1945 to 1947, Sullivan was a member of Boas' New York modern dance company, the Boas Dance Group, before she returned to Montreal to teach modern dance and to choreograph. Many of Sullivan's dances, including *Dualité* (1947) and *Dédale* (1948), are considered to be classics. In the mid-1950s, Sullivan left dance to raise her children and to concentrate on her visual art endeavours. After a twenty-year hiatus, Sullivan began to choreograph again and her early works were rediscovered by a new generation of Quebec choreographers and dancers.

Despite being at the vanguard of modern dance in Canada, Sullivan is best known for her association with the Automatists, a multidisciplinary group of sixteen Montreal artists led by Paul-Émile Borduas. Between approximately 1941 and 1955, the group met to discuss art, politics and to encourage one another in their respective artistic activities. Aesthetically, the Automatists were influenced initially by Surrealism as they believed it was possible to access the unconscious by spontaneously creating art unfettered by preconceived ideas, self-censorship or revision. Unlike the Surrealists, however, the Automatists felt that spontaneity could best be expressed through non-figurative art. The Automatists' rejection of traditional art was also a rejection of the conformity espoused by the dominant sources of political authority in Quebec at the time – namely the Roman Catholic Church and the provincial government headed by Premier Maurice Duplessis.

On February 16, 1948, Sullivan gave a lecture at the home of fellow Automatist members, Pierre and Claude Gauvreau. In her paper, which she titled "La danse et l'espoir" ("Dance and Hope"), Sullivan denounced "academic" dance – dance that is static and favours the mechanics of technique over emotional expression. Instead, Sullivan advocated applying automatism to dance in a kinetic equivalent of the spontaneous creation practiced by the Automatists in their visual art. The political imperative underlying Sullivan's text was a belief that creative spontaneity can and should extend beyond the individual and beyond art to encompass the collective of humanity; according to Sullivan, dancers have the potential to initiate and to participate in social change.

Sullivan was invited to include "La danse et l'espoir" in the Automatists' manifesto, *Refus global* (*Total Refusal*), which contained nine essays on art and politics and was published on August 9, 1948.[1] Sullivan's essay is the only contribution by a woman and the only article to address the potential of dance within the Automatist aesthetic and ideological prescriptives. As a result, "La danse et l'espoir" is one of the first political treatises on dance written in Canada.

Allana Lindgren

---

[1] The text of "Dance and Hope" which follows was translated by Ray Ellenwood and published in *Total Refusal* [*Refus global*]: *The Complete 1948 Manifesto of the Montreal Automatists* (Toronto: Exile Editions, 1985). The text of "Dance and Hope" has been edited slightly by translator Ray Ellenwood in accordance with the wishes of Françoise Sullivan.

Dance and Hope

Françoise Sullivan

More than anything else, dance is a reflex, a spontaneous expression of intense emotion.

People have found in dance a way of satisfying an inner need to feel in touch with the universe.

The dancer, becoming one with motion, is at the turning point of all four dimensions. Within the bounds of the human body, there is infinite variety, which draws sustenance from the core of life itself.

This idea leads to the notion of an evolutionary force in dance, and we must reject as profound error any obsession with dance as something static and unchanging.

Academic dance, the kind we still see most often today, is out of date. The pleasure it offers the spectator is purely visual, depending on exceptionally skillful leg movements and ignoring the rest of the body as it strives to break the laws of gravity.

Confined to old-fashioned methods, the dancer becomes a mechanical instrument executing senseless movements, and the choreographer repeats, in a facile, parched language, things already said. The result is pure dance, art for art's sake; an expression of decadence, petrification and death.

Dance loses its human character, loses everything that allows it to convey the intensity of life, loses feelings and aspirations which are as much individual as social. It becomes a series of acts in opposition to life.

Dance loses its poetic foothold in reality, and consequently so does mankind. Academicism is a vicious circle.

Fortunately, life is stronger than death and has a way of springing back. Energies long stifled eventually find healthy ways of liberating themselves, and with redoubled strength.

Seeds were sown near the turn of the century by a few pioneers. Urgent need burst under pressure. Isadora Duncan, Jaques-Dalcroze, Mary Wigman and others worked out their theories almost simultaneously, from different perspectives but all in agreement concerning essentials.

And today, in dance, we have returned to the magic of movement, the same magic which arouses natural and subtle human forces, aiming to excite, charm, hypnotize and startle our sensitivities.

11

Statements of Belief

What we must do is reactivate the surcharge of expressive energy stored in that marvellous instrument, the human body. We must rediscover, in the light of our present needs, truths known to ancient, primitive and oriental peoples, truths made concrete in the dances of shamans, whirling dervishes or Tibetan tumblers, truths striking our senses through specific means. Dance fulfills its destiny when it is able to charm the onlooker, making use of the body to transport him back to the most subtle notions. To reach that point, we must challenge the human organism and not be afraid to go as far as we must in the exploration of our total being.

Starting from a basic assumption of the fundamental unity of the human being, and considering present scientific thinking, we seek to rediscover the location of those points of emanation which are the source of emotion and physical effort. Modern science shows that those points coincide.

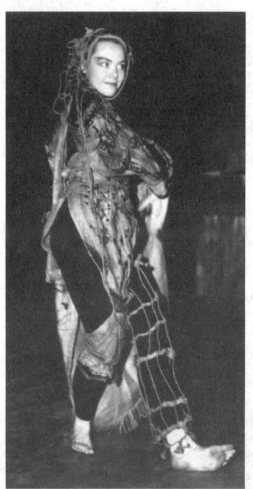

Sullivan's *Black and Tan*, 1949.

Thus we move from the inward out; from intuition and obscure feelings outward into the external matter from which art draws its form (time, space and weight, in this case). We must begin again at the beginning, since our decadence has thrown us so deeply into chaos.

We learn from the history of civilizations that dance and religion were closely allied in the beginning. A common culture linked everyone. A fresh, original energy kept people united in a common faith. Systems of thought were constructed around the mysteries and cycles of life, and all activities flowed in the same direction. There was a sense of wholeness in the unity of activities and relationships.

Man danced to celebrate births, initiations, marriages, death, wars, victories, defeats, changes of season, planting, offerings and sacrifices. Dance was an integral part of human life.

Religious morality and practice influenced the form that dance took, and religion made use of dance because it had incantatory power, because of its ability to sweep men away, transport them to the heart of divine mysteries; because of its magic effect on the people. Dance was infallibly linked with all religions because of its ability to arouse this mysterious side of human nature.

The Christian church was no exception. From the moment it began to spread, Christianity introduced dance into its religious ceremony.

Today there is a separation between chancel and nave, but such was not always the case. At certain times, the worshippers used to cross that barrier and enter the chancel in order to participate in dances for which the priest acted as chorister or leader. The rhythmic recitation of the psalms corresponded to a dramatic action, and the dances were the movements of a chorus.

There were also meetings where men and women gathered in the desert to dance and seek salvation.

Once installed as a sacred rite, dance evolved in a climate of settings, costumes, aromas – in short, the most favourable surroundings. In Egypt, astronomers would decide on the date, time and place of such spectacles, influencing ways of thinking through their hermetic knowledge.

In Bali, a play entitled *Tjalonarang* is performed during the night, when magic influences are strongest, with the culminating scenes coming around midnight.[1] The presentation takes place near a cemetery, because that is where witches are generally found. *Tjulonarang* is often performed during times of sickness. But the presentation is fraught with dangers because the magic it contains can be dangerous as well as protective. Besides, its great antiquity and its links with ancestor-worship make it extremely potent, magically. Often, performances of *Tjulonarang* cannot be given outside the village because of the terror the play arouses. Putting so much magic in action, even through the medium of the shades, could provoke a disaster, so very expensive and special offerings are made on these occasions.

I give this example from Balinese drama because it is well known how integral and crucial a part dance plays in Bali, and it gives a clear notion of the violent, obsessive power dance can have over people.

In the course of its evolution, however, faith and passion ebbed out of dance. According to some mysterious and fatal mechanism, it became profane. For a while, it carried on with reckless abandon, embodying a kind of liberation. At the time, it seemed to be going through a renaissance, but appearances were deceiving. Excessive refinement paved the way for decadence, inevitably, and now, alas! we have nothing left but meaningless gestures of degenerate grace. Our chorus girls are a far cry from the choirs of Byzantium. And so we have no respect for dance, even if we love it.

---

[1] For further information see Beryl de Zoete and Walter Spies, *Dance and Drama in Bali* (1938; reprint, New York: Oxford University Press, 1973).

Following this decline, form alone remains, trying desperately but vainly to entertain, graced with nothing but appearance, unconvincing. Petrification is complete and dance perishes with its civilization.

Once we have made a link between dance and the cosmos, we can understand why it is up to far-sighted individuals, artists, to envision the way, and for initiates to map it.

Today there are those who believe in a revolution to transform the world. The instrument of change will be instinct, and part of our effort must now be directed to unearthing that instinct so long stifled.

Fortunately, there are the basic needs of life, irresistible forces; there is hope, and there is also science, which is wrong to isolate itself but should, instead, take the place it used to have in religion and magic. All our forces must be directed towards liberation, towards a rediscovery of ecstasy and love.

Let us turn to the depths within man, the realm of the unconscious with its impulses, desires, appetites and phobias. If we allow less importance to reason, and open up to the unconscious forces within, we are apt to awaken that which is not yet clear, but felt, and ripe enough to surface. The true and profound treasure to be found in the unconscious is energy. Master of all internal forces, a portion of the cosmic energy, it is the motive power behind our actions. Sensitivity to one's inner nature and attention to the world of dreams can bring one in touch with some levels of the unconscious. So the observation of antiquity has taught us.

Therefore, the dancer must liberate the energies of his body through movements which are spontaneously dictated to him. He can do so by putting himself in a state of receptivity similar to that of a medium. Through the violence of the forces at work, he may even reach a trance-like state and make contact with the points of magic.

Energy causes the need, need dictates the movements. Because the motor phenomenon and the concept are inseparable, they lose none of their value and efficiency.

This is how we can penetrate the mystery of where emotion is located in the body, and we will learn how that special tension is born which can fully express an emotion.

Through automatism, the dancer rediscovers in his body these points and tensions, and as he follows his own individual impulses and dynamism, his work goes beyond the individual towards the universal. Emotion governs everything, not only centring on determined points in the human body, but launching that body into time, space and gravity. This can also take place in the interaction of group formations.

Thus the aim of the dancer is to arrive at a perfect co-ordination of all these elements. What matters is that the emotions or tensions which govern rhythms

Sullivan's collaboration with photographer Maurice Perron,
Danse dans la neige, 1948.

and form should be animated by the same breath.

Rhythm is a part of even the simplest forms of dance. It arises internally and its foundations are physiological and organic. We must distinguish these natural rhythms from influences that tend to block their expression, and we must make the physical elements stand out and be noticed, along with the whole gamut of psychological factors. If we liberate, then control momentum and elasticity, we can show the prototypes of various emotional rhythms.

We must establish, by and for rhythm, an education which provokes in the dancer the need and spontaneous power to exteriorize felt rhythms. And finally, we must discover the effect of these different rhythms on the onlooker, because these rhythms are among our most efficient forces of communication.

Rhythm becomes part of a dynamism whose aim is to trigger psychological forces, and it breaks down resistance. It attaches past movements to present movements and makes connections with movements to come.

Statements of Belief

Man, through his physical and psychological structure, embraces the width, height and depth of space, thus giving a human meaning to those dimensions. In a delineated area, objective space and dream space are united like soul and body. Space takes on a new meaning. Crossing that area is no longer a matter of chance, but of the use of chance. A series of positions are shared with one or more dancers and the way this animated plasticity unfolds communicates to the onlooker the emotions and sensations dictating it.

The law of gravity is another factor to be considered in dance. The dancer plays with his weight by falling, leaping, balancing, by the simple fact of standing, by wobbling, by whirling, etc. He can follow his impulse and make himself very heavy or very light, not by tricks designed to escape the laws of nature, but through the harmonious use of those laws.

If the dancer obeys a rhythm which is related to the stuff of dreams, how can he form part of a communicating expansion, along with other dancers? Precisely by putting his forces in play, his deeply felt emotions. If the dancers want to form an emotional unit, they must be liberated and disciplined in the same direction, in accordance with the potentialities of their art. They must also be steeped in a communal ideal, which will be linked to the social conditions or needs of the time, social needs which are felt and recorded by the dancers' sensibilities, and not abstractly defined. Dance places itself at the interior of the cosmic rhythm by making its connection through the sensibilities of the time. Powerful emotive shock will also accede to the cosmic rhythm. This union of sensitivity and emotion will point each individual towards a common goal and will make the group a living entity, one single body.

Human energy is the common denominator and source of all this life. By going from an interior rhythm to a rhythm imposed from outside through a play of interchanges, the dancers take part in the creation of a world, help build it, then make it evolve.

It is a reality materialized by dancers who follow their dreams and allow the inherent forces in their nature to well up, causing reactions in the other dancers by the variety of values, intensities and situations provoked. Conflicts will be triggered and a drama will be born through the mysterious symbiosis of sense and form.

A universe is created, an entire world breathes. The spectator witnesses an efflorescence of life taking shape before his eyes. He can be moved by the pathos, or transported by ecstasy. The spectacle must act upon him, change something in him. That is the source of its usefulness, of its magic.

It must be clearly understood that the dancer does not choose a type of dance; this is not a question of ethnology, but of contemporary life.

Art can only flourish if it grows from problems which concern the age, and is always pushed in the direction of the unknown. Hence the marvellous in it.

I have tried to clarify some tendencies of dance today, talking about details which could only interest our own age. These mysteries impose themselves on us like a vision of doors long closed on rooms concealing unused treasures. When we do attain a knowledge of these things, we will have to abandon the old techniques to take up the new. Form varies constantly, but something eternal, drawn from the dances of all time, is added to consciousness, polishing a new facet of the diamond of human activity.

Sullivan Speaks Fifty Years Later

On November 7, 1998, York University acknowledged Sullivan's prolific contributions to dance and visual art by awarding her an honorary degree. Sullivan's Convocation Address to the Class of 1998 is a fitting companion to "La danse et l'espoir." Both find inspiration in past art forms and styles while acknowledging the continual need for art to regenerate itself. Both emphasize the potential for the individual artist and the arts in general to be the quintessence of societal vitality. Finally, both identify emotion as the core of creativity.

I would like to thank York University as I am deeply honoured to receive this degree today. I realize on this occasion that, like many people receiving honours, one's first thoughts go to mother and father. There is a wish to share the pride with them, even posthumously. They had so well encouraged me in my ventures. And as I feel close to my family now my mind turns towards my friends from the Automatist years, because of those seven years we experienced as a group at the awakening of our consciousness in the art world and social awareness, interestingly through an exploration of the unconscious in our own practice. The fiftieth anniversary of the *Refus global* makes it timely.

Refus global is the title of a collection of texts by some of the Automatists and the manifesto signed by Borduas and the fifteen members of the group. It aimed, in its prophetic writing at "disturbing" the heavy drowsiness of the province. The freedom we were appropriating in our art we wanted to extend to all aspects of life for everyone.

We were fifteen artists in our early twenties who signed and participated in the manifesto, and seven of these were young women. In 1948 this fact appears highly significant in showing the modernity of the group. We were painters, poets, dancers, an actress and a designer – this also speaks of the multi-disciplinary dimensions of our activities and numerous initiatives.

Not only a poetic text and not a political pamphlet either, it remains mysterious with a life of its own, and it still attracts attention. Recently author Pierre Vadeboncoeur wrote in *Le Couac*: "If we consider the manifesto as historical it is that Borduas and his group, their works and this text represent, retrospectively, perhaps the clearest symbol of freedom of the spirit in the history of our own culture. It is not a meagre title."

Statements of Belief

Though [we were] a multidisciplinary group, painting remained at the forefront. The advances made in art at that moment are worth mentioning. Influenced primarily by the Surrealist movement, the Automatists soon moved away from the illustration of dreams, inventing new nonobjective forms dictated by the plunge onto the unconscious which had become the focal point of our research. It was also about painting in its self-sufficient forms, in its formal innovations. This adventure led to new directions foreseeing the modernist movement. It is interesting to note that some all-over paintings (meaning a composition without a focal point) were done by some in the group and exhibited as early as 1946, slightly before Jackson Pollack's drippings in New York, a fact highly worth stating. Poetry, dance, theatre were also making advances. We did not need international recognition to feel part of the great avant-garde.

Fenêtre abandonnée, bloquée et débloquée, Greece, 1978.

As for myself, at that time, deeply involved in choreography, I was trying to equate in dance the breakthrough happening in painting. My adventurous spirit has led me towards both choreography and the visual arts and, to this day, I continue my passionate journey. I think of it as a destiny. Always, since a childhood fascinated by the arts, I figured my share of work in society to be invested in art. Destiny brought me to recognize in Borduas the exemplary master, the artist whose work is synonymous with vision and courage. I aspired to become this artist and employed myself at inventing my art at the possible limits of myself.

The artwork stands on the edge where the constants in the human spirit meet the social world in its ongoing evolution. It is in the nature of our perceptions to reveal what, otherwise, would lie hidden. If we speak of the distress in the world, we can become more aware and better attuned for changes. And as we move into a new millennium we have to accommodate ourselves to the new facts that drastically alter our lives. Art continues its role. I think, in retrospect, that our century has acted as a preparation to this passage into the year 2000. Great inventions found a parallel in the arts, in the name of electro-acoustic music and abstract painting, in concrete poetry and contemporary dance, in philosophy, cinema and photography. It occurred all over for those attentive to the phenomena.

I am deeply involved in painting, and, though at this time painting is in a serious crisis, I still believe in the ongoing capacity of painting to generate meaning anew. Painting is a phoenix. At Concordia University, where I teach, there are more and more young women and young men wanting to paint. An auspicious sign. In my approach to guide them I turn to their inner necessities, to that which captures the pulse and essence of an epoch. The focus lies on painting as an art, in its creative and ever evolving ways. So, students are urged to include more historical awareness and social empathy in their work, but that must be translated into the demands of painting. If the evaluating and controlling intelligence dominates the emotional experience, the work ceases to project the experience. It resists. The work wants to be tactile. It wants to be sensed, to be felt deep inside. Painting is difficult, painting is fascinating, and it offers the painter an enormous challenge, that of doing painting that compels conviction. We will.

Danse dans la neige, 1948.

Grant Strate: An Introduction

Born Dec. 7, 1927, Grant Strate has led a multifaceted career as dance educator, administrator, choreographer and writer. He studied modern dance with Laine Metz in Edmonton, Alberta, and after earning a law degree from the University of Alberta, he was admitted to the bar. In 1951 he was invited to become a charter member of the newly founded National Ballet of Canada, where he served for twenty years as soloist, resident choreographer and assistant to artistic director Celia Franca. He left the National Ballet in 1970 to found Canada's first university dance degree programme at York University in Toronto. In 1980 he joined Simon Fraser University in Vancouver to become Director of the Centre for the Arts.

Strate was founding chair of the Dance in Canada Association and directed the four National Choreographic Seminars convened between 1979 and 1991. Throughout his career he has worked as a guest teacher and choreographer in various Canadian centres as well as in the United States, Copenhagen, Stockholm, Antwerp, London, Hong Kong, Taipei, Chengdu and Beijing. In 1997 Dance Collection Danse published his *China Dance Journal* (Toronto: Dance Collection Danse Press/es, 1997) after his most recent visit to China, where he was appointed artistic advisor to the Sichuan Dance Academy in Chengdu.

Now retired from Simon Fraser University, he continues to teach and choreograph. He has created numerous ballets over the years for dance companies and schools, including the National Ballet of Canada, the Royal Swedish Ballet, the Juilliard Dance Department, the Laban Centre for Movement and Dance, Dancemakers, Dansepartout and the Beijing Dance Academy.

He has published a number of articles on dance and cultural policy issues in addition to his memoirs (Toronto: Dance Collection Danse Press/es, 2002). He was a member of the Federal Task Force on Professional Training in the Cultural Sector and recently joined the Dance Steering Committee of the International Baccalaureate Organization. Strate has received various honours and awards including the Jean A. Chalmers Award for Creativity in Dance (1993), the Order of Canada (1995), the Governor General's Performing Arts Award (1996) and an honorary Doctor of Laws from Simon Fraser University (1999). He currently serves on the boards of the Vancouver Dance Foundation, which was charged with the task of completing a building for Vancouver's professional dance sector, and the Dancer Transition Resource Centre in Toronto. He chaired the World Dance Alliance Americas third Assembly in Vancouver in 1997 and is now president of that organization.

Selma Landen Odom

Canadian Dance in Progress:
A Personal View

Grant Strate

This essay does not purport to give a complete survey of the seminal influences in Canadian choreography since the late 1960s, nor does it pretend to be a definitive scholarly analysis of the cultural and economic context. Its intention is simply to provide a piece of this complex mosaic from the necessarily limited perspective of my own experiences. These experiences include my entry into the National Ballet of Canada at its inception and my twenty years there, first as dancer, later to become resident choreographer and assistant to the director. They also include a barrage of exciting events and impressions during five months in New York in 1962-63, followed by a four-month grand tour of the European dance scene. Other travels pertain, particularly a year spent teaching and choreographing in Antwerp (1966-67) and three months choreographing for the Royal Swedish Ballet (1968-69). The long period spent in university dance since 1970 has been formative as a time for consolidation of my views on the creative process. And the four National Choreographic Seminars, which I directed at York University (1978), Banff Centre for the Fine Arts (1980) and Simon Fraser University (1985 and 1991), provided an opportunity to help catalyze the ever-changing choreographic scene.

I do not refer here to the huge foment out of Quebec, a phenomenon about which much has already been recorded, and I only briefly acknowledge the very productive contributions of Peter Boneham through the creative lab of Le Groupe de la Place Royale (now Le Groupe Dance Lab). This omission should not be interpreted as negation of their importance in the grand scheme of things. Indeed, a total survey would heap credit on these developments as well as on the host of choreographic workshops presented by almost every professional company, and also acknowledge the encouragement provided by the Canada Council for the Arts and several provincial arts councils (one must particularly praise the accomplishments of the Ontario Arts Council).

My personal view is subjective; it could not be otherwise. It has been formed by every experience encountered throughout my life, and these experiences are not just limited to dance, or art for that matter. I entered the Canadian choreographic stream precipitously, vaulting from a budding law career into the National Ballet of Canada in its founding year, 1951. Celia Franca invited me to join as a dancer on the slim evidence of two solo works of my own choreography (dare I call it that?) danced for her in lieu of an audition. She saw choreographic potential but made it clear that it would be many years (five, in fact) before I would be allowed to create for the company, that preparation for choreographer status must be long and arduous and based on a thorough understanding of the ballet vocabulary. Many years later, in quite another context, I was to hear the same words expressed by Dame Ninette de Valois, further supporting this view of the choreographic process current in ballet circles at the time. That view included the basic premise that you must not begin to invent until you have been steeped in the tradition of classical ballet, and that after years of training and dancing in works created by others a novitiate might be welcomed into the hallowed halls of Terpsichore as a choreographer, if one's credentials included genius as well as an encyclopedic knowledge of the classical code. After all, this was how Sir Frederick Ashton, Antony Tudor and Sir Kenneth MacMillan reached the top of their field.

Too much time has passed for me to remember how I felt about the process of becoming a choreographer as explained to me in 1951. I doubt that I knew enough to venture an opinion. It was splendid enough that I was chosen at all but, in retrospect, I suspect Celia (Miss Franca to us then) was so hard up for dancers that she would risk hiring someone, with no ballet training and an unproven talent for making dances, in the wild hope that she might be vindicated later for her rash decision. She and I have not actually sat down to discuss the results of the next twenty years of my tenure with the National Ballet of Canada, but possibly we would agree that a contribution was made. This period produced as many abrasions and cultural irritations as one would expect from the entry of a Western Canadian, possessed of few traditional attitudes, into the highly distilled British atmosphere of the National Ballet of Canada in its early years. In spite of, or, more likely because of this collision of values, I was able to formulate my own view of the creative process, a view which I now realize owes as much to my experience in that traditional framework as to my own external investigations.

By 1951 Canadian dance already had a history but I knew nothing of it. Until then, my total dance experience had been a year of tap-dance lessons at age six (a post-Depression phenomenon, since my father was reduced to selling vacuum cleaners and landed a sale to a tap-dance teacher who couldn't pay); participation in the University of Alberta Ballet Club where a group of us, who should have known better, performed without benefit of training; and an exciting couple of years working seriously with Laine Metz, a newly arrived refugee from Estonia, who had studied and worked with Mary Wigman in Germany. My first formative roots, therefore, were influenced by mid-European expressionistic modern dance. My first exposures to ballet, inadequate as they were, pretty well convinced me that ballet was silly and superficial, an opinion that resurfaces from time to time on very bad days or in the presence of very bad ballet.

Through my first ten years with the National Ballet of Canada, basic training and performing necessarily happened concurrently, leaving me little time and energy to grapple with issues of art expression as they might or might not apply to ballet. Much of what I was experiencing was still at odds with earlier preconceptions, but I was in no position to challenge it. It bothered me very much that I was labelled immediately as unmusical. There was much talk about "musicality." A dancer seemed to be regarded as musical if the movement responded sensitively to the intent of the composition, and the best of choreography was considered to be a visual illustration of the musical form. Given these criteria, Franca was certainly very musical and Tudor, one of my first profound influences, was a masterful user of music, although he, along with Ashton and Balanchine, managed to present the dance as an equal partner rather than as a slavish interpreter of music.

Grant Strate at the National Ballet of Canada.

It was certainly true that I heard music and eventually used music differently from many others in the field. Very early in my choreographic career, I had the luxury of having original scores written for my ballets. Harry Somers wrote the first two scores and our work process was truly collaborative. It was not a case of laying a soundscape over pre-planned choreography, as now happens so often in the contemporary dance scene, nor was it an attempt to illustrate a predetermined score. It was a mutual investigation of possibilities. The use of music and its relationship to movement still concerns me, as does the whole area of interdisciplinary performance so current today, but these are only a few of the questions that began to formulate in my mind during the early years of my career. Others included the degree of autocracy, seemingly essential to the effective direction of a ballet company; the conditions dancers were expected to accept for the opportunity to dance; the place of the individual in an art form where a corps de ballet is an essential component; classicism versus romanticism, versus the blasphemies of contemporary dance; and, above all, the place of the creative artist in an atmosphere of constant financial crisis and box-office considerations. After years of my own work and over twenty years spent in universities, where the social responsibility of art is much discussed, the biggest question still remains – for whom does the artist work?

This highly personal introduction is meant only to sketch out some background for my own aesthetic point of view and my great interest in the creative process, which led me into directions coincident with the accelerated evolution of Canadian choreography, particularly during the 1970s. At that time the dance explosion fostered so many new ideas and shattered so many preconceptions about the making of dances. In 1962, as one of the first recipients of a Canada Council A Grant (Brian Macdonald preceded me by one year and our travels were almost identical), I found my nine-month leave from the National Ballet of Canada to be a liberating experience that affected everything that followed. Much that occurred during that tour and later travels prepared me for a career change. I had no idea what form that change would take, but by 1970 I knew that twenty years with the National Ballet of Canada was more than enough time spent in a classically based company. There is no rancour in saying this, nor criticism of the direction set for this fine company. It was simply no longer my direction. The change came, fortuitously, by my accepting the invitation to design and direct Canada's first degree programme in dance. I was given the rare opportunity to establish a curriculum from scratch and to test some of my own educational and creative theories. The dance programme at York University was effectively launched with the advice and assistance of several new colleagues met in London and New York. These people included Norman Morrice, Peter Brinson, Martha Hill, Lincoln Kirstein and Selma Jeanne Cohen. More than thirty years later, the impact this programme has had on Canada's emerging and unique dance identity is a matter of record but, in the beginning, I could only speculate.

In retrospect, my entry into the university dance scene was as extraordinarily peculiar as my entry into the dance profession in 1951. During my two decades with the National Ballet of Canada, university dance programmes were regarded as places to experience dance recreationally or scholastically. Dance people, who found their way into the profession through the usual route of ballet training within a professional academy, could not conceive of any other productive route, nor could I. The decision to found the York programme was a leap of faith. Jules Heller, Dean of the Faculty of Fine Arts, talked me into it by supporting my firm belief that a university dance programme should assist and extend the profession and not create an arcane countercultural product, with no roots in the past and no potential for the future. As far as I knew at that time, the various university dance degree programmes, all of them in the United States, fed people into recreational streams as a part of physical education and incestuously back into the university system. My ignorance of dance in universities was appalling.

The York University dance programme was influenced very much by my five-month residency at the Juilliard School of Music, where, I believe, I formulated my educational philosophy for dance. In any event, the founding of the York programme was predicated on the following beliefs:

• Dance movement, its exploration and discovery, should be the central component of all streams of dance education. The experiencing of the feelings that dance evokes enriches the understanding of this art form whether as dancer, choreographer, notator, therapist, historian, teacher or critic.

• Creativity deserves high priority in the university setting. The experience of moving is not enough in itself. The student dancer should have the opportunity to learn compositional crafts while working toward eventual empowerment over the material; toward an idiosyncratic, individualized art statement, reflective of its heritage within an original framework.

• Bodies are fundamentally the same, made up by the same skeletal and muscular architectures and bound by the same laws of space, time and gravity. That is not to say there are not extreme variations in physical capacities and motivations, but the fundamentals of dance training are common denominators within the widely differing aesthetic objectives of modern dance, ballet and jazz, to name the most usual forms of western theatrical dance. Therefore, ballet and modern dance training should be able to co-exist symbiotically and in equal measure.

• The educated dancer is potentially a better dancer, certainly a better artist. Physical training and a liberal arts education may be integrated to the betterment of professional dance.

• Dance scholarship in areas of history, criticism, therapy, notation and analysis, viewed from the perspective of our contemporary world, is important to the better understanding of dance's roots, the guarantee of a healthy future and the rationalization of dance as a primary art form on a par with music and visual art.

• Experimentation/research is as necessary to the arts as it is to the sciences. Professional dance schools and companies do not have the means and often not the inclination to experiment, to pursue new ideas and direction. Universities, not only provide opportunities for research, they demand it as an essential responsibility of faculty. What better setting is there, then, for the advancement of dance creativity?

• Audience development is very much a process of rationalization and communication. Dance is regarded, too often, as an ephemeral, spontaneous activity with few, if any, intellectual underpinnings; quite simplistic compared to literature, drama and music. It certainly seems to be devoid of the long commentaries attached to works of contemporary visual art and perhaps this is best. Even so, the educated dance student, cognizant of dance's past and curious about its future, is better placed to carry the word and to strengthen the profile for those whose eyes fail to understand. More importantly, perhaps, is the prospect of raising standards within the rarefied ecology of dance itself, by the sort of self-criticism and comparative thinking associated with university education. The fact that many manage to graduate without experiencing these values should not diminish the potential for raising standards and thus gaining a more enthusiastic and loyal audience base for dance.

• Dancers should prepare to build their own spheres of activity and not wait to be discovered. They should assume responsibility for the evolution of the art form and should be encouraged to become masters of their own fates.

Not all of these beliefs were well formulated during my brief time at Juilliard but the seeds were certainly planted then. In the early 1960s, New

York was already firmly established as the dance capital of the world; Paris and London had already given over this honour, Copenhagen was too small to ever claim it, and Moscow and Leningrad were too isolated to be in the running. By comparison to anywhere else, New York was a cauldron of dance ideas and a huge magnet for talented artists. The dance underground was vibrantly alive. The establishment was being embraced internationally. Artists could work and live on almost any income or in any physical circumstance. The avant-garde was noisily blasphemous and politically insolent. At that time Martha Graham, already well past her prime, was hailed throughout the world for her fine dancers and her uniquely sculpted choreography. Merce Cunningham was collaborating with leaders of the new music, visual art and theatre. Paul Taylor was entering a successfully productive period. Balanchine was churning out a dazzling array of contemporary works to the surprise of those beginning to think of him as a passé traditionalist, and the Henry Street Playhouse had become an idea incubator for the likes of Alwin Nikolais and Murray Louis.

Although I had visited New York briefly, in 1961, to sneak a look at the Balanchine repertoire, I had few connections and no friends there. So the bleak, rainy day of my arrival in November 1962 for an extended stay was more than a little intimidating. I knew Tudor through his work with the National Ballet of Canada, mounting several of his masterpieces (*Gala Performance*, *Lilac Garden*, *Dark Elegies*, *Offenbach in the Underworld*), so the next day I zeroed in on his class at the Metropolitan Opera House to watch the great teacher in action. Then something happened which changed the course of my life and could very well have ended a budding career. For Machiavellian reasons, no doubt (a Tudor trait), he asked me to teach his advanced ballet classes at Juilliard for the next three months while he flew off to Stockholm. He was then the artistic director of the Royal Swedish Ballet and was expected to be there for a part of each year. It mattered not, to him, that I was inexperienced; possibly that was the very non-credential he was seeking. Whatever his reasons, I accepted the teaching position as well as a commission to create a ballet for Juilliard and I was precipitously launched into a hotbed of iconoclastic young bloods who questioned, prodded and cajoled at every step of their emerging careers. What a shock after my years with the National Ballet of Canada, where English rules of decorum and behaviour prevailed, and where directors, teachers and students inhabited clearly defined hierarchical positions.

Juilliard students taught me much of what I now know about teaching. After each class, they took me out for coffee to discuss the strengths and weaknesses of the class. By the time Tudor arrived back all was proceeding very well indeed, much to his surprise I believe. Juilliard had an amazing line-up of teachers at that time. Master teachers such as Tudor, José Limón, Anna Sokolow, Pearl Lang, Margaret Craske, Alfredo Corvino, Louis Horst and Paul Draper worked under the able, but seemingly chaotic direction of Martha Hill. Martha Graham also taught from time to time. When not there,

26

Graham was always well represented by teacher-dancers from her company, past or present. Of these Robert Cohan, Helen McGehee and Ethel Winter were most notable. Dance composition was heavily emphasized, and almost all of the modern and ballet staff taught it. Horst continued to reduce students to trembling masses of ectoplasm. Corvino and Tudor had as much to say about choreography as Limón and Sokolow. The atmosphere was charged with creativity. The presence of a number of autocratic giants with various approaches to dance-making tended to neutralize dogma. My time there was a tremendous unleashing of the imagination. Previous ideas I harboured about choreographic process were either corroborated or annihilated by the Juilliard experience. The fact that I was there to work and not just to observe earned for me a number of new colleagues who contributed in important ways to the early years of York University's Department of Dance and the National Choreographic Seminars.

By any measure of assessment, the four National Choreographic Seminars must be judged as landmark events in the evolution of Canadian choreography. The list of choreographers, composers, musicians and dancers who attended is now long and impressive. Many careers and collaborations were launched. New ideas and directions were fed into the established order and the new breed of independent dancer-choreographers gained support and impetus. All of the Seminars were led by Robert Cohan, whom I regard as the rarest of artists in his ability to guide other choreographers to express their individual concepts in their own ways, without imprinting his own aesthetic stamp. In my estimation, this ability is essential for the success of any creative process and is one seldom found in artists of established reputation. Cohan, whom I first met at Juilliard, went on to found and direct the London Contemporary Dance Theatre and firmly established American modern dance in England. He had been one of the first choreographic directors of the European Gulbenkian Choreographic Summer School, an annual event originally supported by the Gulbenkian Foundation. Together with John Herbert McDowell, a prolific dance composer associated with the Paul Taylor Company and many other New York choreographers, Cohan developed the approach to the cultivation of dance makers begun by Glen Tetley, an approach that met with considerable success in England.

The Gulbenkian Choreographic Summer School, in London, was the model for the four National Choreographic Seminars. It was through Peter Brinson that I first heard of these English courses. He was, at that time, the director of the Gulbenkian Foundation and had been one of the people who advised me when I planned the York University dance programme. He was also a guest lecturer at York during the programme's first five years. It was during these years that the Gulbenkian Choreographic Summer School was founded as an annual event with Brinson's active support and involvement. In brief, a number of practicing choreographers were matched with an equal number of composers to work with a crew of dancers and musicians under the direction of a master choreographer and musician-composer to explore creative possi-

27

bilities, free of product deadlines and in isolation within a pressure-cooker time frame. Tetley, Cohan and Norman Morrice were among the first to act as choreographic directors. McDowell and Adam Gatehouse were the first music directors.

As I was much impressed by what I knew of the Gulbenkian workshop, I hoped to begin such a process in Canada. It was clear that there would be no support from the Canada Council, for complicated reasons worthy of another autobiographical chapter elsewhere. With the blessing of York University, the encouragement of the Ontario Arts Council and the hard cash of about forty artists, who paid up front for the experience, the first National Choreographic Seminar was held at York University in the summer of 1978. Cohan was contracted as the choreographic director and, as it turned out, Gatehouse from London served as music director. All arrangements had been concluded with McDowell, but at the last minute, his health, long a problem, prevented him from attending. It was risky business financially. There was no Canadian angel to compare with the Gulbenkian Foundation, and unlike the English workshops, where artists were invited to participate with all expenses paid, the choreographers, composers, and even the dancers and musicians were expected to pay a hefty fee for the privilege of working to the point of utter exhaustion. Of course, many were successful in obtaining funds from arts councils and in this respect the Canada Council did give indirect assistance. Even so, there was much scrambling to bring this very expensive venture to a reasonable level of accountability, a condition that was finally reached through a greater contribution from York University than first projected.

Tedd Robinson at the National Choreographic Seminar, Banff, 1980.

My original intention was that the Choreographic Seminars should occur every other year for three times, as I believed that the Canadian talent pool was not large enough to justify an annual event. Given the organizational difficulties and high costs, I certainly did not anticipate the time, energy and inclination to work beyond that objective. I also believed then, as I still believe, that even good ideas become obsolete in time and there should be no attempt to perpetuate the Seminars for their own sake. They should occur only when there is pressure from the ground to offer them. As it turned out, the second Seminar was at the Banff Centre for the Fine Arts, two years later, and the third and fourth, offered at Simon Fraser University, occurred five and six years later respectively.

While the magic formulae for successful creative processes continued to be invoked by Cohan and colleagues, the texture of the experience changed from Seminar to Seminar, in response to evolving choreographic trends in the Canadian scene. The Seminars at York University and the Banff Centre for the Fine Arts put emphasis on dance technique and music-dance interaction with more than a glimmer of influence from south of the border, particularly from the Judson Church movement. McDowell, who was present at the Banff Centre, extolled the virtues of taking wild chances and accomplishing brilliant failures. The Banff event was less formal, less cautious and more adventurous than the first, but then we had more confidence in the process by then. For the 1985 Seminar at Simon Fraser University, we added a theatre component to the mix of collaborative possibilities, with five actors and a theatre director joining the ensemble. Dance theatre, much impelled by Pina Bausch and other European choreographers, had reached a critical mass in Canada, so the addition of theatre artists was logical; troublesome to begin with, but the marriage was happily concluded. The last Seminar in 1991 attempted to introduce video as a working partner of the creative act. In theory, this was an excellent and timely idea but, in practice, there was not enough time to devote to this complicated medium to accomplish more than a glimpse of the ultimate potential for video dance. Video dance remains a current interest without sufficient opportunities to learn enough about the technology to tame the beast in the cause of productive collaborations. The Dance and the Camera workshop, at the Banff Centre for the Fine Arts in the fall of 1992, under the accomplished hand of Bob Lockyer and organized through the auspices of Le Groupe Dance Lab and the Banff Centre, made a very good start in this direction. But video dance is an area that requires more attention.

For all that the four Seminars accomplished, one condition prevailed that saddened me. Despite my urgings and haranguings, the Seminars attracted very few ballet choreographers and dancers. Renald Rabu, James Kudelka and Howard Richard were exceptions, but even they attended in the belief that they were descending into hell. It was always my belief that the process of creating dance should be the same for all types and styles of Western theatrical dance. While the material might vary significantly, the path to effective communication should be the same. Creation has always been given high priority among modern dancers and there are very few who do not aspire to be choreographers. Not so with ballet dancers, most of whom think a choreographer has a responsibility to show them off well. Ballet choreographers are regarded as people set apart who have a talent for putting steps together in charming or virtuosic ways. The material used is too often predetermined from the classical code of movement. Creation is about invention. Movement creation is about invented movement and the best of choreographers – modern, ballet, jazz or whatever – understand this. It is a shame that more ballet people did not avail themselves of the opportunities provided by the Seminars. It is little wonder that ballet companies are now looking to modern choreographers to feed their repertoires with new ideas. There are efforts now in the United States like the Carlyle Project to encourage and cultivate ballet choreographers through specially designed creative processes. It still distresses me that attitudes persist to insulate ballet from the barefoot crowd.

The National Choreographic Seminars reflected a burgeoning interest in choreography and a new independence for choreographers. Although they were organized to some extent on European models they had very specific Canadian roots. Up until 1973-74 choreography was largely imported or choreographers grew up as I did under the protective umbrella of an established company. At this time, with the example of York's new degree granting programme, several universities introduced dance programmes or accelerated existing ones until eventually dance degree status was given to the University of Waterloo, the University of Quebec at Montreal (UQAM), Concordia University and Simon Fraser University. Many other colleges and universities added dance to their curricula which contributed to the influx of educated dancers determined to make a creative statement without expecting to attach to the existing establishment. A large group of independent artists was generated and whether or not this will in time be assessed as a plague or a benefit, the profile of Canadian dance has, as a result, changed drastically since the early 1970s.

There were other important contributing factors, of course. The Fifteen Dance Lab was born in Toronto in 1974 parented by Miriam and Lawrence Adams, two ex-National Ballet dancers who were determined to provide opportunities for emerging dancers never available to them in their own dancing years. Motivated by considerable altruism and a healthy dollop of anger they provided a space; cramped, square and very very black, where anyone who had something to present was allowed to go public. This venue gave a boost up to many "young Turks," a number of whom have gone on to make a considerable mark. One remembers early works of artists such as Christopher House, Terrill Maguire, Marie Chouinard and Jennifer Mascall to mention only a few.

The year before Fifteen Dance Lab began saw the founding of the Dance in Canada Association, an umbrella organization to speak for dancers from all parts of Canada. It was first articulated at a meeting convened by the Dance Office of the Canada Council. A steering committee of four was struck to assess the feasibility of a national organization. The Dance in Canada Association was formed by a painful process of incorporation and the new creature soon became troublesome to Council by widening its definition of "professional" to include almost everyone self proclaimed as such. By the end of the 1980s the Dance in Canada Association became a pale shadow of its earlier proactive period and has since disbanded, but in the beginning it was a vital entity which spoke effectively, if sometimes loudly, for dance as it was to become rather than for what it was at the time. As a member of the steering committee and its first chairman, I was very close to the dynamics for change struggling for legitimacy and recognition within a fairly conservative and elitist established order. A true dialectic ensued. The annual conferences were welcomed as occasions for the interchange of ideas and presentation of the best and the worst of new choreographic ideas. The evening performances were marathon displays of individual indulgences among which many a fresh seed was discovered. Assessments of the past seldom make laudatory comments about cultural service organizations, perhaps because they existed only to serve. I maintain that the Dance in Canada Association, in its early years, should be given high marks for the part it played in a quickly evolving scene. And it should be remembered that at its first meeting of directors it was firmly resolved that the Association should never attempt to justify its own existence, that it should die when there was no longer a need. And die it did, but I would have preferred it to have happened more elegantly.

The Canada Dance Festival was first ably organized by Mark Hammond and Cathy Levy in association with Dance in Canada. For the first time assessments were made about the stage worthiness of the works of the organization's membership, and trouble was the inevitable result. Levy took over two years later and continued to present an all-Canadian dance festival where aficionados and dancers congregated to check out the newest and presumably the best of contemporary choreography. The Festival serves the community well by providing opportunities to be showcased before discerning audiences and critics, but already there is a clamouring, fractious, subterranean pressure from all those not chosen just at the time when the Festival is forced to make the window of opportunity smaller because of funding cutbacks.

In recent years attention has been directed from the finished choreographic product to the process of its creation. Le Groupe Dance Lab, under the paternal leadership of Peter Boneham, was the first professional company to redefine its mandate to give priority to the mentorship of young choreographers. The touring circuit and the theatre space were forsaken in favour of in-studio presentations of experimental works in progress. The Toronto Dance Theatre, Contemporary Dancers of Winnipeg, Danse Cité in Montreal and Main Dance Place in Vancouver provide opportunities for emerging choreographers to experiment with the guiding help of established choreographers, and Bengt Jörgen has developed a process for ballet choreographers in his company now resident at George Brown College in Toronto.

Statements of Belief

We can be justly proud of the growth of Canadian choreography since 1960. It has been remarkable. Contemporary dance has found a Canadian identity without completely killing its European and American roots. Asian influences are just beginning to impact in line with a rapidly changing demography. Quebec has produced contemporary dance that commands considerable international attention for its indigenous invention. New dance in the West is distinctly different from that in Central or French Canada. Ontario is experiencing a resurgence of creative energy. Much of this progress was due to government granting agencies during twenty years of economic growth that lasted until the mid-1990s. More importance has been given to choreographic development by designations made by provincial and federal funding programmes and the prestigious awards given annually by the Chalmers Family and Clifford E. Lee Foundations.

Inevitably, when the pendulum swings it tends to swing too far, and we are suddenly faced with a country with a relatively small population base abounding with choreographers at various levels of accomplishment and talent. The future is bleak indeed for many of them as funding for the cultural sector will most certainly continue its savage decline. The arguments we have always raised to justify the legitimacy of art and a healthy growth pattern are no longer effective in a society where health care, pensions and old age security are being eyed as potential targets to reduce the deficit. Cultural austerity is happening at a time when mankind needs the humanitarian values commensurate with art practice and consumption, but sadly, few of our leaders are willing to share this view. Let us hope present economic realities will not continue long into the future, but, in the meantime, we must anticipate a culling of the field. Artists will not be able to depend on government to supplement their livelihood as they have in the past. We are entering a period where resourcefulness, real talent and new methods of delivery will count for more than they have in the past three decades.

But evolution never occurs in a continuous ascending line. There is many a plateau and valley along the way. Being the optimist I have always been, I believe the creative process made in the art of dance will not be lost, that a consolidation of past achievements is appropriate and that we will soon see another productive era to match the one just past, one in which I have had great pleasure participating.

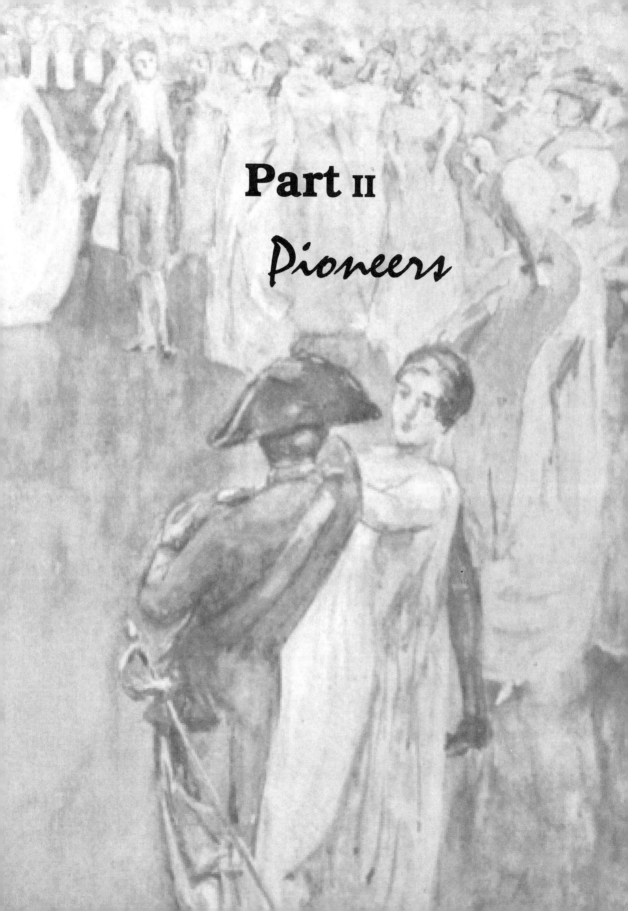

Part II

Pioneers

Portrait believed to be Anne Fairbrother Hill.

Anne Fairbrother Hill:
Canada's Chaste and Elegant Dancer

Mary Jane Warner

Anne Fairbrother Hill was born into a family of theatrical entertainers on July 15, 1804 in London, England.[1] As a child she was trained by her father, the pantomime artist Robert Fairbrother, and by her older sister, Mary, a dancer at Drury Lane. Anne was typical of many show business children who began their careers as dancers and pantomime artists, developing into exceedingly versatile performers. As she matured, she honed her considerable acting skills, and in later years she specialized in character roles, especially comedy parts. She served as mentor for many a stage-struck actress, for early in her career Anne Fairbrother Hill had discovered a flair for teaching: she trained a number of promising amateurs in addition to tutoring her own children for the stage. She was a highly intelligent woman of great charm and compassion, but most importantly, she was a survivor who could make the most of any situation.

In the early years of her career, Anne Fairbrother Hill was a successful actress-dancer on the English stage, somewhat overshadowed by her actor-manager husband, Charles Hill. During the initial years of their marriage, her life necessarily revolved around her husband's somewhat erratic career and the responsibilities of raising her three youngsters, but she still found occasional opportunities to appear on the stage. When the family settled in America during the 1840s, Anne Fairbrother Hill became the backbone of the family, and she seemed to thrive amidst the constant trials of performing under less than ideal conditions. Undaunted by the untrained amateur performers who often fleshed out acting companies in the Canadian towns the Hills visited, she graciously encouraged these novice thespians in their amateur theatricals, for she realized these enthusiasts were not competitors, but staunch supporters of the professional theatre. For some Canadian performers training was based almost entirely on watching and imitating seasoned professionals such as the Hills, and playing minor parts in touring productions after only a sketchy rehearsal.

Probably the greatest influence in Anne Fairbrother's life was her father, "Bob" Fairbrother (1767-1841). He trained her as a dancer-pantomime artist and also instilled in her the moral fibre to cope with the innumerable challenges that would mark her life. Bob Fairbrother began his own career as a

---

[1] An earlier version of this essay first appeared in *Theatre History in Canada* 12: 2 (Fall 1991); reproduced by permission of the Association for Canadian Theatre Research.

dancer-acrobat in his teens and became an established pantomime artist appearing regularly at both London's Sadler's Wells and Drury Lane theatres. He was one of the first teachers of the brilliant clown Joe Grimaldi; through his friendship with Grimaldi, Fairbrother met his own wife, Mary Bailey, whom he married in 1794. In addition to his pantomime and dancing skills, Fairbrother had a good head for business; he became a kind of confidant and general secretary to Richard Brinsley Sheridan, the manager of Drury Lane, serving as go-between in many of Sheridan's business dealings. Fairbrother was clearly comfortable with all levels of society from royalty to the lowliest theatrical apprentice, and he was popular with everyone according to his obituary, which claimed that "disinterested devotion to the services of others was his predominating characteristic, indeed his good will extended to all" (*Spirit of the Times* 13 Mar. 1841: 24).

Bob Fairbrother's likeable personality was a valuable commodity for his large family, which grew to four girls and three boys.[2] His first daughter, Mary Emma, was born soon after his marriage, and other children followed in quick succession. Anne (originally christened Amelia) and her twin sister, Sophia, were born in London in 1804. Although Bob Fairbrother took on extra jobs to feed and clothe his large brood, he still had considerable difficulty making ends meet. Anne grew up in a household that was always short of funds, and she contributed to the family upkeep. By the time the twins were two, they had already appeared on stage as babes-in-arms, and their older sister, thirteen-year-old Mary, was an official member of the Drury Lane corps de ballet. Anne's first official appearance was at Drury Lane as Cora's child in *Pizarro* (*Clipper* 20 Dec. 1890). All the Fairbrother youngsters appeared as pages and children whenever parts were available, but their best opportunities were as elves and fairies in the ever-popular Christmas and Easter pantomimes. Anne and the other youngsters received on-the-job training from their father and elder sister, but the family could call on a wide network of theatrical acquaintances for advice and guidance.

The Fairbrothers faced a serious setback, however, when Drury Lane Theatre burned down on February 24, 1809, and they had to scramble to find work in other theatres. When Drury Lane eventually reopened in October 1812, their friend Sheridan was no longer in charge. Although Mary Fairbrother still performed in the corps de ballet, it appears that the Fairbrothers were out of favour with the new management. Sheridan, however, wrote to Thomas J. Dibdin, the assistant stage director at Drury Lane, urging him to employ Bob Fairbrother: "I will pledge my life for his zeal, integrity, and ability in whatever he may be employed. What the line is in which he may be made most useful, Mr. Ward is most competent to explain. I say

---

[2] The following sources give biographical background on the Fairbrother family: Highfill vol. 5 (1978: 138-40) and Disher (1934). The parish register for London, Lambeth St. Mary gives birth dates for three of Fairbrother's daughters: Mary Emma (ca. 28 Sept. 1794) who in later life became a successful dramatist and translator; the twins, Sophia and Amelia (ca. 15 July 1804) who became dancers. The fourth daughter, Caroline, was also a dancer. The Fairbrother sons also entered the theatrical profession: Samuel Glover was a theatrical publisher; Benjamin Smith was a stage manager; Robert was a theatrical printer.

nothing of his large family, many of whom are qualified to give fair assistance to the theatre" (Highfill vol. 5: 139).

Evidently the plea was at least partially successful, for the Fairbrother girls began appearing frequently at Drury Lane in such works as Oscar Bryne's ballet *Bridal of Flora* and the popular pantomime *Harlequin Horner*. During their formative teen years, the girls likely attended the London Dance Academy established by former Drury Lane ballet master James D'Egville. The academy had been founded during the Napoleonic Wars to train dancers as replacements for the then-usual French ballet dancers. The Fairbrothers' apprenticeships were further augmented by attending performances at Drury Lane and elsewhere to see leading entertainers of the day, such as the great tragedian Edmund Kean, the clown Joe Grimaldi and the renowned Sarah Siddons.

The family fortunes improved substantially when they joined William Moncrieff's new troupe at the recently opened Royal Coburg in 1818, as did Mary's new husband, the actor Joseph Ebsworth, an old friend from Drury Lane. Also joining the troupe was fifteen-year-old Charles Hill, whom Anne would eventually marry.[3] Although the Royal Coburg was built by wealthy subscribers, it soon became the haunt of a rough and boisterous crowd that thrived on melodrama and spectacle. At the Coburg, Anne and Charles grew into seasoned professionals capable of playing to both royalty and a drunken mob. Anne danced in the corps de ballet most of the time, but occasionally she was given a small solo. When the Royal Coburg was dark, she sometimes found work at the nearby Surrey Theatre, another bastion of melodrama, or at Sadler's Wells, managed by old family friend Grimaldi.

By the mid-1820s the Fairbrother troupe had dissolved: Anne's three sisters had headed north to Edinburgh's Caledonian Theatre, while she had remained in London, appearing at both the Surrey and Sadler's Wells theatres. A talented dancer and actress, she was assigned both principal dancer roles and minor speaking parts such as Janetta, the niece, in Dibdin's *Elfrida of Olmutz* (playbill 18 July 1825).

Anne and Charles Hill were married around 1826. Soon afterwards, the young couple followed the trail of many ambitious performers by playing the provincial circuit – Bath, Cheltenham, Brighton – to gain opportunities in major roles that would enhance their reputations. But Anne Hill's own career was clearly curtailed by the birth of her first child, Charles Barton, in 1827, soon followed by two more babies, Rosalie and Robert. The subsequent years were difficult for Anne Hill as she attempted to balance the demands of wife and mother with her own ambitions as a dancer and actress.

By fall 1830, the Hills had returned to London, where they could count on family help in looking after their three lively youngsters. The Surrey Theatre became their new headquarters when Charles Hill was engaged to play both

---

[3] According to his "Obituary" (*Clipper* 3 Oct. 1874) he was the son of the celebrated Covent Garden tenor John Hill. When his parents left England on European tours Charles was left in the care of Charles Kemble's brother-in-law, theatrical manager Vincent De Camp, who encouraged young Hill's career as an actor.

romantic leads and eccentric character parts.[4] Anne's brother, Benjamin Smith Fairbrother, was stage manager there, and now and then Anne Hill performed alongside the Surrey's resident dancer, Mlle Rosier. Clearly, Anne Hill was the equal of Rosier, but family responsibilities permitted only rare appearances in short divertissements – perhaps a stately court minuet and gavotte or a flamboyant Spanish fandango. She could be counted on for special benefit performances, and during the busy-but-profitable pantomime seasons, she usually tackled a major part like Flirtella in *Cinderella* (playbill 7 Nov. 1831).

Once the children were older, she returned to the theatre full time. Since opportunities were limited at the Surrey, however, she rejoined the Drury Lane corps de ballet in the spring of 1833. The Romantic ballet movement was in full flight after ballerina Marie Taglioni had astounded audiences as the ethereal Sylphide in 1831, and Fanny Elssler, Taglioni's rival, would shortly capture hearts with her voluptuous, exotic Spanish *Cachucha*. These popular ballerinas were pushing dance technique to new heights with the introduction of extensive pointe work and virtuoso technique. The theatre was bustling with dance activity as leading choreographers, François Albert, André Deshayes and Filippo Taglioni created stunning new ballets. Although foreign dancers again dominated the dance scene at Covent Garden, Drury Lane and the Italian Opera House, English dancers such as Anne Fairbrother Hill were given abundant opportunities in the corps and in minor solo roles. On stage Anne Hill watched and absorbed the popular Romantic style, which she would perform herself on her return engagements to the Surrey and later in the provinces and in America.

She was a quick study and progressed rapidly through the Drury Lane ranks to become one of sixteen principal female dancers. During her first season back at Drury Lane in 1833, she danced with ballerina Pauline Duvernay in the popular *Maid of Cashmere* and was featured as Louis in *Les Pages du duc de Vendôme*. Between seasons at Drury Lane, she returned to the Surrey, where Charles Hill had been promoted to stage manager. There she tried out her newly learned dance variations and further developed her growing skills as an actress. Her children were also becoming seasoned performers. In August six-year-old Charles Barton and four-year-old Rosalie were featured in *Children of the Wood*, soon after, little Rosalie was given the honour of a benefit performance, with the entire Hill family performing *Ivanhoe*. The Hills also starred in the pantomime *Whittington and his Cat*, with Charles in the dual role of Dick Whittington and Harlequin, Anne as Columbine, and young Rosalie as Fairy Busy Bee. Anne Hill supervised her children's training and thus discovered she had a love and flair for teaching.

Reestablished in London, the Hills moved over to Covent Garden to join other members of the Fairbrother family; Anne Hill became one of the twelve principal female dancers – a remarkable status for an English-born dancer.

---

[4] Although Charles Hill's "Obituary" states he was stage manager at the Surrey Theatre for four successive seasons beginning in 1831 he was not appointed stage manager officially until 1833 (Surrey playbills).

Although she was assigned some solos and duets, the opportunity to watch and learn from famous guest ballerinas – Marie Taglioni, Pauline Duvernay and Fanny Elssler – was equally valuable. Unlike most of her colleagues, Anne Hill was given both speaking and mime roles, especially during the pantomime season. No longer in the first blush of youth, she was billed as Miss Cehill to camouflage her marital status whenever she played opposite her husband, as in the dual role of the heroine Alice and Columbine in the Christmas pantomime *Harlequin Guy Fawkes* (Clapp 1899: 151).

Although Anne Hill's career was flourishing once again and her son Barton was showing promise in children's parts, her husband's career seemed at a standstill. He was no longer stage manager at the Surrey, and at Covent Garden he played mostly secondary character roles. Again the Hills left for the provinces, where Charles Hill was better able to gain employment as a stage manager. In the fall of 1837 they were at Gloucester and its companion theatre at Cheltenham; Charles was stage manager and principal actor, and Anne was principal dancer. Although short-lived, the engagement gave her the opportunity to polish the new repertory that she had picked up at Covent Garden. The following season the Hills moved on to the Brighton Theatre Royal. The theatre management was in poor shape when they arrived, and things went from bad to worse over the next two years. Charles Hill was often ill, the performers went unpaid for weeks at a time and the hours were long. One actor stated in a letter: "The hard work is awful – 3 pieces a night 6 nights a week and a change of performance every evening – from 10 to 4 is the usual length of our rehearsals & what with the studying parts we have scarcely time to fold & direct a newspaper much less a letter" (quoted in Barker 1980: 31).

Nevertheless, Mrs. Hill threw herself into the venture, using the opportunity to expand her dancing and acting repertoire still further. She performed lead roles in *Jersey Girl*, *Grace Darling* and *The Dumb Girl of Genoa*, and she was Columbine in the Christmas pantomime. New dances – *Cracovienne* and *Pas Circasian* – were added to her growing repertoire. She trained the ballet corps and mounted new ballets. One of her most ambitious projects was the restaging of *The British Bayaderes* in November 1838. The East Indian dancer Amani had captivated audiences with her troupe of "Authentic Bayaderes," so much so that London's Adelphi Theatre mounted their own British version. Since Anne Hill had relatives working at the Adelphi, she made several visits to learn the ballet drama before restaging it in Brighton with herself in the principal role of the lead slave girl.

But her endeavours could not salvage the Brighton troupe as conditions deteriorated still further. In spite of her own popularity with both Brighton audiences and company members, her own benefit was ruined when the disgruntled band left the theatre after the overture to protest their unpaid salaries. Unable to pay the bills, the Hills and their two youngest children fled to America, leaving the acting manager E.T. Holmes in charge. Safely on his way, Mr. Hill sent a letter to Holmes informing him that he was seeking profitable engagements in America that would allow him to return to England to meet all his liabilities.[5]

Upon their arrival in America, Mrs. Hill was at the peak of her dancing ability, balancing considerable technical skill with a flair for interpretation. She had an extensive repertoire of popular divertissements and an engaging personal style which could enchant both the sophisticated theatregoer and the country farmer. Few writers give clear descriptions of her dancing, but some sense of her dance style and versatility can be gleaned from her repertoire. She often performed two very popular British dances – Sailor's hornpipe and Highland fling. Both dances required quick, sparkling footwork, precision, tiny beats, little springs and stamina. The gesturing legs were always kept below forty-five degrees, giving the dances a feeling of lightness coupled with modesty. Occasionally she performed one of the court dances that had continued since the seventeenth century – minuet, gavotte or allemand. In these elegant dances, which she often performed within the context of a specific play, erect carriage of the upper body was essential as well as the ability to execute controlled, slow movements in intricate patterns. She added to her repertoire regularly and was attracted especially to the divertissements associated with Fanny Elssler, which called on her dramatic powers. Anne Hill added the *Cachucha*, Elssler's most famous dance, to her own repertoire soon after it was introduced to London audiences; she performed it and other Spanish dances regularly throughout the remainder of her dancing career.[6] The French writer Théophile Gautier provides a tantalizing description of its creator in the dance:

> She comes forward in a basquine skirt of pink satin trimmed with wide flounces of black lace.... How charming she is, with her high comb, the rose at her ear, the fire in her eyes and her sparkling smile. At the tips of her rosy fingers the ebony castanets are aquiver. Now she springs forward and the resonant clatter of her castanets breaks out; she seems to shake down clusters of rhythm with her hands. How she twists! How she bends! What fire! What voluptuousness! What ardour! Her swooning arms flutter about her drooping head, her body curves back, her white shoulders almost brush the floor. What a charming moment! (quoted in Guest 1970: 75-76).

Anne Hill's husband was versatile also, moving easily from stage manager to major character roles. Most important for the success of their American adventure, they carried the stamp of stage experience in some of London's most revered theatres. The Hills hoped that their American venture would be short-lived and financially successful; instead the trip marked the beginning of long careers in America.

The Hills made their American debut at New York's Park Theatre in Morris Barnett's burletta, *Capers and Coronets*. Although Charles Hill had the

---

[5] Barton Hill remained in Brighton at the West Street Academy to complete his education (Clapp 1899: 151-52).

[6] The *Cachucha* was first performed in Paris in the full-length ballet *Le Diable Boiteux* on June 1, 1836, with Fanny Elssler in the lead role of Florinda. The divertissement was introduced to London by Pauline Duvernay several months later (Guest 1954: 72).

misfortune to replace the popular actor, Richings, Mrs. Hill fared better, with one reviewer stating she "was much his superior as an artiste, an excellent comedienne, doing a French character in broken English inimitably well, speaking the language like a native and dancing with exquisite grace and lightness. Youth and beauty only were required (and she was not very aged or very ugly) to have made her one of the most charming and effective, as she was one of the most versatile and useful actresses" (Ireland 1866: 335-36). She quickly became a favourite entr'acte dancer at the Park, delighting audiences particularly with her interpretation of Fanny Elssler's *Cracovienne*.[7] The divertissement was especially suited to Anne Hill's lively personality. *The London Times* provides a vivid description of the dance:

> There she comes with her little military jacket, and her soldier's cap, and her long plaited tails which dangle down her back, and her neat little boots, and the little brass heels which click so prettily to the music – and her *entrée* is a triumph! It is really a dance of character, the talents of the danseuse and the pantomimist being completely blended together. When she first bounds on it is as if she were springing with joy among a circle of admirers. She stops short, she assumes a military stiffness, but it is in the happiest spirit of irony. Now she seems only lazily beating time, and now she rushes along as if seized by the joy of the moment, and not knowing how to contain her delight. Then, when at the conclusion of the *pas* she trots along the lamps in that orderly fashion, and takes leave of the public in right military salute, the impression she conveys is unique (23 Mar. 1840).

In late autumn, *Masaniello* was revived especially for her to play the challenging role of the dumb girl Fenella. The part called on all her talents as a dancer, mime artist and dramatic actress. That winter, the Hills embarked on a tour of the East coast, which included appearances in Baltimore, Boston and Philadelphia. Not until the 1842-43 season did the Hills return to New York, this time to the less prestigious Bowery Theatre, but this engagement, like so many others, did not prove financially successful.

The Hills were persuaded to travel north to Montreal to join their friend John Nickinson's troupe at the Theatre Royal. The move marked the beginning of the most successful decade in their careers as mature artists. Again Mrs. Hill was singled out at their debut performance, with the Montreal *Gazette* declaring she was "the most graceful dancer we have seen for many a long year, and on every night of her appearance has astonished and delighted the lieges of Montreal by her charming performances on 'the light fantastic toe'" (30 June 1843). The French-language paper, *La Minerve* remarked, "Above all Mrs. Hill, both as a dancer and actress always ellicits applause ... Mrs. Hill is always exceedingly gracious and attractive" (6 July 1843; translation from the French by the author). Nickinson planned his seasons to appeal to both English and French audiences; a popular choice was *Capers*

---

[7] According to Guest (1970: 104-25) the complete ballet, *La Gipsy* including the *Cracovienne* divertissement was first produced in London. Two months later, on Sept. 26, 1839, Anne Hill added it to her own repertoire at the Brighton Theatre Royal. Elssler had made her American debut in the *Cracovienne* several months before Anne Hill arrived in America.

and Coronets, featuring Charles Hill as a French ballet dancer. Throughout the summer audiences were treated to a veritable feast of popular ballet divertissements by Mrs. Hill including *La Cachucha*, *Pas Espagnole* and another Elssler dance, *La Smolenska*, which was "a young girl's dream of love, beginning with a tremor of the feet which gradually spread to the whole body. Then, to a lively, bouncing rhythm, she darted, like some frightened animal....

Typical nineteenth-century building, Toronto.

In every movement there was an easy, voluptuous freedom" (Guest 1970: 116). On a few occasions, she even danced a variation from *La Sylphide*, a work usually performed by a more delicate, ethereal dancer than Anne Hill. Praise continued for her with the *Gazette* commenting that "Mrs. Charles Hill danced *El Jaleo de Xeres* with her usual grace, the audience testifying their gratification with a perfect shower of bouquets" (1 Aug. 1843).

Pleased with their Montreal reception, the Hills remained in Canada, recognizing that the community could not yet sustain a year-round professional company. Always an astute businesswoman, however, Mrs. Hill placed notices in both the *Gazette* and *La Minerve* before the end of the theatrical season, informing readers that "Mrs. Hill plans to open a dancing school for young ladies in this city." More extensive advertisements quickly followed:

> Dancing for Young Ladies. Mrs. Charles Hill, Professor and Teacher of Dancing and the Calisthenic Exercises. At the request of several Families, respectfully announces her intention of opening an ACADEMY for the above elegant accomplishments. Having conducted similar establishments in London, Bath, Cheltenham, and Newcastle-Upon-Tyne, with eminent success and unqualified satisfaction to her Pupils, their Parents and Friends, Mrs. Hill can confidently recommend her system for the speedy acquirement of excellence in every branch of BALLROOM DANCING.... The strictest attention paid to the deportment and address, by the practice of easy and graceful Calisthenic Exercises, as recommended by the first Medical men for expanding the chest, and improving the health and spirits (*Gazette* 26 July 1843).

By early August, she had rented a suitable building and within six months her young charges were ready to demonstrate their skills at a Public Ball in the New Saloon at the Theatre Royal (*Gazette* 4 Jan. 1844). The Hills' income was further supplemented by renting out the practice rooms to colleagues from the Theatre Royal for music lessons. The Hills remained in Montreal for two more seasons. Both were willing helpers of the local amateurs in their own theatricals, but professional work was extremely limited, especially after the demolition of the Theatre Royal in the spring of 1844.

With the Montreal venture looking decidedly less promising and restless for better theatrical opportunities, the entire Hill clan set out on an extensive tour of Canada West that included visits to border towns in the United States.[8] Their teenage children took an active part, Barton and Rosalie playing supporting roles, and younger son, Robert, who showed no inclination for acting, served as treasurer. Equipped with "a new and elegant Portable Vaudeville Theatre Painted expressly for him by Mr. James Lamb of the Montreal New Theatre Royal," the Hills visited towns both large and small – Woodstock, London, Chatham, Brantford, Paris, Galt, Guelph, Hamilton and Toronto (Cobourg *Star* 9 Aug. 1846). On the whole, audiences were enthusiastic, particularly as regards Mrs. Hill, with the Chatham *Gleaner* stating:

> The people of Chatham enjoyed the richest treat that they ever experienced in this place.... *Hasty Conclusions* had the effect of making every one in the theatre who witnessed the performance come to the hasty conclusion that as long as the Hills played in Chatham they would be duly appreciated and admired.... The Polka was deservedly encored, and that charming Danseuse, Mrs. Hill, vastly enchanted all.... A duet by Mr. C. Hill and his charming daughter was enthusiastically encored (22 Sept. 1846).

A travelling correspondent for the Hamilton *Spectator* also commented favourably that "as usual the dancing of Mrs. Hill was the chief feature, but the other performances were equally creditable." The same writer also included a review from the Galt *Courier:*

> A family of Theatrical performers named Hill made us a rapid visit this week, giving us two nights' amusement in Mr. Young's elegant new assembly room. We had been so long destitute of any public exhibition ... but the one thus presented to us in our destitution was not only excellent in its selection, but well played having all the advantage of novelty, taste, good costume, thorough stage management, and accurate knowledge of stage effect, the result could only be what it was, a couple of evenings of intense gratification and delight.... The dancing of Mrs. Hill was on all hands allowed to be exquisite, and the other performances exhibited genuine fun, humour or pathos with like intensity (quoted in *British Colonist* 2 Oct. 1846).

Late in the tour the Hills reached their final destination, Toronto. But after only a brief season, including a benefit for Mrs. Hill in which she was called on to encore her Highland fling, the Hills returned to their Montreal headquarters for the winter.

The following spring the Hills joined George Skerrett's theatrical troupe. Skerrett had managed Montreal's Olympic Theatre for two seasons and was slated to run the new Theatre Royal when it was completed later that summer.

---

[8] In spring 1846 Charles Hill combined a New York engagement at the Greenwich Theatre with meeting his eighteen-year-old son Barton, who had recently completed his education at the West Street Academy in Brighton, England (Clapp 1899: 151-52).

In the interim, Skerrett put together a touring company, with Charles Hill as stage manager, and headed for Toronto. Skerrett had played Toronto before, but this time he employed a new strategy of alternating weeks in Hamilton and Toronto. It was a strong stock company, with visiting stars and the enticement of two outstanding dancers: Mrs. Hill and a talented young American, Sallie St. Clair. The Toronto *Examiner* remarked that "the style of these ladies is widely divergent, but each has its claim to appreciation" (8 June 1847). Although both dancers scored personal triumphs, the season was another financial failure. After the 1847-48 Montreal season Skerrett disbanded his troupe.

With limited opportunities in Montreal, the Hills again struck out on an extensive tour to Canada West. They played Kingston to crowded houses; the *British Whig* reported that "they are highly accomplished comedians, and whatever they attempt is done with the greatest neatness. Their children are treading in the footsteps of their accomplished parents" (1 July 1848). Visits to Sackett's Harbor and Watertown followed, then the Hills worked the towns along the north shore of Lake Ontario – Belleville, Cobourg and Port Hope – reaching Hamilton by early September. Perhaps attempting to attract a more conservative public, Mrs. Hill was billed as "the unrivalled danseuse, [who] will introduce her chaste and elegant dances" (*Spectator* 27 Sept. 1848). The engagement culminated with a benefit performance in which Mrs. Hill again danced the Highland fling, always popular with the numerous Scottish audience members, in the farce *The Highland Reel* (*Spectator* 7 Oct. 1848).

The Hills continued their tour with an unfortunate trip across Lake Ontario to Rochester, then returned to Kingston for a short season with the Garrison Amateurs, culminating on January 9, 1849 in a "complimentary benefit to Mr. Charles Hill and his family, who have suffered greatly, both in body and purse, from the rascalities of the Rochester folks" (*British Whig* 15 Jan. 1849). While Mrs. Hill returned to Montreal to run her Dancing Academy, Charles and Rosalie went off to assist the amateur Brockville Thespian Society launch their first season.

That winter riots in Montreal over the passing of the Rebellion Losses Bill and street disturbances kept audiences away from the theatre. With no theatre work available, the Hills decided to cut their financial losses and move to Canada West. At first they may have intended to settle in Kingston; Barton, who had been working as a printer in Toronto, joined them there, and the family troupe was augmented by two singers from New York. Their son Barton's acting talent was clearly evident; the *British Whig* reported that "Mr. Barton Hill, who did 'Box' is rapidly improving in his profession, and bids fair one day to rival his father, who is really one of the best general actors left upon the English stage." The notice continues "Mrs. Hill was as pert and merry as usual, and Miss Rosalie looked and played as charmingly as ever" (6 July 1849). The Hills played Kingston through July and August, but a cholera epidemic kept audiences away, despite the patronage of John A. Macdonald.

In the fall the family settled in Toronto, for they had already tested the waters and found them favourable. The town's population was now 25,000 and the recent transfer of government from Montreal to Toronto promised further growth. As Toronto was a garrison town, both military and government officials would be likely to sponsor benefits and employ the Hills in their own amateur productions. The central location was also ideal for touring to the small towns in Canada West and to American cities such as Buffalo, Rochester and Cleveland. The Hills joined Charles Kemble Mason's newly formed theatrical company at the Royal Lyceum, a troupe composed mainly of performers who had been stranded when cholera had ravaged Toronto that summer. The new ensemble made its debut on September 25, in the popular farces, *The Honey Moon* and *The Young Widow*, starring the four Hills. Barton soon left for Pittsburgh to join another troupe as their romantic lead, but the remainder of the family stayed.

Following her usual practice, Mrs. Hill advertised the opening of her dance academy "during the Fall Season for all the Fashionable Ball-Room Dances including the Redowas, Celarius, Valse à Deux & Valse à Cinque Temps" (*British Colonist* 5 Oct. 1849). Around mid century, the ballroom repertoire was at its largest and most varied; anyone aspiring to society had to be an accomplished social dancer. Torontonians flocked to Anne Hill's new academy and she quickly procured a larger space. Her life, like that of most women in the theatre, was exhausting. Monday and Wednesday mornings, she taught adults; "juveniles" attended classes on Wednesday and Saturday afternoons. On Tuesday and Thursday afternoons, she taught at Madame Deslandes' Academy (*Globe* 18 Dec. 1849). She was also available to teach private families and to visit schools in either town or country. From time to time, she travelled to Hamilton by coach or steamer to conduct classes. In her few remaining daytime hours, she rehearsed new productions and her evenings were often consumed by performances in professional and amateur productions.

The 1849-50 season was particularly rich in dancing opportunities for Anne and Rosalie Hill. The Italian Ballet Company, starring Giovanna Ciocca, had performed several well-known ballets – *La Sylphide*, *Gitana* and *Giselle* – during their short Toronto season, and the Royal Lyceum's manager, Mason, capitalized on this new audience interest by mounting several works that called upon all the Hills' dancing skills. *The Fancy Dress Ball* consisted mostly of popular ballroom dances that had evolved in the mid-1840s: the Valse à Cinq Temps, the Bohemian Redowa and the Hungarian Polka. The production also served as an advertisement for Mrs. Hill's dancing academy, where many of the same dances were taught. The same bill included Joseph Coyne's farce *Lola Montez* with Mrs. Hill as the exotic and notorious Spanish dancer (*British Colonist* 5 Oct. 1849). This role called for her to perform a series of Spanish dances, in which she excelled. Other plays, including *Virginius*, *The Merchant of Venice* and *Rob Roy*, showed the Hills as fine dramatic players.

Mason gave up the Royal Lyceum and dismissed his players at the end of the season, but an amateur troupe was hastily assembled by T.B. DeWalden, a former member of Skerrett's company. Charles Hill was appointed stage manager, and he, Anne and Rosalie played many of the lead roles. The amateurs performed regularly, and their season featured a "Testimonial to Mr. DeWalden," which starred Mrs. Hill in one of her most famous roles in *The Whistler, or The Fate of the Lily of St. Leonards*. This was a part she had "sustained for more than 300 nights in the principal theatres in the United Kingdom" (*British Colonist* 22 Apr. 1850). Since professional engagements were limited, Charles Hill and young Rosalie undertook some touring to nearby small towns such as Barrie, Whitby and Peterborough. The Barrie *Magnet* billed their production as a "Serio-Comic Mono-Dramatic Lecture on the influence of Music, Dancing and the Drama ... interspersed with Historical and Biographical Anecdotes, English, Irish, Scotch, French and other national Serious and Comic Songs" (4 Apr. 1850).

In August 1850 the Royal Lyceum changed hands again, but the new manager, T.P. Besnard, engaged Mrs. Mossop from New York's Park Theatre and the three dancing Kendall sisters as his stars, and the Hills were relegated to secondary roles. At the close of the season, Charles Hill joined the National Theatre in Cincinnati, while the two women remained behind to run the academy, appearing periodically in amateur productions (Shortt 1982: 16). The following spring, Charles Hill rejoined Besnard's troupe for a final season with his family. Again minor stars were imported, and the Hills were used as supporting players in both serious dramatic works and lighthearted farces.

Ultimately, however, their Toronto venture failed. By July 1851 all four Hills were back in Montreal at Skerrett's tiny Bandbox Theatre, along with Olivia Crook, "a favourite singing comedienne and operatic artiste" whom Barton Hill had recently married. Both senior Hills were nearing fifty and Anne Hill's dancing days were over. Invariably resourceful, she had prepared well for that eventuality; she had expanded her acting range considerably during her years in Canada. Always a delicious soubrette and perky comedian, her dramatic range now included supporting roles in serious dramas. She moved easily from playing the comic servant girl, Lucy, in the farce *Young Widow* to the noble Lady Capulet in *Romeo and Juliet* to the Scottish Helen McGregor in *Rob Roy*.

The family troupe, however, was gradually dissolving. Barton Hill was already in steady demand as a leading man and went on to a successful career as a theatrical manager. Rosalie soon left the stage to marry and settle in Hamilton. Anne Hill spent the summer of 1851 in Montreal, reunited with her youngest son Robert, who had begun his own successful career as an accountant. In September she played a short engagement in Quebec City before joining her husband and son in Philadelphia (Wilson 1935: 692).

The senior Hills travelled widely in the 1850s, mostly in the United States, with occasional forays into Canada to visit their children, Robert and Rosalie, usually in conjunction with a brief theatrical engagement. In 1854-55 the Barton and Charles Hills were reunited in New Orleans, where they played at the Academy of Music. For the next three seasons, Anne Hill played various theatres managed by E.A. Marshall in Washington, New York and Philadelphia.

In November 1858 Charles and Anne Hill played a short season at Toronto's New City Theatre, Ontario Hall, then from 1859 to 1861 the Hills joined their son Barton Hill at the Holliday Street Theatre in Baltimore.

In 1862, during the American Civil War, the Hills returned to Montreal. Charles Hill found it increasingly difficult to obtain acting engagements and retired around 1866 on a pension from the American Dramatic Fund. He died September 23, 1874, at the age of seventy, at the home of his daughter Rosalie, in Jersey Heights, New Jersey. Around 1862, Mrs. Hill joined Buckland's company at the Montreal Theatre Royal, where she specialized in playing old women. In addition to her professional work, she continued her usual pattern of assisting local amateurs with their productions. Her last engagement was in 1890 with the Holman Opera Troupe. She died on December 4, 1890 of Bright's disease, at the home of her granddaughter in the village of St. Antoine near Montreal (*Clipper* 20 Dec. 1890).

During her many years in Canada, Anne Hill made an invaluable contribution to dance training and to the development of knowledgeable dance audiences. Her popular dance academy exposed many citizens to excellent ballroom dance instruction in addition to supporting her family. The quality of her ballroom instruction permitted many citizens in Toronto, Hamilton and Montreal to enter society confident of their dancing abilities and secure in the accompanying social graces. Some devotees, such as Toronto's Mr. Robertson, went on to open their own dancing schools. She gave fledgling dancers sufficient training to enable them to appear on stage in the corps, and possibly helped to establish dancing as an acceptable profession. In addition, her own performances educated audiences in the nuances of the ballet repertoire, ranging from traditional hornpipes and Highland flings to the ethereal sylph variations of the Romantic ballet.

Finally, she set an example of graciousness and respectability, which demonstrated that dancing was permissible in polite society. An announcement that appeared in the *Patriot* on May 27, 1851, encouraging readers to attend Mrs. Hill's final Toronto performance, gives valuable insight into her special contribution to Canadian theatre:

> Both in public and private life she has won the esteem of all, not merely by her grace and elegance and consequent success in this department, but also by her extreme good temper, good sense and kindness of disposition. As a performer her merits are well known; but the extent of her histrionic exertions in favour of others is known only to a few. If there be, on the part of the public, the real desire to reward as well as praise, Mrs. Hill's benefit ought indeed to be a bumper.

References

   Newspapers consulted between 1800 and 1890: *British Colonist* (Toronto), *British Whig* (Kingston), *Clipper* (New York), *Examiner* (Toronto), *Gazette* (Montreal), *Globe* (Toronto), *Magnet* (Barrie), *Patriot* (Toronto), *Spectator* (Hamilton), *Spirit of the Times* (New York), *Star* (Cobourg). Playbill collections were used extensively from the British Library, Theatre Museum, Victoria and Albert Museum, London; Metropolitan Toronto Reference Library, Toronto.

Barker, Kathleen. 1980. "The Decline and Rise of the Brighton Theatre 1840-1860." *Nineteenth Century Theatre Research* 8: 1, 29-51.

Chaffee, George. 1943. "The Romantic Ballet in London: 1824-1858." *Dance Index* 11: 9-12, 120-67.

Clapp, John B. and Edwin F. Edgett. 1899. *Players of the Present*. Reprint New York: Benjamin Blom, 1969.

Conroy, Patricia. 1965. "A History of Theatre in Montreal Prior to Confederation." Master's thesis, McGill University.

Disher, M. Willson, ed. 1934. *The Cowells in America: Being the Diary of Mrs. Sam Cowell*. London: Oxford University Press.

Findlater, Richard, ed. 1853. *Memoirs of Joe Grimaldi, by Charles Dickens*. Reprint London: MacGibbon and Kee, 1968.

Graham, Franklin. 1897. *Histrionic Montreal: Annals of the Montreal Stage*. Reprint New York: Benjamin Blom, 1969.

Guest, Ivor. 1954. *The Romantic Ballet in England*. Reprint London: Pitman, 1974.

Guest, Ivor. 1970. *Fanny Elssler*. London: Adam and Charles Black.

Highfill, Philip. 1978. *A Biographical Dictionary of Actors, Actresses, Musicians, Dancers, Managers, and other Stage Personnel in London, 1660-1800*. Vol. 5. Carbondale: Southern University Press.

Ireland, Joseph N. 1866. *Records of the New York Stage from 1750 to 1860*. 2 vols. Reprint New York: Benjamin Blom, 1966.

Kendall, John S. 1968. *The Golden Age of the New Orleans Theatre*. New York: Greenwood Press.

Shortt, Mary. 1982. "Touring Theatrical Families in Canada West: the Hills and the Herons." *Ontario History* 74: 1, 7-25.

Smith, Solomon Franklin. 1868. *Theatrical Management in the West and South for Thirty Years*. Reprint New York: Benjamin Blom, 1968.

Wemyss, Francis C. 1852. *Chronology of the American Stage from 1752-1852*. Reprint New York: Benjamin Blom, 1968.

Wilson, Arthur H. 1935. *A History of the Philadelphia Theatre, 1835 to 1855*. Reprint New York: Greenwood Press, 1968.

Professor John Freeman Davis:
Nineteenth-Century Dancing Master

Kathryn Noxon

Professor John Freeman Davis (ca. 1835-1916), a pioneer of Canadian culture and a talented composer, devoted many years of his life to the art of social dance.[1] His career brings focus to the period between Confederation in 1867 and 1900, which were important years for Toronto. As a musician Davis composed pieces for social dancing, and as a dancing master Davis was an accomplished teacher who also published his own dance manual. These achievements allowed him to hold a respected position within society, although his name and contributions to dance and music are not widely remembered today. Throughout his working life, he was able to base his long-term success on insight into the popular tastes of the day, and he survived in the arts by calling on his multiple talents during a time of rapid social change and growth. His ability to fill two public needs, meeting the growing demand for sheet music and teaching people the latest and most popular dances, were his main accomplishments.

Davis was born in Oakville, Ontario, a small town situated between Hamilton and Toronto. Originally from Belleville, Ontario, his father Charles Davis was one of the first shoemakers in the town of Oakville, where he established his business in the 1830s (Mathews 1953: 68, 408). His mother, Eliza Rose, died when John was still an infant and so he was raised by his father's second wife, Mary Ray (Davis Dyk 26 Feb. 1985). As part of his early education, Davis attended the Gore District Grammar School in Hamilton, the same school attended by educator Egerton Ryerson. Attendance at the school allowed him to get away from his many half-siblings, and gave him a solid academic training that formed the base of his "liberal education" (Adam, *Toronto Old and New* 1891: 139). According to local historian Mercer Adam, a liberal education was defined at that time as an education fit for a gentleman which led to the general enlargement of the mind. Although Charles Davis owned considerable land, there is no indication that his son studied music in Europe or even the United States. He probably received his musical training from a member of his family or he may have been self taught.

Biographical information on John Freeman Davis' early life in Oakville is not available, but his later years and the lives of his "dancing family" are well documented. According to Mercer Adam, he went to Toronto in 1855 and

---

[1] Much of the biographical information in this essay is based on an interview with Carolyn Davis Dyk, the great great granddaughter of John Freeman Davis. I wish to thank Ms. Davis Dyk for generously sharing her knowledge and material on the Davis family.

John Freeman Davis.

married his first wife, Ruth Ann Cunnyworth in 1860 (1891: 139). Their fourteen-year marriage produced six children. The eldest son, Charles Freeman Davis (1863-1928) later became a Toronto dancing master in his own right. Charles ran away from home at the age of thirteen to live with an aunt in the Buffalo area near the Erie Canal. After enlisting in the U.S. Navy, and pursuing various endeavours, he settled in Kansas City, where he married Martha Jane Piper. Following severe losses in a fire, his father arranged for the couple's return to Toronto in 1887. Charles began assisting at his father's dancing school, but within two years he opened his own school, the West End Academy, in direct competition with his father. Charles' dancing academy continued for over thirty-five years. After Ruth's death, John Freeman Davis was married a second time in 1876, to Sarah Keys. Around the turn of the century, his wife Sarah and, later, two of their children, Elsie and Albert, began assisting at the Davis School of Dancing. His wife and children kept the school going after his death in 1916.

In the 1850s when Davis arrived in Toronto, the city was becoming more interested in music and there was a growing demand for musicians to play in local bands for concerts and other social events. Foreseeing the growing prosperity of Toronto, the "Queen City of the West," Davis left Oakville and settled in Toronto at the age of twenty. He established his school of dancing as early as 1859, just four years after arriving in Toronto (*Toronto City Directory* 1894). Though there is no conclusive evidence, his association with dance may have begun at that time as a musician for local dances, as an accompanist for dance classes or as a dance pupil. It is probable that his musical career led to his dancing profession, but his dance teaching career was not firmly established until the 1870s.

Several books written about Toronto dealing with the last half of the nineteenth century provide an impressive image of the young city. Historian Arthur Lower states in *Canadians in the Making* that "Toronto was western, new, energetic, optimistic and equipped with all the talents" necessary to make it one of the "most orderly, well-governed, moral, highly civilized towns on the continent" with its "high concentration [of] business ... religious and educational activity." Toronto was a bubbling centre of expansion and growth in the

50

late nineteenth century. After Confederation in 1867, the city changed at an amazing rate and by the end of the century there were paved streets, streetcars, electricity, Massey Hall and department stores such as Eaton's and Simpson's. This rapid expansion meant financial growth, especially for the middle and upper classes. During this time there was a surge in the arts, and the growing population took an increasingly active interest in music, dance and theatre. Affluent members of society often learned social etiquette, music, dancing, singing and drawing through an acceptable school or with one of the many new private instructors in the city (Lower 1958: 306-7).

In the nineteenth century, according to music historian Helmut Kallmann, many struggling musicians left Canada for the United States or in frustration turned "to more lucrative trades" (1960: 122). It appeared that Davis would do the same. During this time, he dabbled in various occupations such as oyster dealer, fruit dealer and tobacconist (*Toronto City Directories* 1868-1872). After this slight wavering, Davis never looked back, for his knowledge of music allowed him to expand and diversify his horizons in order to survive as an artist. Like other Canadian musicians of the time, Davis composed sporadically (Logan 1913: 487). Though he did not become an internationally known composer, he had a considerable reputation in Toronto, Oakville and Hamilton. His music was popular enough to allow him to compose and publish works for local use for almost twenty-five years. The increased interest in music and musical education made it possible to compose popular pieces of music that ensured a small financial return (Ford 1982: 61). Between the years 1873 and 1896 Davis wrote several musical scores consisting of "polkas, lancers, rockaways, waltzes, two-steps, and other dances published by Nordheimer, Claxton, Whaley Royce, and Davis" (Kallmann 1981: 256). During this time "the bulk of the published Canadian music consisted of music in the patriotic and so-called light or popular vein – marches, galops, waltzes, quadrilles, and songs which were turned out in great numbers by amateurs as well as musicians specializing in this type of music" (Kallmann 1960: 258).

In 1873 Davis opened a music store at 177 Yonge Street called The Musical Hall.[2] He ran the store for only two years but it was a productive time for him musically (Kallmann 1981: 256). During these two years he published his first three pieces of music written for the piano, the favoured instrument of the era (Ford 1982: 60). In 1873 he published the "Great Pacific Lancers" and the "Eureka Quadrille." The third piece, the "New Premier Galop" (1874) became one of his most famous works. The "Eureka Quadrille," written for the Victoria Dancing Assembly, came with dance instructions.[3] These musical pieces indicate Davis' interest in and knowledge of dancing. This sheet music, typical

---

[2] Davis may have opened his store first at 316 Yonge Street, but within a few months it moved to 177 Yonge Street. Information on the name the Musical Hall comes from a page of advertising attached to Davis' sheet music for the "Great Pacific Lancers." Many of Davis' compositions are available on microfilm at the Metropolitan Toronto Reference Library.

[3] Other examples of Davis' musical compositions include: "The Prairie Settlers' Song" (1882), "The Call to Arms Polka" (1885), "La Frolique" (1885), "A Corker Bicycle Song" (1895) and "The Lawn Tennis Dance" (1889).

of the type of music then being produced and published, was of the "short, popular song or dance type" and was inexpensive to print (Ford 1982: 57-58). Advertising was usually included, which gave Davis the opportunity to

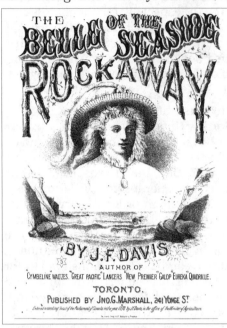

proclaim himself composer, publisher and owner of a store that dealt in "Piano-Fortes, Organs, Melodeons, Violins, Band Instruments of all Kinds, Foreign and American Sheet Music and Music Books, Instruction Books, &c." Davis also composed "Cymbeline Waltzes" (1877), "Belle of the Seaside Rockaway" (1878), "My Pupils' Favorite Jersey" (1883), "Romanisca" (1887), "The Jersey Ripple" and "Gavotte Lancer" (undated). Often "compositions [were] written to celebrate some social or political event" (Logan 1913: 487). The "New Premier Galop" (1874), for example, was written as a tribute to the Honourable Alexander MacKenzie and the "New Premier Two-Step Jersey Caprice or Cycle (New Dance)" (1896) honoured the Prime Minister Wilfred Laurier.

Dancing masters of the late nineteenth century taught men, women and children of the middle and upper classes. Knowledge of the most popular and fashionable dances was of prime importance, but dancing masters offered much more. As custodians of social mores, dancing masters taught etiquette and deportment, for the art of dancing included the important ability to conduct oneself properly at a ball or other social events. They also frequently taught gymnastics and calisthenics for health and stamina. Davis recognized the potential for dancing teachers to fulfill all of these functions as Toronto expanded socially and culturally. By 1875, buoyed with the success of his first three pieces of dance music, Davis began advertising in Toronto newspapers and Toronto city directories as a teacher of dancing. His original school called the Fashion Hall Dancing Academy was located on Adelaide Street East (*Toronto City Directory* 1876).

In 1878, at the age of forty-three, Davis published his first and only dance manual, *The Modern Dance Tutor; or, Society Dancing*. A typical instruction book of the nineteenth century, it emphasized etiquette and deportment, along with detailed explanations of the steps and figures for the dances popular at the time. His manual was a straightforward, no-nonsense guide to social behaviour, good manners and technical dance instructions. The contents are listed as: "Descriptions of all the Latest Fashionable and Popular Dances, viz:–'2 Step Rockaway,' '3 Step Rockaway,' '4 Step Rockaway,' 'Glide' Waltz, and 'Triune' Glide; also, Grand Square in the Lancers." This tiny book, measuring approximately five by five-and-one-half inches, was seventy pages in length and was published in Toronto by Hawkins & Co., Chromatic Steam Printers.

The title page of *The Modern Dance Tutor* tells the reader that Davis had a private academy at 80 Wilton Avenue, Toronto, Ontario, Canada. Davis respectfully dedicates the book "to the Six Thousand and Odd Pupils, who have received instructions from me during the past eighteen years." Here again Davis suggests that his school began around 1859 or 1860. In the one-page preface, addressed to the public, Davis modesty indicates that other authors were "freely consulted, especially in the matter of etiquette and deportment," without mentioning them by name. In this preface, Davis writes that his format for conveying information in his dance manual is original, and he compares it to a "catechism." He also mentions that it is the first book to contain descriptions of the rockaways and triune glide and the latest changes to lancers and quadrilles. For beginners in dance, Davis recommends the aid of a master in learning the rudiments of the art. Davis follows with a three-page introduction which extols the virtues of dance for exercise and enjoyment for all ages.

The manual contains five illustrations. The first shows four squares to demonstrate the positions of the four couples when performing a grand square in the quadrille (31). The second is a figure drawing showing four couples positioned for quadrilles (33). The next two line drawings demonstrate elements of timing for the polka and the glide waltz respectively (48 and 52). The last illustration is a detailed "Waltz Diagram for Learners" (56). Davis also includes a chart entitled "Diagram, or Scale Showing The Different Kinds Of Dances Suitable To The Various Kinds Of Dance Music" (66).

POSITION IN QUADRILLES.

Illustration of the positions for four couples for a quadrille from Davis' book *The Modern Dance Tutor*, 1878.

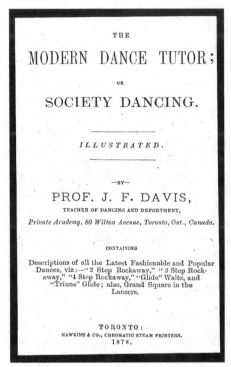

THE

MODERN DANCE TUTOR;

OR

SOCIETY DANCING.

ILLUSTRATED.

—BY—

PROF. J. F. DAVIS,

TEACHER OF DANCING AND DEPORTMENT,

Private Academy, 80 Wilton Avenue, Toronto, Ont., Canada.

CONTAINING

Descriptions of all the Latest Fashionable and Popular Dances, viz :—"2 Step Rockaway," "3 Step Rockaway," "4 Step Rockaway," "Glide" Waltz, and "Triune" Glide; also, Grand Square in the Lancers.

TORONTO:

HAWKINS & CO., CHROMATIC STEAM PRINTERS.
1878.

The main text of the book emphasizes social etiquette and deportment necessary for giving or attending a grand ball or evening party. Information is given in the format of questions and answers. Following this section the book gives dance instructions beginning with the basic five positions of the feet, and how to bow and courtesy. Next, instructions are given for the various dances like quadrilles, lancers, polkas, glides and rockaways including some musical information. Davis concludes with recommendations for improving one's dance style. The last pages in the book promote his private dancing academy and list his latest published dance music.

His booklet and others written in the era such as John Hart's *Canadian Ten Cent Ballroom Companion and Guide to Dancing* are excellent sources of information on contemporary social behaviour and attitudes as well as Canadian social dances of the time (Hart 1871). In Davis' opinion *The Modern Dance Tutor*, selling for only forty cents, surpassed all others (*Globe* advertisement 28 Nov. 1879).

The Modern Dance Tutor was a stabilizing factor in Davis' career. The manual would have increased his reputation and status as a teacher of dance, not only with the public but also with his peers in Toronto and elsewhere, notably in the United States and England. In his advertisements in following years, we see Davis claiming that he is capable of dealing with every aspect of his profession. In the *Globe* newspaper in 1879, Davis announced his reopening for the season as follows: "after great demand; for 18 years, he has taught dance and is known as the top waltz, glide, and general dance instructor of Toronto; his aim to give lessons theoretically and practically in the shortest time possible, though with greatest knowledge" (1 Jan. 1879). A review of his book stated that it is a "wonderful little book which includes 'mysteries' of grand balls, evening parties, the bow, the curtsey, the glide, the Boston, and the grand square; the style entirely the profs own! Alas for Fanning!" (*Globe* 6 Jan. 1879). Brose Fanning formerly taught dancing in Ottawa under the patronage of the Governor General.

Davis' musicality helped him teach timing and rhythm, and the combination of his abilities in music and dance gave him an edge over his competitors. In 1878, in one of his advertisements, Davis boasted of his knowledge of many of the latest dances, and claimed that he could teach eleven dances in six weeks. Some of these dances included the triune glide, Boston glide, New York glide, rockaway, polka, redowa, quadrille and lancers (*Globe* 2 Nov. 1878). He proudly quoted one of his admirers as saying, "I really think he can make a stick dance" (*Globe* 1 Feb. 1879). Davis took this as a generous but well-deserved compliment.

It appears that Davis ran a very successful dance academy for over forty years, and had a satisfying career in music and dance for over half a century. According to many advertisements Davis placed in the *Globe*, he was a popular teacher, continually boasting of the number of pupils he had taught and claiming to be Toronto's favourite teacher. He was the dancing teacher at the principal "Ladies' Schools" in Toronto and one in Hamilton. He also taught at several private residences in both cities, including that of Lieutenant-Governor Macdonald (*Globe* 1 Oct. 1880). Davis' success may be attributed to his method of teaching which stressed a simplified system, along with his abilities as a teacher.

There is evidence that Davis also taught stage dancing, not a common practice at that time in Toronto. From 1877 to 1879 and again in 1888, Davis' academy was located in the Grand Opera House building on Adelaide Street West (*Toronto City Directories* 1877-88). It was a prestigious location giving Davis ready access to any actresses, actors and other entertainers wanting to learn social or stage dancing. Teaching stage dancing to theatrical personalities would in turn have helped spread his reputation. In 1894, Davis still claimed to be a "Teacher of Artistic Society and Stage Dancing," though he was no longer located at the Opera House, but at Wilton Avenue (*Toronto City Directory* 1894).

Though the title "Professor" was commonly adopted by dancing masters of the time, it appears that in Davis' case he had good reason to use the title. One of his death notices states: "He held diplomas and certificates from the National American Dancing Association, the United Professional Teachers Dancing Academy, Western Association Normal School Masters of Dancing, and in 1900, at sixty-five years of age, he was awarded the Grand Prize Diploma of the Paris Universal Exhibition" (Davis Dyk 1985). Davis was strongly affiliated with these dance associations. In 1891, he attended the eighth annual convention of the National Association of Teachers of Dancing of the United States and Canada, held at Providence, New Jersey, from June 9 to 12. The conventions allowed dancing masters to set standards concerning such issues as "position of the feet, arms, hands, &c., preparatory exercises, attitudes, steps and movements." At this particular convention Davis submitted a new dance for approval called the "Curio," a polonaise and gavotte. The "Curio" was approved (Crompton 1984: 29). In 1888 Davis became vice-president of the American National Dancing Association and in 1894 vice-president of the National Association of Teachers of Dancing of the United States and Canada (Davis Dyk 1985).

Mercer G. Adam, in *Toronto: Old and New*, credited Davis with being "originator of a number of popular dances, including the Jersey Ripple, Le

Bronco [sic], Eureka, Gavotte Lancers and others; composer of 'fancy dances' for 'kermesses'; instructor of instrumental music, calisthenics and dancing, and inventor of 'a method by which the acquisition of new dances is greatly simplified'" (139). Clearly, recognition in this book affirmed Davis' social status in the community, for those Torontonians he listed had established "reputations, and fixed places in the society they themselves had built" (Lower 1958: 307). Davis was the only dancing master to be included.

Professor John Freeman Davis, composer and dancing master, can certainly be acknowledged for his contributions to his community and its arts. Davis' chosen profession allowed him many years of productive service to his community. Living and working in his chosen city, Toronto, he established a solid reputation and position amongst his fellow Torontonians as well as nationally and internationally. At his death in 1916, his academy was the oldest in the city. The Davis family continued to carry on the dance tradition. With the help of his wife Sarah and their two children, Elsie and Albert, the Davis School of Dancing was able to continue teaching social dancing using the Davis method for many years after his death. His son, Charles Freeman Davis, an established dancing master in Toronto for over thirty years, further demonstrated the enduring Davis spirit and commitment to the arts. Davis and his family helped build early Toronto society and its culture by encouraging and teaching social dancing, thus contributing to the Canadian dance heritage.

References

The *Globe* (Toronto) was consulted for the years 1877 to 1881. Also consulted were the *Toronto City Directories* (1868, 1872, 1873, 1876, 1877, 1879, 1888, 1894), and the John F. Davis Sheet Music Collection on microfilm at the Metropolitan Toronto Reference Library.

Adam, G. Mercer. 1891. *Illustrated Toronto: The Queen City of the West*. Toronto: J. McConnitt.

Adam, G. Mercer. 1891. *Toronto, Old and New: a Memorial Volume Historical, Descriptive and Pictorial ... With Some Sketches of the Men Who Have Made or Are Making the Provincial Capital*. Reprint Toronto: Coles Publishing Co., 1972.

Crompton, Robert M. 1984. *Dancing: A Journal Devoted to the Terpsichorean Art, Physical Culture and Fashionable Entertainments*. Reprint Toronto: Press of Terpsichore Limited.

Davis, John F. 1878. *The Modern Dance Tutor; or Society Dancing*. Toronto: Hawkins & Co.

Ford, Clifford. 1982. *Canada's Music: An Historical Survey*. Agincourt, Ont.: GLC Publishers Limited.

Hart, John. 1871. *Canadian Ten Cent Ball Room Companion and Guide to Dancing*. Toronto: Wm. Warwick.

"John Freeman Davis." 1992. *Encyclopedia of Music in Canada*. 2nd ed. Toronto: University of Toronto Press.

Kallmann, Helmut. 1960. *A History of Music in Canada 1534-1914*. Toronto: University of Toronto Press.

Logan, John D. Sept. 1913. "Canadian Creative Composers." *Canadian Magazine* 41, 486-94.

Lower, Arthur R. M. 1958. *Canadians in the Making: A Social History of Canada*. Don Mills: Longmans Canada Limited.

Mathews, Hazel C. 1953. *Oakville and the Sixteen: The History of an Ontario Port*. Toronto: University of Toronto Press.

Interview
Davis Dyk, Carolyn. 26 Feb. 1985.

Toronto Armouries, site of the Victorian Era Ball.

The Victorian Era Ball

Janet Wason

"The greatest function ever held in the social life of Canada," trumpeted the *Globe* (29 Dec. 1897). "The most brilliant social function given in Toronto since the famous Dufferin ball," cried the *Star* (29 Dec. 1897). In a more restrained yet equally laudatory vein, the *Mail and Empire* reported, "The event that took place last night ... eclipsed all previous efforts of its kind, and it must rank in Canada as a historic incident" (29 Dec. 1897).

The event which aroused so much enthusiasm in the Toronto newspapers was the Victorian Era Ball, the fancy dress ball which was held in Toronto on December 28, 1897, as the city's final celebration of Queen Victoria's Diamond Jubilee. Its main feature was a brilliant spectacle with six large groups, costumed to depict various aspects of Victoria's reign, performing historical dances such as the Lancers, Old-fashioned Quadrille and other square or figure dances. The groups in turn represented The Empire, Victorian Costumes, Literature and Music, Science and Inventions, Art, and Sports and Amusements. Over 400 guests took part in the three-hour performance, with 2000 other invited guests, many of whom were also in costume, sitting in galleries around the room. After a midnight supper there was dancing for all. This took the form of the current dances, which, with the exception of a single Lancers, were all couple dances such as waltzes, two-steps and polkas.[1]

I first found out about the ball when I came upon the commemorative album while browsing in the John Robarts Library at the University of Toronto. Designed as a souvenir of the performance rather than an accurate record, the *Book of The Victorian Era Ball Given at Toronto on the Twenty Eighth Day of December MDCCCXCVII* contains fifty-one pages of drawings of ladies and gentlemen in their historical, symbolic or fanciful costumes. These individual and group portraits captured the excitement the ball engendered among the people of Toronto and started me on my quest to discover more about this spectacular event. I was to find extensive contemporary documentation, enough to draw a comprehensive picture of the ball and add to our knowledge of social dance practices in late-nineteenth-century Toronto.

The introduction to the album indicates that the motivation for this ball went beyond mere social entertainment. The editor was James Mavor, a professor of political economy at the University of Toronto, who, in addition to

---

[1] A copy of the dance programme for the Victorian Era Ball is included in the Aberdeen Papers (Vol. 12: Lady Aberdeen's Journal, 1898-1899) at the Public Archives in Ottawa. The programme lists the order of the performance on the left side and the general dances on the right.

his work in politics, enthusiastically promoted art and literature. His purpose in compiling the book was to give Canadian artists an outlet for their work, for, as he wrote, "the growth in Canada, and especially in Toronto, of a large group of artists ... is so recent that its existence has, perhaps, hardly been suspected" (unpaginated [v]).[2] Proceeds from the sale of the book were to go to a worthy cause, to the fund for the establishment of the Victorian Order of Nurses.

The album embodied a civic interest which echoed discussions about the ball in the local press the previous year. Further research confirmed that this dance event was indeed used for a variety of political and social purposes. My intent here is two-fold: using the available sources, I give as full a documentation of the dance event as possible, from the earliest preparations through to the ball itself. I also attempt to identify the impact of the ball on various levels of Toronto's society as seen through contemporary eyes.

Overall, the commemorative album was an excellent starting place for my research, since the text yielded vital information such as the date and place of the event, the nature of the central performance, the names of the participants and the characters they played and, most importantly, the name of the organizer, Lady Ishbel Aberdeen. Armed with this information I then searched the Toronto newspapers, notably the extensive social columns in the *Globe* and *Saturday Night*, for descriptions of the ball. The wealth of information was truly astounding, for the papers avidly followed the ball's progress during the five weeks after the first announcement of this "ball of unique character" appeared in the *Globe* on November 17, 1897. The social columns kept Toronto informed as arrangements were finalized, or fanned curiosity with hints about the exciting new dances and costumes. Alongside such lighter matters, the newspapers also printed a few articles describing the benefit the ball could bring Toronto's businesses.

Lady Aberdeen, wife of the Earl of Aberdeen (Canada's Governor General from 1893 to 1898), was an acute observer who recorded her activities for the reading pleasure of relatives in Britain. Her journals contain her motives for holding the ball and details of its preparation. The journals were edited and published by John Saywell as *The Canadian Journal of Lady Aberdeen, 1893-1898* (1960). Her original manuscript includes a photograph of her daughter Marjorie, in costume, and a copy of the dance programme. Lady Aberdeen's scrapbooks contain pertinent clippings, culled from a large number of newspapers.[3]

Taken together, contemporary descriptions paint a vivid and almost complete picture of the Victorian Era Ball and its background. Noticeably absent are descriptions of the old-fashioned dances which constituted the main performance and any information on the orchestra. However, while

---

[2] Among the seventeen artists included were E. Wyly Grier, Farquhar McGillivray Knowles and Beatrice Sullivan.

[3] See the Aberdeen Papers (Vol. 27: Newspaper Clippings, Nov. 1897-Feb. 1898).

twentieth-century dance historians may yearn for details about the dancing itself, contemporary observers were more concerned with the visual aspects of the ball, such as the beauty and originality of the costumes and the symbolism behind the decorations. The only dance description I found was that of the march, which contained obvious symbolic designs in the floor patterns, but to date we remain ignorant of the precise structure of the other dances. Consequently, we can only speculate that in all likelihood the choreography of the dances reinforced the themes of the ball in ways similar to those of the costumes and decorations.

Fancy Dress Balls During Victoria's Era

The Victorian Era Ball followed in the popular tradition of fancy dress balls with the performance of old-fashioned dances. Books such as Ardern Holt's *Fancy Dresses Described or What to Wear at Fancy Balls* (1884) provide ideas for costumes and suggestions for specially arranged dances such as a hunting quadrille, in which the dancers might appear wearing the hunting dress of an earlier period. Indeed, Lady Aberdeen's choice of a lavish fancy dress ball was an appropriate way to celebrate the Diamond Jubilee, for in her early years as monarch Victoria herself used such balls as a means of reinforcing British identity. Soon after she came to the British throne, Victoria followed in the footsteps of her Tudor and Stuart ancestors, reviving the tradition of royal entertainments. Between the years of 1842 and 1851, she gave three costume balls designed to be "not only glittering spectacles and illustrations of the history of the country, but also opportunities of employment for the half-starving working classes" (Finkel 1984: 64).

Two thousand members of the aristocracy were invited to the first Bal Costumé which was held on May 12, 1842 at Buckingham Palace. The chosen theme was fourteenth-century England during the reign of Edward III (portrayed by Prince Albert) and his consort Phillipa of Hainault (portrayed by Queen Victoria). As added entertainment, over 100 of the elite of the aristocracy had organized themselves into four groups or quadrilles. Each quadrille was designed around a theme such as the fashions of the French court and each was headed by a lady prominent in the fashionable world. A souvenir book was published to mark the grand occasion. This format of select members costumed according to a central theme and performing for their peers was to be repeated at fancy dress balls throughout the century, as it was at the Victorian Era Ball. As we shall see, Lady Aberdeen's motives and methods followed the best Victorian traditions when she organized her ball over fifty years later.

Victoria's Bal Costumé was so successful that three years later she offered a second one, Le Bal Poudré, which featured the decades of the 1740s and 1750s, during the reign of George III. For the third Bal Costumé in June 1851, Victoria chose to revive the Britain of the 1660s and 1670s, the time of the Restoration of Charles II. After this last event, royal interest in historical revivals of the glorious past waned, possibly because England faced growing prosperity and a brilliant future.

By 1897 Victoria had reigned over the British Empire for sixty years. Her Diamond Jubilee was celebrated throughout the year. London thronged with loyal subjects who came from all over the world to pay homage to the Queen. The excitement generated by this momentous occasion gave rise to all kinds of elaborate parties. Costume balls had remained a fashionable and popular entertainment, and so when the Duchess of Devonshire, a leading member of the aristocracy, wished to add to the celebrations, she chose to make her grand ball "fancy dress" (Murphy 1984: 47). The theme of the Devonshire House Ball was allegorical or historical costume before 1815. As in Victoria's first Bal Costumé, some of the guests formed themselves into groups organized around a central idea such as Queen Guinevere and the knights of the Round Table. Lady Aberdeen may have known of this lavish tribute to Victoria and may very well have created her own Canadian ball to rival or even surpass the British offering.

Toronto itself was no stranger to fashionable amusements. While the nation of Canada was only thirty years old in 1897, the city of Toronto had been established for over 100 years. York, as it was known to its first English settlers, was "from the first the abode of the most cultured and aristocratic society of the new Province" (Mulvaney 1884: 116). Included in this society's diversions were costume balls, such as the one given by Mr. Galt, Commissioner of the Canada Land Company, and Lady Mary Willis in 1827. The Dufferin Ball mentioned by the *Star* at the beginning of this paper was the fancy dress ball given by the Governor General, the Earl of Dufferin, in Ottawa in 1876. It was such a success that it was cited as the epitome of social events by a generation of party-goers. The Victorian Era Ball, however, far outstripped any other fancy dress ball in the cohesiveness of its conception and the magnificence of its theme.

Ishbel Aberdeen and Preparations for the Ball

Governor General and Lady Aberdeen took their position as Victoria's representatives very seriously, actively participating in many areas of Canadian life.[4] They accomplished this in one way by setting up house for a few weeks in each of the provincial capitals, giving entertainments of their own, at which they could meet a broader spectrum of Canadian society than they could in Ottawa. The Victorian Era Ball was held during the Aberdeen's temporary residence in Toronto.

Lady Aberdeen had a history of using social occasions for political and other purposes. For example, during Lord Aberdeen's service as Lord Lieutenant of Ireland in 1886, she held a ball at which an Irish jig was performed and all the guests were required to wear clothes made of Irish material (Saywell 1960: xx). In Ottawa in 1896, she mounted a Historical Fancy Dress

---

[4] Among Lady Aberdeen's accomplishments were the establishment of the Victorian Order of Nurses and the formation of a Canadian branch of the National Council of Women.

Lord and Lady Aberdeen with their entourage as they appeared on the night of the ball. Lady Aberdeen's gown is of royal blue velvet, the petticoat of cream Irish poplin, embroidered with gold in a Celtic design, and her train is lined with crimson satin. Drawing by George A. Reid.

Ball in order (as she writes February 3, 1896) to "divert Ottawa gossip at least into past times away from ... the everlasting discussion of hockey and winter sports varied with Ottawa society scandal" (Saywell 1960: 317). According to the *Book of the Victorian Era Ball*, Lady Aberdeen's purpose in holding it, besides the obvious celebration of the Jubilee, was to give social life in Canada the same flair possessed by other parts of the Empire and also to provide intellectual stimulation. She had been told that a big ball would give more pleasure to the people of Toronto than anything else, and she therefore searched for an appropriate theme: "[A] great big Ball to which all the world and his wife is asked seems always a meaningless & ponderous affair the main features of which are its size & its supper. Then a Fancy Dress Ball without any central idea has too much of the Carnival about it.... Canadian History had been the pivot of our Historical Ball at Ottawa & of our Dramatic scenes at Montreal & so we must have something different" (Saywell 1960: 446).

Lady Aberdeen borrowed her idea for the ball from a pamphlet by a Mrs. Archibald of Halifax on "Victorian Era Parties."[5] George Robert Parkin, the principal of Upper Canada College, suggested that the ball portray achievements in the Victorian era rather than each of the six decades as she had originally planned. This modified idea was greeted with enthusiasm by the

---

[5] I have been unable to locate this work. Information from the card catalogue at the Metropolitan Toronto Library suggests that Mrs. Archibald was a member of the Nova Scotia Historical Society.

"Toronto great ladies," as she called them, in their first meeting on November 18, 1897, only five weeks before the ball.[6] In fact, there was so much interest that instead of there being only one dance to illustrate each period, there had to be four or five included in each, so that more people could take part. Each group was therefore divided into four or five sets of sixteen people, corresponding to the number of couples in a double set of a figure dance. Each set was placed in the charge of a lady who was responsible for choosing her dancers, and organizing and rehearsing the dance. The careful organization by Lady Aberdeen and her committee contributed much to the ball's success.

I have found little information on the preparations for the dances; however, one newspaper does mention that rehearsals for Mrs. Cawthra's Picture set took place at the Forresters' Hall, where the choreographer, Mr. MacDonald, had his academy. The dances were arranged by a dancing master, or possibly by the lady in charge, to express the set's particular theme. The *Mail and Empire* for December 18, 1897 attributed the choreography of two of the dances to professionals. Toronto's Professor John Freeman Davis arranged the quadrille for the Empire set of the Victorian Costume group. He later advertised this fact, quoting reviews that praised the dance above all others, and indicating that he would be teaching the dance in his Wednesday classes (*Saturday Night* 8 Jan. 1898). Mr. Roy Macdonald, from Montreal, whose father had been dancing master to a number of Canada's Governors General, directed the minuet for the Painting and Acting sets (Saywell 1960: 8). The rest of the choreography is difficult to attribute. Although the *Montreal Star* described Roy Macdonald as "superintending" all the dances, other newspapers identified a few of the ladies, for example, Mrs. Sweny or Mrs. Arthur, as having arranged their dances (21 Dec. 1897). For example, the columnist for *Saturday Night* reported "by the way, I hear Mrs. Sweny has invented an electric dance for the ball, which is creating great interest and is sure to be lively" (11 Dec. 1897). This suggests that these women played a more active role than the other women who were merely "in charge" of their sets. Unfortunately, the creators and the dances themselves must remain a mystery until more information can be uncovered.

The costumes were the highlight of the ball and although the details remained unpublished until after the event, the newspapers kept the public up-to-date with the latest developments: "Costumes to be worn at the Victorian Era Ball are to be gorgeous and costly beyond anything seen in a Toronto ball-room. The leading *modistes* are working night and day at splendid array for the gay pleasures, from her Excellency of Aberdeen down to the twittering *debutante* who dreams of a minuet of fairies and a march of nymphs" (*Saturday Night* 25 Dec. 1897). Much of the discussion had centred around the controversy over the use of rented costumes. The social column for the *Globe*, "Chitchat," announced that one entrepreneur had made arrangements

---

[6] *Globe* (20 Nov. 1897) The women were from families prominent in government, business and society, including Lady Kirkpatrick, wife of the former Lieutenant-Governor of Ontario, Mrs. Nordheimer, Mrs. John Cawthra, Lady Gzowski and Mrs. S. Denison.

for a New York costumer to provide a supply of costumes appropriate for the occasion (7 Dec. 1897). However, less than two weeks later, the writer of that same column crusaded on behalf of the seamstresses, exhorting the public to invest in locally made costumes: "It seems a pity that those who can give a little time and consideration to the work of planning out and arranging suitable costumes at the coming Victorian Era Ball should instead content themselves with renting these garments, thus, possibly depriving our merchants and seamstresses of the benefits which might otherwise accrue to them from the holding of this function" (*Globe* 16 Dec. 1897). Apparently such opinions had the desired effect, for *Saturday Night* reported that a similar suggestion had been "universally accepted" and added that one textile merchant was said to have commented that Lord and Lady Aberdeen "have won the thanks of that portion of the community known as 'trade,' on which our prosperity and comfort so largely depend" (25 Dec. 1897).

The ball was held in the drill hall of the Toronto Armouries, which, because of its size (280 feet by 125 feet), could be divided comfortably into two rooms: the ballroom and a supper room which sat 500 people at a time. Architects and decorators, electricians and carpenters were all involved in the conversion of this military hall into a pleasure palace. A large team of workmen was employed to lay the hardwood dance floor and to install the kitchens and furnaces. The heating arrangements were so successful that following the ball *Saturday Night* printed a short article describing the make of the furnace and the contractor (1 Jan. 1898). Mrs. Arthur, a member of an old Toronto family, and an artist who had been involved with pageants all her life, decided to dispense with the usual decoration of bunting. Instead, she created the feeling of a garden party with festoons of green hanging from pillars and electric lights in pink globes (Saywell 1960: 447). Before returning to Ottawa, Lady Aberdeen presented Mrs. Arthur with a diamond ornament in recognition of her help with the ball (*Mail and Empire* 1 Jan. 1898).

English Canada was immensely loyal to Queen Victoria, and this feeling was evident in the ball. The theme of loyalty to the Empire was carried out mainly in the decorations, such as the arches representing the "three great colonies" of India, Canada and Africa (*World* 29 Dec. 1897). Other imperial motifs were to be found in the shields bearing the names of the minor colonies and British possessions which were hung at various points along the walls of the ballroom. The cover of the dance programme, in white and gold on a background of imperial purple, showed the British Empire as a heart sending up life and strength into the imperial tree (*Saturday Night* 1 Jan. 1898). Apparently the design, by Mr. R. Holmes, the drawing master at Upper Canada College, attracted considerable attention. As a personal touch, Lady Aberdeen's court dress, made by Stitt, presumably a Toronto couturier, was in the British colours of red, white and blue (*Globe* 29 Dec. 1897).

The Ball

The evening was arranged in four sections. Once the 2000 costumed guests were seated in galleries around the room, the vice-regal party made their solemn procession down the centre of the room to the dais to "God Save the Queen." As well as the Aberdeens and their attendants, the procession consisted of trumpeters, the master of ceremonies and dignitaries, such as the Governor of Manitoba, the Lieutenant-Governor of Ontario and the Queen's aide-de-camp, together with their wives and attendants.

Then occurred the main feature of the evening. Over 400 people took part in the performance, which lasted three hours. Each of the six groups consisted of the dancers and various attendants, such as chaperones, pages, a herald and a standard bearer. The order of performance was the same for each. The trumpets blew to signal the appearance of the group; once the dance was finished, the group proceeded to the dais led by the standard bearer. There the group's herald introduced the dancers by name and by character to Lord and Lady Aberdeen. As Lady Aberdeen recounted later in her journal: "There was never a hitch which was certainly more than we expected when we had the rehearsal the night before & when all seemed dire confusion. One dance finished & the next came on like clockwork & between each all the participants were introduced by their real & their assumed names by the respective heralds, the standard bearer of the group standing opposite us & we standing on the lowest step of our broad stairs below the throne" (Saywell 1960: 447). After the performance, there was a midnight supper of soup, quail, "hot little beef things," cold meats and many desserts. To accommodate the 2500 guests, the meal was served in four sittings. Catering was entrusted to the firm of Harry Webb and Company, who managed to provide a sumptuous repast, the tea room refreshments and the waiters, china, glass and linen for less than a dollar a person. The bill was $2100 for 2500 people. Later the company could state in their advertising that they were under the patronage of their Excellencies (*Saturday Night* 15 Jan. 1898). The rest of the evening was devoted to general dancing.

The first to perform was the Empire group, led by the Canadian contingent. This set wore costumes portraying the country's natural resources of land, mines and fisheries, with a nod to the aboriginal peoples in the form of the Cree chief. For example, the Aberdeens' daughter, Lady Marjorie Gordon, as the Forests of Canada, wore a dress trimmed with pine trees and snake fences with a chipmunk and pine tree perched on her shoulders. The other sets wore the native dress of the continents they represented. The only description that I have found of a dance and its music has been of the march, the dance of the Empire group. After the bugles sounded, as they would before each dance, the four sets, North America, Europe, India and Australia, and Africa, came in couples from the four corners of the room into the centre (*Mail and Empire* 29 Dec. 1897). There they performed their figures while the band played patriotic airs, such as "Rule Britannia" and "The Maple Leaf" (*Globe* 29 Dec. 1897). The figures began with a St. George's cross which changed into a circle formed of pairs, then divided into four on each side. Other such formations followed until the pairs met again and proceeded to the dais where they were presented to the vice-regal party. The use of the march as the opening dance of the ball follows the practice common in social dancing.

After the march, Lord Aberdeen read a telegram from Buckingham Palace, an act which reinforced patriotic feeling among the assembled guests: "His Excellency stepped to the front of the dais after the Empire March & announced that he had informed the Queen about the Ball which was to take place & that he had that afternoon received a telegram which indicated that her Majesty's thoughts were with us – he then suggested we should all unite in singing God Save the Queen & as with one spontaneous impulse all rose to their feet & sang. It was an impressive moment, as all present felt it to be & one of those moments which do much to seal a nation's loyalty" (Saywell 1960: 449).

Next to perform was the Victorian Costume group, portraying four periods beginning with the Empire period and ending with an Aesthetic set complete with calla lilies carried by the women. Contemporary observers agreed that the Empire set, who portrayed characters such as the Duke and Duchess of Clarence, and Lord and Lady Jersey, was composed of some of Toronto's loveliest women. Indeed, it proved to be the "beauty set" of the ball (*Mail and Empire* 18 Dec. 1897). The group danced the Old-fashioned Quadrille, all the sets performing to the same music at the same time. This format of all sets dancing at the same time was carried through for each group (*Globe* 27 Dec. 1897). Evidence suggests that while the type of dance was the same, the figures for each set were different.

While most of the performers were members of Toronto's elite, Lady Aberdeen, as leader of all Canadian society, invited Trinity University and the Toronto University Women's Literary Society to make up sets in the third group, Literature and Music. As their subjects, Trinity chose the poet, Robert Browning, and the Women's Literary Society portrayed characters from the Drama and George Eliot. Their dance, the Lancers, was arranged by Professor and Mrs. Wright and a Miss McMicking (*Varsity* 13 Jan. 1898).

That the University women regarded the invitation as a chance to show Toronto that they, too, had much to offer is evident from the column "The College Girl" for December 2, 1897 (*Varsity*). The author refuted the prevailing idea that college girls were bluestockings, utterly inept at anything to do with polite society: "That this is utterly false, we who are college girls know, but we may keep on saying so till we are old and grey and it will do no good, unless we do something to prove that our higher education only enables us to play our part in society … more gracefully." They must have played their part successfully, for in her letter of thanks, Lady Aberdeen wrote, "the set-up of the characters was charming, and the drill was very good" (*Varsity* 13 Jan. 1898). Music in the Victorian Era was represented by characters from Gilbert and Sullivan operas.

Members of the Inventions set from Science and Inventions. Drawing by Clara Hagarty.

The fourth group of Science and Inventions portrayed technological progress during the Victorian era, choosing as their subjects the Post Office, Electricity and Inventions. Progress was expressed not only in the themes, but by the contrast of old-fashioned elements with the modern versions. For example, the women of the Invention set, who portrayed Air Power, wore little windmills perched in their coiffures, and the propellers of the modern air-motor attached to their waists. The gentlemen were dressed as telephones. One observer noted: "The set for inventions was danced to represent a mill-wheel. The ladies had skirts of white accordeon [sic] plaited chiffon that in different parts of the dance were caught up imitating the sails of a wind-mill as they whirled quickly round, coloured lights being thrown on them as they danced" (*Sesame* Jan. 1898: 58).

In the Electricity set the ladies, in white and silver with powdered hair, carried electric wands which were fed from storage batteries in their costumes. They represented the new light of electricity, whereas the men in old-fashioned watchman's dress represented the old light. The herald, dressed as the stereotypical Chinaman, stood in the centre of the set during the dance, representing the still lower light of the Chinese lantern. Their dance was a country dance, arranged by Mrs. Sweny, the lady in charge of the set.

The Electricity set. Drawing by Sydney Strickland Tully.

The last two groups to perform were Art, with its Picture and Stage sets appropriately dancing the minuet, and Sports and Amusements performing the traditional finishing dance, Sir Roger de Coverley. Besides the usual pastimes of yachting, games, hunting and highland sports, this group included the time-honoured amusement of harvesting, complete with Miss Manitoba drawn into the ball room on a Massey-Harris reaper, decorated with wheat, sunflowers and poppies. This contemporary touch contrasted with the old-fashioned shepherdess garb of the women, once again pointing to the achievements of the Victorian era.

Reactions to the ball were ecstatic, with reviews appearing in newspapers as far away as Vancouver and New York (Vancouver *World* 8 Jan. 1898 and New York *Home Journal* 8 Jan. 1898). In Toronto the front pages of the major newspapers carried full descriptions of the event, with inner pages devoted to supporting material such as illustrations and editorials. Costumes, both those of the performers and of the other guests, were described in vivid detail for the benefit of those unable to attend: "The inventions, with the boys in brown and black, coiled wires about their necks and electric bells sounding on every

The Picture set during their march before the vice-regal party. The dancers depicted characters from paintings exhibited at the Royal Academy during Victoria's reign. Drawing by George A. Reid.

hand, escorted pretty girls in snowy, accordion pleated frocks, almost compelled one to cry 'Hello!'" (*Saturday Night* 1 Jan. 1898).

Mention also was made of the dancing, usually to contrast the grace of that performance with the boisterous renditions more commonly seen on the dance floor, such as the "pretty little Gilbert and Sullivan set, whose dancing was delightful and made some of us groan for the Lancers one sees in general" (*Saturday Night* 1 Jan. 1898). The dancers were so well received that some of the sets were repeated during a ball at the Pavillion on January 11, 1898. Proceeds from that event went to the Ladies' Work Depository (*Globe* 12 Jan. 1898). Absent were the "smart Londoners and gorgeous Hamiltonians." The Londoners, some of whom were members of the 48th Highlanders, took part in the Hunting and Highland Sports sets.

The newspapers were quick to point out the underlying significance of the ball. Toronto's *Globe* pointed out that the tradespeople as well as guests benefited from the occasion: "seamstresses, carpenters, electric light employees and a host more, have been decidedly the gainers also by the holding of this ball" (29 Dec. 1897). The reporter also praised the ball's intellectual and artistic excellence ("evident from the plan of the character dances") and acknowledged Lady Aberdeen's role in the production. Indeed, in the midst of all the enthusiasm I have found only one dissenting voice in a letter to the editor which complained that the many who purchased costumes for the ball were really spending money that should go to pay their butcher's bills (*Star* 28 Dec. 1897).

The Victorian Era Ball was a complex, many-layered event significant on a number of levels. The form was that of a fancy dress ball, but the many symbolic costumes, historical themes, the commemorative album, and even the use of a triumphal chariot, evoked the spirits of pageantry and Renaissance spectacle. This spectacular occasion, put on by the elite of Toronto society for other members of the upper class, was calculated to place the young country of Canada on the social map. On the other hand, this elite entertainment affected the lives of many of Toronto's population, for the newspapers were unanimous in their praise for the monetary benefit it brought to the trade and service sectors. On another level, the ball, with its groups of dancers symbolizing the achievements during Victoria's reign, both in Canada and throughout the world, served to affirm Toronto's place in the British Empire. It celebrated English Canada's ties with Britain and the country's role as one of the great colonies of the greatest Empire they had ever known.

The Victorian Era Ball was shaped by, and reflected, its social context. Conversely, with the money generated in Toronto, the opportunity for local artists to display their talents and the monetary support for social agencies, it was also a clear case of a dance event affecting society at large.

Postscript

Since this essay was written two notable exhibitions have shed further light on the history of fancy dress balls in Canada. *Toronto Dancing Then and Now*, co-curated by Jennifer Rieger and Mary F. Williamson, was held at the Metropolitan Toronto Reference Library in 1995. Cynthia Cooper curated *Dressing Up Canada: Late Victorian Fancy Dress Balls* for long-term exhibition at the Canadian Museum of Civilization (1997 to 1998). In addition, Helmut Kallmann recently published a collection of vintage Canadian piano marches and dances.

Pioneers —————————————————————

The Groups and Their Organizers

Group I The Empire
The March

North America	Government House
India and Australia	Government House
Europe	Mrs. Nordheimer
Africa	Mrs. P.D. Crerar

Group II Victorian Costumes
The Old-Fashioned Quadrille

First Period	Lady Kirkpatrick
Second Period	Mrs. Hardy, Mrs. F. Grant
Third and Middle Periods	Mrs. Edgar
Fourth (Aesthetic) Period	Mrs. Walker

Group III Literature and Music
The Lancers

Scott	Lady Thompson, Mrs. Law
Rudyard Kipling	Miss Kingsmill
George Eliot	Toronto University Women's Literary Society
Browning	Trinity University
The Drama	Toronto University Women's Literary Society
Gilbert & Sullivan's Operas	Mrs. Irving Cameron

Group IV Science and Inventions
A Country Dance

Electricity	Mrs. Sweny
Post Office	Miss Kingsmill
Inventions	Mrs. Cattanach

Group V Art
The Minuet

Pictures	Mrs. John Cawthra
The Stage	Mrs. Walter Barwick

Group VI Sports and Amusements
Sir Roger de Coverley

Harvesting	Mrs. Arthur
Yachting	Mrs. Ross
Games	Mrs. J.K. Kerr
Hunting	Mrs. Carpenter
Highland Sports	48th Highlanders

References

Primary source materials consulted were the Aberdeen Papers (Manuscript Division, Public Archives of Canada) and the Victorian Era Ball, 1897 (Ephemera Collection, Public Archives Library). Newspapers consulted between November 1897 and January 1898 included *College Topics* (Toronto), *Evening News* (Toronto), *Globe* (Toronto), *Herald* (Montreal), *Home Journal* (New York), *Mail and Empire* (Toronto), *Saturday Night* (Toronto), *Star* (Montreal), *Star* (Toronto), *Varsity* (Toronto), *World* (Toronto) and *World* (Vancouver).

Aberdeen and Temair, Marquis and Marchioness of. 1925. *We Twa: Reminiscences of Lord and Lady Aberdeen*. Vol. 2. London: W. Collins Sons & Co. Ltd.

Adam, G. Mercer. 1891. *Toronto, Old and New: A Memorial Volume Historical, Descriptive and Pictorial ... With Some Sketches of the Men Who Have Made or Are Making the Provincial Capital*. Reprint Toronto: Coles Publishing Co., 1972.

Aria, Eliza. 1906. *Costume: Fanciful, Historical and Theatrical*. London: Macmillan & Co.

Book of the Victorian Era Ball Given at Toronto on the Twenty Eighth of December MDCCCXCVII. 1898. Toronto: Rowsell & Hutchinson.

Cooper, Cynthia. 1997. *Magnificent Entertainments: Fancy Dress Balls of Canada's Governors General, 1876-1898*. Hull: Canadian Museum of Civilization with Goose Lane Editions.

Dendy, William. 1978. *Lost Toronto*. Toronto: Oxford University Press.

Finkel, Alicia. 1984. "La Bal Costumé: History and Spectacle in the Court of Queen Victoria." *Dress* No. 10, 64-72.

Glazebrook, George P. de T. 1971. *The Story of Toronto*. Toronto: University of Toronto Press.

Gwyn, Sandra. 1984. *The Private Capital: Ambition and Love in the Age of Macdonald and Laurier*. Toronto: McClelland and Stewart Ltd.

Holt, Ardern. 1884. *Fancy Dresses Described or What to Wear at Fancy Balls*. 4th ed. London: Debenham and Freebody.

Kallmann, Helmut, ed. 1998. *Piano Music III: Marches and Dances*. Ottawa: Canadian Musical Heritage Society (Vol. 22).

Lancefield, Richard T. 1897. *Victoria: Sixty Years a Queen, A Sketch of Her Life and Times*. Toronto: C.R. Parish & Co.

Mulvaney, C. Pelham. 1884. *Toronto: Past and Present. A Handbook of the City*. Reprint Toronto: Ontario Reprint Press, 1979.

Murphy, Sophia. 1984. *The Duchess of Devonshire's Ball*. London: Sedgwick & Jackson.

Pioneers ————————————————————————————

Rieger, Jennifer and Mary F. Williamson. 1995. *Toronto Dancing Then and Now*. Toronto: Metropolitan Toronto Reference Library.

Saywell, John T., ed. 1960. *The Canadian Journal of Lady Aberdeen, 1893-1898*. The Publications of the Champlain Society, XXXVIII. Toronto: The Champlain Society.

Schneider, Gretchen. 1987. "The Duchess's Ball." *Dance Chronicle* 10: 2, 236-41.

"The Victorian Era Ball." Jan. 1898. *Sesame* 1: 2, 56-61.

Withington, Robert. 1920. *English Pageantry: An Historical Outline*. Vol. 2. Cambridge: Harvard University Press.

Maud Allan:
Misunderstood?

Carol Bishop

It is the perceived wisdom, first perpetrated by contemporary critics and dancers and subsequently accepted, often without consideration, by dance historians, that Maud Allan (1873-1956) was not a legitimate pioneer of Western early modern theatre dance, but rather an exploitive imitator. This essay, based on research over an extended time which included the compilation of an original choreochronicle and a study of her choreographic and performance styles, presents evidence which challenges the perceived notions concerning Allan. Once the facts have been examined, it is clear that, at best, she has been misunderstood and, at worst, misrepresented. It is first necessary to establish some pertinent biographical details which shed light on Allan's behaviour. The following provides essential background and contextual information to help understand Allan's artistic motivations.

Maud Allan was a true citizen of the world: born in Toronto, Canada, she moved to San Francisco at the age of five and finished her musical education in Germany. Ulla Maude Durrant, as her birth certificate states, was born in Toronto on August 27, 1873. She was the second child in the family and her older brother, William Theodore Durrant, had been born in 1871. For as yet unknown reasons, her father, William Allan Durrant, moved with his wife and two children to San Francisco at the end of 1878. During their California years both Allan and her brother received excellent educations. Although her parents came from a working class background, they made considerable effort and sacrifice to ensure that their children received the best possible education. Both Durrant children were among the first graduating class of the three-year general arts programme at Cogswell College, which had been established to provide young Californians with practical occupational training in addition to the traditional academic pursuits and physical culture.

Throughout her childhood, Allan studied the piano. From an early age she had shown musical talent, and she progressed to lessons with Professor Eugene S. Bonelli at the San Francisco Conservatory of Music. Allan credits Bonelli with encouraging her to go to Europe to complete her musical training. She taught Saturday morning music classes for children while still at school. Between the time she graduated from Cogswell College in 1891 and her departure for Europe in 1895, she was registered in the San Francisco Directory as a music teacher working from her parents' home. Living at home and giving lessons would have allowed her to save money for further studies abroad.

Maud Allan, ca. 1910.

On Valentine's Day, 1895, at the age of twenty-two, Allan embarked for Germany. In April she was accepted as a student at the Berlin Koenigliche Akademishe Hochschule. On April 15, 1895, just two months after Allan left home, her brother was arrested in San Francisco and charged with the murder of two young girls. Durrant's trial during the summer of 1895 received massive press coverage including daily reports in the *International Herald Tribune* read by the ex-patriot American community in Berlin. He was found guilty and after exhausting all appeal attempts, Allan's brother was hanged in San Quentin jail on January 7, 1898. Throughout this traumatic time, Allan remained in Germany. In later years she attempted to distance herself from Theodore Durrant by adopting a stage name and representing herself as an only child.

While her family endured the years of Theodore's trial and the shock of his execution, Allan struggled along with her music studies in Germany. In the summer of 1901 after six years of intermittent study in Berlin, her musical talent was sufficient for her to be accepted into the elite circle to study with the great pianist, composer and teacher, Ferruccio Busoni (1866-1924). Busoni was a German-Italian who had been a child prodigy and travelled extensively as a youth. He moved to Berlin in 1894 and was based there except for a period in Switzerland during the First World War. Throughout his career he spent short periods of time teaching master classes; in Weimar in 1900-01, in Vienna in 1908 and during his final years at the Berlin Academy of Arts. By all accounts Busoni was open-minded about music and endorsed emerging twentieth-century trends in serious music. For example in his Berlin concerts, he premiered works by Bartók and Sibelius and the German premieres of pieces by Debussy and Franck. It is significant to note that Allan also favoured these composers amongst others when choosing music for her dances. Even more significant is the fact that Allan was the first dancer to commission original dance music from Debussy.[1]

---

[1] In 1910 Allan commissioned Debussy to compose the score for a ballet, *Khamma*, based on a scenario written by her and William Leonard Courtney, the drama and literary critic of *The Daily Telegraph*. Debussy failed to fulfill the contract, composing only three dances of the six or seven in the original scenario.

Busoni had been invited in 1900-01 to give advanced classes for pianists in Weimar carrying on the master-class tradition of Franz Liszt. In July and August, 1901 Allan was one of a group of privileged students who studied with Busoni. He became a mentor to Allan and their friendship continued until his death in 1924. It was after Allan's Weimar summer that she decided to give up her dreams of becoming a concert pianist and instead turned her attention to dance.

Allan struggled for nearly five years before achieving recognition as an early modern dancer. She was thirty years old at the time of her debut on December 24, 1903 at the small hall of the Vienna Musikverein. It is significant to note that she premiered at such a prestigious Viennese performing hall with various musical notables such as Joseph Joachim in the audience. The next day the *Illustriertes Wiener Extrablatt* reviewed her two-hour "performance of musical impressionistic mood settings" to the music of Bach, Beethoven, Chopin, Mendelssohn and Schumann. Reporting that she danced before an invited audience of artists, writers and patrons of the fine arts, the unidentified critic named her as a rival to Isadora Duncan.

She premiered her signature work *The Vision of Salomé* on December 28, 1906 at the Carl Theater in Vienna. It was constantly in her dance programmes from its debut to the end of her 1910 North American tour. After that date she performed it infrequently during her 1913-14 Far East tour and for a brief period in New York in 1916. Anyone who refers to Maud Allan as "the Salomé dancer," however, overlooks the fact that *The Vision of Salomé* was her chef d'oeuvre for only a four-year period in a performance career that spanned three decades.

Indeed, Allan spawned many imitators herself, and a Salomé craze swept the stages on both sides of the Atlantic. After Allan's unprecedented success at London's Palace Theatre in 1908, other London music halls were quick to react to Allan's popularity. The Alhambra presented a parody called *Sal' Oh-My* while at the Queens Theatre, a Miss Phyllis Dare and a chorus of little girls, all dressed in replicas of Allan's Salomé costume, presented their own parody. These British parodies are noteworthy for several reasons. In no way was Allan a unique target for this particular form of British humour. Parody and satirical cartoons are indigenous forms of wit. However, this legacy of ridicule may have unwittingly played a part in diminishing perceptions of Allan's serious intent as a dancer. Other cultures, notably North American, may have missed the subtlety of this peculiar form of British culture and misconstrued good-natured parody for contempt of Allan's performances.

The story of Salomé, with its intimations of incest and intrigue, was an inspiring topic for various artists around 1900. Oscar Wilde's play *Salomé* (1892) and the fascination with all things oriental gave the impetus not only for Richard Strauss' opera of 1905 but also for a number of dances. Loie Fuller took the role of Salomé on several occasions. In Russia the Imperial censors had banned Ida Rubinstein's 1908 attempt to produce Wilde's play with her *Dance of the Seven Veils*. However, Rubinstein did perform the *Salomé* dance

Allan's *The Vision of Salomé*.

which Michel Fokine had choreographed in a single performance in Russia and remounted this production in Paris in 1912. If Allan's *Salomé* dance is placed in a chronological context with other dances using this subject matter, it can be shown that with her 1906 debut of *The Vision of Salomé,* she was among the first Western early modern theatre dancers to explore the Salomé theme.

Due to her brother's crimes, Allan was stranded in Germany for thirteen years without financial support from her family. She immersed herself in German life, learning the language, studying music and after 1901 becoming intimately involved in the intellectual circle surrounding Ferruccio Busoni. The Berlin of the 1890s was a boom-town full of new buildings and vitality. It was the theatre capital of Germany for both commercial cabaret style theatres and experimental avant-garde companies. Allan was an active participant in Berlin cultural life. She described the impact of seeing the Max Reinhardt production of Wilde's *Salomé* in an interview in the *London Weekly Dispatch*: "It was splendidly done, but there seemed something lacking. There did not seem enough character in Salomé. Much as I admired the great actress in the title role, I could not help thinking that another interpretation might be given. There and then I determined to try what I could do" (15 Mar. 1908).

Before World War I, a cultural movement labelled as early German expressionism evolved. Art historians credit a group of Dresden artists (Die Brücke) as the first to articulate in a 1906 manifesto the expressionists' aims to achieve freedom of life and action against the well established older forces. This fascination with the expression of the creator's "inner life" and rejection of the establishment soon transferred to other art forms such as literature, theatre and music. Arnold Whittal, in a discussion of expressionist music describes "the essential subjectivism" of all the expressionist arts and the artist's intention to express himself as intensely and directly as possible without reliance on traditional accepted forms (1980 vol. 6: 333). Allan's dance with its attempt to express emotion through movement and the rejection of balletic tradition shares certain common characteristics with other forms of early German expressionist arts.

There was a manic depressive quality to early German expressionism. Sexual themes in art and literature, involving a disturbing element of violence, were prevalent in Germany at the turn of the twentieth century. According to the cultural historian Modris Eksteins, in his study of the birth of modernism, this obsession with sexual violence was more sustained in Germany than elsewhere. "From Frank Wedekind's Lulu plays, which celebrated the prostitute because she was a rebel, through Strauss' Salomé, who beheaded John the Baptist because he refused to satisfy her lust, to the repressed but obvious sexual undercurrent in Thomas Mann's early stories, artists used sex to express their disillusionment with contemporary values and priorities and, even more, their belief in a vital and irrepressible energy" (1989: 83).

A point of significance concerning the German expressionists' philosophy was their enthusiasm and interest in experimenting in a variety of art forms. Furness observes that "many of the expressionists, rather like the German romantics a century before, had stressed the ultimate union of all the arts and perhaps with more success, had demonstrated this in their achievements" (1973: 15). He cites the Austrian composer, Arnold Schoenberg, who possessed talents both as a painter and a musician. Another example was the artist Paul Klee, who was proficient enough as a violinist to have considered a career as a concert performer. In this context, Allan's transference from one performing art to another is more understandable.

At this time in German life, a youth movement embraced physical culture, dress reform and a freer sexuality as a protest against what was perceived as the prudery of middle-class mores. "The youth movement, which flourished after the turn of the century, revelled in a 'return to nature' and celebrated a hardly licentious but certainly freer sexuality, which constituted part of its rebellion against an older generation thought to be caught up in repression and hypocrisy" (Eksteins 1989: 83). An appreciation of the human body with an emphasis on lack of taboos and social restrictions led to acceptance of the styles of dance practised by Isadora Duncan, Ruth St. Denis and Allan.

It would be perverse not to acknowledge the influence of Duncan on the development of Allan as a dancer. By 1904 Duncan had established a school in the Berlin suburb of Grunewald. Earlier in 1903, she had published her theories of dance in both German and English in which she described the dance of the future "whose body and soul have grown so harmoniously together that the natural language of that soul will become the movement of the body" (1903: 24-25). It is highly unlikely that Allan was not influenced by Duncan, although she denied any such connection. The very fact that Allan was living in Berlin at the same time that Duncan was performing and publishing her dance manifesto makes such a denial suspect.

Throughout her career, Allan bore the stigma of being described as an imitator of Isadora Duncan. This raises the issue of intellectual property.

Allan's *Spring Song*.

Duncan was an acknowledged and recognized source of inspiration to a variety of dancers, choreographers and theatre directors such as Vaslav Nijinsky, Michel Fokine and Gordon Craig. While it is obvious that Allan was aware of Duncan's work and philosophy of dance, is it not conceivable that Duncan was one of many sources of inspiration which together formed the dance ideas of Maud Allan? Would it not be possible that her mentor, Ferruccio Busoni and the stimulating and challenging ideas of early German expressionism would have had an equal influence on Allan's evolution into a dancer?

It is harder to write off Allan as an imitation Isadora Duncan when evidence is set forth and examined. Allan's great musicality was acknowledged by many critics, which is hardly surprising when one realizes the depth of her training. In her autobiography she described her dance method as "turning big themes into movement" (1908: 77). Of the fifty-four known dance works in her repertoire, forty-eight took the title of the music indicating that the music played a predominant role. Indeed, dance historian Elizabeth Kendall goes so far as to postulate that Allan's choice of serious classical music may have influenced Duncan's own musical choices. She suggests that Duncan may have been "pushed towards using classical music by the example of another American girl dancer, Maud Allan" (1979: 67).

Why then was Allan perceived by some critics of her time and dance historians as a music hall vulgarian while she considered herself to be a serious artist? This is the crux of the issue – Allan's own artistic intent contrasted to her critics' and audiences' perceptions of her performances. Although she may have sincerely believed in the integrity of her art, her choice of subject matter and costume may have been the unintentional cause of the misunderstanding of her serious intent. If she deliberately chose to titillate her audience with dark sexual overtones and glimpses of naked flesh, then the accepted view of Allan would be accurate. But if she was an advocate of German expressionism and a believer in dress reform and freer attitudes, then she has been misunderstood. Allan's personal life contributes to this paradox.

Unlike Duncan, who as a proponent of dress reform wore free-flowing street clothing, Allan presented herself off-stage as the epitome of conventional Edwardian style with dresses nipped in tightly at the waist and huge overblown hats. Allan's endorsement of German expressionism in her artistic life, while at the same time clinging to conventionalities in her personal life, adds to the confusion.

Any discussion of audiences' perceptions in the context of Allan's performances must acknowledge the male gaze theory of representation which, simply put, offers a subject/object model of the performer/spectator relationship. The spectator, traditionally male, is in a position of power while the performer, in this case Allan, is placed in a passive role. No doubt there was a strong element of sexualization by many of the male spectators who had come to expect a suggestive or coquettish display from Victorian music hall dancers. However this male gaze theory becomes problematic as the majority of Allan's audience were female. A more significant factor is that nearly all the critics at the time were male.

Ann Daly in "Dance History and Feminist Theory: Reconsidering Isadora Duncan and the Male Gaze" discusses the works of a variety of scholars who have developed more complex models going from the two-dimensional to the three-dimensional. In her essay Daly postulates that "Duncan's choreography offered her spectators a new kind of meaning and demanded from them a new way of seeing" (1992: 241). She suggests that her performance was "a kin-esthetic experience in which the spectators actively participated" (255). It can be argued that this new way of seeing can be applied to Allan's dances as well.

Historians usually emphasize the fact that Duncan refused to perform in the popular music halls or vaudeville theatres and would only consider legitimate theatres, concert halls or opera halls. Allan, on the other hand, performed in a variety of venues. Although Allan enjoyed her greatest success at London's Palace Theatre, she appeared at numerous prestigious performance spaces around the world. The Russian ballerina Anna Pavlova also appeared regularly on the music hall stage and yet her reputation as a serious artist has not been questioned.

Unlike Duncan and St. Denis, Allan did not import her dance from the New World. Although she was North American by birth, she spent her formative years in her twenties immersed in European culture. It is inconceivable that Allan would not have been greatly influenced by her thirteen years of studying, touring and living alone in Europe. There is no doubt that the dance career of Maud Allan is a conundrum. It is not easy to assess her role in the evolution of early modern theatre dance. When her education, life experiences and the cultural, social and political contexts in which she lived are taken into consideration, she cannot be so easily written off as a mere imitator.

This essay introduces a number of issues which challenge untested information concerning Maud Allan. Hopefully the points touched upon here will stimulate further investigation to help solve the yet unresolved question of Allan's rightful role in the history of early modern theatre dance.

References

This essay is based on research to collect extant primary sources including programmes, visual material, scrapbooks and a plethora of newspaper and journal articles which are scattered throughout libraries both in Europe and North America. It includes an exhaustive search through newspapers and journals spanning the period 1908-1941 at the British Library Newspaper Collection (Colindale). Newspaper reviews from Germany, France, Russia, Hungary and Belgium relating to Allan's early career 1903-1908 were collected and translated. A visit to the New York Public Library Dance Collection yielded much material. As well, I compiled, by cross-referencing programmes with newpaper reviews, the most comprehensive choreochronicle to date documenting fifty-four of Maud Allan's dances.

Allan, Maud. 1908. *My Life and Dancing*. London: Everett & Co.

Bishop, Carol Anne. 1989. "The Artistic Life of Maud Allan." Master's thesis, York University.

Cherniavsky, Felix. 1991. *The Salome Dancer: The Life and Times of Maud Allan*. Toronto: McClelland and Stewart.

Cherniavsky, Felix. 1998. *Maud Allan and Her Art*. Toronto: Dance Collection Danse Press/es.

Daly, Ann. 1992. "Dance History and Feminist Theory: Reconsidering Isadora Duncan and the Male Gaze." In Laurence Senelick, ed. *Gender in Performance*. Hanover: University Press of New England, 239-59.

Duncan, Isadora. 1903. *Der Tanz der Zukunft*. Leipzig: Eugen Diederiche.

Eksteins, Modris. 1989. *Rites of Spring – The Great War and the Birth of The Modern Age*. Toronto: Lester & Orpen Dennys Ltd.

Furness, R.S. 1973. *Expressionism*. London: Metheun & Co. Ltd.

Kendall, Elizabeth. 1979. *Where She Danced*. New York: Alfred A. Knopf.

Whittal, Arnold. 1980. "Expressionism." In Stanley Sadie, ed. *The New Grove Dictionary of Music and Musicians*. Vol. 6. London: Macmillan Publishers Ltd.

Hector Charlesworth and E.R. Parkhurst:
Looking at Dance in Early Twentieth-Century Toronto

Norma Sue Fisher-Stitt

The seeds for this essay were sown with an investigation into the Toronto performances of Anna Pavlova, the famous Russian ballerina who is remembered for her determination to take ballet to all corners of the earth. In Keith Money's book *Anna Pavlova: Her Life and Art* (1982), Toronto, Canada is listed as one of the stops on her North American tours. Being a Torontonian interested in dance, my curiosity was aroused. How many times did Pavlova visit Toronto? Where did she perform? Did other dance companies have engagements in the city? Answers to these questions were sought through a search of Toronto's early twentieth-century print media, where I soon discovered the columns by E.R. Parkhurst and Hector Charlesworth. Parkhurst was the music and drama critic for the *Globe* from 1898 to 1924; Charlesworth was the assistant managing editor of *Saturday Night* magazine from 1910 to 1926. Both these sources provide consistent information pertaining to the performing arts in Toronto during the first quarter of the twentieth century. The *Globe* featured a daily "Music and Drama" column, while music and drama criticism had been part of the weekly *Saturday Night* magazine format since its founding in 1887. The reviews written by Parkhurst and Charlesworth between 1910 and 1924 provide a window through which the performances by Pavlova and other dancers can be observed.

Edwin Rodie Parkhurst was typical of the model Torontonian of his day: British by birth, Protestant, conservative in outlook and interested in music. Born in Dulwich, England on June 1, 1848, he came from a musical family and studied violin under George Hart, a well-known London violin dealer. As a member of a chamber music trio comprised of himself, his brother and his sister, he performed around London in the 1860s. He maintained his interest in the violin throughout his life, spending his leisure time playing chamber music among friends. He amassed a collection of chamber music described by Charlesworth, in his obituary for Parkhurst, as one "which in later years grew to be the finest and most complete in Canada" (*Saturday Night* 21 June 1924).

83

Cover of Pavlova company programme, 1924.

Despite his apparent talent, Parkhurst decided that the violin could never offer him financial security, and so he became a shorthand writer. It was in this capacity that he arrived in Canada in 1870, where he was employed by the Grand Trunk Railway as a shorthand writer in its Montreal office. After being transferred to Toronto, Parkhurst left the railway in 1872, joining the newly founded Toronto *Daily Mail* as a reporter. His interest in music led him to report on concerts, although according to Charlesworth, "concerts were so infrequent that a music critic's task was necessarily a side issue." Parkhurst moved to the *Globe* in 1873, then back to the *Mail* in 1876 before returning to the *Globe* in 1898 to assume the position of music and drama critic. Concerts and the theatre were no longer a side issue in Toronto, and the broad range of cultural activities required the attention of a full-time critic. Parkhurst remained with the *Globe* until his death on June 10, 1924, five months prior to Pavlova's final Toronto appearance.

Hector Charlesworth was born in Hamilton, Canada on September 28, 1872. The son of a shoe manufacturer, he was articled as a chartered accountant in 1887. Two years later, he began to write for *Saturday Night* under the pseudonym "Touchstone." His full-time career as a reporter commenced in 1892 and he worked for several Toronto newspapers over the next eighteen years before rejoining *Saturday Night* as assistant managing editor in 1910. Like Parkhurst, Charlesworth studied music in his youth, but his devotion to this art form did not match the enthusiasm of Parkhurst; Charlesworth was also keenly interested in the theatre. Each man's background affected how he chose to report on dance. Parkhurst, the reserved Englishman, was encouraging and positive in his reviews. His reluctance to express a negative opinion sometimes brings into question his ability to assume the role of discerning viewer. Charlesworth expressed his views more forcefully and demanded a minimum standard. The reaction of each of these two critics to the performance by Mikhail Mordkin's Imperial Russian Ballet in 1911 graphically illustrates their divergent styles.

Mikhail Mordkin had been in Toronto in 1910, partnering Pavlova. A graduate of the Moscow Bolshoi Ballet School, he was a member of the Diaghilev Ballets Russes in its 1909 debut season in Paris, France. After touring North America with Pavlova in 1910, Mordkin returned to Russia to organize another touring company of Russian dancers, billed the All-Star Imperial Russian Ballet. In November 1911, this company performed *Coppélia* at Massey Hall in Toronto. Unfortunately, Mordkin was recovering from an appendectomy and appeared only in the mime role of Dr. Coppélius. The production was further hampered by a lengthy intermission, leaving the audience with a poor impression of the company's integrity and standards. Parkhurst, ever the gentleman, did not harshly criticize the performance in his *Globe* column of November 10, 1911. Preferring to give polite suggestions, he dismissed any negativity he may have felt with the statement that "Russian dancers have an extraordinary vogue both in Europe and America." Charlesworth was not as sympathetic, and began his review with the caustic remark that "the general impression of the critical public appears to be that it paid $3 for a $1 show." Demonstrating greater insight than Parkhurst, Charlesworth offered another reason for the Mordkin company's comparative lack of success: "The primary cause for this craze is the fact that Anna Pavlova is a Russian. It was her lovely personality, her superlatively fine talent that turned the eyes of the world toward Russia as the home of dancers. Without Pavlova, Russian dancing suffers from an evaporation of public interest. It is the woman, not the nation, that sets our hearts aflame.... When Pavlova comes back, one predicts another outburst of enthusiasm for Russian dancing, but not until then" (*Saturday Night* 18 Nov. 1911).

Charlesworth's dry sense of humour added a sparkle to his columns that brings a smile even today. In the early months of World War I, a certain Dr. Graves accused Anna Pavlova of once having been a Russian spy. Charlesworth delightfully put into context the outlandishness of such a proposal:

> The same Dr. Graves ... announced that the first step that would be taken by the Ottomans would be the blowing up of a lock in the Suez canal. His prophesy has not been verified for a reason that is conclusive: there are no locks in the Suez waterway. It happens to be a sea-level canal cut through the desert. So we may pardonably doubt his statement that Madame Pavlova ever served as a Russian spy. Even if she had ... it would prove her to be the most wonderful woman in the world, for a lady who could keep herself in such a sublime state of suppleness, grace and expressive "fitness" and devote her leisure to mastering the intricacies of international politics, would be Nature's chiefest miracle (*Saturday Night* 21 Nov. 1914).

In contrast, Parkhurst seldom dealt with performers' personal lives; he was more interested in providing educational details than in communicating what he considered to be idle gossip. Parkhurst supplies dates and numbers – crucial materials for researchers. Charlesworth transports today's reader back to the time in which he wrote. For research purposes, both columns have merit. Charlesworth's reviews are more descriptive and place dance within the larger context of the theatre, while Parkhurst's columns, with previews

Mikhail Mordkin, *Bacchanale*, ca. 1910.

heralding forth-coming performances, relay valuable information.

Several weeks prior to each of Pavlova's Toronto engagements, her name would begin to appear in Parkhurst's column. The date of her arrival, other cities included on the tour, programme and ticket details, plus reviews from newspapers such as the *Brooklyn Eagle* and the *London Morning Post* were all gradually released. In 1910, Parkhurst recorded Pavlova's tour schedule preceding her Toronto arrival. Following their opening at the Metropolitan Opera House in New York on Saturday afternoon, October 15, 1910, the company performed at the Brooklyn Academy of Music that evening. The tour continued with performances at the Lyric Theatre in Baltimore on Monday, in Philadelphia on Tuesday, and in Rochester on Wednesday before presenting matinee and evening programmes in Toronto on the Thursday. The company would arrive by train in the morning, then re-embark after the evening performance in order to reach the next destination the subsequent morning. It is not mentioned whether two performances daily was the norm but this is highly probable, since Toronto, a smaller centre than either Baltimore or Philadelphia, was scheduled for two shows. This information sheds a great deal of light on the daily regimen of Pavlova and her company, the most striking aspect being the pace at which she drove both herself and her dancers. Four years later, her touring schedule appears to have not slackened. In his review of her 1914 New Year's Eve performance in Toronto, Parkhurst mentions that the curtain calls had to be prematurely suspended, owing to the departure of the company train that night.

At the time of Pavlova's first visit in 1910, Toronto was going through a period of rapid expansion. Through annexation, the city's area had almost doubled over the previous five years. The majority of the population was English-speaking, of British descent, and the citizens had developed a reputation for having a keen interest in music. Parkhurst's column reflects this propensity for music, and his by-line beneath "Music and Drama" reads "conducted by E.R. Parkhurst." His column was divided into three sections: Music, The Drama and Vaudeville Houses. A wide gulf separated the fine arts from the popular arts. Concerts, operas and dramas appeared in the legitimate theatres such as the Royal Alexandra or Massey Hall. The vaudeville houses, one being Shea's, presented jugglers, acrobats, comedians, singers and dancers. Dance was considered a popular entertainment, not an art form. Prior to Pavlova's tours, dance in Toronto was usually found in the vaudeville theatres, one exception being when it was performed within an opera.

Pavlova's first Toronto engagement at Massey Hall in 1910 was hailed as both an artistic and social event of importance. Members of the audience included the Lieutenant-Governor and Mrs. Gibson, who were joined by the Governor General and Lady Grey from Ottawa. For Charlesworth, the presence of these eminent persons "was an indication that the long neglect of dancing as an art and end unto itself has been a mistake" (*Saturday Night* 29 Oct. 1910). Parkhurst was less eager to recognize dance as the artistic equivalent of music or drama. His first reaction to the increased interest in dance arising from tours by Pavlova and the Diaghilev Ballets Russes was one of bemusement. After reporting that "the Russian dancers at Covent Garden eclipsed the famous singers," Parkhurst proceeded to state that "it is not likely that the revival of interest in dancing will last very long, dancing can never be a thing of such vital concern to us as it was to our ancestors" (*Globe* 16 Sept. 1911). Parkhurst's reaction is easier to comprehend when one remembers that Toronto society had not traditionally patronized dance. His initial reluctance to accept dance as an art form was probably typical of many Torontonians.

Despite his ambiguity towards dance in general, Parkhurst openly acknowledged his admiration for Pavlova. Having witnessed her perform on October 20, 1910, Parkhurst in his column the next day described Pavlova as "the embodiment of poetry in motion. Exquisitely graceful, she is by turns alluring, seductive, characteristic, pantomimic and clear in interpretation of mood and situation." Aside from these words of praise, Parkhurst had little to say about the dancing. Rather, drawing on his own area of expertise, his review focused on the music within the performance. First praising the quality of the orchestra, he went on to say:

A refreshing feature of the performance was the delightful music with which the dance was associated. There were Polish dances by Glinka and Glazounow, Russian dances by Tschakovski [sic], the Swan Song by Saint-Saëns, the Valse Caprice by Rubinstein, the second Hungarian Rhapsody by Liszt and a Bacchanale by Glazounow, all appropriately and ingeniously illustrated by the dance (*Globe* 21 Oct. 1910).

In contrast, Charlesworth chose to concentrate on Pavlova's interpretation of Giselle. His review successfully combines an outline of the plot with descriptions of the dancing:

The first act of Pavlova's dancing when she tells by action and gesture of the fateful legend which clings about her was remarkably expressive and the mad whirl of her death scene was thrilling. But the second act far surpassed it in interest and poetic quality. It had an eery quality, an illusion that was all the more remarkable since the performance was not given in a theatre and the artificial aids which go to create an illusion were meagre. The dancing of the fairies was a lovely spectacle but the subtle thrill came when Giselle, played by Pavlova, rose from her grave. The sight of Mordkine [sic] as the lover, standing bewildered as his love floated about him with ravishing grace and swiftness was one never to be forgotten (*Saturday Night* 29 Oct. 1910).

Charlesworth's impressions of the performance were far broader in context, making it possible for his readers to imagine the atmosphere created by the artists.

Pavlova's first Toronto appearance was well received, but she did not play to sold out houses. This may be attributed to several factors: the absence of an established dance audience, the large size of Massey Hall, and perhaps the ticket prices. At a time when vaudeville theatres were charging 25¢ to 50¢ for admission, and the legitimate theatres $1.00 to $1.50, tickets for the Pavlova company ranged from 50¢ to $3.00. The inexperienced dance audience was not accustomed to seeing ballet, and Charlesworth admitted that "at the outset, it seemed a doubtful experiment" to bring her company to Toronto (*Saturday Night* 29 Oct. 1910). Despite these obstacles, the response was sufficiently enthusiastic to guarantee Pavlova's return not only during her 1913 North American tour, but many times after that.

Between 1910 and 1924, Pavlova performed in Toronto ten times. Parkhurst, who once had predicted an inevitable decline in the popularity of dance, found himself covering dance more frequently. His understanding of dance grew, but certain preferences remained steadfast. He equated a successful dance performance with its ability to tell a story, and in the *Globe* on December 31, 1913, he praised productions which recalled "the old glories of the dance in the days when the ballet was an essential part of grand opera." Parkhurst's musical knowledge consistently played an important role in his dance reviews. Perhaps it was his method of encouraging the musically oriented Toronto audience to attend Pavlova's performances. On October 24, 1914, prior to her engagement, he wrote in the *Globe*: "For lovers of the best in music the forthcoming appearance of ... Pavlova holds particular interest, for Pavlova's musical program is of as great worth as her terpsichorean offerings." After extolling the "sparkling mellifluous qualities of Gluck, Mozart and Weber," he added his endorsement of Pavlova's skills, stating that "aside from Pavlova's music, her terpsichorean interpretations are in a class by themselves."

Despite Parkhurst's urgings, Pavlova's Toronto performances in November 1914 did not sell out. Public malaise accompanying the recent outbreak of war was deepened by a financial recession. "With the stock exchanges closed, with the ocean commerce at a stand-still because of the German sea-raiders, with general trade dormant, the latter half of 1914 was a dubious period. Recruiting was the only steady activity" (Middleton 1923 vol. 1: 405). The war and recession undoubtedly had an effect on the public's interest in the arts, but according to Charlesworth, even concerts in peace time were susceptible to slow ticket sales. He criticized Torontonians for their apathy toward the arts:

It was a very indignant audience which left the first of the Toronto Oratorio Society's concerts at Massey Hall last Monday night. The indignation was aimed at the Toronto public which preens itself on being musical, and which shamefully neglected the event.... Toronto is not a musical centre in the sense that it is a hockey centre, a baseball centre or a prayer-meeting centre.... Fortuitous circumstances have made Toronto a great centre of musical education and of the music trades, but they have not made it really musical.... The fact is, that of the people who can afford to go to high class concerts, but a thousand or less are interested in music (*Saturday Night* 29 Apr. 1922).

In the fall of 1915, a combined opera and ballet tour, incorporating the Boston Opera Company and Pavlova's Imperial Ballet Russe, began. According to Olive Holmes, editor of *Motion Arrested: Dance Reviews of H.T. Parker* (1982), Pavlova was involved in both the management of the company and in the choice of repertoire. From Parkhurst's columns, we learn that the full company totalled 257 members, including sixty musicians, seventy singers and an unspecified number of opera soloists and dancers. The troupe criss-crossed North America in a twenty-three car train, of which fourteen were reserved for baggage.

This company performed in Toronto on two occasions, at the Arena in October 1915 and at the Royal Alexandra Theatre in January 1916. Parkhurst's reviews focused on the music. Charlesworth, with his broad theatrical interests, addressed the problems that had to be overcome by the company before its Toronto opening at the less-than-ideal Arena: "The main obstacle, and that which must remain, is that Toronto possesses no proper auditorium for operatic productions on so vast a scale. At one time the trustees of Massey Hall had a project for deepening their stage and providing the means whereby grand opera on a metropolitan scale could be seen in Toronto ... but civic indifference ... burked it. The management of the Boston organization therefore found themselves confronted with the necessity of practically building a theatre within the Arena" (*Saturday Night* 30 Oct. 1915).

Charlesworth, like Parkhurst, focused more on the opera than the ballet in his reviews. However, we are provided with some details on Pavlova's portrayal of Fenella in *The Dumb Girl of Portici*, a role captured on silent film in 1916 in the Hollywood version of the opera. Written by Daniel Auber, *The Dumb Girl of Portici* had once been popular in Britain under the title *Masaniello*.

"Masaniello" is chiefly interesting to-day because of the unique experiment of making the leading female character absolutely silent, and calling on her to suggest by pantomime, tragic episodes. The incidental music that he has written for the dumb-show of Fenella is skilful in a degree that moderns are apt to overlook. Fortunate were we in seeing a woman who is not merely a dancer, but truly a great mime, Anna Pavlova, in this role. The auditorium was too vast for everyone to catch the subtleties and amazing variety of her facial expression, yet the significance of her gestures and the marvellous personal magnetism which enabled her to rivet attention on herself while never singing a note, made the performance a unique and valuable memory (*Saturday Night* 30 Oct. 1915).

After her appearances with the Boston Opera, which performed in Toronto in 1915 and 1916, four years elapsed before Pavlova again danced in Toronto. It is evident that difficulties accompanied the 1920 tour – even Parkhurst was faintly critical of the programme. His November 22, 1920 response to the *Egyptian Ballet* was that it was "perhaps a little monotonous in its uniformity of pose and movement." *Chopiniana* also fell short of Parkhurst's expectations, described unenthusiastically in the same column as a ballet "in which, occasionally, the appropriateness of suggestion was attained." During one Toronto performance, Pavlova fell when Alexandre Volinine failed to catch her from a leap. This type of accident, always a risk, is often indicative of exhausted dancers performing below their capabilities. Parkhurst's reaction was echoed by others. H.T. Parker, the music, drama and dance critic for the *Boston Evening Transcript* from 1905 to 1934, brought Pavlova to task on October 26, 1921 for the "late curtain, over-long intermissions, tawdry setting, cramped stage, hard lights, cheap costumes, clumsy, chopped up music, threadbare divertissements and sloppy principals." Pavlova, forty years of age in 1921, had been touring relentlessly for a dozen years. The standards likely slipped gradually over time, sinking to the point where the quality, to some, was no longer acceptable.

Anna Pavlova, *California Poppy.*

Ironically, Parkhurst's best dance reviews were written during this unacclaimed 1921 Pavlova tour. As he and the Toronto audience became more experienced dance viewers, his columns became more sophisticated. Without referring to specific steps, he succeeded in providing an outline of the story by describing the quality of the movement. Parkhurst's *Globe* review of November 29, 1921 enabled the reader both to sense the energy and to visualize the action as it had been perceived by the original reviewer.

> The "Polish Wedding" is set in a picturesque hill country, and round the cottage and tavern doors are enacted scenes of rare beauty and delightful sentiment. The approach of the wedding hour is heralded by the ceremonious arrival of the bridal veil, the rolling of a cask to the cottage door, and by dancing by girls and swains arranged in the richest of colours. As the wedding ceremony is enacted, heads are bowed, but exultant. Then the dance proceeds in real earnest, gaining in abandon.... Couples break from the company and seem the very incarnation of joy. Finally, the tottering old parents of the bride can restrain no longer, and join in the merry rounds.

Parkhurst's subsequent reviews did not match the quality of this 1921 effort, perhaps due to his advancing age and declining health. In the *Saturday Night* obituary of June 21, 1924, written by Charlesworth, he states that Parkhurst "had long since lost all interest in all but the musical aspects of the theatre." Dance, intimately aligned with music, had captured Parkhurst's interest when it was combined with Pavlova's alluring presence. These two elements, the music and Anna Pavlova, made him a willing observer and recorder of dance. His loyalty to ballet is confirmed by the number of reviews and previews he devoted to Pavlova and her companies. Each of her Toronto engagements received at least one review while Parkhurst was music and drama critic for the *Globe*. Charlesworth was less consistent, some Pavlova performances going unmentioned in *Saturday Night*.

The Parkhurst and Charlesworth columns, which cannot justifiably be considered perspicacious, unquestionably provide informative data of interest to researchers. In addition to learning about touring schedules, company size, repertoire, ticket prices and audience reaction, we discover the names of those who performed in Pavlova's companies. Mikhail Mordkin, Laurent Novikoff and Alexandre Volinine all partnered Pavlova at some point. All three were trained in Moscow and danced with the Diaghilev Ballets Russes before accompanying Pavlova on one (in Mordkin's case) or more tours. Ivan Clustine, who also trained at the Moscow Bolshoi Ballet School, was her ballet master from 1914 to 1922, and frequently appeared in the *Divertissements* section of the programme. Two young English dancers, Hilda Butsova (née Boot) and Muriel Stuart, performed leading roles. Muriel Stuart had studied with Pavlova, while Hilda Butsova received her training from Volinine and Enrico Cecchetti, Pavlova's mentor, who also travelled with the company on its 1913 North American tour.

A curiosity is the lack of publicity surrounding the engagement of a performer of Pavlova's stature. Photographs and previews appeared, but there is no indication that either Parkhurst or Charlesworth ever conducted an interview with the dancer. The newspapers never featured photographs showing the arrival of the company's train. The brief time the company spent in Toronto before and after each performance may explain the lack of additional materials which would be of such interest today. Canadian journalistic practices of the time may also be a factor.

Did Pavlova influence the development of dance in Toronto? In 1910, the year of her first Toronto appearance, two advertisements for dance schools were placed in *Saturday Night*. The Margaret Eaton School offered classes in physical culture, while Miss Sternberg taught dancing, physical culture and fencing in addition to a ladies' class in society dancing. Music schools far outnumbered dance schools, a situation that remained constant throughout the years of Pavlova's visits. However, an increased interest in classical ballet is evident from the classes offered by various dance teachers. For example, over the course of Pavlova's Toronto engagements, the content of Miss Sternberg's classes changed radically. In 1915, fencing and physical culture were replaced by classical, national and modern. By 1923, classes were offered in classical, national, interpretive, folk and modern. Pavlova's reper-toire likely led to the increased interest in classical and national, while the emergence and subsequent touring of dance companies under Ruth St. Denis, Ted Shawn, Doris Humphrey and others elevated the profile of interpretive and modern dance. This shift and expansion in the dance curriculum is indicative of a growing public awareness of theatrical dance forms. Not only were Torontonians seeing new dance forms, but they also wanted to learn more about them, to experience them personally. It was, however, a slow building process. By 1923, when J.E. Middleton's *Municipality of Toronto* was published, Pavlova had danced in seventeen performances during eight visits to Toronto. Still, within the fine arts section of this two-volume work, dance receives no mention. The reader is informed of the Toronto Conserv-atory of Music, the Mendelssohn Choir, the Oratorio Society, church choirs, chamber music organizations, theatres, art galleries and architecture, but dance is ignored. It is impossible to ascertain whether the author did not consider dance generally to be one of the fine arts, or if it was his opinion that the quality of dance performed by Torontonians did not merit that description.

Pavlova heralded the dawn of a new age of theatrical dance in Toronto. The growing popularity that began with her continued into the 1930s and 1940s when teacher-choreographer Boris Volkoff flourished, and led eventually to the founding of the Toronto-based National Ballet of Canada in 1951. Dance in Toronto continued to expand after that, the city becoming home to numerous modern dance companies, independent dancer-choreographers, and profes-sional level dance schools. Pavlova's legacy is clear. Can this be said of Hector Charlesworth and E.R. Parkhurst? Have they had an enduring influence? Parkhurst's contribution to dance rests in his changing attitude toward the art form and in his efforts to report on dance regularly and with integrity. In the end, both these critics concluded that dance deserved representation in their columns. The willingness of these two music and drama critics to not only accept dance, but ultimately to promote it, could only have had a positive effect on their readers, encouraging them to attend performances. Their legacy lies in public recognition of dance as a valid artistic form, worthy of attention and public support.

Chronology of Anna Pavlova's Toronto Performances

Date	Theatre	Other Principals	Ballets Presented
20 Oct. 1910	Massey Hall	Mikhail Mordkin	*The Legend of Azyiade, Divertissements* (mat)
			Giselle, The Legend of Azyiade, Divertissements (eve)
30 and 31 Dec. 1913	Massey Hall	Enrico Cecchetti Laurent Novikoff	*The Magic Flute, Invitation to the Dance, Divertissements* (30 eve)
			Oriental Fantasy, Paquita, Divertissements (31 eve)
14 Nov. 1914	Massey Hall	Ivan Clustine Serge Oukrainsky Alexandre Volinine	*The Fairy Doll (Puppenfee), The Dance of Today, Divertissements* (mat)
			Flora's Awakening, The Dance of Today, Divertissements (eve)
21-23 Oct. 1915 (with Boston Opera Co.)	The Arena	Alexandre Volinine	*Dumb Girl of Portici* (21) *Carmen* (22)
			Madame Butterfly (opera) *Snowflakes* (ballet) (23 mat) *The Love of Three Kings* (opera) *Elysian Fields* (ballet) (23 eve)
18, 19 Jan. 1916 (with Boston Opera Co.)	Royal Alexandra	Vajinsky	*I Pagliacci* (opera) *Coppélia* (ballet) (18)
			Madame Butterfly (opera) *Snowflakes* (ballet) (19 mat)
			La Boheme, Divertissements from *Carmen* and Spanish dances (19 eve)
20 Nov. 1920	Massey Hall	Marie Gleneva Alexandre Volinine	*Thais, Snowflakes, Divertissements* (mat)
			Egyptian Ballet, Chopiniana, Divertissements (eve)
28, 29 Nov. 1921	Massey Hall	Hilda Butsova Laurent Novikoff Muriel Stuart	*The Fairy Doll, The Polish Wedding, Divertissements* (28)
			The Magic Flute, Amarilla, Divertissements (29)
3 Apr. 1922	Massey Hall	Hilda Butsova Laurent Novikoff	*Chopiniana, Fairy Tales, Divertissements*

93

Pioneers

		Muriel Stuart Mlles. Cabeluezo, Griffith, Glynde and Cole	
19, 20 Nov. 1923	Massey Hall	Hilda Butsova Laurent Novikoff Mr. Oliveroff	The Magic Flute, Amarilla, Divertissements (19)
			The Fairy Doll, The Magic Flute, Divertissements (20 mat)
			The Polish Wedding, Chopiniana, Divertissements (20 eve)
14, 15 Nov. 1924	Massey Hall	Laurent Novikoff Mr. Oliveroff Muriel Stuart	Invitation to the Dance, Autumn Leaves, Divertissements (14)
			Coppélia, The Fairy Doll (15 mat)
			Coppélia, Flora's Awakening (15 eve)

Pavlova's company had a large repertoire of *Divertissements*, including *Bacchanale, The Swan, Valse Caprice, Gavotte Pavlova, Bow and Arrow, Anitra's Dance, Dance of the Hours, Voices of Spring* and a Kopak dance for seven male dancers. Several *Divertissements* were performed on each programme.

References

Charlesworth, Hector. 1910-1924. "Music and Drama." *Saturday Night*. Selected columns.

Charlesworth, Hector. 1928. *More Candid Chronicles*. Toronto: The Macmillan Co. of Canada.

Kallmann, Helmut. "Edwin Parkhurst." 1992. *Encyclopedia of Music in Canada*. 2nd ed. Toronto: University of Toronto Press.

McLean, Maud. "Hector Charlesworth." 1992. *Encyclopedia of Music in Canada*. 2nd ed. Toronto: University of Toronto Press.

Middleton, J.E. 1923. *The Municipality of Toronto: A History*. 2 vols. Toronto: The Dominion Publishing Company.

Money, Keith. 1982. *Anna Pavlova: Her Life and Art*. London: Collins.

Parker, H.T. 1982. "Anna Pavlova." In *Motion Arrested: Dance Reviews of H.T. Parker*. Olive Holmes, ed. Middleton, Connecticut: Wesleyan University Press.

Parkhurst, E.R. 1910-1924. "Music and the Drama." Toronto *Globe*. Selected columns.

"Parkhurst, E.R." 1912. *The Canadian Men and Women of the Time*. 2nd ed.

Music and Movement:

The Overlapping Careers of Madeleine Boss Lasserre and Saida Gerrard

Selma Landen Odom

In an old notebook, brief directions describe a movement improvisation: "A group bending down. Saida center, higher than others. Hands in cuffs behind back. Try to get out of them. Finally drop down, dead. Resurrection. Do not tell them what to do, play it for them."[1] With the students responding in movement to the teacher's piano improvisation, this scene concluded a Dalcroze Eurhythmics lesson given at the Toronto Conservatory of Music in November 1929.

Madeleine Boss Lasserre, the teacher who specialized in the new method of music training based on physical experience, had recently turned twenty-eight. Several students in her advanced class (five women and one man) were older than she was, but one was definitely younger. Still in high school, sixteen-year-old Saida Gerrard worked hard to master the most challenging exercises of counterpoint, polyrhythm and syncopation. With her classmates, she explored Bach Inventions and other musical forms by walking, running and gesturing. She also played piano and studied dancing.

Teacher and student shared a passion for music and movement. For a few years their paths were closely intertwined, and they even reversed roles briefly, when Lasserre took or observed Mary Wigman-style modern dance as taught by Gerrard in the 1930s. Then they diverged. Lasserre, an immigrant from Switzerland, continued to teach Eurhythmics in Canada, while Toronto-born Gerrard made a distinguished career as dancer and choreographer in the United States. Yet they managed to keep in touch for many years. Gerrard periodically contacted her former teacher when she returned to visit, and each took great interest in the other's work.

I learned of their relationship from both of them, first from Lasserre, with whom I had many meetings between 1979 and 1998, when she died at the age of ninety-six, and subsequently from phone interviews with Gerrard, who now lives in Los Angeles. In the past year, I've spent a lot of time looking through

---

[1] This essay is largely based on Lasserre's notebooks, clippings and related materials, which I am organizing for future deposit in Special Collections of York University's Scott Library.

Madeleine Boss Lasserre, ca. 1925.

Lasserre's notebooks, which span almost sixty years, from the beginning of her professional training in 1918 through her retirement in 1977. They reveal the excitement of ideas that came to her as she taught her earliest students such as Gerrard and also, amazingly, that she still wrote "New!" by exercises she gave in her final years of teaching. I rely on Lasserre's meticulous records and both women's collections of clippings and programmes for details of the stories that follow.

Madeleine Boss was born in Neuchâtel, Switzerland on October 5, 1901. Her father was a teacher; her mother died when she was young. She received initial instruction in Dalcroze work through her public school music programme. At barely eighteen, she followed the suggestion of Mlle Virchaux, her piano teacher, that she go to Geneva to study with Émile Jaques-Dalcroze (1865-1950). Dalcroze, a noted composer, had developed a method of music education that involves the whole body in experiences of listening and moving. After his music training in Paris and Vienna with composers Gabriel Fauré and Anton Bruckner, he became fascinated with rhythm during a year he spent in Algeria. During the 1890s, he searched for ways to help his conservatory students in Geneva respond to music more accurately and expressively. Experimenting with exercises of walking and breathing, beating time, gesturing and improvising, he pursued the origins of music in the human body, the original musical instrument. From these beginnings, he and his colleagues pursued movement and improvisation as creative approaches to learning. Their teaching influenced music, dance and theatre education in schools around the world. In English-speaking countries, the Dalcroze method came to be known as Eurhythmics, an invented word that means good rhythm.[2]

When Madeleine Boss studied at the Institut Jaques-Dalcroze from 1919 to 1922, her peers in the professional training programme came from many countries. Most were women, not quite as young as she. Those wishing to teach

---

[2] For further information on Dalcroze and Eurhythmics, see Odom (1992, 1995 and 1998b).

the method were expected to achieve a high level of musicianship by studying rhythmic movement, solfège (sol-fa singing exercises) and improvisation as well as "plastique animée" (movement composition), body technique, anatomy and physiology, theory and notation, harmony, pedagogy, piano and choral singing. She studied extensively with Dalcroze's assistant Paul Boepple, a gifted choral conductor who premiered Honegger's *Le Roi David* in that period. Another influence was Annie Beck, a teacher at the London School of Dalcroze Eurhythmics, who came to choreograph productions in which Boss performed. Beck was highly regarded for the movement she created for several of Dalcroze's collaborations with Adolphe Appia, whose architectural stage designs are considered landmarks in the history of modernist theatre (Odom 1998a). Boss took the part of a nymph in one of these, *Echo et Narcisse*, in 1920.

With her Dalcroze certificate in hand, Madeleine Boss was qualified to begin practicing a new profession. She spent a year in Paris and then, eager to work abroad, she made her way to Canada in 1924. She first lived with a leading Toronto family, teaching their fragile child at homes on Wellesley Place and the western shore of Lake Simcoe. She intended to leave Canada the following year to take a Dalcroze position at the Maret French School in Washington, D.C., when one day she met a handsome older man at a figure skating class. She stayed to marry Henri Lasserre, who turned out to be a fellow Swiss who was teaching French at Victoria College of the University of Toronto. A first cousin of Appia and like him a native of Geneva, Henri Lasserre was a former lawyer and fine amateur cellist. He had devoted his inherited wealth to promoting cooperative living and enterprise ventures in Switzerland (Thomson 1949: 1-21) before moving to Canada in 1921. His organizational experience no doubt helped in his wife's efforts to establish an association to build interest in Dalcroze Eurhythmics in Toronto.

The Margaret Eaton School, the institution that was established as The School of Expression in 1901, announced as part of its reorganization in October 1925 that Madeleine Boss Lasserre would join the faculty. According to the 1925-1926 season brochure, she offered classes for adults and children of different ages in a "method for the development of muscular control, rhythmic sense, musical feeling and self expression through music." Lasserre quickly earned the respect of one of her first adult students, Duncan McKenzie, then Director of Music for the Toronto schools, who believed the method could be applied for all ages in the music classroom. Her work was a welcome addition along with folk dancing and Russian ballet, since the Margaret Eaton School emphasized dramatic literature and, increasingly, physical education. This unique school merged with the University of Toronto in 1941 to become the School of Physical and Health Education (Jackson 1953 and Byl 1992).

Several newspaper accounts enthusiastically described her first public demonstration on April 7, 1926. In the words of the *Toronto Telegram* writer, "a group of happy children" capably showed the work's merits: "The music to which they marched or danced was much more than sound to them. They moved to its rhythm, but they also answered instinctively its other messages.

When it was loud their groupings were far flung and bold in contour, when it grew softer, they drew together, and when it was at its softest they became a sort of whispering fairy ring, fleet-footed and ready at the first breath of crescendo to widen out again in their gambols. And changeful rhythms – from triple to duple, simple to compound – sudden sforzandos, smooth legatos, jerky mazurka accent, or even the hesitancies of syncopation, found them always ready. Their little ears were quick, but their bodies and limbs were not a pulse behind" ("Yenmita" [Edward W. Wodson] 10 Apr. 1926).

In 1927 Lasserre joined the Toronto Conservatory of Music, later called the Royal Conservatory of Music, where she taught for fifty years. There she led hundreds of people into the world of music, using movement and singing to teach the basics of rhythm, pitch, shadings and form. Agile and lithe, she stepped back and forth from her piano on a platform to the floor of the large room where her classes learned music by moving barefoot. Anyone interested could visit the "open" lessons she gave at the beginning of each month. With her students, beginners to advanced, Lasserre also presented demonstrations twice a year, which were attended by prominent musicians as well as proud parents. Sir Ernest MacMillan, conductor of the Toronto Symphony Orchestra, endorsed Eurhythmics as "one of the best means of learning to *live* music, of developing concentration and physical grace, and of illuminating the study of musical form" (undated signed statement in the Lasserre collection).

In her engaging introductions she would say, in one way or another, "What you are going to see is not a performance of a prepared programme but a series of spontaneous reactions. Our aim is to show you the way we work rather than the results of our work."[3] Then she would lead the students through a sequence of exercises and studies of increasing difficulty, usually involving several levels of children in various sets of coloured tunics. The major critics Lawrence Mason, Hector Charlesworth and Augustus Bridle wrote frequently about her early work. "Music of Muscle and Mind," was the title of an article by Edward W. Wodson, who described how Lasserre's advanced students "translated music played on the piano into terms of muscular movement; they painted crescendos and diminuendos by eloquence of gesture that couldn't be misunderstood. They sang intervals and scale phrases that proved infallibly how thorough their knowledge of tonalism and harmony is" (*Toronto Telegram* 14 Nov. 1930).

The future poet Dorothy Livesay took an evening course Lasserre taught for University of Toronto students around 1930 at Annesley Hall, the Victoria College women's residence. Livesay later wrote, "I believe this kinesthetic activity strengthened my feeling for rhythm in poetry. But it did not change my stiff, uncoordinated body movements. I remained too self-conscious to let go and dance. Instead, the words did that" (1991: 91). Lasserre enlisted her help to arrange publicity for special events of the Dalcroze Eurhythmics Association: "Ask Dorothy Livesay about article – *Varsity* or any other paper or magazine," she wrote opposite one of her lesson plans.

[3] Lasserre's collection includes handwritten notes for well over 100 demonstrations she gave with her students between 1926 and 1967. She held open classes in lieu of demonstrations between 1968 and 1977.

Several times, Lasserre brought her former teacher Paul Boepple, then head of the New York Dalcroze School, to give demonstrations. A large audience attended the first of these on March 29, 1928 in Convocation Hall at the University of Toronto. Lasserre arranged to send her best students to complete their professional training with him and later with his successor Hilda Schuster in New York. In 1932 she herself returned to Geneva for several months to be examined for her diploma, the highest credential obtainable in Dalcroze work, which is awarded to the experienced few who are deemed capable of training others to teach Eurhythmics. Needless to say, she earned it with ease.

Young Saida Gerrard also left Toronto for further study, going to New York on the strength of an article she read in *Dance Magazine*.[4] Born on April 9, 1913, she was the daughter of Russian immigrants who were keen music lovers and amateur musicians. Her first dance teachers were Maude McCann and Nora Griffiths. As a young child she had seen Pavlova and later the Isadora Duncan Dancers from Moscow as well as the "gorgeous" women who came with Boepple from New York to participate in his Dalcroze demonstration. In 1931 Gerrard began two years of study on scholarship at the newly opened Mary Wigman School in New York, where Hanya Holm was her main teacher. Interestingly enough, both Wigman and Holm, leading exponents of modern dance in Germany, had extensive Dalcroze backgrounds as well as grounding in Rudolf Laban's space theories and improvisational practices (Odom 1986).

Gerrard eventually studied ballet with Margaret Craske and trained at the Humphrey-Weidman School and with other modern dance leaders such as Fe Alf, Sarah Mildred Strauss, Benjamin Zemach and Martha Graham. Despite her complete immersion in the New York scene, she returned frequently to perform and teach in Toronto during the 1930s and 1940s. In 1934, over 8,000 people attended her dynamic performance of *The Sorcerer's Apprentice* in the first season of the immensely popular Promenade Symphony Concerts conducted by Reginald Stewart at Varsity Arena. Of course she remembers that Madame Lasserre, as she called her, attended. Edward W. Wodson wrote that Gerrard's "technique is notable, perfect synchronization of muscular movement with the most sensitive appreciation of music's rhythmic life, and light and shade" and that she produced a "stark and very intense realism" (*Toronto Telegram* 28 Sept. 1934).

For a two-year period after her father's death, Gerrard committed herself to creating a school in Toronto, and despite the constraints of the Depression she succeeded in attracting ninety students. She taught children, adults and professionals from 1934 to 1936 at her Toronto Studio of Modern Dance, first on Grenville Street and then on the top floor of the Hermant Building downtown, where her studio had tall windows looking out over Lake Ontario. She also taught at the University of Toronto through the drama extension course. Her classes in technique, improvisation, percussion and group work prepared ensembles of dancers who performed at venues such as the Art

---

[4] Much of what follows is based on my telephone interviews with Saida Gerrard and materials in her file at Dance Collection Danse, Toronto.

Saida Gerrard, ca. 1935.

Gallery of Toronto, where at the invitation of painter Arthur Lismer she first presented *Songs of Unrest* in 1935.

The same year, Herman Voaden invited Gerrard's group to take part in his famous experimental Play Workshop series at Central High School of Commerce. Her dance chorale *Death and Transfiguration*, set to music by Richard Strauss, was billed as "an experiment in dance drama." It included bold expressionist light and colour effects by Voaden. For a Promenade Concert in 1935, Gerrard choreographed and performed *Hunger*, a solo set to an original percussion score, the polka from Weinberger's *Schwanda* and *Negro Spirituals*. For Gerrard that period in Toronto meant being part of a "small vibrant group in the arts, people who had something to say, who wanted to make things better for everyone. We wanted content [in our work], to wake people up" (23 Sept. 1999).

Three pages in one of Lasserre's notebooks give insight into what Gerrard taught in her modern dance classes of the 1930s. It is almost certain that Lasserre participated in these experiences herself because of the very brief way she wrote them down. Had she been observing, she would have made more complete notes, as she did in various other situations. According to Lasserre, Gerrard's technique work included "all kinds of ways of walking: carried away with one's weight, legs leading, shoulder leading, hip leading, etc. Diagonally, turning around, squaring steps, very high or very low, etc." Similarly, she noted down directions for exploring what could be done with other parts of the body, such as "in and out" movements, rotations and "figure 8s" for the shoulders and hips. Lasserre also described many of Gerrard's improvisation ideas. Here are several examples:

– Feet rooted to floor on a wide base – work oneself up to a frenzy.

– 2 groups attacking each other and retreating. No leader but feel in group and act accordingly.

– A wall and a prisoner trying to get out. Wall reacts to movement of soloist and

100

finally breaks apart if prisoner is the strongest.

– Each one is a tree – one or two spirits are wandering about seeking refuge. Trees call them but reject them when they come near.

– Walking in all kinds of soil and surroundings. In a barrel – under a very low ceiling – on slippery soil – in deep water, etc.

– Wake up to 2 forces – one dragging you to pleasure and satisfaction of your instincts – the other being all inspiration to do bigger and higher things – the struggle it produces.

– Architecture – feeling lines (monuments, buildings) individually and in groups.

Ray W. Harris, in an article titled "Saida Gerrard – Genius Terpsichorean," wrote around this time that she "was the first to plant the seeds of a modern dance movement in this country. Slender and graceful, young and soft-spoken, with compelling unwavering eyes like stars of flashing blue, her brow clear and broad, her beautiful pale face electrifying in its cameo-like transparency, this girl with the body of a young goddess looks in every respect the genius whose unique endeavor places her among the leaders in her art. It is when she talks of her beloved dance in her own cultured manner that one meets the philosopher, the idealist, and submits willingly to her claims. For a great dancer is also a philosopher, and Saida Gerrard is as eloquent and convincing in her speech as she is in her dancing" (clipping from unidentifiable periodical ca. 1935).

Gerrard made New York her base from around 1936 through 1951. During this period, she danced and choreographed actively, working extensively as a soloist with Charles Weidman and on specific concerts with many other American dance notables including Louis Horst and Hanya Holm. In New York she choreographed *Sea Shanties* and *Waterfront Hornpipe* for a Works Progress Administration concert in 1937 as well as a dance version of *The Grapes of Wrath* (ca. 1940) and *Hostage, 1942*. In 1938, the Toronto Skating Club produced Gerrard's *The Machine*, set to a score by the noted young American composer Wallingford Riegger. She again returned to Toronto in 1949 to produce dances for Max Helfman's highly acclaimed choral tone poem *Di Naye Hagode* (*The Glory of the Warsaw Ghetto*), in which she herself performed the role of the heroic seventeen-year-old who was the last defender in the 1943 uprising. Dancers from the New Dance Theatre appeared with her in this work as well as in *The Lonesome Train* by Earl Robinson, both supported by the full force of the Toronto Symphony and the Jewish Folk Choir. This programme was repeated the following year in Toronto and later in Detroit and Chicago productions. It was her association with Helfman that led to her creating "a series of dances on Hebraic themes" in California (Dougherty 1963: 16).

From the 1950s through the 1980s, Gerrard led an active career in Los Angeles, where she directed modern dance companies and choreographed films, operas, plays and revues. She taught modern dance and composition at Eugene Loring's School of American Dance as well as the University of Southern California and the University of Judaism. Occasionally her groups shared programmes with the Charles Weidman and Gloria Newman companies. In the 1960s she took modern dance for the first time to rural areas of the West Coast, touring seven states from Washington to Arizona.

Meanwhile, Lasserre worked unceasingly in Toronto to introduce people to Eurhythmics, giving countless demonstrations and short courses for teachers' organizations, the Women's Art Association, Hart House Theatre and music groups of all kinds in Ontario. By the time she retired in 1977, Lasserre had taught several generations at the conservatory and the University Settlement School of Music, where she worked as a volunteer. Drama specialist Toby Ciglen says she was "always a part of my life, always my teacher, like a second mother" (19 Nov. 1998). She vividly remembers sitting on the floor and listening as Lasserre would "dissect the thematic strands or draw diagrams in different colored chalks to show us how the lines of music of a Bach Invention would chase each other." Toronto textile artist Temma Gentles remembers her many years of study with Lasserre: "Music just flowed out of her fingers. She could improvise and do all kinds of things. The music was just there, like speaking, and to me it was a miracle" (21 Oct. 1998).

Gordon Jocelyn, one of the first music education students at the University of Toronto in the late 1940s, took her course instead of physical education. He found her energy at the piano "overwhelming," especially the way she could respond to the class moving on the floor. But she could move, too; "it was a two-way thing" (23 Oct. 1998). All four of his children, including the late artist Tim Jocelyn, studied with her. Her student Donald Himes went on to earn his certificate at the Institut Jaques-Dalcroze in Geneva and returned to a multi-faceted career in music and dance as well as Dalcroze and Feldenkrais work. He taught Eurhythmics in "the first class at the newly-opened National Ballet School" in 1959, with Veronica Tennant among his students (Jackson 1977: 23-24). Himes taught the work while he also trained as a modern dancer and worked as accompanist at Patricia Beatty's New Dance Group studio in the mid-1960s; later he danced and taught for many years with Toronto Dance Theatre.

Donna Wood, who studied with Lasserre beginning in the 1940s, became an international leader in early childhood music education. Ruth Pincoe eventually became a musicologist and editor, cataloguing the Glenn Gould papers for the National Library. She was a Lasserre student around the same time as Abigail Hoffmann, later the Olympic track star. Megan Follows, the actress of *Anne of Green Gables* fame, was one of Lasserre's students during the last years of her teaching. These are just a few of the many whose lives she touched. She delighted in the imagination of her children, but then too it was her own playful spirit that reached out to excite them. Her lesson plans are filled with ideas based on animal movements, such as "frog and mouse (ABAB form)," spider and fly, flamingo and fish, ponies, caterpillar, woodpecker, snake, turtle, tiger and "wise old owl." She also used seasonal themes such as shoveling snow, melting snowmen, April rain and raking leaves. Tucked into her teaching notebooks are many examples of clumsily written notation exercises with charming drawings and stories. One girl who drew a tiny piano with a large keyboard wrote, "Madame Lasserre, I love you."

Her collection of playbills shows her ongoing fascination with opera, theatre and especially dance. She saw the Toronto appearances of Irma Duncan with the Isadora Duncan Dancers, Wigman, Kreutzburg and Georgi, La Argentina, Graham, Shawn, the Ballet Russe de Monte Carlo, the Sadler's Wells Ballet and the Canadian Ballet Festival in 1949. She was well into her nineties when she finally gave up her symphony subscription, but she lived independently until a week before she died. Thanks to television, her interest in music and dance never waned, and in retirement she had time to read passionately. When I last saw her in June 1998, she handed me, as usual, a little pile of newspaper clippings, this time about the Canada Dance Festival.

Lasserre was a fount of wisdom who encouraged me in my long-term project to study the Dalcroze method's history. In our many conversations, she more than anyone else helped me understand the core teaching practices, the personalities, the politics and the significance of this work. When she moved to a smaller place in 1988, I persuaded her not to dispose of her notebooks, groundplan sketches for works by Bach, photos, pamphlets, playbills and two films. Shot outdoors in the late 1930s and 1940s, these silent films show classic Dalcroze exercises such as leading and following with a partner, conducting with the body (a leader directs the group's movements) and her choreographic studies in which she herself is one of the tunic-clad participants. Currently I am organizing this collection, which is a remarkably complete record of a teacher's life work.

In doing so, I've learned from a file of correspondence called "Dalcroze Prof[essional] Course" the story of something she did not discuss, which must have been a disappointment in an otherwise satisfying career. The most influential music leaders in English-speaking Canada knew and supported her teaching. In 1951 Dr. Arnold Walter, head of the Royal Conservatory of Music, wanted to establish a Dalcroze department at the University of Toronto, of which the conservatory was then a part. Even though a second Dalcroze diplomate, Brenda Beament of Ottawa, was willing to teach in the proposed programme, negotiations with the Institut Jaques-Dalcroze were not successful. Dalcroze had died in 1950, and his successors would not approve a programme without the hiring of an additional specialist from Geneva. There was no chance of raising sufficient funds for this purpose, however. In 1953 Walter became the president of the International Society for Music Education (ISME) and soon changed direction. He helped to arrange a special scholarship for Canadian violinist Doreen Hall to study with Carl Orff in Salzburg, after which she led a successful programme for thirty years at the University of Toronto. Together they established Orff-Schulwerk in North America.

In Canada today music education is typically based on the approaches of Orff and Kodaly, although Louise Mathieu teaches Dalcroze work in the music faculty at Laval University in Quebec and there are a number of qualified specialists who teach in conservatories and schools in Toronto and other major cities. Was Lasserre bitter about the missed opportunity for Dalcroze professional training in Canada? She seems to have closed the file and moved on, continuing to teach the method she loved and believed in so much. To the end of her life, she maintained close relations with her Dalcroze colleagues, especially Nelly Schinz and Mathilde Reymond-Sauvain, whom she had known since childhood, and the intrepid Edith Naef, who at over 100 years old still taught a class of mature women, her former students, at the Institut Jaques-Dalcroze in Geneva.

There is another story of something that did not happen in the 1950s, this one concerning Saida Gerrard. In 1956 Ettore Mazzoleni asked her to return and establish a modern dance department at the Royal Conservatory of Music. Unfortunately, no position would be available until the following year for Aube Tzerko, her husband who was also from Toronto and a noted pianist, having studied in Germany with Artur Schnabel. So they decided to stay in California. For many years he taught the most elite piano students at UCLA and the Aspen Music Festival in Colorado during the summers (Chodos et al. 1996: 37-40). Saida Gerrard also taught musicians at Aspen almost up until Tzerko's death in 1995. She gave them "not just a workout but dance, so they could experience basic movement, the quality and stepping" of various historical dance forms (22 Oct. 1998).

Going separate ways but remembering each other, Lasserre and Gerrard explored music and movement throughout their long, fruitful careers. The teaching and learning they shared in Toronto when both were young are what explain the intensity of their bond. In the performing arts people rarely forget their earliest connections, the teachers and peers with whom they spend the long hours of training necessary to master skills and embody knowledge. Even more, they treasure the moments of improvisation and discovery when they extend themselves into the unknown. That is the adventure implicit in Lasserre's notes for the improvisation quoted at the beginning: "Do not tell them what to do, play it for them." Working together in movement, people can find out who they really are.

References

This essay is based on Madeleine Boss Lasserre's notebooks, unpublished papers, drawings, correspondence, clipping files, scrapbooks, programmes and playbills, photographs and films (which will eventually be deposited in Special Collections of York University's Scott Library) and clippings, programmes and related materials in the Saida Gerrard file at Dance Collection Danse, Toronto.

Anon. 7 May 1927. "Note and Comment [on Madeleine Boss Lasserre]." *Saturday Night.*

Anon. Mar. 1935. "Saturday at the Art Gallery – An Impression." *The Curtain Call*, 1-2.

Bridle, Augustus. 30 Mar. 1928. "The Poetry of Motion in Intricate Dances." *Toronto Daily Star.*

Bridle, Augustus. 7 Apr. 1928. "Dalcroze Eurhythmics Still Experiment." *Toronto Daily Star*.

Bridle, Augustus. 28 Sept. 1934. "Turn Away Thousands as Prom Hits Record: Saida Gerrard Is Popular in Remarkable Debut Dances." *Toronto Daily Star*.

Byl, John. 1992. "Margaret Eaton School, 1901-1942: Women's Education in Elocution, Drama and Physical Education." Ph.D. dissertation, State University of New York at Buffalo.

Chodos, Gabriel et al. "Aube Tzerko: Sound, Fury, and Passion." Nov.-Dec. 1996. *Piano & Keyboard* 183, 37-40.

Cohen, Nathan. ca. Mar. 1949. "The Choir Excels Itself." Clipping from unidentified newspaper in Gerrard file, Dance Collection Danse.

Connolly, Kate T. Oct. 1928. "Madame Madeleine Boss Lasserre: Canada's Only Eurythmics Teacher." *The Canadian Magazine*.

Dougherty, John. Mar. 1963. "Saida Gerrard Discusses 'The L.A. Problem.'" *Dance Magazine*, 16, 67.

Gerrard, Saida. 19 Apr. 1935. "The Dance." *The Jewish Standard*, 13.

Harris, Ray W. ca. 1935. "Saida Gerrard – Genius Terpsichorean." Clipping from unidentifiable periodical in Gerrard file, Dance Collection Danse. Reprinted in *Dance Collection Danse News* 39 (1994).

Irving, Allan et al. 1995. *Neighbours: Three Social Settlements in Downtown Toronto*. Toronto: Canadian Scholars' Press Inc.

Jackson, Dorothy N. R. 1953. *A Brief History of Three Schools: The School of Expression, The Margaret Eaton School of Literature and Expression, The Margaret Eaton School 1901-1941*. Toronto: University of Toronto.

Jackson, Graham. Summer 1977. "Graham Training Settles in Canada." *Dance in Canada*, 21-24.

Johnston, Richard. 24 Mar. 1950. "Music in Toronto: Jewish Folk Choir under Emil Gartner Offers Interesting Program." *Globe and Mail*.

Lasserre, Madeleine Boss. Winter 1931. "Dalcroze Eurythmics and Musical Education." *Conservatory Quarterly Review* 13:2, 45-46.

Livesay, Dorothy. 1991. *Journey with My Selves. A Memoir 1909-1963*. Vancouver: Douglas & McIntyre.

MacMillan, Ernest. Undated signed statement on "Dalcroze Eurythmics" in Lasserre collection.

Mason, Lawrence. 31 Mar. 1928. "Dalcroze Eurhythmics." *The Globe*.

McCarthy, Pearl. 28 Sept. 1934. "Music Lovers Sit on Railings at Promenade Symphony Jam." *Mail and Empire*.

Pioneers

Odom, Selma Landen. 1986. "Wigman at Hellerau." *Ballet Review* 14:2, 41-53.

Odom, Selma Landen. 1992. "Dalcroze Eurhythmics." *Encyclopedia of Music in Canada*, 2nd ed. Toronto: University of Toronto Press.

Odom, Selma Landen. 1995. "Dalcroze Eurhythmics as an Oral Tradition." In *La Memòria de la Dansa*. Barcelona: Association Européenne des Historiens de la Danse, 31-38.

Odom, Selma Landen. 1998a. "Dalcroze's Dutch Collaborators." In *Dance in the Netherlands 1600-2000. New Directions in Historical and Methodological Research*. Amsterdam: Theater Instituut Nederland, 65-73.

Odom, Selma Landen. 1998b. "Émile Jaques-Dalcroze." *International Encyclopedia of Dance*. New York: Oxford University Press.

Thomson, Watson. 1949. *Pioneer in Community: Henri Lasserre's Contribution to the Fully Cooperative Society*. Toronto: The Ryerson Press.

Wodson, Edward W. 14 Nov. 1930. "Music of Muscle and Mind." *Toronto Telegram*.

Wodson, Edward W. 28 Sept. 1934. "Wigman Dance Delights Folk at Prom. Fete." *Toronto Telegram*.

"Yenmita" [Edward W. Wodson]. 10 Apr. 1926. "Dalcroze System Lesson." *Toronto Telegram*.

Interviews

Beament, Brenda. Various interviews between 1983 and 1998.

Ciglen, Toby. 19 Nov. 1998.

Gentles, Temma. 21 Oct. 1998.

Gerrard, Saida. Telephone interviews: 22 Oct. 1998, 3 Dec. 1998, 15 June 1999, 23 Sept. 1999.

Himes, Donald. Various interviews between 1972 and 1999.

Jocelyn, Gordon. 23 Oct. 1998.

Lasserre, Madeleine Boss. Numerous interviews between 1979 and 1998.

Lasserre, Monty. Various interviews between 1998 and 1999.

Pincoe, Ruth. 19 Apr. 1999.

Wood, Donna. Various interviews between 1982 and 1998.

Creating a Canadian Imaginative Background:
Herman Voaden and Symphonic Expressionism

Anton Wagner

In his influential 1864 essay "The Function of Criticism at the Present Time," Matthew Arnold suggested that critics should always seek "to learn and propagate the best that is known and thought in the world, and thus to establish a current of fresh and true ideas" (1968: 28).[1] For Arnold, a period of "true creative activity" and the development of new artistic forms was directly linked to the "current of fresh ideas" provided by genuine criticism.

In Canada during the first three decades of the twentieth century, artists faced almost insurmountable obstacles to the creation of a distinct indigenous art. The country lacked a large educated public supportive of indigenous creation, significant government or private support of the arts, and a basic cultural infrastructure that could produce an artistic flowering through the stimulus of new ideas and artistic forms. Artists themselves had to establish links to international artistic currents and determine which forms and ideas to incorporate into their artistic practice in Canada.

The attempt by Herman Voaden (1903-1991) to establish a distinct, multimedia "Canadian 'Art of the Theatre'" reveals the rich and complex intermingling of Canadian and international cultural influences during the 1920s and 1930s. Voaden's attempt to create in Toronto a "symphonic" theatre art form in which dance movement was an integral part also reveals the tremendous challenges faced by artists to win critical and public support and to transform artistic ideas into actual artistic expression.

Ann Saddlemyer, in her essay "Thoughts on National Drama and the Founding of Theatres," suggests that Canadian drama is characterized by "arriving, exploring, questioning, and, above all, by celebrating the discovery of *place*" (1982: 193). In English Canada, however, this discovery and imaginative recreation in dramatic terms of Canadian life, nature and its effect upon human character is a relatively recent phenomenon. In the preface to the

---

[1] For Arnold's influence on Canadian critics, see the introduction and essays on Hector Charlesworth and Lawrence Mason in Anton Wagner, ed. *Establishing Our Boundaries: English-Canadian Theatre Criticism* (Toronto: University of Toronto Press, 1999).

1901 edition of his poetic drama *Tecumseh*, first published in 1886, Charles Mair asserted that "our romantic Canadian story is a mine of character and incident for the poet and novelist, framed, too, in a matchless environment. The Canadian author who seeks inspiration there is helping to create for a young people that decisive test of its intellectual faculties, an original and distinctive literature – a literature liberal in its range, but, in its highest forms, springing in a large measure from the soil, and tasting of the wood" (3).

Yet, despite Mair's belief in the rich imaginative sources for literary achievements to be found in Canadian nature, such achievements were slow to emerge in the field of drama. Harcourt Farmer, writing in the *Canadian Bookman* as late as 1919, still called for "national interpretation in terms of individual expression through drama" and asked "where are the Canadian playwrights? I mean persons of Canadian descent, or adoption, who have written plays the subject matter of which deals with some intrinsic part of Canadian life, past or present, and whose plays are directly artistic representations of Canadian life, or interpretations of Canadian temperament" (55).

The scarcity of English-Canadian playwrights until the 1920s cannot be explained solely by the absence of professional, or even significant amateur, theatres producing indigenous dramatic works. Perhaps of even greater significance was the lack of psychological identification and imaginative "oneness" between Canadians and their physical environment. Robertson Davies has commented on our British cultural influences in particular, noting that "Canada did not cease to be a colony, psychologically, until long after I was born [i.e. 1913], and in matters relating to the arts its colonialism was absolute" (1982: 41). He wrote:

> A national culture arises from the depths of a people, and Canadians knew where those depths were, and certainly it was not here. There were too many Canadians who were physically loyal to the new land, but who remained exiles in matters of the spirit. You might as well have asked for an indigenous form of government, or an indigenous religion, as ask for Canadian art. Theatre, music, and literature did not originate here. They came from home, wherever home might be (41).

It is precisely this imaginative and spiritual identification with Canadian nature, expressed in a non-realist representational form, that the Group of Seven sought to achieve in painting in the 1920s and Herman Voaden attempted to express through "symphonic expressionism" in the 1930s.

Cultural Influences

Voaden's non-realist, multimedia production and playwriting style was a complex synthesis of international and Canadian cultural influences filtered through, and pouring out of, Voaden's own highly subjective and mystical artistic sensibility. These influences, beginning with his initial modern drama studies at Queen's University (1920-23) and concluding in 1943 during the altered cultural climate of the Second World War, shaped both the external form and inner content of Voaden's productions.

While completing his M.A. thesis on Eugene O'Neill at Queen's in 1926, he assimilated the vocabulary of the fluid non-realist production style of the European expressionist and expressionist-influenced theatre and dance and their frequent theme of creating a higher social order and human being. Thomas Wilfred's demonstration in Toronto of his colour organ, the "clavilux," had already suggested to Voaden in 1924 how the combination of music and coloured lighting could transform the stage into a visual counterpart of the central character's emotions.

Voaden was directly influenced by Gordon Craig's stage designs and Adolphe Appia's use of light on plastic surfaces. In 1929, he built a Craig-inspired permanent unit setting, designed by Lowrie Warrener, consisting of steps, curtains, platforms, pylons and screens, for productions at the Central High School of Commerce that was used until the mid-1930s. Richard Wagner's music dramas, which he saw at Bayreuth in the summer of 1928, were an inspiration through their synthesis of scene, music, poetry and a heroic conception of life, as were Max Reinhardt's productions through their blending of music, dance, mime, dramatic light and colour.

Influenced by these modern stage techniques, Voaden attempted in his own non-realist multimedia stage language of the 1930s to substitute the beauty of lighting, music, dance movement, sculptural groupings and settings, and nearly chanted speech for the literary qualities of conventional drama to achieve, in an abstract symphonic fusion, Walter Pater's "condition of music." Pater had suggested that all art aspires to the condition of music, leaping from the chains of the concrete and material into its own world to become a direct expression of spiritual reality. In his symphonic expressionism, Voaden similarly attempted to create "a new elevated composite musical speech" and a theatre "where design and colour can meet music, language, dance – all the arts – in an utterance of symphonic quality" (Voaden notes 1939).

On a formal and thematic level, Voaden's non-realist stage language enabled him to reject what he perceived as the "pessimistic coarseness" of Naturalism. He sought instead to embody the transcendence of life and death that he found in the symbolic and mystical conception of dance movement by artists he saw perform such as the Isadora Duncan Dancers (1924) and Anna Pavlova (Massey Hall, 1929) and, on a literary level, in the beauty and spirituality of poetic, romantic and symbolic drama by playwrights such as Rostand and Shaw. In forming his own mystical beliefs, he was strongly influenced by the idealistic philosophy of Carlyle and Shaw's philosophy of creative evolution, the neo-platonic transcendentalism of the English Romantic poets, Blake's communion with God through art and the imagination, and Whitman's example of a new, heroic, universal self-expression.

Yet, Voaden's symphonic expressionism was much more than a mere confluence of European and North American theatrical and literary models and philosophic thought. His artistic and spiritual search for meaning reflected, and grew out of, the English-Canadian cultural nationalism of the 1920s and 1930s in which artists and intellectuals, several of them leading theosophists, sought to forge a Canadian national identity based on, as Mair had suggested, an imaginative identification with the Canadian landscape.

It is doubtful that Voaden would have developed his symphonic expressionist aesthetic without the artistic and philosophic inspiration of the Group of Seven painters, their artist friends such as Roy Mitchell and Bertram Brooker, and critical supporters and popularizers such as Augustus Bridle and F.B. Housser. By their non-realistic representation of the Canadian landscape that they (particularly Lawren Harris) sanctified to the level of the spiritual, the Group of Seven demonstrated to Voaden how he could express his own spirituality and cultural nationalism through the "earth resonances" of his physical environment. Standing before J.E.H. MacDonald's 1921 *Solemn Land*, for example, invoked in him "austere and lonely music richly coloured – the vastness of a cathedral design – I see this state in terms of dance – against such a background – I can hear a chanting of voices – singing – or verse speaking." It was on such a "plane of the sublime – the exalted – the lyrical – that all the arts reach the condition of music – melt and fuse into each other!" (Voaden notes 1934 and 1939).

Creating a Canadian Imaginative Background

Voaden had met Arthur Lismer in fall 1928 through Lismer's art education work at the Ontario College of Art. Through Lismer, he met the other members of the Group and F.B. Housser, whose *The Group of Seven: A Canadian Art Movement* (1926) Voaden studied with great enthusiasm while writing his first northern nature plays in 1929-30.

Lismer was sympathetic to Voaden's non-realist aesthetic and praised his innovative directorial work. "This is an experiment that might catch on," he noted in 1929 of Voaden's production style, expressing a modernist theatre aesthetic similar to Voaden's own conception of "symphonic theatre." "In the theatre all the arts meet ... expressive illusion is as much an aim of the designer as of the producer or the actor. Music and light, speech and colour, setting and the written word, all are inseparable and co-operative elements in production," Lismer stated in an article on stage settings for the *Canadian Forum* (293).

In his own critical writing, Voaden championed the non-realist aesthetic and cultural nationalism of the Group and urged the Canadian little theatre movement to follow its example. In a December 1928 *Canadian Forum* article analyzing the conditions necessary for the creation of a national culture, he asserted that "the time for colonial dependence and slavish imitation is gone in art, as in politics" (106). He wrote:

> Canada has a definite part to play in the world. The artists, notably the Group of Seven, were among the first to strike out boldly. They carved new materials out of our landscape and evolved a different technique to handle them. It is probably true that the painters are the heralds always of wider and more far-reaching artistic developments. They make us artistically aware of a new scene. This new scene must produce its effect on character, and both scene and character are immediately at hand for the novelist, poet, and dramatist.

Lawren Harris had discussed the need for original indigenous creation in drama – and for finding vision, conviction and collective purpose in one's own land – in a 1923 essay entitled "Winning a Canadian Background." In this review essay of Merrill Denison's play anthology *The Unheroic North*, Harris noted the necessity for authentically depicting the effect of the natural environment upon human character through artistic self-expression that would result in the creation of a Canadian imaginative "background." "We in Canada are only commencing to find ourselves," Harris stated, and he continued:

> People from other lands come to us already sustained by rich stable backgrounds, thinking that these can also sustain us. It is not so. We are about the business of becoming a nation and must ourselves create our own background. This can only mean a complete exposure of every phase of our existence, the building of a unique structure utilizing all our reactions to our environment (37).

In a 1925 essay on Canadian art published in the *Canadian Theosophist*, Arthur Lismer provided a detailed analysis of the Group of Seven's belief in the creative relationship between spirituality, our physical and imaginative "background," idealism and non-representational art. "Art is not so much a form of technique as it is a form of intuition. It is feeling rather than action. It is a consciousness of harmony in the universe, the perception of the divine order running through all existence," Lismer suggested.

> The artist sensitive to rhythm, the beat of life, creating in space and time the image of his reception of this order, projects his vision in the eternal language of line, tone and colour, and creates not an imitative outward appearance of the common aspects of life, but an inner, more noble life than yet we all know. To do this the artist at some period in the existence of a nation must become conscious of his background or environment. All great schools of art commence with this desire to project the background – the setting, as it were, on which a later generation of creative artists will put into form and colour the humanity that acts its drama of life (178).

Such an intuitive perception of a divine universe, what Richard Maurice Bucke, Whitman's Canadian biographer, at the beginning of the century called "cosmic consciousness" (1901), not only stimulated individual artistic creation but – through the artist – a national artistic and spiritual identity. "A nation's artists are true nation builders," Lismer stated in his 1925 essay:

> They re-create in terms of line and tone and colour the aspects of nature, and excite the consciousness of the participator or spectator into kinship and response.... This design, or form, of our country is its character, the elemental nature which we recognize as one recognizes a familiar loved shape. It partakes of our own character, its virility and emphatic form is reflected in the appearance, speech, action and thought of our people. It is the setting for our development, firing the imagination, establishing our boundaries. It is home land, stirring the soul to aspiration and creation. The physical universe exists to the artist as to the religious devotee as a means to ecstasy (178-79).

Herman Voaden incorporated these concepts of the crucial role played by the Canadian natural environment and its imaginative background in the creation of a national art and identity into his own aesthetic theories, playwriting and critical writing. "The true Canadian stands as such in relation to his environment," he stated in a planned 1930 article for the *Canadian Forum*.

> The unifying thing in Canada – in Canadianism – is our background. When our people belong to it – where they accept it and live from it – where they are content with it and do not yearn for other lands, be they England, Ireland, Russia – they are our people. They are Canadians.

> And this is the only way in which we will create a national art and literature of our own. The first step is to become aware of this background – to interpret its moods – to accept it as a new thing – self-contained – not to be interpreted in the spirit of another land or people or art (Voaden Papers).

This emphasis on dramatizing Canadian nature and its psychological and imaginative effects upon human character led Voaden in 1929 to advocate the folk play as an initial stylistic choice in the development of a Canadian national drama. Although imbued with the aesthetic of the non-realist modern art theatre, he himself wrote four realistic dramas, *Northern Storm* in 1929, *Northern Song* and *Western Wolf* in 1930, and *Wilderness* in 1931, after having written the symbolist *The White Kingdom* in 1928 and then the highly expressionist *Symphony* in 1930. In 1932, he embarked on his decade-long non-realist symphonic expressionist phase with *Rocks* and *Earth Song*.

In his 1929 "Plea For a Canadian Folk Drama," Voaden echoed the Group of Seven's concern for developing an "aesthetic awareness" of one's environment. "The problem of the dramatist as well as the artist is to apprehend the spirit of a certain environment," he suggested.

> The forces of nature and the currents of human life in the north are, in many cases, lowly and tragic, sombre and immense. Harsh, bleak, crouching, majestic wind and light-swept. Establish a oneness between character and natural current.

> The majesty of mountains, desert vastness of the prairies, clean harsh ruggedness of northern Ontario and Quebec, bleak and lonely Labrador coast. In each of these locales a definite impress upon character. These scenes call for intense imaginative realization. The despair of interminable swamps and dark foreboding lakes – the moody suicide.

By the end of the 1930s, Gwen Pharis Ringwood had indeed begun to develop a distinguished body of prairie folk plays celebrating the struggle of men and women with their natural environment in dramas such as *Still Stands the House* and *Dark Harvest*.

A Canadian Art of the Theatre

By the beginning of that decade, however, Voaden was already advocating a non-realist aesthetic for "the creation of a Canadian 'Art of the Theatre'" which he himself began to implement with his multimedia symphonic expressionism two years later. His 1929-30 national playwriting competition, for which

112

J.E.H. MacDonald served as one of the judges, required an exterior setting for the plays based on a Canadian painting so that the dramas would reflect "phases of Canadian life in Northern Ontario ... in character and atmosphere" (Competition Regulations 1930: 84). The thrust of his 1930 introduction to the anthology *Six Canadian Plays* resulting from that playwriting competition is the belief that we must perceive the Canadian environment, particularly our northern regions, with new eyes and artistically interpret that perception in new and original forms of expression.

However, his introduction emphasizes the necessity for an additional element besides the call for an original perception and artistic expression of Canadian nature – an idealism and spirituality not attainable within the confines of the realistic folk drama genre. "The few volumes of Canadian plays already published," Voaden stated in 1930, "are Canadian in the sense and to the degree that the authors are Canadians and are writing about the locale in which they have lived. This is not enough. There must be dedication, a faith and idealism to give unity and purpose to creation" (xv).

It was such "dedication and absorption in a soil and people" that Voaden felt distinguished the Irish Literary Renaissance and its dramatists, Yeats, Lady Gregory and Synge. They were "inspired by a common vision and an enthusiasm for a land and people with which they felt a spiritual 'oneness'" (xvi). Citing Lawren Harris' 1928 essay "Creative Art and Canada," Voaden asserted that the birth of a Canadian national theatre and drama could result, like the Irish Literary Renaissance, from such a "spirit of dedication" combined with "keen observation, sympathetic study and patient 'awareness' of a new environment." Such creative birth, as Harris had stated, "needs the stimulus of earth resonance and of a particular place, people and time to evoke into activity a faculty that is universal and timeless" (xv).

For Voaden, as for Harris and other members of the Group of Seven, Canadian nature had not only a physical but also a metaphysical and spiritual dimension that reflected and shaped human character and artistic expression into a spiritual "oneness" (Wagner 1985: 195-96). "Many of us are beginning to experience as [Whitman] did, the spell of the great unclaimed areas of rock and tree wilderness that border our civilization," Voaden stated in *Six Canadian Plays*.

> We are aware of something vast, unsentimental, challenging, and spiritual in our land. The wilderness is becoming part of us. We are drawn out to meet it in spirit.... We must feel the "earth resonances" and spiritual emanations of our soil and natural forms. Our innate ideality should force itself on our art, changing our expression till it is in line with our fundamental character (xvii, xxiii-xxiv).

It is primarily to express this idealistic and spiritual dimension that Voaden advocated the creation of an original non-realist, multimedia art form instead of conventional realistic drama or romantic dramatizations of frontier life. Such a Canadian "Art of the Theatre," he believed, would constitute "a tradition in the staging of plays that will be an expression of the atmosphere and character of our land as definite as our native-born painting and sculpture."

> If the strength and individuality of the work of our painters – their artistic achieve-
> ments in form, rhythm, design, and colour, and their spiritual contributions in
> austerity, symbolism, and idealism – if these can be brought into our theatre and
> developed in conjunction with the creation of a new drama that will call for treatment
> in their spirit and manner and be closely allied to them in content and style, we shall
> have a new theatre art and drama here that will be an effective revelation of our own
> vision and character as a people (xxi).

Voaden sought to introduce "the atmosphere and character of our land" in his plays through the use of setting and plot – dramatizing the Muskoka, Haliburton and northern Algoma and Lake Superior countryside and its effect upon Canadians – through verbal imagery and thematic development, and sensorially through his multimedia production style. As Sherrill Grace asks in "A Northern Modernism, 1920-1932: Canadian Painting and Literature," "Voaden's theatrical dilemma comes down to this: how does the playwright dramatize the north and its impact upon human beings?" She notes, "Briefly, what he sought was a non-realistic use of light, music, staging, and dialogue which would enable him to express his vision of a harsh and violent but transfiguring northern landscape, a landscape profoundly influenced by Lawren Harris and the Group of Seven" (1984: 116-17).

New Artistic Concepts and Actual Stage Practice

Voaden's first attempt to dramatize the North primarily through dance movement – in his and Lowrie Warrener's 1930 expressionist *Symphony: A Drama of Motion and Light for a New Theatre* – provides a vivid example of the difficulties faced by artists in the 1930s to transform artistic ideas into actual reality. Voaden had met Warrener, a protégé of the Group of Seven and one of Canada's earliest abstract painters, after seeing Warrener's Gordon Craig-inspired stylized setting for *Antony and Cleopatra*, directed by Carroll Aikins at Hart House Theatre in April of 1929 (Mason in *Globe* 23 Apr. 1929: 14). In the summer of 1930, he travelled with Warrener to Port Coldwell in northern Ontario and to Vancouver via the Canadian Pacific Railway "to absorb this Canadian background" and to draw artistic inspiration from the Canadian landscape while writing their "painter's ballet," *Symphony*. The work portrays an Everyman figure on a pilgrimage that concludes in his death and mystical transformation in the North. The five movements of the drama – "A Large Eastern City," "The Northern Wilderness," "Fishing Village on a Northern Lake," "A Prairie Farm," and "The Mountains" – reflect their impressions of Canadian nature frequently influenced by the Group of Seven (Wagner 1983).

Symphony is unique in twentieth century Canadian drama for its imaginative conception and scope. The play, completely without dialogue, is more akin to a scenario for a dance drama or an expressionist silent movie.

Requiring a symphonic orchestra, a "trained ballet," and an "ample and well equipped stage with exceptional lighting facilities," the work was clearly beyond the capacities of the then contemporary Canadian amateur stage and probably even of the American professional theatre.

The work's first movement, "A Large Eastern City," is the most expressionist section of the drama, a nightmarish depiction of physical and spiritual squalor and depravation. According to Voaden's published stage directions, which are quoted in italics throughout this essay,

The interior of the apartment is dimly lit. Its deep recesses are lost in gloom. Low music with a primitive rhythm is heard as grotesque forms stagger in and out of the light, clutching each other and swaying dizzily as if dancing. Huge shadows play about the room. The scene takes on an impression of sensual, sinister drunkenness (Voaden 1993: 138).

The focus of the scene is on the excessive materialism, approaching idolatry, of city life and on the sensual depravation this materialist pursuit engenders. The only individualized character is the representative Man figure whose dishevelled hair, haggard face and eyes of a madman express the effect of this urban environment. The other figures in the scene are an undifferentiated collective mass whose faces

show dissipation, lust, greed and desire. Swaying drunkenly and moving slowly the masses unite at the steps, climb them and wind through the city like a dark serpent, twisting and disappearing into the night.

The masses ritually worship "an ominous disk" which "half rises in the gloom above the buildings." The mysteriously flashing disk is revealed to be the huge steel-grey tickertape machine of a stock exchange that drives its worshippers to destruction.

Terror turns to panic, the music swells, and the shapes and figures, moved as if by an unseen force, rush up the steps, face each other, hesitating for a moment as the disk flames into a red ball of fire casting a light that flows down the stairs, to meet them, are dawn together at the foot of the stairs, and in a body follow the light that seems to pull them up and suck them into the disk. These shapes and figures are followed by lines of worshippers, who rush into the disk, impelled by the same magnetic force. All are picked up and whirled dizzily in a circular motion from the top of the disk to oblivion in the void below.

Symphony's fourth movement, "A Prairie Farm," is an extended dance drama with contending representational characters such as light green grain figures, grotesque sales agents, brown sun figures, heat waves, winds and fear forms. Man, dressed as a farmer, sows his grain but is eventually defeated by hail and heat.

Lights come up showing the grains, motionless and brown on the ground, with the heat waves fading into the wings and the farmer standing hopeless, looking as though the blood had been dried up in him and he had become a part of the grains. Lights go out and come up on a bare stage, with the farmer standing, in a drooping crucified

posture, with a yellow light playing about him. On all sides of him the great dry
plains stretch away endlessly.

In August 1930 Voaden described *Symphony* to his fiancée Violet Kilpatrick
as a "pantomime emotional colour music choral rhythmic light dance drama
without dialogue" and as "a Canadian rhythmic-dance-colour-music-light-
pantomime drama, without need for dialogue or poetry or libretto, and
requiring only more careful restatement and a musical score to be complete."
He submitted the work on November 5, 1930, to John Murray Gibbon, himself
a librettist, publicity agent for the Canadian Pacific Railway, and organizer of
the CPR's Canadian Folksong and Handicraft Festival in Quebec City and
other music festivals along the CPR line. Gibbon, who had supplied Voaden
and Warrener with free tickets for their trans-Canada journey, wrote Voaden
on January 2, 1931, regarding *Symphony* that "I do not see how we could
make any use of the latter, as it does not appear to have the slightest relation to
the Canadian Pacific Railway, which is essentially an optimistic undertaking
and could not be identified with anything so gloomy and morbid, quite apart
from the question of cost of production."

Realizing the impossibility of finding a production for *Symphony* on the
non-professional indigenous Canadian stage, Voaden turned to the American
professional theatre. He submitted the scenario to the Neighbourhood
Playhouse in New York at the end of November 1930 and, hearing of planned
productions for the Chicago Exposition, to the noted stage designer Norman
Bel Geddes. Bel Geddes replied January 6, 1931, stating that he found the play
"most interesting." "It offers great pictorial opportunities for staging. My chief
regret was a lack of grip and power in the action itself. I have taken the liberty of
forwarding it to Mrs. Claire Reis and Leopold Stokowski, who are the leading
factors of the League of Composers. They do one or two productions annually
on a large scale with the Philadelphia Symphony Orchestra and if interested
are the most likely people to help you."

Writing Claire Reis on January 21, 1931, Voaden suggested that
Symphony offered "unusual pictorial opportunities for staging. It represents a
very sincere attempt to combine music, design, the dance, and pantomime in a
single synthesis. If successfully produced, it should be the most notable of all
experiments made in this direction, to date." When, in 1934, the Canadian
composer Percival Price won a Pulitzer Prize travelling scholarship for his
romantic *St. Lawrence* symphony in four movements (Islands, Rapids,
Flatlands, Mountains), Voaden thought he had found his composer for
Symphony. Writing Price in spring 1934, he referred to his five-week stay at
the Kurt Jooss Folkwang dance school in Essen, Germany, in 1933 and
pointed to Jooss' acclaimed *The Green Table* as a model for creative
collaboration. The highly theatrical dance piece had been choreographed and
danced by Jooss in collaboration with his composer Fritz A. Cohen. "The
result was a ballet representing a perfect fusion between the two arts – a ballet
which indeed constituted a new art form." Voaden suggested a similar
collaboration between himself, Price and the dancer-choreographer Boris

Volkoff. "I am interested in experimental light and staging, and feel that I can add considerably in the way of visual background – the vital light and meaningful colour of the painter – to the production."

Symphonic Expressionism

Unable to find a production for *Symphony* – the work remains unproduced to this day – Voaden abstracted and severely reduced dance movement when he staged his first "symphonic expressionist" productions, *Rocks* and *Earth Song*, in 1932. Instead of dancers, he used lighting to express human emotions and action and to represent Canadian nature. "The North is viewed as a participant in the action, an unseen actor," he wrote in a manifesto published in the Toronto *Globe* explaining his new production style. "The cyclorama lighting, which is also a constant variant in both intensity and colour, expresses the North. The whole movement of the lighting is symphonic. It should be considered as an actor, the personified North" (Voaden in *Globe* 23 Apr. 1932: 18).

Voaden's 1934 Queen's University production of *Rocks*.

Voaden highly stylized and abstracted *Rocks* from his previously realistic play entitled *Wilderness*, written and produced at George Pierce Baker's graduate playwriting class at Yale University in 1931. In abstracting the characters and action of the play – the story of a young woman in the north country whose lover, Blake, is lost in a winter storm – Voaden stripped realistic movement and physical gestures from the waiting Mary and Blake's mother and assigned these to six kneeling dancers. As he indicated in his *Globe* manifesto, "two groups of dancers are employed to provide the rhythmical counterpart of, and complement to, the speeches. Their movements, restricted and severely formalized, express in motion the fluctuated feelings developed in the course of the play."

In December of 1932, Voaden directed his most abstract and symbolic work, *Earth Song: A Drama in Rhythmic Prose and Light*, for the Sarnia Drama League. He again explained his non-realist symphonic expressionist aesthetic to his Toronto public in another manifesto published in the *Globe* December 17. In his "Creed for a New Theatre," he stated in part his multimedia production style: "Let us bring to the theatre the solidity and power of sculpture and architecture, the glory of painting, the spiritual immediacy of music. Let us restore to it the greatness of poetry, dance and ritual it once knew."

117

Arthur Hay and Pam Haney as Adam and Eve in Voaden's *Earth Song*, 1932.

Voaden had cut his initially conceived use of dancers for *Earth Song* and, as in *Rocks*, instead used vastly increased lighting and a cyclorama to create moods, action and heightened emotions. Critics commented favourably on the sculptural use of the two lead actors, their "plastic poses" and "telling silhouette effects." In the December 17 *Sarnia Observer*, W.E. Harris wrote of Arthur Hay and Pam Haney as Adam and Eve that "their great economy in the use of motion and their careful silhouette posing not only portrayed the careful direction of the author-producer but also gave much of the effect that would be produced if trained dancers of the Russian school were doing the parts."

Earth Song does conclude – to the accompaniment of Brahms' *First Symphony* – with an ecstatic dance by the two lovers in a ritualistic celebration of life and the eternal universe itself. Voaden's stage directions state:

> *Eve Dances. Adam, in a moment, also is drawn into the rhythm of her exultant motions. The dance is measured, ritualistic, yet intense and excited The light behind them grows in intensity. Finally the sun appears, rising to silhouette their figures. The dance mounts in ecstatic triumph to a climax, Adam drawing Eve to his side. Their voices mingle and are lost in the blaze of light behind them. The rest of the stage darkens. The sun becomes the earth-flame in which the two ecstatic figures lift their strength in the theme gesture – one in their passionate assertion and radiant acceptance of life.*

The great degree of abstraction and symbolism in *Earth Song* puzzled audiences and critics. While appreciating the beauty of Voaden's technical effects, they were unsure of the meaning of the drama. Lawrence Mason was one of the few critics who believed that Voaden had achieved (particularly through the use of music) a dramatically meaningful synthesis of form and content. In his December 24 *Globe* review, he stated that the musical selections from the First and Fourth Brahms symphonies "were so felicitously chosen and timed that the emotional impact of the words and scenes was immensely enhanced."

Moreover, largely under the catalytic influence of this overwhelming music, the miracle of synthesis veritably took place: all the various component parts of the production actually fused and blended in a unified whole, and the audience received from this highly complex and multiform display of all the arts an impression full, rich, and diversified, while yet at the same time clear, single and homogeneous.

Mason called the Sarnia Drama League production of *Earth Song* "an unusually significant event." "It launched a new art form, struck a valiant blow for experimentalism, and proved triumphantly the falsity of the claim that Canadian Little Theatres are physically and economically unable to put on anything but conventional realistic productions."

A Means to Ecstasy: The Fourth Dimension

When he reviewed *Rocks* in the April 23, 1932 *Toronto Star*, Augustus Bridle quoted Voaden stating that he "got the idea from studying pictures of the Group of Seven" and observed that "the set – just a few low bare rocks – looks like some modern paintings."

But Voaden had not looked to the Group of Seven for a mere external imitation of their non-realist painting style in the formulation of his own theatre aesthetic. Like many European and North American artists since the beginning of the century, he sought to create through his symphonic expressionism a spiritual evocation of the infinite space and cosmic consciousness of a "fourth dimension."

Lawren Harris – in his 1928 "Creative Art and Canada" essay cited by Voaden in *Six Canadian Plays* – outlined the evolution of his own painting style and that of other members of the Group from the initial depiction of "Nature's outward aspect" towards such a "fourth dimension."

According to Harris, the painters developed through their northern painting expeditions "a long and growing love and understanding of the North in an ever clearer experience of oneness with the informing spirit of the whole land and a strange brooding sense of Mother Nature fostering a new race and a new age." They moved from "a period of decorative treatment" towards a greater "intensification of mood that simplified into deeper meaning and was more rigorously selective." "The next step," Harris asserted, "was a utilization of elements of the North in depth, in three dimensions, giving a fuller meaning, a more real sense of the presence of the informing spirit." Harris concluded:

Let me here suggest that a work in two dimensions may contain an intimation of the third dimension and that a work in three dimensions may contain an intimation of the fourth dimension. To-day the artist moves toward purer creative expression, wherein he changes the outward aspect of Nature, alters colours, and, by changing and re-shaping forms, intensifies the austerity and beauty of formal relationships, and so creates a somewhat new world from the aspect of the world we commonly see; and thus he comes appreciably nearer a pure work of art and the expression of new spiritual values (1928: 185).

119

The painter, novelist and playwright Bertram Brooker had already experimented with the creation of a fourth dimension in his dramatic writing – what he referred to as "psychodrama" – just prior to the First World War and, more successfully, in his non-objective paintings beginning in the early 1920s (Wagner 1989; Zemans 1989).

Although Brooker succeeded in capturing a metaphysical fourth dimension in his painting, particularly in the stunning *Sounds Assembling* (1928), he was never fully able to develop his dramatic ideas because he lacked a theatre company with which he could experiment. His most successful productions, *Within: A Drama of Mind in Revolt* and *The Dragon: A Parable of Illusion and Disillusion*, were staged in 1935 and 1936 by Voaden in his symphonic expressionist style. Brooker's initial 1929 notes for *The Dragon* refer to his intention for "the whole thing to be written in the Tree of Death style – broken rhythms – fourth-dimensional feeling – even in the mouths of the humans" (Grace 1985: 20 fn. 18).

Voaden was greatly stimulated by Brooker's nationalistic 1929 *Yearbook of the Arts in Canada*; however, he was even more directly inspired at the end of the 1920s by the experimental theatre director and theosophist Roy Mitchell.[2] Mitchell's expressionist and symbolist productions at the Arts and Letters Club in Toronto (1911-15) and his experimentation with stage lighting while artistic director of Hart House Theatre (1919-21) frequently featured the collaboration of Arthur Lismer, Lawren Harris, A.Y. Jackson and J.E.H. MacDonald as set designers (Usmiani 1987).

Mitchell, too, strongly believed in the mystical power of the fourth dimension. "I offer the theory of a fourth world, into which the theatre can initiate its devotees," Mitchell stated in his 1929 *Creative Theatre*, pointing to the *paradosis*, the miraculous revelation of the ancient mysteries. "It is as if filling the senses with form and sound, stirring the emotions in sympathy, and shaping ideas to one intense accord, they made for their witnesses a causeway into an inner world where they rested in a lightning flash of communion" (6-7).

For Voaden theatre was also "our Gateway to the Divine," as Mitchell had stated in his *Creative Theatre*. And, like Harris, Voaden used three-dimensional elements, particularly simplified symbolic stage settings and actors in sculpted tableaux illuminated by brilliant white or coloured lighting, to evoke a fourth dimension – what Voaden referred to as "moments of intuitive illumination" and "moments in which perfection is glimpsed." In another manifesto, printed in the programme for *Hill-Land* under the title "The Symphonic Theatre" and published in the December 8, 1934 Toronto *Globe* as "Toward a New Theatre," he asserted that symphonic expressionism could create these glimpses of perfection:

---

[2] On Mitchell and theosophy, see Usmiani (1987). A mystical religious movement combining Eastern and Western religions and philosophies, theosophy posited an idealist neo-platonic world view finding ultimate reality in a metaphysical, rather than material, existence. It perceived the artist as a priest-like, visionary "seer" rather than simply as a craftsman.

by intense, slow and lovely picturization – by translating ordinary stage movements into those of ritual and rhythm, by introducing music, dance and choral comment to sustain and lift the moment to complete significance.

Such a theatral language will be capable of supremely exalted statement. It will have music's power of lifting into sudden glory; the lyrical sweep – "the Apollonian glow" – of poetry; and the novel's capacity for reflective comment and varied interpretation. With these it will combine the color and design of painting, the form and mass of sculpture and architecture, the movement and loveliness of dance.

Symphonic expressionism, with its aim to "open wide the doors of beauty and imagination" and to provide "lyrical intensity," "spiritual release," "uplifting vision" and "flashing revelation" was, like Mitchell's *paradosis*, itself a fundamentally religious and aesthetic ritual. The multimedia language of Voaden's symphonic theatre was, like Harris' use of light in his symbolic spiritual paintings, a means of attaining the greater metaphysical reality of the beyond. Reviewing Voaden's 1936 symphonic expressionist drama *Murder Pattern* on CBC radio in 1981, the actress Barbara Chilcott could still recall more than four decades later that "I remember being taken as a child to see one of Herman Voaden's productions ... I recall only space, light, hangings and draped figures. I felt I was being drawn into a strange, lonely magical place and I've never forgotten that extraordinary feeling of 'otherness'" (17 Feb. 1981).

Artistic Collaboration in Dance

Of all the dance Voaden saw in Europe in 1933, he was most influenced by Kurt Jooss' "famous and terrible" dance drama *The Green Table*, "a stern and beautiful indictment of war and politicians," whose combination of dance, music and mime he perceived as approximating his own concept of symphonic theatre. Already working on *Hill-Land*, he based that play's Death Figure on Jooss' own powerful performance of Death in *The Green Table* and also assigned greater movement and participation in the play's action to his choral figures.[3]

When B.K. Sandwell reviewed *Hill-Land* in the December 22, 1934 *Saturday Night*, he congratulated Voaden on his ability to get "dignified ritual movement out of his performers." But he also noted:

while it is undoubtedly possible to raise immensely the significance of a given plot by means of either free dance action or rigid ritual movement, we must remind Mr.

---

[3] During his stay at the Folkwang dance school in 1933, Voaden attempted to interest Kurt Jooss in *Earth Song*. Writing Violet Kilpatrick from Essen March 5, he reported that "Since I came here several of Jooss' group have been interested in *Earth Song*. Yesterday I brought three or four of the Brahms records, and this morning worked out a plot of the play. This afternoon, with Leeder and Jooss' ballet teacher, I went over the plot, some of the dialogue, and the music with Jooss. The result – an interesting four hours discussion. But for the present the matter is closed. Jooss does not believe in my 'symphonic' conception – thinks one hears no music when one watches a great dance etc. – that good music, with its far-reaching imaginative stimulation – should not be confined to a human-made visual interpretation. We could never do it together – for at times I would suppress all dance – make it merely picture and sculpture." Despite Jooss' rejection of his symphonic expressionist aesthetic, Voaden described *The Green Table* as an example of "the symphonic theatre of the future" in his article "Toward Theatral Dance," *Toronto Globe,* June 17, 1933 and in "Dance of the Theatre: Impressions of the Dance in Four Countries," *The Dancing Times* No. 274 (July 1933).

Voaden that the first of these is an art requiring long years of apprenticeship and great natural ability, and that the second is a tradition requiring centuries for development. The pantomime of the ballet is one of the most highly finished arts of our age, and has as its aim precisely that lifting of the significance of a momentary and particular action to eternal and universal validity; but its practitioners know its limits, they know that little can be attained without years of practice.

Voaden drew his performers and technical staff – Sandwell referred to "an unusually able and faithful band of workers, both on and behind stage" – from the students he taught as Head of English at the Central High School of Commerce in Toronto and from more experienced former students and adults of his Play Workshop. He did collaborate with professional dancers when possible and used even amateur performers in patterned stage movement and pantomime before large audiences.

Voaden was attracted to modern dance because he believed that "to suggest the tragic retreating tide of life toward death and then the slow, mounting, ongoing thrust, wave upon wave, to the final transfiguration, the gut or centre-outward movements of the modern dance were best." As in the 1930 *Symphony*, he attempted to create in the 1935 *Dance Chorale* (choreographed by Saida Gerrard with Gerrard as the lead dancer) a new dramatic art form through the synthesis of music (Richard Strauss' *Death and Transfiguration*) and dance-mime. "With the 'motion choir' and the light colour-orchestration we accompanied the solo dancer to her death and then to her transfiguration. There was no plot; it was a pure dance-music-theatre experience following the pattern of death and new life" (Voaden 1975: 77, 79).

Many critics in the 1930s commented favourably on Voaden's multimedia stage experiments. Lawrence Mason, in his February 15, 1935 *Globe* review, called his production of *Dance Chorale* "an exquisite symphony of sound, color and movement." Voaden's most successful dance experiment was *Romeo and Juliet* in 1936. First staged by the Play Workshop at the Central High School of Commerce, approximately twenty brief scenes from Shakespeare's drama were presented in pantomime and tableau to the accompaniment of Tchaikovsky's *Romeo and Juliet* overture. Over 5,600 persons saw Voaden's second production as part of Reginald Stewart's Promenade Symphony Concerts at the University of Toronto Varsity Arena on June 25, 1936. In his *Toronto Star* review, Augustus Bridle called Voaden a genius and stated that his symphonic theatre "was last night lifted for 20 minutes into Reinhardt dimensions. The pantomime was a rhythmic color harmony that might have been a credit to Ballet Russe."

Voaden staged the Canadian premiere of T.S. Eliot's *Murder in the Cathedral* at the 350-seat Convocation Hall at Queen's University on August 7 and 8, 1936, and, for three performances, at the 2,700-seat Massey Hall on October 30 and 31 the same year. B.K. Sandwell, in his August 15 *Saturday Night* review, called the Queen's premiere "a most noteworthy production of a truly wonderful play." Though sceptical of his symphonic expressionist aesthetic, even Sandwell declared that "Mr. Voaden's methods are right for

Voaden's staging of Eliot's *Murder in the Cathedral*, 1936.

this play. He seeks to combine the two plastic elements of highly controlled and varied lighting and highly patterned choric movement (almost but not quite dancing) with the auditory element of spoken verbal beauty." Pearl McCarthy, in the October 31 *Mail and Empire*, called Voaden's production "a definite milepost in Toronto's stage initiative." "The acting was beautiful. We have seldom seen the spirit of event and thought so embodied in muscle, posture and rhythm of movement. The chorus, functioning like an interpretive ballet in movement as well as in speech lines, had an astounding degree of artistic finish."

Because of his skill as a lighting designer, Voaden began assisting Boris Volkoff as lighting consultant for productions of his Canadian Ballet in 1938. Already in 1936, he had suggested the lighting scheme for Volkoff's Indian dance *Mon-Ka-Ta*, staged at Hart House Theatre and at the 1936 Olympics in Berlin. In October of 1938 Volkoff suggested that he and Voaden collaborate on a production of Maeterlinck's *Sister Beatrice*. Volkoff worked as associate director for Maeterlinck's symbolical drama, directed by Voaden for the Central High School of Commerce Annual Concert in February of 1939 and as a Play Workshop entry in the Central Ontario Region Dominion Drama Festival at Hart House Theatre in March of that year. Janet Baldwin played the part of the Holy Virgin.

Using a core of dancers from their forthcoming *Sister Beatrice* production, Voaden and Volkoff also collaborated on *A Cosmopolitan Christmas* for the Arts and Letters Club Christmas Dinner Programme in December of 1938. Produced by Voaden with Bertram Brooker as arranger, the production, described in the playbill as a "national representation" in Four Ballet Scenes of variations on the theme "In Dulci Jubilo," featured thirteen dancers from the Volkoff Ballet and "primitive American, French, Russian and Spanish" music composed by Percy Faith, Viggo Kiel, Ettore Mazzoleni and Sir Ernest MacMillan.

But Voaden's biggest opportunity to collaborate with a professional composer and trained dancers – as Jooss had for *The Green Table* – came with the production of his autobiographical drama *Ascend As the Sun*, staged at Hart House Theatre in April of 1942. Godfrey Ridout composed the music for a choir of six women's voices, trumpets, percussion, harmonium and

Members of the Volkoff Ballet in Voaden's *Ascend As the Sun*, 1942.

piano. Dances were choreographed by members of the Volkoff Ballet. These included Patricia Drylie, Mildred Herman (later world-famous as Melissa Hayden) Natalia Butko, Alla Shishkina, Dorothy Dennenay, Gabrielle Hayne, Rita Warne, Cliff Toner, Raymond Chernysh, Lloyd Thornton and Peter Zradowsky.

Ascend As the Sun dramatizes the first seventeen years in the life of David Branton, an Everyman figure Voaden intended to follow in a subsequent cycle of plays. He used the forestage of Hart House Theatre to represent the realistic interior of the Branton home and other locales and an upstage inset stage on which dancers, allegorical figures, choral voices, music and light visually and aurally suggested not only the dreams and subconscious of the young David and his mother but also a higher metaphysical reality.

J.E. Middleton, in his April 25, 1942 *Saturday Night* review, noted this use of a dual stage to suggest the realistic and symbolic dimensions of Voaden's "drama of man's rise from the earth to an ultimate super-humanity." "The structure of the work is unusual, almost eerie," Middleton declared. "On the fore stage are enacted the undramatic and almost commonplace events of dawning life. A dream stage is behind, the curtains revealing from time to time a great projection-screen for a very delirium of rich lighting. Before this in half-silhouette are statuesque groups, supposedly illustrating the spirit of each scene, and supplementary dance-figures by the Volkoff ballet, stylized, but intense in beauty and charm."

The evolution of mankind towards "the kingdom come on earth" is dramatized in the first choral dance of the play, which he describes in the stage directions:

The stage is dark when the curtains open. Steps lead upward among stylized forms. As the eye accustoms itself to the shadows, the Dancers of the ballet are seen, in huddled, grief-stricken attitudes.

The Dancers stir. In their attitudes and movements they suggest defeated crusaders, hapless builders, tragic believers, pilgrims, warriors for truth, sainted sweet martyrs. Cymbal crash. A promethan dancer leaps among the figures on the stage, inspiring them to begin their upward march. The dance begins. The Dancers struggle toward higher levels up centre, and off to the right and left. There is a big processional feeling in the scene. Figures march against the sky, which brightens with morning light. The dance comes to an end in a crescendo of triumphant music and movement, both based on long, measured, triumphant phrases, developed with majestic power.

In the April 14 *Toronto Star*, Augustus Bridle praised the work's "superb" allegorical dances. "The first dance was a rhythmic scenario for the birth of the hero: a mere prelude to a cycle of glorious tableaux and dance-pantomimes in which the author-director's genius for lighting, color and statuesque groups of figures reached a climax. The dances, all devised by the Volkoff artists, supervised as to theme-illustration by Voaden, are beautiful and significant enough for any opera house. With almost perfect art the mobile figures expressed the various nuances of the argument in evolving phases of young David's life."

Other critics also praised the dance component of Voaden's symphonic expressionist production. In the April 14 *Globe and Mail*, Hector Charlesworth, the dean of Toronto theatre and music critics, called *Ascend* "a unique example of experimental theatre" and noted that "the many tableaux are beautifully presented by the Volkoff Ballet." Rose Macdonald, in the April 14 *Toronto Telegram*, similarly praised *Ascend* for its "beautiful interweaving of the arts of theatre convention, of the dance, of music, of mime."

Ascend As The Sun.

Ascend was technically the most complex production of all of Voaden's multimedia works. The programme for the drama lists twenty-three actors, eleven dancers, ten singers and musicians, and fifteen persons on the staging, lighting, make-up, and costumes and masks crew. Insufficient rehearsal time and the difficulty of co-ordinating such a large number of performers and technical staff in an eighteen-scene drama accounted for the slow pace of the three-hour opening premiere noted by the critics. When Voaden forwarded copies of the Toronto reviews to W.E. McNeill, Vice-Principal of Queen's University, on June 12, 1942, he wrote that "they are all too laudatory: the production was not a completely good one, and dance and music were both too boldly treated to fuse into a single whole for many in the audience."

Kurt Jooss has stated regarding the shaping of *The Green Table* that "I think the whole process of conception of the libretto took about ten years" (Markard 1985: 49). Voaden's collaborative process with Godfrey Ridout and the Volkoff dancers for *Ascend* had only been for a few months so that the written text, staging, dance and music – unlike with most of Voaden's other symphonic expressionist productions – did not emerge from a single creative matrix as had occurred with Jooss and *The Green Table*.

By the beginning of the 1940s it also became difficult to stage the kind of "art" theatre Voaden was producing. In addition to the rise in realism in theatre as a result of the movies, the Second World War also made the idealism of his "theatre of beauty" increasingly untenable. Members of his Play Workshop enlisted in the military and most amateur companies suspended their activities during the war. Voaden retreated to his base at the Central High School of Commerce, staging in March of 1943 the dance drama in two scenes, *The Masque of the Red Death*, based on the short story by Edgar Allan Poe.

He attempted to continue collaborating with other artists, however. Godfrey Ridout again composed the music for piano and percussion instruments. Grace Docter and Marie Lauder choreographed the dances, except one choreographed by Volkoff. Rose Macdonald noted in her March 6 *Telegram* review that "the stately court dances are skilfully counterpoised with the performance of tumbling clowns and with a beautiful saraband, this last danced by Natalia Butko (the choreographer for her interpolation, Boris Volkoff, director of the Canadian Ballet Theatre [sic])."

In its use of music, dance, mime and omission of dialogue, *The Masque of the Red Death* recalls the 1936 dance drama *Romeo and Juliet* and also resembles the 1930 *Symphony*. The "spectral" Death Figure who appears intermittently during the time of plague, evoking fear and bravado, also evokes *The Green Table* whose Death figure Voaden had incorporated in *Hill-Land* and, as The Destroyer, in *Ascend As the Sun*. However, *The Masque* contains no hint of the transcendence of death that characterizes the majority of Voaden's works. The very grotesqueness of his adaptation can be seen as a poetic metaphor for the slaughter and devastation of the Second World War. But such a larger symbolic interpretation was not perceived by the small number of critics who reviewed the production.

Critical Receptions

Both before and after the Second World War, Voaden never achieved general critical acceptance for his unconventional non-realist playwriting and symphonic production style. The British adjudicators of the Dominion Drama Festival competitions in the 1930s criticized his plays for their lack of dramatic action and movement and for subordinating the actor to Voaden's multimedia "orchestral" stage language.

Voaden's staging of Carl Sandburg's poem *Upstream*, 1932.

Malcolm Morley, in the 1935 competition, found *Hill-Land* "a highly static representation, an elaborated tone poem" (7 Dec. 1935). Allan Wade, adjudicating in 1936, thought *Murder Pattern* "had something of the effect of music on me" but echoed Morley by declaring that the thrust of Voaden's symphonic expressionist production style "was away from rather than towards drama as I believe the Festival conceives it to be."

Even after his plays began to be published for the first time in the mid-1970s, a number of literary critics, unaware of the spiritual thrust of Voaden's theatre aesthetic, evaluated his play texts as conventional dramatic literature instead of semiotically as image theatre and judged his work a failure (Leggatt 1980: 139, 141; Goldie 1977: 239-40). Voaden replied to this criticism in 1981 by suggesting that his multimedia plays could be properly assessed only in performance, that "the text was no more than half what the audience saw and heard," and that his plays could only be understood from within the context and conventions of his symphonic expressionist aesthetic (Voaden 1981: 156).

Such an assessment of Voaden's plays in production began at the end of the 1980s with Heinar Piller's dynamic revival of *Murder Pattern* in Toronto in 1987 and 1990. By the 1990s, increased scholarly assessments of Voaden also led to a greater critical appreciation of the artistic value of his multimedia works. Alexander Leggatt concluded in *Later Stages* that "any view of Canada that has no room for Voaden's key idea, the spiritual exaltation inspired by the land, is a sadly diminished view." "Above all, Voaden's determination commands respect. At a time when it must have been tempting to abandon Canadian theatre as a lost cause, Voaden had a positive, clearly worked-out vision" (1997: 341).

Just before his death on June 27, 1991, Voaden completed introductions and detailed stage directions for his plays for the anthology *A Vision of Canada: Herman Voaden's Dramatic Works 1928-1945* published by Simon & Pierre in 1993. A reading of these texts suggests that when he concluded his first major creative period in 1945, Voaden had largely achieved, in his own characteristic manner, the imaginative challenge he had perceived facing Canadian dramatists at the beginning of the 1930s. As he concluded his Introduction to *Six Canadian Plays*:

Pioneers

The challenge to our dramatists is to seek an ever varying expression of our life, in poetry and symbolism as well as prose and realism; and to join hands with our painters, sculptors, dancers, and musicians to create new combinations of the arts, lifting them all to inspired levels of beauty and significance in which they may be universal, being the reflection of the vision and beauty of a new people in a new land (xxiv).

References

Arnold, Matthew. 1968. *Essays in Criticism* 1st series. Sister Thomas Marion Hoctor, ed. Chicago: University of Chicago Press.

Bridle, Augustus. 23 Apr. 1932. *Toronto Star*.

Bridle, Augustus. 26 June 1936. "Imagination Lifts Big Proms Crowd: Performance Last Night Triumph of Great Music and Plastic Art." *Toronto Star*.

Bridle, Augustus. 14 Apr. 1942. *Toronto Star*.

Bucke, Richard Maurice. 1901. *Cosmic Consciousness: A Study in the Evolution of the Human Mind*. Philadelphia: Innes.

Charlesworth, Hector. 14 Apr. 1942. *Globe and Mail*.

Chilcott, Barbara. 17 Feb. 1981. "Review of *The Developing Mosaic: English-Canadian Drama to Mid-Century*." CBC Radio "Stereo Morning."

"Competition Regulations." Feb. 1930. *Ontario Secondary School Teachers Federation Bulletin* 10: 1.

Davies, Robertson. 1982. "Mixed Grill: Touring Fare in Canada, 1920-1935." In L.W. Conolly, ed. *Theatrical Touring and Founding in North America*. Westport, Connecticut: Greenwood Press.

Farmer, Harcourt. Apr. 1919. "Play-Writing in Canada." *Canadian Bookman* 1.

Goldie, Terence William. 1977. "Canadian Dramatic Literature in English 1919-1939." Ph.D. dissertation, Queen's University.

Grace, Sherrill E. 1984. "A Northern Modernism, 1920-1932: Canadian Painting and Literature." *The Literary Criterion* 19: 3-4.

Grace, Sherrill E. Spring 1985. "'The Living Soul of Man': Bertram Brooker and Expressionist Theatre," *Theatre History in Canada* 6: 1, 3-22.

Harris, Lawren. Feb. 1923. "Winning a Canadian Background." *Canadian Bookman* 5. Reprinted in Anton Wagner, ed. *The Developing Mosaic: English-Canadian Drama to Mid-Century*. Toronto: Canadian Theatre Review Publications, 1980.

Harris, Lawren. Dec. 1928. "Creative Art and Canada." *McGill News*. Reprinted in Bertram Brooker, ed. *Yearbook of the Arts in Canada 1928-29*. Toronto: Macmillan, 1929.

Harris, W.E. 17 Dec. 1932. *Sarnia Observer*.

Housser, F.B. 1926. *The Group of Seven: A Canadian Art Movement*. Toronto: Macmillan.

Leggatt, Alexander. Fall 1980. "Playwrights in a Landscape: The Changing Image of Rural Ontario." *Theatre History in Canada* 1: 2, 135-48.

Leggatt, Alexander. 1997. "Plays and Playwrights." In Ann Saddlemyer and Richard Plant, eds. *Later Stages: Essays in Ontario Theatre from the First World War to the 1970s*. Toronto: University of Toronto Press.

Lismer, Arthur. 15 Feb. 1925. "Canadian Art." *Canadian Theosophist* 5, 12.

Lismer, Arthur. May 1929. "Stage Settings for High Schools." *Canadian Forum* 9.

Mair, Charles. 1901. *Tecumseh, a Drama (Second Edition) and Canadian Poems*. Toronto: William Briggs.

Markard, Anna and Hermann. 1985. "Background of the 'Green Table.'" *Jooss*. Cologne: Ballett Buhnen Verlag Rolf Garske.

Mason, Lawrence. 23 Apr. 1929. "Gordon Craig's 'Macbeth.'" Toronto *Globe*, 14.

Mason, Lawrence. 24 Dec. 1932. Toronto *Globe*.

McCarthy, Pearl. 31 Oct. 1936. *Mail and Empire*.

Macdonald, Rose. 14 Apr. 1942. *Toronto Telegram*.

Macdonald, Rose. 6 Mar. 1943. *Toronto Telegram*.

Middleton, J.E. 25 Apr. 1942. *Saturday Night*.

Mitchell, Roy. 1929. *Creative Theatre*. New York: John Day. Facsimile edition Westwood, New Jersey: Kindle Press, 1969.

Morley, Malcolm. 7 Dec. 1935. "Toronto Festival." *Saturday Night*.

Rutland, Enid Delgatty, ed. 1982. *The Collected Plays of Gwen Pharis Ringwood*. Ottawa: Borealis Press.

Saddlemyer, Ann. 1982. "Thoughts on National Drama and the Founding of Theatres." In L.W. Conolly, ed. *Theatrical Touring and Founding in North America*. Westport, Connecticut: Greenwood Press.

Sandwell, B.K. 22 Dec. 1934. *Saturday Night*.

Sandwell, B.K. 15 Aug. 1936. *Saturday Night*.

Usmiani, Renate. Fall 1987. "Roy Mitchell: Prophet in Our Past." *Theatre History in Canada* 8: 2, 147-68.

Voaden, Herman. Dec. 1928. "A National Drama League." *Canadian Forum* 9.

Voaden, Herman. 1929. "Plea For a Canadian Folk Drama." Collegiate Notebook, Herman Voaden Papers, York University Archives.

Voaden, Herman. 1930. "Article for the Forum – Canadianism – Art and Literature." In large diary/notebook marked "Cross Canada Summer, 1930." Herman Voaden Papers, York University Archives.

Voaden, Herman, ed. 1930. *Six Canadian Plays.* Toronto: Copp Clark.

Voaden, Herman. 23 Apr. 1932. "Canadian Plays and Experimental Stagecraft." Toronto *Globe.*

Voaden, Herman. 17 Dec. 1932. "Creed for a New Theatre." Toronto *Globe.*

Voaden, Herman. 17 June 1933. "Toward Theatral Dance." Toronto *Globe.*

Voaden, Herman. July 1933. "Dance of the Theatre: Impressions of the Dance in Four Countries." *The Dancing Times* No. 274.

Voaden, Herman. 1934 and 1939. Notes for a Winter 1934 speech to his Play Workshop, and 1939 speech on art and the symphonic theatre to the Women's Art Association, Toronto.

Voaden, Herman. 1975. "Symphonic Expressionism." Unpublished typescript.

Voaden, Herman. Fall 1981. "Forum." *Theatre History in Canada* 2: 2, 156-58.

Voaden, Herman. 1993. *Symphony: A Drama of Motion and Light for a New Theatre.* In Anton Wagner, ed. *A Vision of Canada: Herman Voaden's Dramatic Works 1928-1945.* Toronto: Simon & Pierre.

Wade, Allan. 1936. Adjudication sheet for *Murder Pattern.* Herman Voaden Papers, York University Archives.

Wagner, Anton. 1983. "'A Country of the Soul': Herman Voaden, Lowrie Warrener and the Writing of *Symphony.*" *Canadian Drama* 9: 2.

Wagner, Anton. Fall 1985. "Herman Voaden's 'New Religion.'" *Theatre History in Canada* 6: 2, 187-201.

Wagner, Anton. 1989. "'God Crucified Upside Down': The Search for Dramatic Form and Meaning," In "Bertram Brooker and Emergent Modernism." *Provincial Essays* 7: 38-51.

Wagner, Anton, ed. 1999. *Establishing Our Boundaries: English-Canadian Theatre Criticism.* Toronto: University of Toronto Press.

Zemans, Joyce. 1989. "First Fruits: The World and Spirit Paintings." In "Bertram Brooker and Emergent Modernism," *Provincial Essays* 7: 17-37.

Evelyn Geary:
Versatility in Motion

Mary Jane Warner

Evelyn Geary's story is similar to those of many dancers born at the turn of the century.[1] She received an eclectic dance training at a local Toronto school, then began her professional career while still in her teens. Like many young girls, she was inspired to pursue a dancing career after seeing the famous ballerina Anna Pavlova perform during one of her frequent tours that included Toronto, between 1910 and 1924 (Fisher-Stitt 1994: 51-63). Following the end of World War I, women experienced considerably more freedom including obtaining the right to vote in 1921. But, despite Geary's success as a professional dancer, as soon as she married she was expected to settle into the routine of wife and companion. After World War II she re-entered the work force when her marriage ended.

In the early twentieth century numerous theatres were built across North America to show silent movies augmented by live performers, ranging from singers, dancers and comedians to animal acts. The number of theatres and the sheer quantity of shows presented provided ample work for all types of entertainers. With the release in 1927 of the first talking picture, *The Jazz Singer*, followed by the stock market crash in 1929, live theatre declined (White 1993: 175). In the 1930s the Great Depression meant fewer people could afford to attend any form of theatre. In response, movie theatre managers cut expenses by eliminating live entertainment and only showing movies. In the mid-1930s, however, more intimate nightclubs emerged which offered entertainers alternative venues for their talents.

Geary's dance career followed the rise and fall of the movie theatres quite closely. Along the way, she worked with several men who had a substantial impact on the Canadian entertainment business: Jack Arthur, who earned the title "Mr. Show Business"; Leon Leonidoff, who choreographed at Toronto's Uptown Theatre before becoming senior production director at Radio City Music Hall; and Boris Volkoff, who is sometimes referred to as the father of Canadian ballet. Geary found that the determination and discipline she developed as a youth helped her through difficult times. She was flexible, always ready to try something different, from being a "swing girl" to taking up a new career as a bookkeeper. Geary recalled her life as a dancer with considerable fondness, but she never dwelled in the past, rather she enjoyed each new experience in her long and fruitful life.

---

[1] Much of this essay is based on various interviews with Evelyn Geary, and the materials she donated to Dance Collection Danse.

Evelyn Geary in Winnipeg, 1926.

Early Life

Geary's English grandfather worked as a sailor before immigrating to Canada in 1874. He found work in Toronto as a tailor; his son Henry Edward "Harry" later entered the tailoring trade also. In 1908 young Harry married seamstress Elizabeth "Bessie" Sarah Howden, originally from a well-to-do Scottish family. The couple moved into a house on Booth Avenue in the Beaches area, where their only daughter Evelyn was born eleven months later.

The early twentieth century was a prosperous time for many Canadians. Between 1901 and 1911 the population increased by over one third, with many immigrants coming from Europe. Trade grew between eastern and western Canada; Toronto became the heart of a large industrial region centred in southern Ontario. The country rejected a reciprocity treaty with the United States in 1911, while seeking less control from Britain. In an era of growing nationalism Canadians began to develop their own art forms (Careless 1970: 314-20).

In this climate of growing confidence, Evelyn's early childhood was uneventful with no hint of a flair for show business. She attended the local public school, where she did well academically, but, from her earliest moments she wanted to take dancing lessons. Since her parents were not well off, she had to wait until a doctor recommended lessons to improve her fragile health. After considering various teachers, Bessie Geary settled on Titchener Smith's Apollo School of Dancing, which had recently relocated to 731 Yonge Street, opposite Loew's Uptown Theatre (Warner 1995: 71-74).

By the time Evelyn began her studies with the handsome and dignified Titchener Smith around 1918, he was giving instruction in "classical, toe, national, interpretive, folk, character, tap and social dancing" (advertisement in Geary scrapbook). Every Saturday Mrs. Geary took nine-year-old Evelyn by streetcar to Titchener Smith's studio. Dressed in a pink chiffon practice dress made by her mother, and wearing socks and ballet slippers tied with ribbons, Evelyn revelled in these classes and thought of little else between lessons, even trying out new steps on her daily walk to school. Although her mother immediately recognized her talent and ambition, her father did not become convinced until considerably later.

After she had been studying for several years, Titchener Smith informed Evelyn that she was ready to learn a solo; thus arrangements were made for private lessons at an additional fee. In his 1923 recital she danced *The Dragon Fly* solo as well as appearing in several group numbers. Titchener Smith recommended his most talented students for occasional paying dance jobs. One of Evelyn's first such appearances was at the Canadian National Exhibition in September of 1922, as one of twelve ballet dancers chosen to appear with the De Feo Grand Opera Company. She was so elated by these early dance engagements that she developed the habit of recording her dancing engagements and fees in a small notebook which still survives today. Soon she was performing "Fancy" and "Toe" dancing at garden parties, fall fairs, Masonic Temples and Rotary Clubs throughout the Toronto area.

Dancing in Pantomimes

In 1922, she auditioned for the pantomime *Cinderella*, to be produced by the Vaughan Glaser Players at the Uptown Theatre.[2] Although the Uptown had opened in 1920, it did not achieve success until the American actor-manager Vaughan Glaser began operating a repertory company there. Soon after taking over in 1922, he decided to produce a typical British pantomime for the Christmas season that would appeal to both children and adults. He hired the experienced British pantomime producer, George Vivian, to oversee the production of *Cinderella*. It required nearly one hundred performers, including over thirty children between the ages of eight and twelve. Evelyn went along to the audition out of curiosity. The youngsters were asked to perform several dance routines, but as the combinations became more complex, all dropped out, one by one, until only Evelyn was left dancing. She was cast, along with a number of other children, as a "toe fairy." After two weeks of rehearsal, the pantomime opened on Christmas Day and ran until January 11, 1923.

Her experience in *Cinderella* confirmed Evelyn's desire to be a dancer, and she continued to find every opportunity to perform. Her career was not all smooth sailing, however. Several months after appearing in *Cinderella*, she was scheduled to perform with eight other girls in a fashion show at Shea's Hippodrome Theatre. Since this engagement necessitated her leaving school at 2:30 p.m. for one full week, as a courtesy, Mrs. Geary informed the school's principal, but he opposed Evelyn's absences. Mrs. Geary countered by having Evelyn attend school only in the morning during the week of the show, but the truant officer called at their home. Mrs. Geary became incensed; the *Toronto Star* got hold of the story which was picked up by papers across Canada and the United States. Since Evelyn was a good student academically with medals for excellence in attendance, conduct and punctuality, the matter was soon dropped by both sides to avoid further embarrassment. She felt "relieved" to enter high school one year later.

---

[2] See Gerald Lenton-Young, "Variety Theatre," and John Lindsay, *Turn Out the Stars Before Leaving* for further information about Toronto theatres at the turn of the century.

Even before graduating from public school, Evelyn decided that she needed a theatrical agent. One day the precocious youngster went downtown alone to find one. Taking along some photographs of herself in dance poses, she was successful in securing a contract with a theatrical booking agency. Her bookings took her across Toronto to many small movie houses, such as the Christie, Oakwood and Beaver, which could not afford a major headliner but needed to offer some entertainment along with the featured silent movie. Although Mrs. Geary was not a "stage mother," she did watch over Evelyn and accompanied her when she was scheduled for an evening performance. Generally, Evelyn was engaged by a movie house to perform for three nights in three different dance numbers. Although her first performances consisted mostly of Fancy and Toe dancing, her numbers soon became more varied. One routine was a lively tap number danced in an evening suit with tails and top hat. She also had a Spanish dance, an Italian tarantella and a gypsy dance in her repertoire, but her favourite numbers were performed on pointe. She usually made $3.00 to $5.00 per night, a substantial amount for a young teenager still in school. The money paid for her dancing lessons and costumes, but a portion was deposited regularly into her own bank account. At sixteen she had saved enough to purchase her own car.

During the summers she danced at outdoor parks and in the autumn at fall fairs in the small communities surrounding Toronto. As the pantomime season approached the following year, her mother suggested that Evelyn not audition so she could spend Christmas day with relatives. At first she agreed, but on audition day she wandered over to the Uptown to see what was happening. Before the audition began, George Vivian whispered that he had a nice speaking part for her. She could not resist this opportunity and went through with the audition. Her mother was none too pleased but accepted the situation. Evelyn played "Boy Babe" in *The Babes in the Wood*; other principals were Lorraine Mitchell as the "Girl Babe," Fred Walton as the "Dame" and Vaughan Glaser as the "Wicked Baron." The show opened for a three-week run on December 25, 1923, running until mid-January, with both matinee and evening performances most days. Evelyn received $25.00 per week, reflecting her status as a featured performer required to act as well as sing and dance. This pantomime was also an elaborate and expensive production, boasting fourteen massive stage sets, ranging from a depiction of the theatre's stage door to the castle of the Wicked Baron. Thirty youngsters performed in a "Ballet of Birdland" and in a "Fairy Ballet."

During the 1924 season Evelyn appeared in *Aladdin and The Wonderful Lamp*. By then, Vaughan Glaser's Repertory Company had moved to the Regent Theatre on Adelaide Street, after Glaser had objected to the exorbitant rental fees charged by the owners of the Uptown. The lead dancer was Helen Codd, a Toronto dancer and teacher specializing in toe dancing (Warner 1995: 55-62). In *Aladdin*, Codd had a ballet number and a more exotic routine as a slave girl. When she was injured, Evelyn, who often watched from the wings, was asked to replace her; she went on with no rehearsal. Although she did not perform the identical steps, she had a good sense of style and knew the general shape of the dances.

In the summer of 1925 she obtained an engagement at Scarborough Beach. Opened in 1907, it had an open-air stage with a bandstand beside it. Comedians, musicians, singers and dancers entertained there regularly until it was demolished at the end of the 1925 season. Sunnyside, which opened in 1922, was a larger and even more popular entertainment site complete with musical rides, games and a restaurant for dinner and dancing (Filey 1996: 22, 46-54). In 1926, Captain Merton "Mert" W. Plunkett, founder of the Dumbells, erected a small building with an outdoor stage located at the water's edge with seating for 300 people (Earle 1956). The stage was used by the Merrymakers, a group consisting of the Dumbells and a small orchestra, plus singers and dancers. Evelyn danced in these productions throughout the 1926 and 1927 seasons.

From observing other dancers, Evelyn decided that she had learned all she could from Titchener Smith and transferred to a new teacher in Toronto, Russian-born Leon Leonidoff (Warner 1995: 75-77). His Russian Ballet School of Dancing was on the second floor of the Massey family's former mansion located at Wellesley and Jarvis Streets. Classes were $1.50 each, plus $.75 for a half hour toe class, a rather hefty price in the 1920s. Leonidoff's assistant teacher and dancing partner was Detroit-born Florence Rogge, who had studied in New York with two exponents of the Italian style, Elizabetta Menzeli and Luigi Albertieri. The classes offered by Leonidoff and Rogge were quite different from those taught by Titchener Smith. They used French terminology for dance steps, unlike Titchener Smith, who followed the American practice of using English names. The one-hour classes were disciplined and demanding. There was a lengthy barre beginning with slow careful pliés in all positions, followed by tendus, dégagés, rond de jambes, développés, petits battements and grand battements. Leonidoff constantly stressed careful footwork and turnout. At the end of the barre, the class did stretching exercises before moving to the centre to execute long, slow adages to strengthen their balances.

The final portion of the class was devoted to allegro with combinations becoming increasingly complex. Generally new combinations were taught each day, but more difficult exercises were repeated for several days until the students had mastered them.

Following her success in *Aladdin*, Geary began working at the Regent Theatre, recently refurbished to serve as the flagship for the newly formed Famous Players chain. Jack Arthur, whom Evelyn had known from infancy, produced the stage shows, and Leonidoff, her current dance teacher, arranged the dance numbers. She appeared in several musicals there including *Going Up*, *Princess Pat* and *Madame Sherry*. The culmination of Leonidoff's Toronto efforts came in 1926, when he introduced a corps of dancers at the Uptown Theatre. These young women did everything from ballet to chorus-line routines similar to those performed by the English Tiller Girls. By that time, however, Evelyn had begun touring with Captain Plunkett's shows and did not become an original member of the Uptown troupe.

Cross-Canada Touring

Evelyn had offers to join touring shows, but her mother felt that she was too young. When she was invited to join *Three Little Maids*, produced by Captain Plunkett, Mrs. Geary reluctantly agreed to let her daughter join the tour after receiving assurances from Plunkett that she would be well chaperoned. She was offered a salary of $50 per week and billing as a specialty dancer. The show went into rehearsal in late 1925 before opening in Ottawa on November 23. It was a typical 1920s musical comedy with a slight pretext for a story but featuring many song and dance numbers choreographed by Leonidoff, assisted by Rogge. Once again Geary was given an additional speaking and singing role when another performer became ill. Reviewers especially liked the show's dance numbers, singling out Geary as "exquisite in smart and intricate jazz toe dance" (newspaper clipping, Geary scrapbook). Of the many routines she performed, she remembered this number best. It was a perky dance filled with vigorous moves including cartwheels, splits and a spectacular ending in which she travelled downstage kicking her leg back to touch her head sixteen times. The company travelled across Canada by train, first to the west coast, then doubling back to take in the Atlantic before ending in mid March with one-night stands in several small Ontario towns.

The following year she toured Canada in Plunkett's *Revue of 1926*. The dance numbers were again choreographed by Leonidoff and Rogge. Geary performed a lyrical solo to Offenbach's "Barcarolle" called *Belle Nuit*. One of the most ingenious numbers in the Revue was *Card Dance* featuring Geary as the Queen of Hearts and two other dancers as the King and Knave of Hearts. The number, with its "quaint stiff maneuvers, their coy pantomime all served to endear the act to the audience" (Geary scrapbook). Leonidoff later used the same routine for the Radio City Ballet.

New York City

In the fall of 1927, Geary was invited by her aunt and uncle to drive to New York with them as companion to her cousin. In New York the family attended a show at the recently opened Roxy Theatre. It was a typical Roxy production consisting of a first-run movie, plus a live show with top entertainers and dancers (Francisco 1979: 4-7). Geary was enthralled by the opulence of the theatre and the quality of the ballet numbers produced by her former teacher Leonidoff. She sent a note backstage telling him how much she had enjoyed the show; two days later he phoned to invite her to join the Roxy's ballet troupe immediately. Leonidoff often commented that he found Canadian dancers better trained than their American counterparts, so it is not surprising that he contacted Geary. She arrived at the stage door the following morning with neither dance clothing nor work permit. But that evening she went on, with a dancer coaching her, whispering, "If you see a space during the number just move into it."

The Roxy's ballet and precision dancers worked seven days per week, doing four shows weekdays, and five on weekends and holidays. The theatre was well equipped with a staff cafeteria, sleeping area, and a small infirmary with a nurse always on duty and a doctor on call. Every morning the dancers rehearsed the show scheduled to open on Friday, then they did the first show before returning to the rehearsal hall. Following the second show, they had a three-hour break over the dinner hour, before the first evening show; then, between the first and the last show of the evening the dancers attended a final rehearsal. It was after eleven before the weary dancers were free to leave the theatre.

Geary danced in the ballet unit under Leonidoff, not in the precision line directed by Russell Markert. Occasionally she worried about her legal status, since she didn't have a work permit, but Leonidoff was good to his former student, often selecting her to perform in additional numbers. After eight months Geary was exhausted by the relentless pace. With two other Canadian dancers she auditioned for another show. The three disappointed Leonidoff when they gave notice in May 1928. Unfortunately the job fell through. Geary was unemployed for two months until she was offered a job in the musical *Sunny Skies*, produced by the Publix chain. The show featured Cuban entertainer Pedro Rubin, backed by the Pedro Rubin Girls, a line of dancers who performed Spanish-type numbers. The work was considerably easier, since there was no need for ongoing rehearsals after the show opened. The thirty-five week tour took the company across the United States in a comfortable private rail car before finally closing in Denver, Colorado.

On her return to New York, Geary contacted Leonidoff, who offered her a choice of work at either the Roxy or the Fox Theatre in Brooklyn (Morrison 1982). She chose the Fox, which paid better. The Fox's dancers, billed as the Leonidoff Girls, did four shows daily, but after a mere six weeks Geary was forced to return to Toronto because of a severe bout of tonsillitis. She had been away from home for just over one year. During her recuperation she operated a

Toronto newspaper ad for the Uptown Theatre.

dance studio in her parent's attic, but the school did not last long, since Jack Arthur invited her to join the Uptown Theatre in the late spring of 1929.

The Uptown Theatre

The Uptown at Yonge and Bloor Streets was an elegant 3000-seat theatre, north of the downtown core of the city. Since taking over the theatre in 1926, Arthur had maintained high production standards, ensuring that the performers as well as the sets, costumes and lighting were among the best in the city. Although Leonidoff was the Uptown's first choreographer, by the time Geary joined, the choreography was in the hands of a teenaged tap dancer, Jean Hemsworth. Arthur offered Geary a contract as both solo dancer and ballet mistress. She was responsible for setting three routines each week, dancing with the Uptown Girls and performing some solo numbers. Soon after, Hemsworth was transferred to Arthur's theatre in Hamilton, thus giving Geary complete responsibility for the dancing, albeit under Arthur's watchful eye. The Uptown Dancers received considerable attention in reviews: "They must be the fairest dancers in all Canada, these lithe, graceful steppers Jack Arthur has chosen for his ensemble. This week twenty girls form the ensemble and the dancers are more beautiful than ever it would seem. 'A Bowl of Orchids' is the title given this terpsichorean moment and besides the dancers Jack Arthur introduces ... Evelyn Geary and Jean Hemsworth as specialty artists." Numbers were given colourful names such as *Sweet Forget-Me-Not*, *Kaleidoscope*, and *Holiday Frolic* (Geary scrapbook).

The Uptown followed the format used at the Roxy, beginning with several movie shorts, followed by a stage show featuring vaudeville stars plus the Uptown Dancers, who performed for approximately twenty to twenty-five minutes, then concluding with a feature film. The Uptown Dancers originally consisted of twelve dancers plus some extras, but the number was gradually increased to twenty. Most of the dancers were between the ages of fifteen and seventeen; at nineteen Geary was only slightly older than the dancers she directed.

The rehearsal schedule was similar to the Roxy's, but not quite as arduous since there were fewer performances. On Monday the dancers arrived at the theatre around 10:00 a.m. to begin work. After a forty-five minute warm-up, they tried out ideas for the next week's numbers. They did a matinee, then rehearsed until 5:45 p.m. before breaking until the 7:15 p.m. supper show. Most of the dancers ate following this show, then returned to the theatre for the final presentation at 10:30 p.m. Since rehearsals continued throughout the week, the pace was gruelling. If a dancer was injured or exhausted she simply asked for time off, and a substitute was called in to learn the routines for the following weeks' shows until the regular dancer was ready to return. Since Geary was part of the production team, she also participated in planning meetings after the final show every Saturday night. At that time Arthur and his team decided on the theme for the show opening in one week; it was frequently linked to the subject of the feature movie.

In September 1929, Boris Volkoff was added to the rostrum at the Uptown as leading male dancer and ballet master (Collier 1997: 140-44). Although born and trained in Russia, he had spent several years touring the Far East as principal character dancer and ballet master before coming to America. There he joined Adolph Bolm's ballet company in Chicago, but came to Canada to avoid deportation when his visa expired. Volkoff took over choreographing the ballet numbers, but Geary was usually paired with him as a featured dancer. Despite their differences in age and background, the two got on well together. But Arthur had little patience with Volkoff's stubbornness and halting English, so Geary often found herself translating his ideas for both Arthur and the Uptown Dancers. Volkoff was highly skilled in choreographing works that showed off his dancers to advantage, despite the limited technique of some and the short rehearsal period. The works were varied, ranging from the abstract to the highly dramatic. One of Geary's favourite numbers by Volkoff was *Rhapsody Moderne* performed to Gershwin's *Rhapsody in Blue*. In this ballet the corps danced to the faster musical sections while Geary and Volkoff performed a pas de deux to a slow section in the music.

The Depression Years

Soon after Volkoff's auspicious beginning in Toronto, the New York stock market crashed on October 29, 1929, sending shock waves throughout the world and triggering the Great Depression. Rising unemployment inevitably had repercussions on theatre attendance. In spring 1930, Arthur decided to end his association with the Uptown and move downtown to the Imperial Theatre, taking his musical director and dancers. Volkoff instead opened his own dance studio and asked Geary to join him. The school was located on the third floor at 771 Yonge Street. It was a large, attractive studio with two dance practice rooms, dressing rooms, office and reception area, plus a one-bedroom apartment where Volkoff lived. Volkoff taught the more advanced ballet students while Geary was responsible for tap, musical comedy, stretching and limbering and pointe classes as well as children's ballet. The youngsters responded to her warm and loving manner instantly, nicknaming her "Miss Dearie." In addition, she managed the office, kept the books, paid the bills and scheduled the pianists.

Volkoff gave his first recital of twenty-four numbers at Hart House Theatre in May 1931. Geary was responsible for seven numbers, including the routines performed by the younger children plus the tap and musical comedy numbers. Geary and Volkoff were featured in two duets: *Polish Dance* and *Night in Russia*. Production standards were high, since Volkoff involved talented people to provide music, sets and costumes. In the next recital the couple performed *Caucasian Sketch*, in which Volkoff played a lad attempting to woo a young maiden. The number was "beautifully danced by Volkoff and Geary. Geary is a captivating artist whose movements are instinct [sic] with beauty, grace and lightness" (newspaper clipping in Geary scrapbook). To conclude the evening, they danced *Holiday in Russia*, joined by four female dancers and a balalaika trio. In their final recital together they danced a *Gopak*. Although Geary enjoyed teaching, she wanted to continue her performing career. Volkoff's school was firmly established and he could manage with the help of others; the two parted amiably to pursue their separate careers.

North America was still in the midst of the Depression, and the number of theatres featuring stage shows was still declining rapidly. In the fall of 1933, Geary returned to New York, since there was little work in Canada. Once again Leonidoff, now production director at the recently opened Radio City Music Hall, hired her as a ballet dancer in the corps de ballet under her former teacher Florence Rogge. At first the group performed only twice daily, but it was so popular that appearances were increased to four daily. Both the ballet corps and the Rockettes, a line of precision dancers, consisted of thirty-six women each. The daily routine was quite similar to that experienced at the Roxy and Toronto's Uptown. However, there was little contact between the Rockettes and the corps de ballet, except when they were all onstage for a large group number. The two groups, at least in Geary's time, tended to dislike each other; she remembered that the ballet and precision dancers wouldn't even ride in the same elevator.

Inevitably Geary grew tired of the intensive routine at Radio City Music Hall, since working seven days each week from mid morning to near midnight left no time for a social life. Preferring touring shows, she joined George White's *Scandals* as dance captain for several months. When this show closed, she returned to Toronto for a visit and was offered a job at the Imperial Theatre. The amount of dancing at the Imperial varied from week to week depending on the headliner. At a time when the dancers were disgruntled with the attitude of the current headliner, a telegram arrived inviting all the dancers to join the touring show *Let's Cheer*, beginning rehearsals the following morning in New York. Geary and the others packed their trunks and made their way to the train station for the overnight trip, leaving the Imperial's management to engage new dancers.

Let's Cheer travelled across the United States, eventually winding up in Texas for five weeks. When the show closed, the seven Canadian dancers returned to Toronto. Soon after, Geary received a call to audition for Buffalo producer David Bines, who was in Toronto to select dancers for Shea's Buf-

Evelyn Geary, ca. 1936.

falo, one of the largest theatres in North America with 4000 seats (*Shea's Buffalo* 1993: 2-3). Bines chose seven Toronto ballet dancers including Geary, who was asked to be a "swing girl." Although not too certain what the job involved, she agreed. Recently a law had been passed in the United States requiring management to give dancers one day off each week. A swing girl was assigned to understudy six different dancers; each day she would fill in for a different one. Since there were three routines to learn each week, the responsibility was daunting at first. Geary was frustrated as she attempted to pick up the movements and places onstage for her six dancers. She turned to another swing dancer asking "How do you do it?" She received a familiar piece of advice: "If you see a spot just move into it." After the first week, she settled in and found the variety rather fun.

One day, however, an immigration officer showed up at the theatre to check on the dancers' immigration papers. None of the Canadian dancers had the necessary documentation, so they were immediately deported. Bines was sorry to lose the Canadian dancers but told Geary that if she could get work papers, he would be delighted to rehire her. Back in Toronto, she busied herself getting her immigration papers. Just over a month later, she made the return trip to Buffalo on New Year's Eve with her green card in hand. The engagement lasted for a number of months, but eventually Shea's also dropped live entertainment and Geary was out of work.

An American friend suggested looking for work in Chicago, but they could find nothing. They took a bus to New York, but Geary was reluctant to ask Leonidoff for work once again. Since her friend had worked in nightclubs, the two decided to find work through a nightclub agency. Their first engagement was in Baltimore before returning to New York in late spring to begin rehearsals for a show that would play the 500 Club in Atlantic City. After her work in live theatre, this engagement was almost a holiday, since they did the same numbers once every night, week after week. After five or six weeks, the rest of the dancers returned to New York, but Geary was transferred to the Ritz Carleton Hotel. Again the dancers were free during the day, doing the same show every night at 11:00 p.m. with headliners such as comedians Milton

Berle and Jimmy Durante. When this show folded in October 1935, the dancers transferred to Ben Marden's Riviera Club in New York, where Paul Whiteman was the orchestra leader. They performed the same show, only twice nightly, throughout the winter. When the show closed, Geary moved to Delmonico's in New York for a couple of months.

Geary returned to Toronto in 1936 for a visit, but soon received a call from a producer who was currently presenting shows at Toronto's Shea's Hippodrome. Since the dance arranger was leaving, Geary was hired as her replacement. She was responsible for setting three numbers each week and performing as one of twelve dancers in the ensemble. The star was comedian Red Skelton, whose sunny personality and wonderful humour kept everyone laughing both on and off stage. After two or three weeks in Toronto, the entire cast boarded the train for Montreal where they performed at Loew's for several weeks before returning to Toronto to begin the cycle once again. When this engagement ended, Bill Beasley, who had recently opened the Top Hat Club at Sunnyside Beach, contacted Geary (Filey 1996: 56). His club became one of Canada's finest supper clubs. In addition to fine dining, there were live shows including eight showgirls who paraded around the stage in ornate costumes, and eight dancers who performed various dance routines. There was a good orchestra so that patrons could also enjoy ballroom dancing. Geary stayed at the Top Hat for several months.

Her final dancing job was at Buffalo's Chez Ami Club where she stayed for a considerable time. On most weekends her boyfriend, Hugh Sumner, drove to Buffalo to visit her. Finally, when the show closed and the dancers were being transferred to another club in Rochester, Geary decided to accept Sumner's proposal of marriage and returned to Toronto.

A New Life

The couple were married on April 14, 1938. Since her husband did not want her to continue dancing professionally, she retired at the age of twenty-nine. Her new life revolved around playing bridge, going to the races and dining out regularly at the fashionable Old Mill restaurant. Unfortunately, Sumner went bankrupt seven years later and the couple broke up. For someone who had been financially independent since her teens, the change in status was difficult. She looked for work and finally was hired by National Trust as a bookkeeper. Once again her determination to succeed came to her rescue. She knew very little about bookkeeping except what she had learned in her brief stint at Volkoff's studio, but she quickly progressed to supervising others and rose to the position of Estates Officer, remaining with National Trust for over thirty years. Following her retirement, she was introduced by a fellow ex-dancer to Alan Moffitt. Geary enjoyed dating this kindly gentleman and the couple married. Through her marriage, she inherited a family of nephews and nieces who helped fill her need for family. The couple enjoyed a happy relationship until his death in 1985. For Geary, her life was filled with wonderful memories. She remembered vividly her days as a dancer, especially the touring, since she felt it was like belonging to one large, happy family. Shortly before her death in February 2004, she commented, "I have had a wonderful life and I wouldn't have wanted it to be any different."

Boris Volkoff and Evelyn Geary, ca. 1932.

References

Several types of materials were used: scrapbooks, notebooks and programmes donated by Evelyn Geary to Dance Collection Danse; specialized collections in the Metropolitan Toronto Reference Library on Boris Volkoff, Vaughan Glasser and Toronto theatres. In addition the *Globe* (Toronto), *Saturday Night* and the *Toronto Star* were used extensively.

Careless, J.M.S. 1970. *Canada: A Story of Challenge*. Toronto: Macmillan.

Collier, Cliff. 1997. "Volkoff, Boris." In Susan Macpherson, ed. *101 from The Encyclopedia of Theatre Dance in Canada*. Toronto: Dance Collection Dance Press/es, 140-44.

Earle, Patrice. 1956. *Al Plunkett: The Famous Dumbell*. New York: Pageant Press.

Pioneers

Filey, Mike. 1996. *I Remember Sunnyside: The Rise and Fall of a Magical Era*. Revised edition. Toronto: Dundurn Press.

Fisher-Stitt, Norma Sue. 1994. "Hector Charlesworth and E.R. Parkhurst: Looking at Dance in Early Nineteenth-Century Toronto." *Canadian Dance Studies* 1, 51-63.

Francisco, Charles. 1979. *The Radio City Music Hall: An Affectionate History of the World's Greatest Theater*. New York: E.P. Dutton.

Lenton-Young, Gerald. 1990. "Variety Theatre." In Ann Saddlemyer, ed. *Early Stages: Theatre in Ontario 1800-1914*. Toronto: Ontario Historical Studies Series, 166-213.

Lindsay, John C. 1983. *Turn Out the Stars Before Leaving*. Erin, Ont.: Boston Mills Press.

Morrison, Craig. 1982. *The Brooklyn Fox Theatre*. Notre Dame, Indiana: Theatrical Historical Society Annual, No. 9.

Shea's Buffalo Performing Arts Center. 1993. Elmhurst, Ill.: Theatrical Historical Society Annual, No. 20,

Warner, Mary Jane. 1995. *Toronto Dance Teachers: 1825-1925*. Toronto: Dance Collection Dance Press/es.

White, Randall. 1993. *Too Good to be True: Toronto in the 1920s*. Toronto: Dundurn Press.

Interviews

The following include the author's personal interviews and others available at Dance Collection Danse.

Geary, Evelyn. Numerous interviews between 1994 and 1999.

Ferry, Jolyne Gillier. Various interviews by Lawrence Adams, Dance Collection Danse between 1994 and 1995.

Leonidoff, Madeleine. Telephone interview by Lawrence Adams, Dance Collection Danse: 2 March 1995.

Spafford, Margaret McBain. Interview by Lawrence Adams, Dance Collection Danse: March 1993.

Boris Volkoff:
Father of Canadian Ballet

Clifford Collier

As a former student of Boris Volkoff, from the fall of 1947 to the spring of 1952, I spent more than five of the best years of my life in his studio at 783 Yonge Street, located near the Loew's Uptown Theatre in Toronto. The wonderful song from *A Chorus Line*, "Up the Narrow Staircase," is especially poignant for me, not only because the studio was located on the top floor reached by climbing up a narrow staircase, but because it became my "home." After Volkoff's death, I found I wanted to share those many happy memories of the man who had such an influence on my life and career and so I wrote the following short piece.[1]

Now acknowledged as the father of Canadian ballet, Boris Volkoff was born on April 24, 1900 (as calculated by today's Gregorian calendar; or April 11, 1900, by the Julian calendar followed in Russia at that time), in the village of Schepotievo, near the town of Tula in then-Czarist Russia. He was the third son of Vladimir Gregorovich Baskakov, a respected tailor and farmer of the district, and his wife Maria Fedorovna Volkova. Boris went to school in Tula and, while growing up, took an active part in the village dance competitions.

His older brother, Igor, was already a successful dancer with the Warsaw State Opera and Variety Company. By the time Boris was eleven, he had rejected the idea of rural life, and so left home to join the small dance company Igor had formed to tour the western and southern parts of the Russian Empire. Igor had already taken his mother's maiden name of Volkoff for his stage name, something which Boris was to do later. Boris' dance debut was ignominious; after forgetting most of the choreography, he climaxed his performance by pirouetting into the orchestra pit. An irate Igor demanded an hiatus in his brother's budding career lest he disgrace the company again, so Boris was sent home, and he went back to school in Tula. He later returned to Igor's company as a character dancer, just before World War I.

With the outbreak of war, the elder Volkoff son was drafted into the Czar's army. The teenaged Boris found himself on his own, dancing with the company that, luckily, spent most of the war years in Baku on the Caspian Sea. There it joined forces with an opera company which performed at the Mailoff Opera House. During those years, Boris studied with Jan-Janowicz and Domaratski-Novakowski while attending school in Baku. By 1918, the company moved on

---

[1] This is a revised version of essays that appeared earlier in *York Dance Review* 3 (Winter 1974), 22-26, and in *101 from the Encyclopedia of Theatre Dance in Canada* (Toronto: Dance Collection Danse Press/es, 1997), 140-44.

Boris Volkoff, ca. 1930.

to Astrakhan. Because of Russia's internal battling, performing life was precarious, so Boris returned home to the quiet farm life of Schepotievo, where at least he would eat regularly. By 1918, he was accepted into the State Ballet School in Moscow, eventually becoming first character dancer with its associated company.

In Moscow, one of Volkoff's first teachers was the choreographer Kasyan Goleizovsky. Volkoff studied with Olga Nekrasova and Alexander Gorsky, between 1920 and 1924, at a school affiliated with the Bolshoi Theatre. Gorsky, like Michel Fokine, was influenced by Isadora Duncan, a reformer who stressed plasticity of movement and complete corporeal expression. Moscow, at that time, had a great variety of private ballet schools, as well as the studios of proponents of François Delsarte, Émile Jaques-Dalcroze and Isadora Duncan, all of whose work had an influence on the academic ballet schools and companies during those years. From 1918 to 1924, as a student and dancer, Volkoff experienced and observed this artistic environment, and here he absorbed the principal foundations on which his later career as a teacher and choreographer was based.

After his graduation, Volkoff joined the Moscow State Youth Ballet, which toured Siberia, the Soviet Far East and China. While on a six-month tour in 1924, he left the company in Harbin, China, and fled to Shanghai, where he signed a one-year contract with the Shanghai Variety Ballet as a dancer and choreographer. The company performed at the Carleton Café, a popular Shanghai nightclub. From that contract, he moved on to work with the local Italian Opera Company, while at the same time he also opened his own school. Involvement with a Mata Hari-like agent resulted in his heading a short-lived group called the Stavrinsky Ballets Russes, which toured throughout the Far East.

When that group disbanded, the determined Volkoff formed another to tour Japan and Hawaii, an easy jump to San Francisco and all the small-town fairs of California and Texas, which his agent next booked for them. Unhappy with this, Boris bought out his contract in 1928 and joined Adolph Bolm, once soloist in Diaghilev's Ballets Russes and Pavlova's former partner. At that time, Bolm operated both a school and a company in Chicago and did extensive work in California. Later, when Volkoff's U.S. visa lapsed, he was told to return to Shanghai or find another country to take him. Bolm advised him that Leon Leonidoff had left Toronto's Loew's Uptown Theatre for the Roxy Theatre in New York City, and that Toronto producer Jack Arthur needed a leading dancer and ballet master. With the help of an English-speaking couple, Volkoff entered Canada illegally and started work at Loew's Uptown in May of 1929.

As ballet master and sole male dancer, Volkoff performed twice a day, six days per week, with Sundays off. Because there was a new show every week, the company rehearsed each morning for the upcoming production, which Volkoff also choreographed. 1930 saw the opening of the first Volkoff ballet school, which operated continuously for over forty years in a variety of locations, but always in the Bloor and Yonge Streets area of Toronto. A number of his studios were gutted by fire. He opened his last studio on Cumberland Street a few months before his death in 1974.

From the very beginning, Volkoff saw a future for ballet in Canada, a vision he doggedly pursued. On his arrival, he immediately attracted the attention of the social and artistic elite. Because this group was not large in Toronto around 1930, everyone knew, or new of, one another. The same people patronized the opera, theatre, symphony and art galleries. Toronto had never before had such a choreographer in its midst. Pavlova and the various Ballets Russes had made their impact on North America, and Volkoff, as a Russian, was lionized. This situation prevailed well into the 1940s. After World War II, with the growth of immigration, the artistic community broadened; this broadening also lessened the early familiarity which helped Volkoff achieve his first success.

Eager to expose audiences to dance, he leapt at every opportunity. One of the first came in 1932, with the offer from the socially exclusive Toronto Skating Club to mount a ballet for their annual carnival. Ballets had been attempted on ice before, but it was left to Volkoff to create full-scale productions of *Prince Igor*, *Swan Lake* and, later, abstract choreographies to the concertos of Rachmaninov and others. From 1932 to 1941, when the war disrupted the carnivals, skaters became his corps de ballet and the current champions were his soloists. The movement was pure Volkoff which, with the aid of skating professional Walter Arian, was translated into terms skaters could understand. Arabesques became spirals, and pirouettes, spins. These skating spectacles, artistically and financially successful, did much for Volkoff's fame, both in the city and beyond. Offered a position in New York to create similar works for professional ice shows, he turned it down. It was not skating he wished to develop but ballet. He wanted to fulfill his dream of a company of young Canadian dancers. Also, as he often stated, he had already had his fill of "those crooks in America."

His school flourished, for it was socially acceptable to study there. Moreover, he was an excellent teacher, able to inspire and develop dancers. By 1935, when he took his Canadian citizenship, he had commenced his annual recitals to show the developing quality of his students to the audiences he was also developing. There was little ballet-going public then; it needed to be

Logo for Boris Volkoff School of the Dance.

nurtured and this he did with determination.

In 1936, Volkoff received an invitation to take a group to the Internationale Tanzwettspiele attached to the Summer Olympic Games in Berlin. Canada's Olympic Sports Committee obtained a mere ten percent reduction on their fares, so the fifteen dancers had to raise most of their travel funds on their own. Covering the majority of other expenses fell to Volkoff. Just before making the trip to Germany, Volkoff married his star pupil, Janet Baldwin, a member of the historically and socially prominent Robert Baldwin family, and the trip to the Berlin Olympics became their honeymoon.

The Canadians had assumed that the dance festival was amateur and non-competitive, so it came as a shock to them when, on arrival in Germany, they realized that they would be sharing the programme with such renowned professional dancers as Harald Kreutzberg and Mary Wigman, among others. However, Volkoff, a pioneer in the field of national expression, had used a Canadian Indian legend for the ballet *Mon-Ka-Ta*, and an Eskimo story for the solo work, *Mala*. The costumes were designed by prominent Canadian artists such as Emanuel Hahn and Elizabeth Wyn Wood, and had authentic musical themes arranged for piano and percussion by Margaret Clemens, his company pianist. The work won approval from the German audiences and other participants in the festival. No prizes were awarded but five honourable mentions were announced and, to their surprise, Volkoff and his Canadian dancers received one of them.

Typically, it was this foreign notice which made Canada realize it now had a ballet company and, on returning home, the dancers were asked to participate more and more in Toronto's cultural life. Their ranks were reinforced by enthusiastic newcomers, all eager to dance. Volkoff's company performed ballets in the operas presented by the Toronto Opera Company; the group showed original ballets at the Promenade Symphony Concerts, held every summer at Varsity Arena; the dancers also prepared their own programmes for Eaton Auditorium and Massey Hall. In 1938, the Olympic dancers became the Volkoff Canadian Ballet and, until the formation of the National Ballet of Canada decimated its ranks, it continued to operate. Volkoff trained such dancers as Melissa Hayden (Mildred Herman), Patricia Drylie and Don Gillies, many of whom later yielded to the talent drain to other countries, a situation which Volkoff decried.

As the Volkoff Ballet grew in the 1940s, so did the regional dance phenomenon. Many new teachers had immigrated to Canada and each contributed to the growth of dance. Isolated, the western cities were forced to develop their own talent, a situation which worked favourably for Gweneth Lloyd and the Winnipeg Ballet. There came a point, however, when this surge of dance activity needed national expression. It was found in the ballet festivals organized by Lloyd, David Yeddeau, Volkoff and Janet Baldwin. The first Canadian Ballet Festival was held in Winnipeg in 1948 and the festivals continued annually except 1951 until 1954, alternating among Canadian cities. These dance festivals so inspired New York critic Anatole Chujoy that he suggested a similar event be held in the United States, which soon developed its own regional ballet festival movement, still going strong today.

The early festivals attracted non-professional groups from all of Canada. Suddenly the young performers realized that they were not working in a vacuum; there were other Canadians who liked to perform. The programming ranged from the classics, *Swan Lake* danced by Irene Apinee and Jury Gotshalks' Halifax Ballet, and *Les Sylphides* by Nesta Toumine's Ottawa Classical Ballet, to original works, many having historical or contemporary Canadian themes. Gweneth Lloyd presented her *Shooting of Dan McGrew* at one festival, while Volkoff created *The Red Ear of Corn* for the one in 1949. Its score, commissioned from Canadian composer John Weinzweig, used a story based on an Iroquois legend that accounted for the growth of red, not yellow, corn. Coupled with the French-Canadian story that the finder of the red ear at a husking bee could choose any bride he wanted, the music and dance blended folk-styles of both cultures.

The Canadian Ballet Festivals were significant in the development of dance in Canada. Without them, it is possible that the National Ballet of Canada might never have been born, for it was to the third Festival, in Montreal, that Celia Franca came from England, to evaluate the state of Canada's dance. Her decision to accept an offer to organize a ballet company in this country was based on what she saw there, and Volkoff welcomed her with open arms. In 1951, the same year Franca founded the National Ballet of Canada, Janet Baldwin and Volkoff divorced. He remarried shortly afterwards and Baldwin went on to make her own name in the Canadian dance world. But with the growth of the National Ballet, Volkoff's name slowly faded.

On June 22, 1973, seven years after the establishment of the award, Government House announced that Volkoff was to be made an Officer of the Order of Canada. Many felt that Volkoff had been unfairly overlooked earlier and his contributions to Canadian ballet ignored. Celia Franca received her honours in the first investiture in December 1967 and, although one cannot

Boris Volkoff's *Mon-Ka-Ta* in Berlin, 1936.

slight her development of a "national" ballet in Canada, Franca's work would have been more difficult if not impossible had it not been for Volkoff's groundwork.

He had assembled the first company of Canadian ballet dancers in 1936, and with this group won acclaim for Canada and praise for his presentations. This was some two years before Gweneth Lloyd and Betty Hay Farrally co-founded their Winnipeg Ballet Club, which became the Royal Winnipeg Ballet, and fifteen years before Celia Franca established the National Ballet of Canada. A generation of young Canadian dancers has grown up unaware of the volatile, unpredictable and sharp-tongued "mad Russian," who never quite mastered the English language but who did father and further the development of Canada's classical dance.

An early interviewer wrote prophetic words about Volkoff: "Pioneer in a thankless task, he is not likely to catch the eye of Ottawa when it comes to ... honour lists, nor would he be likely to appreciate such a distinction.... However Boris is in there punching to establish the right of young Canadians to dance for the pleasure of other Canadians and to prove the country's maturity in spite of itself" (quoted in Collier 1997: 144).

During the forty-four years that Volkoff lived in Canada, he created over 350 separate works. Actively teaching until a fire destroyed his Yorkville studio in November of 1973, Volkoff died of cancer at Sunnybrook Hospital in Toronto on March 11, 1974, aged seventy-three. On March 13th, the funeral service was held at St. Thomas' Anglican Church; his ashes were taken to Lake Temagami in Northern Ontario, the area he loved most in Canada, where he had spent many pleasurable hours fishing, his favourite form of relaxation. A

150

few days before his death, Volkoff donated his papers to the Metropolitan Toronto Reference Library, where the vast amount of surviving documentation can be consulted. His work *The Red Ear of Corn* was reconstructed in 1986 during the Dance Collection Danse ENCORE! ENCORE! reconstruction project.

References

Ayre, John. Spring 1996. "Berlin 1936: Canadian Dancers at Hitler's Olympics." *Dance International*, 14-18.

Collier, Cliff. 1997. "Volkoff, Boris." In Susan Macpherson, ed. *101 from The Encyclopedia of Theatre Dance in Canada*. Toronto: Dance Collection Dance Press/es, 140-44.

Mitchell, Lillian. 1982. "Boris Volkoff: Dancer, Teacher, Choreographer." Ph.D. dissertation, Texas Woman's University.

June Roper, ca. 1934.

June Roper:
Ballet Pioneer in Vancouver

Leland Windreich

In the first three decades of the twentieth century, thousands of little North American girls saw Anna Pavlova or ballerinas of a lesser talent perform in a fascinating stylized kind of dance and were inspired on the spot to study classical ballet.[1] But for those who were indulged with lessons and survived the years of arduous training, opportunities for a career were few in an era when there were no permanent American ballet companies. Compromises had to be made, and the ballet-trained American dancer had these options: to find an alternative medium in the dance, to seek work abroad, or to teach ballet.

June Roper was one of these single-minded dancers. In the course of a short but remarkable career spanning two decades, she took in sequence all three choices.[2] Eventually she turned to teaching during a low point in her activities as a performer and it was as a teacher that she was to realize her talent most fully. Her story is in some respects typical of many American dancers who, frustrated by the paucity of performance opportunities, achieved a high level of creativity in their teaching, producing in their studios a new generation of ballet artists for those companies which began to flourish in America in the 1930s. Her uniqueness lies in the scope of her success and the impact it had upon the American musical theatre of the period – at one time in the 1940s it was estimated that seventy June Roper pupils were performing professionally in New York – and in the link she established between the Ballet Russe companies and her seminal achievements in the development of ballet as a force in Western Canada.

Elizabeth June Roper was born on December 4, 1907, in Rosebud, Texas, at a time and place, and under circumstances, less encouraging than most for one contemplating a career in dancing. Her mother, Elizabeth Woodhead, had been brought up in a strict fundamentalist family in Bury, England, and as a child she had faced a grave crisis when her father caught her dancing in her stocking feet in the attic of the house. For her, dancing came as a natural activity to celebrate her acknowledgment of a world of fairies, and while the household in which she grew up boasted no books other than the Bible,

---

[1] An earlier version of this article was published in *Dance Chronicle* 5: 1 (1987), 105-41. Reproduced by permission of the author.

[2] Most of the information about June Roper's childhood and career as a performer was derived from many casual discussions and one formal interview with her in the period 1978 to 1980, when she was living in Vancouver. Her scrapbooks of photos and clippings were also made available to me, although like so much of the memorabilia collected during a busy career, much of this material is not dated. Thus, a complete documentation of her stage appearances has not always been possible, despite the wealth of material on hand.

doubtless she had found other lines to the folklore of the area. At eighteen she went to Texas to visit an elder brother sent there earlier and his success in the United States, and that of other brothers who had successively emigrated, gave her good reason for not returning to England.

The principal force in Rosebud's Baptist community was George Roper, a widower from Alabama with two young daughters, who was amassing a fortune in cottonseed oil. When he proposed to Elizabeth he promised her a diamond or a holiday in Europe for each child she produced. Four boys and four girls were forthcoming over the next three decades, and Elizabeth June, the last child, was born in her mother's forty-seventh year.

More fire and brimstone descended during Elizabeth's early years of marriage when she was seen by neighbours peering into a barn where a square dance was in progress. Outraged witnesses insisted on her excommunication, but George Roper's threats to remove his financial support from the church soon discouraged any rash action by the congregation. Public abhorrence of dancing was widespread among the fundamentalist Christians of the American South, and the Reverend Mordecai Ham became the prime spokesman in the anti-dance campaigns initiated by his sermons in Palestine, Texas – his pamphlet denouncing dancing, issued in 1914 in a printing of 5000, was reissued in a revised and enlarged form two years later (Ham 1916). Although Rosebud, one hundred miles west of Palestine and forty miles south of Waco, was totally isolated from any contrary influences, the Roper children, who were raised in an enormous house with a staff of black servants, were not restricted from dabbling in the less sensual arts. Twin sisters, Madelyn and Evelyn, studied singing and painting, respectively; June was taught piano; and the boys were given training on various musical instruments.

Each child also had a pony as soon as he or she was capable of holding the reins. Thus, June learned the rudiments of horsemanship early, and her enthusiasm for riding was encouraged by seeing "little girls in big tutus, riding on ponies in the circuses" (Roper 10 Apr. 1979). When itinerant groups of performers would set up tents for small-scale shows in the remote towns of the Southwest, attendance appears to have had the sanction of a community otherwise uncharitable to any form of theatrical presentation. Perhaps the high regard for horsemanship overshadowed any recognition of the exhibitionism so characteristic of the sinful art of dancing.

When June was five, her sister Madelyn was stricken with galloping consumption and was sent to a sanatorium in California. Elizabeth Roper moved to the coast with her younger children and stayed for a time with her brother, David Woodhead. The ambiance of Los Angeles appealed to them, and within a year the Ropers settled in a large apartment. George Roper commuted between their new home and his business interests in the South, and during his absence the family received its guidance from the also staunchly Baptist Uncle David. Certainly Los Angeles, with its innumerable exotic attractions, offered a greater scope for disobedience than Rosebud.

In 1916 Anne Roper, June's eldest sister, procured tickets to a Pavlova performance for herself and June, and the younger child was transfigured by what she saw. Agnes de Mille, who succumbed similarly, and who indeed may have been part of the very same audience in Los Angeles, has captured the essence of the experience: "I had witnessed the power of beauty, and in some chamber of my heart I lost forever my irresponsibility. I was as clearly marked as though she had looked me in the face and called my name" (de Mille 1951: 39). Pavlova's appeal to the American prepubescent girl lay in her personal magnetism, her fleetness, and the affinity she inspired in the young by her own independence and obsessive dedication. With June Roper, as with Agnes de Mille, the preoccupation was fixed, and each child was prepared to make enormous sacrifices and adult commitments. Elizabeth Roper, recalling her own childhood fantasies, understood her child's yearnings but was firm in refusing moral or financial support. On this point she remained adamant over the years; any thought of approaching George Roper for help would have been courting disaster.

But June refused to accept obstructions. A teenaged neighbour who studied dancing with Ernest Belcher in downtown Los Angeles tossed a pair of used toe shoes in the trash container, and the resourceful June retrieved them, cutting them down to size. At age eleven she made her impromptu debut at the family Christmas gathering, accompanied by an ensemble of musically talented brothers and sisters. As she recalled the event, "I took a pair of my mother's brown stockings and a lot of rags, which I dyed green, and put on the cut-down slippers. I was a tree, and I danced to the music of *Trees*" (10 Apr. 1979).

At twelve, June entered the world of commerce and made her services as a baby sitter available, offering free lessons in dancing as part of the package. Since she was fastidious to the extreme, she became popular with mothers in her neighbourhood and her clientele grew. Each session earned her twenty-five cents, and with four assignments behind her, she would take three streetcars into downtown Los Angeles for a class at the Ernest Belcher studios. By 1919 the Ropers had their own house in the West Adams district, and June had demonstrated maturity and independence in her work. Thus, the long absences in town were never questioned. Her mother was aware of June's activities, but made no attempts to prevent them. In the early years of her training June feared the hideous possibility of her father's discovery of her secret; yet she was sufficiently daring to seek out all possibilities for public performance. Amateur nights in the moving-picture houses offered one outlet. Another she initiated herself at a furniture store opening. In a tribute to his teacher, Duncan Noble accounted the event as June Roper told it:

> Wherever she saw a platform she asked to be allowed to dance. Once, at a store opening, when asked what she was going to dance, she saw a copy of the Rachmaninoff Prelude in C# Minor lying on the piano. Being assured that the pianist would play it as her accompaniment, she then made up a story of an escaped dying slave girl for the M.C. to narrate. Since the performance was imminent she needed a costume. Unbeknown to the store manager, who was also the M.C., she went back to

the storeroom and created a costume out of a sack and a length of rope. Of the talent shows she says, "Sometimes I even won the five dollars." Every time she did, it went for more lessons (July 1978: 10).

June Roper, age 14.

Ernest Belcher, an Englishman who had come to Los Angeles in 1916, was an expert purveyor of the Cecchetti ballet method, approaching dancing as a scientist. His didactic approach provided excellent groundwork for the beginning ballet student, and in later years Maria and Marjorie Tallchief would tremble under his exacting tutelage (Maynard 1961: 8-10). Marge Champion, Belcher's daughter, was another product of his teaching. In his enormous classes he mass-trained his dancers; it was not uncommon to find sixty to one hundred students assembled for a lesson. But his perceptive eye could single out the weakness of the individual and the personal correction he offered was invaluable. Because he maintained an employment link to the motion-picture industry, study with him became a means for getting work in the spectacle movies of the era. Ambitious students could thus turn their salaries for film engagements into coveted private lessons, which Belcher offered at the rate of twenty-five dollars per hour.

At twelve, June was one of hundreds of aspiring children in the Belcher studios, but one of the few who came without the support of a stage-struck mother. Belcher had demonstrated no personal interest in her until she was fourteen and had secured for herself an engagement at the Pantages Theatre as a solo dancer in a sketch called *The Goddess of Love*. For the auditions, June commandeered the services of her mother as chaperone, and when the child was accepted, Elizabeth Roper dutifully produced the garment required: a beaded tunic, breastplates with elaborate tassels and a feathered headdress – in all, not unlike the Bakst costume that Zobeide wore in the *Schéhérazade* ballet which Los Angeles had seen in the visit of the Diaghilev company.

"Highly Talented" was the caption over the photo of June in her exotic garb in the Los Angeles *Examiner*, where she is pictured in conjunction with fellow thespians Mrs. Shumway Enderley, "reader, interpreter and harpist," and Marguerite Goetz, "who is giving highly instructive operalogues" (*Examiner* ca.

1919). But such elevated company would not have soothed George Roper; presumably the child and her mother counted on his absence from Los Angeles during this debut and prayed that he did not read the *Examiner*. The account of the sketch reveals that the erotic content was minimal, and that the story involved a romantic encounter not unlike those depicted in current films featuring Rudolph Valentino and Douglas Fairbanks. The photo shows June in a pose suggesting yearning. Her body was still undeveloped, and her arms and legs appear exceedingly long, with her slender feet turned out expressively.

Other assignments followed in vaudeville at the Loew's State Theatre, at the several Pantages houses and at Grauman's picture palaces. Performing opportunities came also through charity bazaars presented in the major Los Angeles hotels, and Belcher began to realize that June was worthy of his personal attention.

In her third year of high school June was able to make more positive moves toward the career she desired. Her father died, thus bringing an end to the need to conceal her activities. With her inheritance she enrolled in a private school where she could study English, French and painting in the afternoons, leaving her mornings free to concentrate on her dance training which began at 7:00 a.m. in the Belcher studios.

Her studies with Belcher brought mastery of basic ballet technique, and through private lessons she acquired profound insight into the mechanics of dancing. Occasional assignments in films helped pay for this personal instruction. A job as stand-in for Billie Dove required that she learn high-diving, and her brothers gave her lessons so that she could take a spectacular plunge into the water at Catalina Island and stab a shark which threatened the heroine of the film.

At sixteen June, who had become an accomplished ballroom dancer and had also mastered the stylized theatrical versions of the major ethnic dance forms, began to incorporate elements from her ballet training into her adagio work. One of her early partners was José Navarro, brother of the film idol Ramon, who worked with her for two months developing a routine which she tried out at her high school's annual show. Her success in training a partner from scratch would be repeated in the years ahead as a performer.

Jack Kinney, a Belcher graduate who was beginning to find bookings in the Eastern nightclub circuits, received an offer of a six-week tour under Pantages for himself and his partner, who was unable to perform the occasional classical ballet number that was required. So Kinney invited June to join them for those pieces which needed her special skills, and the team of Kinney, Lee and Roper set out on a tour which took them to nightclubs in Denver and Chicago. After an engagement at Chicago's Lyric Theatre, Lee abandoned the trio. As a minor, June needed her mother's sanction to perform, and urged her to remain with them on tour as chaperone and mentor. So at sixty-five her mother gave up her comfortable life in Los Angeles to accompany her daughter in a nomadic existence in the United States and Europe for the next seven years.

June Roper and Jack Kinney, ca. 1923.

The team of Roper and Kinney (sometimes billed as June Roper and Jack Kinney, or June Roper and Kenneth Kinney) operated without the services of an exclusive agent and their bookings in the United States were for short-term engagements. From the Lyric Theatre in Chicago they moved to Billy Gallagher's Monte Carlo Club in New York, where they earned the reputation of being "one of the best whirlwind posture and classical dancing teams that has hit the East in months" (New York *Times* ca. 1922-23).

Their New York success was noted by a scout from England, who signed them for a spot at Ciro's Club in London. From that came a three-week engagement at the Kit Kat Club. Each subsequent assignment drew further offers, and there were few breaks in their performing activities, as they accepted engagements in southern France and Spain, where they were signed by the Dutch impresario Tuschinski for the Gaîté Theatres in Amsterdam, Rotterdam and The Hague. As their dancing craft became perfected and their confidence grew, they were able to command increasingly higher fees.

Their stages were to be those of the lavish casinos and nightclubs of Europe – where they presented innovative, characteristically American dances of their own creation – and those of the popular music hall, where their own material would be incorporated into or developed around a specific revue theme.

Three genres of dancing were popular with the performing couples in the musical theatre of the 1920s, which Louis Léon-Martin has designated as *la danse portée*, *la danse espagnole* and *la danse mondaine* (1928: 177-83). The first (often referred to as "classical adagio") involved graceful supported movement and spectacular lifts. The second comprised ballroom adaptations of classical Spanish dances and their Latin American counterparts. The third was drawn from the popular American dances of the current times, such as the Black Bottom, and usually contained elements from negro dancing, which the European audiences, newly exposed to the charms of Josephine Baker and the novelty of American jazz, found enchanting. To their adagio creations Roper and Kinney added acrobatic embellishments, and Roper often incorporated ballet technique into her own performances, some of which were done partly on pointe.

Despite her dedication to the study of ballet, Roper did not attend a performance of a legitimate ballet company from the time she saw Pavlova until 1935, when she was settled as a teacher in Vancouver. Her career in Europe coincided with the last decade of the Diaghilev ballet, but she was exclusively engrossed in the development and performance of her own dances. Often her engagements with Kinney in the major revues would be supplemented by after-hours spots in nightclubs, and their days were taken up with rehearsals, organization of new routines and costume planning. While in Paris, however, she faithfully took class in the studios of Olga Preobrajenska, who was especially noted for her encouragement of strong technique and for nurturing a dancer's unique qualities.

An engagement of several months at the Palacio del Hielo in Madrid gave Roper some freedom to observe the work of others, and she was enchanted by the dancing of Argentinita, whose style and costuming she incorporated into a dance which she performed with Kinney in a Paris revue. But the actual choreography came from a cook in their hotel, who taught them a traditional flamenco routine with a pair of spoons instead of the customary castanets.

Her partnership with Kinney was interrupted for a period of eighteen months when conflicts arose over costs for their costumes. Roper's gowns, costing hundreds of dollars, were a major expense, and several would be required for a season of performances. Kinney, who could manage with the same basic evening wear for most of his numbers, refused to consider an adjustment in the distribution of salaries. While dancing at Les Ambassadeurs, a popular nightclub in Cannes, they were viewed by the German impresario Hermann Haller, who offered them a featured spot in his Berlin revue. Kinney decided to strike out on his own; Roper signed for the Haller Revue of 1925 and proceeded to recruit a new partner.

Her twenty-five-year-old brother John seemed a likely prospect, despite the fact that he had not studied dancing. Tall, handsome and with a splendid figure, he had been her idol during childhood through his determination to resist their father's rigid philosophy. When he received her invitation from Europe, he was working in the California oil fields, but he enrolled in the Belcher studios, and in May 1925, when June Roper and her mother returned to California to plan the debut in Berlin, she had three months to turn her brother into a partner.

They spent their days in the studios under Belcher's guidance, and in the evenings Roper sought out all performance outlets in the community. Amateur nights were popular in the motion-picture houses, and no auditions were required. Their earliest performances were disastrous, but on the fourth try, they began taking prizes.

During her New York engagements at the Gallagher Club, Roper had been approached by a film producer to act as stand-in for the actress Dorothy

Mackaill in a film sequence involving a dangerous dive. For weeks she worked with Kinney to determine the height from which she could be caught without endangering herself. For the Haller Revue, she decided to utilize these skills for the first of the three prescribed dance spots, a romantic adagio called *The College Boy and the Butterfly*. Returning to Berlin in the fall, June and John Roper began training for this act, which would involve a leap from a ten-foot platform into her partner's arms. John Roper had to catch her below the bust and at thigh level; it took them more than a month to arrive at the correct angle and height to make a safe leap possible, working from a chair to the top of an upright piano in perfection of the catch.

Called *Wann und wo*, the 1925 Haller Revue was a lavish production in the style of a Ziegfeld show (Greul 1968: 247). It celebrated the American approach to the musical theatre and featured a troupe of Tiller Girls imported from England. Photographs from the programme attest to the special acrobatic skills required in an elaborately costumed sequence eventually called *Die schönsten Gläser der Welt*. June is shown wearing tights and toe shoes, an embroidered bodice, and a cloche, with gossamer netting draped winglike from her shoulders and forearms. John Roper wears a rugby sweater and satin trousers. In one photo June Roper is shown on pointe and in développé, and in another she is in the same pose while standing erect with her left foot planted in the area between her brother's rib cage and waist; he appears to be supporting her entire weight with a bent forearm.

The *Butterfly* number became the show-stopper of a revue which ran a full year in Berlin, followed by shorter engagements in Vienna and Hamburg. During the Berlin run the new partners also appeared at the Winter Garden. After the tour, John Roper returned to the United States where he applied his newly acquired expertise to devising dance acts for a circuit of nightclubs in the South, and Jack Kinney returned to partner June Roper in new dances featured in the revues of the Casino de Paris. With Mistinguett and Maurice Chevalier as headliners, these shows became the proving ground for a generation of new talent for the theatre and films, as well as providing a stage for occasional appearances by such dancers as Alicia Markova, Anton Dolin, Lisa Duncan and Argentinita (Beaudu 1954: 152).

Roper worked with Mistinguett during this period, coaching her in dance routines and also deportment in her elaborate costumes. The team of Roper and Kinney gained an adoring following in Paris, and news of their skills reached G.B. Cochran, who was sufficiently impressed by their work in one of the fashionable "*dancings*" in 1928 to engage them for his forthcoming revue, *Wake Up and Dream*.

Five numbers that they performed in their act were to be interpolated intact into the free-structured production, but with the stipulation that Cole Porter provide new music for their dances. The inevitable tango, which they had performed to Gade's *Jealousy*, was the most difficult to replicate and the result was called *Agua Sincopada Tango* (Gill 1971: 268). *Wake Up and Dream*, which opened in London on March 23, 1929, was immensely popular, enjoying 263 performances (Eels 1967: 334). The ingenue and singing star was Jessie Matthews, while the Austrian dancer Tilly Losch was the ballerina, dancing in an exotic number choreographed by George Balanchine to the Porter ballad, "What Is This Thing Called Love?" and in a doll-shop sequence borrowed from *Coppélia*. The elaborate sets were designed by Oliver Messel. The show was taken to New York with the same basic cast, where it opened on December 30. But Cochran, requiring a replacement for Jessie Matthews during her assignment abroad, approached Roper with the proposal that she begin training to become an all-purpose musical actress, capable of assuming the leading role in the revue projected for 1930. As Duncan Noble reports, "June was set to learn singing, tap (which she did not favour), acrobatics (she says that tore her body apart) and acting. With her everyday study of ballet – Preobrajenska in Paris, de Valois in London – these added studies began to take their toll. An American vacation was suggested before the new show went in" (Noble July 1978: 11).

During the Atlantic voyage, Elizabeth Roper was stricken with an attack of angina pectoris, which was so severe that the attending physician would not permit June Roper to see her mother for several days. As Roper doubted that her mother would survive the journey, it was an agonizing experience for them both. Roper wired a brother then living in Kentucky to meet the ship, and Elizabeth Roper was taken to a New York hospital, where she remained in critical condition for three months. When pronounced well enough to travel again, Elizabeth was to accompany her son to Kentucky for her recuperation, and June Roper made plans to rejoin the Cochran forces in London. En route to the train station, her mother experienced another attack and was again bedridden – this time for an additional month.

With the second Cochran revue now out of the question, Roper saw her control over her future slipping from her grasp. The weeks of stress began to take their toll and her own fortitude diminished. When Elizabeth Roper was finally able to be moved, June Roper accompanied her on the trip to Kentucky, where she herself collapsed and was hospitalized.

Organic causes were investigated for the symptoms she experienced – pain, depression, anorexia – conditions for which psychogenic causes would be explored in the next generation. In Kentucky an appendectomy was performed, and several months later, when her advanced depression had rendered her nearly speechless, the physicians assumed that they could alleviate her problem by removing her tonsils. Over the next several months her dismayed family shuttled her to various specialists, hoping for a diagnosis which would lead to a cure. Elizabeth Roper, meanwhile, had begun to improve and was to enjoy another eight years of life.

Back in Los Angeles, Roper attempted to regroup her energies and re-establish her dancing career. The effects of the Depression were now felt in Europe, and many of the lavish revues had closed, replaced by motion pictures. In the United States the entertainment field suffered drastic curtailments and many road attractions were cancelled. Hollywood was overpopulated with un-

June Roper, ca. 1927.

employed entertainers with whom Roper now had little stamina to compete. Fitful attempts to work with a new partner would be followed by cycles of discouragement and the periods of depression that plagued her for several years. Her family suggested distractions: one was to visit her sister Anne, who had married a Canadian and now lived in Vancouver. Anne's daughter, Betty Mills, had started dancing lessons and could profit by some expert coaching. Vancouver, with its lovely surroundings, might offer a new perspective, and Anne, who had shared her sister's enchantment with the magical Pavlova in her childhood, was a kindred soul.

Early in the autumn of 1934, Roper packed for a stay of two weeks and drove with her mother from Los Angeles to British Columbia. In 1934 there were dancing schools which offered ballet training in all of the major Canadian cities. Many of the teachers were Englishwomen with no theatrical experience who had mastered a few scraps of basic ballet pedagogy; the more conscientious of these took refresher courses periodically to update their teaching skills. There were also the Russians, some with legitimate and others with more dubious associations with the Imperial academies in pre-revolutionary Moscow and St. Petersburg. British Columbia had a few of each variety, British and Russian, and in some cases the competing factions joined forces. In Victoria, English-born Dorothy Wilson, who had set up an informal dancing studio in 1922 in a church social hall, entered into partnership with Nicholas Rusanoff, "formerly of Imperial Russian Ballet, Moscow, and of London, Paris and New York" (Victoria *Colonist* ca. 19 Sept. 1927). In 1927 they opened the Russian Ballet School of Dancing and began offering professional training. Seven years later Dorothy Wilson would mount Canada's first production of *Coppélia* in Victoria's Royal Theatre (Windreich 1984: 5-6, 8-9).

In Vancouver Boris Novikoff had studios on Granville Street in partnership with Mme. D. Platowa, "late of the Russian Imperial Ballet," and a small concert group which he established made tours down the West Coast. Ballet and acrobatics were offered by, respectively, Nikolas Merinoff and Charlotte del Roy in a school on Dunsmuir Street.

In the 1930s Vancouver received most of its cultural impulses from the western United States. A city of 300,000, it had enjoyed a lively theatrical life since the Klondike gold strikes in the 1880s, and dancing was seen on its many stages in vaudeville and variety performances. Anna Pavlova performed four times between 1910 and 1924, and there had been single visits in that period by Gertrude Hoffman with her pirated Fokine programme, Adeline Genée and Alexander Volinine, and Sergei Diaghilev's Ballets Russes.

Ballet training was popular for the daughters of wealthy families, but they were not expected to make a passionate commitment to the theatre. One who wished she could was Vivien Ramsay, who became an active force in Vancouver's children's theatre and who found expression of her dance enthusiasm in the production of pantomimes. Her friend Yvonne Firkins, a fellow balletomane and a leader in the city's little-theatre activities, proposed a joint effort to develop a school. As she described it later,

> It is just over four years ago, one day in August, that I thought "Why not take a chance and start a School of the Theatre in Vancouver – a school where every branch of the theatre arts can be taught?" My capital was at low ebb, as usual, but my spirits soared high, so I telephoned Vivien Ramsay, herself a very well known dancer in Western Canada and a tremendous enthusiast for the ballet. Would she like to join me in a School of the Theatre and take on the responsibility of organizing the Department of the Dance? Would she! It was the very thing she had been dreaming about for years (Dec. 1940: 4).

Both women had seen Roper's photograph on the cover of the February 1929 issue of *The Dancing Times* and had read about her European career. When Roper's visit to Vancouver was noted in the local press, they agreed that none of the local ballet teachers could offer the kind of high-powered professional training that she might provide. A meeting with Roper convinced them that she was ideal for their purposes. In her chronicle of the school's genesis, Firkins tactfully avoids mention of Roper's delicate state of health and suggests that her presence in Vancouver was due to her being "tired of travelling ... and as she had relatives in Canada, [she] decided to throw her lot in with us for a year anyway" (Dec. 1940: 4).

Firkins and Ramsay set about finding an appropriate location for their school, but they were soon evicted from their first studios for disturbing the peace. A second location, at 712 Robson Street, provided adequate quarters for the B.C. School of the Theatre, which flourished there for nearly a year. The first advertisement for the school was printed in the *Vancouver Province* on September 15, 1934, with reference to Roper as "mistress of the dance" and Ted Cawker as principal instructor in tap dancing, although Cawker was soon replaced by a local athlete, Jerry Mathisen, who specialized in acrobatics. Advertisements appearing a few months later in theatre house programmes note that Betty Mills and Mathisen constituted the "staff of teachers," while Firkins and Ramsay are credited as directors of the school.

Roper's formal introduction to the community took place on November 2, 1934, when she performed at the "Journalists' Cabaret," a benefit held at the Hotel Vancouver Ballroom, in which she appeared with her niece Betty Mills and some of the more advanced students who had transferred from other studios in Vancouver. This performance inspired a number of young girls in the community to begin training with Roper, notably the nine-year-old Jean Hunt from Nanaimo on Vancouver Island, who would commute to Vancouver for a weekly lesson (Hunt 10 Sept. 1984).

Among the children enrolled during the school's initial phase of development were several who would ultimately join professional dance companies: Patricia and Sheila Meyers, whose mother had been a Tiller Girl in the English music halls; Rosemary Deveson, recently arrived from Manitoba and one of the few students who had seen a real ballet performance, on a trip to England five years earlier; and Joy Darwin, who at age four had seen Anna Pavlova's final Vancouver appearance and had surrendered to the summons that earlier had claimed her teacher. For her, Roper's presence in the community made the goal all that much closer. As she recalled years later:

> There had been dance classes for little girls in the Vancouver area, but when June came to British Columbia children had their first opportunity to receive professional training. Miss Roper gave her students the chance to step out of the little girl's Saturday morning dance class mentality into the realm of serious dance. Her rigorous ballet classes gave those of us who wanted to work at it a fine technique. That she succeeded as an inspiring teacher and an exacting task master was shown by the fact that for the first time Vancouver was put on the map balletically speaking, when some of her pupils were accepted by world renowned companies (6 Oct. 1978).

Plans for a comprehensive school of the theatre arts appear to have been abandoned by the directors, who cheerfully promoted the development of the dance programme. As Firkins noted:

> Soon we had considerably over a hundred students, the majority of them studying ballet. At the end of six months we rented one of the largest picture houses in town and gave the first recital. June not only trained all the pupils, but was also responsible for the choreography, and every detail of the staging. Vivien and I, with the help of our seamstress, made the costumes. Far into the night for weeks we stitched and stitched.... But the show was a great success, and quite a worthy forerunner for June's later recitals, which were extremely brilliant examples of excellent training and fine showmanship (Dec. 1940: 4).

The Strand Theatre had been rented for the evenings of May 27 and 28, 1935, and Earle Hill and his orchestra were hired to accompany the dancers. For the revue's title Roper suggested "Stars of Tomorrow," which would serve as a reminder of her objectives in training. For a partner she coached Jerry Mathisen, who appeared with her in an adagio entitled *Nocturne* and with the twelve-year-old Pat Meyers in a number designated as *Adagio*. The balance of the programme offered the kind of material seen in vaudeville and motion-picture prologues, with the inevitable samples of Spanish and currently popular dance forms.

Each student was given a vehicle to reveal her potential, and in these early phases of her teaching career, June drew upon Belcher's expertise for making each dancer achieve a special stage presence by accentuating her inherent charms. Even at this early stage she recognized the ballet capabilities of the Meyers girls, Rosemary Deveson, and the tiny Jean Hunt, who were given assignments in two of the ballet numbers. A tall, expressive child named Rosemary Sankey, who would ultimately become a popular New York model, was given a solo as a dragonfly, reminiscent of the genre popular in the Haller Revue, while Joy Darwin appeared in an ensemble interpretation of *Bolero* – presumably Ravel's.

The first Vancouver visit of Colonel de Basil's Ballets Russes three months earlier had exerted some influence on the programming of this recital. Even more influential, however, had been the impact of the Ballets Russes' individual dancers, who served as tangible examples of what dedicated training in ballet could produce. Tamara Toumanova, Irina Baronova and Tatiana Riabouchinska – still in their teens – provided immeasurable inspiration to the Canadian students. The repertoire, consisting of Léonide Massine's exciting creations in the symphonic and character genres, as well as ballets by Fokine and Balanchine, also gave insights into the broad scope of ballet's theatrical expression.

The visit strengthened Roper's determination as a teacher, for she was both awed by the vitality and glamour of the stars and the diversity of their repertoire, and shocked by the poverty of technique demonstrated by most of the dancers in the ensembles. She soon made it clear that she was not interested in training dancers for assignments in the corps de ballet, thus establishing from the start more elevated goals for her pupils. Furthermore, she realized that it was indeed possible for a dedicated student to equal and even to surpass the technical prowess of those exceptional soloists they had admired in the Ballets Russes. "Russian ballet" thereafter became the specialty of her teaching programme.

Her year as dance mistress with the B.C. School of the Theatre had restored her to health, and with the return of her energies and ambitions, she decided to achieve an appropriate independence. The years of interdependence with Elizabeth Roper had come to an end and her mother returned to Los Angeles. June Roper settled in an apartment in Vancouver's West End and decided to devote her energies to the training of dancers. The Canadian pupils had exceptional innate talents, strong bodies, and the kind of dedication that she demanded. In the fall of 1935 she found appropriate quarters at 887 Seymour Street – two studios adjacent to the Orpheum Theatre. Her commitment to Yvonne Firkins and Vivien Ramsay fulfilled, she inaugurated the June Roper B.C. School of Dancing in the new location. There she would direct the school with a minimum of assistance for the next five years.

Despite the Depression, in the late thirties, Vancouver offered an array of brilliant dance companies from the United States and abroad, and the concert impresario Lily Laverock developed a growing audience for her attractions. Ted Shawn's Men Dancers made their first local appearance at the Empress Theatre in December 1935, and they would return in 1937 and 1939. The de Basil company returned early in 1936, playing to packed houses at the Orpheum Theatre at midnight performances when the motion-picture audiences had gone home. The effect of these performances on the school was immeasurable, as the ranks of students studying ballet grew correspondingly and as boys in the community began to drift into the studios. For example, aware of a vitality generated at the new school, late in 1935 the ten-year-old Audree Thomas transferred from the Merinoff-Del Roy studio, where she studied acrobatics, and her new teacher immediately marked her for a career in ballet.

The Ballets Russes had a particularly strong influence on the kind of dancing and the nature of the productions which Roper would stage for her charges. The year 1936 brought to Vancouver its first exposure to the second act of *Swan Lake* in a superb performance by Alexandra Danilova, while the exotic *Schéhérazade* of Michel Fokine, with Yurek Shabelevsky and Lubov Tchernicheva in the leading roles, was a dramatic revelation. *Swan Lake* gave pupils at the B.C. School of Dancing their first opportunity to see the classical vocabulary expressed fully in a theatrical presentation, thus inspiring new objectives for the year's curriculum. Roper also began to accelerate her pace of training for the ballet pupils.

During the second year of her teaching in Vancouver, Roper made a special trip to Los Angeles to confer with Belcher on the matter of introducing pointe work to the smaller children. He regarded the readiness as a matter of strength rather than of chronological age, telling her that "when the child can relevé with a perfect arch, with the knees tight from the thighs, she is ready for toe shoes regardless of age" (Roper 10 Apr. 1979). Many of her younger girls were thus screened and deemed ready for the transition, one which contradicted most standard programmes of ballet pedagogy at that time – and since. She found the Canadian children exceedingly receptive to a challenge and set high technical goals for them. For their first public appearance on pointe Roper devised an elaborate ballet to show off their accomplishments.

Dream Bird Ballet, incorporating many of the skills she was able to develop in her pupils in a relatively short period of training, was presented as the chef d'oeuvre of her "Stars of Tomorrow" revue at the Lyric Theatre on June 1, 1936. A full orchestra under the direction of Winifred Scott played the music of Offenbach, Tchaikovsky and Ponchielli; costumes were created by Margaret Anderson. Roper's concept and choreography certainly reflected the influence of *Swan Lake* but featured as well many of the devices and tricks used in the Haller and Casino de Paris spectacles:

> In an enchanted forest of a far distant land there are to be found many gorgeous birds of all plumage, having been transformed from beautiful young girls and little children by a sorceress and banished to this far off forest where life is peaceful and undisturbed. Suddenly their peace is shattered by the approach of several hunters, striking terror in them. Little Dream Birds are captured but manage to escape. The Hunters, finding Baby Canaries unable to fly, bear them off with them. Slowly the birds reappear. The stately Bird of Paradise; the Fire Bird and the Silver Pheasant sending forth their challenge, closely followed by the Love Birds. The approach of the Dove is watched by the Chief Huntsman, who upon falling in love with her, carries her away. The Snowy Heron in her regal beauty then appears and having

herself fallen in love with the Hunters expresses the height of her happiness, then calls to her friends and reassures them that the Hunters are so enchanted by their beauty that they need no longer fear them. The Hunters then reappear surrounded by all the birds of the forest dancing in complete unison of enchantment (Lyric Theatre programme, 1 June 1936).

Roper had trained her four huntsmen – Jerry Mathisen, Ernie Grant, Harry Cooper and Malcolm MacGregor – to catch the little Dream Birds and Baby Canaries, who made spectacular dives from the branches of trees. In rehearsal she began by training the youngest girls – those under six – who were fearless when it came to making the plunge into space. These were replaced by the heavier and invariably more cautious girls. Timing was of the essence for the four men, who were obliged to assess each catch in terms of the varieties of weights and physiques that girls of different ages presented.

On the ground twenty girls portraying the baby birds performed on full pointe. The older children were assigned challenging ballet solos. Pat Meyers, who played the Dove, had the coveted duet with Mathisen; Rosemary Deveson, in brilliant plumage, was the Bird of Paradise; and Joy Darwin, the Fire Bird. Rosemary Sankey portrayed the Snowy Heron, dancing to Tchaikovsky's *Troika*.

The balance of the programme offered a potpourri called *Carnival of the Nations*, which served, in true "recital" fashion, to display the less-gifted pupils in dances requiring fewer skills and to afford contrasting challenges to the prize students. It also afforded the kind of variety that was expected by audiences of the era. Roper and Mathisen danced a pas de deux called *Adoration* to music by Borowsky, and Betty Mills performed two solos in the Spanish genre. For the finale eleven girls, including Darwin, Sankey and Pat Meyers, performed a show-stopper: *The Poet and Peasant Overture: A Classical Interpretation in Taps*.

The *Dream Bird Ballet* received lavish praise in the Vancouver press and was repeated for two performances at the Lyric Theatre on December 11, 1936, where it was interpolated into a Christmas extravaganza featuring a pantomime of *The Sleeping Beauty*, which Vivien Ramsay directed.

The arrival of the Ballets Jooss in Vancouver for performances in November 1936 provided a contrast to the florid romanticism which had become the forte of the B.C. School of Dancing in its recitals, but only Darwin saw in these exponents of German expressionism a validity that she could relate to her own ideals. When she made inquiries about the Jooss-Leeder training programme, Kurt Jooss encouraged her to consider joining the company at Dartington Hall in England the following year. Martha Graham's appearance at the Empress Theatre on March 31, 1937, presented another fascinating option. Darwin auditioned for Graham and was accepted for a year of free study, but the prospect of minimizing the expression of the face made her decide to refuse the offer (Darwin 21 May 1979).

Margaret Banks enrolled in Roper's school in 1937 at age thirteen and was noted as a potential ballerina. However, competition among the adolescents

June Roper's

B.C. SCHOOL of
DANCING

887 Seymour Street
Phone: Seymour 8238

★

Specializing in
Russian Ballet, Spanish, Tap,
Character, Adagio.

Miss Roper is a graduate of the famous Ernest Belcher School, a pupil of Ferrari, of New York, and of the Cansinos, world-famous Spanish dancers. As an internationally known Ballerina, Miss Roper has performed as Premiere Danseuse of The Casino de Paris, Paris; The Winter Garden, Berlin; C. B. Cochran's Revue, London, and all the leading Continental theatres.

favouring ballet was strong and Pat Meyers soon became the front runner. Incipient arthritis had made Roper aware that her own days as a performer were numbered, and she began to train Pat Meyers as an apprentice, calling upon her amazing technical abilities and perfect memory to demonstrate difficult combinations to the classes. Pat Meyers would accompany her on annual pilgrimages to the Belcher studios in Los Angeles and to New York for special work in Ballets Russes style with such dancer-teachers as Maria Chabelska Yakovleff, who passed on the refinements acquired in her years with the Diaghilev Ballet.

In Vancouver, Roper had become a respected figure in the community, but she remained so engrossed in her work that she gave herself little time for social life. Her day began at 7:00 a.m. with classes, often continuing through the early hours of the morning, particularly during periods of preparation for the revues. By finding as many performance outlets as the city offered for her pupils, she afforded them regular experience before audiences – exposure which she deemed essential for even the youngest of dance trainees. This regular performing in cabarets, charity shows and nightclubs benefitted everyone: the community became conscious of Roper's abilities as an accomplished teacher and became a supportive audience. Their children were thus enrolled in her classes, and those parents advised by Roper to allow particularly talented pupils to give up public schooling for a full day of dance training were agreeable to the arrangement. Thus Patricia Meyers, Rosemary Deveson, Audree Thomas and others would leave their high schools for a concentrated day of learning the craft of dancing. They would, in time, prove Roper's theory that a finished ballet dancer could be trained in three years of intensive study.

The "Stars of Tomorrow" revue for 1937 was presented on June 1 at the Strand Theatre. On June 5, two of its numbers – *Grand Hotel* and *Romance Ballet* – were offered at the Orpheum Theatre in the form of a prologue to a motion picture. In the longer revue at the Strand, Joy Darwin appeared in a *Slave Dance*, which recalls Roper's impromptu offering at the Los Angeles furniture store during her early years with Belcher. An elaborate showpiece called *Carnival of Venice* had all the trappings of the extravaganzas in which Roper performed on the European stages, described as "a fantasy of song, laughter and dance, a figment of the imagination" (Strand Theatre programme 1 June 1937).

In this number, sea spirits disport themselves among sparkling goldfish beneath the Adriatic. Pat Meyers, Rosemary Deveson and Rosemary Sankey took on this assignment, while the less fortunate Joy Darwin, given the role of an octopus, was required to manipulate long fronds of coarse fabric which extended from her body (Darwin 6 Oct. 1978). The second scene involved an international and historical conglomeration in St. Mark's Square, featuring peasants, gypsies, an organ grinder and his monkey, Mickey Mouse, an Egyptian princess with a retinue of slaves, six baby Egyptians, a Chinese parasol dancer, puppets portraying Pierrot and Pierrette, and a firefly. It ended with a tarantella performed by the assembly.

For the *Romance Ballet* which followed, Roper drew upon light opera for her material. The action takes place in the Austrian court, where three of the Emperor's daughters dance in hopes of attracting "the dashing young Prince of Maurithania" (Strand Theatre programme 1 June 1937). The plot, like those of most of her revues, was simple, romantic and easy to follow. She doted on situations in which cautious infatuations ripen into great loves, with all characters achieving their heart's desires and an appropriate mate. A pas de six to the waltz from *Coppélia* was the highlight of the piece, featuring Darwin, Deveson and Meyers. Devised to show her best pupils at the top of their form, this waltz was repeated often in the cabaret and hotel appearances of Roper's dancers over the next year.

Critics for the Vancouver newspapers were full of praise for the quality of Roper's teaching. Stanley Bligh of the *Sun* marvelled at the *Romance Ballet* for its conception in the classical tradition and the challenges it set up for the ballet aspirants (2 June 1937). F.J. Arendt of the *News Herald* chided audiences at the 1937 revue for reacting indiscriminately to all the dances performed, noting that criteria were required for the proper judging of good dancing (ca. June 1937).

Following the revue, Joy Darwin received a scholarship from Kurt Jooss and was requested to appear at Dartington Hall on September 24 for the opening of the term at the Jooss-Leeder School. At seventeen, and with less than three years of training, she was the first of the B.C. School of Dancing pupils to accept an offer which would lead to an engagement in a professional company. Shortly after her departure, an extraordinarily gifted boy, the eighteen-year-old Ian Gibson, arrived from Victoria to continue his ballet training on a professional basis. Enrolled at age seven in Dorothy Wilson's School of Russian Ballet in Victoria, he had a remarkable natural elevation and a sound training in ballet basics. The role of Franz in Wilson's production of *Coppélia* had given him his first real theatrical experience.

Gibson's appearance at Roper's studios offered her a new set of challenges, for she had in the past trained male dancers to perform well as partners, but had not yet developed the special skills in ballon and elevation peculiar to the male classical dancer. The next year took him to Los Angeles for coaching with Belcher to help him achieve the brilliant technique which would dazzle audiences who saw his superb artistry during a four-year career with the big touring ballet companies, until he joined the Canadian navy – his career another casualty of the war.

The *Sun Ray Gaieties*, an annual Christmas charity performance sponsored by the Vancouver *Sun* for needy families, drew on the talents of all pupils in the local dramatic and dancing schools, and Roper's dancers became part of this city-wide effort, which offered opportunities to perform a broad range of character dances. Roper would devise a suite of national dances around a slight theme, involving flirtation, competition for affections or patience in love rewarded, and the children would learn combinations associated with mazurkas, fandangos, czardas and the like, which would be invaluable for the divertissements they would ultimately perform in ballets by Petipa, Fokine, Massine, Lichine and Nijinska. One principle that Roper stressed with her charges was that nothing in the broad spectrum of dance was impossible to learn; another was that nothing learned should be less than perfectly mastered. A third was that a dancer should be equipped to take on any assignment that might present itself, for a versatile, well-rounded performer is an asset to any company. To this end the students learned as well all the popular dance forms, and in the course of a long recital they might be required to perform a hula, a classical pas de deux and a military tap routine.

With the announcement of the return of Colonel de Basil's Ballets Russes for performances in February 1938, Roper concentrated on preparing her three most promising ballet trainees for an audition. Meyers, Deveson and Sankey were taught fouettés in all conceivable combinations, gaining strength and ease in their execution. The three Canadians were reminded of the romantic qualities of Toumanova in *Concurrence* and the sunny lyricism of Riabouchinska in *Le Beau Danube* when they were urged to achieve a colouring of their dance phrases to make them expressive of their feelings. By the end of 1937, Roper was ready to put her work on the line for the judgment of the celebrated Russians (Arendt Aug. 1938: 531).

On January 30, 1938, Léonide Massine, principal dancer and artistic director of Colonel de Basil's Ballets Russes, left the company after an engagement in San Francisco to form another such organization in Monte

Carlo. Massine, who had helped form the de Basil troupe five years earlier, departed with a number of important dancers and rising soloists. The power structure within the company was changed overnight, and David Lichine, then twenty-eight years of age, stepped into the position which Massine had occupied, becoming in the process de Basil's resident choreographer. With such luminaries as Danilova and Toumanova gone, the de Basil company arrived in Vancouver with reduced forces for three performances in which the works of Lichine would be given prominence.

It was with Lichine, then, that Roper made her initial contacts for an audition, and the choreographer agreed to an audience in the theatre an hour before the curtain. At 7:00 p.m. on February 3, 1938, the American teacher and her three Canadian ballet trainees arrived at the Beacon Theatre, where the girls went through some basic demonstrations on the empty stage. Lichine and Colonel de Basil watched impassively for a few moments before conferring on what they had witnessed. The Colonel wished to see the girls in another setting and suggested an audition at the Roper studios after the performance.

A tense four hours lay ahead as the girls tried to submerge their anxieties and enjoy the performance. *Jeux d'Enfants* brought the exquisite Riabouchinska in the role of the child, while Baronova's phenomenal fouettés as the Top produced waves of insecurity. When the curtain fell on the final ballet, *Cimarosiana*, the girls hurried to the studio and began their warm up with the pianist, Winifred Scott. The guests from the company arrived after midnight, and as Deveson recalls, the crowd was sizable:

> Riabouchinska and Lichine were there, as was the Colonel, and I remember Yurek Shabelevsky – and perhaps Alberto Alonso. And there were my parents and Pat's. We were terribly nervous at first but began to feel relaxed once they made it clear that they liked us. I don't think it even occurred to us that they would ever offer us contracts that evening. We were so young, and it would have been enough to know that they thought we were pretty good (Deveson 6 Sept. 1978; Windreich 1979: 1-21).

In the relaxed milieu of the studio, the visitors urged the three young dancers to explore a broad range of their skills and the audition went on for two hours. At the end of the demonstration, Colonel de Basil approached Roper and praised her endeavours, saying "Never before have I seen such excellent training. Madame, I take my hat off to you" (Vancouver *News Herald* 4 Feb. 1938).

The press for February 4 had full coverage of the audition, and the *Sun* carried the most detailed account. Under the heading "Coming Stars: Two Vancouver Girls Join the Ballet Russe" are photographs of Meyers and Deveson in the ball gowns worn in the last "Stars of Tomorrow" revue. The caption reads: "These two young Vancouver dancers have been awarded contracts with Col. de Basil's famous Ballets Russes. 'The perfection of their technique is absolutely phenomenal,' said the Colonel. 'In 1940 they will be great stars in the world of ballet.'"

The comments of the company principals who sat in at the audition were also quoted: "We have never seen anything like it from girls so young." The

Rosemary Deveson (Natasha Sobinova) and Patricia Meyers (Alexandra Denisova).

article concludes: "Col. de Basil insisted the contracts be drawn up before he left Vancouver and it was not until 5 o'clock this morning that they were approved and signed by parents of the girls."

Sankey was not considered for the company because of her height. Taller than the others, she would enjoy a lively career as a performer on the Broadway stage and with the ballet of the Radio City Music Hall before becoming a successful model.

On February 8 Roper drove Meyers and Deveson, with the latter's parents, to Portland, Oregon, where the girls officially joined the de Basil ballet as apprentice dancers. Within two months they were performing in the corps de ballet as professionals, under the names of Alexandra Denisova and Natasha Sobinova, respectively. This Russianization process was virtually mandatory for all dancers with Anglo-Saxon names who went from the English, American and Canadian studios into the Ballet Russe factions. Only a few, such as

Rosella Hightower, resisted the change and managed to achieve stardom, while some of the promising male dancers were also allowed to keep their identities.

In 1939 Massine's new Ballet Russe de Monte Carlo was the attraction booked for Vancouver performances, and by then Roper's fame as a ballet teacher had spread through the profession. Young Ian Gibson was brought to Massine for an audition and was accepted on the spot after a few basic improvisations. Early in the spring he set out to join the company for its training and rehearsal period in Monte Carlo. Shortly thereafter, Margaret Banks accepted a scholarship to continue her studies in London with the Sadler's Wells Ballet.

On June 6 the "Stars of Tomorrow" revue appeared at the Strand Theatre, offering one of Roper's most popular creations, the *Casanova Ballet*. Set to the Andante movement from Tchaikovsky's Fifth Symphony, the work dealt with the final moments of the eighteenth-century Venetian lover reflecting on his escapades. The ballet called for a number of expressive pas de deux and some new dramatic challenges for the teenaged girls, who were required to portray women of considerable sophistication. Audree Thomas, who was at age thirteen cast as a courtesan, remembers her role as a milestone in her development as a performer (Thomas 19 Oct. 1978). Photographs from the ballet show eight bare-chested men in an arresting tableau suggestive of the ensembles popular with the Ted Shawn company. In the grouping are three men who were assuming responsible roles in assisting Roper in her direction of the school and the revue productions: Duncan MacGillivray, who had begun to teach the classes for the youngest pupils; Louis Hightower, who came from Belcher's studio in Los Angeles to perform and supervise Roper's revue numbers; and William Corey, who would ultimately join the staff of the school, achieving great local popularity as well in a ballroom partnership with another pupil, Peggy Pool.

The outbreak of war in Europe in September dispersed the forces of the two Ballet Russe companies. Colonel de Basil's company was committed to a long season in Australia, and the two Vancouver girls came home from England for part of the winter. For Deveson's homecoming, Roper created a revue number called *Natasha: Russian Ballet*, which was performed as a prologue to the Garbo film *Ninotchka* at the Orpheum Theatre in November. Deveson was partnered by MacGillivray. Featured as second soloist was Rosemary Sankey, who had recently appeared in the Broadway musical *Stars in Your Eyes* under the name Maria de Galenta.

In December, Roper telephoned Lichine in Los Angeles with the hope of placing Jean Hunt in the de Basil Ballet, and the girl was accepted sight unseen. Hunt and her mother proceeded to Los Angeles and sailed for Australia on the *Mariposa* with Lichine and his wife, Tatiana Riabouchinska, Tamara Toumanova and the two Vancouver girls returning to their company.

During the winter, Meyers taught the "Sugar Plum Fairy" variation which was performed in the de Basil Ballet's *Aurora's Wedding* as the ballerina's solo, to Audree Thomas (19 Oct. 1978). It was this dance that she chose for her audition in Seattle with Massine early in 1940 and which got her a contract with his Ballet Russe de Monte Carlo. Like Jean Hunt, who had become saddled with the name Kira Bounina, Thomas was transformed into a Russian following her apprenticeship, drawing the name Anna Istomina.

In 1940 Roper became engaged to Duncan Crux, a prominent Vancouver businessman. At thirty-three, she decided to give up her career in favour of marriage and began to make a practical transition from her heavy programme of teaching and production. Dorothy Wilson, who had toured Europe extensively the previous year, improving her teaching with classes in Dresden with Mary Wigman and in Paris with Preobrajenska and Kchessinska, returned with ambitions to expand her scope as a teacher of ballet. She agreed to buy the B.C. School of Dancing, and her tenure began in the spring. Roper continued to coach her special students and collaborated with Wilson on the "Stars of Tomorrow" revue for 1940.

MacGillivray remained at the school during this transitional year, while Robert Lindgren, a pupil of Dorothy Wilson's who came over from Victoria, received personal coaching from Roper during the last months of her teaching career. In 1941 MacGillivray would be accepted sight unseen at Roper's recommendation by Lucia Chase for a contract with Ballet Theatre, and he would begin a diversified career in the American theatre under the name Duncan Noble. Lindgren auditioned for Massine's Ballet Russe de Monte Carlo in 1941 but could not get a visa to work as a dancer in the United States. After a two-year wait, he was hired at Massine's suggestion by Ballet Theatre, for whom the Russian was then choreographing (Windreich Summer 1978: 17).

In addition to the seven dancers placed in the ballet companies directly by June Roper, others, such as Margaret Banks, Doreen Oswald and Dorothy Scott would join Ballet Theatre after her retirement. Yvonne de Carlo, who turned to Roper for dance training essential for her aspirations to be an opera singer, had been discouraged from any serious pursuit of ballet. For her Roper had advised concentration on her talents for acting and arranged special introductions to people in Hollywood, launching her career in films.

Following her marriage in 1941, June Roper Crux gradually relinquished her ties with the school. In 1945 an article in *Dance Magazine* paid tribute to her contribution as "ballet starmaker" (Coleman Nov. 1945: 12-13, 32), and in the following year she was one of the founding members of the Vancouver Ballet Society. In time, favouring a warmer climate, she made her home in Palm Springs, California, maintaining an apartment in Vancouver for some years. Her younger daughter, Lauren, is a psychotherapist, practicing in California, while the elder daughter, Elizabeth Crux, became an expert ballet teacher and was heir to many of her mother's training techniques, which she used in her studios in Santa Cruz, California, and West Vancouver, B.C. Roper was honoured by the Dance in Canada Association at its annual meeting, held in 1978 at the University of British Columbia, for her outstanding contribution as a pioneer in the evolution of ballet in Canada. In 1982, she moved to Bellingham, Washington, where she lived in retirement until her death on November 21, 1991.

In the 1940s there were few opportunities for permanent professional work in Canada for most of her pupils, and those accomplished graduates who did not favour ballet found employment in Broadway musicals and revues, in Hollywood films, and in nightclub work in the major American cities. During the years of World War II, dancers who could boast training with Roper were welcome in all parts of the musical theatre. It was in the developing American ballet establishment, however, that her effect was felt most strongly. During a visit to Vancouver, Léonide Massine noted to the press that Roper's contribution of talent to the Ballet Russe companies exceeded that of any other teacher in the world (Francis and Francis 6 Nov. 1948: 20).

In the following generation, many of those pupils who had achieved prominence as performers turned to teaching. In 1978, when I received a Canada Council grant to interview the eight pupils who had gone from Roper's classes into the major ballet companies, six were actively teaching ballet in various parts of the United States and Canada. Most of them still gave their pupils the basic barre work that they had learned in their classes with Roper in Vancouver. They agreed on the genius of her methodology and the strength of her convictions that success could be achieved by faith, inspiration, determination and hard work. The marvel of her teaching is today being transmitted to children in various parts of the world where her disciples performed and have ultimately settled to pass on her heritage to their own students.

References

"Advertisement." ca. 19 Sept. 1927. Victoria *Colonist*.

Arendt, F.J. ca. June 1937. "The Week in Music." Vancouver *News Herald*.

Arendt, F.J. Aug. 1938. "Vancouver to Covent Garden: A Canadian Cradle of the Ballet." *The Dancing Times*.

"Attractive Show at Monte Carlo." ca. 1922-23. *New York Times*.

Beaudu, Edouard. 1954. "Parades rythmées et danses au music hall." *Histoire du music hall*. Paris: Editions de Paris, 152.

Coleman, Francis A. Nov. 1945. "June Roper: Ballet Starmaker." *Dance Magazine*, 12-13, 32.

"Coming Stars: Two Vancouver Girls Join the Ballet Russe." 4 Feb. 1938. Vancouver *Sun*.

"Dancers Exhibit Much Competence." 2 June 1937. Vancouver *Sun*.

Darwin, Joy. 6 Oct. 1978. Statement accompanying a letter to Rosemary Deveson.

De Mille, Agnes. 1951. *Dance to the Piper*. Boston: Little, Brown.

Pioneers

Eels, George. 1967. *The Life He Led: A Biography of Cole Porter*. New York: Putnam.

Firkins, Yvonne. Dec. 1940. "Young Dancers' Dreams Come True." *Curtain Call*.

Francis, Margaret and Robert. 6 Nov. 1948. "Ballet in Western Canada Makes Dance World Ogle." *Saturday Night*, 20.

Gill, Brendan. 1971. *Cole: A Biographical Essay*. New York: Holt, Reinhart & Winston.

Greul, Heinz. 1968. *Bretter, die Zeit bedeuten; die Kulturgeschichte des Kabaretts*. Cologne: Kiepenheuer & Witsch.

Ham, Mordecai Franklin. 1916. *The Modern Dance: A Historical and Analytical Treatment of the Subject; Religious, Social, Hygienic, Industrial Aspects*. Anchorage, Ky.

"Home Talents as Headlines." ca. 1919. Los Angeles *Examiner*.

House programme. 1 June 1936. Lyric Theatre. Vancouver, B.C.

House programme. 1 June 1937. Strand Theatre. Vancouver, B.C.

Léon-Martin, Louis. 1928. *Le Music-hall et ses figures*. Paris: Editions de France.

Maynard, Olga. 1961. *Bird of Fire*. New York: Dodd, Mead.

Noble, Duncan. July 1978. "June Roper: Canadian Legend." *Vandance* 6: 3, 10-11.

"Two Vancouver Dancers Will Join Ballet Russe." 4 Feb. 1938. Vancouver *News Herald*.

Windreich, Leland. July 1978. "Vancouver Dancers in the Ballet Russe: Robert Lindgren." *Vandance* 6: 3, 17-18

Windreich, Leland. 1979. "The Career of Alexandra Denisova: Vancouver, de Basil, and Cuba." *Dance Chronicle* 3: 1, 1-21.

Windreich, Leland. Summer 1984. "Canada's First *Coppélia*." *Dance in Canada* No. 40, 5-6, 8-9.

Windreich, Leland. 1999. *June Roper: Ballet Starmaker*. Toronto: Dance Collection Danse Press/es.

Interviews

Darwin, Joy. 21 May 1979.

Deveson, Rosemary. 6 Sept. 1978.

Hunt, Jean. 10 Sept. 1984.

Roper, June. 10 Apr. 1979.

Thomas Ismailoff, Audree. 19 Oct. 1978.

Marion Stark Errington:
From Kilts to Companies
in London, Ontario

Amy Bowring

Several years ago, Canada Post issued a series of stamps honouring four Canadian women. I did not recognize any of the faces but fortunately the stamps were labelled as follows: Pitseolak ca. 1904-1983, Inuit Artist; Adelaide Sophia Hoodless 1857-1910, Family Educator; Marie-Joséphine Gérin-Lajoie 1890-1971, Social Reformer; and Helen Alice Kinnear 1894-1970, Legal Pioneer. Seeing these faces for the first time I wondered why I had never seen pictures or heard of any of these Canadian women. What kind of lives had they led? The accomplishments of Pitseolak, Hoodless and Gérin-Lajoie are all described in detail in *The Canadian Encyclopedia*; however, Kinnear is not included. Does this mean that her contributions to Canadian society are less significant than those of the other women? Or is there simply not enough information regarding Kinnear to include her in an encyclopedia? It is encouraging that Canada Post has issued stamps featuring little-known but significant Canadian women, since there are probably hundreds of Helen Alice Kinnears who have been lost in the annals of Canadian history. These women might have been artists, entrepreneurs, lawyers, doctors, scientists, teachers, pilots, politicians or humanitarians. However, I cannot help but wonder what has happened to all the forgotten Canadian women.

Art historian, author and sculptor Merlin Stone discusses this kind of wondering in her essay "Ancient Mirrors of Womanhood" published in Spretnak's *The Politics of Women's Spirituality*. She states, "There has been an ever growing consciousness of the advantages of being able to personally identify with positive images and role models, in developing the self-esteem that encourages the fulfilment of individual potential. This consciousness has made us increasingly aware of the general lack of strong and positive images of women, in the literature and traditions, both sacred and secular, of our own society. In reaction to these realizations, some of us have been searching in the obscure records of the last few centuries, reclaiming the histories of important women who have been all but ignored" (1982: 91).

In the summer of 1993 I did exactly what Stone is writing about in her essay. I searched in the obscure records of the twentieth century to reclaim the stories of important women in the dance history of London, Ontario, where I

Marion Stark Errington, ca. 1948.

trained in dance as a child. Among the several women that I found were Bernice Harper and Dorothy Carter. Harper was a ballet teacher and choreographer for the London Little Theatre Troop Show during World War I. She was the first Canadian to become a Royal Academy of Dancing (RAD) examiner and one of a handful of Canadians to receive an RAD Fellowship. She retired from examining at the age of eighty-one but continued to teach ballet at the University of Western Ontario. Carter arrived in Canada from England in the mid-1950s with her husband and children. A few years after their arrival her husband died suddenly. She raised two children on her own and established a school of Russian ballet which produced successful dancers such as John Fagan, a former soloist in the Royal Winnipeg Ballet who joined American Ballet Theatre in 1994, Raymond Smith, former principal dancer in the National Ballet of Canada, and Evelyn Hart, principal dancer with the Royal Winnipeg Ballet.

Another remarkable woman in London's cultural history is Marion Stark Errington.[1] There are two main reasons why I focused on her. First, I wanted to search for my own dance roots. The bulk of my dance training from 1978 to 1990 was under the direction of Liliane Marleau Graham at the Woodstock branch of the Errington-Graham Dance Studios, which evolved from the school that Marion Stark had founded around 1917. Secondly, Marion Stark Errington left an extensive collection of notes, newspaper clippings, programmes, correspondence and photographs regarding her contribution to dance in London. Her collection is currently housed at Dance Collection Danse, the archives of Canadian theatrical dance located in Toronto. The information in this essay is drawn from that collection as well as from several recorded oral histories and my personal experiences with the Errington-Graham Studios.

Marion Stark Errington's career in dance spanned over sixty years. A review of her accomplishments makes it clear that she was truly a dynamic and progressive force in London's cultural history. During her seventy-four years she was a student, dancer, teacher, choreographer, artistic director, ballet examiner, businesswoman, wife, mother and role model.

---

[1] Marion Stark Errington was born Marion Stark. Her name changed to Marion Stark Graham when she married Burwell Graham and later to Marion Stark Errington when she married Richard Errington. Liliane Marleau, her colleague and daughter-in-law, added "Graham" when she married Marion's son Ron Graham in 1955.

Marion Stark was born in London, Ontario in 1904. When she was a child she was given some Scottish kilts by her father who felt that since she had these kilts she should attend Scottish dancing lessons; however, he made it clear that she was not to perform in public (Crawford 1 May 1939). When she was thirteen years old her dancing teacher, Alice Henderson, moved away from London leaving her students stranded. The class pleaded with Marion Stark to teach them; she complied and held lessons in her family home while her mother played the piano (Graham 22 June 1993). The piano still resides at the Errington-Graham Studios on Richmond Street in London.

Despite her father's warning regarding public performance, she organized recitals in local high schools. Information on her school's earliest recital is found in a programme dated May 11, 1923. It was a joint performance with the students of local elocution teacher Gwendolyn Anthistle and included mostly national dances such as the Highland fling, Krakowiak, a Spanish mazurka performed by Marion Stark and the *Oriental Fantasy* danced by her cousin, Gladys Tulett.

Since dancing was not considered a suitable career, Marion Stark was sent to the University of Western Ontario immediately following high school. In a 1939 interview with Lenore Crawford of the *Windsor Star*, she recalled, "I was to do anything but be a dancing teacher!" (1 May 1939). She studied general arts for two years but quit in 1926 to marry Burwell Graham. From 1926 to 1928 she and her husband lived in Florida. During this time she danced on the vaudeville stage for the Publix Circuit in various theatres throughout the state, had a baby and continued to run her London school by mailing written instructions to her mother and cousin. Marion Stark's daughter-in-law, Liliane Marleau Graham, commented on Stark's method of operating her school from another country: "She used to write home every day and tell her mother and her cousin what to teach, who to teach, where to tell the pupils to stand. She ran the school from Florida every day for two years and told them what costumes to design and how to make them and what to put on so-and-so and everything, by letter" (22 June 1993). Therefore, when she returned to London her school was still very much intact.

In 1929, while attending dance conferences in New York and Chicago, she discovered just how much she did not know. Liliane Marleau Graham remarked on Marion Stark's trip, "She thought she was God's gift to the dancing world living in London and no competition. And then when her dad sent her to New York and she saw how little she knew it really threw her for a loop. But she didn't do what most people would do, go into another profession. She just picked up her boots and started to learn and just learned everything from everybody wherever she could" (22 June 1993). She became a member of Dancing Masters of America, attended its annual conferences led by teachers such as Ivan Tarasoff and learned from the training programmes created by Ned Wayburn and Louis H. Chalif. By 1930 she had a 250-pupil school in London (Spring Dance Revue programme 14 May 1930).

In the late 1930s her activities grew beyond that of solely operating a school. In 1938 Dr. Harvey Robb arrived in London to assume the position of principal of the Western Ontario Conservatory of Music. He approached her about creating a dance examination syllabus to be affiliated with both the Conservatory and the University. The Western Ontario Conservatory of Ballet was born. The syllabus was designed for the hour-a-week student and was based on the principles of several existing ballet techniques such as Cecchetti, RAD and the teachings of Ernest Belcher (Graham 25 June 1993). A newspaper clipping from the *London Free Press* dated March 25, 1949 shows Boris Volkoff examining the future National Ballet of Canada dancer Colleen Kenney in the Errington studio. In those days the exams ultimately led to an Associate Diploma of the Western Ontario Conservatory of Ballet but today the syllabus includes one more exam, the Gold Medal, which requires the student to perform "The Dance of the Sugar Plum Fairy" from *The Nutcracker*.

In the late 1930s Marion Stark formed the London Ballet Company, which was the first local ballet company (Crawford 1 May 1939). On May 30, 1939 the London Ballet Company presented *Cleopatra* choreographed by Marion Stark and assisted by Richard Errington. This was the second performance of this ballet and the reason is explained in the programme notes: "This company, which received such high praise for its performance with the London Civic Symphony last month, is comparatively young. Mrs. Graham felt that the city of London with such a cultural background would welcome a Ballet Company of its own. The premiere performance, May 1st, was received with such ovation that she was persuaded to present again the Ballet 'Cleopatra'." In her review, Crawford called the ballet an "artistic triumph" and described Errington's performance as "superb" (2 May 1939).

The entrance of Richard Errington marked a turning point in Marion Stark's life. During the next few years he began teaching and managing her school, and her marriage to Burwell Graham dissolved. In 1945 the name of the school was changed to the Errington-Graham Studios; in 1947 the name changed to Errington Dance Studios when Richard Errington and Marion Stark were married.

A decade after the formation of the London Ballet Company came the formation of the Errington Ballet Theatre, which debuted Marion Stark Errington's ballet *Mardi Gras* on June 2, 1948 ("Dance Revue of 1948" programme). Six months later the Errington Ballet Theatre received a civic charter from the City of London during a joint performance with the London Civic Symphony. On December 9, 1948, the London Civic Ballet Theatre was born. That night they performed *Mardi Gras* and Marion Stark Errington's version of Michel Fokine's *Les Sylphides*, which included two extra male roles choreographed by her (London Civic Symphony programme).

There are three important things to note concerning the creation of the London Civic Ballet Theatre. The Erringtons' attitude toward the significance of their company was focused on the company's potential contribution to Canadian dance at large. They viewed the London Civic Ballet as a performance experience that young dancers could use as a stepping stone into the larger companies such as the Volkoff Canadian Ballet and later the National Ballet of Canada (Graham 22 June 1993). Moreover, a civic company meant that open auditions with an outside adjudicator had to be held. Bettina Byers of the Toronto Academy of Ballet often travelled to London to adjudicate auditions ("Ballet Auditions Set for Sunday" 1 Mar. 1953). Finally, Marian Stark Errington's method of learning and staging famous ballets such as *Les Sylphides* must be recognized, especially since it was rather unorthodox. Liliane Marleau Graham described how Marion Stark Errington was able to stage the famous classical ballets: "I know she used to go to see the Ballet Russe. She'd go to Toronto and stay there the whole week they'd be there. She'd see all the performances; matinees, evenings, and she'd write notes. Then she would get Leon Danielian or someone to come and teach the solos to somebody and then she'd have the corps all figured out just from watching it" (22 June 1993). One cannot help but stare in amazement at the cryptic notes that she scribbled in darkened theatres so many decades ago.

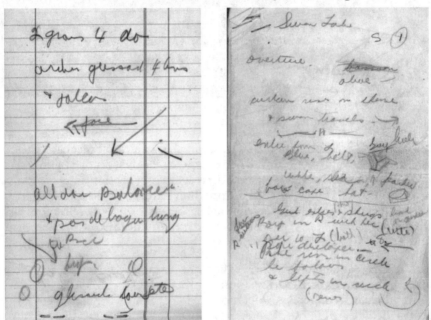

Marion Errington's notes for *Les Sylphides* (left) and *Swan Lake* (right), ca. 1948.

Among other choreographies she created is the comical ballet *Dude Ranch* (1948). The ballet was supposed to be a satire on dances and musicals such as *Oklahoma*; however, judging from interviews with the original dancers and reviews which include a synopsis of the ballet, it seems that *Dude Ranch* was actually quite similar to Agnes de Mille's cowboy ballet *Rodeo* (1942). *Dude Ranch* included a tomboy Rancher's Daughter, Her Society Friends, Cowboys, a Top Hand and some Canadian additions such as The Movie Star On Location and The Mountie (Stars of Tomorrow programme 10 June 1949). The London

Colleen Kenney, Richard Errington and Jean Allison, London Civic Ballet
production of *Les Sylphides*, 1948.

Civic Ballet Theatre performed *Dude Ranch* as its audition piece for the 1950
Ballet Festival in Montreal but was not accepted. The last record of the London
Civic Ballet Theatre in Marion Stark Errington's collection is a programme
from 1954 in which Joey Harris, a Canadian ballet dancer who toured with
Léonide Massine's "Ballet Russe Highlights," was Co-Artistic Director. In this
performance Harris staged Fokine's *Le Carnaval* and his own choreography
Pas de Trois Classique.

While choreographing and directing the company she was still heavily
involved in teaching. In 1952 she founded the Western Ontario branch of the
Canadian Dance Teachers' Association (C.D.T.A.) and was its president for
almost a decade until the Western Ontario branch broke away from the
C.D.T.A. and formed the Associated Dance Educators of Ontario ("Dance
Teachers Pick Londoner" 1952).

In 1955 Liliane Marleau, who had been an ambitious and enthusiastic
student and dancer in the London Civic Ballet Theatre since the late 1940s,
became Marion Stark Errington's daughter-in-law by marrying Ron Graham,
Marion's son by a previous marriage. As the Erringtons grew older Liliane
Marleau Graham took on more responsibilities within the school and eventually
took over. Today she continues to operate the Errington-Graham Dance Studios
in London and its branch studios in Woodstock, St. Thomas and Sarnia.

In 1978 Marion Stark Errington died, marking the end of an era in London's cultural history. The year 1978 also marks the beginning of my dance training and association with the Errington-Graham school. I regret that I never met this dynamic woman. Harris described her as a shrewd business woman (2 July 1993). In an interview with Pauline Gailbraith and Cathy Cave, original members of the London Civic Ballet Theatre, they recounted that she was a flamboyant and excitable but very professional woman who often wore red dresses. According to Liliane Marleau Graham, Marion Stark Errington frequently carried a cigarette holder sporting an unlit cigarette. Liliane Marleau Graham goes on to say that she was a "very positive woman, a leader, not the love of everyone, but she was a fair, just person" (22 June 1993). A letter from Ken Baskette, manager of the Grand Theatre, is filled with words of admiration and he thanks her for doing the work of ten.

During her lifetime, Marion Stark Errington took on the multiple roles that many women have performed in the past and will continue to perform in the future. She demonstrated independence by defying her father's rules regarding public performing. She showed determination by learning everything she could about dance in order to pass it on to others. She displayed progressiveness by forming the first ballet company in London. She exhibited leadership by creating the Western Ontario branch of the C.D.T.A. And she showed a deep commitment to London and its cultural community by making dance in London one of the most significant parts of her life for over six decades. Thanks to the extensive collection Marion Stark Errington left of herself and the memories and lessons that she implanted in dancers across Southwestern Ontario, Marion Stark Errington will not become one of the numerous forgotten Canadian women.

References

"Ballet Auditions Set for Sunday." 1 Mar. 1953. Clipping from unidentified newspaper in Marion Errington Collection, Dance Collection Danse.

Baskette, Ken. ca. 1950. Undated letter to Marion and Dick Errington. Marion Errington Collection, Dance Collection Danse.

Crawford, Lenore. 1 May 1939. "Finds Most Pleasure In Oriental Dance." *Windsor Star*. London Public Library Scrapbooks Vol. 33: 2.

Crawford, Lenore. 2 May 1939. "London Ballet Debut Is Artistic Triumph." *Windsor Star*. London Public Library Scrapbooks Vol. 33: 3.

"Dance Revue of 1948." 2 June 1948. Programme. Marion Errington Collection, Dance Collection Danse.

"Dance Teachers Pick Londoner." 1952. Clipping from unidentified newspaper in Marion Errington Collection, Dance Collection Danse.

Eber, Dorothy Harley. 1985. "Pisteolak, Ashoona." *The Canadian Encyclopedia*.

Pioneers

"London Ballet Company." 30 May 1939. *Cleopatra*. Programme. Marion Errington Collection, Dance Collection Danse.

"London Civic Ballet Theatre." 20 Mar. 1954. Programme. Marion Errington Collection, Dance Collection Danse.

"London Civic Symphony." 9 Dec. 1948. Programme. Marion Errington Collection, Dance Collection Danse.

McCallum, Margaret E. 1985. "Gérin-Lajoie, Marie-Joséphine." *The Canadian Encyclopedia*.

"Recital." 11 May 1923. Programme. Marion Errington Collection, Dance Collection Danse.

"Spring Dance Revue." 14 May 1930. Programme. Marion Errington Collection, Dance Collection Danse.

Stamp, Robert M. 1985. "Hoodless, Adelaide Sophia." *The Canadian Encyclopedia*.

"*Stars of Tomorrow*." 10 June 1949. Programme. Marion Errington Collection, Dance Collection Danse.

Stone, Merlin. 1982. "Ancient Mirrors of Womanhood." In Charlene Spretnak, ed. *The Politics of Women's Spirituality*. New York: Anchor Books, 91-96.

"Volkoff to See London Dancers." 25 Mar. 1949. *London Free Press*.

Interviews

Interviews conducted by Amy Bowring for Dance Collection Danse:

Gailbraith, Pauline and Cathy Cave. 12 Aug. 1993.

Graham, Liliane Marleau. 22 and 25 June 1993.

Harris, Joey. 2 July 1993.

Stories of Dancing Women in Alberta

Anne Flynn

Writing women's lives is an honour, and I feel privileged that Alice Murdoch Adams, Dorothy Ward Harris and Ruth Carse consented to our interviews and to letting me write about them. I became interested in biography when my own parents were approaching their eighties, and I realized that I needed to get all the stories straight because there was going to come a time when I wouldn't be able to say "tell me that story again." I gave my mother and father blank journals and asked them to write down their family histories. My father began in earnest and out came the many-decades-old crumbling leather file bags filled with yellowing papers. My mother hasn't started yet.

So many dancing stories have vanished. Too many. As I became more and more aware of how little has been written about Alberta dance history, I decided that as I had presented blank journals to my parents, I could simply ask these legendary women to tell me their dance stories for the record. So, in the spirit of celebrating the professional accomplishments of all women and of resurrecting the details of dance history, here are the individual stories of three women who were extremely active in shaping the development of the Alberta dance community from the 1920s to the 1990s. Alice Murdoch Adams worked between the late 1920s and the 1950s; Ruth Carse began her professional career in the late 1930s and retired in 1986; and Dorothy Harris was active from 1949 to 1990. They cover a span of sixty years of dance activity in the province and their stories are important resources of information about the cultural heritage of Alberta.

Alice Murdoch Adams

Alice Murdoch Adams was the recipient of the first Alberta Dance Award given by the Alberta Dance Alliance in 1989. When she was told that she would be receiving the award, she wanted to know why anyone would want to do that. After all, she hasn't been active in the dance community since the 1950s. Murdoch agreed to accept the award as long as she didn't have to make a speech, and in return the dance community was able to learn about the life and work of one of its earliest pioneers.

Born on March 5, 1908, in Edinburgh, Scotland, Murdoch immigrated with her family to Canada when she was three years old and settled in Cranbrook, Alberta. They returned to Scotland in 1914 for a year, and that is when Murdoch took her first Highland dance classes. Her family settled in

Alice Murdoch Adams.

Calgary when they moved back to Canada permanently, but Murdoch did not resume her dance studies until junior high school. She then quit school so she could work to pay for dance classes.

Murdoch's first teacher was Jean Gauld, under whom she studied Highland dance for almost ten years. Murdoch remembers that as an advanced student she often taught the first part of class because Gauld was late; eventually Murdoch became Gauld's assistant. Typical of dance schools at that time, Gauld's studio was in her home. In 1926 when Murdoch was just eighteen she began her travels which would lead her to London for ballroom, Paris for ballet, Scotland for Highland, to the Denishawn School in Los Angeles, and to New York and Seattle. These trips were her first opportunity to train in forms such as ballet, tap and ballroom, and it was the start of a lengthy career as a dancer, choreographer, costume designer, teacher and businesswoman.

In 1927 Murdoch opened the Alice Murdoch School of Dance located first in her family's basement and then in several locations in downtown Calgary. Other than Penley's studio, which offered ballroom, Murdoch's school was the only one in Calgary. She offered classes in ballet, tap, acrobatics, Highland, character, ballroom and even exercise classes for adult women. Initially, Murdoch taught all the classes herself from 4:00 to 10:00 p.m. weekdays and all day Saturdays. The school had approximately 200 students who ranged in age from three years to adults. After several years downtown, Murdoch's parents helped her to buy a house on Fourth Street at Fourteenth Avenue S.W. where she could live and teach. Murdoch's own family lived in the back of the house and basement while the living room served as the studio. In addition, Murdoch eventually opened a branch of her school in Lethbridge that was run by her assistant Lola Strand, though Murdoch would travel to Lethbridge on the train to teach on a regular basis. She also taught regularly in Stavely, Claresholm, Vulcan and Drumheller. When asked what would happen if she got sick, Murdoch responded that she never got sick, or if she did, she just kept on teaching.

Murdoch spent every summer taking classes in New York. She studied at the Ned Wayburn School of Dance, learning all the latest steps and styles, and at the Andalusian Academy of Spanish Dancing. She recalls the rompers they wore in dance classes, and how they would wring them out and hang them to dry, changing in-between classes. She also mentions that her mother insisted she wear a money belt under her dance rompers which meant that her money was always wet. Murdoch had two aunts who lived in the greater New York vicinity and she would stay with one or the other of them until she got settled into a place in Manhattan closer to the studio. These summers in New York provided Murdoch with new teaching material, new music and, very importantly, new dance shoes; Mr. Capezio, the world famous dance shoe-

Typical dance belt with money pocket, Lester Ltd. Catalogue, Chicago, 1935.

maker, made Murdoch's shoes. Murdoch laughed when she told me that her first two children were born in August so as not to interfere with either her annual trek to New York or her teaching schedule. Murdoch also spent some time studying in Los Angeles and Seattle, but most of her training took place in New York.

From 1927 to 1949 the Alice Murdoch School of Dance was a very active place. Around 200 students visited the house weekly to take class. Sundays were reserved for rehearsals and the basement change room seconded as a reading room stacked with dance magazines. Murdoch was a prolific choreographer who created hundreds of dances in twenty years. She held an annual recital or revue that in 1943, for example, consisted of forty-one dances, seven musicians and over 150 performers. These annual reviews took place in the Grand Theatre where they would sell over 1000 seats. She also choreographed shows for the Palace and Capitol Theatres that took place in between the double movie feature. For two years Murdoch created a new thirty-minute show every week for the Capitol Theatre that was supposed to relate in some way to the theme of the movie. For all these shows and revues, Murdoch designed and cut the patterns for the costumes while parents and other helpers did the sewing and construction.

Perhaps one of the most unusual aspects of Alice Murdoch's career was the period during World War II when she choreographed and produced shows to entertain the troops. Murdoch estimates that between 1939 and 1943 she and her students performed close to 400 shows in towns throughout Alberta. The materials for costumes and sets would come from a major sponsor such as Birk's or Eaton's; the government paid for transportation and food; and the performers volunteered their time as part of the war effort. Adams Radio Parlours, her husband's store, sponsored Murdoch's show. The performers travelled by bus and would generally return to Calgary immediately following a show, arriving home in the early hours of the morning. Murdoch's son Ryan began touring with the show as soon as he was old enough to play the accordion. Also during these years Murdoch's group would perform shows at country and town fairs around the province.

In 1949 Murdoch had three vertebral discs removed and this in combination with other factors marked the finale of the Alice Murdoch School of Dance, the Grand Theatre revues and an entire era of dance making and teaching. However, the work would continue through Murdoch's sister Jean and later through her own daughter Vicki. Murdoch's sister Jean was seventeen years younger and Alice was her dance teacher. Jean Murdoch became a competitive Highland dancer and even travelled to Scotland to compete in the world championships; she won several world titles. So when Murdoch closed the doors to her studio, her sister opened new ones in another Calgary house renovated to accommodate a studio and there she began to train Murdoch's daughter Vicki Adams Willis.

Alice Murdoch thought that she was through with the dance world in 1949. She had worked seven days a week for over twenty years and raised two children. Her husband encouraged her to hang up her dancing shoes and put up her feet. So, when her third child Vicki was born in 1950, Murdoch had no intention of involving her in dance. This, however, was not to be the case. Vicki saw her Aunt Jean teaching classes and she begged for lessons. By the time she was in university, Vicki also was travelling to New York and Europe in the summers to study dance, returning to Calgary to teach and choreograph. Vicki Adams Willis taught jazz dance in the Faculty of Fine Arts at the University of Calgary for fifteen years before leaving in 1989 to work as artistic director of her company Decidedly Jazz Danceworks. The enormously popular company runs a large community school in their studios on Fourth Street S.W. across from Murdoch's first home and studio. The dance styles have changed and the music too. Rompers have given way to spandex and cotton-lycra. But something in the spirit of Alice Murdoch's work is kept alive every time her daughter begins that familiar count to eight.

After Alice Murdoch's retirement from the school she remained involved in dance for many more years. When her other daughter Sharon wanted to leave Calgary for several years to pursue skating, Murdoch took over classes at the school so Sharon would be free to go. Murdoch stayed active as a choreographer until 1990 doing productions for a variety of community groups, in particular, for the Rotary Club. Murdoch choreographed the annual President's Ball for the downtown Rotary Club every year from 1951 to 1990 for which she was given their service award. Alice Murdoch Adams died on November 18, 1997 at the age of eighty-nine.

Ruth Carse

In September 1991 the Alberta Ballet celebrated its twenty-fifth anniversary at a gala performance with guest appearances by the Royal Winnipeg's Evelyn Hart and the National Ballet's Rex Harrington. Tickets sold for $133 including GST. Ruth Carse founded this company in the 1960s when dancers, choreographers, composers, costume designers and musicians worked for free. The volunteer dance company survived on the energy of its participants, its audiences and the undaunting determination of Ruth Carse.

Ruth Carse.

Carse was born on December 7, 1916, in Edmonton, Alberta and was one of five children. Her father immigrated to Canada from Scotland in 1905 and settled in Edmonton, where he met Carse's mother whose family managed the boarding house where he lived. When Carse expressed interest in taking dancing lessons, her father saw to it that she study Highland dance. At age six, Carse began studying with Madame Boucher, who rolled back the carpets and taught classes in her living room. Chairs were used as barres. Carse came to realize much later that Madame Boucher was in fact teaching a system of training based on the British Ballet Organization Syllabus.

As Carse's interest and skill in dance grew, she left Madame Boucher's living room and began studying at the Kinney School of Dance, which was run by two sisters, Marian and Dorothy Kinney. Marian had studied in Toronto with Boris Volkoff, a Russian dancer-choreographer who directed a ballet school and company. Throughout her teenage years, Carse danced at the Kinney School and began performing. At the age of twenty-one, Carse was encouraged to continue her dance studies, which meant leaving Alberta. Carse reminisced that her father wagered a $100 bet that she would be back home in a month. Carse won the bet.

In 1937 she moved to Toronto to study with Volkoff and eventually became a soloist with the Volkoff Canadian Ballet. Carse danced with the company for ten years, performing regularly in Toronto, touring in Ontario and participating in the Canadian Ballet Festivals in 1948, 1949 and 1953. The extraordinary thing about these ten years is that none of the dancers was paid. They all had daytime jobs and rehearsed and performed at night and on weekends. Carse started working in the checking department of a Toronto advertising firm and eventually became manager of the department while maintaining the position of soloist in one of Canada's original ballet companies. During this time, Carse also went to England every two years to study.

One of Carse's contemporaries was Mildred Herman (Melissa Hayden), who went from Volkoff to New York, where she began an illustrious career as a soloist for the New York City Ballet. While Carse's greatest interest in dance had always been teaching, she decided in 1949 that she should take the plunge and see how she would fare as a dancer in New York. Soon after her arrival in New York, she was given a partial scholarship to the prestigious School of

American Ballet and so was exposed to new styles of ballet training. Carse also auditioned for dance work whenever possible and was hired by the Yiddish Theatre in Brooklyn, where she danced in a new musical every week. She recalled this time with great fondness and said that the dancers were treated "beautifully." She also remembered her time with the Radio City Ballet, where she worked for two years, as being quite luxurious. First of all she was actually being paid to dance. The dancers performed in four shows a day, each of which lasted ten minutes, and they had professional dressing rooms, costumes, makeup and even hairdryers. During breaks between shows Carse would travel uptown to Carnegie Hall on the bus, wearing full stage makeup and dark glasses, to take ballet class. Then, one day Carse received a phone call from the stage manager of the Volkoff Canadian Ballet who encouraged her to fly to Toronto to audition for the brand new National Ballet of Canada. Carse auditioned, was hired, and went back to New York to finish her contract with the Radio City Ballet before returning permanently to Canada.

Carse's career at the National Ballet only lasted three months. She recalled that director Celia Franca was not very pleased when Carse made the decision to resign. From 1952 to 1954 Carse remained in Toronto and began studying the British-based Royal Academy of Dancing (RAD) training system at the Canadian School of Ballet under Gweneth Lloyd. Eventually Carse started teaching the RAD system in the Toronto area which marked the beginning of a forty-year teaching career. During this time Carse also appeared in a number of CBC television variety shows. In the summer of 1954, while she was studying in England, an unfortunate accident, which resulted in a torn Achilles tendon, became the end marker of her performing career. Shortly following the accident, Carse was asked to come to Edmonton to teach for her friend Muriel Taylor, who was on maternity leave from the studio she operated. Edmonton became Carse's home for the duration of her life.

In addition to teaching, Carse began choreographing almost immediately after her return to Edmonton. She did the choreography for musicals such as *Oklahoma*, *Brigadoon* and *South Pacific*, which were produced by the Edmonton Light Opera Company. She also started a group called Dance Interlude which eventually would become the Alberta Ballet. Dance Interlude toured throughout the province beginning in the town of Tofield. By 1960 Dance Interlude was renamed the Edmonton Ballet and in 1966 became the Alberta Ballet Company. It was not until 1971, however, that the company became fully professional which meant that salaries were paid. Up until that time Carse and the dancers trained, rehearsed and performed without remuneration.

Also in 1971, the Alberta Ballet Company School was established and Carse became its director. The school and the company operated together until the late 1970s when they separated for administrative reasons, though the school was still the primary training ground for future company members. In 1974, Carse became an examiner for the RAD which required considerable time and travel; she resigned as artistic director of the company. In 1976

Brydon Paige was appointed artistic director and his association lasted for over ten years, when he was followed by Ali Pourfarrokh as artistic director. Carse continued teaching for the school and examining for the RAD until she retired in 1986. She taught, coached, adjudicated and consulted while also spending winters in Hawaii.

She was the recipient of a number of awards and honours including the Order of Canada, and in 1989 she received the prestigious Dance in Canada Award for outstanding contributions to the dance. Recognized by her colleagues as one of the major pioneers of professional dance in Canada, Ruth Carse returned to her home on the prairies to build a company and a school. Guided by her muse and strengthened by the support of her family, she just kept dancing, and dancing and dancing, until her death on November 14, 1999 at the age of eighty-two.

Dorothy Ward Harris

Dorothy Harris taught dance at the University of Alberta for twenty-six years before retiring in August 1990. Among the first group of dancers to hold a full-time position in a Canadian university, she is a bold pioneer in the field of dance education. Her teaching brought her into contact with thousands of students, some of whom have gone on to successful careers as both performers and teachers. She has worked in provincial, national and international organizations and most people in the field of post-secondary dance education know her name.

Dorothy Ward Harris was born on May 28, 1925, in Edmonton, one of three children. Her family moved to Trail, British Columbia for several years but by 1932 they were settled in Calgary. At age eight Harris began taking dance classes at the Alice Murdoch School of Dance, where she studied ballet, tap and acrobatics at a cost of $5.00 for twelve lessons. She studied with Murdoch for about seven years during which time she performed in the annual revues at the Grand Theatre, in Christmas and New Year's Eve shows and with Murdoch's touring group to county fairs around the province. Harris was especially talented in acrobatics due partially to extraordinary back flexibility. Murdoch choreographed several solos which Harris often performed. Harris remembers those days with enormous affection. She recalls having to heat hair curling irons on Bunsen burners in the basement of the Grand Theatre and receiving chocolate or flowers as payment for performing. Her mother constructed all her costumes based on the patterns designed by "Miss Murdoch." When she entered Crescent Heights High School, Harris thought that her dancing days were over, but while she participated in a whole new variety of activities, she also continued dancing in high school productions of operettas and musicals. When Harris was in grade twelve, her family moved to Edmonton and Harris followed reluctantly. She entered the University of Alberta the following year and completed a Bachelor of Arts degree in 1946.

Dorothy Harris.

During university, Harris spent two summers attending a recreation leadership programme at Mount Royal College in Calgary. She learned to teach Swedish gymnastics and a wide variety of other activities and became interested in recreation studies. After graduation from the University of Alberta, Harris worked at the University Library for a year, and in the summer of 1947 she began studying recreation at the University of Minnesota. It was at this time that she took her first modern dance class. That fall, Harris decided to pursue a Master's degree in physical education at the University of Wisconsin, where she was admitted pending the completion of one year of undergraduate physical education courses. Harris remembers this year as the one that changed her life. She took a dance course with Margaret H'Doubler, a prominent American dance educator who was largely responsible for the establishment of the first university degree programme in dance in the United States, and she was hooked. Dance became her central focus once again and she would spend the next forty years completely engaged in the dance world. Harris completed two years of study at the University of Wisconsin and then accepted a university teaching position. In the fall of 1949 Harris began teaching in the physical education department at the University of Arkansas. She taught courses in dance, soccer, volleyball, softball and ran a number of extra-curricular dance programmes, which included ballroom, square dance, creative dance for children and a performing group called Orchesis. The same year Harris met and married her husband. After two years at the University of Arkansas, Harris accepted a position at Arkansas State University where she had similar responsibilities. She stayed for one year and then taught at the high school level for one year. Harris and her husband then moved to Colorado Springs where they started a family; between 1955 and 1961 Harris had four children. She also taught high school for one year in Colorado Springs.

In the early 1960s the family returned to Edmonton, and Harris found work in both the library and registrar's office at the University of Alberta. A student assistant who worked with Harris brought news one day that the physical education department was hiring someone to teach dance and Harris immediately applied. She was hired on a part-time basis at first and in the fall of 1965 she became a full-time faculty member. This was the beginning of a twenty-six-year career as a dance educator, which would take her all over the world and into contact with thousands of students.

Harris' greatest affinity is for modern dance, but she has taught a wide variety of dance forms. Soon after she joined the faculty she designed a movement course for drama students to satisfy their physical education requirement. She remembers this course with great fondness. Having also started the performing group, Orchesis, which produced an annual concert, Harris recruited a number of dancers from this movement course including Peggy Baker and Brian Webb, both of whom have continued on to successful dance careers. By the early 1970s, however, the drama department would not allow students to participate in Orchesis and the movement course was moved from physical education to drama. Harris regarded this as a tremendous loss and the end of a very exciting time in dance education at the University of Alberta. In the mid-1970s Harris and her dance colleagues tried to win support for a degree in dance, but the university did not support it. Dance would remain as only a small part of the overall physical education curriculum and so Harris simply continued working with whatever resources and energy were available.

The number of people holding full-time appointments and teaching dance in universities was minuscule in the 1960s. Most of the appointments were in physical education, and so it is not surprising that Canada's first national dance committee emerged from the Canadian Association of Health Physical Education and Recreation (CAHPER). In 1965 the CAHPER Dance Committee was formed and its first national chairperson was Rose Hill, a professor at McMaster University in Ontario. Harris was part of this inaugural committee and in 1969 she became national chairperson. She held this position for four years and recalls that the committee's most significant accomplishment was the organization of the 1971 Binational Dance Conference which took place at the University of Waterloo in Ontario. This was the first attempt to bring together dance academics from Canada and the United States, and while the conference organizing committees were drawn from among 400 American dance academics, Canada had eighteen organizers. Harris recalls that the conference was highly successful and the group of Canadians in attendance created bonds that lasted.

In addition to the CAHPER Dance Committee, Harris served on the board of the national Dance in Canada Association from 1979 to 1983 and was part of the conference organizing committee for the 1975 conference held in Edmonton. The organization honoured Harris with a Service Award. Harris was also treasurer of Dance and the Child International from 1978 to 1982 and was part of the organizing committee for its 1978 Edmonton conference. Involved at both the national and international levels, it is no surprise that Harris would turn her attention to the local scene and in 1979 she instigated a meeting of the Alberta dance community, sponsored by Alberta Culture, which resulted in the formation of the Alberta Dance Alliance, a provincial non-profit service organization. Harris served on the board of directors from its inception in 1979 to 1987.

On August 31, 1990, Dorothy Harris retired from the University of Alberta. She continues to live in Edmonton and is involved with two dance-related business enterprises. She is still attending conferences, writing about dance, thinking about dance and living a life that is moved and inspired by the magic we call dance.

Conclusion

These three women were childhood dancers who all began their training in the living rooms of three other women, who likely began their training in the living rooms of three other women. Dance, in many cultures around the world, is passed on from one generation to the next in informal contexts and as part of a whole range of learned cultural traditions and attitudes. In Canada, it is largely through the work of such women that the experience of dance continues to touch our lives.

Reference Note

These three biographical sketches were written based on oral interviews that I conducted with Alice Murdoch Adams, Ruth Carse and Dorothy Harris in August 1991 in Calgary, Alberta. During each interview we perused substantial collections of newspaper clippings, programmes, posters and other historical fragments. The interviews were audio and video taped. At that time, I was extremely new to dance history and was being guided largely by an impulse to simply gather the stories from these individuals before it was too late. I hadn't thought through the theory or methodology in any systematic way, but just went ahead and talked to these women. Adams, Carse and Harris each received a written copy of her biographical essay to review before publication. A different version of these biographical essays first appeared under the title "Prairie Pioneers: Canadian Women and Dance" in the anthology, *Women and the Arts* (Calgary: University of Calgary Press, 1993). Shorter biographical entries also appear in the *Encyclopedia of Theatre Dance in Canada/Encyclopédie de la Danse Théâtrale au Canada* (Toronto: Dance Collection Danse Press/es, 2000).

Part III

Politics and Perseverance

Stepping Out:
A New Look at Canada's Early Ballet Companies, 1939 to 1960

Cheryl Smith

After extensive research on the early years of the Royal Winnipeg Ballet, the National Ballet of Canada and Les Grands Ballets Canadiens, it seemed that the *only* factor they all had in common was the unlikeliness of their founders starting a professional ballet company. In Winnipeg, a company emerged from the efforts of two English dance teachers, neither of whom had any intention of starting a company nor even any professional performing experience. In Toronto, three society women decided to start a national ballet company, although none of them had much expertise or knowledge about ballet at the time. And in Montreal, Les Grands Ballets Canadiens emerged from a pickup company of dancers who worked on television, and who were led by an impoverished young immigrant to Canada.

On closer study, however, it became clear that there were some similarities in the founding of the companies. First, all the founding artistic directors were exceptional teachers and leaders. Second, these women benefitted greatly from the help of a group of dedicated patrons. The written history of ballet in Canada has focused much attention on the first of these important factors: the talented and visionary artistic directors who led the companies through their difficult founding years. These histories, as written by Max Wyman, Herbert Whittaker, James Neufeld and Roland Lorrain, celebrate the leading women while briefly acknowledging the people behind the scenes. Little is known of the patrons, friends and volunteers who sustained the companies through their critical years. Who were these supporters and how did they help the founding artistic directors?

While the word "patrons" suggests a very wealthy donor, it is used here in a more modest sense; although all three Canadian companies were indeed helped by rich donors, their financial contributions were not nearly as great as those given by the patrons of Diaghilev's Ballets Russes or the New York City Ballet. More interesting in Canada was the unheralded work done by those I have called "practical patrons." These patrons were volunteers who performed very practical duties for the companies: in Winnipeg they were a part of the artistic team that put together the shows, and later these and other patrons literally took over the Winnipeg Ballet when it looked like the company could not continue otherwise. In Toronto, a network of volunteers in National Ballet

Founding directors of Canada's early ballet companies (l. to r.): Betty Farrally, Gweneth Lloyd, Celia Franca and Ludmilla Chiriaeff.

Guilds raised money, sold tickets and organized hospitality for the company in Toronto and on tour so that any revenues could go toward paying artistic expenses. And in Montreal, Les Grands Ballets Canadiens' patrons were quite different from the hands-on volunteers in Toronto and Winnipeg, but they were "practical patrons" as well; these patrons were the young producers at the French CBC TV (Société Radio-Canada) who commissioned ballets from the fledgling Montreal company.

If, in the past, the history of Canada's ballet companies has been written with the artistic directors in the spotlight and the patrons somewhere behind the scenes, now it must be seen as a partnership. It was indeed a partnership, a kind of waltz involving two quite different parties, one a dance visionary who could skillfully execute the steps, but new to the scene otherwise. The other partner, the patron, was not quite as comfortable in the spotlight, but was nonetheless pleased to pay the artist's way into the event, introduce her around the room and provide her with the space to do her work. Like any true partnership, power was shared. Sometimes the artist led, and sometimes the patron had control, depending on the circumstances. Over the following pages, the different "waltzes" of the Winnipeg, Toronto and Montreal companies will be explored.

Winnipeg's Artistic Team

The founders of the Royal Winnipeg Ballet were Gweneth Lloyd and Betty Farrally, two English dance teachers who came to Canada in 1938. Within a few months, they had met their patrons and set up a small performing group. Gweneth Lloyd was born in September 1901 into a middle-class family near Manchester. She grew up during an exciting time for women: the fight for women's suffrage was (largely) won in 1918; greater numbers of women were being accepted into the universities and professions; and dress reform meant women were no longer confined by corsets and long skirts. Although Gweneth Lloyd took "fancy" dancing lessons from local teachers throughout her childhood, the seminal event for her occurred when she saw the original Ballets Russes company perform in London in 1918. The performance had a profound and lasting effect on her: "Everything had been pastel before, and suddenly there was all this brilliance. I knew nothing of ballet as such, because I'd only done fancy-dancing, but I knew this was what I liked" (Wyman 1978: 13).

Still, dancing was not considered by her family to be a respectable profession, so instead of pursuing dance studies in London, Lloyd attended one of the physical education colleges for women. These schools trained young women to be gym mistresses through a rigorous programme of pedagogy, Swedish gymnastics and sports. Although "physical culture" was a pre-occupation of the era, some contemporary writers were dismayed by women's involvement in sports, believing that it made women less feminine and perhaps even contributed to fewer women marrying and having children. Nonetheless, Lloyd thrived in this challenging and even controversial environment, and when she graduated in the early 1920s, she took a position as a gym mistress on one of the Channel Islands. Around the same time, she began taking lessons in Revived Greek Dance, which was an English version of Isadora Duncan's modern, barefoot dancing. Lloyd was very excited by the naturalism and sense of freedom offered by this new style of dancing. Despite her family's doubts about dance as a career, she decided she would pursue her interest in dance after all.

Gweneth Lloyd went back to London to continue her studies of Greek dancing with the British teacher Ruby Ginner, and while she was there she took up ballet and other kinds of dance. Although Lloyd was by then too old to start training as a dancer herself, she still made a careful study of the various dance techniques, and finally opened a dance school in Yorkshire along with another teacher in 1927. The school was a great success, but after ten years, Lloyd was looking for a new challenge. She went to Winnipeg in the summer of 1937 to visit friends who had settled there, and when she was told that there were few qualified dance teachers in the city, she became excited by the possibilities. Lloyd left the Yorkshire school and moved to Canada the following summer along with a young teacher from the school, Betty Farrally.

Winnipeg was a sprawling city of about 300,000 in 1938, its population fanning out from the intersection of the Red and the Assiniboine Rivers. European settlement had begun there with French fur traders in the eighteenth century, and it remained a small settlement until the late nineteenth century. The city really hit its stride in the decade before the First World War, when the population was growing at a healthy rate and Winnipeg was home to a host of wealthy families. In 1913, Winnipeg was Canada's third most populous city, behind Montreal and Toronto. As the largest economic centre for many miles in any direction, Winnipeg had no immediate urban competitors and was therefore the centre of cultural and sporting activity for the region. The city's geographic and cultural isolation proved advantageous for the growth of the arts: there was no other city with which to compete or split resources; audiences were more grateful because they could not depend on entertainment from outside; and a consistent vision could be nurtured without too many outside influences. Not surprisingly, locally produced amateur theatre and music were well supported, as were the touring professional groups which visited Winnipeg.

When Gweneth Lloyd and Betty Farrally stepped off their train in the spring of 1938, they entered a city just beginning to emerge from a catastrophic economic depression. As the main shipping point for Western Canadian crops, Winnipeg had been hit especially hard by the collapse of grain prices in the late 1920s and the crop failures that followed. The women had to contend with another serious issue when they arrived: despite Lloyd's and Farrally's prior belief that ballet teaching was nonexistent in Winnipeg, they discovered two dozen dance teachers in the city, some of whom taught ballet and did not appreciate more competition. Undeterred, the two women set up a dance school modelled after the one in Yorkshire, and they ended up forming a small amateur performing group, the Winnipeg Ballet Club, to help their dance school business at the same time. The two women formed the performing group because they reasoned that it would be difficult to attract students to ballet lessons when Winnipeggers, as a result of the economic depression (and later the Second World War), had so few opportunities to see the art at its best: with costumes, live music, scenery and professional dancers, all in a theatre setting.

Starting rather modestly, Lloyd and Farrally began putting on studio demonstrations with the help of a small group of "practical" patrons. These talented community volunteers helped the group produce very professional looking shows for the first ten years. Who were they? First, there were the young local dancers, few of whom had much dance training. Most had backgrounds in athletics. Then there was John Russell, a young professor of architecture at the University of Manitoba, who designed and built most of their early sets. David Yeddeau, a multi-talented theatre man, did publicity, stage management, tour management, makeup, ticket sales and some design, and Constance Sinden, known as "Sindie" to everyone, was their expert seam-stress and wardrobe mistress. Two well placed art lovers, Lady Margaret Tupper and Mrs. Muriel Richardson, gave money and/or used their social connections for the company's benefit. They were helped too by the enthu-siasm of the local newspaper critic, Frank Morriss. Lloyd, Farrally and this dedicated community group formed a stable team which kept the company going through its early years. Their enthusiasm during the first decade is illustrated in this recollection by David Yeddeau: "We had no sense of the future – we were simply doing shows to entertain the public. We were a big success, you see – we'd finish one show and immediately start work on the next. The ballet was our life" (Wyman 1978: 41).

And what did this team produce? Full length ballet classics were avoided. Undoubtedly this was due to the lack of well trained classical dancers and Lloyd's own lack of experience with such ballets, as well as her appreciation of the need to educate, entertain and enlarge her audiences. Lloyd created all the early ballets herself, and within a few years, she and her collaborators had developed a successful "mixed repertoire" formula that has been passed on even to the present day company. They would start the evening with a white ballet (something for the ballet lovers), then follow with something more challenging (probably abstract and more modern), and finally, end with a full company comedy or drama that sent people off smiling (this was "something for the husbands"). Overall, then, there was "something for everyone," from first time attenders to seasoned dance watchers. During an average year, two or three of the comedy dramas, one white ballet and one modern work were created.

New works were a collaborative effort, starting with Lloyd, Farrally and Yeddeau. Often Yeddeau would tell Lloyd that a new white ballet or a new comedy was required for the upcoming season, and she would set to work to find some music. Her choreographic method was to sit with a record player, playing the music again and again with her eyes closed. She would move the dancers in her mind's eye and then write down the movements in ordinary ruled notebooks, using stick figures for the steps on the right side of the page, floor plans on the left and music counts running down a central column. Lloyd's technique of creating without the dancers (or without working it out on her own body) was considered unusual. Most choreographers came to the studio with their ideas and the music, and would move the dancers around, as a sculptor works with clay. As a result, for most companies, creating a ballet could be a long, expensive process, because the "tools" or materials required for the creative process were skilled human beings. Furthermore, the work could not be done just anywhere – it required a large space with heat, light and mirrors. Lloyd, however, disapproved of "wasting everyone's time" by choreographing in the studio and considered her solitary method the most reasonable way to proceed. Reasonable it may have been, but it was also a feat of concentration and focus.

Although she made a number of classical white ballets, Lloyd's most interesting works were her comedy dramas and modern ballets, because they were unusual in both movement style and subject. Up to that time, ballets were usually romantic fantasies. In contrast, Lloyd was inspired by subjects closer to her own life: literature, music, nature and popular culture. The titles of some of her ballets illustrate the point: *The Wise Virgins*, *Through the Looking Glass* (inspired by *Alice in Wonderland*), *An American in Paris*, *The Planets*, *Dionysos*, *Pleasure Cruise*, *The Shooting of Dan McGrew* and *Chapter 13* (based on an American crime novel). Lloyd was a prolific choreographer: she created thirty-two original ballets in fifteen years, more than most choreographers can achieve over a lifetime of making dances.

When Toronto dance historian and choreographer Anna Blewchamp worked with movement from Lloyd ballets for an Expo '86 multimedia presentation, she saw many similarities in movement style with a contemporary of Lloyd's, the American modern dance pioneer Doris Humphrey. Blewchamp called Lloyd's work "radical and imaginative" for its time, specifically citing Lloyd's "integration of different movement techniques, ... [which] did not become a common feature of contemporary dance until the 1950s and 60s."

Blewchamp continued, "Modern dance vocabularies are now commonly integrated with ballet techniques. In the 1940s, Gweneth Lloyd integrated the Ruby Ginner method of Revived Greek Dance, which she refers to as 'natural movement,' with ballet (Cecchetti and Royal Academy), mime, national and social dance" (Blewchamp: 1-2). Musically, too, Lloyd cast her net wide. Whereas the repertoire of other ballet companies showed a preponderance of certain composers, such as Tchaikovsky, Delibes, etc., Lloyd rarely used the same composer twice, running the gamut from the classicists to contemporary boogie-woogie. Lloyd's lack of performing experience, gym teacher training and "something for everyone" philosophy have been viewed as liabilities in more recent times, with some critics denigrating her choreography as "home-spun" and amateurish despite the wonderful reviews she received during the 1940s and early 1950s (Wyman 1978: 27). On the contrary, Blewchamp's research and the company's successes indicate she had a sophisticated under-standing of her audiences and her dancers. She came late to the serious study of ballet, but she was an intelligent, creative woman who bravely became a choreographer because she needed material for her performing group.

Notwithstanding Lloyd's surprising ability to create ballets, the first decade in Winnipeg is at its core a story of voluntarism. Lloyd and Farrally lived off the income from their teaching, not from the fledgling company, and they provided dance training and rehearsal space at no charge; John Russell designed sets on his own time and had them constructed by his students at the University of Manitoba for course credit; costumes were cut and sewn by volunteer seamstresses; dancers came to the studio after school or work, rewarded only with a takeout snack of cinnamon buns or Chinese food if the rehearsals went especially late; Madge Tupper and Muriel Richardson organized teas or receptions to raise money when it was needed; *Winnipeg Free Press* critic Frank Morriss helped them by providing publicity and glowing reviews. This remarkable web of volunteers was held together by the great charm of Lloyd and Farrally, their friendships with all the collaborators, the company's successes, and the fun, creative atmosphere that surrounded the enterprise.[1]

After ten years of growing success and recognition, the company had transformed itself from a tiny entrepreneurial operation into a more public organization. The Winnipeg Ballet was attracting national attention through

---

[1] The smallness of the artistic team is made clear when one realizes that of those few unfamiliar names listed as set designers, costume designers and scenario composers, they can virtually all be linked to someone who was a part of the key artistic team. For example, Shirley Russell, the wife of John Russell, designed the costumes for two productions in 1943. Credit for a scenario in 1941 was given to Peggy Jarman, the daughter of Lloyd's friends, the Jarmans. Costume designs for *The Wager* were done by Mary Morriss, probably a relative of *Winnipeg Free Press* critic Frank Morriss. Frank Morriss himself was virtually a member of the inner circle: he reviewed the Winnipeg Ballet's shows, wrote preview publicity articles, and contributed to their house programme, as well as being a good friend to Lloyd and Farrally. In fact, when Lloyd left Winnipeg in 1951, she was seen off at the train station by just two people, Farrally and Morriss. Madge Tupper herself designed the costumes for a 1941 ballet. On occasion, Josephine Blowe (Joe Blow) was given credit for a scenario or set design. This was a droll pseudonym for Betty Farrally which was used whenever she felt her name was showing up too often in the credits. The ballet family in the first decade was small and intensely committed.

short tours east and west and through the Canadian Ballet Festivals, which had originated in Winnipeg in 1948. In fact, debts from the first Festival were still on the company's books a year later and the company couldn't afford to make the trip to Toronto for the second Canadian Ballet Festival which was being held in Toronto in the spring of 1949. The whole financial side was becoming a burden on Lloyd and Farrally; they needed immediate help to clear their debts and buy train tickets to the upcoming Festival. In the end the money was found and the company was able to participate in the Festival. Furthermore, the company's repertoire was changing from its entire dependence on Lloyd's choreography to contributions by a small group of Winnipeg Ballet alumni. The company had reached an important stage but in order to develop further, it had to have its dancers working full time at dancing, instead of working as clerks and housemaids during the day and coming to the studio at night. The only way to do this was to register the company as a non-profit organization, which would allow a group of citizens to assume the company's debt and conduct the critical fundraising activities.

Although they were concerned about losing their autonomy, Lloyd and Farrally were even more worried that the company would go bankrupt. They reluctantly agreed to register the Winnipeg Ballet in February 1949. Lloyd's fears were soon realized when, under the new arrangement, her position became increasingly one of an administrator answering to the Board of Directors. She left quietly in 1950, tired and unable to work in the changed organization, although she said her departure was strictly for personal reasons. After Lloyd left the company, the Board of Directors deepened its involvement in the details of managing the company. With Lloyd gone, and no real management structure to support the group, the Board plunged in, raising funds, arranging publicity, making souvenir programmes and negotiating fees for tours – the Ballet's managers and advocates were no longer mainly from the studio, but from the Boardroom.[2] The company's practical patrons had taken over. The community partner was going to lead for awhile.

The Winnipeg Ballet's Women's Committee, led by the indefatigable Lady Tupper, was critical to bringing in the money to pay the dancers and subsidize the shows. They organized the membership campaigns, special events and made personal donations too. Women's Committee members produced children's Christmas shows and secured scholarships from other women's organizations (such as the Junior League, sororities and the I.O.D.E.) for needy dancers. They addressed and stuffed thousands of letters before Winnipeg shows and produced the house programmes. Finally, these women refurbished the Wardrobe department, sold candies and cards at Christmas and organized bridge parties, galas and screenings of ballet movies.

The early 1950s were years of competition and hard feelings between the Winnipeg Ballet and the newly established National Ballet company, as they both struggled to stay afloat and present themselves to the public as the

---

[2] Farrally continued to run the studio side of the company, but she was also running the school and raising a child. She became artistic director in 1955.

Lloyd's *Kaleidoscope* (l. to r.): Arnold Spohr, Betty Farrally and David Adams, 1945.

leading Canadian company. Although it seems unlikely today, the Winnipeg company was able to make a good case for its superiority at the time. After all, they were the oldest company, with a repertoire of original Canadian ballets, and a solid group of dancers who had been acknowledged by critics as the best all-round group for years. As a part of this competition between the two companies, Madge Tupper pulled some strings and obtained permission for the Winnipeggers to add "Royal" to the existing name in February 1953.[3] This was a great coup because it made the Winnipeg Ballet the first "Royal" ballet in the British Commonwealth, preceding even England's own company, then called the Sadler's Wells Ballet. Both the Royal Winnipeg Ballet (RWB) and the National Ballet worked to establish volunteer committees in Western Canada

---

[3] It is not clear exactly how Lady Tupper obtained the company's royal charter. As Max Wyman told it, Lady Tupper used her contacts in Ottawa. Tupper had just returned from a trip to New York in November 1952 with a contract from a major U.S. agent to tour the U.S. the next season. Wyman goes on, "Almost certainly she clinched it with a promise to make the company internationally saleable by arranging to have it designated 'royal,' because as soon as she was back from New York she announced to the press that the tour would probably be undertaken under the name of the *Royal* Winnipeg Ballet. 'However,' she added, in her supremely offhand way, 'permission must first be obtained to *use* the title.' She made it sound like a routine matter: in fact, there were only two other 'royal' companies in the world, in Demark and in Sweden. But, by leaning on her contacts in the Royal Household and in the retinue of Governor-General Vincent Massey in Ottawa, Madge Tupper pulled it off. 'She had her pressure points in Ottawa,' Kipp recalls, 'and she knew how to use them'" (Wyman 1978: 83).

204

to help them build audiences and sell tickets when they were touring there. Not surprisingly, in the West, the Winnipeggers prevailed with better audiences and more active support. Still, the great distances between western cities and Winnipeg's modest industry and population meant the RWB was constantly in debt. On the artistic side, the Winnipeg company was enjoying gratifying success. During the early 1950s, they were offered major European and U.S. tours. They were performing for CBC television and the National Film Board, competing with the National Ballet for the best dancers and keeping their own group of dancers intact. The Winnipeggers were confident they could maintain a leading position in the country.

However, in the spring of 1954, the RWB suffered a terrible blow. In the evening and early morning of June 7 to 8, the company's studios were destroyed in an enormous fire. Sparked by faulty wiring in another building down the block, a small fire was turned into a catastrophe by high winds. By morning, five downtown office buildings had been destroyed, including the RWB's headquarters, containing its costumes, sets, music scores and choreo-graphic notebooks. By the time Betty Farrally was alerted, at six in the morning, it was too late; if anyone had thought to call her earlier, they could have saved everything before the fire spread to their building.

The RWB would rebuild but its dreams were different. The company had lost its position as Canada's leading ballet company to the hard driving and geographically advantaged National Ballet (perhaps even before the fire), and the RWB would never really challenge the Toronto company again. In 1954, the RWB's Board of Directors regrouped and, after some debate, decided that the company must rebuild on a more modest scale. Because of the size of their home city and their distance from other centres, they could not compete with the National Ballet. They went back to first principles, the ones on which Lloyd and her patrons had built the company. They would remain a small company which presented entertaining, mixed repertoire shows, often in communities which didn't have a chance to see quality dancing otherwise. Even such a small company was a burden on its local patrons, so they found stability through long tours in Canada and especially the United States. They could play the big cities, but their bread and butter would be to specialize in smaller places. The RWB survived and thrived because they balanced the budget with touring for more and more weeks out of every season.

The RWB began as a modest, community level project by a couple of dance-loving entrepreneurs. Gweneth Lloyd and Betty Farrally did not carry with them the heavy legacy of ballet tradition and elitism. They loved dance of all kinds, were excited by their new country, and they put those two elements together with good sense and imagination to create something quite original. Lloyd's artistry has not always been fully appreciated, but it is clear now that her uniquely varied background and training had the dual effect of producing strikingly original work and ballet accessible to a large audience. With their relatively small population base, Winnipeggers in much greater proportion had to be enticed into supporting the Ballet. By necessity and inclination,

Lloyd and her team brought them in through their educational approach and entertaining programmes.

The extraordinary efforts of community volunteers are also critical to this story. From its first shows, the company was able to mount professional level productions because it had a team of highly skilled "practical" patrons behind it. This handful of friends and collaborators supported the company through its struggling years of training dancers and audiences, into an era of much wider community support. Still struggling to pay its bills through the early 1950s, the company was nonetheless a source of great pride as the leading ballet company in Canada, and the community "owned" it, rallying behind it at critical moments. Though never really the "civic project" that its friends hoped it would become, the Ballet carried on, an enduring example of the importance of citizen volunteers in the survival of Canadian cultural institutions.

The National Ballet's Practical Patrons

The National Ballet of Canada had its first performances in November 1951. The company's creation was most interesting in that the founders were not choreographers or dance teachers, but instead three well-to-do Toronto club women. In the midst of the excitement over the 1949 Canadian Ballet Festival in Toronto, Aileen Woods, Pearl Whitehead and Sydney Mulqueen were approached by local ballet teacher and choreographer Boris Volkoff with the idea of founding a national company based in Toronto. Volkoff and his wife, the dancer Janet Baldwin Volkoff, had done a great deal of the pioneering work for such a company over the previous fifteen years, but as their dream finally bore fruit, they were left on the sidelines. The National Ballet's founding patrons had already made some preliminary decisions about the nature of their company and the type of person they wanted to lead it; it was to be modelled on the British Sadler's Wells Ballet company and it would be led by someone from outside Canada.

Who were these founding women? Pearl Whitehead was an experienced, "professional" volunteer who had held executive positions (including the presidency) of the Toronto Symphony Women's Committee over the previous decade. She was married to the lawyer and civil servant R.B. Whitehead, and lived in Toronto's exclusive Rosedale neighbourhood. Whitehead's neighbour was Aileen Woods. Woods' family was wealthy because they owned York Knitting Mills, which produced Harvey Woods products. She was interested in music and had been a board member for the 1949 Ballet Festival in Toronto. Woods brought in her old school chum, Sydney Mulqueen. Woods and Mulqueen had a history of volunteering, having worked together at the service-men's canteen in Toronto during the Second World War.

Why did these comfortable matrons decide they should start a national ballet company? Put simply, they thought the city (and the country) needed a new ballet company and they felt they were the people who could do it properly

206

(Whittaker 4 May 1992).[4] Some critics have suggested that jealousy over the Winnipeg company's success during the late 1940s prompted the women to found the Toronto company. Alternatively, these women may just have been energetic culture lovers who saw the chance to initiate something important.

The women's work did not take place in a vacuum. In fact, the company was founded in the midst of two broad trends: a growing interest in ballet and a wave of Canadian cultural nationalism in the years after 1945. Canada had come out of the war proud of its enormous contribution and with the position of the third most active trading nation in the world. For the first time, Canada was a world leader in economic terms. But some people argued that this was not enough. In his 1948 book, *On Being Canadian*, the wealthy arts patron and diplomat Vincent Massey declared that it was no longer acceptable for Canadians to be "too busy conquering the wilderness" to think about higher education and the arts. It was time to show the world that Canadians were a "unique and refined people" who deserved their place among the most successful nations (Massey 1948: 37). As Canada's leading cultural nationalist, Massey chaired the Royal Commission on National Development in the Arts, Letters and Sciences, which held hearings throughout Canada in 1949-50. The resulting report stressed the need for some kind of national organization to support the arts. A few years later, in 1957, the Canada Council was established. No doubt the National Ballet's founding women were well aware of the Massey Commission's activities as they began planning their ballet company in exactly the same years. The women's initiative was a part of a larger movement toward professionalizing the arts and creating national institutions.

The other broad trend in which the women worked was a growing interest in ballet. During the late 1930s, ballet companies visiting Toronto had played for only three nights and did not sell out the seats; ten years later, touring companies stayed for two weeks and sold out (Callwood 1 Mar. 1949: 16-17). This was mainly due to the efforts of Ernest Rawley, the manager of the Royal Alexandra Theatre (Whittaker 1967: 56). Only New York and Chicago supported longer runs by touring ballet groups. In November 1951, a *Globe and Mail* columnist commented: "In Toronto, at least, people have been going kind of ballet balmy the past couple of years and scrambling for tickets for visiting companies with a fervour that used to be reserved for Grey Cup finals" (Tumpane 15 Nov. 1951).

Beyond Toronto, these were also the golden years for Broadway and Hollywood musicals, most of which used ballet-trained dancers. In 1948, a ballet movie called *The Red Shoes* was a major success in North America and Great Britain. During the 1940s and 1950s, many books on ballet appreciation were being published in England. Even women's fashions were influenced by the popularity of ballet – the silhouette of 1950s dresses was very much like a

---

[4] The women probably did not realize the difficulties they would encounter, nor the length of time they would have to keep up the work. According to an early Board President, Mabel Hees, the Ballet's first supporters would never have started the National Ballet if they had known what it would entail for them, but once it was underway they had a "tiger by the tail," and didn't dare let go (Hees letter, National Ballet Archives).

long tutu and ballet slippers were popular as ordinary footwear. Further indication of the ballet boom was that in 1949, Toronto ballet teachers reported keeping waiting lists of up to 300 students (Janet Baldwin [Volkoff] Collection, CFRB Interview 25 Feb. 1949). That same year, the Canadian dance teachers formed their own professional association in Toronto, the Canadian Dance Teachers' Association.

Aside from the larger interest in ballet, a direct impetus for the Toronto women was the success of the leading British ballet company, the Sadler's Wells, in its Toronto performances of 1949. At that time the women went to see Ninette de Valois, the director of the Sadler's Wells, and she encouraged them to found a ballet company, confirming their view that they would have to have someone of unquestioned ability from outside Canada. Eventually, de Valois recommended Celia Franca, whom she said was "probably the finest dramatic dancer the Wells has ever had" (Whittaker 1967: 16).

Celia Franca was born in 1921 in London, England. She began dancing at the age of four, eventually winning scholarships in both dance and music which permitted her to attend the best schools. Franca began working professionally at fourteen, and went on to dance with Ballet Rambert, Sadler's Wells, Ballets Jooss and the International Ballet. By all accounts, she had tremendous talent, a combination of a superb choreographic memory, a thorough understanding of music and a genius for the dramatic. On de Valois' recommendation, the women sent a letter to Celia Franca inviting her to come to Montreal for the Third Canadian Ballet Festival in November 1950. Franca agreed to come, and although she was disappointed in the technical level of the dancers, she saw potential and agreed to come to Canada to survey the possibilities, arriving in 1951. Within a few months, the group of supporters formalized themselves as a Board of Directors and began fundraising in earnest. Celia Franca organized a summer school, making valuable contacts and earning a small profit (which went toward the new company). She then travelled across Canada auditioning dancers; she gathered a few, but several of her original company came from Volkoff's Toronto studio. In November 1951, the National Ballet gave its inaugural performance, less than a year after Celia Franca's arrival in Canada.

And what kind of ballet did they produce? In contrast to Lloyd's original mixed repertoire policy in Winnipeg, Celia Franca's preference was to have a repertoire based on the classics, "recognized masterpieces, works by which audience and critics could judge you" (Whittaker 1967: 50). She rejected a repertoire that was tailored to suit the existing facilities and skills. In the first few years, the company danced classical excerpts and full-length classics including *Coppélia*, *Giselle*, *Nutcracker* and *Swan Lake*, as well as new, short Canadian ballets and the works of contemporary English choreographers such as Antony Tudor. Franca was able to mount the large classical works very early on because the company's leading dancers (Franca herself, Latvian immigrants Irene Apinee and Jury (Juris) Gotshalks, and Canadians David Adams and Lois Smith) could dance the most demanding roles while the rest of the company grew into the repertoire. From the first performances, the critics noted Franca's ability to instil in the company the dignity and reserve of classicism. Franca believed the dancers would soak up the classical style by doing the master works, and then after a few years Canadian choreographers would emerge from that base.

From the earliest months, the National Ballet's community side was strong and savvy. The Board knew that if they were going to receive support as a National Ballet, they had to make themselves as "national" as possible.[5] The Board of Directors correctly anticipated a good deal of resentment from other parts of the country toward a Toronto company calling itself "national." The 1952 Chairman of the Board, Mabel Hees, recalled:

> The National aspect of the Ballet Guild concerned me from the beginning, perhaps because my husband was in federal politics and I knew something of the interregional stresses and strains in Canada and also how much Toronto was resented, indeed hated by people all over the country. The Toronto angle had to be played down, yet, we knew, and it has been proven, that Toronto would be our mainstay financially and in many other ways too. *How* was an early, pressing problem, i.e. no support till the company had appeared in a particular area and no money to send it there without that support. Always in debt, the Board continually had to balance the present against the future, to undertake money losing tours to build support for the future (Hees letter; author's emphasis added).

After the pride and excitement of the National Ballet's first official performances, the Board of Directors of the National Ballet could pause but briefly to marvel at what they and Celia Franca had accomplished already. They had a ballet company, with a strong, glamorous leader and a prestigious Board. However, a company of this size was expensive, especially since all the dancers and staff were to be professional from the outset (unlike Winnipeg where everyone had been a volunteer over the first decade). Few large donors had materialized to help pay the bills, and if the National Ballet was to survive and become a truly national company, they would have to gather national support: they would have to get out on the road. Their first short tour followed the company's premiere performances.

Although a tour can bring financial losses, it can also be the way to make a company financially viable. A ballet company needs a large initial investment (for studio rental, dancers' salaries for weeks of rehearsal time, rights to music and choreography, orchestration, music copying, sets and costumes), which is best offset by performing the new work(s) for as long as possible. However, a home city can only support a limited run of any one programme of works before a new one is required. Touring is a way to continue deriving income

---

[5] Most national arts organizations at that time were based in Ottawa or Toronto and few travelled around the country. The list includes the Royal Canadian Academy of Arts (1880), the Royal Conservatory of Music of Toronto (1886, until 1947 known as the Toronto Conservatory of Music), the National Gallery (1913), the National Museum (1926), the National Film Board (1939). Outside Ottawa were CBC radio (1936), the Dominion Drama Festival (1932-39 and 1947-78) and the Canadian Opera Company, known at that time as the Opera Festival Association (1950).

National Ballet of Canada, *Nutcracker*, ca. 1952. Irene Apinee centre.

without making the investment required for a new ballet. While often physically arduous, tours also provide dancers with what they want most: the opportunity to perform as often as possible. Furthermore, successful tours across Canada would build audiences and show the federal government, from which the Board had already requested grants with no success, that the company was truly a national enterprise. Touring was the answer, but virtually all of the Ballet's supporters were in Toronto, and the company barely had enough money to pay for dancers, musicians, production crew, sets and costumes, let alone transportation, hotels, meals, advertising and the other costly elements of touring. Canada, with its relatively small, far-flung communities, was a particularly costly place to tour.

In order to meet some of these pressing needs, the National Ballet Guilds were developed by Woods, Whitehead and Mulqueen, and by a fourth woman, Mabel Hees. Volunteers, mainly women, joined local National Ballet Guilds to raise funds and standing for the company year-round, and to provide a "soft landing" when the company came to their community on tour. The "soft landing" could mean everything from booking the theatre and selling the tickets to billeting and feeding the company members in their homes. Although some of the Guild branches, particularly in Western Canada, were very small and not able to help much, the branches in Ontario and Quebec were very successful. In 1957, the National Ballet Guilds' paid membership consisted of 3,000 people in twelve cities, of which approximately seventy per cent were women (Griffin letter to Canada Council, National Archives of Canada). The efforts of the Toronto and Windsor Guild branches will be examined here in some detail as a window into this intriguing group of "practical" patrons (National Ballet Archives: for Toronto report, see Toronto or London branch records, and for Windsor, see Windsor branch).

The Toronto Branch of the Guild was very active, concerning itself with selling tickets, fundraising, publicity and hospitality. For example, during the 1954-55 season, the members of the ticket-selling committee had managed to sell almost $10,000 in seats at the Royal Alexandra Theatre, or about one quarter of the potential sales. The membership committee's fifty-five volunteers had canvassed over a thousand people and raised $9,850 from 515 members. The project committee had raised almost $8,000 through two events, a fashion show and a supper dance with the theme of "A Night in Nassau." The entertainment committee had organized two luncheon meetings and a backstage reception for 500 members to meet the dancers after a performance. Toronto Guild members had secured donated food, decorations, prizes, halls, or made the food and decorations themselves for these events.

The publicity committee had supported the branch's fundraising projects by sending out press releases to radio programme directors, announcers, women's commentators and television stations. Guild members arranged for the students of the Ontario College of Art to go to the National Ballet studio to sketch dancers in rehearsals; the best of the sketches were then displayed in downtown cinemas. The publicity committee had also persuaded several professional window dressers to create displays in downtown retail stores to advertise the company's upcoming shows.

Branch members also cared for the dancers, arranging luncheons and birthday parties for company members at the studio, and doing most of the cooking themselves to keep costs down. As the number of matinees increased, Franca asked the Toronto Guild members if they could arrange a supper for the dancers at the theatre between afternoon and evening shows, and thereafter a hot chicken dinner was provided for the dancers on matinee days. On other days, branch members laid out sugar buns, cheese biscuits and fruit. The Toronto Branch's contributions were substantial; if the labour and hospitality of these "practical patrons" had not been donated, the company could not have paid for it.

In September 1956, Margaret Reid and three friends founded the Windsor Branch. Over the first year, these four volunteers signed up 167 members. The Windsor Guild raised $1,000 in donations annually, and they billeted dancers, arranged local transportation, undertook local publicity and provided a post-performance supper and party for the company. Other activities in the early years included lobbying the local television station to broadcast a National Ballet performance, lectures on ballet at the University of Windsor and the YWCA, a fashion show of fur and jewellery, the declaration of a Ballet Week in local schools and libraries with related activities, a garden party, cocktail party and tea and, not least, a scholarship fund for one promising dancer per year. During the National Ballet's very difficult financial circumstances through the mid-1950s, the Windsor Branch became guarantors (along with over a hundred individuals, mainly based in Toronto) of an annual loan that the Ballet required to begin operations each autumn, and which was paid off as fundraising and box office monies began to roll in. Each year, the guarantors were asked to donate a part of their notes, and to act as guarantors for the following year. Eventually, the Windsor Branch took on the responsibility of presenting the company's Windsor shows, with all the risks that this entailed. By the early 1960s, the company performed for a full week in Windsor, and averaged ninety per cent attendance (National Ballet Archives).

As the Toronto and Windsor examples demonstrate, the National Ballet Guild branches played a critical role in the early years of the company. Several thousand Guild members, mainly women, worked in their local communities on behalf of the struggling "national" company. Their continuing work meant the National Ballet had a base of "practical patrons" who would provide what the ballet could not afford – publicity, accommodation, meals, parties – as well as a modest yearly donation. They put a local face on a Toronto-based enterprise; the Guilds helped the Ballet avoid some of the resentment that Mabel Hees and others had feared would cripple it. Besides the two communities discussed here, the Ballet's Board of Directors could, after ten years, point to a network of Guild organizations in Ottawa, Quebec City, Sherbrooke, Montreal, London, Belleville, Hamilton, Kitchener-Waterloo, St. Catharines and Calgary.

The branches worked autonomously, using their knowledge of local conditions to sell the company. The National Ballet head office used the branches to contact important local media and groups that might buy blocks of tickets; local Guilds could help with decisions on ticket prices, and avoid conflicts with local events. The Montreal and Quebec Branches stressed the necessity of bilingual materials if the National Ballet was to make any headway in their cities. The Ottawa members worked on confirming the attendance of certain key government figures and diplomats, whose presence would turn the performances into a more chic event, thereby helping ticket sales (Elspeth Menendez [Mrs. C. James] letter, National Ballet Archives). Ottawa's fledgling Guild also worked to overcome significant resistance to the Toronto company:

> The National Ballet had always faced in Ottawa the problem of undefined but nonetheless palpable hostility created by the decline of its own local ballet enterprise which had for many years commanded the loyalty of those most interested in ballet as an art. It is only fair to say the local practitioners and their supporters regarded the National Ballet as a peculiarly Toronto organization which had come lately into the field and by virtue of the name it had chosen to adopt had arrogated to itself an authority and status not particularly flattering to the pretensions of the National Capital. Against this feeling it was necessary to make head with as much tact as possible (Hughes letter, National Ballet Archives).

The Guilds' work was not radical in itself when one reflects upon its nature, nor upon the social position of the women involved. As in the past, middle and upper class women played a large role in the support of culture in

212

their communities. Much of that support by the Guild rank-and-file was an extension of traditional domestic tasks – holding teas, preparing food, organizing parties, hosting visitors in one's home; the Ballet's needs dovetailed nicely with what these women could offer. Moreover, any Guild-related forays into the public realm were eminently respectable because the activities were sponsored by leading community women, they were voluntary, concerned art and culture and were "for the good of the community." Funding scholarships for young ballet students was another logical extension of women's traditional involvement with children and education.

What is surprising is the scale and importance of the women's work in the practical survival of the National Ballet. The gendered character of the art made leading positions unattractive for men (or made women more appropriate leaders), and so provided unique leadership opportunities for the women: they made deputations to local government and corporations, acted as guarantors for loans and headed up mixed committees of men and women. Ballet has a reputation as an elite art form, with the implicit assumption that the company's supporters would just write a cheque if the company encountered any problems. The company did encounter serious financial difficulties and they were occasionally helped by the intervention of a few wealthy patrons, but equally important were the very practical ongoing efforts of these women-centred Guilds. The example of the National Ballet Guilds demonstrates that traditional women's skills, organizational networks and women's media (i.e., print and radio aimed at a female audience) were powerful in themselves. However unglamorous or underappreciated it often was, women's practical patronage had an enormous impact on the survival of this fledgling "national" cultural enterprise. When federal funding became available through the Canada Council in 1957, the Guild branches were proudly touted as evidence of the National Ballet's truly national support.[6]

In 1959, critic Nathan Cohen paid tribute to Celia Franca's progress with the National Ballet after its first "dismal" shows: "With no support behind her except the enthusiasm of a group of women, and lacking sound financial backing let alone a couple of experienced ballet dancers, Miss Franca was nevertheless able to build her company on a solid artistic foundation" (Cohen 1959). The "enthusiasm of a group of women" took the National Ballet very far indeed.

Montreal Networks
A National Ballet Guild was established in Montreal in the early 1950s and the Toronto company made regular appearances in Montreal; however, despite their best efforts, the English-style National Ballet company did not do well in Montreal. Les Grands Ballets Canadiens, a company which was more closely tied to French Canada, became Montreal's own company. Les Grands Ballets Canadiens did not become established with the help of volunteers, as

---

[6] Although the company had more professional managers to do much of this type of work through the 1960s and 1970s, the Guilds were still a vital force for decades. Several Guild branches survived into the 1980s, although the Toronto Guild, now called the Volunteer Committee, is the only one still existing.

213

the Winnipeg and Toronto companies did. Instead, the company found a few important though not necessarily wealthy patrons early on, and with them became a part of a larger wave of French Canadian nationalism to which they contributed and which in turn protected them.

The great irony of the founding of Les Grands Ballets Canadiens was its beginnings as a very non-traditional ballet company in a most traditional society. Throughout the nineteenth and early twentieth centuries, French Quebec was dominated by a deeply conservative Roman Catholic church. In addition to its many parishes throughout the province, the Catholic church also ran the basic social institutions such as schools and hospitals, giving it an exceptional degree of influence in people's ordinary lives. Another strong and conservative influence came from Maurice Duplessis, Quebec's leader from 1936-39 and again 1944-59. Although Duplessis led the province during a period of prosperity, he is most well known for his old-style paternalism, his disregard of civil liberties and his harsh response to industrial strikes. During the 1940s and 1950s, this profound conservatism of both the church and state met with resistance. Small pockets of dissent grew, especially amongst trade unionists, intellectuals and artists, who wanted to see greater freedom in everyday life.

One of the key events in this backlash occurred in 1948, when the Automatists, a group of Montreal artists including dancer Françoise Sullivan, published a manifesto called *Refus global* [*Total Refusal*]. Led by painter Paul-Émile Borduas, the group denounced "the suffocating power of establishment thinking" in Quebec. Although the immediate effect of the manifesto was to cause the termination of Borduas' teaching contract at an art college in Montreal, in a larger sense it was a harbinger of the Quiet Revolution, Quebec's great transformation during the late 1950s and 1960s in which the French-speaking population began to challenge the conservatism of the church and state, as well as the dominance of English Canadians in business circles. The phrase that was often used was that Quebeckers wanted to be "masters in our own house" (maîtres chez nous). The history of Montreal's Les Grands Ballets Canadiens is tied to this revolution because the founder, Ludmilla Chiriaeff, became an ally and collaborator with many French-Canadian intellectuals and artists at a time when French-Canadian nationalism was beginning its ascent.

Montreal already had a healthy amateur dance scene during the 1940s. There were a number of very good teachers whose students went on to dance in New York and elsewhere, but there was no stable professional company. In 1952, dancer Ludmilla (Otzup-Gorny) Chiriaeff settled in Montreal. She was born in Latvia in 1924 into a family who had had to flee the Soviet Union because her family had fought with the White Russian army during the 1917 Revolution. The family eventually settled into an expatriate community in Berlin, where her father, Serge Gorny, established himself as an importer-exporter. Until then he had been a poet and mining engineer. Gorny's lingering health problems meant that he often worked from home, so a steady stream of expatriate Russians visited the family. These visitors included many famous writers, artists and performers, including the choreographer Michel Fokine.

Ludmilla attended a Russian school in Berlin where she studied six languages: French, German, Russian, Latin, Greek and English. At the age of seven, she took up ballet lessons with a former dancer of the Bolshoi Ballet, and she later danced professionally in small roles with de Basil's Ballets Russes while the company was in Berlin. Ludmilla Otzup-Gorny continued to dance professionally through several years of the Second World War, although she spent the last months of the war in a forced labour camp. Eventually she made her way to Geneva, Switzerland, where she taught ballet, danced leading roles with the local company, married an expatriate Russian set designer, Alexis Chiriaeff, and had two children. In 1951, she immigrated to Canada.

Ludmilla Chiriaeff arrived in Montreal in the depths of the winter of 1951-52, along with her husband and two young children. At the time of her arrival, she was almost nine months pregnant with her third child. They arrived very late at night and needed to find a hotel. While her husband and children had a meal in a diner, Ludmilla Chiriaeff walked outside to see if there was a hotel nearby. She looked one way up St. Catherine Street and down the other. There, on a marquee was her name, Ludmilla Chiriaeff. She stared at it, transfixed. Finally, she realized the sign was on a movie theatre that was showing a dance film she had made in Europe several years earlier. She decided it was an omen that her destiny would be in Montreal. Throughout the trying years ahead, Chiriaeff was sustained by her strong religious beliefs and by her sense that her survival through the war was "not for nothing." She believed that "one is born for a purpose. I believed, from a child, that my purpose was the ballet and I accepted it willingly and with love but my work as a dancer was so often interrupted that I began to wonder if ballet was in truth the purpose of my life.... It was only then that I knew what my purpose was intended to be – not to perform but to work for the ballet of French Canada" (Maynard 1971: 56-58). Throughout the history of Les Grands Ballets Canadiens, Chiriaeff was driven by this extraordinary sense of purpose and by a very practical need to provide for her family, both of which propelled her forward when others might have found the circumstances intolerable. She would have to work very hard, but Chiriaeff had personal motives to succeed. She believed she had found a home: "Some people come to earn money and then leave again. Others become Canadians to get a passport. I really wanted to integrate. Be accepted. I was an orphan on the national level. To be accepted by a country where you feel at home, this is to be adopted by a family and to finally have a feeling of belonging to a nation" (Lemelin 1978, translation by the author). Chiriaeff was absolutely determined to stay, integrate and succeed.

A few days after her arrival, Chiriaeff met a woman who was a producer with the new CBC television in Montreal, called Société Radio-Canada (SRC), which was to go on the air several months later, in September 1952. Chiriaeff was asked to do an audition, so only a few weeks after giving birth, she scraped together the money to rent a studio and cut up some curtains for a costume. Chiriaeff did a short "Gypsy" dance for the cameras and was then contracted to hire more dancers and create one ballet per month on SRC. This was soon increased to several contracts per month as Chiriaeff began to do short pieces for variety, children's and other shows. Chiriaeff had found her patrons, and they were at SRC.

As Chiriaeff soon learned, SRC produced innovative television. Lacking other models and with a new freedom from Quebec's traditional elites (funding was from federal, not provincial sources) new ideas could be explored with less regard for the usual conservative constituencies. In fact, television became a forum where traditional ideas were challenged by leading journalists, artists and intellectuals, and its effect could be huge because it reached so many people at once. SRC was able to play an important role among French Quebeckers (and in the Quiet Revolution) because it was so well tuned to its audience. A large percentage (near 75%) of its programming was custom-made for Quebeckers, in contrast to the situation in English Canada, which broadcast many American imports, roughly two thirds of the schedule in a 1956 survey (Rutherford 1990: 80). The French service did not have the luxury (and crutch) of prepared television from France because French television developed very slowly. Furthermore, the French-Canadian producers of programmes working in Montreal knew little about the television product that already existed and did not wish to know any more (Stewart 1986: 28). They had made a conscious decision to create their own kind of television and solve their own problems without referring to American or other models. SRC also had the enormous advantage of a large and captive market. For several years, the CBC/SRC had a monopoly on television broadcasting in Canada, and this was particularly effective in places like Montreal, which lacked any large American cities nearby that might offer a service to compete for viewers. The province was large and Quebeckers acquired televisions at an even faster rate than Canadians elsewhere (Linteau 1991: 287). So for both structural and content reasons, the SRC thrived and enjoyed considerable popularity in Quebec.

Journalist and politician Gérard Pelletier, among others, has spoken of the excitement, the euphoria around SRC television in those early days, and there were some very good reasons for the enthusiasm among those who produced the cultural programmes (Pelletier 1983: 175-79). First, the creative people were in control, rather than the bureaucrats who subsequently became more powerful in a few years' time. As an example, during this "golden age," many of Ludmilla Chiriaeff's shows were produced by Pierre Mercure or Gabriel Charpentier, two of Quebec's most successful young classical music composers. It would be difficult to imagine such collaborations today because television producers are rarely accomplished artists themselves. Another reason for the excitement was that everything had to be produced quickly, so there was a good deal of improvisation and intensive collaboration by artists from different disciplines. Most television producers were new to the medium and caught up in anticipation of its possibilities. In fact, very few producers had even come over from radio because the CBC/SRC, fearing a devastating effect on its radio service, made the move from radio to television financially unattractive. So, the powerful producers of the era were from varied backgrounds, but not from television or radio. Best of all, there was money available to do all this work: many Quebec artists were able to make a living from their art for the first time.

SRC offered an eclectic roster through the week, with one night featuring wrestling and the next night highbrow shows like *L'Heure du Concert*. There was huge diversity in the programming as SRC tried to serve its many "publics." Over the SRC's first fifteen years, a significant percentage of its resources was devoted to bringing elite culture – music, theatre, dance, opera – to Canadian viewers. The CBC/SRC became the largest employer of artists in the country. From the perspective of these artists, who found lucrative, innovative work, an audience and a community of other artists, this was indeed a golden age. For a few years, the performing arts of the concert hall were a featured part of the television schedule; but ironically the highbrows, whom the CBC/SRC was partially trying to serve, tended to be scornful of television and preferred to absorb their culture in the traditional way in a concert hall or theatre.

What kind of ballet did Chiriaeff create in those early days of television? Generally, she didn't do large scale traditional ballets with dozens of dancers, as in *Swan Lake* or *Giselle*. Chiriaeff had not danced in these classics herself and had a preference for other choreographic styles. In Montreal, Chiriaeff customized her ballets according to the type of show for which she was contracted, be it variety, concert or children's shows. For evening variety shows such as *Porte Ouverte*, *Tzigane* and *Shalimar*, which offered a mix of popular music, dance, and comedy, Chiriaeff would produce short, lively works. The variety shows were less concerned with bringing ballet to their audience than they were with pure entertainment. Chiriaeff and her dancers saw them as a means to an end; as she said in a 1971 interview, "On Monday [the night for variety shows] we danced to eat ... on Thursday [the night for *L'Heure du Concert*], we danced for love of the ballet" (Maynard 1971: 56). For children's shows, such as *Boîte à Surprise*, Chiriaeff spoke to the camera, taking the role of the teacher as she described a little about the history of dancing from, perhaps, medieval times, with a short piece to demonstrate her points, or she would create a ballet to illustrate an old Quebec folk tale.

Dancing for television was hard work. In the early days, the shows were all live, so whenever the performance was scheduled (afternoon or late evening) the dancers had to be supple and energetic. As in any film production, there were many technical requirements, and dancers recalled rehearsing the ballet full out again and again for technicians who were setting the lighting and for the director who was choosing camera angles. This would not have been so bad except that often much of this rehearsing was done on the same day as the performance. They had other difficulties: the stage floor was small and made of concrete rather than wood.[7] Dancing on television was also difficult because it meant dancing for a cool, impersonal group of cameramen and technicians, instead of a live audience where one could expect some reaction, some clapping

---

[7] The CBC was compelled to install a proper dance floor by George Balanchine in 1956 because he refused to have his company, the New York City Ballet, perform on anything but a sprung wooden floor.

Eric Hyrst's *Drawn Blinds* (l. to. r.): Sheila Pearce, Ludmilla Chiriaeff, Eva von Gencsy, choreographed for television, 1954.

or laughing, a connection between performer and audience. As well, the movements themselves had to be more subtle because television amplified small gestures and facial expressions, so the kind of broad movements which might be required on stage had to be toned down, as did stage makeup and costumes.

The greatest surprise television held for Chiriaeff and her dancers, however, was that many viewers thought their dancing and costumes were offensive, even obscene. Although the Ballets Chiriaeff, as the company was then called, was somewhat sheltered from the complaints because they were directed at the SRC, the dancers still had to live in this conservative environment – in Montreal during the 1950s, for example, women were not allowed to wear pants or shorts in public (Lawrence 22 Feb. 1995). In the early years, the church kept a close eye on what appeared on television; before every appearance of Les Ballets Chiriaeff, a member of the clergy came to the television studio to ensure that the company's costumes were not too revealing to go on the air.[8]

On a more positive note, Chiriaeff's dancers had steady work in a high-profile medium. They were performing constantly, in all kinds of new works

[8] The main concern seems to have been the women's breasts and legs; however, on at least one occasion, a man's costume was deemed offensive because his genitals were too obvious in his tights, so he had to wear a kind of diaper underneath.

modelled on their own personalities and bodies, and they could be seen by thousands of people at once. After the first few years, SRC began to shoot the ballets live to tape, so although there was still a great deal of pressure to get it right (given the inability to edit), the dancers at least benefited from seeing themselves when the dancing was actually broadcast. Chiriaeff's dancers were also part of the great cauldron of creativity at the SRC in those days, when all kinds of artists were thrown together with some money and a deadline. Many dancers spoke of their excitement in working with other Quebec artists, designers, singers and actors on the various productions. They felt they were at the centre of something unique. They believed they were opening Quebec up to the influences of the outside world, while at the same time exposing Quebec's unique culture to the world. They were pioneers of television and of ballet, improvising and educating, collaborating with other artists. It was an exciting time and place for such artists.

Ludmilla Chiriaeff's association with SRC was a great stroke of fortune; her SRC producers became her practical patrons. Nearly destitute when she arrived in Canada, it could have taken her years to build up a group of dancers and supporters, and to raise the money to mount a professional show, which required costumes, decor, musicians and a theatre. Under the wing of the SRC much of this was provided for her, and it was of high quality. She had an immediate, regular income and desirable status (as a teacher and contractor) among the city's dancers. Her producers and colleagues were some of Quebec's leading composers, designers and musicians. Despite her minimal financial resources, Chiriaeff was able to make a good start with her patrons' help. Furthermore, there was a confluence between what Chiriaeff could offer artistically and what was needed for television. She couldn't offer the great ballet classics because she hadn't danced in them; she was more comfortable with the shorter, dramatic works of the Ballets Russes or the modernism of German expressionist dance. Yet, her nontraditional repertoire was not a disadvantage. Her creations were more suited to the time slots available on television, and were probably more dynamic on a small screen than the classics. Furthermore, at SRC, Chiriaeff was sheltered from opposition to her work. Certainly, she still had to contend with ignorance of ballet and outright opposition from conservatives, but she had stumbled upon Quebec at a golden moment for the arts, when the social order was loosening up, and when federal money provided opportunity.

Admittedly, there were a few problems with starting a ballet company for television. One of the disadvantages of Chiriaeff's early work was that it was being put out indiscriminately into thousands of homes to indifferent and sometimes even hostile viewers. If she were producing for a more traditional theatre setting, Chiriaeff could rest easy in the knowledge that her audience members were familiar with the art, and indeed were even devoted enough to pay to see it. On television, she had no real feedback. She had to speak meaningfully to a huge cross section of Quebec society, from neophytes to longhairs, with little idea of what they knew, what they enjoyed, what they wanted. Producing for television rather than the stage meant working much more quickly than was comfortable, and Chiriaeff found herself constantly simplifying and explaining her choreography. She had to work within the bounds of religious censors. SRC provided her sets and costumes, but they also owned them and unfortunately they had a policy of destroying the sets immediately after the broadcast. Her work was not lost, but it was not a tangible creation like a musical score on a piece of paper; rather, it was preserved in the minds and bodies of her dancers. Chiriaeff could reconstruct her ballets. But if she decided to cut her ties to SRC, she would have to start from scratch in practical ways, with no costumes or sets sitting ready in the back room. Chiriaeff had another worry – her legacy as a choreographer: she was like a composer on a new instrument, breaking new ground but not at all certain that others would view the work as legitimate.

In 1955, Chiriaeff did a couple of live performances with her troupe in Montreal. It was a pleasant change from the pressure of creating and performing for television. Much to her surprise, the critics and others exclaimed how pleased they were to have a ballet company that they didn't even know they had. Chiriaeff discovered then that the highbrow audience, the audience who would actually come out and pay for a live ballet performance, was not watching her on television. Television in those early days was not so omnipresent as it is today, and at first many people refused to get a TV because it was considered too lowbrow. Sensing that her television company didn't have a great future and knowing that she herself was becoming exhausted by its demands, she decided to transform her group into a more traditional live performing company and founded the new company, Les Grands Ballets Canadiens, in 1957. With her new company, Chiriaeff continued collaborating with the Quebec composers, designers and musicians she knew from SRC, but she needed to find supporters in the wider community too. Again, Chiriaeff found her patrons, in this case a Board of Directors composed mainly of French Canadians, who were lawyers, accountants and teachers she met through teaching ballet to their children.

Chiriaeff had an uncanny sense for finding the right community to promote her work. At first, this little "community" consisted of just three or four fellow artists, young French-Canadian composers who also happened to be some of the leading producers for the new SRC television out of Montreal. Within a few years, Chiriaeff's community had become a whole cadre of Quebec's leading artists from every artistic discipline; through collaboration with various artists on SRC shows, Chiriaeff and her dancers had become a part of a much larger artistic awakening in the province. Soon, all of Quebec would experience an even larger awakening, an overturning of traditional conservative structures and a movement of openness to the world and pride in Quebec. And Chiriaeff was tied in with the community who led this "Quiet Revolution." The small group of French-Canadian professionals who helped Chiriaeff launch Les Grands Ballets Canadiens in the late 1950s were in the leading classes of Quebec during the 1960s. Chiriaeff managed to keep her group at the centre of several of Quebec's most important communities. Furthermore, the leading ballet company of Quebec, depicting French-Canadian stories, promoting French-Canadian dancers, music and design, could not be ignored by the Canada Council, however reluctant the Council was to support another large ballet company.

In 1972, a critic wrote of Chiriaeff: "[Her] influence on dance in Quebec is pretty well all-pervasive. She is the single leading luminary and she has adopted the particular mystique of her adopted land with a great passion. In a sense, she is more French Canadian than the French Canadians" (quoted in Fulford 1977: 93). Chiriaeff's destiny was in Quebec, as she had believed it would be. In the end she had founded a traditional ballet company, but she had done it through television, with the help of a handful of influential French-Canadian artists and professionals.

Conclusion

The contributions of Lloyd, Farrally, Franca and Chiriaeff to ballet in Canada are enormous, and must be acknowledged with gratitude. However, the historical narrative must also be widened to examine the communities, the boards of directors, producers, volunteers and audience members, who sustained the women and their ballet groups. Too often, the history has been written without a full appreciation of these fundamental supporters. The Winnipeg Ballet Club, for example, went through its first decade as a wholly voluntary operation. In Toronto, the National Ballet Company began as an idea of three society women who decided the city needed its own ballet and then set out to find a suitable artistic director. Once Celia Franca had arrived and assumed command of the artistic side, the three women built up an impressive network of National Ballet Guilds. These Winnipeg and Toronto volunteers were practical patrons, because their contributions were usually given in practical ways: by sewing costumes, making sandwiches, putting up posters, painting sets, stuffing envelopes. During the time when the companies could not afford a proper administrative structure to support the artistic side, volunteers did that vital work for years.

Ludmilla Chiriaeff's company was the smallest of the three, and she never developed the same organized groups of volunteers that were found in the other two cities. She relied instead on her television producers to provide her with access to an audience, a venue, music, costumes and sets; they were practical patrons of another sort, not writing personal cheques or making sandwiches, but rather patrons who put the resources of a large institution at Chiriaeff's disposal over her company's first five years. Later on, she was helped in practical ways by her Board of Directors, who aligned her with a segment of French-Canadian society who became influential in the 1960s.

Canada did not have a royal court or dozens of wealthy art patrons to tempt an ambitious artist into setting up a ballet company. But when four talented women immigrated to Canada and began the arduous task of building

221

the country's premier ballet companies, they didn't have to "waltz" alone. They had Canadian partners, practical patrons who found ways to support the women, often times with money but also with hospitality, volunteer labour and social influence. Perhaps these stories lack the glamour inherent in the histories of the old European companies, but practical patronage gave each of the companies a firm base on which they have thrived, even to the present day.

References

This essay is based on research in several Canadian archives including Dance Collection Danse (files on Gweneth Lloyd, Betty Farrally, Bernadette Carpenter); Metropolitan Toronto Reference Library, Special Collections (Janet Baldwin [Volkoff] Collection, Boris Volkoff Collection); National Archives of Canada (Canada Council Collection); National Ballet of Canada Archives (Box Aileen Woods Early Correspondence Files, Box Bob Turnbull Donation); Société Radio-Canada Archives (Biographical file on Ludmilla Chiriaeff, General file on *L'Heure du Concert*).

Blewchamp, Anna. n.d. "The Dance Education of Gweneth Lloyd." Unpublished essay, Dance Collection Danse.

Callwood, June. 1 Mar. 1949. "Ballet Rally." *Maclean's Magazine*.

Cohen, Nathan. Apr. 1959. "Celia Franca's Plans." *The Dancing Times*, 345.

Fletcher, Sheila. 1984. *Women First: The Female Tradition in English Physical Education 1880-1980*. London: Athlone Press.

Fulford, Robert. 1977. *An Introduction to the Arts in Canada*. Toronto: Copp Clark Publishing.

Lemelin, Mireille. Oct. 1978. "Ludmilla Chiriaeff." *Chatelaine*.

Linteau, Paul-André, René Durocher, Jean-Claude Robert, and François Ricard. 1991. *Quebec Since 1930*. Translated by Robert Chodos and Ellen Garmaise. Toronto: James Lorimer & Co.

Massey, Vincent. 1948. *On Being Canadian*. Toronto: J.M. Dent & Sons Ltd.

Maynard, Olga. Apr. 1971. "Purpose: Ludmilla Chiriaeff and Les Grands Ballets Canadiens." *Dance Magazine*.

Neufeld, James. 1996. *Power to Rise, The Story of the National Ballet of Canada*. Toronto: University of Toronto Press.

Pelletier, Gérard. 1984. *Years of Impatience 1950-1960*. Translated by Alan Brown. Toronto: Methuen.

Rutherford, Paul. 1990. *When Television Was Young: Primetime Canada 1952-67*. Toronto: University of Toronto Press.

Smith, Cheryl. 2000. "'Stepping Out': Canada's Early Ballet Companies, 1939-1963." Ph.D. dissertation, University of Toronto.

Stewart, Sandy, 1986. *Here's Looking at Us, A Personal History of Television in Canada*. Toronto: CBC Enterprises.

Thistle, Lauretta. Fall 1976. "The National at 25, Myth Fact and Fancy." *Dance in Canada* No. 10, 6-8.

Tumpane, Frank. 15 Nov. 1951. "Ballet Balmy." *Globe and Mail*.

Whittaker, Herbert. 1967. *Canada's National Ballet*. Toronto: McClelland and Stewart Limited.

Wyman, Max. 1978. *The Royal Winnipeg Ballet, The First Forty Years*. Toronto: Doubleday Canada.

Wyman, Max. 1989. *Dance Canada, An Illustrated History*. Vancouver: Douglas & McIntyre.

Interviews

Chiriaeff, Ludmilla. Montreal. 14-23 Feb. 1995.

Lawrence, Sheila. Montreal. 22 Feb. 1995.

Whittaker, Herbert. Toronto. 4 May 1992.

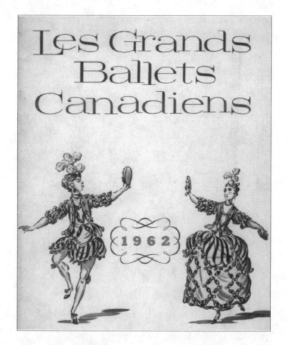

Souvenir programmes for the 1962-63 seasons of the National Ballet of Canada, the Royal Winnipeg Ballet and Les Grands Ballets Canadiens.

The Ballet Problem:
The Kirstein-Buckle Ballet Survey for the Canada Council

Katherine Cornell

The "ballet problem" was a term whispered by officials in the halls of the Canada Council in the early 1960s. As a result of the presumed ballet problem, the Council commissioned a Ballet Survey in 1962; much of this essay is based on correspondence and assessors' reports located in the Ballet Survey file. Peter Dwyer, the Arts Supervisor responsible for overseeing the Survey, hoped the Survey would answer the question: should the Canada Council fund only one ballet company? Much of the attention focused on the National Ballet of Canada. Two foreign ballet experts were finally selected to conduct the Ballet Survey. Lincoln Kirstein, co-founder of the New York City Ballet, characterized the National Ballet of Canada as "inadequate," while British ballet critic, Richard Buckle, found it "dowdy." In the end Kirstein's and Buckle's reports were submitted to the Canada Council but were never released, and their recommendations were not implemented. Since then, the Ballet Survey has been virtually forgotten.[1]

The Survey cost the Canada Council $15,000, which in 1962, was a significant portion of the money allocated to dance by the Council (Ballet Survey 1962). It appears that the Survey occurred because certain bureaucrats in the Canada Council wanted reassurance from abroad to determine which Canadian ballet companies were viable and worthy of funding, yet the assessors' recommendations were never directly applied because of the implications for the personnel involved in the Council and in the companies. They all had different visions of what dance in Canada should be, so the inevitable solution was "laissez danser."[2]

In the early 1960s the three officials most involved in the granting process

---

[1] This essay is a condensed version of my Major Research Paper for the M.A. in Dance at York University. Cheryl Smith includes a detailed chapter entitled "The Infamous Survey" in her recent University of Toronto Ph.D. history dissertation, "'Stepping Out': Canada's Early Ballet Companies, 1939-1963." Remarkably, Smith and I were both inspired to investigate the Ballet Survey because of a footnote. The footnote appeared in a seminal article about the first ten years of the Canada Council written by Jack L. Granatstein (see references).

[2] "Laissez danser" appeared to be the path of least resistance when it came to the ballet problem. The chapter on ballet in the Canada Council's 1963-64 *Annual Report* used the term "Laissez danser" (leave them to dance) to characterize the bureaucrats' frustration with the ballet problem. See *The Canada Council Annual Report for 1963-64* (Mortimer Ltd. 1964), 17.

for ballet at the Canada Council were Claude Bissell, the President; Albert Trueman, the Director; and Peter Dwyer, the Arts Supervisor. Dwyer, an Oxford graduate and playwright, had worked in British military intelligence prior to immigrating to Canada to take a position in security sections of both the Canadian Research Council and the Privy Council offices. He joined the Canada Council in 1958 (Cornell 1998: 7).

Of the three bureaucrats, Dwyer took the most interest in the ballet problem, since he had the unenviable job of administering the entire Arts Section (Woodcock 1985: 57-60). After establishing granting procedures in 1957, the Canada Council gave the National Ballet $50,000 (with a guarantee of another $50,000 in 1958); the Royal Winnipeg Ballet $20,000; and the Council also offered to fund Les Grands Ballets Canadiens even though it had not yet applied for funding (Granatstein 1984: 454-57). As historian J.L. Granatstein explained, "Excellence was the goal but regionalism was a fact of Canadian life" (449). In a sparsely populated country, access to the arts became a primary tenet of the Council. The Council's initial generosity led to repeated requests by the National Ballet for additional funding, which the Council funding met, thus encouraging the company to make further requests. During the 1958-59 granting season, the National Ballet received $85,000, the Royal Winnipeg $32,600 and Les Grands Ballets Canadiens $8,000 (Canada Council 1960: 21). (For the companies' complete budgets for this year see figure 2). Despite increased funding, the income gap between what the Canadian ballet companies made at the box office and their expenses continued to widen.[3]

The ballet problem included several complex issues, among them regional representation and artistic standards, but, in 1959, the Council's main concern was the financial instability of the three ballet companies. This had led to the commissioning of the Kenneth Carter Survey of 1959. Despite his lack of background in the arts, Carter, an eminent Toronto accountant, assessed all three companies' records, audiences and markets; he also commented on the current state and the future of ballet. He suggested that the Toronto-based National Ballet appeared the strongest of the three. At the conclusion of his report, Carter acknowledged that ballet "clearly require[s] the continued support of the Canada Council" (Carter 1959).

After the publication of the Carter Survey, the National Ballet successfully applied to the Council once again for an emergency grant of an additional $20,000 to add to their initial operating grant for 1958-59. Then, in 1960, only months after they had been awarded an $85,000 operating grant for the 1959-60 season, the National Ballet again asked the Council for assistance to address the company's $180,000 deficit. At this point the Council refused, because it could not justify assisting the company without further investigation. Carter suggested that Guy Glover, a noted Canadian arts critic, begin a critical investigation into the artistic quality of the National Ballet.

---

[3] Baumol and Bowen demonstrated in their research on the performing arts income gap that "the live performing arts cannot expect to pay for themselves without subsidies." See *Performing Arts – The Economic Dilemma* (1966: vii).

As a result Glover was commissioned to write a report on the state of Canadian ballet. In addition, Dwyer, under instructions from the Council's director Trueman, also wrote to Lincoln Kirstein, the wealthy co-founder of the New York City Ballet, in August 1961, about the advisability of conducting a survey. In his letter Dwyer stated that, at present, Canada's three ballet companies "lack clear artistic policies, sufficient discipline in training, and adequate standards of decor and costumes" (Ballet Survey 1962). Kirstein responded with a range of grand suggestions, going so far as to suggest that "an Administrator would be hunted by the Canadian Mounties" to administer a proposed Canadian ballet academy. The density and intricacy of Kirstein's response affirmed Council administrators' intention to form a Ballet Survey committee. And so the Survey was born.

Dwyer corresponded with various people in the ballet world, first to get advice on potential committee members and then to invite certain experts to join the committee. Fernand Nault, an internationally recognized French-Canadian dancer and teacher working with American Ballet Theatre, was among those invited to join the survey committee. Dwyer succinctly summarized the ballet problem in a letter to Nault: "The difficulty which we face is to provide subsidies to three companies out of an amount of approximately $150,000 a year. Indeed the question is whether the country as a whole can in fact afford three separate companies, and in particular whether it can afford the extremely expensive National Ballet of Canada" (Ballet Survey 1962). Dwyer's intentions were clear, to limit the grants for the ballet community to one exclusive company. In a letter to Council President Bissell, in May 1961, Dwyer proposed restructuring the funding to support one truly national institution entitled "Ballet Canada." This conglomerate flagship company would tour the nation and act as ambassadors for Canada abroad. Dwyer probably felt his plan would be economically preferable to the assortment of dancers assembled within the three existing institutions (Ballet Survey 1962). This idea seemed logical and feasible in principle but, as anticipated, the three companies raised some serious objections.

According to correspondence in the Ballet Survey file, the Council was eager to get George Balanchine on side as a member of, or consultant to, the Ballet Survey committee. Dwyer felt that Balanchine's opinion carried great weight in the dance community and was necessary for a survey of this magnitude. In a November 1961 memo to colleagues at the Canada Council, Trueman stated that Fernand Nault, a French-Canadian dancer and ballet master from the American Ballet Theatre; Guy Glover, a Montreal dance critic and film producer; and Tom Patterson, founder of the Stratford Shakespearean Festival, along with Richard Buckle, British dance critic, would form the Survey committee even though some of them had not responded in writing to the request. Balanchine and his associate Kirstein, if they agreed, would act as consultants to this committee of four (Ballet Survey 1962). Dwyer and Trueman quickly discovered that administering a committee of this stature was problematic because the eclectic experts did not "see eye to eye with others" (Ballet Survey 1962). Balanchine suggested that his approach did not coincide with that of any of the other possible candidates who were untrained in Russian ballet technique (Ballet Survey 1962). It seemed that Balanchine did not want to work with this committee.

As a result, the direction of the Ballet Survey changed drastically. Dwyer never informed the other committee members in writing of Balanchine's views. Luckily for Dwyer, most of the Canadian contingent of the proposed committee dissolved without Dwyer having to explain to them that they lacked authority next to the international prominence of Balanchine and Buckle. Only Glover's involvement in the Ballet Survey continued to prove awkward for the Council, since he had already expressed willingness to participate. Eventually Balanchine's schedule became a huge impediment to the cooperative endeavour. He finally sent Kirstein in his place, apparently unaware of how contentious the situation would become with Kirstein involved. The addition of Kirstein compounded the project because "his vast disapproval of all the works of the National Ballet of Canada [was] so well known that his association with any group of advisers would be very badly received" (Ballet Survey 1962). Regardless of the opposition, Peter Dwyer succumbed to the pressures and agreed on individual reports from Kirstein and Buckle.

The debate surrounding the National Ballet dominated Council corre- spondence about the ballet problem. Bissell stated that "the National Ballet [was] presumably happy about the prospect of facing very high-level criticism" (Ballet Survey 1962). Arthur Gelber, President of the National Ballet Board of Directors, held a distinctive status during this Survey because the ballet problem could be summarized in one unspoken question: could the Canada Council afford the National Ballet? Gelber, an inaugural member of the Board of Directors of the National Ballet and its President from 1961 to 1963, devoted his life to Canadian culture from the inception of the National Ballet in 1951 onwards. Later he served as both Director of the Ontario Arts Council and the National Arts Centre. He assumed a key role in the ballet problem as defender of the National Ballet's reputation.

As founding artistic director of the National Ballet in 1951, Celia Franca modelled the company directly after Ninette de Valois' Sadler's Wells Ballet. Positive initial reviews encouraged the young company; notably Lois Smith and her husband David Adams promptly became the most popular leading dancers. The novelty of the company's original accomplishments soon wore off and "stringent criticism of its shortcomings became the dominant public tone" (Neufeld 1996: 80). By 1960 journalists like Lauretta Thistle, of the *Ottawa Citizen*, began to question supporting the National Ballet with public funds. Thistle stated that "any group which has got up to an annual budget of $857,000 and still has an artistic policy as muddled as the National Ballet's should be forced to stop and consider its position" (*Ottawa Citizen* 13 Feb. 1960: 22). Regardless of the criticism, supporters of the National Ballet pressed for increased funding as a solution to their artistic needs. The company aspired to the total

$150,000 designated for dance at the Canada Council.[4] The National Ballet of Canada Board believed that this support could solve the company's problems.

The relationship between the Royal Winnipeg Ballet and the National Ballet of Canada was adversarial from the start. Franca ignited the rivalry between the Winnipeg Ballet and the future National Ballet when she wrote of the 1950 Ballet Festival, which featured Canada's only professional dance institution – the Winnipeg Ballet – stating that "there is evidence of some bad training" and there were few dancers of professional calibre (quoted in Swoboda Fall 1995: 13). Then, during the National Ballet's 1954 tour of the United States and Western Canada, sponsorships dwindled and Franca appealed for funds from the stage, even in Winnipeg. This action incited Gweneth Lloyd to purchase space for a letter in the *Toronto Evening Telegram*, on January 25, next to the National Ballet's performance advertisements, reminding the ballet-going public that "While it is regrettable that one company finds itself unable to remain solvent despite generous public support, it would be more regrettable that the hard-working young dancers should be misled and disillusioned regarding their opportunities in the future" (Neufeld 1996: 55). This letter sparked controversy and considerable commentary. The writer Wendy Michener observed in *Canadian Forum* that "Canadian ballet will not have a leg to stand on unless the two legs can refrain from kicking each other" (Mar. 1954: 277). Michener concluded by saying there appeared no reason for both companies not to exist in a country as vast as Canada. The rivalry for support continued, to a certain extent because of the very existence of the Canada Council with its competitive evaluation policies.

Many people associated with the National Ballet felt it could rightfully assume a place as the only Canadian dance institution, despite its problematic financial history, and perceived artistic shortcomings. Even when Kirstein became an assessor, the National Ballet still defended its claim. The Board solicited the opinion of British journalist A.V. Coton of *Dance and Dancers* magazine on both the National Ballet and the Royal Winnipeg, to reassert publicly that the National Ballet maintained international standards (perhaps anticipating an unflattering assessment from Kirstein). Coton had nothing but praise for the National Ballet's production of Balanchine's *Concerto Barocco*. This endorsement from abroad reinforced the company's cause. Coton also countered the entire purpose of the Ballet Survey by stating in the *Toronto Star*: "I was equally surprised to find that some Canadians appear to think [three companies] is too much ballet for one country" (24 Feb. 1962: 27). Gelber then defended the National Ballet's claim to the largest percentage of funding during the Buckle-Kirstein Survey, because he firmly believed that the Canada Council would allocate the support its title denoted. The National Ballet had everything to lose in the Ballet Survey, and the Royal Winnipeg Ballet and Les Grands Ballets Canadiens had everything to gain.

---

[4] Franca admitted in the draft version of her report at the Annual General meeting of 1961, that the tenth anniversary season had been a disaster and that the company desperately needed both artistic and financial rejuvenation (See Neufeld 1996: 79-80).

Politics and Perseverance ─────────────────────────────

Kathleen Richardson, a member of the Winnipeg Ballet's Board of Directors, President of the Board from 1957 to 1961 and an influential patron, did not really play an integral role in the Buckle-Kirstein Survey, because she concerned herself mostly with the Winnipeg season. Arnold Spohr, the new Artistic Director and a former danseur with the Royal Winnipeg Ballet, brought the company into a new era of recognition but he, too, was more concerned with the company's immediate needs than its place in Canadian dance at the time of the Ballet Survey. Spohr scheduled an impressive season, which included Balanchine's challenging *Pas de Dix* and Agnes de Mille's *The Bitter Weird*, a balletic version of the musical *Bridgadoon*.[5] The 1961 season irrevocably changed the Royal Winnipeg Ballet for the better. One of the Vice-Presidents characterized the company's activities by saying "we've turned the corner" ("Bolshoi Duo, DeMille Ballet Coming to RWB" 10 Aug. 1961: 72). Most impressively the season's loss was only $4,732.[6] The Royal Winnipeg Ballet kept to itself and catered to a western audience by frequently using original choreography that concentrated on local themes, by recruiting guest performers known to their audiences and by dancing within their financial means (Wyman 1978: 112-13).

The Royal Winnipeg Ballet united the community. Co-founder Gweneth Lloyd has been credited with bringing ballet to the Canadian west and creating a western Canadian style of ballet. "She made out of nothing and sold to the people of Winnipeg, Manitoba (a city whose motto is 'Commerce, Prudence, Industry' and whose escutcheon displays one buffalo, one locomotive and three sheaves of wheat) the Ballet: a traditional, glamorous, sophisticated, complicated art-form. Winnipeg loved it" (Fulford 1977: 96). Beyond being the local politicians' pride, the Royal Winnipeg Ballet fostered Canadian content in its repertoire as well. Ballets, such as Lloyd's *Shadow on the Prairie*, spoke to the average person as well as to the intellectual. The company demonstrated its commitment to the community by encouraging Canadian talent such as Brian Macdonald, Don Gillies and Arnold Spohr (Morriss 13 Aug. 1960: 8-9). For their twenty-first season, in 1959, the company celebrated in the Legislative Building, with the dancers performing alongside the Winnipeg Symphony. This event also demonstrated the Royal Winnipeg Ballet's devotion to Manitoba first.

Both Richardson and Spohr appeared, by and large, uninvolved with the Ballet Survey. Very little correspondence appeared in Dwyer's files from Winnipeg. Many journalists, like James Lorimer writing for *Performing Arts in Canada*, recognized that "ballet in Winnipeg has relied on large private

─────────────────────────────

[5] De Mille was also considered as a possible member of the Ballet Survey committee before she committed to working with the Royal Winnipeg Ballet as a guest choreographer.

[6] The Royal Winnipeg Ballet's deficit had been $15,014 the previous year and in comparison with the National Ballet's deficit of $202,065, the deficit was minimal. Records of the National Ballet's deficit appear in the "National Ballet of Canada Administration file, Financial Statements, 1959," National Ballet of Canada Archives. Reference to the Royal Winnipeg Ballet's deficit appears in "Bolshoi Duo, DeMille Ballet Coming to RWB," *Winnipeg Tribune* (10 Aug. 1961), 72.

contributions to continue"(1962: 49). But Richardson and Spohr did not react to the whole affair as did the National Ballet or Les Grands Ballets Canadiens, perhaps because they knew the Royal Winnipeg would survive even if the Canada Council funds ceased. In conversations with Buckle, Spohr did not seem concerned about the Council's questions or money. Richardson said she did not care what happened elsewhere in Canada, she only cared about Winnipeg (Ballet Survey 1962). Critics enjoyed the company's work, especially the Balanchine and de Mille choreography. According to James Lorimer, Herbert Whittaker of the *Globe and Mail* aptly summarized the Royal Winnipeg Ballet as "a Canadian ballet company which has been buffeted about but, in struggling to survive, has evolved its own style. It is neither English, nor European, nor for that matter, a reflection of the ballets of the United States." It is a conglomeration, how typically Canadian (Lorimer 1962: 49).

Like the Royal Winnipeg Ballet and the National Ballet, Les Grands Ballets Canadiens had a feisty, dominant immigrant woman at the helm. Ludmilla Chiriaeff founded Les Ballets Chiriaeff and her school in the early 1950s to produce ballet initially for the *CBC Concert Hour* television programme. "The group quickly developed a reputation for innovative choreography in the new medium and attracted the interest of no less a figure than Balanchine. Chiriaeff's pioneering work soon became a significant part of Québecois cultural self-expression" (Neufeld 1996: 91). Even though Chiriaeff's company was the youngest in Canada, she defended its right to equivalent public support when the Ballet Survey began. The link she established with Balanchine's company would prove very profitable when the reports were finally submitted.

Chiriaeff began her company on the television screen and this strategy soon emerged as a highly advantageous decision on her part. The group cultivated its following before it even stepped into an expensive theatre. The company represented the French-Canadian culture through dance; the Quiet Revolution and the empowerment of the French-Canadian people occurred at the same time as Chiriaeff was establishing her company. She astutely pro-grammed ballets with French-Canadian themes along with contemporary classics. For example, during its first incorporated season in 1957 and on Saint Jean Baptiste Day, no less, the company premiered the highly popular *Suite Canadienne* ("Chiriaeff, Ludmilla" 1993: 269). Chiriaeff, like Lloyd, employed Canadian themes and choreographers over the classics, and this strategy served the company well, especially in the eyes of the Canada Council.

Chiriaeff, knowing that it would take many years to produce highly trained dancers, established a professional school, L'École Supérieure de la Danse, at the same time as the company in 1957. She trained her students in the Russian ballet tradition but in a Canadian context. Of Chiriaeff's style and dancers, Herbert Whittaker stated, "while it may not be essentially French or very Grand it is undeniably Canadian" (Wyman 1989: 86). Les Grands Ballets Canadiens' inauguration made a definite impact, due in part to Canada Council funding from the onset, but primarily because of Chiriaeff's keen professional sensibilities as translated into the company's early productions.

Politics and Perseverance

The strengths and shortcomings of all three institutions were well known when Glover, and then Buckle and Kirstein embarked on their task of assessing Canadian ballet. "By the early 1960s, Les Grands Ballets Canadiens had become a strong regional company, competing with the Royal Winnipeg and the National Ballet, not only for the attention of the Canada Council, but also for the financial support of the public and patrons. The two smaller companies could claim a clearly defined regional base and regional identity" (Neufeld 1996: 81). Les Grands Ballets Canadiens and the Royal Winnipeg Ballet carved out a niche and identity for themselves while the National Ballet floundered despite strong local support. The Council questioned if the National Ballet could live up to its name. It also wondered if either of the two regional companies had the potential to overshadow the others and become the only bone fide recipient of ballet grants from the Canada Council. Each organization had its own explanations for why it deserved the blank cheque: we're the biggest; we're the oldest; we're the best. The assessors had to decide, individually, if any of these claims had validity.

Glover was Canada's authority on dance in the 1950s. A Montreal-based critic, he knew many Canadian artists because of his work with the National Film Board. In 1950, Glover assumed the role of adjudicator for the third annual Ballet Festival held that year in Montreal.[7] Unlike many other Canadian newspaper journalists, he was not afraid to be critical of Canadian ballet, regardless of the age of the institutions he critiqued. He said of both the National Ballet and the Royal Winnipeg Ballet in 1953 that the "companies themselves [were] lulled into security by the praises of local critics and the uncritical applause of local audiences" (1953: 509). Statements such as these caught the attention of individuals at the Canada Council.

Glover's experience as a dance adjudicator and writer made him an obvious candidate to sit on the committee for the Ballet Survey. He submitted an initial report to Dwyer early in 1961, from research he had already conducted in late 1960. It is still unclear if Glover even knew that his comments would ultimately not be circulated as part of the Ballet Survey. In his fourteen-page report, Glover commented on the National Ballet's performances and then briefly on Canadian ballet in general. He believed both the Royal Winnipeg Ballet and Les Grands Ballets Canadiens responded to provincial audiences with more success than the National Ballet. Accordingly, Glover recommended that no further aid be considered for any company unless recommended by an artistic advisory committee. He urged the Canada Council to create this committee including non-partisan ballet critics, professional writers, dramatists, designers and artists. He then suggested that blanket "no questions asked" operational grants had proven part of the ballet problem and, as a result, he felt that Canada Council grants should be given only for specific projects, training and touring. Finally, Glover stressed his

---

[7] The Canadian Ballet Festival Association began in 1948. The group created an annual event where all of Canada's aspiring professional dancers could perform on the same stage. The first two festivals were held in Winnipeg (1948) and Toronto (1949).

hope for further unity and communication between the amateur and professional dance communities in Canada (Ballet Survey 1962). In the end, as the only Canadian critic involved in the Ballet Survey, he voiced some well-founded criticisms of the country's largest company; his corresponding recommendations supported, in detail, his unique understanding of the Canadian condition, a point of view neither of the well-known foreign assessors could provide.

Certain individuals at the Canada Council did not appreciate Glover's comments about Canadian ballet. Bissell's statement, in a letter dated May 1961, characterized his belief in the regional predispositions of Canadian critics: "I know of no particular reason why one should pay too much attention to the Montreal critics. What I suggested ... was that [the office] should try to compile representative criticism from the United States, where, presumably, the comments would be free of the kind of national bitterness that so often affects the Canadian scene. Mr. Glover's comments are certainly magisterially impressive, but I am wondering whether he does not represent the apex of preciosite" (Ballet Survey 1962). Ultimately, we may never know why Glover's report was disregarded, but an examination of the Buckle-Kirstein Survey proves that Glover's assessment had validity; his observations were paralleled in the reports of Buckle and Kirstein.

Buckle, an old school chum of Dwyer's, placed himself in a difficult situation by agreeing to participate in the Survey of Canadian ballet. He knew that Dwyer wanted only one ballet company left standing in the end. If Buckle criticized the National Ballet of Canada, he might as well have said the Sadler's Wells did not produce anyone of worth. If he denigrated the work of the Royal Winnipeg Ballet, he might as well have said the Queen had no standards. Needless to say the British connection made his job more difficult than that of the other critics. Dwyer desperately needed a "big name" in British ballet included in the Ballet Survey to satisfy the companies under review and especially Gelber of the National Ballet. Buckle provided a knowledgeable, experienced and internationally respected point of view. His diplomatic observations of the individual companies and his summary on the future of Canadian ballet correlated in many ways with the general Canadian critical opinion and in particular with Glover's initial assessment.

Buckle's conclusions characterized his acute awareness of the politics of the situation. He outlined five possible solutions to the ballet problem, each of which addressed the bureaucrats' and/or assessors' concerns.[8] Buckle's five points diplomatically addressed the other proposals at hand, often playing the role of devil's advocate. For example, point number two stated that removing funding from any of the three companies would be inhumane at this stage of development, which opposed Kirstein's suggestions to form a new company located in Montreal; and point number three explained why merging the three

[8] There is no documentation in the Canada Council files about whether Buckle knew of the other reports or opinions but his conclusions certainly intimate that he was well aware of the entire situation.

companies into one would be a financial and political nightmare, which contradicted Dwyer's original intentions to end up with one company. In the last paragraph of Buckle's report, he recognized what he saw as the crucial issues: full-time employment for Canadian dancers, honourable recognition of the pioneers and a need to consolidate their work. This eloquent, polite and diplomatic essay completely supported Glover's criticism, but it contrasted with Kirstein's report in tone, if not in content.

Kirstein formulated his feelings about ballet in Canada well before he submitted his final report in 1962. When the suggestion of a survey first arose, Balanchine's name surfaced at the top of the wish list, primarily because of his knowledge and international clout. Dwyer originally contacted both Balanchine and Kirstein in the summer of 1961. Kirstein burned his undeniable bias into the page of a letter he sent Dwyer in August of that year. The language of the letter itself took on a condescending tone, with comments that sent shock waves through the Council and all who read it. First, he asserted his belief in the necessity for one Canadian ballet company. Remarkably he felt none of the three existing companies were worthy. He frankly stated that all three should be cut off from public funding. Kirstein thought it the best alternative for Canadian ballet and used analogies like the starvation of sickly fruit to save the young sapling. His letter must have alerted Dwyer and the other bureaucrats to his opinionated point of view, especially about the National Ballet of Canada. The criticisms in his report did not waiver much from his original attitude when first contacted about the possibility of participating in the Survey but, at the same time, his final recommendations approximated Glover's conclusions, with an American touch of egotism.

Not surprisingly, Kirstein felt that Les Grands Ballets Canadiens, with its Russian heritage, had the most potential of the three companies. He prescribed that Canadian ballet start over again with Montreal as a focal point because of "its spiritual proximity to New York City and State" (Ballet Survey Buckle Survey 1962). He also outlined five steps for the future of Canadian ballet as it stood in the triumvirate format. First, he wanted a committee of sponsors and bureaucrats instituted, in an effort to circumvent any further competitive or regional issues. Secondly, he insisted that an inventory of acceptable choreography for Canadian ballet companies be outlined. Thirdly, he fervently recommended the participation of good Canadian composers, poets and painters in the future. Fourthly, and most importantly, Kirstein suggested performances "in a different center each year of a combined season, showing the best works of each company, plus one pool-work combining the best of the whole Canadian ballet world." And finally, he predictably suggested a universal switch from the British method of training to the Russian. These recommendations, along with his comments on the companies, did not stray far from Glover's or Buckle's reports.

After a year of correspondence, a multitude of meetings and $15,000 worth of advice, the Canada Council chose to ignore the recommendations of Buckle and Kirstein. The preliminary comments on the unfinished assessments, located in the *Canada Council's Annual Report of 1962/63* terminated the public discussion of the Kirstein-Buckle Ballet Survey. Presumably written by Dwyer, the six-paragraph summary assumed a poetic tone: "Someone has said that rumour is like a little wind. In the world of ballet it is a gale. We wish we could temper this wind ... we might summarize our purpose by quoting Mallarme's *L'Après Midi d'un Faune*: "Ces nymphes, je les veux perpetuer" (14).

Lauretta Thistle, of the *Ottawa Citizen*, aptly concluded the purpose of the Kirstein-Buckle Ballet Survey and its end result in her 1964 article for *The Ballet Annual and Year Book*: "The unspoken question behind the Canada Council's attempt at an impartial investigation of these companies was whether one of them was worthy of a virtual monopoly on Council funds, that is of being elevated to real 'national' status. Evidently the Council has decided not" (67). The Survey itself has drifted from public memory. Later changes in Canada Council policy would be its greatest influence and legacy. The Ballet Survey helped to establish the patterns that would be used in granting public sponsorship to ballet. From 1962 onwards, the three flagship ballet companies received grants conforming generally to the 50%, 25%, 25% split, first utilized in 1963 (Neufeld 1996: 244). If a company's status was ever in question again, it would be assessed individually on artistic merit by a jury of peers. The Kirstein-Buckle Survey affected the history of Canadian ballet because the three critics rejected Dwyer's notion of exclusive funding for a single national company. Today Canada proudly presents several distinctively Canadian ballet companies of international standard, which few people realize could have been eclipsed if Dwyer had solved the ballet problem.

Figure 1: Chronology

Oct. 1958	Peter Dwyer writes Kenneth Carter regarding financial Survey
Jan. 1959	Carter Survey submitted
Nov. 1960	Glover attends National Ballet performances in Montreal
Jan. 1961	Glover submits his Report
May 1961	Canadian Conference of the Arts meeting held in Toronto
	Bissell writes Dwyer
	Dwyer responds to Bissell's letter
Aug. 1961	Dwyer writes Kirstein for advice on the ballet problem
	Kirstein responds to Dwyer
Sep. 1961	Dwyer starts to search for potential jurors
	Canada Council Press Release announcing the Ballet Survey
Nov. 1961	Trueman's memo to the Council, listing committee members, and Balanchine and Kirstein as consultants to the Ballet Survey
	Canada Council Press Release about Balanchine's participation
	Dwyer's assistant sends a letter to Glover about visiting Winnipeg
Feb. 1962	Canada Council Press Release about Buckle's visit
	Buckle travels to Ottawa, Toronto, Montreal and Winnipeg
Mar. 1962	Balanchine declines and Kirstein travels to Montreal, Toronto and Winnipeg to attend performances
	Canada Council's Annual Report of 1961/62 released
Apr. 1962	Buckle submits his report
May 1962	Kirstein submits his report

Figure 2:

This chart appears on page 21 of the *Third Annual Report of the Canada Council* for 1958-59. The material was compiled by Kenneth Carter. I assume this is the most accurate depiction of the three companies' finances at the time despite some minor contradictions in newspaper articles.

	Expenditure	Revenue	Operating Deficit	Donation	City Grants	Provincial Grants	Canada Council Grants
National Ballet	$608,090	344,312	213,778	111,577	18,000	-	85,000
Royal Winnipeg Ballet	$115,215	47,711	67,504	33,484	-	-	32,600
Les Grands Ballets Canadiens	$34,021	5,675	28,346	2,135	3,000	5,000	8,000
TOTAL	$757,326	447,698	309,628	147,196	21,000	5,000	125,000

236

References

Arah, Jessica. 1993. "Chiriaeff, Ludmilla." *Internatonal Dictionary of Ballet.* Vol. 1. Detroit, MI: St. James Press, 268-70.

"Ballet Makes the National Scene." Mar. 1961. *Performing Arts in Canada* 11: 1, 2-3.

Ballet Survey. 1962. File RG63. Volume 1348. National Archives of Canada.

Ballet Survey Buckle Survey. 1962. File RG63. Volume 1348. National Archives of Canada.

Baumol, William, and William Bowen. 1966. *Performing Arts – The Economic Dilemma.* Cambridge, Massachusetts: Massachusetts Institute of Technology.

"Bolshoi Duo, DeMille Ballet Coming to RWB." 10 Aug. 1961. *Winnipeg Tribune,* 72.

The Canada Council Annual Reports for 1959-64. 1960-64. Ottawa: Canada Council.

Carter Survey (Ballet). 1959. File RG63. Volume 1351. National Archives of Canada.

Cornell, Katherine. 1998. "The Ballet Problem: The Issue of Exclusive Funding in the Dance Office of the Canada Council." Major Research Paper, York University.

Coton, A.V. 24 Feb. 1962. "U.K. Critic Looks at Our Ballet." *Toronto Star,* 27.

Coton, A.V. June-July 1962. "English Critic Praises Concerto Barocco Ballet." *National Ballet News* 3: 3, 1.

Fulford, Robert. 1977. *An Introduction to the Arts in Canada.* Toronto: Copp Clark in association with the Citizenship Branch, Department of the Secretary of State of Canada and Publishing Centre, Supply and Services Canada.

Glover, Guy. Spring 1951. "Reflections on Canadian Ballet, 1950." *Canadian Art* 8: 3, 115-19, 125-27.

Glover, Guy. 1953. "Ballet as a Canadian Art." *Queen's Quarterly* 60: 501-13.

Granatstein, Jack L. Dec. 1984. "Culture and Scholarship: The First Ten Years of the Canada Council." *Canadian Historical Review* 65: 441-74.

Lorimer, James. 1962. "Royal Winnipeg Ballet." *Performing Arts in Canada* 1: 3, 48-49.

Michener, Wendy. Mar. 1954. "Ballet in Canada." *Canadian Forum* 33: 277.

Michener, Wendy. Apr. 1956. "The Canadian Ballet." *Canadian Forum* 36: 14-15.

Morriss, Frank. 13 Aug. 1960. "Royal Ballet of the Prairies had Danced to Maturity." *Globe and Mail*, 8-9.

Neufeld, James. 1996. *Power to Rise*. Toronto: University of Toronto Press.

Swoboda, Victor. Fall 1995. "The Third Ballet Festival." *Dance International* 23: 3, 10-13.

Thistle, Lauretta. 13 Feb. 1960. "Getting Unwelcome Reputation As Repository For Cast-Offs Of 30s." *Ottawa Citizen* 22.

Thistle, Lauretta. 1964. "Ballet in Canada, 1962-63." In Clarke, Mary and Arnold Haskell, eds. *The Ballet Annual and Year Book 1964*. London: Adam and Charles Black.

Woodcock, George. 1985. *Strange Bedfellows: The State and the Arts in Canada*. Vancouver and Toronto: Douglas and McIntyre.

Wyman, Max. 1978. *The Royal Winnipeg Ballet: The First 40 Years*. Toronto: Doubleday.

Wyman, Max. 1989. *Dance Canada: An Illustrated History*. Vancouver: Douglas and McIntyre.

The History of a Devolving Nationalism:
Three Dance Films of the National Film Board of Canada

Jody Bruner

Nationalism is a powerful ideology that both unifies a country by minimizing differences within it and maintains that country's autonomy by highlighting differences between it and other nations. This essay looks specifically at the varying degrees to which three National Film Board of Canada (NFB) dance films, *Ballet Festival* (1949), *Shadow on the Prairie* (1953) and *Pas de Deux* (1967), have perpetuated the goals of Canadian national interest. Produced at different moments in history, they reflect an increasingly centrifugal nationalism. This discussion proceeds, first of all, by considering the historical and political circumstances surrounding each film. In each case, these circumstances are translated into nationalist policies. In looking at these films I am particularly interested in nationalist cultural policy, especially legislation concerning the National Film Board. Finally, I look at the particular films in question, with an interest in how they each reflect the prevalent national mood.

There are two principal ways in which traditional cultural nationalism in Canada works to both unify the country, and protect it from infiltration from the United States: on the symbolic level nationalism fosters the myth of the North, and on the practical level the nation controls the media. The myth of the North promotes a sense of national unity, identity and pride. Carl Berger, in "The True North Strong and Free," an essay found in *Nationalism in Canada*, describes the history and characteristics of this phenomenon. The myth of the North was first stated coherently by Robert Grant Haliburton, who lamented the fact that Confederation had been created with as little excitement among the masses as if a joint-stock company had been formed (Berger 1966: 5). For Haliburton, Canada's northern qualities assured its future as a dominant nation, and should be celebrated. The very fact of northernness connoted strength, hardiness, vigour and purity. Canadian northernness defined Canada against America and the South. According to the myth, southernness connoted effeminacy, voluptuous living and the degeneration of character. The myth of the North also allowed for greater unity between the French- and English-speaking Canadians, who were naturally divided by language, religion and origins, because both showed a fitness and willingness to cope with the harshness of the climate.

Not only is Canada a northern country, it is also vast and sparsely populated. This geographical and demographic characteristic is a huge challenge for the goals of nationalism. Western Canadians, for example, may have more in common with their neighbours in the United States than with their compatriots on the other side of the continent. Canadian nationalism has traditionally dealt with this by centrally or federally controlling the communications media. Also, by prohibiting or limiting American ownership and control of media in Canada, public ownership provides a way of protecting that unity from the threat of cultural absorbtion and invasion by the United States. I will explore some aspects of the history of one such publicly controlled communications medium: the National Film Board of Canada from which all three films have emerged.

The birth of the NFB was possible because of the psychological state of the nation. It was born at a time when Canada had a strong sense of self-esteem and independence. In the years after the First World War, Canada slowly evolved away from the traditionally strong identification with Britain and began to identify itself as a North American nation. Ramsay Cook, in "Landscape Painting and National Sentiment in Canada," an essay in *The Maple Leaf Forever*, explains that although prior to World War I Canada identified strongly with Britain, participation in that war led to a sense of revulsion towards Europe coupled with a sense of pride in Canada's contributions to and achievements in the war effort. There was a conviction that Canada's domestic concerns, including the need to restore national unity, needed first priority (1977: 174).

Along with a greater sense of a national self, Canadians also recognized a need to nurture that fragile self by protecting it from influences coming from beyond the borders of the nation, particularly from the United States. Cultural nationalist efforts during the years between the two world wars shared a strong belief in the importance of federal state action, particularly in the field of communications policy, and were derived from a fundamental commitment to public as opposed to private ownership. This tendency towards public ownership was attractive not only because the state had the resources to finance cultural survival, but also, in Cook's words, because "a statist or socialist approach to culture would in itself be evidence that Canadian culture is different from the free enterprise culture of the United States" (Bashevkin 1991: 9). One such cultural nationalist endeavour led to the establishment of the NFB.

The following brief sketch of the history of the NFB is largely drawn from C. Rodney James' *Film as a National Art* and from D.B. Jones' *Movies and Memoranda*. The medium of film was first used by the Canadian government as a national instrument to promote trade. To this end the Motion Picture Bureau (MPB) was established in 1923 as an arm of the Department of Trade and Commerce. By the mid-1930s the MPB had stopped developing because of

240

the financial restraints of the Depression and because its director, Captain Frank Badgley, had no interest in either the art or the social utility of film. But the wider possibilities of film were recognized by Ross McLean, who was private secretary to Vincent Massey, then High Commissioner to London. McLean had met John Grierson, the organizer of the Empire Marketing Board and the General Post Office film units in England, and became interested in Grierson's philosophy of the public responsibility of the motion picture. McLean convinced Massey to allow him to prepare a report on film developments in Canada and Britain. McLean's report urged that changes be made in the activities of the Bureau, and concluded with the recommendation that Grierson be invited to Canada to make a survey of the situation and to prepare a report including more specific recommendations.

Grierson's report, prepared in 1938, essentially criticized the MPB's lack of centralized power and purpose. He pointed out that there was no comprehensive sense of propaganda for Canada, and recommended a propaganda policy that would assure that the idea of Canada would be dramatized and brought into the imagination of the home country, that information about Canada would then become an integral part of the public's general knowledge, and that direct trade publicity would then be organized to make the fullest use of the pro-Canada sentiments thus created (James 1977: 672-73).

Grierson was asked to implement his recommendations, which resulted in the legislation of the 1939 Film Act. This in turn led to the establishment of the National Film Board in 1941. The mandate of the NFB was to help Canadians in all parts of Canada to understand the ways of living and the problems of Canadians in other parts. Although when attempting to implement his recommendations, Grierson had to deal with the negative forces of the vested interests of certain government departments and commercial filmmakers, he enjoyed the full support of Prime Minister William Lyon Mackenzie King. Mackenzie King saw that a strong National Film Board could help solidify and strengthen a national Canadian identity, and protect it from the threat of engulfment by the United States. According to Jones, Grierson recalls Mackenzie King commenting to him: "Wouldn't it be a great pity if Canada were to lose her sense of dependence on the Mother Country only to fall into a sense of dependence on ... 'our good neighbour to the South?'" (Jones 1981: 22).

Within months of the passing of the Film Act in 1939, Hitler moved his troops into Poland and World War II began. This meant very rapid and urgent growth for the film board, for it became an important vehicle for communication on matters of war, a source of information for citizens, and a tool of propaganda for the government. *Canada Carries On* (CCO) was the first of several film series designed for theatrical release. Its function was to dramatize all aspects of Canada's war effort. It was produced from 1940 until 1959, and *Ballet Festival*, released in 1949, is from this series. The earliest examples of CCO aimed to educate and unify the country for the war effort, and to boost morale. After the war, the new role of CCO was to interpret the whole of Canada in all its aspects. In doing this, the series became less of a newsreel, and

Volkoff Canadian Ballet dancers at the 1949 Canadian Ballet Festival held in Toronto at the Royal Alexandra Theatre.

concentrated mainly on individual feature stories. All the films in this series (including *Ballet Festival*) generally started with a concept or message, which is supported with commentary, stock-shot footage and scripted action.

Ballet Festival is an example of the post-war feature story style. It is highly interpretive, with the ubiquitous narrator explaining the value and significance of the festival for the audience. The film opens with a shot of the Royal Alexandra Theatre, the festival's venue, on opening night. Two young female dancers are running through the night and enter the theatre by the stage door. They give their names "Lillian Jarvis" and "Katherine Stewart" to the stage manager as they rush by him and dash into the dressing room, where the door slams on the camera. The dressing room, viewed briefly from without is full of excited women all preparing for their performance. The narrator then exclaims, "Made it! And just in time, too!"

We next see shots of various preparations for the performance. We see the audience purchasing their tickets, filing in, taking their seats and glancing impatiently at their watches. The dancers are seen putting on their greasepaint and costumes. They warm up in the wings, and we hear the orchestra warming up in the pit. During all this, the narrator continues:

Tonight of all nights, opening night, is no time to be late! Not with the house packed to the gods, and a full symphony orchestra and a real professional stage. The very same stage where Pavlova has danced and the Ballets Russes and the Ballet Theatre! Using these very dressing rooms! All those famous professionals from London and Paris and New York. What are people who have seen them going to think of schoolgirls and stenographers from Vancouver and Winnipeg and Hamilton? Just amateurs from Toronto or Ottawa or Montreal.

At this point, we hear the call: "Onstage for *Sylphides*! Onstage everybody!" The narrator continues, taking us into the final nervous thoughts of the young sylphs: "Almost curtain time. Suppose somebody falls, or something slips. In front of all those people. Suppose you forget what to do?" Finally, the lighting technician turns on the stage lights, and the curtain rises on *Les Sylphides*, a fragment of which is captured on film. With this performance of a great classic ballet, we see that indeed the young stenographers and schoolgirls can take their place with pride on this "real, professional stage."

With *Les Sylphides*, the Canadian dancers satisfactorily meet the benchmark of professionalism set by the foreign professionals. But the narrator's text stresses that these dancers and choreographers have also made their own uniquely Canadian contribution to dance. We learn that the Winnipeg Ballet presented an entirely Canadian Ballet (*Visages*), of which a lengthy section is shown, and that this ballet was a huge success.

The success of the festival is emphasized with shots of the dancers receiving congratulatory long distance phone calls from proud parents, opening boxes of flowers and reading telegrams. During this, the narrator explains that "the folks back home, even those who find little appeal in the ballet are caught up in the general enthusiasm, proud of their success. And proud they should be.... Hard work and determination and self-discipline are not only the basic qualities of good dancers. They are also the qualities of good citizens. And in dance after dance, all the week of the festival, these young performers demonstrate the qualities of both."

More fragments of the actual dancing are shown in extremely abbreviated although energetic form, with a bit more time allotted to Boris Volkoff's *The Red Ear of Corn*, another featured Canadian piece. What finally remains with us, as the curtain closes on closing night, are the words of the narrator, who says: "It's been a week of ovations for company after company.... It's been a week of achievement for their teachers who brought the discipline and the joy of the great tradition of ballet to Canada and whose dream is to develop out of the Canadian character a distinctively Canadian dance, a professional Canadian company and an appreciative Canadian audience." As the dancers leave the stage after their last curtain call, the narrator reminds us that "the festival is only a beginning, but it is a beginning to be proud of."

As an expression of nationalism, *Ballet Festival* is both shrill and heavy-handed. First of all, it unabashedly taps into the notion of the superiority of the northern race that accompanies the myth of the Canadian North, as described by Berger, and transforms it into a blatantly propagandistic message. The narrator of *Ballet Festival* stresses the typical "northern" qualities of the Canadian dancers ("hard work and determination and self-discipline") that make them such promising dancers and model citizens.

Not only does the film use the qualities of Canadian dancers to exemplify the qualities of good citizens, it also uses the fact of the Ballet Festival as a means of justifying Canada's nationness by associating it with a venerable past. In his introduction to *The Invention of Tradition*, Eric Hobsbawm explains that this is a typical device used by modern nations to validate themselves. One method for achieving this end is the grafting of new traditions onto old ones. In this light it is interesting to note that the aspect of newness is emphasized in the script of *Ballet Festival*. The Festival is heralded as "Canada's First National Ballet Festival."[1] "The Festival is only a beginning," the narrator informs at the film's conclusion, "but it is a beginning to be proud of." The newness of the invention is not enough in itself; it must also be associated with "tradition," which, for Hobsbawm, is characterized by invariance and continuity. The film script not only highlights the newness of ballet in Canada, but also overtly taps into the European tradition of classical ballet and aligns the Canadian dancers with this tradition. Recall that near the beginning of the film, the narrator tried to evoke the feelings of the young participants as they attempt balletic classics on "a real professional stage – the very same stage where Pavlova has danced and the Ballets Russes and the Ballet Theatre, ... all of those famous professionals from London and Paris and New York...."

The film not only manipulates the myth of the north and the tradition of ballet to suit its nationalistic agenda, but it also manipulates the actual dancing to a similar end. Although two original Canadian works are showcased (*Visage* by Gweneth Lloyd and *The Red Ear of Corn* by Boris Volkoff), they are manipulated to meet the overtly nationalist agenda of the film. While more is shown of them than of the other pieces, they are not permitted to speak for themselves choreographically, but are used to demonstrate the positive audience response, suggesting the tremendous success and achievement of native Canadian ballet. For example, the narrator announces *Visage*, a clip of it is shown and then he exclaims, "Canadian Ballet! What did they think? They loved it!" while the camera scans a wildly applauding audience.

But aesthetic weaknesses of *Ballet Festival* reflect the internal problems of the NFB during the late 1940s, and not any general post-war floundering of Canadian nationalism. Once the war ended, the NFB had to regroup for peace-time film production. The period between 1945 and 1950, when a new film act was passed renewing support for the NFB, was very difficult. Much of its funding was cut back. Also, the NFB was undergoing three different investigations. It was charged with leaking classified information in its production of films for the Department of Defence, and underwent a painful

───

[1] A previous Festival had been held in Winnipeg in 1948; however, the media tend to identify the 1949 Festival as the first despite the fact that the souvenir programme titles the 1949 Festival as the second.

244

investigation by the RCMP which resulted in the discharge of three employees. Woods-Gordon, a management consulting firm, was meanwhile conducting a thorough examination of the NFB's administrative structure and functioning. Also, the Massey Commission was exploring the involvement of government in the arts, and commercial film producers were putting pressure on the government to allow them a chance to produce the government films that were exclusively produced by the NFB. The Film Board's future looked awfully bleak in the winter of 1949-50, the same year *Ballet Festival* was produced. Although the very fact of this film's existence must be credited to the wave of nationalism that gave birth to the NFB in the late 1930s, its weaknesses as a film are due to the malaise that the NFB was undergoing in the late 1940s.

In the meantime, according to Paul Litt in *The Muses, the Masses and the Massey Commission*,

[a] confident and ambitious Canadian nationalism had grown out of the great accomplishments of the nation during World War II and the new international prominence Canada enjoyed in the postwar world. National confidence was expressed and reinforced by developments ranging from the admission of Newfoundland to Confederation to legislation making the Supreme Court of Canada the court of final appeal in the land. For a generation weaned on the "colony to nation" theme of progressive national independence, it seemed that Canada had finally come of age constitutionally, diplomatically, and militarily. A cultural nationalism that cultivated a unique cultural identity was an appropriate capstone for the nation-building process (1992: 17).

It was the task of the 1949 Royal Commission on National Development in the Arts, Letters and Sciences (known as the Massey Commission) to explore the state of Canadian culture and recommend ways in which the government could assist in its development. The findings of the Massey Commission, not surprisingly, recommended reinforcing and broadening the Canadian tradition of public commitment to the arts, letters and sciences. *Shadow on the Prairie* rides the wave of this generally euphoric nationalism and benefits aesthetically from the renewal of government support for culture.

While the Massey Commission can be seen on the one hand as a response to growing Canadian pride and nationalistic fervour, it also grew from a typical Canadian anti-Americanism. Specifically, there was a perceived threat of cultural invasion from the United States in the form of television. Although by 1949 television was not yet officially introduced in Canada, there were more than 45,000 sets situated in homes along the southern border receiving American programming (Shea 1952: 21). One of the most pressing concerns that the Massey Commission faced was to deal with whether or not, and the degree to which, television should be controlled by the government-controlled broadcasting corporation (the Canadian Broadcasting Corporation) that controlled radio.

Aside from reflecting the traditional Canadian requirement for unity and protection from the United States, the impetus behind the Massey Commission also reflects a new, more centrifugal and international identity. In *Culture in Canada*, a booklet written by Albert Shea with the express purpose of explaining the findings of the Massey Commission to the Americans, this perspective is stressed. Shea comments that the strong protectionism of the report can be understood as a declaration of cultural independence from the United States. He justifies this by arguing that Canada's cultural immaturity is due to the fact that it had always been heavily influenced by the United States without being critical enough of the influence. But he stresses that the defensiveness of the report should not be interpreted as anti-American in sentiment, but rather as a defence of the values of the whole Western world against the threat of communism. He writes:

> If we as a nation are concerned with the problem of defence, what, we may ask ourselves, are we defending? We are defending civilization, our share of it, our contribution to it. The things with which our enquiry deals are the elements which give civilization its character and meaning. It would be paradoxical to defend something which we are unwilling to strengthen and enrich, and which we even allow to decline (1952: 12).

Meanwhile, the NFB emerged from its post-World War II malaise significantly strengthened by the new 1950 Film Act. The RCMP investigation of the security leak ended with the release of the three employees who were considered security risks, and the NFB was considered purged. The Woods-Gordon study sympathetically revealed the difficulties under which the NFB had to operate. Because the findings of the Massey Commission were not published until 1951, the Woods-Gordon study was more influential in the drafting of the 1950 Film Act. Nevertheless, the findings of the Massey Report would support the nationally unifying function of the NFB. The Film Act in general gave the NFB greater strength, flexibility and access to funds while limiting government involvement. Its newly defined purpose was to "produce and distribute and to promote the production and distribution of films designed to interpret Canada to Canadians and to other nations," signalling a more international horizon than that of the 1939 Film Act. Also, the NFB was encouraged to "engage in research in film activity and to make available the results thereof to persons engaged in the production of films" (James 1977: 709). This provision led to the growth of film study and technical development and also improved the creative standards of the NFB's films.

Post-1950 films were distinctly different from the earlier NFB films. *Shadow on the Prairie* (1953), benefits directly from the increased artistic freedom of the NFB. It was produced and directed by Roger Blais. Blais, along with Bernard Devlin, was responsible for the production of French-language films, the need for which was stimulated by the coming of French language television in 1952. The Canadian Broadcasting Corporation (CBC) was unable to fill, by itself, the daily demand for hours of original French-language material, so the NFB filmmakers were appealed to for help. There was suddenly room for the filmmakers to participate, experiment and try out new ideas. Devlin and Blais did not agree on the appropriate direction to follow.

246

Blais favoured cultural programming such as adaptations of literary works by Canadian authors and a showcase for the performing arts. This was typified by his short-lived five-part series *Horizons* (1953), of which *Shadow on the Prairie* is a part. This film was adapted from the staged ballet which was choreographed by Gweneth Lloyd for the Winnipeg Ballet in 1952. The *Horizons* series also included a dramatized extract from a novel by André Giroux, an extract from a novel by Hugh MacLennan, a rehearsal of a new composition by Harry Somers by the Montreal Symphony and a mime performance by Guy Hoffman. Devlin favoured a regular television news reportage, which finally won out, mainly because it was cheaper to produce.

Shadow on the Prairie begins with the following narrative: "From the history of the Canadian West comes this story of young settlers on the raw, new prairie. Friendly neighbours welcome them with the gift of a sapling tree, symbol of hope in a tree-less land, sad symbol of a remembered home to a young wife." The second part tells us what becomes of the wife: "Winter brings hardship and loneliness. Neither her husband's love, nor her neighbours' friendship can help the young wife. Gradually terror of the frozen wasteland destroys her mind. In a climax of despair her wedding chest provides a last tragic refuge." The camera remains on the set, providing various shots but never intruding on the sense of a stage production. In the right foreground of the set there is a large covered wagon. At the rear left there is a house represented in minimalist and abstract terms. The doorway, for instance, is represented by a primitive freestanding archway. The backdrop represents an expansive prairie landscape that is also rendered in a minimalistic fashion. The dancers are costumed in simple country style. The women wear dresses that reach to mid-calf with geometric designs at the hem. The men wear pants with either fringed jackets or flannel shirts.

The ballet begins with the wife sitting by the covered wagon. Her husband enters by their house, and they dance together. Soon their friends and neighbours arrive bearing gifts and a group dance ensues. This dance is characterized by simple movements such as running and skipping steps, stamping feet with elbows stuck out to the side, running while clapping in time to the music and swinging partners. This country dancing, or square-dance feeling is reinforced by the music which has a folksy syncopated feel to it. The energy is high, and there is a sense of a great deal of space being covered. This is also true for the dancing of the husband and wife. Their dancing is more complex and difficult than that of the ensemble. Although the movement is clearly drawn from the vocabulary of classical ballet, it is markedly simplified, possibly to express the unaffected simplicity of life on the prairie. The wife wears soft slippers, not point shoes. She dances with a lyrical freedom of the torso, unlike the typical rigidity of the ballerina. She rounds her back forward and backward. Her arms generally are fully extended (not rounded as in conventional ballet) and sweep and circle with her torso in all directions. Her legs likewise reach in all directions. Also, she seems to cover a great deal of space; she seems always to be running from position to position. This sense of

Gordon Wales and Carlu Carter in *Shadow on the Prairie*, 1953.

space and freedom likely corresponds to the vast nature of the prairie landscape itself. The movement quality of the second part is similar to the first, but the wife's dancing becomes more violent and unpredictable as she loses her mind.

Shadow on the Prairie exhibits aspects of the Canadian national myth of the North, but in a much different way than *Ballet Festival* does. Actually, *Shadow on the Prairie* doesn't really deal with the North directly, but with rural life. In "The Myth of the Land in Canadian Nationalism" in *Nationalism in Canada*, Cole Harris points out that the northern Precambrian Shield, although firing the imagination of Canadians, is actually not a reality for most. Only a handful have ever lived there. He explains that because farming was, until recently, the principal Canadian occupation, the Canadian character has been drawn more from its agricultural background than from any contact with the Shield. Accordingly he deals with the conception of farming and agriculture in Canada. He specifically describes how it derives from the Canadian myth of the North, and differentiates it from the myth of the land in the United States, concluding that "if there is a myth about Canadian agriculture, it is about the toil and uncertainty of farming in a harsh environment, and this is a very different myth from any in the United States" (1966: 34). This myth is precisely what is dealt with in *Shadow on the Prairie*, which, as we have already seen, tells a tragic story "from the history of the Canadian West" about "young settlers on the raw new prairie."

The use of the myth of the land in *Shadow on the Prairie* is more in keeping with the way it is used in other Canadian arts, especially literature. In *Survival*, Margaret Atwood claims that each country has a single, unifying and informing symbol at its core, which functions like a system of beliefs that holds the country together. The central symbol for Canada is survival. This characteristic preoccupation with one's survival corresponds to a preoccupation with the obstacles to that survival. Accordingly, in *Shadow on the Prairie*, the young wife is preoccupied with the loneliness and terror associated with surviving on the prairie. While in *Ballet Festival* the myth of the North is manipulated to reinforce the positive qualities of the ideal Canadian citizen, in *Shadow on the Prairie*, the use of the myth is more in keeping with the way it is used in literature, and allows for what is defined by Atwood as a typically Canadian tragic ending: the failure to survive.

Shadow on the Prairie exhibits a much different treatment of the actual dancing than was found in *Ballet Festival*. In the latter film the dancing was manipulated and placed at the service of the nation, while in the former, the nation is at the service of the arts. *Shadow on the Prairie* provides some explanatory comments, but generally allows the choreography to speak for itself. The camera is unobtrusive, contributing to the overall mood of the composition, and there is no interpretive narrator.

The final film considered in this look at the function of nationalism in Canadian dance films is *Pas de Deux*. Produced in 1968, it was directed by Norman McLaren and received considerable acclaim, winning over twenty awards and honourable mentions. Whether seen from a historical perspective or thematically, there is little about this film on the surface that can be called nationalistic. I have interpreted it as an expression of high-technology, in this way aligning it with new technologies of television and computers which were widely perceived in the 1960s to be a threat not only to traditional forms of nationalism, but to traditional ways of living in general.

McLaren had a long and fruitful career at the National Film Board. His relationship with the NFB was very special. The nature of this relationship is described in a 1970 interview with Alan Rosenthal, published in the *Journal of the University Film Association*. In response to Rosenthal's question about how much personal freedom McLaren was allowed in his choice of subject, McLaren replies: "Towards the end of the war ... I was free enough, although it all depends on how free you mean. For instance, someone had recorded a number of French Canadian folk songs, and we were asked to make films, illustrating them. In that group of films, I was not 'free' – the theme was set for me. But apart from those, I've been free ever since – and I mean real freedom. I don't have to submit a script or a treatment before starting a film, but I do have to make a budget estimate and give a two or three line description of what the film will be about" (Rosenthal 1970: 8). Since it is categorized with his post-war films, *Pas de Deux* can only be perceived as representing McLaren's views, and not those of either the NFB or those of the government that funded it.

No discussion of McLaren can be complete without a consideration of his technical inventiveness. He is credited with rediscovering and popularizing many lost animation techniques, which had been introduced by early film pioneers, as well as with inventing many of his own. His passion for and curiosity about technique was usually what inspired him to create.

Pas de Deux is no exception. It was born of a desire to explore a kind of movement quality suggested by a technical procedure that involved multi-plying and superimposing live action film using an optical printer. The possible effects are numerous and are integrated into the narrative of the film.

Single frame from Norman McLaren's *Pas de Deux*, 1968.

McLaren began by experimenting with filmed samples of simple movements, and finally chose ballet as a vehicle to showcase this technique. For *Pas de Deux*, Ludmilla Chiriaeff choreographed a ballet to suit the needs of the experimental technique, which was performed by Vincent Warren and Margaret Mercier, and filmed in slightly slowed motion, in black and white. The dancers wear white leotards against a black background and are severely edge-lit. In most shots they appear to be nothing but an outline, at times appearing to be a series of simple white line drawings against a black background. This serves to emphasize the featured special effects.

The ballet tells a very simple love story. It begins with a shot of the woman lying on the floor. She seems to awaken and gradually rises to her feet. She begins to dance, first alone, and then in various ways with her double. For instance, the dancer ends a phrase and freezes. Her double continues from the frozen position and performs another phrase. The dancer in turn dances the same phrase as the double and joins her image. In another instance, the woman dances in opposition with her double and the two images overlap in interesting and beautiful ways. At this point in the narrative, the man enters. She becomes more interested in him than in her narcissistic double, and they gradually fall in love. As their passion and love grow, the technical dimension becomes more prominent and complex. The most characteristic effect of this second part is achieved by exposing the same shot onto itself several times, but delaying or staggering each exposure by a few frames. This technique causes a simple port de bras to seem like the opening and closing of a fan, and a series of jumps or lifts across the screen to seem like moveable sculpture. One particularly striking effect was achieved by starting with a shot of the man kneeling on the ground while the woman strikes a simple arabesque en pointe in front of him. He turns her around by her supporting leg while she sustains the arabesque, creating a kind of human kaleidoscope. Because the complexity of human beings in a relationship is signified by the complexity of the filmic technique, one could say that in *Pas de Deux* the medium is the message.

Marshall McLuhan's *The Medium is the Message*, written while he was the director of the Centre for Culture and Technology at the University of Toronto, was published in 1967, the same year that saw the release of *Pas de Deux*. With the advent of television, there was suddenly a glut of information available to the viewer. This new technology not only permitted access to a huge amount of information, it also required the consumer to process this information in a different way. In his book, McLuhan gleefully heralds the age of "electrical technology" which was replacing the older "mechanical technology." In the age of mechanical technology the predominant medium was the printing press. Printing created the portable book which people could read in privacy. Printing therefore led to the cult of individualism, and promoted the pre-dominance of the private, fixed point of view. Translated into social behaviour, these trends led to an attitude of detachment and non-involvement. But electric technology abolishes these divisions between individuals. Its ascendency heralds "a brand-new world of allatonceness." This was exemplified in 1967 by the technology of television. "Television demands participation and involvement in depth of the whole being. It will not work as background" (1967: 125). McLuhan declares that because of this kind of technology traditional ways of defining ourselves socially are no longer valid; "we now live in a global village ... a simultaneous happening" (1967: 63).

Melville Watkins, in his 1966 article "Technology and Nationalism," addresses the implications of McLuhan's ideas on the notion of nationalism in general and Canadian nationalism in particular. He suggests that traditional nationalism is a symptom of print, understood as that sense of common identity that flows from print technology. Nations that are formed by print's mechanical technology are self-absorbed, detached and uninvolved with other nations. Electric technology, by encouraging the individual to seek involvement in the community and crave collective goals in a world that has shrunk to the size of a village, casts the inner-directed individual adrift and exposes the superficiality of old social forms, including conventional nationalism. The trend to collectivity will lead, Watkins says, to the eventual dissolve of national borders, with growing emphasis instead on localized planning on the one hand and the rise of international organizations on the other.

Watkins points out that Canada is sadly vulnerable to the decentralizing threat of electric technology because it is a weak and tenuously held-together nation at the best of times, and has to overcome not only the problem of having two national languages but also has to bridge a vast, sparsely populated land.

But he claims that "what is required is for us to take seriously the idea of mankind as a concept transcending nationalism.... The compelling need for the future is not for national societies in a world community – desirable though such a social system would be today – but rather for a world society fit for a global village" (1966: 301).

Seen together, then, these three films can be seen as embodying a trend of Canadian cultural nationalism. *Ballet Festival* is intensely nationalistic, with a shrill urgency that harkens back to the ultra-nationalistic needs and concerns of the war years. *Shadow on the Prairie* displays a far more sophisticated form of nationalism. It reveals dance that artistically explores aspects of the Canadian experience, and is comparable to parallel endeavours in other art forms. It corresponds in Canada's national history to a time when Canada had arrived and was confidently exploring and questioning its national and international identity. *Pas de Deux* emphasizes technical wizardry. It participates in the international or extra-national dialogue encouraged by the possibilities of electronic technology. In this way, *Pas de Deux* finally suggests the possibility of the end of the nation-state in general, and specifically the end of the Canadian nation-state that gave birth to it.

References

Anderson, Benedict. 1991. *Imagined Communities: Reflections on the Origin and Spread of Nationalism*. London and New York: Verso.

Atwood, Margaret. 1972. *Survival: A Thematic Guide to Canadian Literature*. Toronto: House of Anansi Press Ltd.

Bashevkin, Sylvia B. 1991. *True Patriot Love: The Politics of Canadian Nationalism*. Toronto: Oxford University Press.

Bennington, Geoffrey. 1990. "Postal Politics and the Institution of the Nation." In Homi K. Bhabha, ed. *Nation and Narration*. London and New York: Routledge, 121-37.

Berger, Carl. 1966. "The True North Strong and Free." In Peter Russell, ed. *Nationalism in Canada*. Toronto: McGraw-Hill Company of Canada Ltd., 3-26.

Blais, Roger, film dir. 1949. *Ballet Festival*. Montreal: National Film Board.

Blais, Roger, film dir. 1953. *Shadow on the Prairie*. Montreal: National Film Board. Originally choreographed by Gweneth Lloyd in 1952.

Bruner, Jody. 1990. "Norman McLaren's *Pas de Deux* from a Canadian Dance History Perspective." Unpublished essay.

Clarfield, David. 1987. *Canadian Film*. Toronto: Oxford University Press.

Cook, Ramsay. 1977. *The Maple Leaf Forever: Essays on Nationalism and Politics in Canada*. Toronto: Macmillan.

Harris, Cole. 1966. "The Myth of the Land in Canadian Nationalism." In Peter Russell, ed. *Nationalism in Canada*. Toronto: McGraw-Hill Company of Canada Ltd., 27-46.

Hobsbawm, Eric. 1983. "Introduction: Inventing Traditions." In Eric Hobsbawm and Terrence Rogers, eds. *The Invention of Tradition*. Cambridge: Cambridge University Press, 1-14.

James, C. Rodney. 1977. *Film as a National Art: NFB of Canada and the Film Board Idea*. New York: Arno Press.

Jones, D.B. 1981. *Movies and Memoranda: An Interpretive History of the National Film Board of Canada*. Ottawa: The Canadian Film Institute.

Litt, Paul. 1992. *The Muses, the Masses, and the Massey Commission*. Toronto: University of Toronto Press.

McLaren, Norman, film dir. 1967. *Pas de Deux*. Montreal: National Film Board. Choreographed by Ludmilla Chiriaeff.

McLuhan, Marshall and Quentin Fiore. 1967. *The Medium is the Message: An Inventory of Effects*. New York: Bantam Books.

Rosenthal, Alan. 1970. "Norman McLaren on *Pas de Deux*." *Journal of the University Film Association*, 8-15.

Shea, Albert A., ed. 1952. *Culture in Canada*. Canadian Association for Adult Education.

Watkins, Melville. 1966. "Technology and Nationalism." In Peter Russell, ed. *Nationalism in Canada*. Toronto: McGraw-Hill Company of Canada Ltd., 284-302.

Nesta Toumine, ca. 1949.

Nesta Toumine's Legacy:
From the Ballets Russes
to the Ottawa Ballet

Rosemary Jeanes Antze

It is a curious moment, to be confronted with an earlier period of one's life and to find it turning into history.[1] This occurred for me in 1994, during a dance history class at York University, in which guest professor Rhonda Ryman was teaching a square dance from Nesta Toumine's *Maria Chapdelaine* (originally titled *Marie-Madelaine*). Ryman was able to reconstruct this excerpt from an original Canadian ballet choreographed in 1957, using the Labanotation score created in 1986 during the ENCORE! ENCORE! Reconstruction project (Ryman 1994). Selma Odom had invited me to the class to add my perspective as a former student, dancer and researcher of Nesta Toumine (1912-1996), a pioneering figure in Canadian dance.

This experience set me thinking about the legacy of a dance teacher and choreographer. Although certain elements of Toumine's choreography had been preserved in a notated score and brought to life again in a reconstruction, the steps and choreographic patterns seemed a faint and partial image of the ballet I had known. On the one hand, I was gratified that Madame Toumine, as teacher, choreographer and artistic director, was no longer overlooked as a significant player in the Canadian dance scene. On the other, I was struck by a loss of the essential flavour of her work which once permeated the atmosphere of her studio, set the tone for rehearsals and animated company performances.

The question arose, what else is needed to preserve and communicate a fuller picture of a dance, a choreographer, an era? How quickly even the recent past, which took its life in the studio through the immediate interaction between choreographer and dancers, and existed in those fleeting moments of performance, is relegated to the memory of those who participated directly in it as performer or spectator. As one who had spent a large part of my training and apprenticeship for the stage under Toumine's tutelage, I began to recognize the impact of her attitudes towards dance in shaping my own. In her relationship with her students, she nurtured the individual in each of us while also introducing us to the larger world of professional ballet that had been part

[1] This is a revised and expanded version of an article published in *Dance in Canada* 49 (Fall 1986), 4-10. Research for the original project was supported by an Explorations grant from the Canada Council.

Born Nesta Williams, she used Toumine when she married. While dancing for the Ballets Russes de Paris, she used the Russianized name Nesta Maslova.

of her early career. As students, we not only learned and performed the classical repertoire, but also ballets by great choreographers of the post-Diaghilev era who had influenced her own ideas on choreography. In class we were inspired by her stories of great dancers she had known, making the daily routine of a dancer more than just a technical training ground. The "studio" became a second home where we rehearsed and socialized nightly and through the weekends; several generations of dancers as well as her two sons grew up overlooking Rideau Street, under the almost parental eye of Nesta Toumine. Only many years later did I realize that what so fascinated me in my graduate research concerning the teacher-student relationship in India, actually existed to a very large degree in my own dance heritage.[2] So I will include some account of rehearsals at the Classical Ballet Studio, as well as details of the company's repertoire and the scope of its annual performance season.

In addition, to understand Toumine's place in the continuity of ballet tradition, it is crucial to look back to her formative years and early career. The world of dance that came to life in Ottawa from 1947 and continued up to the late 1970s, embodied in Toumine's particular approach, took its roots and drew its inspiration from her fourteen years away from Canada. In working with her dancers, she tapped the knowledge of English and Russian ballet that she had gleaned from her studies in England, from her professional work with many leading choreographers of the day and from her performing with several post-Diaghilev Ballets Russes companies. Toumine's sense of ballet, its relation to contemporary music and to strong design elements, its subject matter that ranged from the dramatic to the abstract, was cultivated during her years in Europe. This vision of dance that she brought back was gradually recreated with her own dancers. To present this aspect of her artistic formation, I will revisit my earlier essay concerning her life story.

---

[2] In my thesis "Tradition and Learning in Odissi Dance of India: Guru-Sisya-Parampara" (Jeanes [Antze] 1982), I examine the teacher-student relationship in its widest cultural sense. Then I present my research on how the *guru-sisya* paradigm is understood in Odissi dance, both as it was in the adoptive mother-daughter relationship of traditional temple dancers and also in the rapport between contemporary gurus and their students learning the renewed classical style.

My experience with Madame Toumine as artistic director began when I was invited to work with her company in children's roles in *The Nutcracker* during the Christmas season of 1961, and in *Maria Chapdelaine* in May 1962. I had the thrill of swinging on the arm of David Moroni (later premier dancer with the Royal Winnipeg Ballet and now director of the school) as one of a pack of wolves moving in to kill Jean, the romantic lead. Rehearsals took place in the spacious second floor studios on Rideau Street where her school had moved the previous year. The senior dancers became a "Concert Group" and would work on into the evenings after the daily advanced ballet class. Then on Saturday and Sunday afternoons dancers would be called at various hours for full company rehearsals.

These long rehearsal hours provided a stimulating education in dance, in part because there were opportunities to watch senior dancers, led by Joanne Ashe and David Moroni, rehearsing their roles. By the early 1960s, Toumine had trained a full generation of dancers since her first foray into teaching in 1946. The more talented dancers were committed to her dream of a professional company in Ottawa. By 1961 the Classical Ballet Concert Group of Ottawa had twenty-five members, who worked at office jobs or attended university locally in order to be able to devote their evenings and weekends to dance. With the National Ballet of Canada in Toronto and Les Grands Ballets Canadiens in Montreal still in their first decade, the Ottawa dancers expected to become the next professional company, especially since, unlike the other companies, the director was a native of her city, Canada's capital, and the talent was home grown.

Although Toumine was very much an Ottawan, the source of her vision was the Ballets Russes companies with which she had worked in Europe and New York. We danced the classics, *The Nutcracker*, *Swan Lake* Act II, *Giselle* and *Coppélia*, as she had danced them. As a teenager, I had the privilege of learning *Les Sylphides*, *Les Elves* and *Prince Igor* at only one step removed from their creator Michel Fokine, since Toumine had rehearsed these ballets under his direction.

This direct link with the legendary figures of the Diaghilev era was also sustained by her husband, Sviatoslav Toumine. A former dancer with Anna Pavlova and with the original Ballets Russes, he would come to the studio on weekends when he was home from his design job in New York. In his capacity as Artistic Director of the company, he sat in on rehearsals to develop his scenic and costume designs for Nesta Toumine's choreography. He also brought a critical eye to our dancing; it was especially evocative the way he would comment on how a great ballerina of the past, perhaps Alexandra Danilova, had danced a certain role. The famous Russian dancers, many of whose autographed photographs lined the walls of the studio entrance and sitting areas, came alive for us in a gesture or story, which in turn inspired us in our own dancing. When Mr. Toumine took on character roles such as Dr. Coppelius in *Coppélia*, his sense of stagecraft and the dramatic, animated our performances and provided continuity with the past.

Politics and Perseverance

An important feature of Nesta Toumine's versatility as a director was the dual nature of her repertoire. Her company performed the classics and significant recent ballets that she remounted from memory. Yet she also produced a steady flow of new works that ranged from the dramatic *Medusa* to the abstract *Gymnopédies*, from *Pas de Quatre*'s characterizations of the rivalry amongst the ballerinas of the Romantic era to the technically demanding *Shostakovitch Ballet Suite*.[3] These ballets were already part of her repertoire of over forty works when I joined her company in the mid-1960s. In addition, I remember the excitement of walking into the studio and being part of the choreographic process. It was impressive how well she knew the music before she began creating on her dancers, and how she drew her inspiration from a variety of sources, such as Rodin's sculptures of the *Burghers of Calais* for the groupings in her *Holberg Suite*.

She was also a master at using her resources to best advantage and at bringing out the special talents of her dancers. In the French-Canadian story ballet *Maria Chapdelaine*, she created a number of dramatic roles for members of the family, in which the acting talents of mature performers who played Maria Chapdelaine's parents contributed to the atmosphere on stage. She cast a young boy, who was an exceptional step dancer, in the role of Maria's brother and gave him opportunities to display his virtuosity in the middle of the square dance, just as might happen in a rural Quebec dance party. She put great effort into coaching her performers to animate their characters, while she also choreographed challenging sequences for her stronger classical dancers.

By the 1960s, Toumine's company had a busy annual schedule with performances almost every month. The 1963-64 season exemplifies this period, with each engagement generally involving several shows. In October of 1963, the Classical Ballet Concert Group performed the second act of *Coppélia* and *Medusa* in the Second Annual Performance of the Performing Arts. In November, a group of dancers appeared with the Laurentian Junior Music Club and in the Orpheus Operatic Society production of *The Music Man*. In December, Toumine took a break from her traditional annual *Nutcracker* and mounted a mixed programme of *Coppélia*, *Medusa* and premiered her own choreography of *La Bayadère* and *The Legend*. The company travelled to Deep River to perform in January, and dancers were also invited to perform a Can-Can for the Annual Press Club Ball. In February, the company appeared again in Ottawa, adding *Les Valses* to the mixed programme. Toumine choreographed the Orpheus production of *Brigadoon* in April. May brought more touring to Hawkesbury, July saw several performances at Carleton University, and there were an additional three at the Lakeside Festival in August.

As full as this year seemed, more ambitious plans took the company into its 1964-65 season. The Ontario Arts Council helped support a tour to western

[3] Susan Toumine, former wife of Nesta Toumine's son Lorne, has recently remounted several of her ballets including excerpts from *Shostakovitch Ballet Suite* at the Banff Centre Summer School.

Ontario, to Fort Frances, Port Arthur (now Thunder Bay) and Sudbury. There was also an initiative to revive the spirit of the early Canadian Ballet Festivals that had taken place between 1948 and 1954, and to bring more dance to Ottawa. In April 1965, Toumine and her company hosted eight American companies and the Canadian Junior Ballet from Toronto at the Sixth Northeast Regional Ballet Festival. More than 300 dancers participated in this international event designed to promote and develop ballet on the continent.

In just under twenty years, Toumine had built up all the elements of a professional dance company. She had trained dancers, developed a large and varied repertoire, collaborated with other performing and musical groups in the capital and cultivated audiences both in Ottawa and surrounding centres. Her reputation had also spread to the United States through her participation in regional ballet festivals, for which Anatole Chujoy, editor of *Dance News*, sang her praises. Igor Youskevitch invited her to mount two of her works for his company Les Ballets Romantiques for performances in Washington.

Toumine's dream and aspirations of a fully professional company would never be realized, however. Ottawa was just not the place to be, now that Canada had three ballet companies. Granting agencies at the time thought that was quite enough. Dancers who had placed their hopes in Toumine's vision began to look elsewhere for ways to pursue careers in dance. It is remarkable that amongst dancers who worked with her in the 1960s, over twenty went on to dance with other professional companies, both in Canada and in Europe. What is especially poignant is that Toumine had everything but financial support. In order to put her contribution in a larger frame, I will return to her beginnings as a dancer and trace the development of her career.

When Anna Pavlova danced her *Snowflake Ballet* at Ottawa's Russell Theatre in 1920, a small girl in the audience made up her mind that one day she would wear a long white ballet dress and marry a Russian. In an interview, Toumine looked back on her seven-year-old self with a chuckle. "It was rather strange that it came out that way!" Not only did her romantic vision catapult her into the glamorous world of the Ballets Russes companies of the 1930s and 1940s, it also returned with her to Ottawa where she founded the Ottawa Ballet Company in 1947 and where she continued to teach until her death in 1996. How did a small Ottawa girl, who described herself as "knee-high to a grasshopper" when she made her stage debut as a "merry little dancer at the end of a line" in a musical show directed by ballroom master, Professor Sinclair, develop and sustain an international dance career? Why was her company that flourished in Ottawa during the 1950s, 1960s and into the 1970s, unable to find an ongoing place in the development of Canadian dance?

Nesta Williams was born on October 28, 1912, in Croyden, England. Her father was Canadian but her English mother wanted to return home for the birth of her eleventh and last child. In 1913, Nesta and her mother returned to Ottawa to join the rest of the family. Inspired by performances of Pavlova and Mikhail Mordkin at Ottawa's Russell Theatre, Toumine's mother sent her youngest children to learn dance. At the age of four Toumine began lessons in

Fancy Dancing in the huge ballroom of the former Ottawa Racquet Club. She remembered that while the mothers watched from the balcony, "we girls, in our prettiest starched dresses with large sashes, perfected the curtsey, rocked our dolls to lullabies and entwined our feet in Irish jigs."

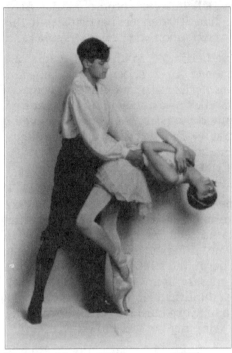

Nesta and Lorne Williams, ca. 1925.

Soon she moved on to more serious fare with Gwen Osborne, who also taught other future professionals, Betty Lowe and sisters Nora and Patricia White (later Patricia Wilde).[4] Osborne had undertaken studies with Russian dancer and teacher Konstantin Kobeleff in New York, but she was also very interested in barefoot dancing that derived from followers of Isadora Duncan. Soon Toumine and her brother, Lorne, were dancing two to three times a week, and preparing recital dances such as the 1926 *Gavotte* that Osborne modelled after Pavlova's famous duet.

When Nesta was sixteen, her eldest sister took her on a trip to England to provide some distraction following the death of their mother the previous year. She and her friend Betty Lowe plucked up their courage and took classes with the Russian teacher, Nicholas Legat. Toumine remembers how wonderful it was, to join in a class with professionals, such as Russian dancers from de Basil's company, including the baby ballerinas Tamara Toumanova, Irina Baronova and Tatiana Riabouschinska. Through the early 1930s, Toumine continued her studies in London and began auditioning for dancing work. In 1934 she was hired for her first professional engagement in the musical *The Golden Toy*, choreographed by Ninette de Valois. She recalled playing two shows a day for six months, "posing amidst artificial lakes, fountain and little mountains, and dashing back and forth between the three revolving stages." Once she had made her way into the theatrical world, other engagements followed, with the Carl Rosa Opera Company, as the head ballet girl in the pantomime *Cinderella* in Manchester and in a film with Anton Dolin.

While earning her living on the stage, Toumine turned her attention to serious training in the Cecchetti method with Margaret Craske. After a year of syllabus work, she took her examination before a committee which included the noted dance critic, Cyril Beaumont. With this solid technical grounding, its

---

[4] Betty Lowe went on to dance with Colonel de Basil's Ballets Russes de Monte Carlo and the Original Ballets Russes companies under the name of Ludmilla Lvova, while Patricia Wilde became a ballerina with George Balanchine's New York City Ballet.

emphasis on good placement and on the rationale behind each exercise, she was able to fill in certain gaps in her training. She also hoped it might prove useful when she was ready to return to Canada to teach.

Romantic interest in a young czardas dancer, Sviatoslav Toumine, led Toumine to audition for the Ballets Russes de Paris, a small touring company. So in 1936 Toumine landed her first real ballet job and set off on a tour of the British Isles. Working with the company came as a shock. "I was given costumes and told to fit them myself," she remembered, "then quickly thrown into the repertoire." Many of the dancers were Russian and to fit this stereotype, Toumine was compelled to change her name to Maslova, which means butter. The financial backing of the organization was precarious; for the six-month tour the dancers received their full salary only twice and then were stranded in Belfast when the money ran out. Sviatoslav Toumine cut his losses and joined René Blum's ballet for a tour of South Africa while Nesta Toumine went home to Canada to see her family.

The next year marked her big break. Toumine had returned to Cecchetti classes in London when, one Saturday afternoon, a cablegram arrived from Paris. It read, "Come at once. Slava." Borrowing the fare from a friend, Toumine took the boat-train from London to Paris, where she met up with Sviatoslav Toumine now with the Ballets Russes de Monte Carlo. The story was that an English girl had come down with the measles and a replacement was needed in a hurry. After a flurried audition with the ballet master, she began rehearsals for the second act of *Swan Lake*. "I was just put in according to height," she recalled, "and off I went." Toumine's quickness in learning new parts and her adaptability soon made her a valuable member of the company. "If anybody was sick, the ballet master would call, Williams! So-and-so's sick tonight. You dance!' And I'd learn the part before the performance or during intermission." This skill, combined with a photographic memory, earned her first-hand knowledge of a great many roles, both female and male. And this knowledge stayed with her and later provided the basis of the early repertoire for her Ottawa dancers.

Her first year with René Blum's Ballets Russes de Monte Carlo was spent touring throughout England and Scotland. Then the company settled in its official home, the elegant and intimate theatre of the Monte Carlo Casino. The programme for the month-long season in April 1937 included the ballets *Coppélia*, *Casse-Noisette* (*The Nutcracker*), *Les Elves*, *Prince Igor* and *Petrouchka*. Toumine danced in every ballet. There she was, at the heart of the ballet world, beginning a period of work and apprenticeship under the major creative figures of the day – Michel Fokine, Léonide Massine and, later, George Balanchine. Reminiscing about these great choreographers, she characterized Fokine as the most exacting. He would change details in *Les Sylphides*, such as nuances of the arms, musical timing, or the way he arranged the corps de ballet according to height, each time he set the ballet on a different company. As rehearsal director, he had no patience with lateness and once made a tardy dancer rehearse her part as a Furie on the floor, still dressed in her sleek black

261

suit. During performances Fokine watched and took notes from the centre box of the house. "Once in *Schéhérazade*," she related, "he noticed a boy over-playing an amorous caressing motion, and immediately rushed backstage, caught the fellow by the ankle and pulled him out of the act." More usually he would restrain himself until the ballet was over, but did not hesitate to give corrections or even to rehearse certain bits during the intermission. Only when he was satisfied would he allow the dancers to change into their costumes for the next ballet.

Massine, in his approach to the creation of a ballet, was apparently very different. He was much freer and more receptive to ideas from the dancers. Toumine described him in rehearsal: "He would give you a skeleton, then a dancer might do something he'd like and he'd work from there." With Balanchine, it was his great musicality that she recalled, particularly in the early masterpieces, *Serenade* and *Jeu de Cartes*. Late in her career, Toumine also performed in Agnes de Mille's *Rodeo*. Working with such a range of choreographic approaches and thematic material enriched her understanding of composition and choreographic styles.

During these years Toumine described her life as a "gypsy existence." The Ballets Russes spent much of the year touring, initially in Europe and Britain. When World War II broke out Toumine was working in Paris. She remembered that the director of the company simply returned the dancers' passports and left them to fend for themselves. She and an American friend just managed to get permits to leave the city and were able to arrange passage to New York from Rotterdam. There they went immediately back to rehearsals with Massine who had formed a brand new company and was preparing for a South American tour. Colonel de Basil, on the other hand, saved the Russian male dancers, including Sviatoslav Toumine, from being drafted into the army by forming another company and heading off on a tour of Australia. For the next two years Toumine and her "romantic interest" danced with rival groups, the Massine Ballet Russe de Monte Carlo and the de Basil Ballet Russe. Once the couple met only for twenty minutes in the rush of Grand Central Station when Sviatoslav gave her an engagement ring.

In the fall of 1941, the two companies chanced to cross paths in Toronto. Sviatoslav Toumine was visiting her backstage, when the company manager pointed them out to a photographer as an item for a publicity story. They had carried on their romance over six years, at times from opposite sides of the globe, for brief periods dancing together, then being separated first when the Ballets Russes de Paris was disbanded, then by the outbreak of war. They had planned to marry in Paris, but couldn't get authorization. In Toronto, the reporter took matters in hand. Because the couple did not have the time to go together to City Hall, he arranged the licence, took photographs of them buying the ring and Toumine's hat. So at noon on September 18, 1941, Nesta Williams married Sviatoslav Toumine. Slava went on to Chicago with his company, but soon afterwards flew back to New York to join his wife in Massine's company.

Toumine's two childhood fantasies had now become reality. She had indeed worn many a long white ballet dress, plus a few bizarre outfits designed by Salvador Dali for Massine's *Bacchanale*. She had also married a Russian who, when she founded her Ottawa company, provided original designs to complement her choreographic ventures. The early years of her marriage were spent in New York. However, the summer heat prompted her to take her two young sons home to Ottawa in 1946. There, Yolande Le Duc, another former student of Gwen Osborne, invited her to teach a guest class at the old "Y" gymnasium on Metcalfe Street. Once she began teaching, choreographing and directing followed naturally. Classes went so well that Toumine and Le Duc decided to mount a performance, and the Ottawa Ballet Company made its debut at the Capitol Theatre on March 12, 1947. The choice of ballet for that first performance drew on the strengths of Toumine's professional back-ground and set the company's future course. The opener was *Les Sylphides*, in which she had danced under Fokine's eye, while the second work, *The Nutcracker*, became an annual Christmas event, inaugurating a holiday tradition that spread across the continent.

The first performance was no small affair. More than forty dancers graced the stage, amidst the "futuristic settings" created by Sviatoslav Toumine. Guest artists from New York, including the young Svetlana Beriosova, later ballerina with Britain's Royal Ballet, took principal roles in both ballets, and Ottawan Jean Stoneham, later ballerina with the Royal Winnipeg Ballet, made her debut in the Valse in *Les Sylphides*. The next day, *The Evening Citizen* devoted its whole entertainment page to the performance, proclaiming the success of the company with the headline, "Ottawa Thrills to Choreographic Perfrmance [sic] of Ballet." The display of six photographs suggests a remarkably professional-looking group of dancers, while two full columns of review, unsigned, praise every aspect of the production.

By its next season the company was able to turn to "home-grown" Jean Stoneham to dance the title role in *Giselle*, opposite Vladimir Doukodovsky, premier dancer of the original Ballets Russes. Sviatoslav Toumine played Hilarion. Toumine created her first original work, *Once Upon a Time*, set to Strauss waltzes, in which she herself danced. Then in March 1949 she added a second work, *Sonata in C Sharp Minor*, to the repertoire. This programme was under the musical direction of Eugene Kash, in whose popular young people's concerts the dancers also participated. That same week, the company travelled to the second Canadian Ballet Festival in Toronto to join nine other Canadian groups in the week-long event at the Royal Alexandra Theatre.

Anatole Chujoy, the editor of *Dance News*, was invited to come from New York to write reviews of the Festival for the *Globe and Mail*. He rated the Ottawa Ballet Company among the top three Canadian companies, together with the older and comparatively more established Winnipeg Ballet and the Volkoff Canadian Ballet. He praised the Ottawa dancers' performance of *Les Sylphides*: "Not only did they execute the required pas with care and love, they were in the style of the great master's work, no easy task for young dancers."

Toumine's *Marie-Madelaine*, 1956. Centre: Joanne Ashe; right: Elizabeth Shelton.

He also remarked upon Toumine's "choreographic inventiveness" in *Sonata in C Sharp Minor*. Later, in *Dance News*, he noted her company's "attentive and loving consideration of the classics ... through which it fulfils an important mission in the general scheme of Canadian Ballet." It is ironic that two and a half years later, in November of 1951, Celia Franca launched the National Ballet in Toronto with two of Fokine's works, *Les Sylphides* and "Polovtsian Dances" from *Prince Igor*, which were also in the repertoire of the Ottawa Ballet.

After the success of 1949, Toumine split with Le Duc and moved into the next decade as director of the Classical Ballet Company. She developed her dancers' repertoire equally in the classics, notably *Swan Lake* and *Coppélia*, and Fokine's *Le Spectre de la Rose*, *Les Elves* and "Polovtsian Dances" from *Prince Igor* and in new works. Her company continued to attend the annual Canadian Ballet Festivals until their demise in 1954, including hosting the fifth one in Ottawa in 1953. In 1955 she also organized a special gala evening as a benefit performance to aid the Royal Winnipeg Ballet whose scenery, costumes, music, recordings and photographs had all been destroyed by fire the previous year.

In less than ten years since her return to Ottawa, Toumine had trained dancers capable of fulfilling her vision of a professional company. Sviatoslav

Toumine contributed striking and innovative designs for decor and costumes, and Eugene Kash conducted a live orchestra for performances. The company had also built up a loyal following among Ottawa audiences so that Toumine was ready to break loose from the more cautious approach of remounting the classics. In 1956 the company presented the premieres of four original Canadian works: two story ballets, *David* and *Marie-Madelaine*, the latter with an original score composed by Hector Gratton, and two shorter works, *Pas de Deux* and *Les Valses*.[5]

Now the Ottawa company was on the brink of becoming professional. On a shoestring budget, Toumine selected her twelve most senior dancers to form the Classical Ballet Concert Group and, by 1959, managed to put them on a monthly salary. That year *The Ottawa Citizen* reported that "The Classical Ballet Concert Group is moving into the big-time." The article noted that with its core of dancers, "the company was capable of producing 24 ballets, complete with music, sets and costumes, at a moment's notice." By drawing on dancers from the school, it could mount another sixteen works. The dancers' schedules became hectic, with weekend touring around the Ottawa Valley, a series of Saturday afternoon performances for children and gala performances at Christmas. In addition, the Concert Group was the only Canadian company invited to the first Northeast Regional Ballet Festival in the United States.

Through the early 1960s the company maintained its high profile in the Ottawa region and at American ballet festivals. A full-page spread in *The Ottawa Citizen* on February 17, 1961, announced a three-month spring tour, made possible by a small grant from the Canada Council, with a mandate "to take ballet to communities which see few formal performances." The seven photographs in the newspaper convey the range of the company's repertoire, from *Pas de Quatre* with its four ballerinas evoking the delicate lithographs of the Romantic era to Toumine's *Gymnopédies* with its leotard-clad dancers in abstract poses that might be found on ancient Greek vases. A picture of *The Nutcracker* reveals Sviatoslav Toumine's surreal decor, while photographs of Joanne Ashe and David Moroni in a new ballet, *The Seasons*, show their pure and expressive lines. Later that year the company travelled farther afield, to the United States in May and to Quebec City in August.

Government support of the company reached its peak in 1964, when a $3,000 grant from the Ontario Arts Council subsidized a week-long Christmas tour through northern Ontario. Ottawa's profile as a centre for dance was greatly enhanced the following spring when the company hosted the sixth Northeast Regional Ballet Festival. Up to the mid-1960s the Classical Ballet Concert Group grew steadily in reputation, because of the breadth of its repertoire, the high quality of its productions and the skill of its dancers. Toumine recalled that there were three times when her company was close to

---

[5] *Marie-Madelaine* was reconstructed in 1986 during the ENCORE! ENCORE! project under the name *Maria Chapdelaine*. For more details, see Rhonda Ryman's article "Impressions of a Reconstruction: Capturing the Essence" in *Canadian Dance Studies* 1 (1994), 89-106. During the 1960s, Toumine changed the ballet's name from *Marie-Madelaine* to the title of the original story by Louis Hémon.

becoming fully professional. But each time something went wrong. "I can't tell you what it was, because I was never interested in the business side at all. I had the dancers, and we could have gone [on tour]. If we could have paid the dancers, we could have gotten more dates; we could have been on the road." In an interview Ottawa dance critic Lauretta Thistle confirmed that Toumine "was too much a creator. She just wasn't up for the whole social whirl involved in launching a ballet company. As a director she preferred to immerse herself with her dancers in the studio."

On the other hand, it is probable that the small size of Ottawa was also a factor in the disappointments, since private funding was a less available option than in the larger centres. The situation was significantly different in Toronto where a provisional board of directors actually initiated the invitation to Celia Franca to found a national company. Throughout the 1950s there was also growing competition for limited public arts funding, with the National Ballet of Canada just getting off the ground in 1951 and Les Grands Ballets Canadiens beginning in 1957. These events, coupled with the fact that the newly formed Canada Council held firmly to the view that three ballet companies [including the Royal Winnipeg Ballet] were plenty for a country with Canada's population, made prospects look dim.

During all the years of creative endeavour, Toumine took no salary for her work as director or choreographer. She drew on volunteers and on the resources of her school for the necessary support. Once her students were accomplished and committed enough to join the company, she generally waived their tuition fees. It was in her dancers that she saw her strength and the potential for realizing her dreams of a permanent company. With performers like her leading lady and "right hand," Joanne Ashe, a fine technical dancer who had turned down several offers from other Canadian companies in order to stay in Ottawa, Toumine saw a bright future for her company.

Until the 1960s Toumine's dancers did stay in Ottawa, taking office jobs or pursuing university degrees that would permit them to dance each evening and on weekends. But when their hopes for a professional company in Ottawa began to wane, they started to move on. David Moroni, who developed into Toumine's premier danseur during his twelve-year association with her studio, left for the Royal Winnipeg Ballet in 1963. He was soon followed by Toumine's niece, Marilee Williams, as well as by Joan Askwith, and in 1970, by Victoria Pulkkinen, who later danced with John Neumeier's Hamburg Ballet. Alistair Munro (who subsequently became a principal dancer with the New York Metropolitan Opera Ballet) and I joined the National Ballet of Canada, as did Christopher Bannerman, who went on to dance and chore- ograph with England's London Contemporary Dance Theatre. The Toumines' son, Lorne, danced with Les Grands Ballets Canadiens, as did his first wife, Susan Toumine, and Richard Sugarman. Carol Barrett became a leading dancer with Manchester's Northern Dance Theatre and later joined the London Festival Ballet. Several other former students won contracts with other companies, including Les Feux Follets. Despite the loss of so many of the dancers she had been preparing to meet the demands of her choreography, Toumine persevered. Striving to maintain momentum, in 1965 she changed the company's name to Ballet Imperial. Her company had the distinction of performing at Expo '67 in Montreal, and later that year she mounted a full-length production of *Cinderella*, set to Rossini's score. The company continued to be invited to American regional ballet festivals until 1977.

Until she gave up the management of her school in 1990, Toumine went daily to her studio to teach a new generation of students, often saying, with a voice tinged with both nostalgia and determination, "if only I had the dancers, how much more I could do." For the next five years and into her eighty-fourth year, Toumine continued to teach as a resident guest of Dance Educators of Ontario, in the studios where her dreams and dancers had come to life. Nesta Toumine passed away in Ottawa on February 1, 1996. Those former students and friends who gathered, with her sons, to pay tribute to a great lady of dance, remembered her studio as a second home, her company's repertoire as a remarkable artistic formation and her training as the basis for a lifelong love of dance (*The Ottawa Citizen* 3 Feb. 1996).

Nesta Toumine began dancing long before professional ballet existed in Canada. She travelled to Europe, danced internationally for over a decade with the major companies and choreographers in the 1930s and 1940s, and then brought that experience back home. For fifty years she shared her dance knowledge through her teaching. Her greatest dreams lay in her belief that she had all the expertise to found a permanent ballet company in Ottawa. From the late 1940s to the late 1970s, all the ingredients of this vision materialized and her company became a vital player of dance in the capital and in surrounding regions.

To create and sustain a performing company, on virtually no budget for over thirty years, is no small achievement, especially at a time when dancers were accorded even less recognition than they are today. Although no company survives as a testament to Toumine's labour of love, her influence persists through the dance world in the ongoing work of her students. Lauretta Thistle, who as dance critic for *The Ottawa Citizen*, watched and wrote about the company for many years, had a good vantage point from which to assess Toumine's contribution to Canadian dance. In an interview in 1983, she observed that Toumine's teaching produced dancers "with a very good, strong, basic technique, and dancers who were malleable, hence their success in other companies." Thistle also commended the Classical Ballet Company for keeping Ottawa audiences familiar with the classics, yet for provoking their imaginations with new works. She praised Toumine's judgement as a director who knew her audiences, and "could put together a well-balanced program," as well as her skillful way with her dancers: "She stayed within their limits, so that the company always looked good." Thistle characterized Toumine as a skilled choreographer, rooted in the classics. "She knew how to use the classical vocabulary to great effect. There were moments of great beauty.... I remember catching my breath at one or two lifts." Thistle singled out a short

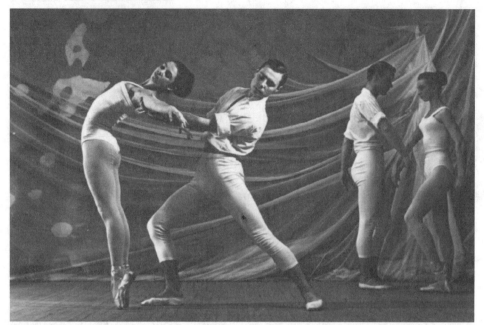

Carla Katznelson, Frederic Braun, Immo Tilgner and Marilee Williams in Toumine's *Gymnopédies*, 1960.

work, *Gymnopédies*, as "one of her most successful creations." Premiered in 1960, an abstract work for three couples set to the music of Satie, "it was a modern ballet, slow and lyrical, a beautifully sculptured work. This was one of her most successful creations; it stayed in the repertoire for years."

As one of Toumine's former students, I recall the atmosphere of the dance world she created in her studio. Until 1990 the paintings and designs by her husband looked down from the foyer walls of the Classical Ballet Studio. Signed photographs of great ballerinas of the Ballets Russes era lined the walls of the office, and a frieze of photographs of her dancers, in her own ballets, led towards the studios. In the heyday of the studio, there was always a sense of openness. Master teachers in other dance styles came to teach and we were urged to attend their classes. These artists included John Stanzel and Eva von Gencsy who came from Montreal to teach tap and jazz respectively. Brenda Beament specialized in Dalcroze Eurhythmics, which was especially recommended for younger students' musical development. Biroute Nagys taught modern for several years, as did LaVerne Mikhail who came from Sarah Lawrence College to teach Limón technique. All of these teachers were also invited to choreograph, so the dancers' range of movement was stretched beyond the bounds of classical ballet. It was also at the studio that I first saw Bharata Natyam, the classical style of India, when, in the late 1960s, Anne-Marie Gaston (Anjali) gave a demonstration.

The ballet world never seemed small or enclosed at the Classical Ballet Studio. In these times when links to community are being re-examined as

268

crucial to the survival of our arts, Toumine's work in Ottawa seems exemplary. She drew men into the dance world, inviting the small boys from the acting classes at the Ottawa Little Theatre to perform in her *Nutcracker* and then offering them free classes when they were tempted to stay on for more. She worked collaboratively with the Ottawa Orpheus Society, lending her dancers and her choreographic expertise to such musicals as *Can Can*, *Brigadoon* and *The Music Man*. She contributed dances to French Theatre productions of Molière's *Le Bourgeois Gentilhomme* and to Edgard Demers' children's production of *Blanche Neige et les Sept Nains*. And when the Ottawa Press Club needed a class act for its Press Club Ball, Toumine staged a rousing Can-Can. Though generally her musical accompaniment was taped, there were always dedicated pianists for class, rehearsals and some performances. Yet there were also occasions when she worked with live orchestra, and even times when we danced with the bells of the carillon of the Peace Tower on a makeshift stage on Parliament Hill. No opportunity for performing was passed up; each new venue developed artistry in the dancers and spread the delight of the dance to wider audiences.

No dancer with the desire to dance and the willingness to work was turned away or discouraged. Toumine's ballets showed her well trained classical dancers to good advantage, but also drew on the strengths of mature performers and varied body types. Character roles in her story ballets came to life with actors whom she taught to dance; young performers with other skills found expression in the French-Canadian step dancing so central to the mood of *Maria Chapdelaine* or in the Highland dances of her Scottish *Legend*. Even those who went on to excel in other fields in the arts, such as concert pianist Angela Hewitt, recall the spirit and love of performance that were so vividly embodied in all Toumine touched.

At the Classical Ballet Studio, three studios vibrated with dancing, while the excitement of the stage emanated from the back room filled with costumes and sets. Toumine's dedication to her art, manifested through late nights spent in long rehearsals, always leading to the next performance, inspired many a young person to dance. This love of dancing, passed on to students in Ottawa for nearly fifty years, and continuing through her former dancers now teaching across Canada and beyond, will surely carry Toumine's legacy into the future.

References

During the research, the author consulted programmes, newspaper articles, reviews and personal letters in the collection of Nesta Toumine now deposited with Dance Collection Danse Archives. Other resources include films of several ballets by Nesta Toumine in the collection of Albert Davy, and the author's own experience as a student and dancer with the Classical Ballet Studio from 1959 to 1967, as well as programmes and clippings in the author's personal collection.

Politics and Perseverance

Antze, Rosemary Jeanes. 1986. "Nesta Toumine: Classical Ballet on a Shoestring." *Dance in Canada* No. 49, 4-10.

Antze, Rosemary Jeanes. 1991. "Apprenticeship: Oriental Examples." In Eugenio Barba and Nicola Savarese, eds. *A Dictionary of Theatre Anthropology: The Secret Art of the Performer*. New York: Routledge.

Anderson, Jack. 1981. *The Ballet Russe de Monte Carlo*. New York: Dance Horizons.

Demers, Edgard. 1996. "Nesta Williams Toumine (1912-1996) Legacy of a Luminary Lady." *Dance Collection Danse News* No. 42, 1, 6.

Jeanes, Rosemary. 1982. "Tradition and Learning in Odissi Dance of India: Guru-Sisya-Parampara." Master's thesis, York University.

Rowe, Andrea. 29 Oct. 1990. "Madame Toumine: The Dance Goes on for Teacher at 78." *The Ottawa Citizen*.

Ryman, Rhonda. 1994. "Impressions of a Reconstruction: Capturing the Essence." *Canadian Dance Studies* 1, 89-106.

Tam, Pauline. 3 Feb. 1996. "Trained in Europe, Ottawan Pioneered Ballet Education." *The Ottawa Citizen*.

Interviews

Thistle, Lauretta. 17 Oct. 1983.

Toumine, Nesta. 22 Aug. 1983, 25 Sept. 1983 and 17 Oct. 1983.

Politics and Dance in Montreal, 1940s to 1980s:

The Imaginary Maginot Line between Anglophone and Francophone Dancers

Iro Valaskakis Tembeck

A metaphor taken from history books will serve as a graphic image to direct the ensuing discussion of Montreal's dance past. The Maginot Line was conceived by French war minister André Maginot to block off possible German invasion. It acted as a fortification of the eastern and north-eastern borders of France from 1927 to 1936. Since the Maginot Line did not extend into the Belgian-French frontier it was easily penetrated by German forces in 1940, and the Germans were thus able to invade France after all. What the French thought was a foolproof way to preserve their territory from foreign invaders turned out to be ineffectual.

When applied to the dance scene in Montreal, the metaphor of the Maginot Line can help to explain that cultural insularities existed in this city, invisibly segregating French Canadian dancemakers from their Anglophone counterparts. Age-old societal tensions between members of Canada's two founding nations had created isolated cultural pockets in the city with few people transgressing the language and social divide. St. Lawrence Boulevard, acting as the city's geographical centre, in fact separated the Anglophone west end from the Francophone east end. It became an invisible tacit frontier. One cannot therefore speak of Montreal's choreographic past as being one single history. Many different histories occurred simultaneously and were perceived differently by the various cultural sectors. With the accession of the Parti Québécois to the political scene in 1976, the promotion of the "French Fact" and the cultural distinctiveness of French Canadian society became an uppermost concern. In the dance picture that meant that the contribution made by English Quebeckers to local dance history became obscured, while other pioneers of dance history were deemed more important to remember and emphasize. The following essay uses an ethnographic approach and reflects on several moments of Montreal's choreographic past. These moments illustrate both a cultural selective blindness and the varying perceptions of our dance heritage.[1]

---

[1] This is a revised version of a paper first published in the *5th Hong Kong International Dance Conference July 15-28, 1990*, Conference papers vol. 2, 261-73. Reproduced by permission of the author.

Politics and Perseverance

The methodology applied here is inspired by French historian Michel Foucault's groundbreaking theories. In his *Archéologie du Savoir* (1969), he stressed the importance of looking at history not in the customary way of examining what has existed throughout the ages. Rather he dwelled on the importance of what had ceased to exist, or what in fact had been "silenced." History to Foucault was to be an analysis of the discontinuity of events, of those "silences" of history which revealed specific mind frames and evolving social values dictated by those in power. As Marietti explains, Foucault's New History approach examines "what has been done *and undone* [emphasis mine], what has been announced and denounced" (1985: 7). This theory rests on questioning facts which are no longer considered indubitable and which are now explained under a different light. Foucault's revisionist method proves that history is no longer absolute and one sided. Multiple readings of historical events are indeed possible. Such new interpretations make use of other disciplines such as the social sciences to expose the underlying politics and *mentalité*, or specific social attitudes, that have shaped past events.

In reconstructing the past, the historian fashions a picture based on interpretation. All historiography is an interpretation of facts; conclusions are drawn as a result of the particular lens that has been selected. As historian Henri Irénée Marrou maintains, with many others, the limits of history are its arbitrary explanation of what has come to pass (1954: 162-96). The operative term here is "arbitrary." Explanations are arbitrary because they are coloured by the personality, knowledge and particular stance of the historian-onlooker. He will start with a hypothesis and will set out to prove it by adopting a specific path of inquiry. Furthermore, there is in this task of writing history a creative element of intruding into unknown territory because of a hunch or a yet unproven belief. The historian's task then is to find the necessary arguments to prove the stance he has already adopted. In the ensuing essay, I use this conceptual framework to present idiosyncratic moments in Montreal's professional dance past.

Unlike the United States, Canada does not have a melting pot, preferring to adopt an official policy of multiculturalism. The majority of Canadian society, however, is affected by a duality provided by the two founding nations, the French and the English, which have spawned separate cultures and lifestyles. The country's geographical vastness offers communication problems from the standpoint of transportation as well as from psychological and ideological dimensions. To these two dominant cultures one must add the diverse cultures of neo-Canadians, all of them making up Canada's demographic reality. This multi-faceted reality cannot be avoided when investigating the history of an art form beyond the mere chronology of events. It, in turn, dictates that an ethnographic perspective be adopted in the inquiry.

Curiously enough, it was not in the more sophisticated centres of Montreal and Toronto that the first professional dance company was launched but in the prairie land of Manitoba. The Winnipeg Ballet Club (later renamed the Royal Winnipeg Ballet) was created in 1938, closely following the birth of the San

Francisco ballet, the first West Coast company in North America. Yet a full twenty years separate this first founding from that of a sister company in Quebec. Montreal-based Les Grands Ballets Canadiens was incorporated in 1957, a telling time lapse which immediately underlines the culture lag that was then experienced by all of French Canada.

Cultural Dependencies, Anachronisms and the Distinctness of Quebec Society

Quebec's short-spanned dance history displays several anachronistic patterns. In the first place, the rise of modern dance in this province coincided with that of classical ballet. Such a paradoxical twin birthing process caused two otherwise rival art forms to evolve parallel to each other. These two dance genres were often found to be complementary as they proceeded along their respective paths of growth. As an offspring of Europe, Canada held on to Old World aesthetic values, too often looking for inspiration to London, sometimes to New York, for its cultural role models; Quebec artists had the added burden of looking to their own particular mentor: Paris. These influences affected the Canadian aesthetic sensibility. Of the three major Canadian ballet companies Les Grands Ballets Canadiens, located in Montreal, seems quite Latin and European in both style and temperament, thus setting it apart from its sister companies the National Ballet of Canada and the Royal Winnipeg Ballet, which respectively reflected from the beginning a more definite British and American image.[2] These different cultural dependencies underlie the country's two major sensibilities and are the result of distinct lifestyles and value systems.

Unlike the rest of the Canadian federation, French Canada was held under the strict, tight fist of the reigning Catholic clergy. Under its hegemony Quebec dance experienced a continuous uphill struggle to overcome official and popular prejudice regarding its practice. Numerous edicts proclaimed by Quebec's ultra-conservative Catholic Church emphasized the evils of dancing, which were believed to breed promiscuity and sinful behaviour among Catholic youths. It was as late as 1952 that Cardinal Léger partially lifted the ban on dance by accepting folk dancing as a legitimate social activity. Ballet, modern dance and ballroom dancing, however, were still peripheral to the social structure, and in reality it was only during the 1980s that dance finally moved out of the fringe to weave itself into Quebec society. Its place, nonetheless, is far from being a coveted one when compared to the other arts, which still enjoy greater recognition to this day. If music and theatre managed to be sporadically tolerated in French-Canadian traditional society, dance, unfortunately, due to its primary emphasis on the expressive body, could never hope to be so sanctioned. Its survival testifies to sustained disobedience of clerical will.

[2] By the 1990s, however, the respective images of these companies had altered with new artistic direction: Lawrence Rhodes, at the helm of Les Grands Ballets, brought in a new repertoire of American and European contemporary choreography; James Kudelka, since 1996 Artistic Director of the National Ballet, known for its productions of the ballet classics, favoured contemporary creations by himself and other Canadian choreographers.

Politics and Perseverance

Elsie Salomons.

The modernization of Quebec society, in fact, meant its secularization, and the Catholic stronghold mainly affected the French sector. Education was separated into two school boards: Catholic and Protestant. Whoever was not born a Catholic was to be raised in the Protestant school system regardless of race or creed. Such segregation and cultural duality was thus encouraged from birth, and the differences in the experience of growing up were increasingly apparent in the two separate sectors of Quebec society. Divergent upbringings indeed coexisted in Montreal, nurturing the *Two Solitudes* so aptly described in Hugh MacLennan's novel of 1945.

Montreal's professional dance grew by fits and starts, always remaining on the fringe. The details varied, however, depending on which aspect of society or subculture one examines. When dance programmes started appearing in institutions of higher learning in the French-Canadian educational system during the mid-1960s, this development was considered to be quite avant-garde for Montreal. Unknown to most people, however, McGill University had been offering six credited courses in dance in its Physical Education Department since 1929, a fact which becomes all the more significant when one realizes that the first university dance degrees were awarded in the United States in 1928. McGill held a progressive stance not only in relation to Quebec's or Canada's cultural landscape but also a broader international perspective. Graduates from the McGill Physical Education Department during the early 1930s went on to introduce modern and creative dance in high schools of the Protestant school board in Montreal. Pioneering efforts in this field were made particularly by Elsie Salomons (1914-1999). Yet her work, like that of her colleagues, was consistently ignored or remained unknown. McGill, being a Protestant bastion, naturally followed the liberal-minded ideology of *mens sana in corpore sano* (a healthy mind in a healthy body). Why have these facts been ignored by both the dance community of Montreal and the general public? The answer is simply that *Montreal's choreographic history has mainly, if not exclusively, focused on the knowledge of the French-Canadian lineage.* The contributions made by English Quebeckers to dance history seem to have been rendered unofficially invisible, or erased from memory, or even disguised with time.

A possible reason for the historical silence that obliterated the work of some pioneers can be found in the increasing prominence of dance professionalism in Montreal, which coincided with a major cultural revolution in

Quebec, triggered by French-Canadian left-wing intellectuals in the late 1940s. Militant waves were about to disturb Quebec's social structure; among the militants were radical artists who rebelled against cultural imperialism and what they considered to be an obsolete system of values. They rallied together and published a manifesto known as the *Refus global* in 1948, the ripples of which were felt even in the unlikely and budding field of dance. The sense of urgency felt on the part of French-Canadian intellectuals and dancemakers was not felt to the same degree by English-speaking dance artists who had not lived through the same cultural tensions and social repressions.

The shock waves engineered by these Québécois artist-rebels launched a protest for artistic independence from foreign prototypes or models. Meanwhile, elsewhere in Canada and even in English-speaking Quebec, artistic colonialism remained and models from abroad kept being carefully reproduced. The neighbouring United States also acted as a cultural Leviathan surreptitiously influencing its northern geographical partner. Canadian identity had yet to be defined, as Edward McCourt pointed out so well in an essay prepared for the Royal Commission on National Development in the Arts, Letters and Sciences, better known as the Massey Commission, which undertook a comprehensive analysis of the state of Canadian culture (1951: 67-82).

The dominant theme arising in the aftermath of the *Refus global* was the re-appropriation of French Canada's cultural roots. Quebec's Quiet Revolution started in the 1960s and its well-defined political stances generated specific social changes. Likewise, in signing the manifesto, artists rejected all external influences and opened wide the doors of innovation in what became known as the Quarrel between the Ancients and the Moderns in this national search for artistic freedom and identity.

Two of the artists who signed the *Refus global* manifesto happened to be dancemakers. Françoise Sullivan and Françoise Riopelle were to explore new types of dancing based on spontaneity, individual expression and the collaboration between art forms. Their approach, which naturally shunned all past traditions, based itself on the precepts of the new Automatiste school of art launched officially during the late 1940s in Quebec.

Since dance as an art form had never had the chance to establish itself permanently in Montreal, it had no tradition to speak of, and hardly any frames of reference were available to the general public or even to the practitioners themselves. Although Montreal had always been the first port of call in the North American touring circuit for national and international companies such as the Ballets Russes and the Ballets Jooss among others, this type of entertainment catered mostly to the cultured elite, the majority of whom came from the English sector of town.

By refusing to adhere to any dance code or convention, French-Canadian dancemakers of the late 1940s forged a peculiar situation. No real chronological caesura was experienced since there had not been any *sustained* effort in professional dance prior to this anarchic stance. This rebellious action

Carmen and Maurice Morenoff, ca. 1926.

constituted more of a *cultural embargo* towards past historical assets which were at best, embryonic. An odd case of consecutive virgin births stem from this point onwards in Montreal dance; virgin births which, in refusing to come into contact with external influences, have reached the proportion of cultural amnesia. Furthermore, in wanting to achieve the peerless status of originality, dance artists have at times suffered the need to reinvent the wheel.

Maurice Lacasse-Morenoff (1906-1993) was among Montreal's veteran pioneer dancemakers. A real dyed-in-the-wool French Canadian, he started to dance at the age of six at his father's studio. Adélard Lacasse had opened a ballroom dance academy as early as 1895 in the east end of town, which was then solely a French district. His son Maurice took over the school in the 1930s, adding ballet to the already established curriculum of ballroom dances. Maurice was completely self-taught, having learned ballet with the help of a handful of technical manuals on the subject. Such unorthodox training and other eccentricities take on additional significance when one realizes that he never considered even observing a class – let alone taking one – in other Montreal studios to verify his purely literary or theoretical knowledge of ballet.

Another tendency at that time was to adopt Russian names to emulate Diaghilev's blockbuster company. Thus Maurice Lacasse became Maurice Morenoff when he and Carmen Sierra, his wife, muse and dance partner, embarked on a five-year tour of North America from 1926 to 1931. Together they danced his "toe tap and acrobatics" routines in many of this continent's well-known vaudeville theatres and nightclubs, and it is precisely on account of his theatrical flair and show-business expertise that he is best remembered in Montreal.

Despite the fact that Morenoff benefitted from adequate experience gained from both his North American five-year tour and his annual stagings of musicals for the Variétés Lyriques (the Montreal small-scale equivalent of Broadway shows) from 1936 to 1951, he was consistently disregarded by the Montreal dance community. He was practically ostracized and was considered an oddball because of his eclecticism.

Morenoff's contribution to dance history was hence marginalized. He was labelled as an entertainer, a wizard at adagio partnering who could never reflect the high seriousness of the art of dance. He was, nonetheless, responsible for spawning the first generation of male ballet dancers of Montreal, who subsequently succeeded in acquiring international reputations. Fernand Nault, ballet master at American Ballet Theatre for twenty-two years and later artistic director and choreographer-in-residence at Les Grands Ballets Canadiens, is among the most striking examples. This was an important feat, first because of the clergy's generally negative attitude towards dancing, and secondly because choosing dance as a masculine profession was even more disapproved.

Working in another part of town along this invisible Maginot Line were several immigrant dance artists. Most of them were central European dancer-choreographers who had come with impressive cultural baggage and credentials. Yet they worked alone in Montreal, quietly endeavouring to build their own following. These European dancer-choreographers felt equally at home in both ballet and the German style of *Ausdruckstanz*, which they had practised prior to their arrival in Montreal. One of them, Ruth Abramowitz Sorel, a former Wigman dancer, alternately billed her company under the names of Les Ballets Ruth Sorel or the Ruth Sorel Modern Dance Group, illustrating once again that the lines between rival disciplines of ballet and contemporary dance were easily transgressed in Quebec.

An important link to German Expressionist dancing therefore existed in Montreal in the work of such artists as Ruth Sorel and Elizabeth Leese. Leese had studied at Dartington Hall in England and had been a member of the Swiss dancer Trudi Schoop's company. Yet this direct link was never explored nor exploited in order to nurture growth. Each dance school of the city worked single-handedly at building its own audience. Mutual indifference was felt among the various schools of dance and recitals were hardly attended by disciples of other schools. The choreographic explorations conducted by these dance artists remained available only to a specific sector of the general dance audience, which itself was quite small. Much ignorance, often self-inflicted, and little bilingual publicity of events, characterized Montreal's dance scene.

Meanwhile, the first generation of local dancers nurtured by Morenoff, as well as the artist-rebels who had signed the *Refus global* manifesto, all went into a self-imposed exile by the end of the 1940s. Not finding sufficient stimulation in Montreal to quench their artistic thirst for the New, they left for such international cultural centres as New York and Paris.

Demographical Survey of the Dance Scene in the 1950s and 1960s

Statistically, few native Montrealers founded dance companies in Quebec, although Jeanne Renaud, as founder in 1966 of Le Groupe de la Place Royale, is a notable exception. A quick survey reveals that Les Ballets Jazz de Montréal was created in 1972 by a triumvirate which included a Hungarian refugee (Eva von Gencsy), a Parisian-Moroccan émigrée (Geneviève Salbaing) and a Haitian

Eva von Gencsy, 1963.

(Eddy Toussaint). Toussaint later severed his connections with Les Ballets Jazz in order to found his own company, Le Ballet de Montréal, in 1973. Furthermore, Les Grands Ballets Canadiens was founded in 1957 by Ludmilla Chiriaeff, a White Russian, whose earlier company, Les Ballets Chiriaeff, mainly performed on television during the mid-1950s. The now-defunct Entre-Six founded in 1974 had the American Lawrence Gradus at its artistic helm. As for the city's second oldest modern dance company, Le Groupe Nouvelle Aire, it was founded in 1968 by Martine Époque, a French woman from Provence, while another short-lived modern dance troupe, the Contemporary Dance Theatre, was launched by Mexican born Hugo Romero in the same period.

It was only during the 1980s that newly formed companies were finally being headed by Montrealers and French Canadians such as Paul-André Fortier, Jean-Pierre Perreault and Ginette Laurin. Critical and public opinion have been quick to crown them as the true exponents of an indigenous Québécois style of dancing for various reasons. Both Toussaint's company and were considered by experimental dancemakers (who, after all, constitute the bulk of the dance community in Montreal) to be too commercially oriented, since they provided a more popular type of entertainment. As for Entre-Six and Groupe Nouvelle Aire, these two companies had disbanded. Romero's quick stab at contemporary dance-making was also short-lived. Lastly, when Le Groupe de la Place Royale chose to relocate in Ottawa in 1977, it could no longer directly contribute to the Montreal scene.

The aftermath of the *Refus global* manifesto brought a certain dismantling of Montreal's fragile dance scene. Because of the iconoclastic stance that had been adopted, there was no collaboration between different dancemakers, no channels of communication, and no institutional support structure. What inevitably emerged was a *tradition of no tradition*, making the historian's task of documenting the historical events and establishing their lineage doubly difficult. An imaginary wall indeed severed the city in two, splitting it right at St. Lawrence Boulevard which, as the geographical nerve centre of the metropolis, determined that the West side was English while the East side belonged to the French. In analyzing Quebec's dance history, one can easily see it as a case of a historical chain made up of missing links with little cultural interface occurring. Spontaneous generations spawned further spontaneous generations and virgin births, a potential choreographic lineage was deftly nipped in the bud and consecutive revolutions substituted for evolutionary growth.

Confronted by such a peculiar cultural and artistic landscape, how can one explain the sustained prominence of Les Grands Ballets Canadiens through several decades? Its mandate from the beginning was never merely classical, for it chose a loose and eclectic repertoire quite unlike the purist angle adopted by the National Ballet of Canada. Les Grands Ballets Canadiens favoured the neo-classical genre, modern dance, experimental works and museum pieces alike. Its parent company, Les Ballets Chiriaeff, had arisen out of the need to meet the many choreographic contracts granted to Chiriaeff by the nascent television network in Montreal. The exposure brought about by these television shows improved the image of both dance in general and this company in particular, and partly explains the resiliency and survival that this company and its subsequent offspring experienced. Dance was introduced into people's homes via the television screen and it, in turn, educated its public. In so doing, it greatly helped define dance as an art form and as a profession. Chiriaeff, the right person at the right time, was henceforth dubbed godmother of professional dance not only for providing regular salaries to many starving dancers but also for helping to give a more legitimate status to this occupation.

Cultural Dualities, Historical Breaks and Ironic Twists

Les Grands Ballets' broad artistic vision does not particularly reflect a Québécois sensibility, either in choreographic treatment or in thematic concerns. Nevertheless, when the rise of nationalism spilled over onto the performing arts scene in Quebec, the company strategically required its dancers to alter their names to more French-sounding ones, because it had been unofficially denounced as not sufficiently representative of the French-Canadian identity. During the 1970s, Sacha Belinsky became Alexandre Belin, Roslyn Faierstein was billed as Roseline Forrestier and Sylvia Kinal became known as Sylvie Chevalier. If the previous generation headed by the Lacasse-Morenoffs had sought Russian-sounding names to emulate Diaghilev, we now witness a fascinating reversal in this conscious gesture to frenchify stage names. Another interesting departure from the norm is that Les Grands Ballets, with its non-traditional approach to repertoire, deliberately avoided nurturing stars of international stature comparable to the National Ballet's Karen Kain and the Winnipeg's Evelyn Hart.[3] Paradoxically, Montreal's 1980s cult figures tended to be picked from the otherwise unlikely field of modern or experimental dance. Margie Gillis, a latter-day Isadora Duncan, was awarded the Order of Canada in recognition of her role as this country's cultural

---

[3] Although Anik Bissonnette and Louis Robitaille do have a star following in Montreal, they gained their popularity as offsprings of Toussaint's company. It was the public who continued to hail them as stars once they became part of Les Grands Ballets rather than company policy favouring star status and divas.

ambassador at the relatively young age of thirty-three, while Louise Lecavalier, a post-modern dancer with Edouard Lock's La La La Human Steps, received a Bessie award for outstanding performance.

When the separatist Parti Québécois acceded to power in Quebec in 1976, it was responsible for drafting this province's first government dance policy, which stressed nearly unilaterally the need to encourage French Canada's dance heritage. The angle adopted by this policy implicitly discarded the work of previous cosmopolitan pioneers such as Ruth Sorel because it did not illustrate specific Québécois concerns. The policy also stressed the creation of new choreographic works and not the reconstruction of past masterpieces. Further insularities become apparent at this point and they, in fact, created a second cultural embargo.

Quebec's cultured elite of the last two generations, for the most part, consisted of wealthy, educated English Canadians who had been part of a separate educational structure. Access to information in all fields including dance was easier on this continent for English-speaking intellectuals. French-Canadian society was ruled by linguistic enclaves and narrow-minded religious upbringing. Misconceptions and factual misrepresentations abounded. To illustrate this particular *mentalité*, many Québécois mistakenly interpreted the fact that most dance studios were located in fashionable and upper class WASP Westmount as a sign of snobbery. Yet practical considerations dictated the choice of a Westmount location over that of other ones in the city. Located within the city but identified as a separate borough, Westmount did not fall under the municipal laws which required all dance schools to pay an extra entertainment tax. Thus Westmount studios were able to escape further taxation which would have created an additional economic burden for poverty-stricken artists. Such a misunderstanding is indicative of the unnecessary communication barriers existing in the city, which stretched the Maginot Line dividing the dance community in Montreal even further.

The Metaphor of the Maginot Line

The actual Maginot Line did not stop the Germans from invading France. When this metaphor of an invisible demarcation is applied to Montreal theatre dance, many similarities become apparent. After thirty years of rejecting European, particularly German, influences, Quebec modern dance has now come full circle. Present dancemakers unconsciously looked to Pina Bausch and to Reinhild Hoffmann for their role models in the late 1970s and early 1980s, little knowing that Kurt Jooss, who was the mentor of these avant-garde *Tanztheater* choreographers, had disciples of his school right here in Montreal several decades earlier.

Both Elizabeth Leese and Ruth Sorel had trained and danced with the masters of German Expressionist dance before their arrival in Canada. They had tried to establish schools in Montreal, yet their work quickly sank into oblivion. Ironically nevertheless, it was this very tradition that was now being

280

Jeanne Renaud, Le Groupe de la Place Royale, ca. 1966.

sought by the present generation, which had no inkling that this tradition had actually been on hand in the past. Ironies keep increasing when we realize that today Quebec dance is acknowledged internationally because it is no longer considered insular or hermetic and has finally shown some kind of allegiance to trends which can be recognized by an international public.

Previously, Montreal's choreographic tendency in the early 1980s had reflected local thematic concerns and an absence of any acknowledged universal style of movement. Critics were baffled, not having any lasting reference points to latch onto nor any thread of continuity; instead they were confronted with hermetic works which often reflected a closed-in culture. By the late 1980s Montreal's dance theatre exponents showed a more European sensibility. They had become more organized, had adopted a better publicity strategy and were ready to discover and to relate to what was happening elsewhere. These current choreographers are the heirs of Le Groupe de la Place Royale and Groupe Nouvelle Aire, the two founding institutions responsible for spawning this city's modern and post-modern dance lineage.

Further dichotomies and discrepancies can be sensed in the choreographic lineage stemming from these two parent companies. Nouvelle Aire and its progeny tend towards a more European sensibility, particularly in respect to dance theatre and social critique. Place Royale, on the other hand, seems more American, because of its tendency to adopt Cunningham's autonomy between art forms and its clear advocacy of abstract and linear imagemaking. Paradoxically, however, Place Royale was the spiritual heir of those artists who had been involved with the *Refus global* manifesto in praise of artistic independence from cultural imperialism of any sort. Their ironic rapprochement with an American school seems at this point to disavow these previous principles.

As for the rival group, Nouvelle Aire had been founded by Martine Époque, the French woman who acted as surrogate mother for many of the present generation of indigenous dancemakers. They, in turn, adopted the dance-theatre approach using themes that were at first too culture-specific. Topics such as liberation from sexual taboos, the gay movement, and other provocative subjects had already been forgotten in the arts elsewhere by the late 1970s and early 1980s, at the time when they were emerging prominently in Montreal. These French-Canadian dancer-choreographers posed as agent-provocateurs, and severely criticized their own society's extremist morality. Such choreographic themes and treatments triggered as a rebellion against Catholic upbringing could not have arisen elsewhere in Canada, since other provinces were not subjected to rigid Catholicism. The existential anguish Quebec dance betrayed in overthrowing past values was doubled by the struggle to come to terms with a still-unformed new set of guidelines.

Ironies and dualities, historical anachronisms and breaks, parallel tracks and twin births. Such are the terms that describe the overall picture of the growth of professional dance in Montreal. Today Quebec dancemakers seem to have shed their previous radicalism and donned a mellower and more structured approach which, as a result, brings them more into the international limelight. Sombre content is becoming less important and form is finally being developed. Baffled dance critics, not knowing how to interpret this proliferation of original dance styles have coined it "*le nouveau bouger*," which can be translated as "the new way of moving" for lack of a better term. There is a return to a technique of sorts, and there are conscious or unconscious borrowings from a variety of other schools that, as in the case of most other current post-modern trends, result in a pastiche or collage of the old and the new. Montreal dance is just entering its adult phase; its dance artists, after having consciously refused to be either British or French or European, are now revealing themselves to be North American. Their new post-modernist aesthetic displays high tech, fast-food, video-clip and design approaches, along with an androgynous mentality more fitting to today's North American society. They are now able to communicate on a world-wide scale, for they seem to be talking a dance language that is recognizable. Their collective efforts are thought by some to have forged a Quebec school of dance, an issue that would easily provide an interesting departure point for a long-winded research into the origins and characteristics of the "Quebec style."

Broader issues are raised by this case study. One of them involves the close interaction of politics and artistic events. The other deals with the dance historian's delicate task.

Art and Politics:

1. Art often arises out of radical, left-wing militantism, as a protest against archaic values. It frequently thrives on conflict, whether internal or external, and it is through the careful analysis of this conflict that an understanding of the art form may be reached.

2. Adopting a socio-economic and cultural perspective seems necessary in certain cases in dance history. Contextualizing is often the key towards understanding the role of an art form within a particular society.

3. Some political artmaking can be as totalitarian in attitude, even when left-wing, as arch-conservative regimes are expected to be. Information and knowledge concerning the past can be filtered by both extreme positions thus lending a bias to the recording of past events and altering our perception of history in the process. The cultural embargo and selective amnesia experienced by theatre dance in Montreal is a striking example of such left-wing totalitarian mentality.

4. Cultural segregation does sometimes occur in a society and it can exist over and above the fact that this society is bicultural or multicultural in nature. This case study offers an intriguing example of cross-cultural non-communication. Varying perceptions of historical events yield different factual accounts. These accounts are shaped by aesthetic and political positionings of writers or people in power as they choose to highlight certain events over others. An overall picture made up of several opposing interpretations would be needed to make history transcultural and multifaceted.

5. The filtering of artistic knowledge and reference points can be the result of propaganda favouring one specific aspect of artmaking over another (the New as opposed to the Old or vice-versa). The clergy in Montreal had consistently banned the practice of dance for centuries. Knowledge concerning the choreographic art was therefore sparse. With the advent of radicalism in dance this art form fared no better. The information still remained sparse. By filtering all external influences and role-models, radical dancemakers in Montreal bred and sustained a closet culture. The choreographic lineage of French-Canadian artists was the only one systematically documented or given prominence. Thus, similar totalitarian attitudes are to be perceived in both radical artists and clergymen: they both sought to proselytize even though they approached their propaganda-making from diametrically opposed positions.

6. There is a possibility that the cultural and artistic embargo experienced in French-Canadian dance could have been the result of an *unconscious* ignorance due to communication gaps rather than a deliberate ignoring of

facts. Here again the lack of cross-cultural interaction within the same society is underlined anew. The historical silence which ensued would then have to be redefined as having been unintentional but still a result of societal tensions.

The Historian's Task:

1. In a situation when no history has been written about an art form in a particular culture, one cannot speak of reviewing the facts but rather of uncovering and discovering them (finding as well *where* and *what* they are) before attempting statements of opinion. The historian becomes a historiographer: she has the added burden of being responsible for issuing the actual first drafting and recording of history and her duty is to include as much documentation as is available and reveal as much data as possible.

2. The delicate treading over political time-bombs in revealing past history becomes yet another burden to the normal task of the historian. The question it raises is how much of what has been unearthed needs to be made public in a first reading and drafting of a history of an art form?

3. Likewise, how is the historian to piece together the information concerning a peculiar chain of events when it is consistently filled with missing links? This is where Foucault's method, invoked at the beginning of this essay, proved to be most valuable in providing the necessary analytic framework. It is through the analysis of the silences provided by history that a general path of growth will be perceived. It is what has been discontinued, broken and scattered that is of interest and enlightening, not only what has continued to exist. The historical problem is thus attacked from a reverse angle. Some of the missing links involved mistaken perceptions. The fact that many dance studios existed in the English district of Westmount in the 1940s and 50s was viewed by most French Canadians as a case of catering to the financial elite. Yet the opening of Westmount studios was in order to escape the additional municipal entertainment tax that Montrealers had. Rather than being an act of snobbery, the Westmount studios represented a creative way of erasing this tax requirement and thus helping starving artists save more money. This mistaken perception, however, dissuaded many Francophone dancers from studying in Westmount studios and contributed to thwarting possible growth and interaction among the various sectors of the dance community.

4. Any work of historiography or even dance history is, at best, but an interpretation of events. It makes use of a creative bias provided by the historian-onlooker who will search elements in the events of history to prove the point she has taken. Her work is therefore creative, and like all creative output is, itself, subject to various interpretations and readings. According to Marrou, theory does precede inquiry. The historian then has to fashion adequate tools of investigation as part of his creative task.

Montreal dance history presents a fascinating case study about how to defy assumptions, presumptions and prototypes of historical growth. The topic has required the present historian, who embarked on several years of research in this field, to find an appropriate "other" framework than that one would normally use, one which is more in compliance with the very idiosyncracies it is treating. This history has also proven that dance can very easily become the body politic.

Author's Postscript

Since the 1990s Montreal's shifting dance landscape offers a richer, more complex and diversified picture. Numerous dance styles are now presented by local choreographers, which incorporate ballet, martial arts and ethnic influences, all of these resulting in a hybrid product. Edouard Lock has gone balletic and Paul-André Fortier now draws inspiration from the visual arts rather than from theatre. Relative newcomers – Roger Sinha, José Navas and Irene Stamou – allow their own ethnic backgrounds to permeate their work. Performers display better craft, having honed their technical skills now that technique is back on the scene. There are also several networks, both official and alternative, that broaden communication between artists, and reflect Montreal's changing demographics into a cosmopolitan city influenced by the many cultures that comprise it. The latest irony is that dancemakers today acknowledge the importance of history and now wish to be part of it. This puts the brakes on the previous tendency of a "tradition of no tradition." Retrieving and restaging works created some fifteen years ago is the current new trend among established choreographers. It arises from the fear that their own groundbreaking works will be lost to the younger generations.

Dance in Montreal is no longer in its adolescent stage, but has reached adulthood. What was true in the 1980s no longer really fits the ever-widening and complex portrait. This essay has reflected various choreographic events that prevailed within a particular time-frame and gave birth to idiosyncratic signature styles.

References

Ellenwood, Ray. 1992. *Egregore: The Montréal Automatist Movement*. Toronto: Exile Editions.

Foucault, Michel. 1969. *Archéologie du savoir*. Paris: Gallimard.

Marietti, Angèle. 1985. *Michel Foucault: archéologie et généalogie*. Paris: Livre de poche.

Marrou, Henri Irénée. 1954. *De la connaissance historique*. Paris: Seuil.

McCourt, Edward. 1951. "Canadian Letters." In *Royal Commission Studies: A Selection of Essays Prepared for the Royal Commission on National Development in the Arts, Letters and Sciences*. Ottawa: Government of Canada, 67-82.

Ministère des Affaires Culturelles du Québec. 1984. *Politique de la danse au Québec*.

Politics and Perseverance

Tembeck, Iro. 1988. "Four Decades of Quebec Modern Dance: Maintaining a Steady Independence from Tradition." *International CORD Conference Dance and Culture Conference Proceedings July 13-17, 1988*, 191-207.

Tembeck, Iro. Fall 1994. "Dancing in Montreal: Seeds of a Choreographic History." *Studies in Dance History* 5: 2.

Three Intrepid Montreal Dancers of the 1940s and 1950s

Pierre Lapointe

Studying three pioneers of dance in Quebec, Marc Beaudet, Roland Lorrain and Fernand Nault, was not a haphazard choice. If history is to shed light on our past, people should learn about pioneers in Montreal dance and their contributions, so that they may serve as examples to future generations. This essay traces the careers of three male performers during the period of the 1940s and 1950s. Their determination to pursue their dance ideal reveals steadfastness and willpower, indispensable elements for anyone who devotes himself to an artistic career. Dancers of today perhaps might find them interesting role models.

At the beginning of the 1940s, Beaudet, Lorrain and Nault, who had not known one another previously, found themselves studying ballet at the Morenoff Studio in Montreal. Imagine three adolescents dedicating their careers to dance in that period when dance was burdened by prohibitions from both the Roman Catholic Church and society.

For many years, the Church had disapproved of dance, warning that it would lead to immoral lifestyles and that it was a way of selling one's soul to the devil. Ecclesiastical writings abound to that effect. Part of a lament originally published in 1873 is a good illustration:

> Listen to the regrets of a bewitched young girl
> For she loved dances and parties too much.
> Listen to her sobs, her cries of misery,
> Touched by her unhappiness, be dispassionate.
>
> Ah, my folly gives me absolutely no hope,
> I loved the pleasure of the dance too much!
> For my stupid pride, my lot is that of Lucifer,
> Who fell from heaven to the pit of hell.
>
> Oh! misery, oh! unfortunate mother,
> Why didn't you clasp me to your breast?
> Why did you permit me the party and the ball?
> Your permissiveness was cause of my downfall.
> (quoted in Séguin 1986: 52; translated from the French)

Politics and Perseverance

From the 1930s to the 1980s, the Morenoff Studio was a nerve-centre of French-Canadian dance. Self-taught, Maurice Morenoff had some knowledge of social dance and acrobatics, but classical ballet was a relatively unknown domain for him. Despite his lack of formal training, he was able to devise a programme in classical dance for his students with the help of books and related research. His technique was considered "wooden" in the eyes of purists; however, he succeeded in transmitting to his pupils a very definite love of dance, and his school became a seedbed for dance artists.

In 1947, Alphonse Saumier of the École de Ballet de Sherbrooke, when asked why the majority of students were Anglophones or Jewish, replied: "The reason is simple. The Church threatens to exclude from its midst all those who give themselves to dance" (*La magie du spectacle* 1987). Catholic nuns were particularly hard on young girls who practised dance. Young women who were not Catholics could consider a dance career more easily, for they did not have to overcome as many prejudices. It is not surprising then that, faced with such a negative attitude, the majority of French Canadians refrained from signing up for dance classes. Thus it was indeed courageous of these three young boys to confront the Church's disapproval.

Reflecting on public opinion concerning dance as a masculine activity, Fernand Nault has said: "It was sinful for girls, but even more sinful for boys. It was even a disgrace" (Nault quoted by Brousseau in *La Presse* 27 Oct. 1984). People believed that ballet displayed womanly qualities, but, if by chance a boy turned towards ballet, suddenly the old prejudices resurfaced: "effeminacy," "homosexuality," "perversion," prejudices all equally offensive to the aspiring male dancer. Such an attitude was far from favourable for the growth of professional dance.

Fortunately nowadays people recognize that the male dancer's training is as demanding as that of an athlete. Just like the athlete, the dancer practises on a daily basis to develop muscular strength and coordination. When seen in this light, old prejudices may easily vanish. Young people of today have more freedom in choosing a career than they had in the past. In general, what still worries parents is the precariousness, indeed the brevity of a dance career, and the lack of financial security.

But back in the 1940s, the family milieu was not too receptive to the idea of a dance career. If it involved a girl, a family might tolerate such a choice, but when it concerned a boy, there were additional reservations. Considering all these factors, Marc Beaudet's case was quite exceptional. His father, a doctor by profession, was reasonably open to the arts. Besides, Marc's brothers Jean and Pierre were well regarded as musicians. Marc's artistic vocation blossomed easily from this fertile ground. Roland Lorrain and Fernand Nault had entirely different experiences. Lorrain came from a bourgeois milieu and his father was a veterinarian. The family did not favour his aspirations, and he constantly confronted a father who resisted dance. For his part, Fernand Nault sprang from a working-class background in Montreal's East End. His father, a ruggedly masculine type, did not look kindly on his son becoming a dancer. By contrast, his grandmother had married the "fiddler" of the village of Saint-Tite-des-Caps and adored dancing. His own sister Margot was a dance instructor at the Morenoff's studio. That was enough to goad him into becoming a dancer. Nault began to study tap dance with Raoul Leblanc before choosing classical ballet.

These three pioneers of Quebec dance had an almost identical start in dance, having studied with Maurice Morenoff in Montreal, and all three danced in shows produced by Les Variétés Lyriques. Lorrain took the stage name of Nicolas Québec, and Fernand Nault borrowed the name Bill Watson, while Marc Beaudet kept his own name. Following their first stage experiences, Lorrain and Beaudet left for New York to pursue their dance studies. The three dancers were able to create an enviable place for themselves in American and European ballet companies, despite their starting from religious and family constraints as well as the public's low esteem for dance. Who were the audiences for professional dance performances in Montreal? According to journalists of the period, attending shows was mainly the pastime of the wealthy and the upper middle class, which was already an au courant audience. Most people, however, scarcely knew professional dance and only occasionally went to annual school recitals or vaudeville shows.

In the United States at that time, professional ballet was evolving steadily. Several great artists of the Diaghilev Ballets Russes had settled there and contributed to the growth of classical dance in North America. Among them were Mikhail Mordkin and George Balanchine. In 1937 Mordkin founded the Mordkin Ballet, which became Ballet Theatre in 1939. After a European tour in 1957, the adjective "American" was added to the company name to emphasize its national affiliation. Henceforth, the official name became American Ballet Theatre. And Balanchine, together with Lincoln Kirstein, founded Ballet Society in 1946, which went on to become the New York City Ballet in 1948.

The Marquis de Cuevas, arts patron of Chilean origin and married to one of the granddaughters of John D. Rockefeller, followed a similar path. Unlike Balanchine and Mordkin, he was not a dancer himself, yet he donated part of his fortune to Ballet International, the company he founded in New York in 1944. An interesting anecdote about the company's premiere was told by Lorrain. The premiere took place after seven months of rehearsals, and the city's elite attended. From the start, the lack of experience of the corps de ballet was evident, and one ballerina fell, pulling three other dancers down with her. The public, however, already smitten with the youthfulness of the troupe, did not ask for much, and criticism was merciful. Yet from one night to the next, fewer and fewer people showed up, to everybody's dismay. The Marquis later discovered the reason for the shrinking audience. He surprised the box office manager, who was announcing "sold out" on the telephone when really only a few tickets had been sold, hence the lack of an audience. The show disappeared from the billboard after only two months of performances. The season that had opened on October 30 closed December 23, 1944.

Marc Beaudet.

These companies played important roles in the careers of the three pioneers. In 1944, Ballet International was looking for dancers. Lorrain auditioned and was accepted; it was the beginning of an adventure that lasted seven years. Marc Beaudet enrolled at the School of American Ballet with Balanchine as programme director. When Balanchine decided to create a dance company and launched Ballet Society, Beaudet was included. Thus began the first phase of his career, which was eventually to take him across the United States, South America and Europe. As for Fernand Nault, chance truly played into his hands. Ballet Theatre was performing in Montreal during its continental tour when a dancer was injured. Fate would have it that Nault would be chosen as a substitute for a six-week period. Happily for him, this original contract was extended into twenty years with Ballet Theatre.

Marc Beaudet mainly danced in the United States and Europe. He began with Balanchine's Ballet Society and then followed by touring with Alicia Alonso, who was trying to make the art of dance accessible to a wider public. Tours in Cuba, Central America and South America were especially risky. Dancers were transported in wagons, scenery was inadequate, floor boards crashed under the weight of the company, platforms fell in – it was definitely "a tour from hell," in his words. Despite these misadventures, the dancers thought themselves lucky to be able to continue dancing. He ended up finally performing in Léonide Massine's troupe in Paris, Monte Carlo and Florence. When Beaudet returned to Montreal in 1952, he opened a dance studio. The budding television network offered him the possibility of choreographing, but his dreams were more along the line of founding a dance company. Finding himself limited in these career ambitions by growing competition, he accepted a job at the National Film Board.

As for Roland Lorrain, he discovered that he possessed a talent for writing. On his return to Montreal in 1952, and after dancing for seven years with six different companies, he took up journalism, landing a contract with *Le Petit Journal*, for which he wrote a weekly column on the state of dance in Montreal in 1953. Following that, he penned several articles for the dailies *Le Devoir* and *La Presse*. Hired later as a public relations officer at Les Grands Ballet Canadiens, he kept this post for some time. In 1973, the Canada Council gave him a grant that enabled him to write the history of the company and its founder, Ludmilla Chiriaeff, published later that year. This book would be followed in 1985 by his autobiography, which garnered mixed reactions.

Of the Morenoff pupils, Fernand Nault was the one who left the greatest mark on dance in Montreal. He entered Ballet Theatre in 1944, where he was, in turn, soloist, rehearsal director, teacher, ballet master, reconstructor and choreographer. He worked with all the great names of international dance, and a generation of young American dancers came to rely on his excellent visual memory. Returning in 1965 to Montreal, his birthplace, he was invited to share the artistic direction of Les Grands Ballets Canadiens with Chiriaeff and to remount the masterpieces of the world repertoire. He worked as teacher for both the company and school, while also serving as ballet master. But his greatest contribution was as a choreographer, and the continuing success of his *Nutcracker* proves this. Choreographically, *Carmina Burana*, *Symphony of Psalms* and *Tommy* were all key works, both in Quebec and abroad. By bringing a new public to Les Grands Ballets Canadiens, his ballet *Tommy* succeeded in breaking barriers that had hitherto kept men from choosing careers in dance. Today, at an advanced age, Fernand Nault is a no less pivotal dance figure in Quebec. He is the first Québécois to have acquired international status in the world of dance, and his contribution to the development of classical ballet in Quebec remains significant and enduring.

Reflections and Issues

I chose to study these dance pioneers because, for me, it was essential to bear witness to the courage and resolution required of three young men who set forth on an adventurous path without knowing its possible outcomes. People say that faith moves mountains, and this affirmation seems to hold true in their case. Only an undying love for dance could have led these three to follow their dream. For starters, two major hurdles awaited them: the painful financial condition of dancers and the bad reputation attached to the profession. Dance as a career has invariably been discredited and considered a second-rate occupation. That is reflected not only financially but also in relation to the social acceptance of the dancer's profession. Thus, throughout the period when the trio performed in shows at Les Variétés Lyriques, it was a matter of "doing it for nothing" for the sake of gaining valuable stage experience.

As for the social acceptance of the male dancer, this is also far from accomplished: people tolerate these career choices, but very rarely do they celebrate them. The idea that "dancer equals homosexual" is so well entrenched in people's minds that it will be decades before this image will change. Nevertheless, when Roland Lorrain published a series of articles in the 1950s on the Montreal dance situation, he chose to use terms such as "sissies" and "homosexuality," terms which today may seem inoffensive to us, yet were considered crude and provocative in that period.

Fernand Nault.

The term "intrepid" seems to be a good word to describe the three pioneers, since it underlines how they had to overcome numerous obstacles, financial as well as familial and religious, to have an international career in dance. Only Beaudet received financial assistance from his family for his dance training. Lorrain, for his part, made the acquaintance of a sponsor who turned out to be Pierre Elliott Trudeau's mother, who paid for his dance classes. Nault had to rely on himself. Since his family was not well off, there was no question of hoping for family aid. Only in carrying out menial work did he succeed in amassing the funds necessary to cover his dance studies.

It is obvious that in researching an individual's contribution, one must establish the social, cultural and political contexts of the time. In this case, the decades of the 1940s and 1950s are of particular interest, since the period is known as "la grande noirceur" [the great darkness] because of the Duplessis despotism. Ultimately, however, my research bears essentially on the professional identity of the three pioneers and not that era, during which societal prejudices strongly affected the professional development of male dancers. It often happened then that unsophisticated audiences did not know the difference between masculine styles and effeminate mannerisms, with the result that, when a dancer carried out slow and languorous movements, people charged him with being effeminate, which was not at all the case. As for more vigorous movements such as tour en l'air, they were accepted by the public because they were "manly."

In the final analysis, was it chance that launched the respective careers of Nault, Lorrain and Beaudet? In Nault's case, it most certainly was, for he found himself in the right place at the right time. A dancer injured himself; he needed to be replaced right away. Nault luckily obtained the contract that would link him with the American Ballet Theatre for more than twenty years. He has excellent recollections of this entire period, and his anecdotes on the subject are numerous. According to journalist Mathieu Albert, Nault "had to dance on a stage while scenery crashed around him; painter Marc Chagall had to finish painting Nault's costume just seconds before he went on stage, or even worse, the ballerina in her *Swan Lake* tutu surged into the middle of the stage, only to realize several minutes later that the decor around her was for Antony Tudor's *Pillar of Fire*" (*Le Devoir* 10 March 1990).

As for Marc Beaudet, his performing experience resulted from good opportunities that came his way, and he made an honourable career with several different companies. His dream on returning to Montreal in 1952 had been to create a ballet company. Let us remember that in those early days there were no funding institutions and the Canadian Broadcasting Corporation was just starting. After several choreographic efforts for television, he put aside his projected company to accept an offer from the National Film Board of Canada and devoted his time to film production until his death in 1978.

In the case of Roland Lorrain, he worked for six different ballet companies, and on his return to Montreal he devoted himself mostly to journalism with several Montreal newspapers. The three male dancers thus demonstrated varying degrees of accomplishment and professional success. They were far from ordinary figures, given the social context of the time, and for this reason their careers are worth studying. Their image as dancers was doubly marginalized in an ultra-traditional Quebec.

The social climate reigning in Quebec in the 1940s and 1950s was highly charged with religious fervour. The archbishop of Montreal, Cardinal Léger, filled with good intentions, inaugurated his famous radio broadcast *Le chapelet en famille* [The Family Rosary]. Every night at the vesper hour, all Catholic Quebec knelt down to recite prayers. At that time, people traditionally sought approval from the parish ecclesiastical authorities for any and all social behaviour, and anyone who strayed would be denounced. Dancing as a profession was badly regarded both by the family and by the Church. Furthermore, even if interested, boys dared not register in ballet classes for fear of being taunted by their peers, who would not fail to associate dancing with being effeminate. The three young men defied such opinions.

Beaudet, Lorrain and Nault leave a tangible legacy. Beaudet was best known as a dancer and a teacher. He was one of the first to take part in Ballet Society under the direction of Balanchine. Considering the extent of Balanchine's choreographic work and influence around the world, Beaudet could consider himself privileged to have worked under him. When he first returned to Montreal, he devoted himself to teaching and sharing with his students the knowledge he gained from his masters. The training offered at the Studio Beaudet was based on two methods. Beaudet, having studied with Russian teachers such as Balanchine and Massine, followed the Russian method. His associate Paula Dunning from the Sadler's Wells Ballet specialized in teaching the Royal Academy of Dancing syllabus. The core group of professional dancers who studied there included Vanda Intini, Lise Gagnier, Louise Ricard, Françoise Berthier, Geneviève Salbaing, Michel Boudot, Rémi Tricov and John Kelly. Beaudet's teaching experience was short, scarcely three years, but he was much appreciated by his students who, in their turn, became dance teachers.

Writing is Lorrain's best contribution to the Quebec dance scene. His articles in *Le Petit Journal* and *Le Devoir*, the publication of his history of Les

Grands Ballets Canadiens and his autobiography illustrate his commitment. His writings are interesting because they give us a glimpse of the atmosphere that reigned in dance during the period 1953 to 1962. *À moi ma chair, à moi mon âme! du cloître au ballet* [To Me My Flesh, to Me My Soul! From the Cloister to the Ballet] is an autobiography relating his life during his time with different ballet companies.

Of the three pioneers, Nault was the only one to devote his life completely to dance. A self-effacing type, he never sought to push himself forward, for above all, a job well done was what mattered most to him. From the time of his professional debut with American Ballet Theatre, he progressed through the ranks, from the corps de ballet to soloist, and then from rehearsal director to ballet master, enjoying the longest international career on stage of the three pioneers. His first choreographic experiences were with various American regional ballet companies, and, in 1964, he became resident choreographer with Les Grands Ballets Canadiens. The critics reproached Nault for having staged a rock-opera destined for Broadway, in which classical technique was totally absent. *Tommy* was not considered to be a work representative of a classical ballet company. Be that as it may, *Tommy* proved to be a definite financial success and succeeded in filling the coffers of Les Grands Ballets Canadiens.

Nault felt the influence of his background, and several of his works have themes relating to Quebec folklore. Certain features stand out clearly in Nault's choreographic work. His preferred theme seems to be the sacred and spiritual character of dance, which no doubt comes from the fact that he was raised in a traditional Québécois family. Born in the 1920s, in a working-class Catholic milieu, he was immersed in his youth in the religious ambiance of the 1940s, and the influence of religion is reflected in his choreographic work. Moreover, in his private life, Nault is a collector of religious objects. Among other things, he owns a group of icons and angels as well as twelfth-century relics. He admits that several characters in his ballets and the works themselves are filled with religious feeling (Breniel 8 Apr. 1990). Of the three dancers, Nault made the greatest impact on Quebec's choreographic scene. His works are danced around the world. Despite his age, he still pursues his creative work, at a slower pace. His assistant, André Laprise, helps him in this task. Les Grands Ballets Canadiens, Les Compagnons de la danse and l'École supérieure de danse du Québec have all profited from Nault's wise advice concerning their choreography, teaching and artistic planning.

Beaudet, Lorrain and Nault made up the first generation of truly professional French-Canadian dancers in the 1940s and 1950s. They broke the ground and led the way for a second generation of dancers who were active during the period from 1950 to 1965. I should add that this second generation, of which I am a part, did not find a road paved with gold, but the possibilities for training and work certainly were better than those the preceding generation knew. In addition, the male dancer would soon be seen in a better light and recognized as an artist equal to the actor and opera singer.

The arrival of European teachers, the coming of television and the formation of professional troupes – Les Ballets-Québec (1949), Les Feux Follets (1952), the Montreal Theatre Ballet (1956) and Les Grands Ballets Canadiens (1957) – all helped encourage the emergence of second-generation dancers. The latter have enjoyed greater visibility because of, among other reasons, television and a better public image. Furthermore, in a climate more receptive to creation, several choreographers conceived original Québécois works, thus contributing to the development of Montreal dancers and, at the same time, to the evolution of dance in Quebec.

Modern dance, until then in a fledgling state, took off with the arrival of the third generation around 1965. Le Groupe de la Place Royale (1966), Le Groupe Nouvelle Aire (1968) and Les Ballets Jazz de Montréal (1972) were three companies whose mission was to promote modern dance and jazz as an integral part of the artistic milieu. From then on the Montreal scene was in a position to offer a great array of choreographic events, as much in classical dance as in modern and jazz. Today Montreal is known as an important dance centre, and many of its male dancers and choreographers enjoy international reputations.

The work of this trio of bold dancers, and the courage and bravery they have shown, marked a step forward in the evolution of professional dance in Quebec. The diverse structures now in place to support the vocation of the artist, notably specialized theatres, funding agencies and changes in public perception, are several factors that make the dancer's career much easier today.

References

Albert, Mathieu. 10 Mar. 1990. "La timidité incurable d'un chorégraphe." *Le Devoir*.

Breniel, Pascale. 8 Apr. 1990. "La personnalité de la semaine." *La Presse*.

Brousseau, Jean-Paul. 27 Oct. 1984. "Au nom de la danse et de tous ses pionniers." *La Presse*.

Lapointe, Pierre. 1999. *Trois danseurs intrépides: Montréal 1940 et 1950*. Montréal: Les Éditions Francine Breton.

Lorrain, Roland. 1973. *Les Grands Ballets Canadiens, ou cette femme qui nous fit danser*. Montreal: Éditions du Jour.

Lorrain, Roland. 1985. *À moi ma chair, à moi mon âme! du cloître au ballet*. Montreal: VLB éditeur.

La magie du spectacle, 1860-1960. 1987. Sherbrooke: Musée du Séminaire de Sherbrooke.

Pereima, Alex. *Réminiscences*. Undated notes on dance in Montreal. Iro Tembeck Archives, UQAM Département de danse.

Séguin, Robert Lionel. 1986. *La danse traditionelle au Québec*. Québec: Les Presses de l'Université du Québec.

Madame Hylda Davies' dancers in *Ship Ahoy*, Majestic Theatre, Halifax, 1928.

Dance and the Outsiders:
Ballet and Modern Dance Companies in Nova Scotia

Pat Richards

"Boom or bust" seems to be the way to describe the professional and semi-professional ballet and modern dance companies in Nova Scotia. When they were thriving they were supported by the community and praised by the press, but when they died nobody seemed to care or to think them worth fighting for. Why was this? Why did the performing companies arise when they did? Why did they die? Each time a successful dance venture failed was it because there was no administrative structure or money to support it, or because there was no audience support, or because there were no local dancers trained to a high enough level?

The answers to these questions are interrelated but one common thread seems to wind its way through all the scenarios: each time dance has flourished as a serious theatre art it has been nurtured and inspired or pushed along by somebody who has come from outside Nova Scotia, from England, the United States, Latvia, or from other parts of Canada. They came, stayed for varying amounts of time and then left, significantly affecting the dance scene during their stay.

Nova Scotia has a long and rich history of music and dance, as Max Wyman points out in *Dance Canada: An Illustrated History*. The native Mi'kmaq danced here first. When Marc Lescarbot, a Parisian lawyer accompanying the explorer Samuel de Champlain, arrived he devised the first dance-theatre performance in Canada, *The Theatre of Neptune*, which took place at Port Royale in 1604 (Wyman 1989: 20).

When the first settlers arrived, Nova Scotia seemed a rocky and desolate place far away from the cultural centres of the world. It was through music, dance and theatre that they kept their links with home and their traditions alive. The Acadian and Scottish communities, scattered throughout Nova Scotia, danced, sang and played music at most social get-togethers. Ceilidhs, traditional Gaelic dance gatherings, have been, and still are, an essential part of Nova Scotia's Scottish communities, with step dance quadrilles still being performed. These small, largely fishing communities, were relatively poor, so that sharing an evening at home with friends was an inexpensive form of entertainment. People also knew that the chance of their returning home was almost impossible and so they put down roots and tied themselves to this new land. Some settlements in Nova Scotia also had very wealthy residents, often

Hylda Davies.

posted from Britain and France, who tended to their country's interests in the colonies. Most of these people saw their stay in Nova Scotia as a necessary sojourn. These individuals attempted to recreate the cultured life of the European middle and upper classes. The fortress of Louisbourg, isolated on Cape Breton's east coast, had two French dancing masters in residence, between 1720 and 1754, who taught the families of the upper classes. Halifax was an important sea port to the English in the eighteenth and nineteenth centuries, and English officers stationed there amused themselves with balls, musical entertainment and plays. The *Weekly Chronicle* of 1797 had a headline which read "Dancing School," and reported that "Mr. Powell's new room, opened on last Monday's night, his days of teaching are Mondays, Wednesdays and Fridays, except on those Wednesdays and Fridays when his duty calls his attention to the theatre" (quoted in Mullane 1926).

Charles Stewart Powell was the manager of and actor with the Theatre Royale. This school taught the minuet, country dances, cotillions and other "fancy steps."

Arriving from England in 1971, I was surprised to find how sparsely populated Nova Scotia was, how little creative dance was taught in the schools, and in my naiveté I felt like a modern dance pioneer. During my twenty years of involvement with the dance community in Nova Scotia and through my research I have become aware of Nova Scotia's tremendously rich traditional dance and music heritage, and it was against this backdrop that I began to consider dance as a theatre art in Nova Scotia and to wonder why a professional company has never been able to survive here.

Nova Scotia's first dance company for which I have evidence, the Madame Hylda Dancers, developed from a school which was formed in the 1920s after a chance encounter in Woods Brothers, a prosperous store in Halifax. Joy Reddin and her daughter Marguerite were in the toy department making a purchase. The store clerk, Hylda Davies, and Joy Reddin began discussing a dance figurine and then dance in general. Davies was newly arrived from England with her sister Kate. They were dance teachers but had no idea how to get established in their new home. Reddin had been advised by her doctor to enrol her daughter in dance classes to help with the leg problems Marguerite was experiencing as a result of childhood rickets. Reddin offered to call her friends and see if they could find enough young girls to start a class. A few were found but, of that first class, Marguerite was the only one who was to stay on to become one of Davies' most successful pupils. She became known as "that 'star' of ballet dancers who would have made a model for a Greek sculpture" (Tully). In the spring of 1925 Ruth Tully joined the school. Tully was the darling of the Halifax press. She had been performing her own work for several years with George's Juvenile Entertainers, eliciting such reviews as "the gem of the evening was the solo dance by Miss Ruth Tully in ballet costume, who was the personification of grace," and "Ruth Tully, whose graceful ballot [sic] dancing has so often charmed the concert going public of Halifax" (Tully). Mariel Mosher, Greta Rent and Betty Davidson also joined Davies' school in the 1920s. Mosher, one of Davies' featured soloists, later assisted Davies by teaching and choreographing after studying and performing with Albertina Rasch in New York in the early 1930s. Davidson and Tully also went away to study in England and New York but on their return, also in the early 1930s, they left Davies and established their own schools of dance.

Halifax at this time had several theatres with a strong tradition of vaudeville; however, only the Majestic Theatre and the Strand showed moving pictures. In 1926 J.F. O'Connell contracted Davies to present prologues to the movies. The live entertainment was used to entice people into the movie houses. Tully remembers being given a box of chocolates as a performance fee with supper at the Green Lantern on Saturdays. Their success led eventually to two dollars and then five dollars per performance! This contract lasted for twenty-five years (Turnbull 1987: 8). The press of the time commented on the professionalism of the dancers and the high standard of the performance. In 1927 an outdoor concert was held in the Halifax Public Gardens and the page-size advertisements for the event featured Davies and her "Classic Dancers."[1] Another headline said, "The Whole City is Going to See Mme. Davies and her Classic Dancers."[2] Four thousand people crowded into the Public Gardens to see this event which was repeated in 1928 with improved staging and lighting. Davies' dancers were brought to the Canadian public's attention in 1928 when Pathé News came to Halifax to film the dancers. The footage, which unfortunately has not been found, captured the dancers frisking on a sandy beach at Cow Bay. Stills of this film show the dancers in Duncan-style Grecian tunics and barefeet performing interpretive dances. Fortunately one film is still in existence. It was filmed by Mosher's father at the Capitol Theatre and shows a 1935 prologue, danced by Mosher and other Davies dancers.

[1] These advertisements are part of the collection of primary source materials in File MG 20 1870 #1-20, Public Archives of Nova Scotia, compiled by Mary Turnbull and her daughter Kim in preparation for the Dance in Canada Conference in Halifax in 1985. The collection includes clippings from the *Halifax Mail Star* and many other local sources.

[2] It is interesting to note the Greek theme and the outdoor concert, in the style of Isadora Duncan and the whole Rousseau movement. Davies may have seen Canadian dancer Maud Allan perform in London in 1908. Duncan was also performing in London at this time, but the British preferred Allan as she was considered more musical and prettier than Duncan. See Jowitt (1988: 99).

Marial Mosher.

Over the years some of Davies' dancers formed their own schools, after further study in New York and London, or became performers with the Halifax Dramatic and Musical Club, of which Davies disapproved. Davies' studio was closed by 1942, so that when Jack and Zeversa Brayley arrived in Halifax in November 1946 from Montreal with their daughter Sally, who was destined for a career in ballet, they found that there were no studios focusing specifically on ballet. Zeversa Brayley, undeterred, bought a basic ballet book and continued her daughter's training. Fortunately they did not have long to wait. In 1947 Mariss Vetra, the Latvian head of the voice section of the Halifax Conservatory of Music, learned that two Latvians from a displaced persons' camp were performing with the Latvian Exile Ballet in Germany for the allied forces. Halifax at the time had a Latvian Relief Association and the ties between the two countries were quite strong. It was decided that the Conservatory would bring them to Canada to develop a ballet division. The names of these two individuals were Juris Gotshalks and Irene Apinee.

Gotshalks and Apinee had met and studied together in Riga in the studios of the Latvian Opera Ballet School under Harijs Plucis. Gotshalks previously studied with Alexandra Feodorova-Fokina, a Russian-American dancer and teacher, married to the brother of Michel Fokine. After joining the renowned Latvian National Ballet Company, which performed at the National Grand Opera House in Riga, Gotshalks and Apinee quickly rose to the position of soloists. The Latvian National Ballet Company was one of the foremost large-scale ballet companies in Europe prior to 1939 (*Halifax Family Herald and Weekly Star* 3 Aug. 1950). After World War II broke out they were sent to Germany as slave labourers. Fortunately for the pair the Germans recapitulated, allowing Gotshalks and Apinee to raise their status to that of displaced persons. Dance was their passion and they began performing in the camps, eventually joining other Latvian exiles to create a performance ensemble known as the Latvian Exile Ballet. It was also while in the camps that they married and later met Hilda and Alfred Strombergs, who also immigrated to Canada.

The move to Canada was a chance for a new life for the Gotshalks, both in their early twenties. But what a change it was – to arrive in a small city, not speaking a word of English, with the task of establishing a classical ballet school from scratch. In 1948, after their first year of teaching, they presented their initial recital. By this time they had approximately sixty students and all were commended by the *Halifax Mail Star*, June 6, 1948 for their "precision and skill." The *Halifax Mail Star* also noted that at this performance the "Highlights of the evening's program were the dances by Irene and Juris Gotshalks assisted by their pupils. Particularly effective was the pas-de-sclave [sic] ... which closed the program and the charming, Valse Triste.... The dashing fire dance was beautifully interpreted by Irene Gotshalks and drew much enthusiastic applause" from a capacity audience of 1,400 at Dalhousie University's Studley gymnasium.

By 1949 the school had grown to 130 pupils and the end-of-year recital reflected the growing ability of the students. Apinee choreographed a new one-act ballet called *Sally's Dream*, to Franz Shubert's music, featuring Sally Brayley. Also presented on this programme was *Swan Lake*, a choreographic poem in one act. The review of the concert, which appeared in the June 10, 1949 *Halifax Mail Star*, praises the fact that "the brilliant presentation of the ballet *Swan Lake* at the Halifax Conservatory second annual recital of classic ballet before a packed house at the Dalhousie gymnasium Wednesday evening marked the first time that an authentic ballet had been presented in Halifax and won great applause for the directors...." This recital was a landmark event for another reason. The Strombergs were now also resident in Halifax, and Alfred Strombergs had put together an orchestra to accompany this performance (this was the beginning of Nova Scotia's first symphony orchestra). Students from the Nova Scotia College of Art and Design created the stage decor from designs by Ernest Fong, providing a professional atmosphere for the school and its performances. This was also the first year of the Gotshalks' fledgling ballet company, which became known as the Gotshalks' Halifax Ballet. Fifteen dancers were chosen to form the corps de ballet and the Gotshalks' first performance, outside the province, with this corps and Hilda Strombergs as soloist took place on February 10, 1949 in Moncton, New Brunswick. This was the first time that classical ballet had been presented in this city. To Nova Scotia, New Brunswick and Prince Edward Island audiences the company was very exciting and professional but an article in the *Halifax Family Herald and Weekly Star* highlights a problem that the Gotshalks were experiencing; "to the amazement of the Gotshalks they have found themselves pioneers in classical ballet. Things that they took for granted in Europe are not available in Nova Scotia: costume designers, theatrical dressmakers.... 'The Canadians' says Irene Apinee in her delightful accent, 'are wonderful people. But oh, we miss so the art'" (3 Aug. 1950).

The primary purpose of forming the Gotshalks' Halifax Ballet company was to perform at the Canadian Ballet Festival to be held in Montreal in November 1950. The Brayleys, Eagens and Merritts, along with other parents, were keen that their daughters should have this opportunity and so they formed the Halifax Ballet Guild, primarily to fundraise and finance the trip. John Merritt, a

Halifax souvenir programme, 1949.

Halifax surgeon, became the president, Jack Brayley, first vice-president, and Harold Eagan was treasurer. Also part of the first Ballet Guild board were Harry Ormiston, associate treasurer; Maxine Dennis, secretary; and James Myrden, second vice-president. Jack Brayley, with his Canadian press connections, also became the company's unofficial publicist, and Zeversa Brayley and Louise Merritt took on the role of wardrobe mistresses. All these parents were significant figures in Halifax social circles and, to begin with, were very successful in their fundraising ventures. As the productions grew more professional and more lavish the task became harder. Merritt noted in his foreword to *Ballet Cinquante-deux* in 1951 that: "Ballet is being received with enthusiasm across the continent, but at the same time there is a sombre note due to expensive production and continuously rising costs. In other countries the arts have always required financial support in considerable amounts if they were to survive. Up to the present a comparatively small number of people have supported our renaissance. If the public wishes performances of the professional standard such as 'Ballet Cinquante-deux' in preference to the recital type program then a great deal of further financial assistance is imperative" (Merritt 1951).

At first, however, the Ballet Guild was successful and by February 5, 1950, they were ready to present the Gotshalks' Halifax Ballet in *Ballet Premiere*. This performance was to be adjudicated by Guy Glover, representing the Canadian Ballet Festival. The programme consisted of Act I and Act III of *Le Lac des Cygnes* pas de deux and variations, *Sonata Quasi Una Fantasia* and *Don Quixote* pas de deux and variations. The choreography was adapted by the Gotshalks after Lev Ivanovich Ivanov, the Russian choreographer who had often collaborated with Marius Petipa. The company, after a successful audition, left for the festival aboard the train, the Ocean Pacific. All of the money for the trip, the costumes and the hotels had been raised by the Ballet Guild. In a review of the festival written by Glover for *Canadian Art* in the spring of 1951, he said of the *Swan Lake* extract, "this was a charmingly produced classical revival with some fine dancing by Irene Apinee and Juris Gotshalks and some very tidy dancing by a well-schooled, young corps de ballet" (Glover 1951: 127). In this same article he commented on the fact that all the dancers suffered from a lack of performance opportunities and he singled out the Gotshalks particularly.

Here are two young dancers, with formidable technical grounding, who attempt material which is technically beyond almost any other Canadian dancer, yet the relative isolation of their home-base, the lack of frequent opportunity to dance before audiences, the lack of contact with a first-rate *maître de ballet* are rapidly ruining them as dancers of top quality, and both – but Mr. Gotshalks in particular – are developing unpleasing stylistic habits. This is peculiarly distressing exactly because they are so good fundamentally. Their work as teachers has borne excellent results as could be seen in the work of the young dancers in the Halifax Ballet, yet their teaching cannot maintain their dancing. Anyone with a scrap of feeling for good dancing will understand me when I suggest that this situation is tragic (127).

If Glover's opinion is representative of the Ballet Festival organizers it is easy to understand why certain key Toronto dance aficionados decided to bring Celia Franca to Canada. She was to redress this problem by moving all the best dancers in the country to Toronto to form the basis of a new truly national ballet company. In one respect this was admirable, but it virtually destroyed small regional semi-professional ballet companies. It took more than twenty years before Nova Scotia had another ballet company that managed to survive for more than one year. Once the Gotshalks were gone, and after them the Strombergs, ballet went back to being weekly dance classes. Dancers who wanted to perform went somewhere else.

The Gotshalks' Halifax Ballet returned from a successful trip to Montreal and performed the same programme at the Capitol Theatre for the residents of Halifax. The review in the *Halifax Mail Star* of February 6, 1951, includes a photograph of the Gotshalks with Lieutenant-Governor John Alexander Douglas McCurdy and two of their dancers. "Haligonians recognised in their midst to-day the symptoms of a new and rapidly spreading epidemic – balletomania. The numbers so affected are the hundreds who taxed the Capitol Theatre last evening" read the opening paragraph. Also quoted was Glover: "Their [Gotshalks'] *Swan Lake* is without doubt a performance to be seen."

The Ballet Guild had high hopes for their new fledgling ballet company. They hoped it would "encourage Halifax dancers, musicians, designers and choreographers ... enabling them to eventually earn their livelihood in this city and Province and lead to the establishment of a permanent company" (Merritt 1951).

The Gotshalks attended the Canadian Ballet Festival held in Toronto in 1952 with their dancers, but this time they took dances choreographed by Oswald Lemanis who had been a world-famous choreographer with the opera in Riga. He too had left Latvia and was at this time ballet director of the Institute of Musical Arts in Detroit. Lemanis choreographed *The Vision*, extracts from *Don Quixote* and a work called *Fiesta en Seville*. The fact that the Gotshalks were now performing with the National Ballet, invited by Franca, was causing problems at home. Hilda Strombergs had been left in charge of the school, and in the Gotshalks' absence she had been asked to choreograph and provide the dancers for the Halifax Opera Workshop production of *The Marriage of Figaro* and *Bonanza*, a new musical. All was fine until the Gotshalks returned from Toronto and refused to let their dancers do any more performances without their personal approval. Eventually Strombergs formed her own company called Halifax Ballet Theatre, which caused a rift in the community (Bee 26 Dec. 1952). It was the new Halifax Ballet Theatre that attended the 1953 and 1954 ballet festivals. The Strombergs left Halifax later in 1954.

Although the Gotshalks developed the only ballet company in 1949 in Halifax, another studio, the Irene School of Dancing (affiliated with the Maritime Academy of Music) opened and was run by Irene Spence and Herbert Le Frois (*Halifax Mail Star* 8 June 1949). After the departure of the Gotshalks and the Strombergs, the Halifax Conservatory of Music brought Mirdza Grikis Dambergs to Halifax to teach ballet, and later brought David Latoff. They were well loved by their students but did not, however, develop companies.

Modern dance in Halifax grew out of an experimental theatre movement that was blossoming in the late 1960s and early 1970s. There were various groups of dancers, actors, musicians and puppeteers who were exploring mixed-media work and performing it in art galleries and other informal spaces around the province. Judith Garay was involved with these performers and began to teach a movement class for actors. She left Halifax in the early 1970s to study dance in New York, eventually dancing with the Martha Graham Company.

When I arrived in Halifax in 1971 there was some ballet teaching taking place but very little modern. The classes that were occurring were scattered around the city and at Dalhousie University. In December of 1972, the dancers and teachers in the city decided to organize a Graham workshop taught by Norrey Drummond of Toronto Dance Theatre. The workshop was a success and we began to think about organizing a dance co-operative. In the summer of 1973, a second workshop, called "Chance to Dance," was held and from this a group of dancers formed Halcyon, Nova Scotia's first modern dance company. David Weller was the director of the company and its principal choreographer. He had arrived in Halifax from Vancouver where he had become excited about dance through choreographer-teacher Paula Ross six years previously. Also dancing with the company were Anita Martin, Donna Williams and Jeanne Corrigan from the United States, and local dancers: Duncan Holt, Wanda Graham, Ellen Rumm and Sandy Greenberg.[3] The company made its home in shared space in Connor's Carpet Warehouse with the newly formed dance collective, Dance Co-op. The funding for Halcyon came from a Local Initiatives Programme grant, and the company members supplemented their meagre income by teaching for Dance Co-op. During 1973-74 the company toured the province in addition to giving numerous performances in Halifax. The work they created and performed was well received despite the woeful lack of adequate performance spaces. Pier 1 was one such inadequate but important performance space that played a vital role in the development of both experimental theatre and dance in Halifax at this time. In 1974 Weller left Halifax to join Winnipeg's Contemporary Dancers feeling that he was too inexperienced to be the director of a company. Without him and without adequate funding Halcyon dissolved.

---

[3] Jeanne Corrigan later married science fiction writer Spider Robinson and danced professionally under the name Jeanne Robinson.

Dance Co-op continued to exist despite a shoestring budget, no permanent studio space and many staff turnovers. It survived mainly because it was a co-operative and the people who were involved were passionate about seeing dance develop in Nova Scotia, with the ultimate goal of a permanent company. Dance Co-op's dream of a dance company finally became a reality in January 1977. The original title for the company was Dance Atlantic, but everybody just called it the Dance Co-op Company, which remained its name for the two years of its existence. The artistic director was Sara Shelton. A former dancer with Alwin Nikolais and Murray Louis, Shelton had been coming to Halifax regularly to teach modern dance at the summer and winter "Chance To Dance" workshops, and in the fall of 1976 she returned as a permanent teacher and choreographer-in-residence. The original concept for the company was to have eight to ten dancers working in three distinct styles: ballet, modern and jazz; however, this proved to be too unwieldy and the company was pared down to Randy Glynn (later to form his own company in Toronto), Chris Van Raalte, Diane Moore, Saccha Liboiron, Linda Dauphinee and Sheilagh Hunt.[4]

Although the company was in existence only two years it had a prodigious repertoire. Shelton's choreography was a fusion of Nikolais, Louis and contact improvisation; her work "flowed, stopped and went in unpredictable directions" (Thompson 1977). In addition to the crazy eccentricity of Shelton's modern pieces were dances choreographed in the jazz idiom by Mary Turnbull and Penny Evans, more mainstream modern by myself and Jackie Moriarty, and ballet-based work created by Alison Masters.

In Dance Co-op's first year of operation they created a lecture demonstration that toured to schools and a show that they took on the road. In the summer of 1977 they visited thirteen small communities around the province, performing wherever there was space. Glynn remembers one performance at Springhill, where, because there was no suitable covered performance venue, they performed in the middle of the town on a grassy triangle to which the locals drove their cars. They observed the performance through their windshields, and showed their appreciation by honking their horns at the end of each piece. One dance, *Entre Deux*, required Glynn and Masters to run towards each other longingly; however the effect was destroyed when a young boy rode between them on his bicycle! Throughout the rest of 1977 and 1978 the company performed continually in galleries and alternate spaces. The company also travelled to Toronto and Montreal in October of 1978.

Money was always tight however, and there began to be artistic/administrative differences. Shelton was also beginning to do more and more independent performances, eventually collaborating with Jennifer Mascall and later Byron Brown with whom she moved to California. Without Shelton's passion to drive the company, the dancers left for one reason or another and the company ceased to function.

---

[4] The company also had several understudies and three guest performers: Alison Masters, Sekai (formerly Blaine Vaney) and Francine Boucher.

Politics and Perseverance

Following the failure of the Dance Co-op Company there were several bursts of short-lived activity such as Clare Bader's Halifax Dance Theatre in 1979, and Sekai's Sekai and Co., in 1978 and 1979. In 1979 Jeanne Corrigan opened her own school, DancExchange, and formed her company, Nova Dance Theatre, the following year. It is interesting to note that it was at a Halcyon performance in Digby in 1974 that Spider Robinson saw his future wife dance and decided he had to meet her. After Corrigan's marriage to Robinson she lived in the Annapolis Valley where her daughter Luanna and their book *Stardance* were born. While living there she received Canada Council Explorations money to develop a one-woman show called "The Valley Dance Experience." She returned to Halifax in 1978, after studying in New York with Beverly Brown, and moved into a studio space on Hollis Street with Sekai, choreographing and performing with him. This collaboration proved to be temporary, Sekai leaving town shortly afterward and moving to Montreal. Robinson's first performances were under the name Jeanne Robinson Dance Project and were collaborations with Barbara Morgan, Francine Boucher and Diane Moore. She knew, however, that she was going to have a permanent company and that she was going to do it right. For the 1979 Dance in Canada Conference at the University of Waterloo, she arranged a meeting with the Canada Council to find out what she needed to do if she was to become eligible for Council funding. She returned to Halifax, became incorporated, formed a board of directors, hired her first administrator, auditioned for dancers, secured project funding from the province and presented her first fully professional show in April 1981 as Nova Dance Theatre. Her first company included herself, Barbara Fulton, Tish Hopkins, Leta Smith, Duncan Holt and Angela Holt. Robinson had danced with Duncan Holt in Halcyon in the early 1970s.[5]

The reviews of Robinson's debut with her company were positive. Glendon Scott, writing for *Dance in Canada* magazine, concluded, "It was the final piece of the evening, *Stonedrift*, which finally persuaded me that I was witnessing, not merely an evening of enjoyable dance, but the birth of a company" (Scott 1981: 33). Robinson kept Nova Dance Theatre going for six years but at tremendous personal cost, both financially and emotionally. The local audience support for her work was tremendous, she had strong dancers, but she was caught in a Catch-22 situation between the province's then named Department of Culture, Recreation and Fitness and the Canada Council. The Department had a policy that operating funding would be given only to companies that had received the Canada Council's stamp of approval, and if the company could show that they had "bums in seats." However, to qualify for Council funding at the time Robinson was told that she had to meet a "national standard of excellence," translated locally to "Toronto taste," and be doing cutting-edge work, which in Nova Scotia at the time would not draw a large audience (Kelly 18 Oct. 1985). The Department believed in her work and did give Robinson operating grants and by 1986 the chances looked good for

---

[5] After the demise of Halcyon, Duncan Holt moved to Britain, where he met and married Angela, both of them performing with Cycles Dance Company.

Canada Council funding. The Canada Council informed Robinson, by letter, that her fall 1985 and her spring 1986 performances had both met the national standard of excellence but the Council's budget was cut, which meant there would be no support for new companies unless an existing one was cut or died! By 1986 Robinson needed $50,000 for her $170,000 operating budget, but the corporate support that she had been seeking eluded her because she did not have that magical Canada Council stamp of approval. Without this money it was impossible to keep the company together. In an article for *Arts Atlantic* Dawn Rae Downton interviewed the Robinsons as they prepared to leave Nova Scotia for Vancouver. Spider was writing a farewell piece for the local paper: "'Do you think calling this place a snow-choked graveyard of dreams is too much?' he asked. Jeanne didn't think so.... Spider ended his piece with 'On to Vancouver.' He said he might have added 'where I'll probably meet a whole bunch of ex-Haligonian artists earning a living'" (Downton 1987: 2). Downton goes on to say:

> What the community loses is not only an exceptional imagination and will manifested in a more than creditable dance company, perhaps the best and only one of its own it will ever see as funding coffers dry up. With N.D.T. goes its dancers/teachers, the collaborative artists it commissioned, its spin-off projects like last year's eagerly received *Dance Crazy*, and all its interdisciplinary impact in the area. What it loses most, of course, is its own transformation by the dancers' or the choreographers' act of magic.

Nova Dance Theatre survived for six years, a record for Nova Scotia. Robinson left bitter, not at the community, but at the national funding bodies who she felt unfairly penalize those artists who choose to work in small regional areas where they remain in relative isolation, unable to tour to larger centres in order to have their work seen.

Overlapping with Robinson was another enterprise, the Atlantic Ballet Company. In 1982 Marijan Bayer was invited to Halifax to become artistic director of the Halifax Dance School. The old Dance Co-op had by this point undergone major changes including its name. Robinson's school was now the centre for modern dance in the city and the Halifax Dance School focused on ballet, with the beginnings of pre-professional training for young people. In 1983 Bayer brought his company, City Ballet of Toronto, to Halifax, renaming it the Atlantic Ballet Company and adding two local dancers as apprentices. The company performed at Dalhousie University's Rebecca Cohn Auditorium to a sold-out house and toured to Chicago and Bermuda, but by 1984, a Halifax newspaper headline read, "Atlantic Ballet Cancels Season, Future in Doubt." The article by Stephen Thorne begins, "The Atlantic Ballet Company says corporate Scrooges, combined with past management problems, have forced cancellation of its Christmas production of Tschaikovsky's *Nutcracker Suite* and may have crippled the fledgling troupe for good. Just past its first birthday, the ballet has shut down, packed up and gone home. And organizers don't know if they can bring it back" (12 Sept. 1984).

Since the demise of Nova Dance Theatre in 1987 there has been no permanent professional modern dance company in Nova Scotia. Most modern

Jeanne Robinson.

dancers work as independent choreographers and performers. The dream of a dance company is still alive in Nova Scotia but the planning and building towards this dream is taking place slowly and carefully. Halifax Dance School now has a pre-professional training programme with ballet, modern and jazz. It has the Young Company for its senior dancers, performing work by professional choreographers. Dancers are beginning to go on to professional training, and the dance community hopes there will be a dance company in Nova Scotia when they are ready to return.

To return to one of my original questions: Why did the companies arise when they did? First, it was because an exceptional individual, with drive and determination, pushed the company into existence, their energy magnetized those who were here. That compounded energy carried the company along for, in some cases one year, in some, many years. Energy is not the only important aspect, as everyone knows. There must also be infrastructure: a core of dancers from which to draw, financial stability and good administration. All the companies lacked one or all of these aspects. The other reality is that Nova Scotia is a small province, isolated from central Canada. This is positive in many ways; the artists do not follow trends, but seek their own expression influenced by their own experiences here. But it is also negative; the expense of touring makes it impossible to get out and be seen, and to become a national force, a company has to be seen. Developing networks of choreographers and dancers is also difficult with isolation.

Financial support is also central to the survival of any company. No Nova Scotian dance company has received Canada Council operating funding. Most have received some form of provincial funding, although inadequate, and a few have received corporate support. All three are vital to a company's survival here, but the combination of all three requires a sophisticated administrative structure that no fledgling company has. Hylda Davies funded her company because of her contract with O'Connell, and the Gotshalks' Ballet Guild raised funds from local small businesses, but modern dance has had difficulty in attracting corporate support.

There has always been audience support for dance, but without long-term dance companies dance has not grown. Each new company that came along had to start from scratch. Outside companies that toured here were also of no help. Isolation means few companies come, and now the National Ballet of Canada rarely tours to Eastern Canada because it is too expensive and there is no suitable theatre! Many of the visiting modern companies, funded by the Canada Council, killed audiences for modern dance for several years, mainly because the work they performed in smaller communities was inappropriate. These are the same communities that have developed a strong infrastructure of traditional music and dance, but to lay the groundwork for an appreciation and understanding of modern dance as a theatre art takes time. It is interesting to speculate as to whether the other reason modern dance and ballet have not fared as well as traditional folk dance here, is because they are considered elite forms of dance, performed by people with no roots here and therefore not considered relevant to many people's lives.

Finally the one key element is dancers. Davies and the Gotshalks survived the longest because they had a strong core of well-trained dancers, in addition to their choreographic and artistic abilities. Training without a company to aspire to means dancers will leave. A company without a core of well-trained dancers will bring in dancers from outside the province who are likely to leave when their contracts expire. To ensure continuity, dancers need to be able to train here, have a company to aspire to, be able to leave and dance in other places, but know that if they want, they can return. From this pool, new artists will also appear whose roots are here and who will provide the leadership for the future.

Editors' Note

Pat Richards, author of this article, was an influential figure in dance in Nova Scotia from her arrival in 1971 to her death in 1998. She was trained at the Laban Centre in England before immigrating to Canada. She quickly became active in Halifax as a dancer, teacher, choreographer and advocate for the arts. She was very involved in Halifax Dance as a teacher, choreographer, administrator and board member. During much of her career she taught at Dalhousie University in the Faculty of Leisure Studies. She sat on several boards including the Dance in Canada Association, the Association of Dance in Universities and Colleges in Canada, the Canadian Association of Professional Dance Organizations and the Nova Scotia Arts Council. She was also active as a member of Nova Scotia's Education Minister's Advisory Committee on Arts Education and as a member of the work group that created Dance 11, the province's first public education dance curriculum. In 1996 she was presented with the DANS Award, the highest dance award in Nova Scotia for her outstanding contribution to the development of dance.

References

Primary source materials consulted were File MG 20 1870 #1-20, Public Archives of Nova Scotia, housed at the Dance Nova Scotia Archive. This collection of dance materials was compiled by Mary Turnbull and her daughter Kim in preparation for the Dance in Canada Conference held in Halifax in 1985.

Politics and Perseverance

Bee Jr., Jay. 26 Dec. 1952. *The Citadel Reporter*.

Carpenter, Bernadette. 1989. *Spotlight Newsletters 1951-1956*. Toronto: Dance Collection Danse.

Downton, Dawn Rae. Fall 1987. *Arts Atlantic* 8: 1, 2.

Family Herald and Weekly Star. 3 Aug. 1950.

Glover, Guy. Spring 1951. "Reflections on Canadian Ballet, 1950." *Canadian Art* 8: 3, 115-19, 125-27.

Glover, Guy. 1990. *Just Off Stage # 1*. Toronto: Dance Collection Danse.

Gotshalks, Juris and Irene. Scrapbooks. File MG 20 1870 #5-20, Public Archives of Nova Scotia.

Jowitt, Deborah. 1988. *Time and the Dancing Image*. Berkeley and Los Angeles: University of California Press.

Kelly, Deirdre. 18 Oct. 1985. *Globe and Mail*.

Merritt, John. 1951. Souvenir programme for *Ballet Cinquante-deux*, Gotshalks' Halifax Ballet.

Mullane, George. 1926. "The Professional Drama of Yesterday in Halifax, 1787-1870." A paper delivered to the Nova Scotia Historical Society. File MC 100 152 #28, Public Archives of Nova Scotia.

Scobell, S.C. 1953. *Canadian Business Review*, 28-29.

Scott, Gordon. Summer 1981. "Nova Dance Theatre." *Dance in Canada* 28, 32-33.

Thompson. Sally. Feb. 1977. "Review." *Visual Arts News*.

Thorne, Stephen. 12 Sept. 1984. Unidentified Halifax newspaper clipping.

Tully, Ruth. File MG 20 1870 #2, Scrapbooks, Public Archives of Nova Scotia.

Turnbull, Mary. *Dance Nova Scotia Newsletter* 13: 3.

Wyman, Max. 1989. *Dance Canada: An Illustrated History*. Vancouver: Douglas and McIntyre Ltd.

Interviews

Interviews conducted during the 1980s by the author: Zeversa Brayley, Randy Glynn, Wanda Graham, Jackie Moriarty and Jeanne Robinson.

Interviews conducted by Lawrence Adams for Dance Collection Danse: Irene Apinee (1990), Louise Merritt (1990) and Marilla Merritt (1990).

Mary Turnbull interview for Dance Nova Scotia (1985): Dance in Canada Conference Oral Archive Videotape.

Rachel Browne:
Dancing Toward the Light

Carol Anderson

Through the challenges she has faced and her deep, ongoing commitment to her art, Rachel Browne has come to stand as a moral force in Canadian dance.[1] She is a remarkable woman, singular in her courage, her intrepid determination, her unflagging discipline and in what at times has been sheer bloody-mindedness. She is unique among women of her generation in Canada, creating dances regularly for concert performance as she moves into her seventies. Browne has fought her way to this time of her life through doubt, adversity, poverty and active opposition. She has always fought the dance establishment, including that of Winnipeg's Contemporary Dancers, the company she started in 1964, which fired her as Artistic Director and later banned her from entering its studios.

Rachel Browne has fought for recognition, and she fights the passage of time with equal determination. Maintaining a strict daily schedule of strengthening exercises helps her sustain the creative work and teaching which are her life. Browne is dogged and senior. The seriousness with which she weighs moral questions affects every artistic decision she makes. She has enriched those who work with her through her resolute artistic engagement. Yet her present creative state can hardly be called a state of grace.

Browne speaks now in her work about areas which fascinate and provoke her, delving into the primal roots of emotional gesture. She wrestles with the complex tangle of obsession, sweetness, naiveté and toughness which are her nature and the ground of her vision. In her bemused, honest, groping way, her struggle toward an authentic voice makes manifest the evolution of an artist. She just will not quit.

Through the 1950s and 1960s, Browne's complicated woman/mother/leader/dancer/teacher conundrum confounded and occluded her creative urges. She spent long years busy with the demands of Contemporary Dancers. In her earlier periods of creation Browne was tethered by the needs of her company's touring repertory. She was constrained by her desire to fulfil the needs of dancers and of the boards of directors, who have caused her such grief through overzealous involvement with the company she founded. Through an abiding commitment to creating dances, Browne has found a way to create which is not formulaic, but austere, intense and emotionally resonant.

---

[1] Much of this essay is based on interviews with Rachel Browne between 1995 and 1996.

Politics and Perseverance

She has struggled as well with her loyalty to her own training. The formal ideals of ballet became the foundations of her belief in dance. Her early works reflected her respect for these ideals, which had become the creative conventions of the time, by following structural guidelines. They were most often created in relation to existing music. From early days Browne has had a fondness for the voices of women in poetry and song. Folksinger Odetta's songs inspired one of her earliest, and to Browne most enduringly satisfying, suites of dances. Her dances often have drawn inspiration from her favourite poets, Dorothy Livesay or Adrienne Rich. Particular pieces of music, very often solo instrumentals by Bach, have inspired her to move. Her earliest dances seemed created out of a concept of dance as a formal art, a solitary art, somehow isolated from real time. Perhaps this stemmed from her sense of respect for dance as an art with its own "laws" of composition. A more basic exploration of what is expressed through movement came later for her.

Browne's life has had several clear epochs. The roots of her present creation can be discerned in the influences and changes which have marked her life. Suffering seems to have cleared her way to speaking with her true voice. Browne and her work seem raku-fired, earthy, touched with rich, emergent colours and textures. One thing has remained true. She loves dance as her life.

Browne remembers her childhood as a time of indulgence. As an only child, she was spared nothing. Her parents, Russian immigrants, were never wealthy. Browne was born in Philadelphia and grew up in a part of the city called Strawberry Mansion. Her mother, a garment worker, was an independent-minded woman. Browne attended a subsidized day care where her rhythmic talent was noticed, and she was taken to music lessons at the renowned Curtis Institute. Browne studied piano until she was a teenager. Her parents managed to scrape money together for lessons and a piano for her. Browne traces her continuing need for finding solace in nature to her afternoons with her mother in the park. She recalls seeing a dancer dancing on her toes and telling her mother she wanted to study that kind of dancing. From the time she was no more than six, Browne has been dancing.

Browne's parents were politically involved. Her father told her that his wealthy parents had bought his freedom from the Russian authorities and sent him to America. In an interview, she said,

> He read newspapers, and journals, and listened to short wave radio. Whatever he read that came out of the Soviet Union, he believed implicitly that this was truth. My mother was very left wing too. They were on the side of the Revolution as opposed to the White Guard. In the war time, and as far back as I can remember, everything was questioned. I grew up being very wary of the U.S. government. I remember I would try to explain to my friends why communism was better, more humane than capitalism. In junior high I used to go on peace marches and wherever there were protests.

Browne attended Girls' High School, which prepared young women for university. She also attended Sholem Aleichem Folk Shul to learn Yiddish.

She recalls a good deal of discussion about politics there, about the benefits of socialism, and influences from dance and theatre.

Although her parents indulged her, their own lives were edged with tragedy. Her father was an insurance agent. As the area of Philadelphia where they lived began to change from a working class Jewish neighbourhood and fill with black families, racial enmity also moved in. One night Browne's father was brutally beaten while collecting money in one of the very poor neighbourhoods, and never truly recovered his health.

> My mother, right to the end of her life remembered clearly how he came home. She was going to call the doctor and he was saying in Yiddish "Forgive them, they don't know what they're doing." A socialist-communist right to the end.

Browne describes herself, early on, as a "bunhead." She fought a physique, which in her assessment was less than perfect for classical ballet, with constant, obsessive practice. By her teen years she was determined to pursue a career as a dancer.

> I heard of Sunday workshops to be given by Antony Tudor. He was mounting a production of *Les Sylphides* at the Academy of Music with the Philadelphia Orchestra under the direction of Eugene Ormandy. This was an opportunity to work with a great master, so I went to his classes, which I thought were strange and quirky. It was true that he had a very, very sharp side, he could be quite cruel in his criticisms. I remember the kind of direction we got. It was quite a revelation, very sophisticated direction. It wasn't just a bunch of steps, but a certain ambience and mood that we had to capture, very romantic, wispy.

Around 1950 Browne approached Tudor for advice. She feels that he must have recognized where her talents lay, as he guided her toward teachers in New York who were evolving a contemporary way of teaching ballet. One of these was Benjamin Harkarvy.

The day after Browne graduated from high school, she moved to New York. She was seventeen and a half. Browne had many typing jobs to support herself while she made the rounds of the studios. She patched together a schedule of work and two classes a day. Harkarvy was teaching at Carnegie Hall, a honeycomb of studios and studio apartments. Browne describes being constantly starved and exhausted, running from job to class to school, pointe shoes hanging out of her bag, eating lunch from a brown paper bag while she rode the subway.

> I lived a kind of cloistered life. I went to the studio, and then I probably went to work. I practised afterward, always, I practised the exercises I couldn't do well enough in class, to the point of exhaustion. Then I would go to the Automat. I had so little money. Then I would go to work and then back to Carnegie Hall to take my second class. I remember there were some nighttime classes. They were closing up the place but I would still be there in the hallways practising.

Browne went to see the New York City Ballet and the American Ballet Theatre performing at City Center. She avoided modern dance, which she

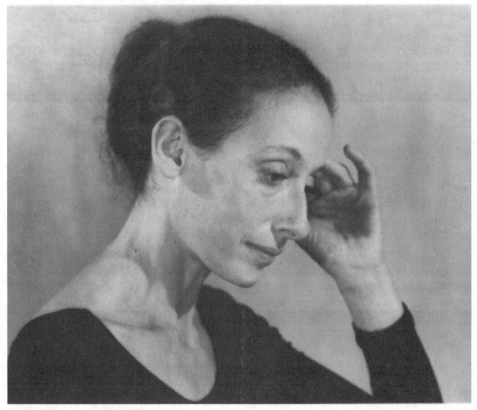

Rachel Browne, ca. 1975.

considered ugly. Browne felt committed to extending her education. Her continuing interest in politics led her to enrol at the Marxist-oriented New York School for Social Research. She met Don Browne, her first husband, in a class there. On their first date they went to the Automat, where you could get food from huge dispensing machines. Browne recalls that he was astonished by how much she could eat. At eighteen, she decided to get married. The Brownes lived at 99 Suffolk Street, a cheap flat in the Lower East Side. Their flat was a firetrap, infested with roaches. Twice they shivered in the street in the middle of the night while firemen put out a blaze. Later Don Browne began to work as a longshoreman, and Browne was thrilled when they qualified to move to a subsidized building in the docks area of Brooklyn. It was clean, complete with beautiful floors, real rooms, and hot and cold running water.

Some of Browne's earliest choreographic experience was gained in New York. She was an earnest young woman, eager to put her political convictions to work. She recalls that she and a group of friends formed a group called The New Century Dancers.

> The deal was, anybody that came to the group had to be enlightened in terms of believing in socialism – socialism or communism, not capitalism.

She remembers the director, Irving Burton, with the wry observation that although the group was composed of women, they appointed the one man as director. Years later Burton's niece Rosalind Newman was invited by Browne to create a work for Winnipeg's Contemporary Dancers. Burton choreographed some politically oriented modern dance which Browne remembers being quite strong. She recalls presenting a work of her own, one of the first made for the group, set to Mozart country dances. Complimented by Benjamin Harkarvy, who was surprised by her musicality and choreographic talent, she recalls not seeing any real contradiction between her politics and her dancing. "It was possible," she says, "to be an enlightened ballet dancer."

Browne attended a round of auditions for Broadway shows, for the New York City Ballet and the American Ballet Theatre. Finally, she gained an Equity card after dancing in a summer stock production of *Oklahoma* with reconstructed choreography by Agnes de Mille. The card enabled her to bypass huge "cattle calls" for the relative luxury of auditioning with forty or fifty dancers at an Equity call.

During her New York years Browne danced with the Ryder-Frankel Dance Drama Company. The company performed work by the directors Emily Frankel and Mark Ryder, who created in the modern idiom, as well as by Sophie Maslow, a legendary member of Martha Graham's first companies. They also performed ballets by Todd Bolender and Zachary Solov. The company toured extensively throughout the United States. Browne was ecstatic with this long-coveted opportunity to get her teeth into performing.

> I remember relishing the touring, thinking every performance was heaven. My whole life was geared toward wanting to perform.

Browne's studies in New York continued to excite her. She often took the same class as ballerinas Melissa Hayden and Allegra Kent, as well as with Glen Tetley, Mary Hinkson, Ethel Winter and other luminaries from the Martha Graham Dance Company. Browne attributes a good deal of her musical sensibility to these classes.

> Harkarvy would create combinations that were so musical they just came alive, they sang. He had exceptional taste and knowledge of music – Bach, sometimes Schubert lieder, and I'm sure Mozart, but Bach was a great favourite. It influenced me greatly in my own musical tastes and in the kind of music I chose for classes. I would demand of a pianist that I worked with that they play exceptional music, something that would develop the musical taste of the dancers.

Harkarvy's teaching influenced Browne deeply. In addition to his musicality, she describes his "direct striving for unmannered simplicity," his eye for "uncluttered, organic placement." At his invitation, Browne accompanied Harkarvy when he went to Winnipeg to direct the Royal Winnipeg Ballet in 1957. Browne's sustaining goal had been to dance in a ballet company in New York. She made the decision to leave with great trepidation, telling herself that she would return to New York when her six-month contract in Winnipeg was up. She had worked like a fiend to overcome a physical makeup which was not ideal for classical ballet. In hindsight she says,

> I definitely did not have the kind of limber body that was needed for a real classical
> dancer. I did have good feet. I was very, very musical and highly intelligent and able
> to pick up movement very quickly. Harkarvy, who has exceptional standards in terms
> of the ballet aesthetic, understood my talent. He didn't just see me as a body, he saw
> how I could move, and my expressiveness. That's why he asked me to join the
> Winnipeg Ballet. So I did, in a sense, achieve part of my goal.

Browne never did move back to New York. She stayed on with the Royal
Winnipeg Ballet, rising to the level of soloist. She recalls dancing the Bluebird
variation with Richard Rutherford, dancing to Vivaldi's The Four Seasons in
Gweneth Lloyd's *Romance* and in Brian Macdonald's *The Darkling*. Harkarvy
returned to New York after one season. Eventually, it became clear to her that
she would not be featured in the classics in Winnipeg either. Browne describes
soon figuring out from the casting, though nothing was ever said to her, that
her classical abilities had been assessed and found wanting.

Browne yearned for the classic mode, though friends noted that she had a
real feeling for modern work. The only "barefoot ballet" Browne was part of
was created for the Royal Winnipeg Ballet by Robert Moulton, a choreographer
from Minneapolis. Called *Grasslands*, the work was set to music by Virgil
Thompson. Dancing with the Royal Winnipeg Ballet was gruelling. The
company toured all over Canada and the United States by bus. There were no
rules governing their travel and rest hours. Browne recalls a repeating loop of
travel and one-night stands that left many of the dancers injured and
exhausted. At home too they were overworked. Browne describes rehearsing
all afternoon, and walking – there were no buses – to her inexpensive apartment down by the Assiniboine River, eating dinner, and walking back to the
studio for night rehearsals. When she was twenty-six, Browne left the ballet.

> I left the ballet company which I dearly loved. I was a fanatic, I fanatically loved to
> perform and dance, I was a total bunhead ballet dancer. I just wanted to get up on
> stage in my pointe shoes and do classical ballet, and the more classical it was and the
> more difficult it was the better I thought it was, and the more challenge I felt.

She attributes her decision to leave to her naiveté and to the prevailing
social forces. Women of twenty-six were supposed to have children, and be
happy homemakers.

> I was socialized to think that part of being a whole woman was to have children. So I
> allowed myself to be convinced to adopt our first daughter. And then I felt quite
> strongly that it was very bad to be working, and to go on tour, and so I resigned from
> the Winnipeg Ballet.

Browne was suddenly home with a child. She had no idea what to do with
the baby, and was abruptly and completely isolated from the identity and life
she had worked hard for. She still practised obsessively, willing herself
through her barre in the kitchen, going to company classes and watching
rehearsals, determined not to let her dancer's skills slip away. Ironically, it

was not until after she had left the company that Agnes de Mille came to work with the Royal Winnipeg Ballet. Working with her, getting close to the feisty cowgirl in *Rodeo*, might have changed Browne's devotion to the classical ideal of the ballerina.

I believe the first dance de Mille did for the company was *The Bitter Weird*. My mouth would water when I would see this dance, and I felt so abandoned. I felt as if I were not really human, as if I didn't have arms and legs, being at home.

After a time Browne began to teach. "I just grabbed the opportunity," she says, "because this was a chance to get out of the house." In time she and her husband adopted another girl and had a daughter of their own. Her mother looked after the children.

I always continued to practise even after we adopted the second child and I was very pregnant with my third daughter Annette. I was practising every day. I was practising the day I gave birth. And after, when I was in the hospital, I was doing my exercises immediately, because I was a fanatic. I had this absolute determination to keep my body in shape, to be able to perform, to not miss out on this thing that I desired so much.

Browne taught at the Nenad and Jill Lhotka Ballet School. Since her New York days Browne had been coaching fellow students, helping them refine their technique. She knew she had the analytical ability to be a good teacher. Quite soon, recital time came along. She took the plunge, she recalls, and decided to make some dances for the senior students, choosing some Brahms waltzes.

This time at the Lhotka Ballet Studio was part of the period of my transformation from a kind of ballet mentality to thinking about dance in a new way.

Browne was burning to dance again herself. She heard some music by Odetta which inspired her.

When this first dance came out of my body it certainly was not balletic. It turned out that I had broken that strong connection to ballet because the movement looked, felt, contemporary. It was just from inside, from my gut some place. Many years later I looked at this old choreography and thought to myself that some of my instincts were really right on. It was very naive, primitive-looking choreography. But a lot of what I do today was there, in that early dance.

Browne created a few other dances, including *Turmoil*, set to a piece of music by Béla Bartók, and Browne and the Lhotkas gave their initial performance at the University of Manitoba. Invitations followed from the University of Winnipeg, the old Normal School and several Winnipeg school divisions. Effortlessly, the company bloomed. Browne called it Contemporary Dancers. The company marked its official beginning in 1964.

Browne began to make yearly trips to New York to study the modern dance technique she needed to understand. She studied Graham technique, then Limón and Cunningham. She cites Ruth Currier as an important Limón teacher.

Politics and Perseverance

Rachel Browne, 1980.

Browne was finding her way into a vocabulary and teaching philosophy, which she has continued to develop. Even now, though she no longer takes classes herself, she makes excursions to New York to observe classes and dancers, always calling on Harkarvy.

> I learned from my trips away, and also from the people that I brought in to work with the company. I really started to make a reversal in my whole training, and I became familiar with, and loved, heavy, rough, floorbound movement.

The company began to evolve. Browne juggled the claims of her family, her growing company and her own driving needs. But it was very difficult. Browne's first marriage ended painfully. Custody of Browne's two adopted daughters was given to her ex-husband, and her visiting rights were severely restricted. Browne recalls bitterly,

> I broke the law. I snuck around and found every way to see them. When they started to become young teenagers they voluntarily chose to be with me. There were three or four years that I walked around feeling very depressed, very sad that I couldn't be with my other children.

Browne's mother continued to help, living in a tiny attic apartment near the inexpensive north-end apartment which was Browne's home for fourteen or fifteen years. Browne sustained her choreographic, performing and touring activities, while the company expanded. It was a lonely time for her.

> My focus during all this time, the marriage, the children, the divorce, the separation, was always chiefly on the dance. These years of being on my own did teach me a great deal. They taught me a lot about how to make my own happiness happen and how to be self-sufficient and how to live on next to nothing.

When long-sought support for the burgeoning company did come from the Canada Council, it came in the form of support for Browne's growth as an individual artist. Browne's relationship with the Canada Council was never an easy one. She recalls being awarded an "Arts Grant A" of $25,000 in 1973, which at her manager's insistence went straight into the company's coffers, while the company itself received $6,000 in support.

> I remember feeling very resentful about the fact that they were always very, very complimentary about my dancing. They felt that it had substance, strength, originality, maturity. The dancers, they said, were still young, and rather juvenile and undeveloped, and they need more modern technique.

Browne was the central force of the company in its early days.

In the beginning the quality depended on me a lot – the quality of my work, my dancing and my choreography for myself. This was also what they [Canada Council] would say, especially that my choreography for myself was really substantive, but the choreography I did for the group was sometimes too light or too entertaining.

So compromise for her own path was built right into the beginning of her company's activities, a familiar quandary. In the company situation she had initiated to serve her own creative needs, Browne found herself consumed by motherhood issues of nurturing and providing.

I knew that I wanted to please the audience, and if I just gave them very difficult, serious stuff I would not have an audience. That did influence my choices, and the choice of repertoire.

Ideal dance managers, who have a love for the art, which comes first in all considerations, are exceedingly rare. Browne has had a particularly rough ride with management. Contemporary Dancers' first manager came from a publicity background. Bob Holloway was an excellent booker and produced slick materials for the company's use. Together Browne and Holloway began the School of Contemporary Dancers. The school was started partly for practical reasons, as a way of generating income and of spreading knowledge of dance within the immediate community. The school grew from its initial enrolment of 30 or 40 to a peak size of about 500. In the mid-1990s the school's population had stabilized at 200 to 300.

From the beginning, Browne's care, and possibly the memory of the early encouragement she received in music and dance lessons, cleared the way for very talented students who came through the school. Many were provided encouragement and extra training in preparation for professional careers. People refer to the school as "Canada's best-kept dance secret." Now under the directorship of Odette Heyn Penner and Faye Thomson, two young women hired, encouraged and guided by Browne, the school has quietly flourished, training many future company members and acquiring a reputation for fine teaching. It is one of three acknowledged Canadian training centres for professional contemporary dancers.

Browne was a novice in terms of power within an organization, and recalls virtually handing Holloway power, allowing him to do most of the negotiating with the company's Board of Directors, and with the councils. It is Browne's understanding that he came to think that the company, once it gained momentum, would be better off replacing her.

He felt that I was at my best when the company was really struggling. The company started because I had a real need to dance, choreograph, perform, and if you take away the heart of why the company started, then you take away the company. I started to suspect that things were not so good when he wanted to lock me out of the office ... and not let me have access to certain files.

Browne went to her Board with her grievances, and the Board let Holloway go. A series of managers followed, more distinguished by their lack of knowledge of dance than their brilliance at managing the dance company. Then in 1979 the company hired Tom Scurfield, who came from a background in theatre and the insurance business. He came to grief when he insisted on acquiring full executive powers from Browne's Board of Directors. When Scurfield moved on, the Board hired Evelyn Polish, who came to the company from a background in management and community work. She stayed with the company for ten years.

By the early 1980s, shifting ideas were circulating in the dance world. The Canada Council had identified the creation of new work as the soul of modern dance. Points were going to innovative young creators, and attention was increasingly on the Montreal scene. Contemporary dance, true to its tradition, was being remade, this time by the influence of the radical revisioning of New York's post-modern pedestrianism and the extravagant riskiness of Montreal dance theatre. In this climate of change, management developed the idea that Contemporary Dancers could boost its fortunes with a change of Artistic Director. There was some discontent among the dancers, and the ill intent spread like a prairie fire.

Although she recalls it as a very uneasy time, Browne did not suspect the precariousness of her directorship. Browne, by her own admission never terribly astute politically, was fully occupied with the pressing needs of choreographing and daily company life. But there were warnings. The Board had formed a production committee, which began to insist that its suggestions be taken. One suggestion, put forward strongly by Rick Muller, at that time Board President, was that the company present *Now I'm John*, a piece set to music by John Lennon and choreographed by Lynne Taylor-Corbett, at the National Arts Centre in Ottawa. Browne felt that the work was not strong artistically, and she was out of agreement with the Board's argument that the dance would attract large audiences. But she felt compelled to oblige, and the company did not do well in Ottawa.

The company's turmoil, which became overt in 1981, culminated in Browne's stepping down as Artistic Director in 1983. She was ousted by the Board, and called down by the dancers. She talks about her disbelief when an ally on the Board, Moti Shojani, came to her one evening as she was rehearsing to tell her of the Board's decision.

> It was as if somebody had punched me out, or I had gotten run over by an automobile, or somebody had taken me and hit me forcefully against the wall. I just could not believe it, I was aghast, I was speechless, I was weeping.

But the report of the Board's decision was true.

> The whole Board was won over to the side of Rick Muller and Evelyn Polish, who were convinced that all they had to do was get rid of me and install Associate Artistic Director Stephanie Ballard and the money would come flowing in from the Canada Council.

Browne is thoughtful about this traumatic turning point, and philosophical about the choices she made. She instinctively protected her needs to create and keep dancing. Most certainly, her continuing presence with Contemporary Dancers has affected the big picture of the company's development, and likely ensured its continuing existence. Browne also faced the painful issue of being "outgrown" by the people she nurtured. Just before leaving for the 1983 Christmas holiday with her family, Browne was handed a letter by members of the company to read during the break.

> I didn't open it until I was on the plane to New York. I knew it would not be a good letter. I had heard some secondhand reports from the Board. I don't think that time will ever be duplicated in terms of the trauma I felt. This was a whole long, long listing of negative statements about me and my way of rehearsing dancers, my choreography, my way of teaching, the way I give notes, my organizational abilities, the way I make up the schedule, the way I deal with them. Many of them I brought right through the ranks, right from novices, because I believed in their talent. And all of them had signed, the whole company had signed this letter. I knew that these were my last days.

Although Browne was devastated emotionally, her feistiness and her thoughtfulness came to her rescue. From the ashes of this attack, Browne took a radical position. She assigns importance to the writing of Dr. Albert Ellis, a pioneer of rational emotive therapy, in helping her encompass this traumatic time.

> I remember ... feeling that if I could remember all the reasons why I was okay, that I could survive this, that I could live through this. Part of me knew that what I was reading on this document was kind of a contrived list of disgruntlements, because indeed I was not perfect, but I knew I was damn good in many ways. This loss equalled great sorrow and sadness, but it did not equal major depression, where I could not function. Not to be able to teach, not to be able to choreograph, not to be able to perform, not to be able to take class and exercise. Then what would I do with my life?

And in the contemplation of the awful emptiness that this would bring into her life, she found that there would be ways for her to bring her beliefs to bear.

> If my love of dance were ripped away from me, I could still do something worthwhile and meaningful and good with my life. I would have my family, who I adore. I could devote myself to peace, and to helping other people, and to working against pollution of the environment.

These thoughts comforted Browne, and gave her courage to go on. It is a measure of her generosity and the deep questioning that has guided her that she has since helped some of the dancers who helped to bring her down, when they in turn have faced similar situations.

Meanwhile, Browne's work was woven like a binding thread through the core of Contemporary Dancers. Contemporary Dancers was her home and her means of creating new dances. When the idea of keeping her association with the company seemed a possibility, she became wily. After "resigning," Browne was appointed interim Artistic Director of the company. She agreed to assist the Board in the search for a new director. The company's search broadened outside Canada. Bill Evans, a Seattle-based modern dance teacher and choreographer, was hired. Browne says,

> I hadn't even thought of life after Contemporary Dancers. I thought the end of the world had come. That I'd never be able to choreograph again, to teach, to dance, and so I wanted to hang onto some part of the company even in a compromised position. So I thought if I help to bring in somebody like Bill Evans, then I can talk to him about keeping me on as one of the resident choreographers, and doing some teaching.

Browne speculates that had she left at the time of the coup, she might have been less wounded when she was finally shut out of the company entirely.

> Some people think that when I returned I acted in a very desperate manner. In a way it was a wise thing for me to do. It was very, very hard, but when I think of it now, I was pretty smart to do it because it satisfied some of my intrinsic needs.

At the same time, Browne feels she was badly used by the Board.

> I was a bit of a fool to play into the hands of these Board members. They didn't have to deal with me as Artistic Director because they thought I was a detriment to the company, but they did have the benefit of my intensive knowledge of the field to help them look for a new Artistic Director.

Browne's fortitude and her deep love of dance sustained her. Even through her despair, she worked. Isolating herself in a quiet part of the church which housed Contemporary Dancers, she found solace in creating.

> I remember listening to some music by Bach, and starting to create a solo of mine called *Shalom*, which means "Peace be with you." My dancing of that piece and the performing of that piece did save my sanity. Even though I lost the company I wasn't going to lose dance.

During Bill Evan's season with the company (1983-84), Browne continued to teach for the company and in the school, and created a new work, *A Jest of God*, inspired by Margaret Laurence's novel. As well, she became the company's Development Officer. As a fundraiser she proved valuable to the company, even though she had to deal with Evelyn Polish.

When Bill Evans left the company, Tedd Robinson became the company's new Artistic Director, a position he held from 1984 to 1990.

> Tedd was somebody I had brought to Winnipeg. I brought him up first as an apprentice. Eventually he developed into a dancer and into our resident choreographer.

Browne again turned this new situation to her advantage, ensuring herself another five years of relative quiet. Robinson, a gifted creator, took an increasing share of the focus of the company, and although her work was not primary to the company, Browne still felt some satisfaction in being able to create. Over this period, her considerable success in fundraising earned her new respect in the company.

And from this long recovery curve Browne began to see different possibilities.

> I don't know what bug landed inside my head to make me think, why not try to do some independent work, separate and apart from the company. I thought, the only way I'm going to be able to present some work is to go and apply to the Manitoba Arts Council to do work independently.

Gathering her nerve, she approached the Council, and began to work with a few carefully chosen dancers. Release from her responsibilities at Contemporary Dancers allowed her new freedoms.

> I started from an initial performance, given in 1987, to what I'm doing today, which is a very active life as an independent choreographer. Being kicked out ... allowed me to focus on what I love the most and what I find the hardest, to try to make dances, finally trying to choreograph. Always feeling that I was not naturally gifted at it, that I had to work extremely hard at it to make it work. I just wanted to do it. And I still do.

Rachel Browne, 1996.

For Browne, the final ignominy came during Charlie Moulton's season as Contemporary Dancers' Artistic Director (1990-91). Charlie was the son of Robert Moulton, choreographer of Browne's first "barefoot ballet" with the Royal Winnipeg Ballet. He was a hot, young New York-based post-modern choreographer who had worked with Contemporary Dancers on several occasions, and even danced for a season with the company early in his career. A condition of the contract Charlie Moulton signed with the Board was that Browne, acknowledged since 1983 as the company's Founding Artistic Director, was to be denied access to the studios of Contemporary Dancers.

Browne pointedly ignored this, privately saying that the company would have to throw her out. For some months she kept quiet about her anger at this personal insult, and about her fears that Moulton's attitude would damage the company irreparably. Then in March of 1991 she spilled the beans to the *Winnipeg Free Press*, to the Manitoba Arts Council and to the Canada Council. By now Browne had the support of a group of new Board members, led by Richard Irish, who were eager to preserve the company's integrity and Browne's association with it. The Board fired Moulton. After a lengthy search Tom Stroud was appointed Artistic Director later in 1991. In 1994 the company celebrated its thirtieth anniversary under his direction, the gala programme including a number of works by Browne.

Politics and Perseverance

Browne's own work has continued to deepen. In part to show the value of devotion to an art in performance, she will continue to appear in her own work from time to time. She has always loved being on the stage, though creation is her true priority at this time. Her subject is women, and she expresses her feeling about women being who they are and who they want to be. She looks into dark, quiet moments in the emotional topography of women's lives, of her own long path of motherhood, of daughterhood, of her mother's dying and her early years with her own three daughters. She is interested in the voices of women, in radical feminism, in lesbianism, in all of women's expression.

Later works, *Mouvement* (1992), *Four Haiku* (1993) and *Toward Light* (1995), are radically different from her early work. They are based in her investigation of basic urges, of instinctual, almost animal-like movement. She is not dealing with the pretty and the nice, but with the dark side, with images of grasping and breaking through. The dances are spare and still. Browne has entered a place where she is concerned with capturing intangibles, subtle currents of thought or feeling, in movement. Experiencing the restriction of being drawn by music, she has responded to the "special challenge" of creating in silence and finding appropriate music later.

> I love delving as far as I can go with one dancer and one dance. *Four Haiku* and *Mouvement* are two of the most satisfying experiences of making dances ever. Although very different, I feel that spirit-wise they are connected. With these two dances, I was making a choice to work with mature dancers with whom I share an understanding. I wanted to make a statement about women dancing together and about me, a woman choreographer. I forced myself not to make up any steps. Previously, for weeks or months before, I would go into the studio and master some movement, as a kind of security. I did a lot of improvising, and looked for textures of movement, quality of movement. I chose a theme of earth, wind, trees, water. I decided to work with no music, just the bare elements of the movement. I loved the results.

In 1995 Browne created her first full-length work, *Toward Light*, performed by eleven women of varying ages, including Browne herself. It was performed to a commissioned score for solo piano by Ann Southam and to the Fifth Suite for Violoncello by J.S. Bach. More recently she has been deeply affected by hearing Southam's "Music for Slow Dancing" and "Fluke Sounds," and created *Six Messages* (May 1996) and *Edgelit* (June 1996). She sees these dances as "a slow unfolding of longing," and perceives a certain refinement of movement in them.

Browne must continue to create. She is concerned about being able to keep creating, financially, physically, and about the new challenges which time will bring. But she has found her work.

> I keep on coming back to dances about the life cycle in some form. Birth, death, renewal.

The end of her extraordinary perseverance has been to bring Browne closer to her own voice, to liberate the creative being who for so long gave away her song. Her story has aspects of a mythic woman's journey, like the myths and stories which growl beneath her present work. Rachel Browne is clear and present, committed to this work of dance which she loves so much.

References

Videotapes and a catalogued list of Rachel Browne's choreography from 1963 to 1994 were consulted at Dance Collection Danse.

Anderson, Carol. 1999. *Rachel Browne: Dancing Toward the Light.* Winnipeg: J. Gordon Shillingford Publishing.

Brownell, Kathryn. Spring 1979. "Toronto Dance Festival." *Dance in Canada* No. 19, 19-20.

Enright, Robert. Winter 1982. "Contemporary Dancers: A Prairie Lament becomes a Song of Hope." *Dance in Canada* No. 34, 20-23.

Forzley, Richard. Summer 1985. "Contemporary Dancers Canada: New Directions." *Dance in Canada* No. 44, 4-9.

Good, Jacqui. Winter 1983-84. "Contemporary Dancers." *Dance in Canada* No. 38, 27.

Good, Jacqui. Fall 1989. "Dance-Maker, The Turbulent and Moving Times of Rachel Browne." *Border Crossings* 8: 4, 59-63.

McCracken, Melinda. 1994. "A 30th Anniversary in Winnipeg." *Dance Collection Danse News* No. 36, 4-7.

Noticeboard. Fall/Winter 1977-78. *Dance in Canada* No. 14, 38.

Powell, Johanna. Spring 1975. "Tales of Touring/Histoires de tournée." *Dance in Canada* No. 4, 14-17.

Singen, Kevin. Summer 1978. "Contemporary Dancers." *Dance in Canada* No. 16, 27-28.

Stringer, Muriel. Spring 1982. "Contemporary Dancers." *Dance in Canada* No. 31, 33-34.

Interviews

Browne, Rachel. Various interviews between 1995 and 1996.

The author also consulted Melinda McCracken's interviews with Rachel Browne, June 1994.

Part IV

Visions and Revisions

Re-Placing Performance:
The Inter-Media Practice
of Françoise Sullivan

Karen Stanworth

Performance art exists ambiguously in the space between "high art" and those apparently more populist forms of public expression such as dance, theatre and music. A process with no product, a practice with no remaining evidence, it often proves difficult to retrace the historiographic significance of a specific performance in the development of an artist's body of work. Furthermore, when an artist, such as Françoise Sullivan, produces work within and across both the popular and so-called "high art" forms, it becomes difficult to resolve the perceived contradictions between craft and art, or, between performance and dance. As a consequence, Sullivan's performance pieces of the 1970s have been critically subsumed into her prior art practice. Despite the evidence of site-specific work, of pieces which articulate a particular history and of shifting realms of concern, critics have continued to view Sullivan's performance pieces of the 1970s and her paintings of the 1980s through the lens of Automatisme, which virtually precludes any other interpretations of her work. This essay attempts to address this critical lacuna by retrieving the specificity of her work after 1970, and by examining whether that practice is continuous with the Automatiste stance of the 1940s as evidenced in her writing and in her dance productions.[1]

On August 9, 1948, in Montreal, Paul-Émile Borduas and fifteen Québécois artists, dancers and poets signed and published a manifesto, *Refus global*, which profoundly rocked the socio-cultural foundations of Quebec. The artists involved became known as the Automatistes due to their emphasis on the necessity for "automatic" or spontaneous expression to be manifested in their art. The spontaneous, whether literary or visual, was proposed as a means of counteracting the rules of production implicit in contemporary art and society. The Automatiste manifesto articulated a refusal to accept any personal, social, or aesthetic confinement or preconditions. The lead article of the manifesto declaimed all forms of "intention, the two-edged, perilous sword of reason" and proclaimed the necessity of magic and "objective mysteries" (Ellenwood 1985: 37).

---

[1] This is a revised version of an essay first published in *Tessera* 11 (Winter 1991), 99-108. Reproduced by permission of the author.

Visions and Revisions

The manifesto has been both damned and praised for singlehandedly undermining the cultural status quo in Quebec. The motivations for its production in the summer of 1948 were tied to various personal and professional quarrels, post-war dissatisfaction, local politics, etc. While it has been generally acknowledged that the manifesto was the product of its time and place, and therefore served as a prelude to the Quiet Revolution in Quebec in the 1960s, it has ironically been preserved primarily as an aesthetic and philosophical movement by Canadian art historians. In particular, Sullivan's contribution to the manifesto, the essay "La Danse et l'espoir" [Dance and Hope], has been interpreted as being somehow autonomous from the socio-political aims of the Automatistes. Disconnected from history, the artist becomes the aesthetic pawn of her own writing. Critics seek the writer and dancer of 1948 in all her subsequent production, disregarding the relations between choice of medium, subject/object meanings, socio-cultural context and personal history.

The desire on the part of the Automatistes to overthrow the entrenched relations of power, whether artistic or political, secular or religious, was seemingly informed by a Jungian rhetoric. Borduas' lead text incorporated references to the collective unconscious and psychic energies of the Québécois – references which had appeared previously in Sullivan's public reading of "La Danse et l'espoir" six months prior to the publication of the manifesto (Gosselin 1981: 21).[2] She, in turn, likely developed her notions of how the collective unconscious might be expressed in visual form by drawing on the anthropologically informed dance theory of Franziska Boas in New York and on discussions with her childhood friend and co-signatory of the *Refus global*, the poet and psychologist-in-training, Bruno Cormier.[3]

Sullivan proposed that the modern dancer was capable of discovering a common culture which had been shared by everyone at some undefined point in the past. The body was seen as the storehouse of cosmic energy which was released through automatiste dance. The dancer could go "beyond the individual towards the universal" (Sullivan in Ellenwood 1985: 106). This "universal" or the collective unconscious is articulated through symbolic themes believed to underlie the automatic dance performance. For the Jungian, the symbol expresses the essence of human psychic energy. Some such symbols may be archetypal, that is, they may be derived from mythic themes whose symbolism illustrates universal human history, or, the symbols may have personal significance and reveal the individual unconscious. In the performances in which Sullivan danced alone, as in *Danse dans la neige* (1948), she stated that she was attempting to release her individual psychic energy through movement – movement, which she proposed would symbolize

---

[2] "La Danse et l'espoir" was read at an Automatiste evening at the Gauvreau apartment on February 16, 1948.

[3] Cormier's article "L'Oeuvre picturale est une expérience" was probably in progress before Sullivan's paper was read. It is evident that there was no one source for the expression of collective unconscious in this forum. While Cormier cited Freud in his essay, he referred to ideas which also reveal a Jungian conception of expressive energy of the unconscious, of the cosmos and of archetypes. See Ellenwood (1985: 12, 93-100).

the universal or collective psyche.[4] She also sought to recreate archetypal symbols, as is exemplified by her reference to the "Shadow," defined by Jung as "our other self." The archetypal symbol of the Shadow underlies her performance of *Dualité* in which two dancers, Sullivan and Jeanne Renaud, one in black, one in white, enacted themes of opposition and attraction.

While Sullivan's dance and choreography of the 1940s was undoubtedly Jungian in its automatiste enactment of symbolic, "universal" elements, I question the authority of this interpretation in her subsequent production. In particular, Sullivan's return to the "high art" medium of painting in the 1980s has served to reinforce the tendency to read the predominantly performance and site-specific work of the 1970s as part of an aesthetic, a historical progression from Automatiste dance to contemporary painting. This framing of Sullivan's performance pieces by "high art" functions to reduce them to contributory elements (as part of a progressive history) rather than acknowledging their disruption of an aesthetic purism and their impact upon subsequent work.

Sullivan's *Beware! Beware! His flashing eyes, his floating hair*, 1983.

The critical placement of the artist's contemporary practice within the bounds of her Automatiste stance is exemplified by a recent analysis of Sullivan's painting, in which a critic characterized *Beware! Beware! His flashing eyes, his floating hair* (1983) as exemplary of Sullivan's "desire for tangency with the universe" (Saint-Pierre 1986: 38). The painting depicts a figure with arms outstretched and legs apart, with most of the body weight balanced on one leg (not quite the model of balance represented by Leonardo da Vinci's *Vitruvian Man*). The figure appears to be female. She is framed by a rectangle which is inscribed in a circle, but the rectangle breaks through the confines of the circle at the base. This image is described as "a metaphor of the universe and of pictorical representation, since the artist has made a summary of her own body by placing herself on the canvas.... [This depiction] evokes the excessiveness of the body that merges with the universe." The implication is that the artist returns once more to that notion of the unconscious, now evinced as bodily excess, which is

[4] See M. Bousquet-Mongeau, C. Gosselin and D. Moore, *Françoise Sullivan – Rétrospective* for the most extended discussion of Sullivan's oeuvre prior to 1981.

realized within the collective experience of the universe. However, I would suggest that the represented body contains the potential of self-contradiction in its symbolic and allegorical dimensions. Symbolic of the artist (extending Leonardo da Vinci's *Vitruvian Man*), the body also functions allegorically as gender displacement serves to destabilize the image of man at the centre of a harmonious universe. Breaking through the geometric framing of the body (the rectangle not entirely contained within the circle), the body's transgression is echoed in the emblems of the scorpion and the paint brush which do not belong in the ideal universe proposed by Leonardo. Here, the scorpion, as a sign of astrological identification, is understood as emblematic of the year end, the end of a cycle. Similarly, the paint brush in the extended hand of the artist implies the desire to control or to author her own fate. Furthermore, the face of the artist is darkened by a shadow cast across her visage. Is the masked face a further rebuttal of cosmic harmony? Or does it reinforce a negative interpretation of the presented cosmology? When formal considerations are added to the set of represented relations, such as the ephemeral quality of the drawing of the body as compared to the vehemence of the swirls of paint in her immediate space, then the reading of the image is far more complicated than is implied by the idea that "the excessiveness of the body merges with the universe." Rather than merging, it would seem that displacement or uncertainty of position is the artist's concern in *Beware! Beware!* The irony is further underlined by Sullvian's reference to Coleridge's poem as a source for her title since his literary conceptualization of the unity of the symbol to its referent is so obviously being queried by the artist.

Sullivan's post-1970 production, whether performance or painting, seems to be undermining the Surrealist paradigm "to explore the subconscious and to expand the boundaries of memory as knowledge" (Saint-Pierre 1986: 37). Rather, she appears to be questioning the very rationale of such an inwardly directed approach. It may be that such a challenge would be the inevitable result of her optimistic desire to "unite objective space and dream space" while at the same time insisting that "art can only flourish if it grows from problems which concern the age" (Sullivan in Ellenwood 1985: 115). How can the transcendent transcend the temporal, if it must be situated within it? Sullivan's automatiste desire for cosmic consciousness appears to have been reassessed in the light of temporal realities. In part, this shift from modernist to antimodernist concerns, or from symbolic unity to rhetorical stance, is located in her response to Joseph Kosuth's determination of the death of art.

After reading Kosuth's *The Philosophy of Art* (1969) in which he argued that the world was overstocked with art which was no longer necessary or valid, Sullivan was prompted to face her growing discontent for abstraction which had dominated art in North America for two decades (Gravel 1988: 44-47).[5] Working within an abstract paradigm, Sullivan had been producing minimalist sculptures in the 1960s such as *Aeris Ludus* (1967) which strives

---

[5] Gravel refers to Sullivan's comment on the impact of Kosuth on her thinking about her own art production.

to attain a harmonious whole executed with a few basic shapes unified in orange paint. During an interview in 1972 in which she was defending her abandonment of abstraction, Sullivan declared, "Like many other artists, I was distraught. I had a great love at the depths of my soul for art, but I know I was uneasy to even pronounce the word. An artist consecrates her life to do a job which is nearly no longer plausible. Our world is saturated with art objects. So what do we artists do now? I don't think that artists today are happy because a gap exists between what the artist is doing [minimal/abstract art] and what the artist wants to do" (Sullivan in Toupin 13 Jan. 1973).

In addition to the aesthetic and philosophical impact of Kosuth, it is likely that Sullivan's personal life further pressured her into some form of reassessment. Her biographies, whether copious or brief, all mention her marriage to Paterson Ewen and the birth of their four sons in the 1950s. This personal data remains relevant since this period of alienation from art during the years of 1968-1970 paralleled her estrangement from Ewen. This was also a period of extreme political and social upheaval in Quebec. The student riots in the colleges and universities, the dramatic intervention in the religious control of education and the foundation of the Parti Québécois marked an intense era of cultural change. By 1970, the F.L.Q. crisis with the kidnapping of Cross and Laporte and the enactment of the War Measures Act exemplified the frustration of many Québécois with the status quo. It is no surprise that this was the background to Sullivan's questioning of the unifying potential of art. Sullivan's historic association with the Automatistes arguably set a personal precedent for her in that she was not afraid to challenge established conventions. By 1970, the hegemonic presence of formalism in contemporary art was deemed no longer convincing.

In an interview regarding an installation piece done in 1973, Sullivan declared that she and her contemporaries "are no longer interested in problems of form and colour anymore. We are working at another level" (Sullivan in Toupin 13 Jan. 1973). The need for authenticity in representation was perceived as most pressing. All of Sullivan's subsequent work questions the nature of representation, and particularly that of the human subject. Her practice of the 1970s and 1980s is characterized by a shift from a search for symbolic unity to a fractured discourse of the other realized within a rhetorical stance which appropriates symbolism and allegory in order to challenge representational norms.

The paradigmatic shift which I perceive as having occurred at the inception of Sullivan's self-conscious, anti-modernist practice is actualized by a change from notions of internal coherence in art to explorations of external reference. The breakdown of the modernist conception of art as a "hard-won unity" of surface and spatial tensions resulted in a reconstruction of referentiality in Sullivan's performance pieces, paintings and choreographic work.

Ambiguous and always contextualized physically and theoretically, her post-1970 work implicates one aesthetic practice into another. Her perform-

ance pieces such as the promenade, *Rencontre avec un Apollon archaïque* (1974), are informed by her previous dance experience, and in turn impact upon her later choreography. The dancer who wrote "La Danse et l'espoir" abandons a vision of harmony in order to begin a reassessment of what art means to her. Her "encounter with Apollo" is explicitly referential. It does not exist except as a photographic record. The artist/dancer moves in a choreographed path through Montreal's East End refineries searching amongst the detritus of the industrial age for a sign of classical art. What does the Apollo signify? Or should the question be how much does it signify? The possibilities range from a personal search for traditional values in artistic practice, to a post-modern questioning of the value of representation itself (signified by Apollo) in a world so cluttered that Apollo can be reduced to a simulacrum posted randomly amongst the refineries.

Once again, the response to Sullivan's production was to review it as consistent with Automatisme. In the catalogue from the retrospective exhibition of Sullivan's oeuvre, it was stated that the motive for her "submission"(!) to antiquity in her *Rencontre avec un Apollon* becomes "clear and coherent" when one recalls that she believed in the "rediscovery of the truths already familiar to the ancient primitives" (Moore 1981: 84). However, I would suggest that the parallelism between the use of Apollo and the search for ancient truths is not so apparent, because, as a sign, the Apollo elicits numerous readings, recombines with the new contextualization of the refineries, and cannot be assumed to signify a universal archetype.[6] This questioning of the authenticity of the symbol, its reception and the consequent

---

[6] Indeed, the Apollo image chosen was that of the Belvedere Apollo which was widely admired as the epitome of Classical art in the late-eighteenth and nineteenth centuries. When it was realized that this Apollo was a late Roman copy of a Greek original, the object lost its elite status.

Sullivan's *Rencontre avec un Apollon archaïque.* 1974.

validity of representation appears to inform all the post-1970 work. It is essential to consider Sullivan's performance pieces in light of her conscious choreography of space and time relations in the promenades. It is surely not coincidental that her performance pieces are awkward to categorize as dance or installation.

As a text, *Hiérophanie*, a performance/installation/dance piece of 1979, assists in the examination of the shift in Sullivan's position relative to aesthetic ideologies. *Hiérophanie* was Sullivan's first major choreography since the 1950s. It was characterized by the *derviches-tourneurs* often present in her earlier pieces (notably in the pieces in which she danced herself). Breaking the self-reflexive harmony of her early dance pieces, Sullivan inserted abrupt breaks in the music and in the use of materials (here a long piece of brown paper) which literally cut the movement of the dancers. Rather than the trance-like, automatic dance of the 1950s, *Hiérophanie* was constructed to be deconstructed. An observer wrote that the impact of the dance "was troubling and fascinating," – hardly the reaction of an Automatiste viewer anticipating a recovery of deep emotional resonance achieved through cosmic harmony (Dagenais 3 Apr. 1979). Sullivan was tearing away at the idea of myth, and forcing myth to unveil, to deconstruct its own tautological authority.

Similarly, another product of Sullivan's late 1970s practice centred on constructive/deconstructive activity – the blocking and unblocking of doorways and windows. Once more, the record of these activities is photographic. It is the recording of the act which becomes the artifact. The moment of creative production is further distanced by having the performance and its record occur in Crete (home of many fundamental Western myths), whilst its repro-duction through display was in a North American gallery. The photographs of the *Fenêtres abandonnées, bloquées et débloquées* (1978) were arranged in the gallery in such a way that the observer was forced to experience the event in one of two ways, either reconstructing the blocking by approaching from the end of the photo series which started with a photograph of the empty window, or, by deconstructing the blockage by approaching from the opposite side of the gallery, where the series of photographs commenced with the image of a blocked window. In other words, the observer was choreographed through the exhibition. To what end? This presentation of photographs of the artist's performance becomes another event in its representation. The use of the secondary medium forces the viewer to question what is being represented and to what degree the viewer is constructing the meaning(s) available.

This layering of activity and meaning is also present in a later choreography *Et la nuit à la nuit* (1981). Here again the critical response describes the enactment as a symbolic fertility rite, cites "La Danse et l'espoir" of 1948, and comments that "the archetypal elements which she has used before are found in a moving synthesis, profoundly human" (Moore 1981: 90). Certainly the use of symbolic motifs underscores every move in this production. The use of a nude, pregnant dancer is explicitly referential as she appears at the end of the performance, sedately carrying a basket from which she removes half a dozen young rabbits. While Iro Tembeck has observed that "the dance finishes with this double symbol of fertility," it should not be inferred that the literal symbolism is meant to encompass all potential meaning (Tembeck 1982: 18).[7]

Ironically, Sullivan herself states that *Et la nuit à la nuit* was conceived in a state of semi-consciousness and built around several key images (Sullivan 1981). While the choreographer may or may not have conceived the piece in such a state, the dance itself is performed according to prescribed choreographic directions. It is a predetermined enactment which, regardless of the inspiration, fulfills a specific intention. As such the "automatisme" of its dancers is constrained if indeed it is possible. It is essential here to separate the stated "automatic impulse" of the author-choreographer from the directed movements of the dancers. In fact, Sullivan's choice of symbols and structuring of interactions would not support an unconscious expression but rather a self-aware examination of her world and the power relations of men and women. Nor is it possible to claim that this dance portrays the "hope" of "La Danse et l'espoir." If anything the dance explicitly challenges the reification

---

[7] It is not clear from the text that Tembeck intended this exclusionary interpretation.

336

implied in the potentiality of the feminine archetype, *Le Grand plein* (the reproductive mother).

The three dance segments act out the symbolic relations between Man, symbolized as the River, and Woman, symbolized as the Mountain. The "natural" progression of life is represented in vignettes describing the birth of man by woman, their consequent union, the eventual destruction of both, and the closing scene featuring the pregnant dancer. The dance appears to literally confirm the cycle of life. If, however, the dance is not interpreted in light of the "hope" but in recognition of the shift in Sullivan's art practice (as exemplified above), then the dance could be understood as an allegory of desire. The use of multiple symbols is not necessarily only literal, and the literal and allegorical do not necessarily have to confirm each other. The rhetorical stance implicit in the anti-modern positions evidenced in Sullivan's work since 1970 can again be found in *Et la nuit à la nuit*. There is no hope of breaking the cycle, doomed to repeat itself through birth, union and destruction; continuity may be ironic, satiric or pathetic, and confounds hopefulness. The use of the nude woman reinforces her role as the vulnerable element in the equation. Her pride and self-confidence is misplaced in her destructive fertility. Certainly, it is possible to read this piece as an anti-modern investigation of the human condition and the gender difference which sustains it.

The use of symbols to construct a metaphor which is, in turn, deconstructed by the rhetorical context of the artist and viewer is an ongoing preoccupation in Sullivan's recent work. This brings us back to the question posed at the beginning of this essay – as to whether Sullivan's current art products, paintings or choreographic productions can be judged as continuous with her Automatiste stance of the 1940s.

The nearly pervasive tendency to interpret Sullivan's post-1970 work as somehow contiguous to her Automatiste writing "La Danse et l'espoir" and to her *Danse dans la neige* has created a methodological quagmire for her critics. On the one hand, they admire the consistency of notions of hope, on the other, they try to fit the artwork itself into that interpretation. Once performance is re-placed into Sullivan's oeuvre as an other expression, and not as a replication of prior concerns dressed in a new mode, then it must be acknowledged that the fragmented nature of the work presents anything but a harmonious whole. Whether it is discontinuous dance or torn, unprimed, unmounted canvas which provides the material, it appears that Sullivan's production can no longer be subsumed under the aesthetic umbrella of Automatisme. The artist who refused to accept convention, whether aesthetic, social, or political, in the *Refus global* is still refusing the established categories. I am arguing that in re-placing her performance into her total oeuvre, we can realize a larger appreciation of her contribution to a dynamic cultural expression in Canada, be it achieved through dance, performance, or autonomous art objects.

References

Unique materials were consulted in the Françoise Sullivan file at Dance Collection Danse.

Bousquet-Mongeau, Martine. 1981. "Fenêtres bloquées et debloquées." *Françoise Sullivan – Rétrospective*. Québec: Ministère des Affaires culturelles, 63-78.

Dagenais, Angèle. 3 Apr. 1979. "Françoise Sullivan: un retour à la choréographie." *Le Devoir*.

Ellenwood, Ray, trans. 1985. *Total Refusal [Refus global]: The Complete 1948 Manifesto of the Montreal Automatists*. Toronto: Exile Editions.

Gosselin, Claude. 1981. "Sur Françoise Sullivan." *Françoise Sullivan – Rétrospective*. Québec: Ministère des Affaires culturelles, 7-62.

Gravel, Claire. Mar. 1988. "Françoise Sullivan – la parole retrouvée." *Vie des Arts* 32: 130, 44-47.

Moore, David. 1981. "Françoise Sullivan et l'espoir." *Françoise Sullivan – Rétrospective*. Québec: Ministère des Affaires culturelles, 79-92.

Saint-Pierre, Marcel. Summer 1986. "Françoise Sullivan – La Rhétorique du rêve, The Rhetoric of Dreams." *Vanguard*, 34-39.

Sullivan, Françoise. 27 Mar.-1 Apr. 1981. In publicity statements for *Et la nuit à la nuit*. Le Tritorium, Cegep de Vieux Montréal.

Tembeck, Iro. 1982. "Danse à Québec." *Réflex* 2: 1, 18.

Toupin, Gilles. 13 Jan. 1973. "La Nostalgie de l'Art." *La Presse*.

From Post-Ballet to Post-Modern:
The 1972 Debut of Toronto's Ground-Breaking 15 Dance Collective

Jennifer Fisher

In terms of the theatrical dance world, Toronto was pretty much a two-company town in 1972. There was the National Ballet of Canada, firmly ensconced since 1951, and the strictly Graham Toronto Dance Theatre, attracting a small but devoted audience since 1968. That left a lot of unexplored territory, into which came Fifteen, an ad hoc dance collective that gave its first concert on June 13, 1972.[1]

Named simply for the number of its original participants, Fifteen came from the ballet side of town, but it didn't stay there long. Within a few years, the group evolved into a performance space called Fifteen Dance Lab, where rules were broken, skills were tested and new dance constantly developed. But first came Fifteen's single-evening debut, a sort of post-ballet moment that kick-started Toronto into the post-modern dance era. The recipe for this evolutionary event was simple: take several unemployed, disenchanted ballet dancers and add two iconoclast, ex-National Ballet members named Lawrence and Miriam Adams.

Several Fifteen members had trained at the National Ballet School, some had performed with the company and all had met at the Lois Smith School of Dance, where the Adams were teaching. It was natural, then, that Fifteen's first programme opened with a conventional ballet pas de trois, complete with chiffon, pointe shoes and an onstage pianist dressed in black velvet, playing Ravel. As unofficial mentors to the democratically organized troupe, the Adams dictated no aesthetic rules, but they themselves were ready to leave ballet behind. To this end, they offered the two closing works: Miriam made a witty, acrobatic dance to a poem about yogurt, and Lawrence's piece combined everyday movement, bits of scratched records and a recorded speech by Richard Nixon.

It was because of the Adams that Fifteen began with one foot firmly in the rosin box, while the other dangled tantalizingly over uncharted ground. In the Toronto of 1972, no one had quite understood what kind of dance alternatives there were: before becoming familiar with Fifteen, John Fraser, then dance critic for the *Globe and Mail*, admits that he had thought of himself as "the ballet critic." But with Lawrence and Miriam, he recalls, there was a constant

---

[1] Quotations and information about the formation of Fifteen and its first concert were taken primarily from a series of interviews with observers and participants, and from a few other sources.

Rehearsal of Miriam Adams' *Chairs* (l. to r.): Lawrence Adams, Miriam Adams, Cornelius Fischer-Credo, Cynthia Mantel, 1973.

buzz of excitement and unpredictability. "They were essentially liberating," he says, "getting us out of all the straitjackets. It was through them that I started taking innovation seriously" (19 Nov. 1990).

A few years before, the Adams had had trouble taking dance seriously. Initiating the first Fifteen concert was part of a process that began with their frustration while dancing in the National Ballet of Canada. As a corps member in the 1960s, Miriam had become increasingly unhappy with her career as a swan or a flower. "I didn't want to be a more important swan," she says, "I didn't want to be a swan at all" (27 Sept. 1990). For Lawrence, who is remembered best for his dynamic Mercutio in *Romeo and Juliet*, ballet life took on an even more uncomfortable sameness. He was always casting about for something else to do. One of his official National Ballet biographies said, "A break from [his ballet] career led to a short term in business for himself as a hi-fi technician" (National Ballet press biography. Clippings file, Metropolitan Toronto Reference Library). He was never a narrowly devoted danseur. Whenever the ballet was short of stagehands, Lawrence would volunteer.

In 1969, the Adams left the National Ballet, feeling like small cogs in an institutional wheel that increasingly turned, they felt, just to crank out money. Among their other complaints were the facts that the National Ballet was not especially relevant to Canadian experience; that they were basically employees who had no influence on what they did from day to day; and that their lives were too specialized due to ballet training and the restrictions of company life and touring. Working out how to turn those limitations around for dancers would result in the Fifteen philosophy: to create pieces that contained meaningful ideas; keep costs low and have control over space and repertoire; to become "generalists," who not only danced but took on all other production duties. They called their new vision of the dancer a "dance artist."

The Adams say they were unaware of other dance experimenters in the years leading up to Fifteen's debut – work by the post-modernists at the Judson Church in New York, for instance, or Montreal's Le Groupe de la Place Royale, whose members were also working to redefine dance. Instead, the Adams list their primary influence as a group of visual artists they met through an antique and framing gallery they ran on Toronto's Markham Street. "What was interesting," says Lawrence, "is that they could talk about what they did and we couldn't." "We could talk about dance," says Miriam, "but they could talk about the visual arts in an analytical, interpretive, intelligent way" (22 Nov. 1990).

What the Adams could do to start associating dance with interesting ideas was not immediately apparent, but an opportunity to experiment arose while they were teaching ballet at the school of Lois Smith, a former National Ballet colleague. At the time, Miriam's classes were conventional, but Lawrence was likely to tell everyone to go off and warm up by lying in the sun, always looking for a way to break from routine. His attitude was one of puckish cynicism, asking students why they worked so hard, since they could never make a good living as dancers. But one day, he decided he had heard one too many complaints about how no one could get hired and get a chance to dance. He told them to make their own opportunities: a small theatre could be rented cheaply, he pointed out. They wanted to dance? Why wait for a call from Celia Franca? (22 Nov. 1990).

Original Fifteen member Diane Strickland remembers what happened next this way: "I guess Lawrence just couldn't stand all these young students trying to be swan queens and just being yes people and not thinking. So he took the bull by the horns, just saying, 'You know you can do it. We're going to do a show and everybody's going to be equal, and you're all going to make your own dances, and you're all going to dance in each others' dances, and no, I'm not in charge – you're in charge!'" (24 Nov. 1990).

Almost before they knew it, fifteen people had contributed fifteen dollars, and Lawrence had booked a theatre for a night in a few month's time. Smith loaned her studios for rehearsals, and the first-time choreographers laboured over pieces during evenings and weekends (many of them worked full-time elsewhere). Meanwhile, the Fifteen philosophy was increasingly in evidence, starting with Lawrence's "Just do it, and do what you want" dictum, and extending to the requirement that everyone make their own technical preparations.

Group meetings were held in nearby restaurants or the Markham Street Gallery, and once at the house of the parents of one teenaged member, Cynthia Mantel. Her father, Hans Mantel, who had a video company and taped many later Fifteen performances, recalls that "there was brainstorming and lateral thinking at work, where things were a free for all" (24 Nov. 1990). Sometimes the upcoming programme details were lost in a discussion of what dance really was, recalls original member Ken Peirson (who was later an administrator for several dance companies).

During rehearsals, says Hans Mantel, "Lawrence would test the performers' intentions, to give things shape. He would say, 'Why do you do a posé here?' and make them think." Making dancers – and the audience – think is a recurring theme in all the Fifteen recollections. "We weren't just dumb dancers," says Strickland. "Lawrence insisted we could do anything. He made us think differently ... that the dancer wasn't just an object, and our bodies weren't just for other people to use" (24 Nov. 1990).

With only word-of-mouth publicity, the 104-seat Poor Alex Theatre in the Annex area of Toronto was full on the Tuesday evening of June 13, 1972. Admission was one dollar. The audience received something called a "programticket," a single sheet of silkscreened brown paper that listed five new works, named only with a number (starting at ten and ending at fifteen, with intermission named Twelve). In the casual spirit of the times, only first names of choreographers and dancers were listed. The performance lasted about an hour and a half with one intermission.

From all accounts, the ballet numbers went over well. The first pas de trois was called *Ten*, choreographed by a young ballet dancer, Donna Nickeloff, and described by on-stage pianist James Maybank as owing "a lot to Jerome Robbins' *Dances at a Gathering*" (26 Nov. 1990). There was also a duet about an engaged couple called *Thirteen*, the work of Clyde Robinson. Remembered by several company members as employing conventional ballet vocabulary and mime in a "schmaltzy" way, it was set to Elgar's *Enigma Variations*.

Robinson was also responsible for the only piece on the programme that was improvised: *Eleven* was a solo performed in silence by Clyde himself, dressed only in brief trunks and ankle bells. It has been variously described by company members as "interesting," in that it featured a lot of free-flowing stamping, bouncing, clapping and generally non-balletic movement, or "insufferably long" – more than one observer recalls that the curtain was pulled in order to end it after fifteen or twenty minutes.

Undoubtedly, the most popular work that evening was Miriam Adams' *Fourteen*, an ode to yogurt, which, she recalls, had just started to be marketed in small cups of individual flavours. Lasting only a few minutes, it involved a lot of jumping and tumbling (the dancer, Debbie Smith, had been a gymnast), and what Maybank later called "Twyla Tharpish movement" (26 Nov. 1990). Its score was made up largely of a poem of chanted fruit flavours ("raspberry, strawberry, blueberry, boysenberry ... ") and some sort of orchestrated Beatles music. Most everyone remembers the piece as athletic, clever, satirical and fun, as much of Miriam's later work would be.

Fraser attended the concert but did not review it, at the group's request. He remembers that Lawrence's piece, called *Fifteen*, made a lot of jaws drop, with its solo to a Nixon speech about Vietnam and a lot of apparently non-sequitur stamping and kicking of an exposed wall. It is least remembered in terms of specific movement (though everyone agrees it was not dancerly), but is recalled as the most stimulating, for instance, by Debbie Smith, who went on to dance with several Canadian modern dance companies. For Fraser, who wrote on politics as well as dance for the *Globe*, it was "right up my alley" (19 Nov. 1990).

Another plus that came immediately from Fifteen, recalls Fraser, was humour: "That was the big thing, because modern dance in Toronto was Toronto Dance Theatre, and it was deadly serious – *deadly* serious. The stuff the Adams were bringing in was just a wow. It was suddenly fun to write about humour in dance. Humour at the National Ballet was Puss and Boots in *The Sleeping Beauty* – very saccharine. The whole notion of wit was essentially introduced by Fifteen."

Taken as a whole, Fifteen's first concert seemed a success, and the collective was excited to have pulled it off. Out of their pockets, imaginations and training they had woven a dance event that felt fresh and was appreciated. Lawrence and Miriam Adams had functioned crucially as motivators and innovators, taking dancers who had not previously been in the habit of thinking for themselves and pioneering a non-institutional way of presenting their work.[2] Lawrence was so encouraged, he took the $136 profit from the show and that night booked the theatre for two further dates in July. Several members would not be up to another challenge, and the collective would eventually narrow down to four or five.

But new wheels had been set in motion. "What they did for me they did for basically any small group of people who were exploring in dance," says Fraser. "They loosened us up a lot. Everybody was into liberation those days, and it was extending our own vocabularies and understanding" (19 Nov. 1990).

In 1974, the Fifteen collective became Fifteen Dance Lab, a performing space central to Toronto's alternate dance development. By the mid-1970s the city was enjoying a blossoming of small dance companies and independent choreographers, nourished significantly by graduating students of York University's young Department of Dance. Fifteen Dance Lab closed in 1980, but by that time it had given opportunities to performers such as Margie Gillis, Judy Jarvis, Jennifer Mascall, Judith Marcuse, Jean-Pierre Perreault and many others.

As a kick-start to thrust Toronto into an age of dance pluralism, Fifteen had worked.

Original Fifteen Collective Members:
Lawrence Adams
Miriam Adams
Lucia Barkauskas
Diane Drum (now Strickland)
Cornelius Fischer-Credo

---

[2] At the time of Fifteen Dance Lab's closing in 1980, the Adams said they felt there were plenty of alternative dance spaces available in Toronto, although that number has dwindled since because of rising rents. The Adams now serve an invaluable historical purpose as archivists of Canadian dance through Dance Collection Danse.

Visions and Revisions

Helene (last name lost)
Peter Jones
Cynthia Mantel
Donita Nahon
Donna Nickeloff
Bardi Norman
Ken Peirson
Clyde Robinson
Danny Sandiford
Debbie Smith (now Kaplan)
Pianist at debut concert: James Maybank

References

Adams, Lawrence. National Ballet press biography. Clippings file. Metropolitan Toronto Reference Library.

Chitty, Elizabeth. Spring 1975. "Fifteen is an Amoeba." *York Dance Review* No. 4, 38-40.

Fifteen programme. 13 June 1972. Dance Collection Danse.

"Fifteen Shows Video, by 3 by 4." 1974. Promotional material for a video collective. Clippings file for Fifteen. Metropolitan Toronto Reference Library.

Fraser, John. ca. 1973. "Innovation, experiment from 15 Dancers." *Globe and Mail.*

Jackson, Graham. 1978. *Dance As Dance*. Scarborough, Ontario: Catalyst.

Mascall, Jennifer, compiler. Spring 1975. "Chronology [of Fifteen Dance Lab]." *York Dance Review* No. 4, 40-42.

Wyman, Max. 1989. *Dance Canada: An Illustrated History*. Vancouver: Douglas & McIntyre.

Interviews

Adams, Lawrence and Miriam. 27 Sept. 1990 and 22 Nov. 1990.

Barkauskas Karminskas, Lucia. 21 Nov. 1990.

Fraser, John. 19 Nov. 1990.

Mantel, Hans. 24 Nov. 1990.

Maybank, James. 26 Nov. 1990.

Peirson, Ken. 26 Nov. 1990.

Sandiford, Danny. 26 Nov. 1990.

Strickland, Diane Drum. 24 Nov. 1990.

Moving Forward Looking Back:
Lawrence and Miriam Adams and Dance Collection Danse

Carol Anderson

Before they got into business as iconoclasts, publishers, archivists, impresarios, cultural activists, media pioneers, rescuers of the vanished and champions of the forgotten, Lawrence and Miriam Adams were dancers. Both were members of The National Ballet of Canada. Miriam Adams, a self-described "bunhead," turned in *Nutcracker* performances for seven years. Lawrence Adams was a star, famous for his witty, dangerous Mercutio in *Romeo and Juliet*. When they left the Toronto company, the two were fed up with the rigours of the life and the strictures of the mindset. Over time, the Adams initiated a long line of radical Canadian dance enterprises, culminating with Dance Collection Danse (DCD). Following Lawrence Adams' death in February 2003, Miriam Adams and Amy Bowring have carried on the work of Dance Collection Danse.[1]

Leaving the National Ballet, in 1969, they began teaching at the Lois Smith School of Dance. Soon the Adams started Fifteen, a collection of fifteen dancers, in response to the clamour of dancers needing somewhere to dance besides the ballet. Fifteen gave its inaugural performance at Toronto's Poor Alex Theatre, a tiny alternative space, in 1972. Then as later, the Adams were relentlessly non-curative, refusing to make judgment calls about the quality of the work Fifteen presented. For the first Fifteen performance Miriam Adams choreographed a witty homage to yogurt, and Lawrence Adams presented *Fifteen*. By all accounts this was a jaw-dropping if puzzling work. Distinctly non-dancerly, it was performed by Lawrence Adams, who kicked a ball about the stage space, sometimes accompanied by a tape of Richard Nixon giving a speech about Vietnam.

The Adams made renegade history with Fifteen Dance Lab, a downtown performance space which opened in 1974. Their idea was to create a place where dance artists could afford to present their work. Renovating a former brass foundry on Toronto's George Street to create the city's first alternate theatre for dance, they turned the space into a minimalist forty-one-seat theatre. They maintained a strict laissez-faire policy about the programming. In hindsight, the Adams admit that much of what went on at Fifteen Dance Lab was "awful." But much of it was controversial and forward-looking.

---

[1] The original version of this article was published as "15 Years in 15 Minutes," in *Dance Collection Danse Magazine* 48 (1998).

Exterior of 15 Dance Laboratorium (l. to r.): Stanley, Lawrence Adams, Miriam Adams, Mr. Dog, Jackie Malden, 1975.

During the 1970s Fifteen was a Toronto hotbed of dance innovation, performance art and general hell-raising. The terms "dance artist" and "independent choreographer" were coined by Lawrence Adams to describe the new breed of dance creator and performer emerging from the Dance Department at York University and from new downtown initiatives. Most of the radical choreographers of that era gravitated toward Fifteen, forming a kind of core, among them Elizabeth Chitty, Margaret Dragu, Jennifer Mascall, Peter Dudar and Lily Eng, Anna Blewchamp, Judy Jarvis, Paula Ravitz.

Elizabeth Chitty later wrote: "Lawrence described Fifteen as an 'atelier.' The essence of the atelier concept was that every artist had the right to work in an environment of tolerance to experimentation and failure.... I believe the access offered by 15 shaped the possible. It liberated" (1993: 4).

Fifteen Dance Lab lasted until 1980, during its time presenting 135 artists, among them Toronto radicals as well as Marie Chouinard, Jean-Pierre Perreault and Margie Gillis, Quebec dance artists who later achieved international recognition. Earlier on the Adams had supported the theatre's activities with a picture-framing business which they operated in the lobby during the day. Later, Fifteen became even more sought-after as a venue –

assisted by small grants from the Ontario Arts Council, its main supporter, as well as the Toronto Arts Council, Metropolitan Toronto and Canada Council, it offered choreographers a princely $250 fee, plus 80% of their box office.

The Adams had an ongoing interest in choreography. Miriam Adams created *Another Nutcracker*, a wacky takeoff on the ballet's Christmas confection. Critic John Fraser called Miriam Adam's version "a little bit of pure genius." Feeling the need to put their art in an art gallery, in 1975 they mounted "Mr. and Mrs. Adams Present," a multimedia installation, at A Space, a Toronto alternative gallery. In the same gallery in 1978 Miriam offered performances titled *Watch Me Dance You Bastards*. She also presented work in the Art Gallery of Ontario's important but short-lived choreographic series, and in the INDE Festival, a national festival which paired choreographers and composers.

Cover article from *Canadian Dance News*, August 1982.

During the time they were operating Fifteen Dance Lab, the Adams also published *Spill*, a controversial seat-of-the-pants forum for dance writing. They encouraged dance artists to express themselves in print. In 1980, realizing the need for a monthly newspaper to cover the extensive dance activity across the country, they founded *Canadian Dance News*, a tabloid financed by 1200 subscribers as well as by national advertising. It lasted two years – until the recession of the early 1980s took over and advertisers became hard to find.

Before they closed Fifteen, the Adams originated a proposal to create a facility they called Studio Place. They had identified a Toronto Transit Commission substation on King Street East, in the heart of the St. Lawrence Project in downtown Toronto, as perfect for a space for dance. Working with the renowned architect Ron Thom's firm, they designed a wonderfully flexible facility for performance and media use, which would, as well, be easily adaptable for community use. Their proposal was defeated by Young People's Theatre, richer and more powerful in the city, which developed the space instead. But the Adams' ideas were prophetic; the notion of a multipurpose space for dance is again current in Toronto.

In 1974 the Adams, with videographer Terry McGlade, incorporated Visus, an entity for documenting dance using videotape. Again ahead of their time, they offered workshops to the dance community – how to use a camera, investigating the potential for dance on video – but the city's dance creators were perhaps still too consumed with the pressing concerns of live dance to pursue these directions at that time. Now, "dancefilm" is the hot ticket.

Visions and Revisions

By 1983 Visus had metamorphosed into the Arts Television Centre, which was built by Lawrence Adams and artist-colleague John Faichney. Lawrence spearheaded the fundraising efforts and the Centre soon opened its doors as a mixed-use facility. Operated by Lawrence and John, it was designed to be used by performing artists, and also to accommodate private sector video production for promotion and corporate training.

At the time the Adams operated the Arts Television Centre, they were ostracized by the local video community for their non-purist approach. Their varied base of users at the Arts Television Centre anticipated the present-day search for partnerships between business and the arts, but the 1980s were challenging times for them. The Adams closed the Arts Television Centre in 1990. At the same time, the Adams had foreseen the potential for interaction between media and the arts. Their application for a pay-TV license was short-listed by the Canadian Radio and Television Commission. They proposed to broadcast art films from all disciplines, produce documentaries and offer a local arts report.

Since the beginning of the 1990s, Lawrence and Miriam Adams have striven to identify cultural publishing as a priority of Dance Collection Danse. The Adams were early proponents of the ease and cost-efficiency of electronic publishing. Recently they have come to the conclusion that, along with their ongoing archival work, it is the books they have published which are a confirming strength. By early 1999 Dance Collection Danse Press/es had published sixteen dance titles, with several more waiting in the wings.

Lawrence and Miriam Adams continue to operate with the large aspiration of developing a language for the observation and discussion of dance. They dig deep and don't take short cuts. The ways in which they publish are consistently creative. Their work is their art – there is no separation between them and the large aims which animate them; chameleonlike, they reinvent themselves with new expressions and skills.

Miriam Adams often snaps the photos for the covers of their books. Lawrence Adams is a self-taught desktop publishing wizard. Early in 1997 Dance Collection Danse published *China Dance Journal*, dance statesman Grant Strate's account of a 1996 teaching trip to mainland China. The Adams printed the books upstairs in their house, and put them together in the kitchen. Nine of their other books have also been printed in-house. *Cecchetti, A Ballet Dynasty*, their 1995 publication about Enrico Cecchetti, one of the great classical ballet figures of the twentieth century, won a design award. The Adams do virtually all their own design and layout work. They ship books to England, Australia, New Zealand and the U.S.

China Dance Journal
September October 1996

Grant Strate

Dance Collection Danse's small budget comes from donations and government support. As a non-performance entity, they find it next to impossible to enlist corporate support. Their sustaining energies come from the people who inspire their work. At Fifteen Dance Lab they caught tantalizing whiffs of Canadian dance from the 1930s, '40s and '50s. One day they came across a programme from the 1949 Ballet Festival, which told them that dance had indeed flourished in a nearly forgotten, concealed history. Their 1986 project ENCORE! ENCORE! remounted works from the 1940s by six significant Canadian choreographers, Nesta Toumine, Gweneth Lloyd, Boris Volkoff, Jeanne Renaud, Françoise Sullivan and Nancy Lima Dent. The works were reset on a group of dancers by the original choreographers (some in their seventies and eighties during the reconstruction) and then videotaped.[2] Living history! Just in time, these key

works of art were rescued from oblivion where most dances languish. From this experience was born the Dance Collection Danse identity as a "living museum."

ENCORE! ENCORE! presented a week-long run of a multimedia show at Vancouver's Expo '86. Choreographed by Toronto scholar-choreographer Anna Blewchamp, it was designed to honour the artists and developments of Canadian theatrical dance from about 1900 to 1950. The Adams instituted the ENCORE! Hall of Fame in 1986, launching it with a posh induction ceremony at Casa Loma. On May 5, 1986, they honoured Canadian dance pioneers Fanny and Helen Birdsall, Madame Hylda Davies, Gweneth Lloyd, Jean Macpherson, Dorothy Wilson, Boris Volkoff, and Carmen and Maurice Morenoff as the first inductees to the Hall of Fame.

Jean Macpherson, ca. 1930.

The Dance Collection Danse archives are a key component of the entity's mandate to preserve, communicate and distribute Canada's theatrical dance story. The archives include oral histories, theatre programmes, photographs and negatives, videotapes, news clippings, scrapbooks, posters, biographical information, correspondence, newsletters, choreographic notation, costumes, backdrops, masks and other artifacts. There are about 300 individual portfolios. Through access to the archives, DCD serves researchers, media, writers, scholars and the public. Frequent users include teachers responsible for dance in the Canadian public school curriculum.

During the first fifteen years, Dance Collection Danse's primary research focus was on the period from around 1910 to 1950. As new collections come

---

[2] Boris Volkoff died in 1974, but several dancers who had worked closely with him were available to help set his work.

into Dance Collection Danse's care, research begins to move into the 1950s and 1960s. Several collections are in DCD's expanding electronic archives.

The Adams cluster their collections around people's names. The archives contain materials from many significant figures in the country's dance history including early ballet teachers, early modern dancers, choreographers and company founders. A few of the individuals represented in the archives may serve to indicate the scope of the collection. Boris Volkoff, a Russian teacher active in Toronto from 1929 through the 1960s, was often referred to as the "father" of Canadian ballet, and was artistic director of the Volkoff Canadian Ballet. Rosemary Deveson, Vancouver-born, danced with de Basil Ballet Russes de Monte Carlo from 1938 to 1940. Betty Farrally and Gweneth Lloyd co-founded the Winnipeg Ballet in 1939. Amy Sternberg was a teacher in Toronto from 1890 to 1930. Jeanne Renaud and Françoise Sullivan, dancers, choreographers, were originators of Quebec danse-théâtre. Sullivan is also a painter, and an original signatory of the *Refus global*, the historic 1948 Quebec artists' manifesto. Renaud is founder of Le Groupe de la Place Royale, and a former artistic director of Les Grands Ballets Canadiens. The list of Dance Collection Danse's reservoir of history goes on and on.

Playbills, souvenir programmes, brochures, choreographic notebooks, musical scores, magazines, correspondence, film, videotapes, audio cassettes, slides, photographs, costumes, make-up and other miscellany from various individual collections within the Dance Collection Danse archives.

Always seeking new ways to see and respect dance, recently the Adams have begun to develop "bundles" of information around particular choreographic works. In response to their feeling that it is important to try to recollect what actually happened in dances, in order to develop a context for seeing dance works as works of art, and to address the poverty of original correspondence in the archives, which might provide insight into the process or conditions of choreography, their aim is to collect as complete a context as possible around certain works. The bundles include choreographic notes, artifacts, and impressions through oral history, recollections by dancers, choreographers and audience members.

The Adams also have cultural activists' headgear in their wardrobes. They have been provocative participants in watersheds of recent Canadian dance history. The Last/Lost Dance Symposium, which they organized in 1992, galvanized discussion about the agonies of a disappearing art. They are deeply involved with dance organizations and cultural consulting processes. Miriam Adams has served on the boards of the Toronto Arts Council, the Dance Umbrella of Ontario, Dancer Transition Resource Centre and Artscape. Lawrence Adams was a founding board member of the Dance in Canada Association and is the Chairman of Arts Inter-Media/Dance Collection Danse.

Dance Collection Danse stands alone in Canada, and is the country's only dedicated dance publisher. Unique in the national dance community, the Adams are not agents and not an institution. They are responsive. They work hard and creatively to effect their ideas. They like a good argument. Through all their activities, their "living history," their expanding archives, their biannual magazine *The News*, the oral histories they are amassing, the books they publish – from biography to directories to dictionaries of dance terms – Lawrence and Miriam Adams are quietly building a context of informed history for dance in Canada, a framework other performing arts take for granted.

As Canadian dance continues to bloom in international stature, the Adams' idiosyncratic vision secures its respect at home. They embody creative will in action; their prolific output, on the slenderest of budgets, is nothing short of amazing.

In 1998 Dance Collection Danse celebrated fifteen years of capturing Canadian dance. The Adams remain very dancerly in a way; work hard, work constantly, do it yourself, figure out how to make things happen with the leanest of means. Lawrence and Miriam Adams would probably enjoy a good argument about whether it's dancerly or not – but they're far too busy. Driven by their fascination with the seemingly endless depth of history, old ways coming to light, and new ways of seeing, they keep moving. They leapfrog from past to future, pausing only briefly – to hold up a fresh idea for our consideration, or to winkle out some astonishing new treasure of our dance legacy.

Collage of publications from Dance Collection Danse Press/es: Carol Anderson's *Chasing the Tale of Contemporary Dance Part 2* (2002), Michael Crabb's *An Instinct for Success: Arnold Spohr and the Royal Winnipeg Ballet* (2002), Iro Valaskakis Tembeck's anthology *Estivale 2000: Canadian Dancing Bodies Then and Now/Les corps dansants d'hier à aujourd'hui au Canada* (2002), *Encyclopedia of Theatre Dance in Canada/Encyclopédie de la Danse Théâtrale au Canada* (2000) and Mary Jane Warner's *Toronto Dance Teachers 1825-1925* (1995).

References

Chitty, Elizabeth. 1993. "Lately, I've Been Thinking Again About 15." *Dance Collection Danse News* No. 35, 4-5.

Terrill Maguire:
Choreographer and Instigator

Susan Cash and Holly Small

> Dance has always been something that took up the void where words didn't function. It is something that takes the place of words, that is as valuable as words, that can express thoughts and feelings that words cannot capture, except perhaps in poetry.[1]
>
> Terrill Maguire

The contemporary dance scene in Toronto in the 1970s is not well documented or understood. The groundswell of avant-garde artists working at the time had a significant impact on the direction of dance in Canada. They stretched the definitions of "dance" to the extreme. Like their peers in other urban centres, they questioned traditional dance values, techniques, compositional structures, vocabulary, style, content and venue. They questioned conventional notions of beauty and accessibility in dance and changed the perception of the art form. They challenged the mainstream, company-centred funding policies of the arts councils of the time and effected permanent change in the granting procedures to individual artists. This burgeoning activity was the foundation for the thriving, multi-dimensional independent dance scene we now have in Canada.

Dance artists such as Lawrence and Miriam Adams, Elizabeth Chitty, Margaret Dragu, Maria Formolo, Terrill Maguire, Jennifer Mascall and Sarah Shelton Mann featured prominently at the time and have continued to develop the creative impulses that drew them to dance in the first place. Along with numerous colleagues, they have made their mark in related disciplines such as performance art, writing, visual art, film and video. Their efforts still resonate in the community. The dynamic young artists of today benefit unknowingly from the avant-garde choreographers who shook up the system

---

[1] Quotations are taken from interviews with Terrill Maguire conducted by the authors on July 20 and 21, 1993. The authors have known Terrill Maguire for many years. They grew up as dancers and developed into choreographers under her initial tutelage when they were students at York University. Now they both teach at York and continue to dance and choreograph. Maguire's encouragement and influence on them as artists has been significant. She has offered them many opportunities to present their choreography, including the INDE Festivals of Music and Dance. Holly Small has performed and toured with Maguire on several occasions. Their experiences as students, colleagues and friends give them a broad perspective and deep admiration for Maguire's unique role in the evolution of Canadian dance.

Terrill Maguire, 1978.

thirty years ago. The tremendous freedom of expression they take for granted today is in fact the legacy of the earlier generation.

This profile draws attention to a singular artist whose positive impact has been overlooked. Terrill Maguire was a unique presence in the dance community in the 1970s. She was an extraordinary dancer, renowned for her fluid sensuality and provocative solo choreography. Through time she has also emerged as a catalyst for various collaborative ventures including the production of a major national festival of music and dance. Hers is a compelling story of conflicting passions and politics. She is an enigmatic, controversial personality. She has staunch supporters and equally vigorous detractors, but few can deny she is a true artist.

Maguire grew up in southern California, the eldest of six children. While most of her choreographic career has been spent in Canada, those childhood influences are deeply etched in her work and in her life. Some of her earliest movement-related memories are of playing in the Pacific Ocean – diving into the surf, running with the wind, watching the cloud formations drifting overhead. Nature imposed no formal structures or concepts of discipline and achievement. Her experiences were of joyful movement in harmony with the environment. This heightened awareness of being part of the natural world was further reinforced by her first formal dance training with Gertrude Knight, who taught modern dance in a free-spirited, improvisational way. Knight encouraged her young students to create their own dances, free of any external framework, style or syllabus. Maguire's natural affinity for dance eventually drew her to more traditional training in modern and ballet techniques and, as a teenager, she received private coaching as well as classes from Adele Charaska De Angelo, who had been a dancer with the Ballet Russe de Monte Carlo and the Ballet Company of Radio City Music Hall. In addition to the ballet training, De Angelo also introduced the slender, leggy, young dancer to the mystical and metaphysical writings of Gurdjieff, Ouspensky, Buber and other spiritual teachers. When Maguire was just sixteen years old, De Angelo took her to hear Krishnamurti speak outdoors, under an ancient oak tree in Ojai, California. It would take more than a decade of conventional dance training and various company affiliations before this unique mix of spiritual influences would manifest itself in her work.

Maguire began working as a professional modern dancer even before she graduated from UCLA with a degree in dance. In Los Angeles she trained extensively with Donald McKayle and worked in the companies of Richard Oliver and Marie Marchowsky, a recent arrival from New York described fondly by Maguire as "a ferocious she-devil." Marchowsky was an original member of the Martha Graham Dance Company, who began her lengthy affiliation at the age of fourteen, the youngest dancer ever to join that company. She was intent on transplanting to southern California the harsh disciplinary regime of Graham. She forbid her dancers to take any classes other than those she herself conducted and, in typical Graham fashion, required her company to rehearse long and arduous hours. Since she paid them nothing she had to give them some time off to earn a meagre living. The long months of rigorous training and rehearsal culminated in just two performances, insufficient reward for such devotion. While Maguire was in Marchowsky's company she moved to a rustic cabin up from the coast, in Topanga Canyon, which offered a reprieve from the sometimes abusive environment of the company. Although Maguire was drawn to the purity, clarity and passionate physicality inherent in the Graham tradition, she soon discovered she couldn't bear to leave the mountains and the ocean for the one-hour commute to rehearsals in downtown Los Angeles. So she quit the company.

At that time, she found it a refreshing contrast to work with the wild and wacky Mystic Knights of the Oingo Boingo, a Los Angeles-based company of musicians, dancers and actors whose mandate was the polar opposite of the Marchowsky company. Their work was an eclectic mix of music and movement, employing colourful theatrical effects, intriguing African and Asian instruments and the guerrilla tactics of street theatre. They rehearsed very little and performed all the time in the street, nightclubs, at private parties, galleries, as close to the audience as they could get. Every performance began with a festive parade to gather an audience. Among the company members was Michael Byron, a musician and composer who introduced Maguire to the world of New Music. Oingo Boingo soon began to enjoy success. They received many offers to perform including a prestigious engagement for the Coty Fashion Design Awards at Lincoln Center, which brought the company to New York for a lengthy sojourn. The immediacy of the contact she had with her audience transformed her into a versatile, street-savvy performer. But when she left the group she was hungry to do some serious choreography.

In 1973, Maguire and Byron moved to Toronto where Byron was a graduate student and lecturer in the Department of Music at York University. Maguire started teaching movement classes in the Music Department, which allowed her to pursue her interest in interdisciplinary collaboration. There were a number of other Americans teaching in the Music Department at the time, including Richard Teitelbaum, David Rosenboom, Robin Engelman, Jon Higgins and Casey Sokol. They were influenced by the strong ethnomusicology slant of the programme at York University, and at the same time they were exploring the potential of integrating the art forms of music and dance. The radical ways these artists worked and thought was an inspiration for Maguire. She had grown up in a home filled with a variety of music and had always found working with musicians to be creatively stimulating. This was in the early days of the minimalist movement in the arts and it had an impact on her choreographic methods. She realized that very small and simple movements could be compelling.

The following year, Maguire began teaching in the Department of Dance at York University. It was a hotbed of dance activity which gave her a choreographic outlet and inspired her to work harder than she had ever worked before. It was her first major teaching appointment and she learned as she went along. She taught classes in modern dance which were an eclectic mix of Cunningham, Limón, Horton, jazz and yoga techniques. Her own body seemed ideally suited to the material she taught. She could move freely in the hip sockets and had extraordinary extensions. She liked slow, twisting movements, undulating arms, low grounded shapes, wide lateral weight shifts, multiple rhythms in different body parts, extravagant balances and mesmerizing stillness. What came so easily to her was not always so easily passed on to the less physically gifted dance students.

She also taught classes in dance composition. It was a time when there was only a handful of composition teachers in Canada and the whole area of study was relatively new. Maguire's own early influences were strongly evident in her teaching. Her approach might best be described as non-interventionist. She emphasized the need to work from internal impulses and created a safe environment for those who were really interested in pursuing creative research. Group and individual improvisations were a key element of her course. She assigned studies on a variety of themes such as body isolation, circular movement, stillness, ritual, rhythm, mirroring and chance procedures. She provided her students with a wide-ranging reading list which included all the standard dance composition texts as well as books about music, visual arts, theatre, metaphysics and spirituality. She addressed issues of form and content in an oblique manner. Some students, however, did not connect with her approach which rarely included direct criticism. But, left to their own devices, other students flourished, given the luxury of time and space to experiment freely. She established a collaborative link with the students of Professor Phil Werren's electronic music course across campus. These projects resulted in performances at venues such as A Space and the Music Gallery, which propelled her students into the downtown professional community. In many cases these experiences later led to fruitful, long-term artistic relationships.

Maguire and Byron were married and living, at that time, with visual artist Jacqueline Humbert and composer David Rosenboom in a Victorian farmhouse, surrounded by fields and woodlands, north of the university in Maple, Ontario. Maguire was immersed in a lifestyle that allowed her considerable creative freedom. She began collaborating with Humbert on a work set in the trees on their land. Humbert designed a hammock-like cocoon which hung high in the trees, and created a costume for Maguire of kelly green nylon with secret zippers which contained beautifully painted silk butterfly wings. Maguire hung mysteriously in her cocoon, pulsing with life. As her movement became increasingly urgent, sharp and jabbing, she eased open the zippers to reveal vivid streaks of colour which transformed into huge, wonderful wings as she unfolded her arms. Arching backwards over her net, she emerged fully, dropped to the ground and fluttered away into the woods. Recognizing that nature itself provided an elemental sound score, Byron chose to add only simple percussion that melded with these existing environmental sounds. The work, entitled *Chrysalis*, was a celebration of rebirth and transformation. It was subsequently performed in various other venues and was the subject of an award-winning film by director James Orr.

Just as she encouraged her students to create through ritual, so was she strongly motivated by ritual in her own work. Her next environmental piece was created during the first National Choreographic Seminar hosted by York University in 1978. Maguire participated as a dancer and choreographed her duet *Eclipse*. It was a time when she had the luxury to read and to dream and to use her dreams as source material for her work. She was particularly intrigued by the Druids and their mystical rites. This research culminated in her Summer Solstice ritual which took place in a wooded area on the fringes of the York campus.

Shortly before midnight, the audience was led by candlelight through the woods to an old, gnarled, apple tree in a small clearing. The tree was illuminated by a circle of candles in wine glasses, and laden with fabric sculpture by Carmelo Arnoldin which gave the impression of delicate cobwebs. Nearby, musicians Gordon Phillips and John Kuipers played softly on a gamelan-inspired cluster of percussion instruments. Deeper in the woods, the white-robed figure of Maguire appeared. She moved through the trees, gliding in and out of the open spaces as she gradually drew near to her sacred tree. She circled, paused in a hollow at the base of the tree, and then climbed up into the branches of her partner. She recalls feeling a deep sense of connection with the spirit of this tree. Twisting and wrapping herself around it, she ascended to its topmost branch and, gripping the tree with her legs, she let go with both arms and arched out into space. At just that moment, she saw the full moon rise over the top of the tree as if it was responding, on cue, to some divine lighting designer.

Clearly, Maguire was developing a penchant for site-specific work. In 1979, she was invited to the Yard, a dance artists' retreat on Martha's Vineyard, an island off the coast of Massachusetts. There she created a quartet called *Terradactyl*, with music by Byron. It was performed in an open-sided barn with the stars and the moon as a backdrop.

Groves of sacred trees and unobstructed views of the moon and stars are hard to find in New York City, so when she moved there in 1980 she began adapting her outdoor dances to the dense, urban spaces of Manhattan. She performed at Castle Clinton, in Battery Park with a group of six dancers and three musicians from the Steve Reich Ensemble. In the intense heat, the dancers explored the textures and architectural features of the park – grass, concrete, gravel, stonework, walls, windows and platforms.

Terrill Maguire performing her *Water Sources*, Bell Trinity Plaza, Toronto, 1997.

This initial brush with architectural settings led to the first of what was to be a series of fountain dances. It was set in the Isamu Noguchi Fountain at the Chase Manhattan Bank Plaza in the Wall Street district. She spent hours observing the site, visualizing her dance and planning her choreographic strategy for the large, circular pool with its scattering of volcanic rocks. For security reasons, however, she was allowed only one day to work in the pool. With woodwind player Richard Cohen, she choreographed and rehearsed the fountain dance in full view of passersby and workers in the surrounding office towers. This aquatic experiment appealed to Maguire on an elemental level and she went on to create fountain pieces for groups of dancers at the Canada Dance Festivals held in Ottawa between 1987 and 1992. These fountain dances explored images of mermaids, water nymphs and sirens. They were performed in an ornate Victorian fountain in Ottawa's Confederation Park to the pleasure and astonishment of the many people out to enjoy a summer's day in the park.

Solo work has continued to be an important creative outlet for Maguire. York University was not only a place to germinate ideas but also a platform from which she made her name as a solo dancer and choreographer. In those days, York was one of the centres of dance activity for the Toronto area. It sponsored an important concert series which presented Merce Cunningham, Laura Dean, Meredith Monk, Murray Louis and many other international companies, which regularly drew the downtown dance community up to Burton Auditorium. Maguire was right in the midst of all this cultural stimulation. During her years at York, from 1973 to 1979, she created more than fifteen solo works in collaboration with local composers, which were presented in a variety of alternative venues such as the Music Gallery, A Space and Fifteen Dance Lab.

Distinctive among these works were *Sea Changes*, an impressionistic dance about the sensuous ebb and flow of the underwater world; *Kali*, a fearsome glimpse of the Hindu goddess of destruction and creation; and *Run Ragged*, a loose-limbed, rhythmic response to James Tenney's score. *Passage* is a solo from this period that has stood the test of time. It was originally commissioned by composer Richard Teitelbaum. He challenged her to accompany his music, which was so quiet as to be almost inaudible, with a dance that moved so slowly as to be almost imperceptible. It has become a signature work which she is often invited to perform. In the dance, she makes slow, steady progress on a shallow diagonal from stage left to stage right, passing from a dreamy verticality to a yearning horizontal. The adagio is sparsely punctuated with those seemingly involuntary flicks of hands and feet so characteristic of her work. From the point of view of the audience, it is an enigmatic dance with veiled intentions, perhaps charting the passage from one plane of existence to the next.

In person, Maguire is a woman of medium-build and average height who, in her fifties, still has the vulnerable aura of a flower child of the 1960s. On stage she assumes a statuesque presence. Her body is ageless and perfectly proportioned for dance – long limbs, wide back, expressive torso. Her feet are extraordinary, with sinuous arches and prehensile toes. Her head floats delicately on her long neck. Her steely blue, owlish eyes can be remote and mysterious or penetrating and manipulative. She moves with fluid, boneless ease, describing curves and curling shapes in the space around her.

The ideas brewing in her earlier solos came into clear focus in *Cutting Losses*, an autobiographical dance premiered in Toronto in 1983. The dance includes poetic spoken text which tells of a harrowing incident in Maguire's life. Through sparse, impressionistic images she reveals just enough information for us to grasp her story of being raped by her dance teacher. The experience was so vivid in her own mind that she was able to perform the work with a clarity and conviction that was poignant without being sensational or exploitive.

This piece is essentially a solo for Maguire, with a second dancer appearing intermittently as a shadowy alter ego, at times compassionate, at times aggressive, at times a physical burden clinging to Maguire's back. Composers Harry Mann and John Lang provide live music on clarinet and piano. The music drives the more vigorous, athletic sections of the work and subsides during quieter sections where Maguire describes dispassionately the sensation of the "stiff, grey carpet bristles" pressing into her cheek, or the view, from where she has been forced to the floor, of "dry, brown, brush-covered hills." Choreographically, *Cutting Losses* was not a great departure from earlier works. The movement vocabulary still favoured isolations, languid leg extensions and body percussion. The structure again relied on accumulations, repetition and circular or spiralling floor patterns. Yet the work possessed a more resonant power. The movement was meaningful beyond the representation of broad, abstract themes such as the human journey, rhythms of the sea or mythical goddesses. It engaged the audience on a personal level, unlike earlier solos such as *Marrow* and *Passage* and works to come such as *Hyacinth* and *River of Fire*. Because the work was rooted in a concrete issue about which she had intense feelings, the choreography unfolded with a sense of inevitability, and Maguire performed it with an unprecedented directness and singularity of purpose.

This clarity was also evident in *Only Time To/No Time Not To*, a work which had its intriguing beginnings in the Rosicrucian belief that the earth and moon had once been a single body. The moon broke off and went its own way but the two entities maintained a connection which, for Maguire, was an apt metaphor for human relationships. The child comes from the parent and then separates but there exists a lifelong bond.

She first researched this material at the Newfoundland Sound Symposium, in St. John's, during the summer of 1986 with singer Michelle George and composer Pauline Oliveros. At that time, they were immersed in the work of Jungian analyst and author Marion Woodman, as well as other related writing. Their process was largely intuitive and this first version of the work came very easily. But when Maguire wanted to develop the piece further for the INDE '88 festival of new dance and music, there were some difficulties in the working situation. A Canadian composer was part of INDE's criteria so composer Wendy Bartley was incorporated, replacing the original collaborator Oliveros. As well, George was concerned that the work had become too dance-oriented. When Maguire had it videotaped shortly before the opening, she hated it. She worked fervently, and within a matter of days had changed the entire piece. They managed to produce a compelling work which challenged some perceptions of dance.

The performance began with an image that also occurred in *Cutting Losses*, of one woman carrying another woman on her back. In this case, Maguire is curled on the broad back of George, who sways gently and utters plaintive, breathy syllables. Maguire gestures softly, her arms framing George's head. As she slides to the floor, we are struck by the tall, imposing figure of George which emphasizes Maguire's girlish presence. There is a brief struggle before George loses her maternal hold and Maguire flings herself into wild and convulsive movement. George's extended vocal work rises from guttural rumbling to sorrowful keening, and soars to a high pitched, nasal lament. The dramatic power of the piece seems to come first from her voice and then from the relationship between the two women. The best moments occur when they each surrender to the needs of the work, transcending their individual egos and giving in to the sense of unity or community that is so necessary to human existence. Within the dance milieu, to pair the slender Maguire and large George could be regarded as slightly extraordinary, but their contrasting body types make the work all the more effective. It was Maguire's intention to challenge the conventional portrayal of women in fashion, advertising and music videos, to get past these impersonal, manipulative and false images and offer a realistic alternative. "I think we've had our sexuality taken away from us and now we are told by the media what's supposed to be sexy, what's supposed to be sensual, what we're supposed to look like. Are we so conditioned that the image of a person who weighs more than 104 pounds, or a person over twenty-five years of age being sexual or sensual, strikes us as obscene?"

Maguire is particularly drawn to explore the relationship between sexuality and spirituality. For society in general, these elements are separate but Maguire sees sexuality and spirituality as very compatible as well as very compelling subject matter. Most recently, Maguire has been inspired by *The Song of Songs*, one of the most profoundly sensual and erotic passages in the Bible. Her imagination is captivated by the mythical, archetypal and sacred treatment of sensuality. In September 1993, Maguire completed one section of *The Song of Songs* project in collaboration with singer Alejandra Nuñez and two dancers. This first section, entitled *Crazy To Be Born*, explored one aspect of sensual and spiritual love. It was based on Eduardo Galeano's translation of the creation myth of the Makiritare Indians of South America. In his *Memory of Fire: Genesis*, he evokes a poetic image of the first man and the first woman who dreamed God was dreaming they were to be created. "The man and woman were inside a great shining egg singing and dancing and kicking up a fuss because they were crazy to be born" (*Dancing the Goddess* programme notes, Toronto, 1993).

Maguire began this project with hazy images that gradually came into focus as she developed the choreography in a series of workshops with a group of four dancers, two actors and two musicians. She designed improvisational structures to stimulate the senses, encouraging the dancers to respond on a primal level, to different sounds, smells, textures and images. "I am interested in working with our wild natures that get so stifled and smothered and buried. Some artists like to fall back on a script, story or structure, because it's scary getting out there in unknown territory. But, for me, dependence on such devices prevents the material from finding its own way." An important aspect of her process, at first, is to suspend judgment and simply let the material emerge. Only then does she judge and evaluate, edit and shape the dance.

Visions and Revisions

Out of the workshops came the finished piece that premiered in the full evening programme *Dancing The Goddess* in September 1993 at the Winchester Street Theatre. This was an evening of sacred dance and ritual produced by choreographer Patricia Beatty who, as co-founder of Toronto Dance Theatre, has played a prominent role in Canadian dance for three decades. Beatty provided an outlet for her own work as well as that of Maguire, choreographer Linda Rabin and composer Ann Southam. Beatty and Maguire seem to be on the same spiritual path and share a long-term friendship rooted in emotional, intellectual and artistic support. In Beatty's programme notes, she dedicates the concert "to the sacred feminine in dance and music, celebrating the reverence for the earth, the human body and the joy and nurturance of relationships." All the works on the programme dealt with archetypal themes and had both spiritual and visceral impact.

Crazy To Be Born begins with an image of a bird-like shamaness straddling the entwined forms of the "first man and woman." She is a hawk, a jaguar, a shape-shifter, a god who breathes life into the man and woman. Her gutsy singing, and the seductive undercurrent of percussion from two small shakers she holds in outstretched hands, arouse the two dancers and incite them into wild and abandoned movement. Clad in faun-coloured, suede loincloths, they roll and tumble and furiously kick, discovering each other's bodies and exploring their new-found power to stir up the energy in the space and in each other. The work hovers at an intense pitch, its contained, circular structure drawing the audience into its vibrating sphere. The tangible eroticism is almost cinematic in the way it plays on the senses of the viewer. She expanded on these ideas two years later in *Bloodsongs*, a group dance in which the breathtaking partner work of three grounded couples used sensual lifts often performed on floor level and on the knees.

The bulk of her choreography has been solos for herself and duets, often including herself. This seems to be partly her preference, but also because of lack of funds and resources. Those few group dances that she has produced show another facet of her talent. When other skilled dancers interpret her movement it can be appreciated for its inherent qualities. When she is able to step back from her work and direct the choreographic process, the form of the work emerges more clearly, spatial patterns are more intricate and the dynamic range is greater.

Califia, a refreshingly spirited work for ten female dancers, premiered in 1984 at Premiere Dance Theatre. It is based on a sixteenth-century Spanish account of the mythical island of Califia, an earthly paradise inhabited by a race of Amazon women. The piece opens on a silent, empty stage. Dancers, in short filmy tunics, enter one by one, galloping in circles, transforming the silent stage into a whirlwind of kinetic energy. They seem to be gathering for a ritual. There is a sense of sisterhood underscored with a watchful competitiveness. There is a conflict over the leadership of the tribe, which is accentuated by the strength and directness of each encounter, as they approach and retreat and eventually entwine and arch their bodies. The dance has a persistent ebb and flow. Strong, idiosyncratic solos and duets highlight each dancer, and culminate in a full ensemble series of oddly earth-bound jumps.

In the same vein is Maguire's group work, *Edge of Eden*, commissioned for the first choreographic workshop of the Ottawa Ballet in 1992. This is a romantic, contemporary piece for three couples. Maguire used the balletic abilities of the dancers to develop different possibilities in partnering and, even in this short attempt to work with the stylistic differences, one could see the possibility for distinct and substantial growth. It was hard for her to get these young ballet dancers to express themselves authentically, to adapt to one another in a genuinely sensual way. "They couldn't melt. They couldn't erase the barriers. Then, the one couple that did the best ended up getting together, so at least that was one good result." Perhaps another, more significant result was the infusion of quickness, buoyancy and precision in *Edge of Eden*, which is uncharacteristic of most of Maguire's work.

But Maguire is a matchmaker at heart. Her love of putting people and groups together fuels her creative strategy. In 1985, she founded the INDE Festival to provide performance opportunities for the independent dance community by bringing together teams of choreographers and composers to create new work. The nationally acclaimed festival was initially developed as a biannual event to foster the development of the art forms in new directions. The festival premiered in Toronto at the Great Hall, and subsequent seasons in 1988, 1990 and 1992 were presented at the duMaurier Theatre at Harbourfront.

In articulating her original vision for INDE she touches on many issues important to artists. "I've come to realize we do have something to do with creating the kind of world we want to live in, and I much prefer the world view in which people cooperate with each other and share and give support. And it has certainly been useful for me in the past to have someone give me a push to work with someone I never would have considered otherwise. It's lonely being a choreographer. Why not share the resources and share the endeavour as well?"

She recognized that there are many different kinds of artists. Some are skilled at raising funds, promoting themselves and producing their work, but others, who are just as worthy of exposure, may not present themselves in the same way. The intention was not to create an underdog festival but a festival that balances disparate elements and creates the possibility of cross-pollination in an environment of mutual tolerance and support.

Maguire admits she is a better facilitator than administrator. INDE '92 was marred by a lack of clarity among all the players in reference to financial matters as well as disagreement over the selection of the artists. "Now I don't know exactly what went on with INDE '92, but to reclaim the original vision of INDE I had to restructure the whole thing. I'm not necessarily interested in the Hottest, the Newest, the Latest! That's not what INDE's about." She has incorporated and expanded the mandate to include educational programming and community involvement. She continues to receive resumés and proposals from artists who want to be considered for the next INDE. Evidently the community still needs such a forum, and Maguire is intent on rejuvenating the original spirit by sponsoring workshops and performances throughout the year that will build momentum towards the larger festival and create more performing opportunities for independents.

Maguire feels responsibility towards INDE but not a sense of possessiveness or ownership. For her, it is important that INDE not repeat the same formula year after year but continue to respond to changes in the community and develop in whatever directions seem appropriate to the times. "Part of my mission is to shine the light on those people who are doing wonderful things in the dark, especially the ones who go against the grain or against the norm. If you feel you're not getting any kind of results or rewards or support then you're not going to flourish, you're going to dry up. You're hardly even going to survive."

Maguire *is* a survivor. She is able to turn apparent obstacles into opportunities for growth and change and to juggle her roles as artist, presenter, wife and mother. Maguire has been married since 1984 to David Langer, a television producer/director and former dancer. They have two children. Motherhood, especially, has shaped her current perspective and allowed her to abandon willingly any conventional idea of ambition. For Maguire, competition has never been a strong motivating force. "You compete with yourself as an artist and try to fulfil your own needs and abilities. But it is frustrating because children have overwhelming needs for a long time which can lead to terrible conflicts. It keeps you right in touch with your feelings, right there at home living in your heart."

She didn't know if having children was going to be the end of her creative life in dance. "If it meant that I was to become a mother and all this other stuff was just to recede then that's how I would live my life." But she continues to have creative impulses and like all artists she suffers when prevented from expressing them.

Maguire is a balancer by nature and extravagantly describes her adventures in maintaining her equilibrium. "I sometimes feel I'm walking on a tightrope over a chasm with rapids and sharp rocks and piranhas down below. At least that's what it feels like. I think accepting that I'm in an impossible situation is the best way for me to proceed. But there's a lot of conflict. When you have children you have to nurture them first, then you have to continue to cultivate your relationship with your husband, and finally you try to get to your work which clamours relentlessly for attention. So, it can be absolutely harrowing."

As Maguire walks that fine line balancing her creative and personal needs, she is not without thoughts and hopes for the future of dance. Her work is infused with the inherent power of nature, which she instinctively responded to as a child, and the mystical aspect of the creative process, which she has embraced increasingly later in life. Her mission is to instigate and cultivate new possibilities for dance to play a significant role in the world today.

A Conversation with Christopher House

Francis Mason

Francis Mason (Editor of *Ballet Review*): Where do you come from?[1]

Christopher House: The east coast of Canada, from St. John's in Newfoundland – the most easterly point.

Francis Mason: Did you see any dance when you were young?

House: A little on television, you know, the June Taylor Dancers, and I would change to the other channel. We only had two. A couple of ballet companies came through. I remember seeing some ballet, and thinking how unbelievably silly it was that adults would do that, would behave that way on the stage. And I think it probably wasn't very good, what I was seeing.

So I really didn't have any interest in dance, but I was always interested in the theatre and was pretty actively discouraged from following through on that. I managed to get into some community-type theatre productions as an actor. I mean in the way that all kids make up plays, we put on shows. I was that kind of kid at five or six. By the time I was a teenager I didn't do very much.

Mason: Did you have an impulse to make things up?

House: I think so. But I wasn't sure exactly what. My brother was always interested in architecture. He was a dinky toy fanatic – tiny model cars. They're beautiful English cars that were made of steel. And I guess they're probably quite rare now, because everything's made of plastic. They're beautifully crafted. My brother was a car fanatic. He used to sit in the driveway from the age of four every day behind the wheel of the car. And he got bigger and bigger until finally he was able to pull it in and out of the driveway. He had this car mania. So he used to organize cities with the dinky toys. I designed a lot of environments and buildings in collaboration with him. I think environments would be the only way to describe it, which mostly involved things from the kitchen. I would often get in trouble for pulling everything out of the cupboards – soup cans and pots and pans and scarves and ties for roads and that kind of thing. I think most kids do that.

---

[1] This interview first appeared in *Ballet Review* 20 (Spring 1994), 43-51. Reproduced by permission of *Ballet Review*. Christopher House has served as Artistic Director of Toronto Dance Theatre since 1994.

Christopher House performing his *Encarnado*, 1993.

Mason: The building impulse – architecture – it didn't occur to you?

House: Not really, no. I was interested in music. My mother taught me to play the piano when I was about four or five, so I started musically when I was quite young. But St. John's was not a big cultural city at all. There was a lot of traditional folk art there, but I didn't really have access to that.

Mason: And there wasn't a Shakespeare repertory company or anything like that?

House: No, nothing like that.

Mason: Christmas pantomimes?

House: Well, yes, that sort of thing. But I was not old enough to appreciate what was dying off, and I was at the age where the television culture was coming in. If I'd grown up ten years before I think I would have been exposed to a lot more of the older culture. It's quite a self-contained, Irish-English culture, and I miss that. But I was interested in the theatre. When I went to university I studied political science – at Memorial University in St. John's for a couple of years, and I had some friends who were in the theatre. But I myself wasn't involved in that because I was too busy with my studies, and I thought I would like to join the foreign service and travel around. It seemed like that would be a way to get around the world interestingly. And because I love travelling and I travel a lot. I've since found out from people that I've met in foreign service that it's not quite as glamorous as it seemed – a lot of waiting around at receptions and trying not to drink too much. My father was a doctor and for some reason I thought I didn't want to be a doctor just because he'd been one. I guess you often want to do what your parents don't do.

Mason: Your mother is a musician?

House: An amateur musician, but she mostly stayed at home.

Mason: She knew enough to begin to teach you the piano.

House: Yes, and my older sister and my younger brother. The music wasn't a big deal. We played piano all the time, including at music festivals. I still play the piano. For some reason I can play by ear and my brother and sister don't. In fact, my technical skills were less developed because when I began to work on a piece I would have heard it played around the house, so I could just discover the skeleton and then play it without really learning how to read it as well.

Mason: That's a real advantage.

House: Well, in some ways it's good because it saves you a little time. In other ways it's not good because I would always bomb in the sight-reading exams in the music festivals.

Mason: It's useful for your work now?

House: I can read a score. Sometimes when I'm working on a piece I'll work with the score. In other works it seems inappropriate to use the score, for any number of reasons.

Mason: Did you watch plays at the university?

House: No, I was really enjoying the academic life. And I got a scholarship to go to the University of Ottawa to study French. So I went to their political science department. The University of Ottawa had an unusual theatre department, and I met people who were in it. And then in my final year, because I had been so keen all the way through in my studies, I had already done all my requirements, so I actually graduated in political science by taking theatre courses that final year. And very quickly I realized that this was something that I wanted to do. The movement side appealed to me the most, and the movement teacher also taught modern dance, a woman named Elizabeth Langley, and she suggested that I might want to come to one of her modern dance classes. I was almost twenty. I went to her class. It was Graham-based, because she'd studied at the Martha Graham school. About half of it was based on improvisation, because she was interested in teaching adults how to learn what they liked about dancing and to enjoy their own physicality. And about ten minutes into the class work I realized that this was something extremely important that I'd never experienced.

Mason: She began her class on the floor in the Graham way?

House: She began on the floor and went through the whole breathing process and some of the formal Graham exercises. I said to her, "Oh, I think I want to be a dancer." She discouraged me because she said dance is not a field where you can be sure about what you want to do. But that was how it happened. I very quickly found it was the most challenging thing I'd ever run up against, because I had been quite competent academically. Dance seemed to have every intellectual challenge, every emotional challenge, and every physical challenge. It also had that kind of indescribable thing that sits, I think, in the back of your neck, which has that kind of spiritual excitement attached to it.

Mason: Before, had you been good at games?

House: I was never good at team sports, I had never done any gymnastics. I liked playing soccer, but that was the only team sport. I swam and played tennis and I was always active physically, but not in a committed way. That's one of the reasons why it was easy for me to start dancing at that age because I hadn't had any injuries – the broken legs or sprained ankles from tearing around with footballs and hockey sticks.

Mason: Paul Taylor began dance in his university career.

House: Didn't Taylor swim?

Mason: Yes. You fell into dance because it had its physical side as well as its spiritual?

House: I think probably the initial impulse was the physical excitement of it all. But I guess the thing that appealed to me most was the notion of a suspension of weight, the feeling of falling in different directions and turning to fall and the sensation of suspension in jumping. I took immense pleasure in being airborne, whether it was being airborne before you hit the deck or being airborne before you land from the jump.

Mason: And how you control those things.

House: Yes, how you modulate those things. Different ways to phrase. I guess that is a big impulse to make dances right away, too, because immediately I began to make studies for myself. When I began dancing it was through a looser framework. Probably if I had started at a ballet barre or had learned a very specific kind of technical code immediately, I would have been less likely to do that. Because I was starting in improvisation, I had no idea that I was, you know, an untrained and clumsy oaf.

Mason: Langley let you make studies for yourself?

House: Yes. I feel very lucky that I was introduced to dance that way.

Mason: You could do anything that you thought was possible, and it wouldn't be laughable because it didn't fit in?

House: You go through a period where you discover what a glissade is, what a pirouette en dehors is, without being told what they are. Then when I looked at other dancers I realized that I could do a little work in technical ways, so I began to take formal classes in ballet and modern dance.

Mason: When did you see the first formally staged dance?

House: I came to New York soon after that because I figured New York would be the place to be. Earlier I had seen a production of *Swan Lake* by Les Grands Ballets Canadiens, and I saw some Balanchine early on – *Concerto Barocco* and *The Four Temperaments* by that company. When I came to New York I saw the Graham company and New York City Ballet and American Ballet Theatre. That was about 1977 – at the height of the excitement over Baryshnikov and Gelsey Kirkland and Makarova.

Mason: It was a good time.

House: It was a very exciting time. Suzanne Farrell and Peter Martins at the New York City Ballet! I was really glad to be in New York. I mean, I was a complete beginner, but when I went back to Canada I think I had seen who the important dancers were.

Mason: Did you come to New York to study with anyone?

House: I didn't take classes at the Graham school at that time. There was a woman here named Nikki Cole whom I had met in Canada and she taught an amalgamation of some of the Limón principles and some of the Cunningham principles, and she'd worked with Matt Mattox, that wonderful jazz choreographer. I studied with her, and she did all kinds of very beautiful isolations, not in an especially jazzy way, but she had incorporated these approaches into her work. She was a very inspiring teacher and was very much concerned with phrasing and texture and movement. She could demonstrate so beautifully herself. I think she was a big influence. Perhaps I was attracted to her because I wanted to move that way. I took class with Alfredo Corvino at his studio and at Zena Rommett's studio. She taught a floor barre. It was very good for teaching basic principles of alignment and placement, because you can take a million ballet classes and unless you have the right teacher you're never going to learn how to stand up properly. Zena Rommett still has her studio, and her teaching is somewhat ballet based. You lie on your back and flex your feet and point them and turn out your hip. It's absolutely distilled principles of alignment. Either you were doing it or you weren't. It was very clear and very helpful. I went back to Canada and spent a couple of years at York University in Toronto. Because I had a previous degree I was able to go back into the university system and get support, but do nothing but studio courses. They had a gigantic fine arts complex. I studied ballet, and that's when I started to study Graham technique formally.

Mason: Who was teaching it?

House: Norrey Drummond. She had danced with Toronto Dance Theatre. And Sandra Neels was teaching Cunningham. And a number of people from the National Ballet of Canada. There were some very good teachers.

Mason: So you took a bit of all of this?

House: Less Cunningham, because I was a little afraid of it, and now I kick myself. But you don't do everything. I was attracted to Graham for a number of reasons. One, I felt it was the most difficult because I was very light by nature, and I thought that it would give me some weight and that glorious organic coordination that comes from learning all those floor exercises. I thought that I had to use something like that or I would get stuck as a mosquito for the rest of my career.

Mason: And you began to perform?

House: Yes, there was a fair amount of performing involved too. And by then I was making my own dances and performing them. And in my second year in Toronto we actually put on a production in downtown Toronto. I shared a programme with a couple of other students. It was in a space like The Kitchen or Dance Theater Workshop. I think the production was my idea. I showed three pieces. That was 1979, so I was twenty-three years old. There was a solo for myself to a piece of Irish traditional music. None of these pieces will ever appear again. There was a trio. And the third piece was a narrative piece, based on the brother and sister relationship in *Les Enfants Terribles*. The programme was sold out. Tickets were three bucks. We did three performances. Then I joined Toronto Dance Theatre immediately after that.

World Gone Mad Productions in Association with the Necessary Angel Theatre Company

presents

Three Working

Dances
Choreographed and Performed by
Anita Shack
Christopher House
Joe Bietola

May 18, 19, 20 at 8:30 p.m.

15 Dance Lab
155A George Street
(1 Block East of Jarvis at Queen East)
tickets are $3.00
reservations, call 869-1589

Mason: Had David Earle or Peter Randazzo of Toronto Dance Theatre seen your performance?

House: David Earle came – I'm not sure that Peter came – but I had danced with Toronto Dance Theatre the previous summer, after my first year at York. I took a Saturday class there and liked the atmosphere very much. And really it was David's class. I enjoyed it a lot. And they were looking for some extras for the company's tenth anniversary season at the beautiful Royal Alexandra Theatre. And they were doing a revival of an older piece of his and they needed somebody, a character, I think it was like a reborn king, or something like that, kind of a young king. So I danced with them very briefly. I went on tour with them, and we opened a new theatre in Albany, upstate, the Empire State, I think it was. They thought I would like to go on tour with them for the rest of the year, and I said I'd better come back to school and study because I didn't think I had enough technique yet. So I went back, and I'm glad I did. And for many years I wished that I'd gone back for another year. But they still took me the following spring.

Mason: You earned a Ph.D., as it were.

House: I didn't care about being in the university at all, but I did want to study more. At York there was a ballet teacher named Sandra Caverly who had been in the National Ballet of Canada. She was very interested in Bournonville technique and had done a lot of studies in Denmark. And she taught a kind of Bournonville basic class which I adored. I love that kind of dancing, the style of

370

jumping. I've mentioned the pleasure of suspension – in Bournonville it's so much the same. That probably had a certain influence on the kind of work that I was doing at the time.

Mason: Seeing you the other night on stage, I knew soon who you were because I said to myself, "He seems to know what he's doing."

House: I have a kind of authority in my own work.

Mason: You have to know what you're doing before you can tell anybody else what you're doing.

House: The more performing the better, because I realize that the more I learn and the more people I'm working with myself the more I have to give to them.

Mason: Never stop. Don't stop until you have to. Like Taylor. When you returned to York did you continue to make improvisations and pieces for yourself?

House: A lot, yes. They were just kind of exploring; they were more about me learning how to dance and figuring things out and just exploring my own physicality. Then after my first year at York, Robert Cohan came and did a choreographic seminar. They brought together six choreographers and six composers and a bunch of dancers, and every day a new project is assigned. And I was one of the dancers. So I watched other choreographers struggle for two hours intensively to produce a dance out of a very specific, difficult choreographic problem. Something has to happen. This was in 1978. Then in 1980 another seminar was held in Alberta. Bob Cohan was there to take part, and Todd Bolender from America, and this time I was a choreographer. That was very interesting.

Mason: You were assigned something to do and did it?

House: That's right. It was a horrible experience at the time.

Mason: You worked with a musician who had written something?

House: Yes, a composer. Or you had to do something together, so you'd be given a project to realize. Say: produce a piece that is no more than five minutes long that somehow alters our sense of time. Okay.

Mason: Why didn't Cohan suggest that maybe you should come back to England with him?

House: No, he's very supportive, and I've spent a little time with him since, but he was pretty hard-nosed. I mean he was very forthright with his criticism about my dancing. I think he said to me, "You know, you're pretty good but you could be way better than that." So I got to work. And no one up to that point had really talked to me like that. So I thought it was nice that he'd done that. He made suggestions. He came and worked with members of Toronto Dance Theatre on making dances. They did a choreographic workshop a couple of years ago, and he came and led a wonderful process with them, and he saw a number of my works and gave me some feedback, and I realized that our aesthetic priorities are quite different. It was interesting to be at the point where one realizes that there is no formula. The formula only applies within the system itself. It can't come from outside. Everything depends on the inner logic of the thing itself.

Mason: And being strict about that is not very personal.

House: No. That doesn't win you any prizes. Although I spent a couple of years working very consciously on form, I kept discovering that the only interesting things I did were the things where I would completely mess something up, where I would think I was trying to accomplish something and it would all fall apart, and then just the act of saving it from total chaos would produce something much more interesting.

Mason: What do you mean by "aesthetic priorities"?

House: Well, for example, when Cohan saw my Stravinsky piece *Artemis Madrigals*, he felt in the last movement that on the climax there should be some perfect, beautiful lift. In making up the dance I think he would have set it up in a way so that a lift would have made perfect sense. But I felt that I had organized that whole movement so that when the climax came it would just happen by itself and sort of nothing would be happening.

Mason: As Balanchine used to say, when music is making something big, you don't have to.

House: It's true, absolutely. I think I've learned a tremendous amount from Balanchine and that was in the early eighties when I would come down and study privately with people like Larry Rhodes for a couple of months in the summer. And then I would essentially live at the New York State Theater throughout their season and see as much of that as I could. That was the year before Balanchine died and I continued for a couple of years after that.

Mason: When you went back to Toronto Dance Theatre after a year away, you were dancing in many pieces?

House: Yes, and the company was touring a lot. The first two or three workshop pieces that I did were quite successful. The first piece that I did was taken into the company repertoire right away, which was quite unusual, because there were three choreographers, and they very generously took this piece, which was to two pieces of music by Steve Reich. And I think that hit, balanced the programme in the repertoire, because at the time a lot of people were complaining that the other works were very heavy. So I think that there was a void that my work filled a little bit, perhaps because it was more kinetic and a little more formal.

I became resident choreographer in 1981, which was soon after that. I started to do work with some other companies as well. I've done three pieces for Les Grands Ballets in Montreal, the National Ballet in Toronto and a few other modern dance companies, and last fall I did a piece for a ballet company, Ballet British Columbia in Vancouver.

Mason: And here in the U.S.?

House: I've never worked with any companies here.

Mason: Are there many pieces in Toronto Dance Theatre's repertory by you that we haven't seen here in New York?

House: Yes. Every year and a half I do a programme of my own, actually, just of my own works. The company probably has between twelve and fifteen works of mine. We could do them tonight if we had to.

Mason: The Brahms piece that we saw at the Joyce – *Handel Variations*. How did that come about?

House: That was the first dance that I did where I didn't use the music right away. I worked with the score but the movement was nearly all made in silence. I've stayed with that approach ever since. I was getting too constipated by working with the music. It would just take forever to become satisfied with, like, four bars of music. So I kept not getting anything done. So then I began to use another approach. I know the music. I have the score. This score, visually, is so beautiful, just the way ...

Mason: It looks.

House: Yes, the way it looks. And that itself was very suggestive. So we made the movement vocabulary up in silence, and I think I knew this would probably go here and this would go there, and then once we actually had a kind of, I guess, palette of steps, then our body rhythms started to play. A composer friend of mine told me that he always starts to write a piece and doesn't worry about it, and then once he's halfway through, and the piece is fine – then he goes back and rewrites the beginning. And it's fine. Then he finishes it. So I often do that. I start with just any old thing just to get going. And then once it begins to take on some sort of form, I go back and fix the beginning and then take it. So although the piece is obviously very much tied to the score, it wasn't choreographed right on the piece, actually.

Mason: How big a role do the dancers play in the making of the pieces?

House: They're there and I'm involved in training them as well as David Earle, obviously. They inspire me but I mostly tell them what to do. We don't choreograph by committee.

Mason: You don't say "Let's see what you can do today"?

House: More like, "How do you want to get out of that?" Other choreographers have a different system, and there're a lot of people who turn on the video camera and people improvise and they get wonderful ideas from doing that. But for some reason I haven't gotten to that.

Mason: You're happy where you are.

House: For the time being. I'm not doing any commissions away from the company because I'm going to become its artistic director at the end of this year. I'm focusing on that. I'd like to figure out what I'd like the company to be

373

able to perform with live music. It's really frustrating to have to dance to taped music. Actually so much of our work is musically based and inspired by the relationship with the music. To dance with recorded music is tough.

Mason: Graham and Taylor both did it at the City Center this year, and it was tragic. Of course, you can't hire just anybody to play the Brahms-Handel variations.

House: That's the problem.

Mason: But Stravinsky's *Duo Concertant* for *Artemis Madrigals* is possible. Erick Hawkins has always insisted on live music, even if it's just a drum. He's so eloquent about it. He says you cannot have live dancers and dead music.

House: I'm trying to organize an ongoing collaboration with our contemporary music group in Toronto whom we've worked with before.

Mason: And they can perform with you.

House: They can perform with us. But it's so expensive to work with musicians.

Mason: It's dear, very dear.

House: But the result is three-dimensional.

Mason: Erick Hawkins told me recently when *Appalachian Spring* was commissioned, he and Martha told Copland to use a small ensemble of instruments because the company could find those players wherever it toured. All of the works that Graham commissioned when Erick was in the company were composed for small ensembles that could be expanded – as Copland did later. Everything was tailored for the road.

House: There's an odd thing that happens with the whole Graham school. Because the language is so complete, so organic, and because it feels so good, when people choreograph in that language, they get seduced into what feels good rather than what makes sense. It is odd how few people have come from that tradition who are really interesting choreographers, who haven't some-how made a break with it.

Mason: Like Hawkins, Taylor and Cunningham, who got away.

House: I remember seeing the revival of *Primitive Mysteries* when I was in New York the first time. It is a very formal piece. Why does it have this kind of flat density? Why is it affecting me this way? It wasn't just this sort of big visceral mass of energy that was working in certain theatrical ways. It was actually a piece of architecture. Or each time I watch *Serenade*. I watch it and I'm absolutely mystified by it because I think I know every step in it and every moment of it, and it still takes me by surprise. And that's very exciting.

Mason: Do you work on your own? Do you go into the studio and try things out on yourself before you put them on other people?

House: Sometimes. More likely around my apartment where I'm always smashing into the furniture.

House's *Early Departures* (l. to r.): Bill Coleman, Graham McKelvie, Michael Sean Marye and Christopher House, 1992.

Mason: Tell me about *Early Departures*. It's the best piece on AIDS I've ever seen.

House: Well, it wasn't planned to be a piece about AIDS. We just started to do it, and they knew I wanted to do a piece with four men and, I mean, it's about relationships. Someone gave me a little Penguin book with the Gilgamesh epic in it. I had never read that, so I began reading it. It's an ancient Sumarian legend. It sounds a bit dry, but it's great, very poetic, very beautiful.

Gilgamesh is a hero of the people, and he has this friend who is a wild, wild man named Enkidu who's covered in hair. They go out on adventures together. Enkidu insults a god or goddess and he has to die. And the wounds all cover and fasten around him. And he dies.

Mason: Gilgamesh is devastated.

House: Like Achilles at the death of Patroclus. He falls apart and goes to the ends of the world to find the great wise men who can tell him how this could happen and what is the meaning of life. So I'd been reading this story, and it's filled with the most extraordinary physical images. By coincidence, I had been travelling in Italy and had spent a lot of time in Venice and had fallen in love with those beautiful Bellini altarpieces that always have archangels commenting on the scenes. And the day I came back from Italy I learned a lot about people who were working with AIDS patients, people who are dying, who help, to sort of ferry them on to the next world, through music, and how music has traditionally had this power to help the sick, to soothe people who are dying. And all these things came together.

I started to work on *Early Departures* and I found this extraordinary score by John Rea, the composer, in Montreal, which to him is an evocation of Kubla Khan's funeral procession. Strange decaying sound to it. So that's how we ended up with that piece. Once again I worked without the music because I was discovering the dance language we were going to use: the taking of a pulse, the kind of formality of the dance structure, and then letting it all break down.

I realized it was a piece about many people like me who are not HIV-positive but who are asking, how do we help? I tried to do a couple of narrative pieces, to tell a story right off the bat, and they have always been stinkers. It's not a gift I have. But perhaps I can work with a visual narrative, allow some things to begin to take on their own life. I love ambiguity. That's what I love in Balanchine's work, the poetic ambiguity of it. That's what dance can do best. It can suggest a whole life process without being didactic.

Walking the Tightrope:
Acrobatics and Athleticism on the Montreal Stage

Iro Valaskakis Tembeck

> In the circus the important thing is *how many* balls you juggle. In the theatre it is *how* you juggle them that matters.

This seemingly simplistic statement theatre historian Jane Baldwin made in 1995 might well provide the necessary demarcation line between what constitutes theatre practice and what are essentially spectacular stunts associated with circus type entertainment. Circus acts and gymnastic feats have steadily taken over the Montreal scene over the past ten years, making acrobatic athleticism one of its most recognizable theatrical trademarks. Even when what is shown seems drawn from circus acrobatics and high wire acts – as is the case with Montreal's famous Cirque du Soleil – the urge always seems to be to present an out-and-out innovative, *artistic* product. Cirque's publicity stresses the "new" experience it is offering via a thematically unified theatricality which also incorporates stage design and detailed choreography. But is the real objective the number of balls that are being juggled, or the way they are being handled?

Performance styles created by Gilles Maheu's Carbone 14, Ginette Laurin's O Vertigo and Edouard Lock's La La La Human Steps are explored in this essay. More specifically, I compare three works, one by each of the above named companies, which were premiered around the time when this new performing genre began to be noticed both locally and abroad. Laurin's *Timber* (1986), Maheu's *Le Dortoir/The Dormitory* (1989) and Lock's *Human Sex* (1985) became critically and publicly acclaimed signature pieces stemming from individual artists now in their forties, all Montrealers, yet who hail from different artistic backgrounds. It is my belief that these works laid the cornerstones for respective new approaches that helped fashion and define their makers' personal aesthetic statements. Moreover, these works reveal several similar concerns about staging and theatrical effects.

Interestingly, Maheu is a mime artist turned theatre director-choreographer. Laurin, originally a gifted modern dancer, later became a choreographer, while Lock never danced professionally but was briefly associated with Groupe Nouvelle Aire as a budding choreographer. He brought his knowledge of film techniques such as montage to his choreographic craft. The movement language of these three director-choreographers was developed in these pieces, and their subsequent works to this day continue to be based mostly on what they discovered in these early works.

Since the mid-1980s, stage movement in Quebec, whether in mime and theatre pieces or in plain choreographic fare, is often aggressive, muscular, garrulous and androgynous. It superseded the previous trend, which was minimalist yet message-filled, with arresting images reigning supreme and simple gestures being endlessly repeated. It seemed more important then for the stage to provide grounds for a violently image-filled commentary of social plight. Dance-theatre of Pina Bauschian vintage was the unacclaimed norm. Now, a broader range of movement has been retrieved from Western dance styles, to which is added a great deal of gusto and a chaotic theatricality of vigorous body works that have transformed the stage into a roller coaster experience. These are some of the salient features of the Montreal stage that I shall discuss.

However, this recent trend is not as abrupt an about-face as one might suppose. In fact, Montreal has long favoured the "toe tap and acrobatic" medley of performances since the mid-1920s, as illustrated by pioneer dancemaker Maurice Morenoff (1906-1993). His teaching, just like his recitals, fused different body techniques not only within the same evening but within a single choreography. Another ballet dancer and teacher, Gina Vaubois, opened her own Montreal studio in the 1940s where she regularly taught classical dance alongside trapeze acts. In the middle of her studio lay a thick rope from which aspiring dancers would learn how to be airborne, literally. Vaubois herself had danced in ballet companies in England and had also been a member of a circus. Finally, from the 1920s onwards vaudeville shows in which entertainers would present all sorts of stage numbers or acts, including acrobatics, were the most popular form of entertainment even in Catholic, prudish Quebec. Extraordinary stage acts certainly seemed to fascinate Montrealers then as now.

On a more universal level, the twentieth century witnessed theatre practice becoming increasingly more physical because of its necessity to redefine itself when pitted against film, television and now virtual reality. If film offers escapism into endless dream sequences, television is a one-way mirror where the onlooker can be a non-interactive couch potato. Theatre however uses real bodies onstage, and that fact was the focus around which new performing theories appeared. The teachings of Constantin Stanislavsky in the early twentieth century had placed emphasis on realism and moved away from stilted delivery of lines. The method acting that grew out of his approach directed the performer to find in his/her own life similar experiences to those depicted on stage. These in turn were to be used as a key to make the characters more believable. Antonin Artaud and Jerzy Grotowsky worked along similar lines: it was the *live* performance that provided a thrill, making theatre exciting to watch and perform. Artaud's concept was called "the theatre of cruelty" because it came from the rawness of emotion; this very raw quality was to shake the audience out of its usual passive role. Grotowsky went beyond Stanislavsky and Artaud by adding a truthfulness to the rawness of the performance. Actors took chances and risks, baring their souls in front of the public, thus walking a psychological tightrope. These techniques gave new directions to western theatre productions from the 1960s onwards.

The dance scene was somewhat different, the risk-taking being both psychological and physical. A hundred years ago, physical culture movements in the United States and Germany had spawned twin offsprings, gymnastics and modern dance. By the end of the twentieth century, choreographers seemed to be rediscovering their common origins. Psychological risk had been apparent in the early modern dance when the dancer delved inside herself to express personal, meaningful gestures and to discover new steps. By the 1980s physical risk had come into the picture as dancers incorporated daring steps done at breakneck speed so as to be in tune with fast action video clips and hip-hop culture.

In the Montreal dance scene, the three companies Carbone 14, O Vertigo and La La La Human Steps have intriguing names. They all move away from Montreal's earlier tendency to name a company after its founder-director. Titles are as mystifying as artistic products, willfully shattering any kind of prior expectations for the uninitiated spectator. All three troupes deal with layered perceptions and virtuosic performance. Carbone 14 refers to a carbon dating process used to determine the age of objects. Used metaphorically, it represents the theatre of the "here and now": *today's* theatre, substituting this word for the more usual label of avant-garde or experimental. O Vertigo suggests connotations of dizziness and loss of orientation but also designates a disease experienced by horses which disrupts and destabilizes, thus forcing the animal to keep moving. La La La Human Steps, finally, is a split title. The La La La seems a tongue-in-cheek discarding of required signification while Human Steps stresses the importance of the human element in the performing arena.

Maheu's Carbone 14

Carbone 14, the brain child of Gilles Maheu, epitomized a move that had been emerging in Montreal since the mid-1970s. At that time Maheu, Michel Barrette and others were part of Les Enfants du Paradis, a troupe named after the movie by Marcel Carné, which included mime, street theatre and acrobatics. Maheu, who was trained by Etienne Decroux and Eugenio Barba, founded Carbone 14 in 1982, while Barrette joined the now famous Cirque du Soleil as circus stage director. By 1984 actors in Maheu's *Le Rail* needed to have specific physical conditioning: they had to clamber up nets, swing across ceiling pipes and drop to the ground, which was filled with mud and earth as in war trenches. In *The Dormitory* (1989) nimble performers had to jump over whirling metal beds as in a Coney Island fair, doing daredevil dances. At this point choreography officially entered Maheu's shows. The physicality was close to that which was later associated with England's DV8 and Belgium's

Wim Van de Keybus. Anna Kisselgoff believes Montrealers were the first to make use of hurling bodies as theatrical devices (1990). Other Quebec theatre companies embarked on this same kind of physicality. Dynamo Theatre, whose target audience is teenagers, also created works based on precarious balancing on top of scaffolding, and even the more formalist choreographer Jean-Pierre Perreault had his dancers moving, running, jumping on and off ramps of varying heights in *Joe* (1983), *Stella* (1985) and *Eldorado* (1987). As for Cirque du Soleil, its winning combination was to present astounding circus acts with the only "trained" animals being human beings. Its alchemical brand of theatre focused on a glorious celebration of skill in the realm of acrobatics, high wire acts and bodily contortions all stitched together in a tight choreographic weave with original music to boot. As a genre Cirque succeeded in graduating from fair-type entertainment to "art" without losing its broad appeal.

All of these shows, Cirque du Soleil included, are far from ordinary products and defy regular definitions. Just like Maheu's, Laurin's and Lock's performances, Cirque presents multidisciplinary shows in which brilliant, dizzying, frenzied performers baffle us with their skillful play, forceful imagery and overflowing energy. Maheu best synthesizes this trend:

> We have to rediscover the art of disturbing, of disrupting. I believe in a theatre of emotion, a theatre of the body. The stage is the source of the fire, a hurricane, a storm where primal and dangerous forces clash. Props, action, movement and speech are but the external expression of a hidden discourse, a deeper mystery that is at the heart of any theatre piece and is the true "script" of the performance. The director is both Mephisto and Faust poised at the threshold of this mystery (Carbone 14 Press Release).

To seasoned critics such as Marianne Ackermann, Maheu's theatre is exemplary in proving that the limitations of film can be transcended with live bodies being continuously and admirably transformed on stage (1984).

At times, risk-taking, which is part and parcel of experiencing this brand of theatre either as onlooker-voyeur or as ecstatic performer, is too close to home and the game's bluff is called. One singer relates an accident which occurred on stage during *Le Café des Aveugles/Blind Man's Cafe* (1992) where performers hang from the stage ceiling in Christlike, Dali-esque pictures before dancing a musical chair and table jig in which the objects, not the persons, are being moved around in an unusual rendition of the game.

> Jerry got a chair whack in the back of the head. He fell to the floor but is supposed to be on the floor at that point. So I enter, approach, approach, sing, approach, sing, then see a puddle of blood a meter wide around his head.... I pick him up and he says he's alright. But even as he's telling me he's OK his eyes are rolling back into his head.... The audience is watching all of this. As soon as the scene was done, they brought down the curtain, the ambulance stitched him up and we went on with the show, stitches, shaved spot and all (quoted in Charlebois 1992).

One wonders how much of the thrill of these shows comes, as in the case of

Maheu's *Le Dortoir*, 1989.

circus acts, from the fact that there are no safety nets, that the risk of injury is real. Donnelly sums up the ambiguity of the experience in a critique of Carbone 14 which might also be applied to Lock's type of stage performing: "Whether it is dance theatre, performance art, a rock concert or an acrobatic circus is difficult to say" (1992).

With *The Dormitory* (1989) Maheu had already stepped firmly into the world of dance. Theatre people had viewed the piece as a dance work while dancemakers classified it as a theatre one. In any event the work was mainly featured in dance festivals round the world and confirmed the fact that Carbone 14 was a difficult company to pigeonhole, stemming as it were from mime roots, branching out into spoken theatre, incorporating a new gesture language and finally using singing and music that would best place it in the category of musical theatre.

Another reason for moving away from traditional spoken theatre in Quebec has political implications. As the sole French-speaking entity in the North American continent, Quebec wants both to state its "différence" to preserve its cultural distinctiveness yet also to be popular and exportable throughout Canada and the United States. Language is a barrier whereas movement is a universal mode of communication. Thus, different gesture languages are appropriated by theatre companies for many reasons, one of which is that they provide another way of soul searching. Maheu himself seems aware of this when he says:

> Since the referendum on sovereignty [first held in 1980 and then in 1995 on the question of Quebec's secession from Canada] politically aware members of the audience sought to rediscover themselves as individuals via avenues that included

381

theatre. It was this new combination of self-reflection and an international taste that formed a nurturing milieu for a new theatre. [I parallel] Québec with postwar Poland and Germany where people were closemouthed. In the past fifteen years though, people have turned to themselves in an effort to find out why. And this ... is the beginning of creativity (quoted in Aaron 1987).

In other words, political uncertainty and identity crises have helped foster this new kind of theatre focused on much physical action, strong images and less word play.

Lock's Human Steps

Edouard Lock's signature style seems by fever possessed. In 1985 he took his audience by storm as he premiered *Human Sex*, consecrating Louise Lecavalier as a soon-to-become cultural icon like Madonna. There he launched his lightning-paced, risk-filled pieces featuring unbridled bodies used as human missiles. His is an aesthetic of excess where extreme images, break-neck transactions and nonstop delirium elicit visceral reactions to this rock and dance show. In fact, one of his later pieces was renamed *Infante: Destroy* (1991). In Parisian slang the word destroy means extreme. Action-packed though the product might be, it sends shock waves to its spectators due to the realization that this type of dance is based on real physical risk. However, beyond subscribing to the punk aesthetic and the current trends of break-dancing and video clips, Lock's philosophy is also clearly thought out: "There are two kinds of shows: charismatic ones and empathic ones. The first pretends to show perfection and desirability and admiration. The second has to do with problem-solving. Uncertainty is the name of the game in this case" (my free translation from the French quoted in Pontbriand 1991).

For Lock the physical being on stage is the biggest attraction. Dancing defies death, the death of gesture just as the death of life. To him dancing is found midway between a whisper and a shout (in Pontbriand 1991), his particular brand of theatre being definitely the latter. He believes the public reads violence in his works because it is forced to reconsider its own perceptions of the body: "Speed breaks the lines, the proportions, the form. What we arrive at is a flow which is much higher than beauty, proportion or aesthetics, the beauty contest words so freely associated with dance" (in Pontbriand 1991).

Yet with increased velocity comes the risk of accidents, so working without safety nets becomes the implicit assumption. Injury, he says, "is a form of anarchy, of breaking the line" (in Pontbriand 1991) and again "acrobatics is a precise measure whereas dance is anarchy" (quoted in Asselin 1987). Lock is therefore using his art as a subversive force exposing and exploiting the body's fragility, extending its parameters with apparent recklessness. And his muse, Louise Lecavalier, is not exempt from injury.

From *Human Sex* onwards Lock, rather than defying gravity, chooses instead to give into it, smashing his dancers' bodies on the floor. This gymnastic hurling arises from the fascination of our inability to suspend. He

Edouard Lock and Louise Lecavalier in Lock's *Human Sex*, 1987.

therefore pays tribute to the fall, seeing falling as an act of freedom from gravity's restrictions. His arresting barrel rolls which have become his trademark serve the same purpose: they upset the usual vertical balance of a dance performance and destabilize the eye of the beholder. The hyper-kinetic dance style is built around the fall, its champions therefore becoming fallen – or hell's angels. Ironically, Lock's previous piece was named *Businessman in the Process of Becoming an Angel*.

In *Human Sex* gender roles are reversed. It is not a piece about sexuality as such, but about gender: about perceiving a neuter gender, "a human sex." Thus, Lecavalier sports a fake mustache and her partner Marc Beland is outrageously made up. Nonetheless, the androgynous quality goes beyond that cosmetic addition and in the midst of the onslaught of memorable images the last one particularly stands out: Lecavalier hoists her partner over her head tossing him in a heap across the stage before she crumbles to the floor. Obviously she is not the frail consumptive beauty of the Romantic ballet. Her body is made of granite, the result of countless hours of Nautilus-type training. We are confronted here with a new model of beauty, a hermaphroditic one which inspires awe in its spectators. Was not that part of the circus experience, too – gasping at the strongest man on earth, the fattest woman, the tiniest dwarf, etc.?

Ginette Laurin's O Vertigo

Traditional gender roles are also revisited in Laurin's milestone *Timber*. This seventy-minute piece is a compendium of all her freshly minted devices: the high energy, flamboyant movement in which she introduced athleticism on the theatre stage; the astonishing physical work performed by petite dancers, who lift tall men as though it were a run of the mill activity; the intricate landings and rhythms. With Laurin, everyday movement such as playful mimickings, shufflings and runs are "poached" from daily life and transformed into a spectacular mould. Risk-taking is part of her kinetic research since she was a gymnast during her teens. Her dancers, like those who perform for Lock or Maheu, need good cardiovascular training and daring. They all must transcend human limitations in performance, accomplishing their own marathons. The set for *Timber* consists of scaffoldings, platforms and staircases of various levels. Dancers throw themselves off these makeshift cliffs, trusting they will be caught by their partners in extremis or maybe they will just have to continue rolling once they hit the floor. *Timber* explores falling, taking Humphrey's choreographic principle of fall and recovery many steps further. It is in direct contrast to mainstream dance's urge for flight. Here we are exposed to chartered flights of fantasy in which whirlwind motions are executed with split-second timing but less rapidly, thankfully, than in Lock's choreographies. Her approach is more subdued, yielding better nuance. To train for the piece the dancers took parachute lessons and were taught by real stunt men. As Laurin states, "I am compelled to break the boundaries of physical limitations.... An energized body is in itself a poetic object" (quoted in FIND Souvenir Programme 1989: 48-49).

Speed engenders fascination and becomes poetry in the making. Many of Laurin's works have energetic self-explanatory titles: *Crash Landing* (1984), *Up the Wall* (1985), *Timber* (1986) and *Train d'enfer* (1990), which can roughly be translated as "Life at a Fast Forward Pace." It illustrates the contagious Vertigo alluded to in her company's name.

Laurin's gesture language is less bone-crushing than Lock's or even Maheu's. She is alone among these three to have had firsthand performance experience in both dance and gymnastics, the combination which allows her to craft her pieces by experimenting on her own body – something Lock would be unable to do. Moreover, Laurin borrows gestures from all techniques, freely incorporating Tango moves, Flamenco and social dancing to her mastery of both ballet and modern dance. All three directors fly high, metaphorically and physically, breeding a constant sense of urgency in their theatre offerings. Yet Laurin alone keeps refining her movement as she discovers new angles, and she modulates her rhythms. Since *Train d'enfer* she is also developing theatrical themes of loneliness, leave-taking, alienation and incarceration, allowing them centre stage while still continuing her gestural research. In this aspect she seems close to Maheu; at other times one discovers similarities with Lock.

Ginette Laurin, Louise Bédard and Gilles Simard in Laurin's *Timber*, 1986.

Visions and Revisions

Obviously things do not grow in a vacuum and cross-fertilization does take place whether consciously or not. As noted previously, when Les Enfants du Paradis disbanded in the early 1980s, Maheu went off to create Carbone 14 and Barrette joined the fledgling Cirque du Soleil. It was no coincidence that movement experimentation became a prime concern for both of these companies. Laurin for her part performed in Lock's early pieces, dating from the 1970s, which he had crafted from the dancers' improvisations. Furthermore, many dancers have performed in Maheu's *The Dormitory*; some, like Johanne Madore, danced for Laurin before joining the ranks of Carbone 14.

The Montreal hyper-kinetic dance style which became internationally acclaimed is the fruit of the cross-pollination of mime, theatre, dance and circus people. The immediate influences are the specific culture, sociopolitical tensions, the invasion of North American media structures such as video-clips and Much Music channels, breakneck street dancing and, finally, the aesthetic of disposable artistic commodities. This new species of entertainment has set its own artistic standards of theatricality, whether it is Carbone 14's theatre of images, Cirque du Soleil's novel experience or Lock's and Laurin's high-energy acts. Whether the emphasis of this Montreal movement style is on "épater les bourgeois" as exemplified by *how many* balls one keeps juggling or whether it is more concerned with *how* one juggles them is difficult to assess in one sweeping statement. Cirque du Soleil has elevated the genre into artwork, while at times La La La seems to be presenting a three-ring circus, coming just barely short of choreographic bungy jumping. In the end, Montreal's signature stage movement lies midway between circus acts and message-filled theatre fare, part of its attraction arising from its ambiguity and from the thrill generated within the performance arena.

Author's Postscript

By the late 1990s, the Montreal dance scene had shifted its aesthetics somewhat. The signature movement language that emerged in the 1980s in the work of Ginette Laurin, Edouard Lock and Gilles Maheu was highly energetic, with accelerated rhythms and repetitions, which at times dared the body to go beyond its known physical limits. Dancers began to pump iron and undertake cardiovascular training to gain performing endurance for such marathon-type dancing. The works of these three choreographers contributed to drawing international attention to what local critics had coined as "Montreal's new way of moving" [le nouveau bouger montréalais]. The picture was quite different, partly because the choreographers were now older and more experienced, their dancemaking showed less flashiness, more sustained craftsmanship and greater nuance. Moreover, the theatricality that often triggered a dance piece in the past, was now replaced by a renewed interest in the visual arts which yielded a more sedate, less rebellious aesthetic.

Dancers responded by modifying their training methods to include the gentler, deeper work of Pilates in alternation with cardio-pumping. Gilles Maheu came up with two visually arresting pieces *La Forêt* (1994), with real earth and trees providing the setting for the emotional exploration by a young boy, representing innocence, and an old man, signifying experience, in a series of impressionistic tableaux. It was followed by *Les âmes mortes/Dead Souls* (1996), a haunting study of past generations of tenants who had inhabited a now abandoned house. Both these pieces were contemplative in their treatment of life's significance, and both were handled with great sensitivity. Sparseness was now used to present the various evocative images and were not overly repeated as in the more recent past.

As for Lock, his evening-long work of 1998 titled *Exaucé* in French and *Salt* in English, showed some similarities, at first, to William Forsythe's use of abstract and contemporary ballet vocabulary. Lock's company now features several ballerinas, while pointe work and neoclassical lines are incorporated into his new artistic vision. The speed of execution, one of his customary trademarks, is by necessity slowed-down somewhat, since pointe work requires particular balancing feats; in so doing lines became more elongated, and dare one say more "lyrical." Laurin, for her part, showcased *En Dedans/ Inside* (1998) which also revealed a more inward-looking meditative quality.

In the new millennium, the tide seems to have changed heralding a newly found, gentler mode of dancemaking by these three prominent choreographers that also reflects the evolution of Montreal's artistic taste.

References

Aaron, Susan. Nov. 1987. "Carbone 14." *Performing Arts in Canada*, 7-10.

Ackermann, Marianne. 3 Nov. 1984. "Le Rail: A Rare Slice of Life." *The Gazette*.

Asselin, Suzanne. 7 Nov. 1987. "Edouard Lock et La La La Human Steps: Il dérange, bouscule et séduit." *La Presse*.

Baldwin, Jane. 22-27 May 1995. "Meyerhold's Theatrical Biomechanics and the Contemporary Actor: A Synthetic Approach to Actor-Training." A lecture-demonstration presented in the *Actor Actress, on Stage: Body/Acting/Voice*. Annual Conference of the International Federation for Theatre Research. Montreal.

Carbone 14. Undated press release on Maheu's biographical profile.

Charlebois, Gaetan. 13-20 Aug. 1992. "A Physical Attraction." *Mirror*.

Crabb, Michael. August-Summer 1989. "OOO Vertigo. What Makes Ginette Laurin and Company Parachute, Somersault and Dance a GoGo?" *Performing Arts in Canada*, 11-13.

Donnelly, Pat. 19 Apr. 1988. "Maheu Shakes Up Theatre World." *The Gazette*.

Donnelly, Pat. 19 Aug. 1992. "Carbone 14 Mixes the Elements." *The Gazette*.

Godfrey, Stephen. Apr. 1989. "Carbone 14's Gilles Maheu Keeps a Step Ahead of the System." *Globe and Mail*.

Howe-Beck, Linde. 13 Mar. 1986. "O Vertigo's *Timber* Thrilling, Near Perfect." *The Gazette*.

Jackson, Naomi. 1994. "Deconstructing Dance: Edouard Lock's Postmodern Steps." In Selma Odom and Mary Jane Warner, eds. *Canadian Dance Studies* 1. Toronto: Graduate Programme in Dance, York University, 145-48.

Kisselgoff, Anna. 1 Nov. 1990. "Reflections from Quebec on Adolescence in the 60's." *New York Times*.

Lefebvre, Paul and Denis Marleau. 1984. "Cet enfant incestueux." *Jeu: Cahiers de théâtre* No. 32, 49-69.

Pontbriand, Chantal. Dec. 1991. "La Chute du Saut. Interview avec Edouard Lock." *Parachute* No. 64, 5-12.

"Profile of Ginette Laurin." Souvenir programme of the 1989 Festival international de nouvelle danse (FIND), 48-49.

Tembeck, Iro. Mar. 1992. "Oh La la Superman Steps." *Cité Libre*, 31-33.

Tembeck, Iro. 1993. "Tableaux d'une exposition corporelle Made in Québec'." *Les Vendredis du Corps: Le corps en scene, vision plurielle*, 53-70.

Tembeck, Iro. Fall 1994. "Dancing in Montreal: Seeds of a Choreographic History." *Studies in Dance History* 5: 2.

Valaskakis Tembeck, Iro. 1994. "La nouvelle danse montréalaise: ses antécédents, ses perceptions publiques, ses caractéristiques. Un essai de définition." Ph.D. dissertation, Université de Montréal.

Impressions of a Reconstruction:
The ENCORE! ENCORE! Project

Rhonda Ryman

What went on in that barn-like Toronto studio can only be described as a labour of love. From April 14 to May 31, 1986, a group of twelve young dancers and their not-so-young mentors assembled to perform a near impossible task: bringing back to life key works of six pioneering Canadian choreographers.[1] In another field, the task might seem easy enough, but in the world of choreography, with no written heritage, recapturing the elusive elements that gave life to a great work of the past is like putting together a giant jigsaw puzzle with only a few of the pieces. More the challenge! The members of the ensemble gathered together by Miriam and Lawrence Adams, producers of ENCORE! ENCORE!, were equal to the task.[2] But where to begin this adventure? Take one septuagenarian ex-Ballet Russe de Monte Carlo dancer with the grace of a dove and the memory of an elephant, and you are off. Nesta Toumine stunned us all with her incredible recall of *Maria Chapdelaine* (originally titled *Marie-Madelaine*), a work she choreographed, based on the well-known French-Canadian folk tale, for the Ottawa Classical Ballet Company in 1956.

"I didn't realize how much I was going to fall in love with Nesta Toumine," confides Daniel Jackson, who acted as rehearsal director.[3] "I think it was almost love at first sight for practically everyone who was involved in the project. It was a very moving experience. She was a rather super human being who was very involved in the creation of her own project. She had an extraordinary memory. Also, I don't think the piece was as old as the other works and it might have been performed more often." (This is in contrast to other pieces reconstructed, such as Boris Volkoff's *The Red Ear of Corn*, which was created almost forty years ago and performed, in its entirety, only three times.) Jackson continues, "Nesta was more apt to have problems in

---

[1] This is an expanded version of an article first published in *Dance in Canada* 49 (Fall 1986), 19-23, 26-27, which the author revised before Lawrence Adams died in 2003.

[2] Lawrence and Miriam Adams have had a long and active involvement in Canadian dance. Both performed with the National Ballet of Canada, Lawrence as a principal dancer, before founding Fifteen Dancers which became an experimental dance space. They published *Canadian Dance News* in the early 1980s and then created Dance Collection Danse, whose mandate is to promote Canadian dance through collecting and archiving historical material, researching special topics, conducting oral history projects, and publishing in traditional and electronic formats.

[3] Daniel Jackson, formerly co-artistic director of Les Grands Ballets Canadiens, was artistic director of Montréal Danse, a contemporary dance company, from 1986 to 1996.

389

Reconstruction of Toumine's *Maria Chapdelaine* (l. to r.): Chester Fergusson, Angela Borgeest, David Earle, Nesta Toumine, Stanley Taylor.

relation to musical tempos, which were difficult because the piano recordings made for this project followed the musical markings on [composer Hector] Gratton's score. In those days Nesta would have had a live pianist and could have made adjustments as she liked."

The markings on the piano score were more trouble than help. Labanotator George Montague and I had diligently prepared for the first rehearsal by studying the piano score to familiarize ourselves with melodies and plot line.[4] When the action taught in the studio repeatedly conflicted with the word notes on the piano score, we discovered that the notes were made by Gratton and not by the choreographer as we had naturally assumed. Toumine, it seemed, had so widely digressed from the action envisioned by Gratton that he had disassociated himself from the ballet, hence its temporary title change to *Marie-Madelaine*.

---

[4] I coordinated the production of Benesh and Laban notation scores for the works reconstructed by ENCORE! ENCORE! Benesh and Laban are the two most widely used twentieth-century systems for recording dance on paper. The Benesh Institute, London, England, has catalogued over 900 scores by more than 275 choreographers (1955-1985). The International Council of Kinetography Laban has catalogued over 3500 works to 1988. For further information, consult the reference list at the end of this essay.

390

There were the inevitable moments when the music played on, but the movements wouldn't come, and no clues could be found from the score or the press reviews and photographs that lined the lobby walls. At one point, Rosemary Jeanes Antze, a former Toumine dancer and now a dance anthropologist living in Toronto, came in to share her recollections; she helped fill in some critical gaps.

When no flickers of memory surfaced, choreographic director David Earle was at hand to fill gaps or make cuts in the music, always careful to preserve the flavour of the original period.[5] "I felt that the marriage between the choreographic director and the choreographer, on that occasion in particular, was a highlight of the ENCORE! ENCORE! experience," remarks Daniel Jackson.

David Earle's gentle touch sustained us through many a tricky situation, as he mediated between Toumine deep in thought; Jackson operating the tape machine and mapping shots for the videotaping that ended each rehearsal period; and the six dancers who often played two or more roles each.

Since some two-week reconstruction periods overlapped, the twelve dancers were split into two groups. Even works with large casts – *Maria Chapdelaine* (thirty), *Heroes of Our Time* (sixteen), *Shadow on the Prairie* (twenty-five) and *The Red Ear of Corn* (twenty-two) – were set on six well-worked bodies. There were times when everyone was up and dancing to fill in as bodies. Daniel Jackson soon became irreplaceable as Maria's father and David Earle did a cameo appearance as the fiddler in the square-dance scene. Even Toumine pitched right in and was quite prepared to do so, despite a terrible knee problem. Age and physical problems were rarely in evidence as she whipped through the first two scenes of the ballet.

"As we worked on the process," recalls Jackson, "if we needed to have four extra people on the stage, Nesta automatically became two and I became the other two. The word schizophrenia was absolutely epitomized here," he continues, "when we had to take our two male dancers and four females and turn them into snowflakes and double it." Fortunately, the section was all geometric patterns, so it was possible to visualize the missing bodies. Notator George Montague, through his score, was actually the only person who could account for every dancer.[6]

At mid-week, music for the third scene had not yet been recorded. This gave the dancers and the notator a welcome chance to go over the first two scenes. As soon as the music tape was ready, Toumine pressed on, quickly

---

[5] David Earle co-founded the Toronto Dance Theatre with Peter Randazzo and Patricia Beatty in 1968. An active dancer and choreographer, Earle was the company's artistic director from 1987 to 1994 until he stepped down to work as an independent choreographer.

[6] The notation score commissioned for *Maria Chapdelaine* is not available, since Montague assumed a position with the Indianapolis Ballet before he could complete it. Fortunately, I had been notating sections for the rehearsals I was able to attend. From my notes, I was able to put together a rough score which I ultimately used to mount the work for the Carousel Dance Centre, University of Waterloo, in 1987. A videotape of that stage production is housed at Dance Collection Danse.

setting the entire ballet, then going back and filling in details. "She looked forward to the cleaning process," relates Jackson, "to making the movement look like it was supposed to look." This involved time to work on individual passages and to mould character studies. Angela Borgeest and Stanley Taylor alternated with Audrey Brownlow and Chester Ferguson as Maria and Jean, the young lovers. Susan Cash was transformed into an engaging Bébé, Maria's younger brother. Along with Vicki Fagan, they doubled as assorted friends, family, snowflakes, winds and wolves to create a touching portrait of family life and love in rural Quebec.

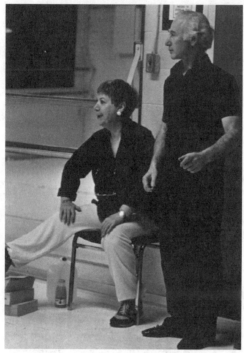

Nancy Lima Dent and Marcel Chojnacki reconstructing *Heroes of Our Time*.

Evolving characterizations through movement was a major focus for Nancy Lima Dent, choreographer of *Heroes of Our Time*. The work was originally done for the 1950 Canadian Ballet Festival in Montreal, with dancers Marcel Chojnacki, Laya Liberman and other members of Toronto's New Dance Theatre participating in its creation. Chojnacki and Vera Davis, another of the original dancers, were on hand for its transformation in the 1980s to a new score composed by Harry Freedman. The original score, a collection of Russian piano music, had gone the way of much of the original choreography, but the statement *Heroes of Our Time* made was clear in the minds of the original dancers.

The work was a commentary on the raging comic-book controversy of the time. As such, some of the dancers found its message a bit dated. Substitute computer games in a video arcade, however, and the deeper theme might seem more contemporary. The action centres on young Binky and his friends, and, on the blurred line between a fantasy life of adult adventure and the childish reality that ends in tragedy.

"In *Heroes*," says Annabel Helmore, the Benesh notator who produced its score, "the specific movement is not so important as long as it is within context, story line and so on. Nancy resisted setting things, tying things down, especially to specific music counts. She wanted the dancers to recreate the character studies, based in what the individuals had to give. The dancers [had to] use a given structure, concept, basic characterization and build from there." Helmore continues, "After the first few days I realized how it was going to work and I had to tear up everything I [had done] the first few days. It was most important to get the structure, contacts, people's locations and inter-relationships and not the specific steps. With the basic concepts and structure, there was a lot of walking around and interaction, and with the score and video, it may be possible to get the essence."

"It was interesting to see this approach to choreography, as an alternative to classical choreography," remarks dancer Sharon Wehner. "I've been looking at it in the context of its time and in conjunction with the other pieces here."

Helmore agrees. "The piece is quite interesting historically, perhaps more so to dancers than to a lay public. Nancy was one of those people who threw away [their] pointe shoes and [were] groping around to fill that void. No other technique was developed in Toronto at that time. Her work was representative of the development of dance at that time. The party scene was based on jitterbug, the social dance of the day."

How then were these dancers able to improvise within that context? Choreographer Anna Blewchamp, there to observe the day's action in preparation for the ENCORE! ENCORE! show at Expo '86 responds, "I expect that the selection of dancers' improvisations was a part of the original process of choreography, not the process of reconstruction." But should or can an improvisationally based piece be set without going through some of that original process?

Using only six dancers created problems. Although all parts could be accounted for in the notation score, Lima Dent had difficulty in visualizing the total action, the interplay of the various personae, so she cut characters. The dancers also experienced problems in creating multiple personalities, although many had emerged by the day of the videotaping.

Helmore offers a unique perspective. "By following through on the characterizations in the notation score," she says, "you can get some idea of the development of each character. This is more possible via the notation score than the video. Although I was having a hard time following the development of the characters through the rehearsal period, I found I was able to get a better handle on them while writing out the score."

A problem common to all the works reconstructed for the ENCORE! ENCORE! project was the lack of a final performance. "Dancers need that concrete deadline to work toward," asserts choreologist Helmore.[7] Without it, many felt slightly disoriented and unfocused. As a result, the videotaping that ended each rehearsal period quickly took on the role of a final performance.

Tapes were made in the Arts Television Centre in Toronto, against a white cyclorama and without sets, costumes or decoration. The floor was gridded into twelve sections: four columns upstage and downstage, and three sections across, corresponding with wings. A single stationary camera was mounted at about seven feet from the stage front, and very full, even lighting was maintained. Since each video was meant to be a documentary, without

---

[7] Traditionally, notators who use the Benesh system are called choreologists.

production elements, props were only indicated, except for utility set pieces, such as a card-table in *Maria Chapdelaine* or a tree in *Shadow on the Prairie*.

Continuously throughout the tape, there is a band on the bottom of the screen. The lower right side of the band displays an index number, starting at zero and counting up, bearing no relationship to time or rhythm. In the centre of the band is a bar counter, a letter or number coinciding with the music score. At the left of the band is the number of the scene or act. Producer Lawrence Adams comments: "In most cases, a bar count is really helpful in that you can follow the video without a music score in hand. For example, some of the counting in the barn-dance in *Red Ear* is quite complex."

Each video begins with a floor plan of the gridded-out stage, shown on a white board, indicating where props are located onstage. A menu is then displayed to list sections of the work and logical breaks in the piece, either scene numbers and breaks, or entrances identified by catchy names that people develop when rehearsing. Beside each section name is the corresponding index number and approximate time on the tape. A lineup of dancers standing behind identifying character names or roles is displayed before each take. Any overture or introductory music runs during the preliminary information; then the dancers are filmed performing the choreography.

If more than six dancers were needed onstage at any time, that section was retaped, preceded by a new line-up of characters. When the dance was symmetrical, as with the snowflakes in *Maria Chapdelaine*, the action on each side of the stage was taped separately to aid people who have difficulty transposing sides. In cases where there was some sort of intricate business, the section was retaped in detail, zooming in more tightly or taping from a different angle. The step-dancing in *Maria Chapdelaine*, for example, was recorded from the knees down to show intricate footwork, with and without the music. Complex scenes were often repeated with fewer dancers for clarity, but, with the index and scene numbers always in full view at the bottom of the screen, perspective could not be lost.

Lawrence Adams hopes to add each choreographer's commentary on a second audio track, without music, describing production elements and dramatic qualities relevant to each section shown. "It helps in getting the quality of the action," he says, "and has an archival value in that you'll hear the choreographer talking you through the work."

One of the most breathtaking pieces unearthed by ENCORE! ENCORE! was a collaborative work by Jeanne Renaud, founder of Le Groupe de la Place Royale, Montreal's first professional modern dance company, and Françoise Sullivan, a prominent French-Canadian visual artist and choreographer. The 1948 duet, entitled *Moi-Je-Suis*, is a surrealistic vision performed to poetry. Renaud and Sullivan, who created the work on themselves, were playing with the correlation, or perhaps more correctly, the co-existence of dance movement and sound. Sounds were created by the poet reading words at an unset tempo, free to repeat any sections any number of times, juxtaposed with sounds

Jeanne Renaud and Françoise Sullivan with dancers Louise Bédard and Ginette Boutin.

created by the dancers' breath, the swish of arms and torsos, or the weight of the steps. The work also built on the wordless rapport between two moving bodies, the entropy created when their energies inhabited merging spheres.

Newly set on dancers Louise Bédard and Ginette Boutin, the work had a fantastic dynamic range. Movements erupted like random electric charges passing from one body to another, then subsided into a stillness, only to be recycled with greater intensity. Key movements such as claps, swings and suspensions were set, as were some stage locations; but the dancers had freedom to vary the speed of the movements and, very often, their size or direction. They could also decide how many times key phrases were performed and, to some extent, the floor patterns. The visual result was often thrilling.

"To me, the original was kind of the birth of chance choreography," Daniel Jackson speculates. "There were days Ginette and Louise took chances that were beyond human belief. I thought for sure someone was going to get an elbow in the mouth. They were just phenomenal. Very hard [to achieve] in the actual end product, however, because of the situation of filming."

Indeed, how should the videotape of an improvisationally based piece be viewed? As the final product? Perhaps it can be seen as one objectification of a choreographic process that can yield a wide range of results.

There would be a danger in looking at the videotapes without referring to the choreographers' notes or the notation score that documents the verbal images and impressions used in setting the work. In this sense, the score serves not only as a record of the structure of the work, but also as archival material which captures certain aspects of the process of its creation. "By looking at the video alone," comments Benesh notator Janis Sandles-Oakes, "you wouldn't get any sense of how that dance should be reconstructed. You would just recreate the outer shell and you may lose what the choreographers were getting at, the essence of the piece."

To ensure that the videotapes are used effectively, supplementary material, such as newspaper articles and reviews, interviews, photographs, set and costume designs, and even old film clips will be available, whenever possible, with each video. Dancers who have used videotapes are aware that there is more to a work than what can be seen on the screen, but the human tendency is to look at the video and believe it. "I know that even when you have a score and a video," laments Sandles-Oakes, "the dancer will say, 'Okay, I'll find it on the video.' The dancer could have been off a beat, or off her dancing on a particular day, but if it's on the video, it's fixed in stone." "The interesting thing about videos that are done in theatres," adds Daniel Jackson, "is that there is a time lapse until the recording sound hits the back microphone. So you can often think that the work is completely off. It's one of the reasons that very few choreographers will allow those performance videos to be seen to represent their work for something major."

That problem is not an issue with the ENCORE! ENCORE! videotapes, thanks to the technical expertise of Michael J. Baker, who was in charge of providing music tapes for the rehearsals and recording them at the video sessions. His composing talents came to the rescue in unexpected ways during the project. Françoise Sullivan did not have a recording or a score for her work *Black & Tan* and had to hum the melody, accompanied by Daniel Jackson and Ginette Boutin. Baker recorded the song, took it away and reset it on his synthesizer, singing it himself. "It was very touching, that experience," relates Jackson. "When Françoise heard it she bawled her eyes out and was thrilled to death. And, of course, everything flooded back into her head and she put the piece together in minutes. She praised that aspect of the organization, because she felt that that was what collaboration was all about. And that, to her, was beyond restoration only."

New collaborations have been born, as well. Daniel Jackson has invited Françoise Sullivan to create a new work on Montréal Danse, the company he and Paul-André Fortier formed. "My mind was made up when I saw her work here," he declares. "She will also do the costumes and the decor, and that's very important, to put that aspect of her art onstage. This has rarely happened. Other great artists have surrounded her pieces, but we wanted her to do a total piece."[8]

For decades, Sullivan has been a well-respected visual artist whose work is represented in major galleries and collections. That talent is evident in the

---

[8] This experience motivated Jackson to present a retrospective programme by Montréal Danse called *Duos*, which remounted six works by Montreal choreographers. The oldest of these, Françoise Sullivan's *Dualité* (1947) was reconstructed during the ENCORE! ENCORE! project (Howe-Beck 1992: 46-49).

intricately formed notations she has made describing some of her works. Most are visual patterns reflecting floor patterns, with word notes. On her first day, she brought them to Benesh choreologist Janis Sandles-Oakes and Labanotator Leslie Johnston and said, "Here, you see. Maybe my notation is better than yours!" Who can dispute that notation done by a choreographer for her own work can best capture its essence? The plans will be included as an appendix to the notation score, because any information that can shed light forms an important part of that score. But, as with any personal notation system, no one except the author will be able to interpret the plans adequately.

Personalized methods of showing floor plans are often used by choreographers as memory aids. Nesta Toumine remarked that she drew plans for many of her works. Gweneth Lloyd was known to keep meticulous notebooks that included floor plans. Tragically, most of these were destroyed in 1954 by a fire which demolished the home of the Royal Winnipeg Ballet. Betty Farrally, Lloyd's long-time colleague and now a consultant on dance at the Banff School of Fine Arts, says that Lloyd was able to visualize her choreography clearly in her mind's eye, "like a filmstrip. She never danced a step when setting her works, but had everything written down: the steps on the right-hand side of a page, mirrored by the floor plans on the left, with the music counts running down a central column."[9]

The choreography of *Shadow on the Prairie* reflects this carefully structured approach. "Gweneth got the idea for *Shadow* from a story she had read, set in one of the Dakotas, about a settler girl from Norway," relates Farrally. "She transplanted the story to tell about a Scottish girl settling in Manitoba. That's why she included Highland steps. The jig is actually set after a Red River Jig. She had a real Selkirk settler come up and teach it to us."

A reconstruction within a reconstruction! How was a group of mostly Eastern born-and-bred dancers of the 1980s to deal with this? Fortunately, a fourteen-minute film of the original twenty-eight minute ballet was made by the National Film Board in Ottawa, only a year after the work's 1952 creation for the Royal Winnipeg Ballet. Lloyd condensed the ballet and new sets were made for the filming. The original cast performed the lead roles: Carlu Carter (the young wife), Gordon Wales (the husband) and Josephine Andrews (the other woman).

The film is a gem, a work of art in itself, but it was not meant to be choreographic documentation. The shifting camera angles and close-ups often intensify the action but hide key details. "It was only half as long as the original, and a lot of the dramatic action had to be condensed," cautions Farrally. "The full ballet has more character development, much greater impact. I remember the premiere in Winnipeg," she continues. "We were all so moved and chilled at that last moment, when the spotlight dies on the chest, that everyone forgot that Carlu was still in there. We barely got her out in time for the curtain calls. From then on, one person was designated to get Carlu out of the chest." Benesh notator Debbie Chapman laughs, "I'll be sure to note that in my score!"

---

[9] Betty Farrally passed away in 1989 and Gweneth Lloyd followed in 1993.

Lloyd, Farrally, Carter, Wales and Andrews, all a lot older but as vibrant as ever, were on hand for the resurrection of this powerful and touching portrait of pioneer life. With choreographic director David Adams and the National Film Board film, they were able to piece together very nearly the entire ballet.[10]

Gordon Wales, still trim and agile, even twenty-five years after leaving the dance world, said it was almost like being in a time capsule, finding himself back in a studio with the same people, doing the same thing. Josephine Andrews, who had also left the profession many years ago, had been terribly concerned that nothing of the original choreography would come back to her. Carlu Carter, who has continued her career in Australia, was eager to begin unravelling the pieces of the puzzle.

Once in the studio, everyone was amazed at how quickly they began fitting together. Nina De Shane, a University of Waterloo ethnomusicologist documenting the project, remarks: "It was a completely natural thing. They had the video, which was a great help, and they had each other. Once the music started, it was just there somewhere programmed deep inside of them."[11]

It was indeed a high point of the ENCORE! ENCORE! project to see Wales, Carter and Andrews stand up and to witness the movements born again in them. "They wouldn't even realize what they were doing," recounts Debbie Chapman. "They would put on the music, watch a bit of the video and, before they knew it, they were dancing parts that weren't on the video. Then they would turn around and say, 'What did I do?'" Daniel Jackson comments, "You could see the essence of the movement through their bodies regardless of the shape they are in now. It's wonderful to see that clarity in someone who has really learned a role well." Once the structure of the work was set, more time was devoted to helping the young dancers develop characterizations. Gweneth Lloyd was very concerned that they get a feeling of the wide open spaces, looking off into the distance, sharing the folksy quality of life in a prairie community. "You are not dancers," she cajoles. "You're people at a square-dance. You're welcoming these people into your community." Very often her body would evoke flashes of movement images – settlers waving to one another or friends reassuring the newcomers – and the young dancers would translate these visions anew.

Andrea Smith and Sylvain Brochu, as the young couple, together with Sonya Delwaide, Manon Levac, Loney Reece and Sharon Wehner, made an attractive corps of settlers, updating the story for this generation. The 1980s look was unmistakably there. Contrast Carlu Carter's long, straight hair with the unisex "frizz" sported by Smith, or Gordon Wales' short, sleek cut with the casual "shag" of Brochu. The bare-footed, unitarded bodies were also markedly different from the slippered, long- skirted females seen in the film. "I

---

[10] David Adams has been a principal dancer in Canada with the National Ballet of Canada, and in England with the Metropolitan Ballet, London Festival Ballet (now the English National Ballet) and The Royal Ballet. He later taught dance in Alberta.

[11] Nina De Shane later became an Associate Professor in the Department of Dance at York University.

Sylvain Brochu and Andrea Smith rehearsing Lloyd's *Shadow on the Prairie*.

thought we should have used skirts so that the girls could get the 'feel' of the movement," relates Betty Farrally. "The sway of the skirts was actually part of the line." For this reconstruction David Adams wouldn't let the girls use skirts, because he wanted to see the lines of their bodies.

Attention to form and technique is a high priority to dancers of this generation. Farrally expresses concern that today's dancers often appear uncomfortable in literal works involving mime or emotional portrayals. "Today's dancers try to analyze everything," she says. "They seem too intellectual, with not enough imagination. Maybe it's because they watch too much TV and don't read enough."

Daniel Jackson suggests that today's training focuses more on technique than acting, leaving the development of characterization up to the imagination and resourcefulness of the individual. Cliff Collier, one of the original dancers in Boris Volkoff's *The Red Ear of Corn*, agrees with Farrally and Jackson. "Dancers of thirty or forty years ago were often dancing actors as much as acting dancers," he reminisces. "It was certainly that way at Boris' studio."

Volkoff's students worked all day to earn a living and rehearsed at night. There were fewer performing spaces and, therefore, fewer opportunities to perform. "In our day," recalls Natalia Butko, "you were lucky if you got onstage at the time of the show. We had no rehearsals onstage or with live musicians. What we lacked in technique we formed with our bodies, our personalities, our exuberance."

"Don't get the idea that we couldn't dance," interjects Gladys Forrester. "Half the original National Ballet came from Boris!" These thoughts were echoed by Isabel Bodkin, Everett Staples and Bill Diver, other former members of the Volkoff Canadian Ballet, on hand to sift through photo albums, press reviews, piano scores and old film clips to fan the flames of memory. There was even an orchestrated 1949 Trans-Canada Network radio broadcast of John Weinzweig's score, with commentary by Fraser Macdonald.

The most important ingredient, however, was missing. Boris, as he is still affectionately referred to, passed away in 1974, leaving a legacy of over forty major works in the minds and hearts of Canadian dancers and balletomanes. The very fecundity that spurred him to produce new works to feed the appetites of the audiences he was developing, prevented any one Volkoff work from enduring. *The Red Ear of Corn*, premiered in Toronto at the 1949 Canadian Ballet Festival, was performed in its entirety only three times, although many considered it his greatest work. Everyone involved in the ENCORE! ENCORE! project had anticipated that *The Red Ear of Corn* would be the most difficult reconstruction and it was. "The work was never really in our muscles," says Gladys Forrester.

Every now and then, however, a glimmer surfaces. "I just had a revelation!" exclaims Natalia Butko. "If things keep coming back to me like this we'll be here another twenty years." She rose from her chair to become Tekakwitha, the intense, young Indian maiden fleeing from her enraged fiancé. Unwillingly betrothed to Chief Renard, she has insulted him by spilling his ritual dinner. She will forfeit her life for the transgression. But how? "I remember that Renard pulled Tekakwitha by her long black hair," reminisces Butko. "I'm sure of that because I had to dye my hair black for this role. I couldn't wear a wig! I remember everyone closing in on me before I am killed," she says, her body shrinking to the floor. "The stabbing was not right out in the open.... I was killed amidst the corn." And from that crimson spot would rise the fabled Red Ear.

Apart from remembering choreographic details, even sorting out the plot line posed problems. The first scene is based on the Iroquois tale described in Louvigny de Montigny's poem *La Légende de l'Epi Rouge*. The second scene, set at a corn-husking and barn-dance, depicts the French-Canadian superstition that good luck comes to the finder of the season's first red ear of corn. Word notes on the piano score, when they could be discerned, conflicted with events described in the poem, in newspaper clippings and in the dancers' memories.

Even the opening was in doubt. "I remember two versions," asserts Butko. "In one, Tekakwitha's friend was alone onstage when the curtain rose, then I made my entrance. In another we were both onstage when the curtain goes up." Cliff Collier remembers the friend onstage sleeping under a tree as the curtain rose. "But," he says, "it was not unusual for Boris to change a work after it was set. That's what was exciting. I firmly believe that if Boris were alive today and had been asked to participate in this, many of the sections would have been changed, because he wouldn't have remembered, or for a number of reasons, such as time constraints or to make improvements. All we can do in reviving *Red Ear* is to give an impression of how Boris choreographed, of what his company would have been like. If we don't get that excitement across, it would be better to let his memory be just that, a memory."

The fragmented but highly animated remembrances shared by Volkoff's dancers leave the impression that his contributions are far too important to leave to the ravages of time. "It's hard to measure the impact of a given individual," says choreographic director David Adams. "It's almost subliminal. Thousands of people have memories of seeing a Volkoff ballet and may have been moved or affected in ways they don't even know. My concern is, what happens when that memory is no longer directly accessible, when there are no direct links to those living traditions?" Faced with the task of extracting from these haphazard recollections something close enough in spirit and style to the original work, Adams admits, "I don't think it is possible to revive the original choreography, so I have aimed to recreate the essence, not the steps."

But just what is that elusive essence and how can it be captured apart from the structure of the work? Some of the essence can be gleaned from a short film clip of the barn-dance, recorded onstage at the 1949 Canadian Ballet Festival. But what did that show of the dance, apart from the obvious charisma of the dancers?

Perhaps his gift for bringing out the inner talents of his dancers was, to a great extent, the essence of Volkoff. Cliff Collier offers an interesting insight: "Boris' style of choreography stemmed from his teaching style. He didn't teach syllabus, but rather Russian style, based on the standard elements of a class – barre, centre, allegro, turns – but, within that formula, no two classes were alike. The same applies to his choreography. He relied on his dancers to learn what he showed them and reproduce it. There was a stylistic quality to Boris' movement that we began to absorb. We wouldn't always know what steps he wanted, but we knew what he didn't want. He had the ability to make the most of his dancers' abilities. The ideas for his dances came about because there was a particular dancer around the studio. Even old pieces might be rechoreographed for a new dancer. He used the stage like he used the classroom. Pattern was very important as in all the Russian ballets. You always thought of the audience in the upper reaches, not at the footlights. The audience could see the pattern, as in the works he did for the ice shows in Toronto. I really think that they were influenced by his ingrained Russian sense of pattern and spectacle."

Gladys Forrester laughs in agreement. "Boris used to block out the patterns first and then ask us to fill in sequences," she recalls. "It was like organized chaos in that he would say, 'I want you to end here and you there,' and we just threaded our way over, picked up a partner and there we were!"

"In this reconstruction," Collier continues, "you have a group of dancers who cannot say with any sureness, 'These are the steps Boris created.' Yet, if they saw a sequence of steps, they could say, 'This is or is not the sort of thing that could have happened here.' All of the other reconstructions have had the original choreographer available. Even if they themselves changed their steps from the original, they are still the product of the original choreographer. When the choreographer has died, it is up to the original dancers to try to get as close to the original as possible, which is valid if [the end-product] is referred to as rechoreographed. We agree that today's versions are not original Petipa or Bournonville but, in essence, the style is there."

Collier continues: "Volkoff style had a bigness, with complicated, but never 'bitty' foot patterns. His dancers used space, travelled. The stance was very open in the arms and chest, with the arms held in a high, open-second position. They had a lightness. They were never 'into the floor,' unless for definite characterizations. Boris himself was a jumper and a turner, even from fifty to sixty. He was not a classical dancer in the 'noble' sense, but he choreographed for girls with the most delicate musicality. He was able to demonstrate this quality to the girls even though he himself was not that type of dancer. He had a real sense of humour. He liked to do the unexpected in his choreography. There could be certain enchaînements which you would expect to continue in a certain way, then there would be a change, a surprise even for the dancers. It seems almost a contradiction, but he was predictable in his unpredictability."

That sense of the unexpected carried through to his use of music. "Boris never worked in quarter notes straight with the music," says Forrester. Everett Staples adds, "Boris' stuff always had such a funny off-beat quality. In *Red Ear*, the count isn't always the same. You had to count. In some cases it was the only way you could get at it, until it got drilled into you." "Years ago," relates Butko, "we weren't used to hearing the kind of music in *Red Ear*. When we first heard the music we thought, 'What? I can't hear the melody, let alone find a count!'"

His students were always amazed at Boris' sense of dance history. In contrast to dancers at that time who rarely read, he was constantly searching for stories to set to dance, from Canadian folk legends to Biblical tales.

Thanks to the input of Volkoff's students, the rechoreographed *The Red Ear of Corn* has some elements that Volkoff talked about including, but never actually had the time or the means to set. "The Indian theme from Scene I is repeated at the end," says Collier. "Boris wanted to show the Indians silhouetted in the background to tie the two scenes together. He also wanted to show a reprise of Tekakwitha's killing behind the barn-dance couple (the lucky boy who finds the red ear of corn and his chosen girl) to reflect how her suffering brought happiness to later generations."

ENCORE! ENCORE! participants examine a video recording (l. to r.): Josephine Andrews, Gordon Wales, Carlu Carter, Sharon Wehner, Loney Reece, Andrea Smith, Sonya Delwaide, Gweneth Lloyd; seated: David Adams, Deborah Chapman.

Betty Farrally endorses the trend toward the use of videotapes and notation scores. "I imagine that the combination of video and notation works best and fastest," she suggests. "You get the overall impression from the video and the details from the notation score." Daniel Jackson adds, "A film or video is the closest thing to conjuring up immediately the visual forms, the final product.... But there is a whole process that goes on beneath. We may not be able to duplicate the finished product, but we may be able to get at it through a process that mirrors the original process."

Notator Janis Sandles-Oakes comments: "The beauty of the notation score is that it easily records the structural details, such as entrances and exits, and basic choreography, things that we spent so much time debating and working out. Good scores also include verbal descriptions and images that help the dancers bring the movements to life. The choreographer is a maker of images, so his words can be a springboard for his images. Even if a dancer falters in his steps, if the image has come across the movements are successful. From the film or video, you can't separate the performance from the choreography. It's like eating a cake and reading its recipe! Every time a work is done it can come out differently. If a basic structure is there in the score, more time can be spent on bringing out the dramatic elements, the characterizations and interplays between characters. The score is like a basic script for a play, what a director and a particular cast do with it is up to them."

This open-minded view is not shared by all. Some dancers and choreographers are protective of their works, fearing that a bad production will reflect on the choreography and not on the particular interpretation. Or they are concerned that a different interpretation would change the essence of the work, even if all the structural elements were reconstructed to the letter.

"I would like to see people be able to get access to all the videos of these reconstructions, perhaps through public libraries," says Betty Farrally, "but then, I suppose, people might want to put them onstage. Only reputable people should be able to do that." Foreseeing this concern, ENCORE! ENCORE! has set up an archive of scores, videotapes and supplementary material, which will be available to schools or companies wishing to stage a work. Paradoxically, the choreographers' rights may be protected more through this process than if the works were not recorded, since documentation is one means of establishing copyright or ownership.[12]

Looking back on the seven-week session, it is difficult to anticipate its overall value or impact. In Daniel Jackson's assessment, "The project will be more meaningful in time, in retrospect. Because we live in a far more technical time, it is hard to know how these pieces will be accepted. Audiences have grown very demanding. They like to see chance choreography, and they like to see things of technical brilliance, so there are a lot of barriers that have to be broken down. I think the interest will come in time, although I feel the project

---

[12] Archival material is housed at Dance Collection Danse, in Toronto. The public is welcome to view the scores and videotapes; however, performance rights must be negotiated directly with the choreographer or copyright holder.

had to be done now. It is dealing with something historical and the importance of it at this particular time is the fact that the project exists, not necessarily that the project be meaningful to everybody across the country. It has to reach out, and people have to see it and consider it for what it is."

The variety of pieces reconstructed certainly gives us an insight into the richness and diversity of the Canadian dance scene in the mid-twentieth century, from the improvisationally based pieces of Renaud, Sullivan, Lima Dent and, to some extent, Volkoff, to the meticulously structured pieces of Toumine and Lloyd. "This was certainly a very worthwhile project," reflects Betty Farrally. "People should know how it all started. A lot of people worked very hard in those early days." David Adams echoes the sentiment. "We want professional dancers of today to realize that important things were going on," he declares. "The dance of today wouldn't exist without the dance of before."

References

Benesh, Rudolf and Joan Benesh. 1956. *An Introduction to Benesh Dance Notation*. London: A. & C. Black Ltd.

Berry, Irmgard, ed. 1986. *Benesh Movement Notation Score Catalogue: An International Listing of Benesh Movement Notation Scores of Professional Dance Works Recorded 1955-1985*. London: The Benesh Institute of Choreology Ltd.

Blewchamp, Anna. Sept.-Oct. 1992. "The Wise Virgins Reconstructed." *Dance Connection: Special Theme Issue on Reconstruction* 10: 3, 40-44.

Brown, Ann K. and Monica Parker. 1984. *Dance Notation for Beginners*. London: Dance Books Ltd.

Elton, Heather. Sept.-Oct. 1992. "Reconstruction: The Archaeology of Dance." Interviews with Lawrence Adams, Anna Blewchamp, Rhonda Ryman, Selma Odom, Deepti Gupta. *Dance Connection: Special Theme Issue on Reconstruction* 10: 3, 22-37.

Horwitz, Dawn Lille. 1988. "Philosophical Issues Related to Notation and Reconstruction." *Choreography and Dance: The Notation Issue* 1: 1, 37-53.

Howe-Beck, Linde. Sept.-Oct. 1992. "Secrets from Montreal's Past." *Dance Connection: Special Theme Issue on Reconstruction* 10: 3, 46-49.

Hutchinson, Ann. 1954. *Labanotation: The System of Analyzing and Recording Movement*. Reprint New York: Theatre Arts Books, 1977.

Hutchinson, Ann. 1984. *Fanny Elssler's "Cachucha."* New York: Theatre Arts Books.

Warner, Mary Jane. 1984 and 1988. *Laban Notation Scores: An International Bibliography*. 2 vols. Columbus, Ohio: International Council of Kinetography Laban.

Gweneth Lloyd and *The Wise Virgins*: Arguments for the Reconstruction of a Canadian Ballet

Anna Blewchamp

In 1990 I began the search for a lost ballet by Canadian choreographer Gweneth Lloyd (1901-1993). Lloyd is best known as the co-founder with Betty Farrally of the Royal Winnipeg Ballet, and during the eighteen years of her association with the company, from 1939 to 1957, after which her works no longer appeared in the repertoire, she choreographed over thirty-five ballets for the company. My reconstruction of her 1942 work, *The Wise Virgins*, was performed in 1992 by the York University Dance Ensemble.[1] During my research period certain elements were brought into focus which clarified many of the distinctive qualities of this elegant choral dance. The exact basis of Lloyd's movement vocabulary was her integration of ballet with the English modern dance form known as Revived Greek Dance. The aesthetics which informed her artistic vision could be traced through her own experiences as both a student of dance and as an educated dance viewer. Her creative ideas coalesced in Winnipeg, and it is unlikely that she could have found so completely receptive an environment anywhere else.

There was, however, another issue, one striking aspect I encountered during research, which increased my determination to restore the ballet as a record of the choreographer's importance. At various times, I was made aware of the oddness of my intentions, as if my desire to reassert the value of Lloyd as a choreographer, rather than as a teacher or company founder, and to reappraise one of her forgotten works of art, was rather a strange thing to do. Quite often I got the feeling that I wasn't expected to find a ballet of any worth, although I might find a charmingly old-fashioned artifact with some scholarly value. This generalization is not meant to deny the encouragement and interest I received from many quarters but is, instead, to acknowledge that there were enough consistent doubts voiced by others which implied that what I was attempting was either impossible or not really worthwhile. I realize now that I had entered into that nebulous area which envelops all artists and works which are "Canadian."

---

[1] A more thorough analysis of the reconstruction and Lloyd's choreographic work can be found in my thesis (Blewchamp 1992).

Gweneth Lloyd, ca. 1942.

Lloyd emigrated from England to Canada in 1938 and is often described as founding the first truly Canadian ballet company. She created works with Canadian themes; she choreographed for Canadian dancers trained in Canada; she helped to identify the national importance of Canadian dance by initiating, with Farrally and the Royal Winnipeg Ballet's manager David Yeddeau, the first Ballet Festivals. If Lloyd the artist can be characterized as "Canadian," does this denote a specific identity? And, if her works are "Canadian," have they any value? In other words, to rephrase Margaret Atwood's two central questions regarding Canadian writing in *Survival: A Thematic Guide to Canadian Literature* (1972), one can ask, "What's Canadian about Canadian dance, and why should we be bothered?" The question "Why should we be bothered?" encapsulates the doubts that were expressed to me. Why bother reconstructing a Canadian ballet at all? In Atwood's case, she can attempt to answer both questions by referring to her own reading of Canadian books. She can base her arguments for a distinctive Canadian literature on numerous examples. (Read the book, compare the book to other books from the same culture, analyze the book in relation to books from other cultures.) With Canadian dance, comparisons have often been made only with artists or choreographies from other cultures. Atwood argues that this is a particularly Canadian trait, and examines "what it means to live in a cultural and economic colony" (1972: 182). She illustrates this point with a quotation from E.K. Brown's essay "The Problem of a Canadian Literature": "A colony lacks the spiritual energy to rise above routine, and ... it lacks this energy because it does not adequately believe in itself. It applies to what it has standards which are imported, and therefore artificial and distorting. It sets the great good place not in its present, nor in its past nor in its future, but somewhere outside its own borders, somewhere beyond its own possibilities" (Brown in Atwood 1972: 183).

It is not how Canadian dance relates to itself and its society, but rather how it stands up to the dance of the Mother country or the Brother country next door. Reconstructing a Canadian work from the 1940s implies immediate comparison with either English or American works from the same period, and the prior assumption is that the Canadian work just cannot be as good. We can attempt to make comparisons within our own culture by reading current texts or by researching contemporary accounts, but we have to believe in their veracity. If we suffer from the colonial malaise described by Brown, we don't trust either of these sources unless they include approval from outside our own borders. This failure to believe in ourselves undermines the very credibility of Lloyd's work in Canada.[2] There is a predominant feature in discussions of Lloyd's work, and it is the emphasis placed on her arrival with Farrally in the wastelands of Winnipeg to bring ballet (in other words, culture) to the uninformed inhabitants. Emphasis is also placed on her ability to create accessible choreographies and balanced programmes for the fledging Winnipeg Ballet company, which in some way made the acquisition of ballet as culture more palatable to Canada's culturally deficient audiences. There is an anecdote attributed to Lloyd, quoted with great regularity, which clearly demonstrates this point of view. The most recent reappearance of this story was published in William Littler's commemorative article which appeared in the *Toronto Star* shortly after Lloyd's death in 1993. "Lloyd, a visiting dance teacher from Yorkshire, fell into conversation with another woman ... in Assiniboine Park. 'How much ballet is there on the prairies' she asked her fellow stroller. 'Ballet?' the woman looked up. 'I've never heard of it.' 'You will,' Lloyd is said to have replied, 'you wait and see'" (10 Jan. 1993).

That this may have happened is not the relevant point; the fact that it is endlessly quoted makes it significant. This statement seemingly gives credence to Lloyd's fierce determination to bring ballet to Canada but it also emphasizes a lack of cultural awareness in the words of the other woman. She obviously represents all Winnipeg, and all Canada. Why is it necessary to reiterate that there was no knowledge of ballet in Winnipeg prior to the arrival of Lloyd and Farrally? (Especially as it isn't true!) Does this help in proving, when Lloyd managed to found the ballet company and create highly successful ballets, that neither the company nor the works were really first-rate? We have already been informed that audiences didn't know what they were seeing, and it's a relatively easy step to include critics in the same category as the audience. I may seem to be exaggerating the importance of this nameless Winnipeg woman, but even now I find I am asked the same central question about Lloyd. It has everything to do with "place," and nothing to do with Lloyd as a creative artist. Why did she choose Winnipeg? The idea that artists from another country would choose Winnipeg as a place to live and work apparently seems hard to comprehend. The implication is that if they do make that decision willingly, then there must be something wrong with them.

How do we then challenge these assumptions? We can't experience the dance itself once its period of immediacy is passed. When choreographies

---

[2] I often wonder whether we allow ourselves to value Lloyd more as the founder of the ballet company because of the undeniability of its economic reality and its real estate. We may still need international approval for the dancers and the choreographers, but can point with total assurance to the reality of the company's budget and buildings. These definitely exist!

vanish from the active repertoire, we can no longer "read" the works as Atwood is able to read works of literature. We can't form our own opinions as to their meaning. We can, however, trust the responses of Lloyd's contemporaries. We can study written reports by critics, and, as I did, we can search out the dancers or associates who knew Lloyd intimately during the period of her greatest creativity. Oral histories that give full value to the subject's point of view have tended to reveal a much more complex and interesting analysis of Lloyd and her work than I have yet found in any more recently published texts on the Royal Winnipeg Ballet. We can also document current works with more deliberation, so that film, video and notation today support the written records of a choreographic work of art.

I was inspired to take the laudatory contemporary reviews of Lloyd's choreography at face value by seeing a small section of the ballet on film. *The Wise Virgins* had been filmed by the National Film Board of Canada in 1945, but the film could not be located. It was probably destroyed much later in a fire at the National Film Board headquarters in Montreal. Outtakes from the editing process had somehow survived, and these were available to view through Dance Collection Danse in Toronto, the "living museum" whose mandate is the preservation, promotion and celebration of Canada's theatrical dance history. Although there is no sound, and the outtakes show incomplete sections, I was struck by the distinctive quality of the movement, by the breadth and sweep of the choreographic design. As there was no known connection between Lloyd and American modern dance, I was intrigued by the modern look of this ballet. Where did her choice of movement or her knowledge of form come from? It became obvious that I would have to locate the development of her creativity within the social and cultural context of her English background, but also place the maturation of her artistry within the cultural context of Winnipeg and Canada. Failure to do this would mean a superficial reappraisal, one which talked of Lloyd only as an immigrant bringing certain "real" values to the colonies, values which suddenly became less meaningful once Lloyd became identified as "Canadian." Lloyd arrived with a substantial background as a teacher which, coupled with an idiosyncratic creative drive, became the basis for experimentation in Canada. Her own theories regarding dance training could be employed, her own innovations in choreography could be explored. The city she chose as her new home was alive with artistic activities, and Lloyd and Farrally were able to draw on many existing resources to support the creation of a ballet company.

Lloyd's choreographies were the outcome of many years of training in diverse areas of physical movement and dance. She was born in Eccles, England, in 1901 and her early years were spent with her grandmother in Cambridge and with her parents in London. In her childhood, she took lessons in social and Fancy Dancing, followed by years of study in physical education and creative movement at the Liverpool Physical Training College. Although she was an accredited physical education teacher, she chose to leave her first job in order to study her real love, dance, with Ruby Ginner at the

Lloyd's *The Wise Virgins*, Winnipeg Ballet, 1942.

Ginner-Mawer School of Dance and Mime in London. There she took the teacher's course in the Revived Greek Dance, and supplemented her training with classes in ballet, Cecchetti with Margaret Craske and the Royal Academy of Dancing (RAD) syllabus with various independent teachers. By the time she arrived in Canada, she was an examiner for the RAD and the Classical Greek Dance Branch (Ginner Method) of the Imperial Society of the Teachers of Dancing (ISTD). During her years in Winnipeg (1938-50) and later in Toronto (1950-57), she often lectured on dance, and would present her students in lecture-demonstrations as a method of showing audiences the potential theatrical possibilities in different forms of dance. She organized professional courses in Winnipeg, which included exams in elementary physiology and anatomy, speech, national dance, mime, ballet, modern dancing and composition. Students also studied the syllabus for RAD exams.

Her own studies were originally undertaken so that she could become a teacher, and in this way she embodied a traditionally acceptable role for women. However, her choice of a career in physical education and dance was closely linked to the change in women's roles which occurred during the early years of the twentieth century. It was a period in which women reclaimed their own bodies and minds, breaking through barriers to assert their right to expressive physical activity as well as to higher education. Lloyd was influenced by a number of independent women, all of whom were visionary in their fields. At Norwood College, as an adolescent, she studied Swedish gymnastics, national dance and free movement with Bertha Knowles, who encouraged her to attend Liverpool Physical Training College. There she came under the influence of Irene Marsh, one of the earliest founders of a training college for women. At Liverpool she also studied national dances, "natural movement," improvisation and composition. Finally, she met Ginner, a woman who developed a new philosophy of movement and composition based on her understanding of ancient Greek dance, which emphasized freedom of movement and expression. All these studies combined with Lloyd's love and knowledge of music, theatre and dance. She learned music as a child, and visits with her family to theatre and ballet performances were regular events. As an adult, she attended every dance performance she could afford, and the period of the 1920s and 1930s was a very exciting and rich one in English dance history. Her own ballets were subsequently highly imaginative and unusual because of her integration of different movement vocabularies and aesthetics. This integration of techniques was noted by journalists and arts writers during the 1940s and 1950s, and was often described as a combination of classical ballet and modern dance. There was a natural progression from Ginner's ideas to Lloyd's development of her own style which, in some ways, mirrors a similar development by American choreographers who were following in the footsteps of Isadora Duncan or the Denishawn school.

In *The Wise Virgins*, there is a striking resemblance to Doris Humphrey's early works, and it is interesting to note how these two choreographers simultaneously devised similar movement ideas. Both were responding to the influence of early modern dance artists in their own culture, and both transformed these influences in individualistic ways. Lloyd is particularly interesting because she tried to create a fusion of "natural movement" with ballet. Guy Glover in *Canadian Art* described it as "an amalgam of straight ballet idiom and ... a free dance technique. This provides ... a flexible and expressive style, which adds eloquence to the upper torso, arms and hands, while preserving ... the strong dynamic of classical ballet" (1949: 152). For the mixed repertoire of the Royal Winnipeg Ballet, Lloyd created works which were traditionally classical, as well as story ballets with recognizable elements such as narrative structures, humour or drama, visually exciting stage settings or well-known music. Her more abstract or modernistic works, which fully explored her own stylistic experiments, often offered a redemptive or transcendent view of the world.

The Wise Virgins, based on the Biblical parable, has a similar thematic concern, the struggle of the Foolish Virgins to enter the Kingdom of Heaven, with an ideal state being represented by two Spiritual Apotheoses. This ideal, to be inspired by something greater than oneself and to excel accordingly, permeated Lloyd's life, and characterized her relationship with her students and to her own choreography. In the reconstruction process, her choreographic methods and the public reaction to her work had to be rediscovered through the primary source of oral histories and the critical response in published secondary sources. The reconstruction itself was, however, the result of studio rehearsals with original dancers; interviews with Lloyd, company members and designers; and research in archives as well as in personal scrapbooks for photographs, films, or choreographic notes. Most of Lloyd's choreographic notes from the 1940s were lost in the 1954 fire which destroyed the studios of the Royal Winnipeg Ballet, but five pages of notation

Rehearsal for the reconstruction of Lloyd's *The Wise Virgins* (l. to r.): Viola Busday Robertson, Margaret Hample Piasecki, Anna Blewchamp, Alvin Tolentino, Lawrence Adams and Lisa Otto, Winnipeg, 1991.

from 1955, with an almost complete section of the female soloist's choreography, were discovered in Toronto in 1992.

It was in the books, magazines and newspapers consulted that I noticed the pervasive influence of the colonial mentality. When Lloyd first arrived in Winnipeg, a great deal of importance was laid on her English background and her status as an examiner for the RAD and a graduate of the Ginner-Mawer School. Lloyd herself quickly became an advocate for Winnipeg, and always wrote or lectured about the value of Canadian dance with little reference to the superiority of dance in England. Critics were quick to applaud the significance of the company as a Canadian group, and to comment on the strengths of other Canadian companies performing at the Ballet Festivals. By the end of the 1940s, a number of arts writers, while valuing the sophistication of Lloyd's choreography, voiced their desire to see ballets with Canadian themes. There were also calls for the creation of a Canadian national ballet. Lloyd appeared to be the obvious choice to head such a Canadian enterprise, but instead a newer import from England, Celia Franca, was invited to form a company which Franca herself saw as being modelled on England's Sadler's Wells Ballet.

An amazing tug-of-war ensued as to which company could call on the best form of approval from outside Canada, with Winnipeg winning hands down by receiving its designation as the Royal Winnipeg Ballet in 1953. Lloyd had choreographed *Shadow on the Prairie* in 1952 and was heralded as having produced a great Canadian masterpiece with a distinctly Canadian theme. Franca intended to develop Canadian choreographies for the National Ballet of

411

Canada. According to Grant Strate as quoted in Max Wyman's *Dance Canada: An Illustrated History*, "she realized this plan was naively out of line with her ambition to create a company of international stature, and it was only a matter of months before she decided to base it on the classics" (1989: 73). Oddly enough, the English were developing national companies of international stature with repertories made up of works by English choreographers, as were the Americans with American choreographers. The 1954 fire, which almost destroyed the Royal Winnipeg Ballet, and subsequent attempts to rebuild with "outsider" artistic directors, left the company and Lloyd's reputation in a precarious state. The company, by the time it had redefined itself under Arnold Spohr's direction during the 1960s, had become determined to gain international status, and also turned to "outsider" choreographers to give validity to the inclusion of home-grown works. In his history of the company, *The Royal Winnipeg Ballet: The First Forty Years*, Wyman describes Lloyd's ballets as "naive creations" (1978: 51). It is taken for granted that she choreographed simple works in keeping with the limited talents of her dancers, and is consequently a complete denial of Lloyd's own standards of excellence. The retrospective view of the company and Lloyd's choreography is that if both were successful in Canada at the time, neither can really have been that good.

To return to the original questions "Why reconstruct a Canadian ballet?" and "What is Canadian about Canadian dance and why should we be bothered?" we cannot identify distinctiveness or include Canadian dance in philosophical or aesthetic discourses unless we know what Canadian dance is and take it seriously. When we rely on current analysis, that speaks arrogantly of the importance of the present over the past without having a past accurately defined, and while our present is qualified by outside approval, we are essentially missing the boat. E.K. Brown writes that "a great art is fostered by artists and audience possessing in common a passionate and peculiar interest in the kind of life that exists in the country where they live" (Brown in Atwood 1972: 181). If this statement is true, we need to be much more aware of the legitimacy of the immediate response to dance in performance. If audiences and writers responded in a certain way at the time, perhaps the link between artist and audience had not then been broken by questions of self-doubt. Dance in Canada continues to be marginalized because we don't trust our own responses to it. We still seek outside verification of its worth and we don't appear to have the ability to create mythologies around our own heritage.

The reconstruction of *The Wise Virgins* joined with other attempts to recognize Canadian dance history, to identify the heroines in our midst. Dance Collection Danse in its ENCORE! ENCORE! project reconstructed a number of Canadian works in 1986, one of which was *Shadow on the Prairie*. Other reconstructions of Canadian works have followed, in particular a series of duets from 1947 to 1983 staged by Montréal Danse in 1992. All this effort is intended to break the pattern of looking outside for reflections of self-worth. By looking at our own dance past, alive again in performance and restored as

412

carefully as we are able, we can chart a sequence of creative events which could only have occurred in Canada. We should "be bothered" because earlier dance artists also explored that "passionate and peculiar interest in the kind of life that exists in the country where they live" (Brown in Atwood 1972: 181). By sharing that interest we can begin truly to ascertain the nature of this Canadian art and we can recognize the traces of its inheritance in the works that are being created today. We can stop attributing each new decade's artists with outside influences, and stop insisting that each new decade's successes, be they artists or works, are definitely real because they have been accepted elsewhere. We can instead understand the traditions, the innovations and the thematic concerns. By reconstructing Lloyd's *The Wise Virgins*, a link in that chain of creativity could be reconnected, a link that could have been forged only in Winnipeg by an artist who saw herself and her creations as "Canadian." Gweneth Lloyd saw "Canadian" not as "something other than" but as something specific unto itself.

Members of the York University Dance Ensemble performing Blewchamp's reconstruction of Lloyd's *The Wise Virgins*, 1992.

References

Anderson, Carol. 1992. *"The Wise Virgins Speaks across Time." Dance Collection Danse News* No. 28, 1-2.

Atwood, Margaret. 1972. *Survival: A Thematic Guide to Canadian Literature*. Toronto: House of Anansi Press Ltd.

Blewchamp, Anna. 1992. "Gweneth Lloyd and *The Wise Virgins*, The Development of an Artist: The Reconstruction of the Ballet." Master's thesis, York University.

Dafoe, Christopher. 1990. *Dancing Through Time: The First Fifty Years of Canada's Royal Winnipeg Ballet*. Winnipeg: Portage and Main Press.

Glover, Guy. Summer 1949. *Canadian Art* 6: 4, 151-54, 180.

Littler, William. 10 Jan. 1993. "Gweneth Lloyd Set our Ballet in Motion." *Toronto Star*.

Lloyd, Gweneth. Spring 1947. "Ballet in Canada." *Manitoba Arts Review* 5: 3, 33-37.

Morriss, Frank. 1939-1955. Various articles. *Winnipeg Free Press*.

Patton, Randolph. Newspaper Clippings 1940-1942. Royal Winnipeg Ballet, Manitoba Provincial Archives.

Wyman, Max. 1978. *The Royal Winnipeg Ballet: The First Forty Years*. Toronto: Doubleday & Company Ltd.

Wyman, Max. 1989. *Dance Canada: An Illustrated History*. Vancouver: Douglas and McIntyre.

Wyman, Max. Spring 1992. "Max Wyman's Notebook." *Vandance International* 20: 1, 35.

Dance Defined:
An Examination of Canadian Cultural Policy on Multicultural Dance

Katherine Cornell

Canadian culture is complex and multifaceted.[1] Unlike the American melting pot, the Canadian mosaic recognizes the distinctive identities of all citizens. Immigrants celebrate their culture within Canadian society instead of being assimilated into the dominant culture, yet this is a policy that caused considerable controversy. Our plentiful mosaic makes Canadian culture difficult to define, but defining it has preoccupied academics, journalists and politicians alike. Multiculturalism, a term utilized by the government beginning in the 1970s, in many ways describes Canadian culture. Joyce Zemans, former director of the Canada Council, states that "though our multicultural policy is admired internationally and considered a model by UNESCO, critics blame the policy for devaluing what it purports to promote, fracturing Canadian society by its insistence on hyphenated Canadians and the creation of 'identity communities'" (1996: 19). Gina Mallet, a journalist formerly with the *Globe and Mail*, defines multiculturalism as "the masochistic celebration of Canadian nothingness" (15 Mar. 1997). As multiculturalism grew in Canada, so too did the number of recognized dance forms. In a 1986 study on multicultural dance in Ontario, dance ethnologist Nina De Shane asserted that the term multicultural dance refers "to any dance traditions other than Western European-based classical genres" (1994: 86).

This essay investigates Canadian cultural policy as it relates to multicultural dance by focusing on three questions: One, who makes cultural policy in Canada? Two, what are the specific policies that evolved to support multicultural dance? Three, why are these policies significant? The research concentrates on Toronto, the largest city in Canada, which is noted for its cultural diversity.

In Canada, like many other countries, there are three tiers of government: federal, provincial and municipal. Each level includes specific ministries responsible for monitoring cultural affairs. "Unlike education, arts and culture is not an area specifically assigned in the British North American Act," thus no one level of government claims constitutional control over arts and

---

[1] This is a revised version of a paper that first appeared in the *Continents in Movement Conference Proceedings*, Oeiras, Portugal, 1998.

culture (Canadian Conference of the Arts 1981: 99). At the federal level, the area of cultural affairs includes numerous issues such as immigration, bilingualism, tariffs and copyrights, along with the visual and performing arts. These broad and diverse areas of responsibility were not lumped together and delegated as the sole responsibility of either the federal or provincial governments. Therefore, in Canada, there are sources of public funding available for artists at all three levels of government. In addition, the primary public funding agencies are situated outside the respective governmental ministries in arm's-length councils who disperse funding based on peer assessment of artistic works. This policy allows the art councils to remain independent from the government and prevents partisan support for specific artists.

The Canada Council began funding artists in 1957 with financial backing from an endowment. Over its more than forty-year history, the Canada Council has been the country's most significant funder of individual artists and arts organizations. Zemans, in an essay on national cultural institutions, explained that "the inspiration and model for the Canada Council, Canada's principal instrument of government support to artists and arts organizations, was British, and a primary impetus for its creation was the domination of American product in the Canadian market" (1995: 147). The Council plays a major role in servicing the arts community, advising on arts policy development and providing artistic networks on both the national and international level. The Canada Council also works in tandem with the provincial arm's-length arts councils and with private foundations to increase the spectrum of support services available to artists. Unlike the federal ministries, the Canada Council "evaluates artistic significance rather than relying on economic impact as the principal criterion for support" (Zemans 1995: 149).

The Ontario Arts Council (OAC), created in 1963, was modelled after the Canada Council. Bill 162 as passed by the Ontario Legislature created a Council of twelve members to "promote the study and enjoyment of and the production of works in the Arts" (Ontario Arts Council 1963: 10). From the beginning, members of the OAC conferred with the Canada Council in order to aid artists not supported by their federal counterpart. Even today both Councils continue to operate at arm's length from government and utilize the artistic community as assessors to assist them in their granting decisions. Communication between the federal and provincial councils remains a vital link to coordinate funding.

Most provincial arts councils, including the OAC, gradually concentrated their funding in specialty areas not addressed by the Canada Council. In 1963, when the OAC began, its Dance Office primarily funded ballet companies with operating grants. Then, in 1974, the OAC requested that dance writer Susan Cohen investigate separating dance grants into those for companies and for choreography. The Dance Office willingly accepted her recommendations to diversify and expand the dance grants thus adapting to the needs of the growing community. When Cohen became the OAC's Dance Officer in 1981, many new initiatives were undertaken: allotting funds to umbrella organizations, servicing specific communities such as Native Canadians; in addition to operating grants, allocating money to established dance companies for specific projects, such as workshops and tours; supporting multidisciplinary endeavours; and funding multicultural dance. The grassroots activity at the provincial level made it a natural place to introduce new policies on multi-cultural dance.

The OAC led the way in adopting programmes geared towards non-Euro-centric dance styles. In 1986, its Dance Office created the Multicultural/Folk Arts Dance Grant. Although this short-lived grant opportunity funded only a few umbrella organizations such as the Native Arts Foundation, it was an important stepping stone towards a more comprehensive policy. The new Culture Specific Dance Grant, created in 1990, met a need within the broader dance community and fulfilled the provincial government's specification for more multicultural policies and programmes. Susan Cohen, the Dance Officer at that time, can be credited with implementing grants to satisfy both native and multicultural constituents. Dance on the periphery of the "mainstream" expanded enormously in the 1980s. Developing a more integrated grant and application process policy became an urgent necessity within the dance community.

Gradually the term multicultural fell out of favour and as a result, in 1990, the OAC enlisted the help of Lina Fattah as the Council's first Multicultural Coordinator. Fattah consulted with artists on the topic of cultural diversity. Based on the results of her survey found in the subsequent publication *Consultations with Artists in a Culturally Diverse Society*, she made three major suggestions which were accepted and adopted by the Council. The artists whom she had consulted felt that the OAC literature did not inform and communicate adequately the information necessary to complete the application process. As a result, the OAC published the *Guide to Grants* and *Understanding the Assessment Process*. Her second recommendation emphasized that jury composition had to represent the diverse Canadian culture. Applicants felt that juries lacked experts within their specific dance fields. The OAC and the Canada Council now require at least one expert from the specific dance field on juries. Her third recommendation concerned Canadian art. Artists involved in the consultations "considered themselves Canadian artists practising Canadian art. They felt that labels such as 'multicultural' or 'ethnic' stereotyped them and excluded them from partici-pation in the general stream of Canadian art. They believed that definitions of what was artistic needed to be broadened greatly. In general, participating artists wanted to access regular OAC programmes and not be slotted in 'multicultural' slots" (Fattah 1990: 2). These consultations with artists directly influenced the creation of the Culture Specific Dance grant in 1990. This grant assisted dance groups in the transition from the multicultural dance stream to mainstream acceptance. However, the Dance Office never intended the grant to be permanent.

As a result of Fattah's consultations and recommendations, Dance Officer Susan Cohen hired Rina Singha, a classical Indian dancer, to coordinate the

Culture Specific Dance Programme. Credibility and flexibility were hallmarks of this programme especially in its first years. The grants targeted individual dancers, schools and organizations, not necessarily professionals, but nevertheless, all met the mandate of enriching their culture and their community through dance, thus establishing a new policy of inclusion at the OAC (Ontario Arts Council 1992: 3). The Culture Specific Dance Programme was eliminated in 1995, along with many other programmes, due to lack of OAC funding. The transitional nature of the grant made it a natural target for cutbacks.

In the introduction to *Consultations with Artists in a Culturally Diverse Society*, the OAC states, "in Ontario, the arts have increasingly become a forum through which distinctive identities can be nurtured and shared. This development – so new in Ontario's experience and yet so ancient in the history of world cultures – brings with it tremendous possibilities for those of us working in the arts field" (Fattah 1990: 21). This statement set the tone for change, which in turn influenced other funding organizations. The OAC's concept of professional dance and the inclusion of performers from diverse cultural backgrounds on juries certainly influenced policy makers at the Dance Office of the Canada Council.

Prior to 1993, the Dance Office of the Canada Council's definition of dance limited eligibility for operating grants to mainstream dance companies. The Arts Awards and Touring Offices, on the other hand, had a less restrictive policy of eligibility for dance. For example, the Menaka Thakkar Dance Company, a Toronto-based Indian dance group, received substantial funding, mainly from the Canada Council Touring Office throughout the 1980s, yet her company was not eligible for an operating grant from the Dance Office (Thakkar 27 Nov. 1997). Anne Valois, then Director of the Touring Office, promoted a sense of openness in all her departments. She recognized that in the 1980s and early 1990s, the Arts Awards and Touring Offices offered the only form of funding for which these performers were eligible. She has continued this openness as current Director of the Dance Office and Strategic Initiatives Unit. William Lau, Chinese dancer and a former intern with the Canada Council, stressed the absolute necessity of the Arts Awards for individual performers, especially those in non-Eurocentric art forms (20 Nov. 1997).

The policy adapted by the Canada Council's Dance Office to promote the concept of greater openness began in 1991, when the Council commissioned Susan Macpherson, a modern dancer formerly with Toronto Dance Theatre and the Danny Grossman Dance Company, to develop an inventory of Canadian cultural dance. Her findings were published in an *Inventory of Dance "Other Forms"* which acted as a who's who directory to the cultural dance sector. Macpherson documented the cultural dance community's opinion of the Canada Council's restrictive definition of dance. She explained that "it quickly became clear that the definition was contentious, to put it mildly" (1991: 4). In her recommendations, Macpherson insightfully listed four issues that emerged as potential problems for the future: the definition of professional dance, the need for a separate office to address the issues of native dance, the question of funding folkloric troupes, and difficulties with the assessment process. The Dance Advisory Committee of the Canada Council, which advises the Dance Office on policy, reviewed Macpherson's report in 1991 (Macpherson 1991: 13-20). She found that prior to 1991 the Dance Office defined a professional dance company as "a company directed by fully trained people, operating on a continuous basis, attempting to employ dancers full time (although it is recognized that dancers might still have to earn a significant portion of their income from other sources), administered by some permanent staff, incorporated as a non-profit organization, and assigned a charity number by Revenue Canada" (Macpherson 1991: 4). Although this definition did not mention style specifically, the requirement of infrastructure made most small dance companies ineligible. It was a pivotal time period for the Dance Advisory Committee that could have been fraught with infighting and competitiveness but, instead, Andrea Rowe, then a Dance Officer with the Canada Council, described the feeling of the committee as collegial regardless of the jurors' discipline background, be it ballet, modern or "other." The "other" sector was represented on the committee by consultants Zab Maboungou, a Congolese dancer working in Montreal, and Maria O'Dole, an associate of the Vinok Folkloric Group from Edmonton (Rowe 27 Nov. 1997). Lau explained that the committee valued these two pivotal consultants, because they embodied the voices of the unheard dancers. The conventionally funded dance companies welcomed the removal of restrictions from the definition of dance for the betterment of the whole community. The new policy in the Dance Office of the Canada Council undoubtedly began with individuals and companies who shared this more open mindset.

The final step towards a more open policy in the Dance Office came from the recommendations of the Canada Council's Racial Equity Advisory Committee. This committee recommended that the Council hire interns for each discipline to represent the interests of minorities in their particular art form. The Dance Office hired Chinese dancer William Lau for the contract position of dance intern as part of the Equity Programme. Lau felt that the requirement of a cultural expert on every dance jury, the hiring of a First Nations dancer to report on First Nations dance, and the information forums held in Vancouver, Toronto and Montreal stood out as the most productive equity accomplishments in dance during his internship. He emphasized that the point of the Equity Programme, for him, was the realization that "sometimes money is not the whole thing, people are looking for recognition ... people are looking for access" (20 Nov. 1997). Negating the traditional definition of dance at the Canada Council clearly made accessibility a priority.

Unlike the Ontario Arts Council, the Canada Council did not instigate a specific grant for multicultural dance forms following the definition change. Instead, the new definition now permitted professional dance companies performing dance styles other than ballet and modern accessibility to operating funding. Previously, they were limited to special funding such as Touring Grants.

These two policies, at the provincial and federal level, legitimized multicultural dance and accepted it as a Canadian artistic endeavour. First and foremost these new policies recognized the prominence of classical and fusion forms of dance other than ballet and modern. Acceptance of these dance forms alone was a huge step towards greater inclusivity. These policies acknowledged the growing prominence of multicultural dance in Canada. The new policies of the OAC and the Canada Council promoted accessibility. Although applications from the multicultural dance community do not outnumber those from ballet or modern companies, they are no longer automatically rejected. These applicants can now expect to be consulted to ensure that a specialist in their style of dance participates in their assessment process. Finally, these two policies helped to alter the concept of Canadian mainstream dance. The lines between dance styles are no longer as rigid or definitive. For example, Toronto Dance Theatre, the largest modern dance troupe in Canada, invited Chandralehka, a world-renowned Indian choreographer, to create a work in 1997. Canadian performers, choreographers and audiences have a broader sense of dance as a result of the openness of the dance community and the Councils that fund them.

The Canada Council's policy was, in some ways, more significant, because a definition cannot be the victim of cutbacks. Although the OAC's Culture Specific Dance Programme did much to open people's eyes to the need for more inclusivity, by labelling and separating cultural dance, the OAC marginalized the recipients and hindered them from symbolically becoming part of the mainstream. The grants were always intended to be transitional, so perhaps, the OAC's Dance Office in fact did accomplish its own goal of recognition of multicultural dance.

The revised policies of both the Canada Council and the Ontario Arts Council have done much to publicly and financially welcome multicultural dance forms into the dance mainstream. Various professional Indian, Chinese and African dance companies now perform alongside modern and ballet companies in the mid-size theatres in Toronto. These new policies facilitated and enabled smaller companies to perform at venues they might not have been able to afford in the past. Accessibility has remained the key issue throughout the past ten years of policy-making in Canada. Although the changes adopted by the Ontario Arts Council and the Canada Council have garnered their fair share of critical attention from the media, the changes have had a positive impact. The Canadian dance community has benefited and extended its scope as a result of these new multicultural policies.

References

Canada Council. 1992. *Recommendations of the Advisory Committee to the Canada Council for Racial Equality in the Arts and the Response of the Canada Council.* Ottawa: Canada Council.

Canadian Conference of the Arts. 1981. *More Strategy for Culture.* Ottawa: Canadian Conference of the Arts.

De Shane, Nina. 1994. "'Multiethnic' Dance in Ontario: The Struggle over Hegemony." In Beverley Diamond and Robert Witmer, eds. *Canadian Music: Issues of Hegemony and Identity.* Toronto: Canadian Scholar's Press.

Fattah, Lina. 1990. *Consultations with Artists in a Culturally Diverse Society.* Toronto: Ontario Arts Council. Reprint 1992.

Macpherson, Susan. 1991. *Inventory of Dance "Other Forms."* Ottawa: Dance Office, Canada Council.

Mallet, Gina. 15 Mar. 1997. "Has diversity gone too far?" *Globe and Mail.*

Ontario Arts Council. 1963, 1986-92. *Ontario Arts Council Annual Report(s).* Toronto: Ontario Arts Council.

Ontario Arts Council. 1990. *Guide to Grants.* Toronto: Ontario Arts Council.

Ontario Arts Council. 1992. *Understanding the Assessment Process.* Toronto: Ontario Arts Council.

Zemans, Joyce. 1995. "The Essential Role of National Cultural Institutions." In Ken McRoberts, ed. *Beyond Quebec: Taking Stock of Canada.* Montreal and Kingston: McGill-Queen's University Press, 138-62.

Zemans, Joyce. 1996. *Where is Here? Canadian Cultural Policy in a Globalized World.* Toronto: Robarts Centre for Canadian Studies.

Interviews

Lau, William. 21 Mar. 1997 and 20 Nov. 1997.

Rowe, Andrea. 27 Nov. 1997.

Thakkar, Menaka. 27 Nov. 1997.

Valois, Anne. 27 Nov. 1997.

Learning Belly Dance in Toronto:
Pyramids, Goddesses and Other Weird Stuff

Kathleen Wittick Fraser

Dance was never a major element of my childhood, and what little I studied I embraced casually and abandoned fecklessly. I took on dance in little nibbles, unwilling or unable to commit to anything. Yet the dance impulse was there covertly, ready to surface when I needed it most, the "most" coming unexpectedly in the form of a life-threatening illness. It was at that time when dance (at that moment manifested in the form of belly dance or *baladi* or Middle-Eastern dance, which are some of this dance's names) took on life-giving meaning. Perhaps this dance was not the main reason I recovered, but its glorious rhythms, movements arising from deep within the body, its groundedness – and above all the joy of its expression – carried me away for six or more hours each week into some place where strength and vitality existed. At that time I was content (and only able) to do and not to think about this dance. Only later did I finally want to know more and to study. I decided on the middle-aged equivalent of running away to join the circus – I left my career to take a graduate degree in dance history, focusing always on my beloved belly dance. Yet, exposed to rigorous scholarship, it took me only weeks to realize that, coming from a starry-eyed vision of beads and glamour, much of what I had learned was a sham.

Introduced to academic dance studies, I realized what had happened. I had learned the form but not the cultural meanings of the belly dance. My experience appears neither unique to me nor to Toronto, for it is at the level of meaning that modern belly dance in North America is all too often problematic. In "Rakassah – an American Middle East Dance Festival: Exoticism and Orientalism in the Twentieth Century," Elizabeth Buck looks at the meanings North American dancers attach to the belly dance (1991). Buck carried out her research, ultimately for a master's thesis, at an annual festival in Richmond, California. Two thousand participants from across North America, mainly American women of European ancestry, attend this event. Buck asks the question why this gala attracts so many and finds her answer partly in the continuing appeal of Middle-Eastern images handed down from the nineteenth century. Both Europe and North America have been fascinated with orientalism, as exemplified by Hollywood's traditional exploitation of the

423

exotic, the extraordinary and the fantastic.[1] Buck found the eclecticism of 1920s Hollywood films, for example costume and dance elements from Morocco and Thailand combined, still at work at Rakassah, in the "American Middle Eastern dance community where Afghani and Tunisian jewellery, Egyptian dresses and Moroccan scarves may comprise a single costume" (1991: 28). She believes the inspiration for these modern costumes may often lie ultimately in the nineteenth-century European orientalist paintings that shaped the West's invented fancies of the East. Images such as camels, pyramids, date palms, scarabs, serpents, scorpions, scimitars and veils appear in the Rakassah festival literature and in the ornaments and props the dancers use to develop their Middle-Eastern masquerade as odalisques, women of harems, village maidens and snake charmers. Buck also found widely varying levels of conceptualizations of the Middle East in the movement repertoires; a few choreographies attempted to have some basis in Middle-Eastern culture, but other presentations were entirely personal and freely interpretive in movement and meaning.

Buck's findings concerning orientalism at Rakassah conform with my experience with belly dance in Toronto during ten years in a dance school. My teacher, Eddy Manneh, despite his Middle-Eastern birth and heritage, seems to have had scant knowledge of the history of the dance beyond a sense of the lives of Egyptian dance stars of the 1940s onwards, and showed little feeling for the deepness of folk dance traditions. Further, his fear lest a student learn outside of his circumscribed framework kept us ignorant of the little good information available, for example the periodicals *Arabesque* and *Habibi* and locally available Middle-Eastern videotapes. He did not allow us to use his collection of dance tapes as study materials, and we saw them briefly and only rarely, at special dance workshops. The lack of access to Middle-Eastern culture was confining. Worse were the orientalized quality to his choreography and his broad hints of the dance's roots in ancient Egypt (for both the solo belly dance and for the folkloric group numbers). This somewhat skewed aesthetic, promoted as deep understanding, was constructed and invented. My training was no better and no worse, however, than the average training for the many Toronto-area women who have embraced this dance form from the early 1970s to the present.

In the school, the students were almost all Canadians of European extraction. We learned both belly dance and folkloric group pieces (that nevertheless incorporated mostly the same belly dance movements) that we performed in school events, and at multicultural festivals, entertainments in hospitals and old age homes and the occasional Middle-Eastern wedding. For the folkloric numbers we dressed in voluminous brightly coloured costumes of vaguely Middle-Eastern appearance, embellished with much glitter, sequins, and loose flying scarves. Almost never were the costumes designed with a

---

[1] In this essay the term carries the connotations developed in Edward Said's *Orientalism* (1978). For another discussion of the term and its derivatives see Boehlke-Muc Votruba (1994: 65 note 1).

particular Middle-Eastern country or region in mind. My teacher's choreography, set on us in class, relied heavily on props such as jars, swords, canes, baskets and tambourines as the identifying feature of the dance. These dances, presented to us as authentic folk dances, actually went through a regular cycle, the individual dance reappearing in the school after about eighteen months, recast slightly to a different Middle-Eastern music piece. The jar dance took us to the well and back; the basket dance took us out and about and round and round; the scarf dance saw us waving coloured ribbons happily; the cane dance had us stepping to beats from Upper Egypt; the straw tray dance led us to the fields to gather vegetables. With swords and boots we became Bedouin women (later called the Ghawazee dance) – fierce and warlike.[2] The dances, never located precisely in time or space, were vaguely "from over there." We, of course, never questioned their authenticity.

School programmes freely made use of orientalist images such as those identified by Buck. Programme covers liberally depicted small drawings of camels, palm trees, sand dunes, and oases with pools. Photos of my teacher in the programme always showed him in flowing Arabic-style robes and headdress. A programme from 1981, for an evening entitled "El Hareem," featured an orientalist nineteenth-century painting on the cover, a reclining woman attended by a black servant. This programme evoked stereotypical images of the East, stating: "It is an ancient tradition among Moslem peoples that the wives and concubines of the Pasha should live in utmost seclusion and privacy. This female world of the harem is therefore a place of high passion, as the women vie for the attention of the Pasha – each one by her beauty and charm seeking to become his favourite.... Exotic, centuries-old customs, which are deeply woven into the fabric of Middle-Eastern life, each has a place in the expression of the dance" (Manneh 1981). While much of the public explanation of our dancing always embarrassed me, I had maintained the hope of a core of authenticity in the choreography. I was unaware then of the need for both form and meaning to be congruent.

Besides the element of orientalism, Buck made a second major discovery at Rakassah, the element of myth, although this finding is implied rather than stated directly. She states that the women at Rakassah made liberal use of mythical characters such as Eve, Cleopatra, Circe and Salomé to explore alternative images of the feminine. Performers also incorporated images corresponding to "enchantress, priestess, siren and muse" (1991: 29). This Rakassah finding has its Toronto counterpart in the school dance manual; one can see here, in print, symbols only inferred in class. Implied was a direct link of present dance practice with ancient Egypt. "Belly dancing has always been a functional dance in all the temples as, whenever you communicate with God, you express your thoughts and ideas with your hands and body. For example, there are rock engravings of ritual fertility dances in most of the museums around the world. As centuries passed, Belly Dancing developed and gained in

---

[2] The female Ghawazee dancers of Upper Egypt have been well researched in the past twenty-five years. They do not dance with swords and wear boots, and their style is not "fierce and warlike."

popularity, appearing in Egyptian tomb paintings as early as 5000 B.C."
(Manneh undated: 3). An elaborate 1988 programme for school presentations
at Carassauga and Carabram showed line drawings of the Egyptian temple of
Karnak, illustrations of pharaonic Egyptian eye makeup, ancient palettes on
which malachite was ground for the eye paste, and a pyramid.[3] The inclusion
of "pharaonic" dances and pantomines in the repertoire always suggested
arcane knowledge on the part of my teacher, supposedly based on his careful
research of ancient dance forms.

The concept of the antiquity of belly dance, and its direct link with women's
public sacred ritual (acknowledged to become individualized, private and
secular in more modern eras) is echoed in most North American dance
manuals and popular publications on belly dance. Serena Wilson, since the
1960s an influential New York dancer and teacher, wrote the first major North
American belly dance manual. Her remarks on the origins of belly dance
represent much of the comments in subsequent books and dance manuals up
to the present. "Is it possible that the first dance ever done by a woman was the
belly dance? If we could peer back through the haze of time and secretly watch
our cave sister, what kind of a dance do you think she would be doing? The
belly dance, of course" (1972: 9). "Belly dancing has always been a *functional*
dance. By this I mean that it has always had a practical *reason to be*. It was
used in fertility rites, and was the first exercise regimen for natural childbirth.
It has been used to make women more attractive sexually, and has been
awarded a role in sex education" (1972: 5).

Recent Canadian thought on the belly dance is no different. In a serious
document on world dance for the Canadian Museum of Civilization in Ottawa,
Carmelle Bégin and Pierre Crépeau include a two-page section featuring
Dahlia Obadia, a Toronto teacher and former performer. Here Bégin and
Crépeau write that "To those with only a casual knowledge of Arab dance
tradition, the term *baladi* is usually considered synonymous with belly
dancing but that art is only one aspect of the complex and subtle
choreographic tradition of the Middle East. When the pharaohs reigned, Egypt
already had a vast array of ritual dance in honour of Hathor, goddess of love,
joy and music. Located on the southern route of Gypsy migrations, Egypt also
adopted certain elements of the sacred dances Gypsies brought with them
from India" (1989: 24). This passage does little to explain and actually
mystifies Obadia's art. This is unfortunate since Obadia has an impeccable
understanding of the dance roots of Egypt and of her native Morocco. The
CBC's "Ladeez and Gentlemen: The Belly Dancer and the Cowboy," in the
prestigious *Ideas* series, regurgitated the same mythical materials, reinforced
by the views of various authorities in the belly dance field (1991). At the 1993
fringe Festival of Independent Dance Artists in Toronto (fFIDA), a local belly
dancer participating in the festival advertised her classes with "Belly dance is

---

[3] Caravan, Toronto's annual multicultural festival, became Carassauga and Carabram as adopted in Mississauga
and Brampton, Ontario.

one of the world's oldest dances. It was originally a fertility rite and birth mime" (Ilana 1993). Is it any wonder that the average amateur dance student believes sincerely that she is reenacting some legitimate approach to the feminine divine, that she considers belly dance inherently sacred?

Against this North American framework of orientalism and myth, what are the meanings given by Egyptians to belly dance in all its professional performance manifestations? My thesis fieldwork consisted of interviews with Egyptian Canadians, living in Toronto but born in Egypt, using the film elicitation technique to explore the paramenters of belly dance and its aesthetic considerations.[4] It was not difficult to achieve a consensus on the modern belly dance in Egypt, for taken as a whole respondents' remarks had a remarkable consistency. From their remarks I isolated fourteen elements to create an aesthetic for the professional Egyptian belly dance performance.[5] The articulated standards encompass not only the visible parameters of the dance (the form) but also, and more importantly, the qualities of the dance performance (the meaning). I found that form can be more or less transplanted; meaning is complex and embedded in a culture. Unlike the many North Americans writing with certitude, all Egyptians interviewed confessed they had no positive idea about the dance's origins; their best guess was that the dance was transported into Egypt from Turkey with the Ottoman conquerors (sixteenth century) and refined in Egypt, blended with local dance styles. There was never a mention of ancient sacred ritual nor of priestesses.

For Egyptians, the elements that give meaning to belly dance lie in four main areas: the entertainment quality of the dance; society's ranking of the arts in general, and of the dancer; and the contexts in which the dance takes place. The purpose and function of the belly dance as entertainment was clearly stated – to bring joy and happiness and evoke in Egyptians an Egyptian experience. Emotional pleasure given by the performance is most important, as important as dancing correctly. The subtle qualities of dancing "Egyptian" and the eroticism desired in belly dancing provide layers of complex meanings to any excellent performances. The dancer is expected to express "Egyptianness," that is her dance should be subtle, gentle, innovative and possess *dala*, the quality of an Egyptian coquette. Charm and liveliness of face contributed to perceived Egyptianness. Respondents saw the sexual nature of the dance as eroticism, and actual words they chose to describe this quality were *dala*, coquetry and sensuality. There exists for Egyptian Canadians a hierarchy of the arts in general, with belly dance having a legitimate, if lowly, place within this hierarchy, clearly separated from the esteemed arts like music. (Folk dance has a somewhat more respectable reputation.) Since belly dance is not

---

[4] This technique uses filmed and videographed dance materials to stimulate critical reactions from respondents. I used videotapes of performances by four Egyptian belly dancers widely acknowledged as stars (Nagwa Fouad, Sohair Zaki, Fifi Abdou and Samia Gamal). I excluded dancers on the wedding and festival circuits. See Nieuwkerk (1998) for this topic.

[5] My research findings and details on the constructed aesthetic can be found in my thesis (Fraser 1991). It was assumed that the opinions of Egyptian Canadians born in Egypt would correspond closely with opinions of Egyptians living in Egypt.

honoured, even its stars cannot perform in locations reserved for the arts, such as the Cairo Opera stage. Thus Egyptian Canadians can express their love for this dance while saying they respect it little.

Generally the belly dancer fares worse than the dance, stigmatized for her assumed immorality, the use of her female body to create the art form, her typically lower-class origins, and the often dubious contexts of her perform- ance. With hundreds of dancers in Egypt only three or four can belong to the elite, the wealthy stars who command huge salaries and hence some pseudo- respectability. All respondents were able to tell me about this acknowledged ranking system of dancers into first, second and third class performers. The latter work in the poorer cabarets and the tourist haunts near the pyramids, and they are, according to one source, only "moving bodies," with the implication that they are no better than prostitutes. Male respondents suggested that men go alone to the small clubs in Egypt, the less-elegant places of entertainment, and that dancers then often pay particular attention to obviously well-to-do patrons. Male respondents also said that men may go to a show with a "line-up of flesh," expecting to go off later in the evening with one of the dancers (Fraser 1991: 88).

There is, thus, a seedy side to this art form that cannot be denied, and, considering that the stars and high-class performances comprise only a small proportion of the total, this element is significant. The noted Lebanese American publisher, teacher and scholar, the late Ibrahim Farrah, had no difficulty valuing all aspects of contemporary performance. He wrote, "when visiting Egypt's *original* Sahara City Nightclub (considered a low-class locale) ... I saw some contemporary dancers who included in their performance the older *beledi* styles. Indeed, the artist who utilizes some of the more traditional styles and the *zar*/dervish entertainers were always my programme favorites – and my compulsive reason to frequent this not so chic, but fondly remembered, haunt" (Sept./Oct. 1993: 6). I had gone out to explore the best of Egyptian belly dance, but respondents made me aware of its underbelly, leading me to understand that belly dance is still locked into certain existing male/female power relations, as was ballet in the nineteenth century. While some involved in the dance, such as Farrah, can accept the dance as it is, others cannot. It is my contention that this aspect of the dance's meaning has led many North American practitioners, seeking self-actualized alternative images of the female self through the belly dance, to reject the dance's sexist connotations and to supply alternate meanings more in line with modern feminism. It is here that the element of myth has proved irresistible.

Changing the meaning of the dance when the meaning proves unpalatable plays a major role in the novel *The Great American Belly Dance* (Gioseffi 1977). Here, the heroine, Dorissa, takes up belly dance after her divorce, finding the dance inspirational and totally absorbing. Studying in New York with a teacher from the Middle East, Aneera Ohanian, Dorissa goes to a nightclub to see her first authentic belly dance performance.

"Aneera's my teacher. I study at her studio," Dorissa said proudly.... The man started to say something, but just then Aneera, with a silver-fringed and red-sequined costume, wrapped in a red veil of sheer material, entered. She circled around the small dance floor a few times, clicking her cymbals and moving rapidly. Then, as the music slowed to a sensuous tempo, she began to remove the red veil that covered her.... Dorissa noticed that she wore heavy eyelashes, bright rouge, and lipstick. Her breasts were pushed up high and together by a red, sequined bra, which drooped beaded tassles from its tips. She looked hard and slick in a way she never looked in class. Going around to the men sitting at the edges of the dance floor, she shook her breasts in their faces or bumped her hips toward their shoulders.

When Aneera came to Dorissa's table and shook her breasts in front of the dark-haired man, he smiled and put a dollar bill in her cleavage. Dorissa, now high on ouzo, felt a sudden fury welling within. She leaped up, snatched the money from the dancer's bosom, and threw it down on the table. Grabbing a dollar from her own purse, she pushed it in Aneera's hand. "What's the matter?" asked the surprised Aneera, recognizing Dorissa as her student. "This dance is a sacred ritual to the Earth Mother goddess, not a cheap burlesque," Dorissa growled to her random companion (24-26).

A complete novice, and a stranger to the culture from which the dance has sprung, Dorissa has recreated the belly dance in another image. While one might dismiss Dorissa as a fruitcake, Gioseffi is an established writer, belly dancer and teacher. How could this line of reasoning, this reference to myth, come about?[6]

Feminist anthropologists of the 1970s had high hopes for the field with the introduction of the variable of gender into anthropological theories. In *Gender at the Crossroads of Knowledge*, editor Michaela di Leonardo writes that in the early 1970s North American feminist writers were examining mid-Victorian evolutionary ideas concerning male rule over women (1991: 8). One article that she cites as seminal to ten years of feminist thought, Paula Webster's "Matriarchy: A Vision of Power" in *Toward an Anthropology of Women*, is useful as a possible explanation for belly dance's recent mythical claims. Webster begins with the conundrum that, "Women in the movement were asking why women had never been politically powerful, why men had always had higher status and why a matriarchy was impossible" (1975: 141). She reexamines the work of Johann Jakob Bachofen, the mid-nineteenth-century theorist who had studied ancient myths and had concluded that in ancient times women held real social and political power over men. This matriarchy, according to Bachofen, ruled through power of the mother, and followed a religion with supreme female divinities and a stress on fecundity rites. Men eventually rebelled, to establish a patriarchy. This new power structure, according to Bachofen, proved his theory, the primitive evolving into the proper order of the world, with men in charge (Bachofen in Webster

---

[6] It would be gratifying to take this extravagant novel as a satire on the belly dance movement's excesses, but in "Ladeez and Gentlemen" Gioseffi demonstrates that she is to be taken literally on her meaning for the dance (1991).

1975: 143). Webster argues that by the standards of modern research Bachofen does not provide suitable empirical evidence for his theories. She concludes rather sadly that, although matrilineages did and do exist, there are no grounds for a prehistoric matriarchy, that is real female power. Unlike many feminist scholars, for example Webster and di Leonardo, who have examined and then discarded mid-nineteenth-century thinking about mythical pre-history, contemporary writers on the belly dance continue with ideas made popular at the time of Bachofen and seemingly revived in the 1960s with a translation of his works (Manheim 1967). Under the impression that concepts such as goddess rule, fertility rites and sacred dances to the feminine principle are past realities to be reinstated as empowering aspects of the modern women's movement, they are recycling nineteenth-century weirdness.

Di Leonardo writes that, "the early 1970s were years of closely linked scholarly and political ferment in the United States," and in this ferment she includes the women's movement (1991: 2). At that time, both popular culture and feminist anthropology were eager to absorb any insights of scholarship on the question of ancient matriarchy. Professional archaeologists, however, did not take up the early feminist questions addressed to their field, leaving writers of popular culture alone to continue their speculations in this area. Di Leonardo identifies an influential early work of popular culture, *First Sex* by Elizabeth Gould Davis, published in the United States in 1971. This utopian book calls for a return to a goddess worship, the coming of a time when female energy will return the earth to peaceful and more moral rule.[7] In her examination of 3000 years of patriarchy and her review of the ultimate tragedy of the lives of all women, Davis does not discuss specific ceremonies of worship nor dance itself. Her basic philosophy, however, is identical to that underlying popular works on belly dance from the 1970s and 1980s and it is reasonable to suppose her work helped inspire this material. Unfortunately, rigorous and sustained dance scholarship on the traditions of the Middle East was then in its beginning stages; there was no adequate data at that time as a balance for these musings from popular writers. Di Leonardo notes that with the increasing specialization in feminist research and the development of radical feminism since the 1970s, the gap between scholarship and popular culture has grown even wider (1991: 8). Present popular writing and popular theory in the field of belly dance seem to show the results of this long non-communication.

Despite the physical fitness explosion of recent years, ordinary North American women are often profoundly limited at the level of kinesthetic bodily expression. Belly dance's continuing popularity, then, reveals women's desire for dance, for dances and for those that express them specifically as female. The nineteenth-century trappings of orientalism and myth heavily bias belly dance in North America from becoming a modern dance for modern women. In Toronto, however, previously referred to Dahlia Obadia some years ago began to question the performance standards of even the stars of Egyptian

---

[7] Davis lists the 1967 translation of Bachofen in her citations.

belly dance. For her the dance still is too feminine, and carries too much of the baggage of generations of performers. She is willing to take risks herself, to express herself as a strong woman. Inspired by the 1993 appearance of Egypt's folk dance Aswan Troupe at Toronto's Canadian National Exhibition, Obadia expressed a wish to create her dance on male dancers' well-defined rhythms. Obadia felt that she could have it all – traditional Jewish-Moroccan, Arabic, Egyptian and modern woman. Keeping some of the core meanings of the traditional dance, she would discard others. She appreciates the mixed Canadian and Middle-Eastern audiences here in Toronto who, she says, are willing to work at understanding dance, for she incorporates a seriousness into her choreography (19 Nov. 1993). This type of building on existing tradition seems promising for the future of all belly dance's practitioners. Unfortunately, Obadia has never mounted a major production using her new values.

Belly dance's unsuccessful attempt to approach the sacred nevertheless points out yet another apparent inherent need in modern North American women. In this area, interesting Toronto experiments are making the sacred danceable and the danceable sacred. Alexandra Caverly-Lowery, dancer and dance scholar, works within the Christian context to create her scripture-based choreography, often for performance in church. At the Winchester Street Theatre in Toronto in September 1993, choreographers Patricia Beatty, Terrill Maguire and Linda Rabin, composer Ann Southam and artist Aiko Suzuki presented an evening entitled "Dancing the Goddess" (Citron 1993: 40). Using Jungian ideas of archetypes, and presented as ritual theatre, the choreographies were based on expressing the feminine principle as divine. In their explorations of the sacred and the dance, Caverly-Lowery, as well as Beatty and her colleagues, are making legitimate statements about these important issues that belly dance cannot make. While it is possible for the meanings surrounding belly dance to change, such a major new use of the dance means that the dance is no longer the same dance, as defined by the present culture from which it comes. Then we can no longer really call it "belly dance." The sole possibility seems to keep belly dance as it is, with the meanings it has legitimately, that is dazzling entertainment, joy, humour, legitimate sexuality, Middle-Eastern connotations and often sleaze and vulgar show. From this base creative artists will allow it to grow, change and flower as it will. Unlike the dances of Caverly-Lowery and others, belly dance does not seem to lend itself to visions of possible futures. For that we need new dances altogether. One thing seems clear from this discussion of modern belly dancing – we need new paradigms for women's dances.

Author's Postscript

Belly dance critics concern themselves with its future not only for Toronto. In my thesis, where I discuss issues of innovations and changes in modern belly dance in Egypt, an Egyptian Canadian woman lamented that while changes do occur, this is not the issue; no one in Egypt tries to make belly dance "better, a liberal art, pure." Another said: "Dancing is not improving; it

Yasmina Ramzy.

has its highs and lows but there's no development of the artists" (Fraser 1991: 104). That nothing important overall was happening to the dance obviously caused them much distress. For belly dance, being static, then, may be just as detrimental as going off in strange directions.

Since I first wrote this article in 1994, singlehandedly Yasmina Ramzy, Toronto dancer, teacher, impresario and choreographer, has persuaded me to change my gloomy overview of developmental changes in belly dance. Her last four major productions have managed to maintain its legitimate meanings yet enhance it with "visions of possible futures."[8] I see four areas in which her choreographic experiments are paying off: fusion, reconstruction, modern authenticity and exploration of myths. The following are some of her recent solo and troupe works.

For "Didi" (*Call of the Nile*), Ramzy sought modern dance's Lisa Sandlos to co-choreograph a contemporary Algerian song with too many Western elements to interpret successfully with a belly dance vocabulary alone. The result was a zany troupe piece crackling with "world beat" qualities. In "Five" (*In Search of the Almeh*), Ramzy and Sashar Zarif placed their two dance traditions side-by-side to music commissioned from Ron Allen. From the poles of Egypt/Azerbaijan and female/male they danced a serious analysis of similarities and differences.

The late, great, Egyptian singer Oum Kulthoum inspired Ramzy's "Huwwa Salih" (*Descent of Ishtar*), performed live with a Middle-Eastern orchestra. It was not billed as reconstruction. Nevertheless as choreographer and soloist, Ramzy fused her dancing with instruments, song and poetry (including George Sawa's able translation provided in the programme notes) to reconnect profoundly with Egypt's great musical heritage of the recent past.

In the witty and sophisticated "Nakarat El-Tabla, or Attacks of the Drum" (*In Search of the Almeh*), Ramzy laid bare the fundamental role of the drum in

---

[8] *Call of the Nile* (Nov. 1996), *Aswan* (fringe Festival of Independent Dance Artists, Aug. 1997), *Descent of Ishtar* (Apr. 1998) and *In Search of the Almeh* (Apr. 1999).

432

Middle Eastern dance music. Through interacting movement and total use of the stage, her troupe visualized both the patterns of the drum's rhythms, and its colours – its three basic sounds of doum, tak and sakkah.

"The Descent of Ishtar" (*Descent of Ishtar*; remounted in *In Search of the Almeh*) used the motif of old myth to illustrate a modern search for the innermost self. Thirty minutes long, with nine separate parts, beautiful costuming, and set to commissioned music by Richard Ferren, this extraordinary theatrical piece is Ramzy's equivalent of Martha Graham's *Errand into the Maze*.

I am impressed; I am encouraged; I am happy.

References

A review was carried out of popular books on belly dance from 1975 until 1990, belly dance manuals produced in North America from 1972 until 1982, and the author's Toronto-based dance collection of newspaper clippings, programmes, school advertisements and flyers.

Ashworth, Marie. 1997. *Belly, You Say*. Videotape. Produced and directed by Marie Ashworth.

Bégin, Carmelle and Pierre Crépeau. 1989. *Dance! Roots, Ritual and Romance*. Ottawa: Canadian Museum of Civilization.

Boehlke-Muc Votruba, Gretchen. 1994. "Ruth St. Denis' Oriental Dances: Early Canadian Impressions." *Canadian Dance Studies* 1, 65-77.

Buck, Elizabeth. 1991. "Rakassah – An American Middle Eastern Dance Festival: Exoticism and Orientalism in the Twentieth Century." *UCLA Journal of Dance Ethnology* No. 15, 26-32.

Citron, Paula. Sept. 1993. "Gaea Consciousness: Dance and the Emerging Feminine Principle." *Dance Magazine*, 39-43.

Davis, Elizabeth Gould. 1971. *The First Sex*. New York: G. P. Putnam's Sons.

Di Leonardo, Michaela. 1991. "Introduction: Gender, Culture, and Political Economy." In Michaela di Leonardo, ed. *Gender at the Crossroads of Knowledge: Feminist Anthropology in the Postmodern Era*. Berkeley: University of California Press, 1-48.

Farrah, Ibrahim. Sept.-Oct. 1993. "A Matter of Study to Fill a Hundred Years." *Arabesque* 19: 3, 6-15.

Fraser, Kathleen. 1991. "The Aesthetics of Belly Dance: Egyptian-Canadians Discuss the *Baladi*." Master's thesis, York University.

Gioseffi, Daniela. 1977. *The Great American Belly Dance*. Garden City, New York: Doubleday & Doubleday.

Henni-Chebra, Djamila, and Christian Paché. 1996. *Les danses dans le monde arabe, ou, l'héritage des almées*. Paris: L'Harmattan.

Visions and Revisions

Ilana. 1993. "Belly Dance Classes with Ilana." Printed Flyer. Toronto.

"Ladeez and Gentlemen: The Belly Dancer and the Cowboy." *Ideas*. 26 Nov. and 3 Dec. 1991. Radio Programme. Canadian Broadcasting Corporation.

Manheim, Ralph, trans. 1967. *Myth, Religion and Mother Right: Selected Writings of Johann Jakob Bachofen*. Princeton: Princeton University Press.

Manneh, Eddy. Undated. "Notes on Oriental Belly Dancing." Toronto: Freddy's Dancing Academy.

Manneh, Eddy. 1981. "Eddy Manneh presents El Hareem." Programme Notes. Toronto: Freddy's Dancing Academy.

Mourat, Elizabeth Artemis. 1998. "The Myth of the Dance of the Seven Veils." Newsletter of the American Academy of Middle Eastern Dance.

Nieuwkerk, Karin Van. 1995. *A Trade Like Any Other: Female Singers and Dancers in Egypt*. Austin, Texas: University of Texas Press.

Shay, Anthony. 1999. *Choreophobia: Solo Improvised Dance in the Iranian World*. Costa Meza, California: Mazda Publishers.

Webster, Paula. 1975. "Matriarchy: A Vision of Power." In Rayna R. Reiter, ed. *Toward an Anthropology of Women*. New York: Monthly Review Press.

Wilson, Serena and Alan Wilson. 1972. *The Serena Technique of Belly Dancing*. New York: Drake Publishers Inc.

Interview

Obadia, Dahlia. 19 Nov. 1993.

The Rebel Goddess:
An Investigation of the Shift in Narrative in Indian Classical Dance

Sarala Dandekar

Amongst scholars of Indian dance, it is widely acknowledged that the push behind the reconstruction of classical dance in the twentieth century began as part of a nationalist movement for independence in India. The movement was supported by an elite class of Indian intellectuals, often educated in Britain, resisting the undemocratic domination by the British Raj. As an integral part of discarding the shackles of colonialism, the intellectual elite turned to India's rich ancient culture to construct and claim a national identity separate and autonomous from "the jewel in the crown," a term often used to describe India's place in the Empire.

India, as a unified geo-political construct, contrasts strongly with the mosaic of regional cultural clusters, each with its own language, religious practices and cultural identity. The national effort to revive regional traditional arts reflected both a rejection of colonial identity and the political need to accept the notion of a single "Indian" cultural identity. By the early decades of the twentieth century, however, the temple dance tradition now linked to shastric (classical) culture had suffered centuries of moral disapprobation. The *devadasis* (temple dancers) were first condemned by missionaries, then by colonial rulers and finally by the Indian government itself. It was important both socially and politically that the re-established "Indian classical dance" forms would equal in sophistication and purity, the "high art" of classical dance culture in other countries. "High art" as defined by Canadian philosopher Francis Sparshott, is representational of a country's official culture. As such, it requires the following qualities: it must be technically difficult to accomplish, exceptional in its aesthetic values, of high prestige and heritage value, and reflect that the country is "civilized enough to appreciate such gifts" (1995: 39). The scholars, patrons and government body (Sangeet Natak Akademi) responsible for officially classifying India's regional dance forms used the term "classical" to separate the dance from its less respectable temple antecedents. As Fredrique Marglin points out, the title Indian classical dance "connotes status on par with Western Classical Ballet" (1985: 2).

One luxury of reconstructed behaviour is the freedom to literally re-create the past. "Restored behavior offers to both individuals and to groups the chance to rebecome what they once were – or even ... to rebecome what they wish to have been" (Schechner 1985: 38). By reinstating dance as a respectable reflection of culture on the pristine setting of the secular stage, the art form became less of a reproduction of past dance rituals and more of an original, creative monument to the ancient traditions depicted in classical sculpture and text.

Indian classical dance as a reinvented representation of national culture creates a cultural unity that never existed geographically or politically until the subcontinent came under colonial rule. In addition, as a high art, Indian classical dance has allowed Indian communities throughout the world to prove that they are "civilized enough" to embrace, celebrate and protect the purity of classical dance performed on national and international stages. At the close of the twentieth century, India's forty plus years of Independence was marked by cultural performances around the world. Indian artists such as musician Zakir Hussein and the sculptor Anish Kapoor have become renowned for their individual artistic vision, independent of any classically "Indian" tradition or cultural community. Indian novelists writing in English have formed a strong part of the contemporary literary elite. Yet for the most part, Indian classical dance remains a taboo area for innovation or personal expression. Over the past several years, a few Indian classical dancers in Toronto presented work that marked a clear departure from the mythic classical narrative and stylized ideal dance persona endemic to the form. This new direction marks an important shift in the perception of Indian classical dance as a vehicle for preserving and presenting classical mythological themes and virtues to an appropriate medium for personal expression. In this essay, I focus on a recent example of these artistic ventures, a dance drama entitled *The Rebel Goddess*, which premiered at the Music Gallery, Toronto, on October 23, 1999, as a focal point for the inquiry into new narrative territories within the Indian classical dance idiom.

Shifting Borders: Indian Dance Community in Toronto

Indian classical dance in Toronto flourishes at the community level. The Indian population in Toronto is large enough to support numerous private dance schools (there are nine schools listed in the 1998 Dance Ontario Directory), and there are frequent community celebrations that provide opportunities for cultural performances by dance teachers and their students. But there is also a recognized place for Indian classical dance performance within the larger, professional dance community of Toronto. Outside of the specifically Indian communities, the nature of the Indian dance community is tenuous. It is composed predominantly of solo artists: one-person islands clumped together rather unwillingly under a vague, community umbrella convenient for categorization and funding purposes within the larger dance community. Although there is little antagonism among dancers, there is little visible support within the community. This relatively solitary stance among the dancers may be due, in part, to the high competition for funding and the fact that most of these Indian classical dancers are trained as soloists and are unaccustomed to collaborative work.

Local, provincial and national arts council grants have established the professional reputation of several Indian classical dancers who, modelling themselves on western dance structures, have their own "companies" and give yearly performances to premiere new works. These companies, as they exist, are made up of groups of student dancers, proficient but still under the wing of their dance *guru* (teacher). The company dancers may or may not get paid for their performances and do not receive a salary. They often have other professions or are attending colleges and/or universities. Student loyalties are strong and the company dancers do not, as a general rule, perform in other Indian classical productions. Frequently dance gurus will bring individual guest artists from India to perform featured roles in their productions and teach workshops in the company and dance school. These guests add to the prestige, amongst the Indian community, of one particular dance school or another.

The Indian dance community in Toronto can be divided into two "generations." The first generation of dancers immigrated to Canada between twenty to thirty years ago and were the first to introduce Indian classical dance to the Toronto dance scene. All of them established schools and teach dance to the children of the Indo-Canadian population as well as performing on a regular basis in dance venues such as Harbourfront and the Betty Oliphant Theatre. They tend to feature traditional repertoire rearranged for a group of students, or new choreography set to traditional music with traditional movement vocabularies. They model themselves on the classical precedent set in India to cultivate elite audiences, small devoted communities, who appreciate the "authenticity" and integrity of their classical performances.

Two of Toronto's first generation classical Indian dancers, Rina Singha and Menaka Thakkar.

Visions and Revisions

The second generation of Indian classical dancers may or may not have been born in India or the Asian subcontinent. Most of them have been raised in Canada, Europe or the United States. They consider themselves firmly multicultural, very much a part of, and at times torn between, the ephemeral world of classical Indian dance and the more immediate global trends. Few of them have established formal schools, although several conduct classes at various studios in the downtown area. They tend to work along similar lines to the independent modern dancers in Toronto. They often freelance for the first generation of dancers as guest artists in their annual productions as well as presenting their own performances, generally in smaller venues such as the Winchester Street Theatre, the Music Gallery and other experimental spaces for showcasing new choreography or work-in-progress. In addition, there is much more ongoing collaborative work done between the second generation of Indian classical dancers. Group projects among these second generation dancers do not carry the same territorial loyalties as do the "company" productions and often dancers and dance students are borrowed from one of the first generation dancer's schools or companies.

When one examines the experimental choreography presented by classically trained Indian dancers in Toronto, the first and second generation dancers seem to deviate from one another quite clearly. Although it must be stressed here, however, that the emphasis on preserving the integrity of the classical repertoire is equally shared by both generations. The difference between these two generations is remarkable and useful when examining the shift in performance narrative from the mythic ideal of Indian high art to the more intimate, quixotic revelations which I will call the Personal.

Among the first generation of Indian classical dancers, experimentation has generally taken two paths: the reinterpretation and restaging of traditional "classical" themes or stories that are well known to Indian communities; or, collaboration with Canadian dancers from other styles (ballet, flamenco, African and Afro-Caribbean, modern). The latter pieces generally deal with themes of cultural exploration: two cultures/dancers meet at a crossroad, bump into one another at merging ceremonial grounds or in more abstract pieces, seek commonality between movement vocabularies as the dancers enter a staged variation of the New World melting pot. Within these collaborations, the Indian dancer rarely steps out of the traditional movement vocabulary, musical constructs, or traditional costume/identity of the Indian classical dance *ideal*. Their dance personae, carefully constructed images cultivated by traditional training, remain intact regardless of the other dancing bodies on the stage. Perhaps the dancers are enacting their own professional history within these pieces: carrying the Indian classical dance form and performance mystique, inflexible and unchanging, into "new worlds."

The second generation has also performed its share of danced cross-cultural encounters, marked at times with somewhat bolder choreography – actual physical contact between the dancers and more adventurous attempts to master choreography and movement from other dance languages. To continue the parallel with professional history, these dancers entered the Toronto scene a good ten years or more after the first classical dancers primed Canadian dance culture for the inclusion of Indian classical dance. Still, the second generation is careful to protect their reputation as classicists even as they embark on experimentation. Along a more interesting vein, the second generation seems to be developing a new form of experimentation that involves an active rewriting of the narrative content of traditional dance themes.

Both generations are careful to present a balanced programme of traditional repertoire and new work. Even at the risk of extending a programme to three hours in length, it seems necessary to present one's ability to execute both the classical and the experimental. This decision is probably influenced most strongly by two factors: the dancer's relative ease and comfort level in presenting traditional work, which rests on decades of vigorous training and the unquestionably high quality of choreography and musical accompaniment; and the taste of the audiences. Audiences attending these programmes are made up of a mixed collection of purists, who may or may not have children training in one of the various dance schools, and supporters of the larger dance community, involved either as performers, educators or funding administrators. The audience's inclinations, expectations and reactions may not always fall into clear cut party divisions, but by presenting both sides of the artistic coin, the dancer has the potential to include and please at least half the audience half of the time.

In the collaborative, experimental work created by the first generation, the illusory and ideal role of the dancer never waivers, although she may be set in a radically different stage context. Within some of the newer choreographic work of the second generation, the dancer challenges the deepest of stylistic expectations, emerging on stage separate and apart from her traditionally performed identity. This has proven to be a provocative and controversial new step. Unlike the interesting juxtaposition of Indian and African dance ritual or the pleasing virtuosity of "competing" Kathak and Flamenco footwork, these new theatrical dance pieces challenge the cultural ideals, gender roles and aesthetic limitations of classical Indian dance narrative within the language and voice of the dance technique itself. Within these experimental works, the personal narrative disrupts the anticipated, spiritually encoded "mythic narrative" of Indian classical dance: the mask is allowed to slip and the spell is broken.

Mythic Narrative

In order to better understand the impact of integrating personal expression within the classical Indian dance framework, it is useful to examine the traditional "frames" necessary in rendering such performances successful. Helena Wulff discusses the frames of performance in her approach to analyzing classical ballet in the twentieth century (1998:105). These frames, which include expected performed behaviour, also describe the elaborate costumes, set designs, lighting, orchestra and audience behaviour that create the drama in its entirety, of an evening at the ballet. She describes the various risks of performance, including a falling set, miscued curtain or light call, and most upsetting of all, the on stage dance injury. Any of these events shatter the performance frames and remind the audience that the fantastic construct of the ballet is not "real." Indian classical dance does not rely upon comparable lavish sets, nor the cooperation of large stage or technical crews. For the most part, the performance relies upon one dancer and four of five musicians to conduct the audience away from the mundane towards a very precise, spiritually inspired world of myth in which the individual seeks and eventually gains communion with the divine. The primary frame in Indian classical dance is the remote, otherworldly performance mystique of The Dancer.

Traditionally, Indian "classical" dances, as opposed to folk dances which are still performed with lavish sets and costuming, were performed for select audiences. Either in the temples or the palace courts, the dance was exclusive spectacle. When the dance forms ascended the national and international stages as high art, the dance scholars, gurus and dancers themselves resisted public consumption, maintaining and controlling how the dance should be perceived and by whom. In keeping with the formal, dignified presentation and spiritual undertones of the narrative, the audience should be both privileged and knowledgeable so as to appreciate the subtle rendering of expressive or abstract movement. Like a painting in a museum, the spectators must educate themselves to gain access to the art. The training is incredibly controlled, with a strong emphasis on a student's devotion to the guru and unquestioning deferral to his authority. The guru shapes the dance persona that the dance student is to assume, to various degrees, within any formal public sphere. For many of the great dancers of past decades, their lives on and off stage, become an ongoing, performed tribute to the guru.

In all of the classical choreography, the individual dancer must, to some extent, submit her own being to the training imposed upon her, she must perform the role of The Dancer. Backstage, the dancers develop personal routines around the physical transformation in the dressing room in order to cultivate a parallel mental process of transformation. Ellora Patnaik, a Toronto based Odissi dancer, explains "putting on the costume is like entering a different body" (Dandekar 1998). Many dancers described the passage from dressing room to stage space as being comparable to entering another world. But, by its very nature performance is not completely transformative. Every performer is in a position or role of "double agency" a state in which they both are and are not the role being performed (Hastrup 1998: 39). In other words, the performer is still in control and aware of the performance of a different identity. (Trance dancing is an example in which the dancer becomes entirely possessed by another identity, but these dances are clearly delineated from any kind of performance.)

In many Indian classical dance narratives, the dancer is in a state of triple agency. At one level she is performing the role of The Dancer from the moment she steps on stage; simultaneously, within any one theatrical dance piece she

Ellora Patnaik.

will change from one character to the next, portraying each through the constant, underlying guise of The Dancer. Finally, hidden from the audience completely, the true performer is monitoring the secondary frames of performance, aware of any piece of jewellery threatening to fly off, mistakes by the musicians and any other obstacle or risk to be negotiated without drawing undue attention away from the performance. Revelation of the person controlling the performance, beneath and within The Dancer, is considered a critical flaw, or disruption of the frame in classical performance. One knowledgeable dance director, upon leaving a programme commented, "Half way through the piece she stopped being Radha [a mythological figure who was the human consort of Krishna] and became a woman with whom I've complained about our children" (Dandekar 1998). The mystique of the performance and the sanctity of the moment was invaded by a moment of realism, a mannerism that struck this audience member as too natural, too reminiscent of the daily persona of the dancer and by doing so, it broke the spell.

Some of the second generation dancers are challenging the need to preserve this spell in performance and rebelling against the idea that the trained dance persona is an obligatory part of their devotion to the dance form, guru and system of performance. This work deliberately crosses boundaries, visual and aural cues, and frames that reassure the audience that the work is within the expected, comfortable realm of tradition. Interestingly, the dancers working in this area of artistic experimentation are firm classicists and assert that experimentation will never replace the beauty and authority of traditional art forms. But, the authority of tradition is not the only valid artistic narrative. It is quite obvious that the ideals of traditionally engendered virtues and classical narrative are not harmonious with the lives and identities of these young, North American artists. That some of these artists have chosen to focus upon the chasm between art and reality within the realm of classical technique presents a new and interesting deviation from the experimental ventures seen in Toronto thus far.

The Rebel Goddess: Personal Narrative and the Classical Framework

The Rebel Goddess, conceived by Bageshree Vaze and created by a cast of five dancers and composer Ernie Tollar, was presented at the Music Gallery, Toronto, on October 23 and 24, 1999. The piece focuses on the crisis precipitated by a creative spirit trapped within the constrictive rules of society. The main character is split into the seeker (the internal "unperformed" self of the dancer, struggling to reconcile taught behaviours with her desire for self expression) and as her foil, the goddess (the product of the seeker's imaginative collapse of her own individual ideals of beauty, perfection and control) played by two separate dancers. Between these two personas, the artist attempts to reconcile various cultural and social ideals of femininity and performance with her own conflicting desires. The artist attempts to please and conform to various cultural pressures yet at the same time honour her subversive urge to flip the power structure and take control of the creative process (to be, in her eyes, the goddess). The role of the rebel, or seeker, brings the personal narrative into the foreground of the dance drama. The other dancers are cast into the roles of caricatures or stereotypes portraying the limitations and rigidly controlled boundaries of trained identity either by cultural or social training, whose aims are to dominate the seeker's creative impulses.

The piece begins with a stylized depiction of a traditional dance class. The female dance student is dressed in a traditional sari. She enters the stage space and bows to another dancer, posed as the goddess Saraswati (goddess of art and culture), who is standing on a raised platform. Then, at the behest of her dance guru, she bows to the figure of Lord Siva, dancing in a ring of fire, before bowing to the guru and beginning class. The goddess figure, alive in the dancer's mind as the ideal of beauty, power and feminity, engages the seeker in non-verbal dialogue through hand and eye gestures and facial expressions that blend the stylized *hasta abhinaya* (communication through stylized sign language and physical expression) of Indian classical dance with more casual, realistic expressions that come naturally to the dancer. The scene challenges the ideal within Indian classical dance based on the Hindu tradition of learning and passing on of knowledge through complete, unquestioning obedience on the part of the dance student. Every time the student is inspired by her own joy of dance to deviate from the repetitive dance exercises, the goddess on the platform approves and encourages her, while the guru goes into pantomimed explosions of temper. While the goddess and dance student have naturalistic dialogue (the confused seeker looking for guidance, the serene goddess reassuring her to follow her heart), the dance guru uses exaggerated, farcical gestures relegating his character into the single-dimensional role of an inflexible, unreasonable dictator.

In the next scene, the rebel-seeker has, with the prompting of the goddess, left her guru. Deviating from the path of dutiful devotee, she wanders into her next phase (the goddess remains on stage throughout the piece but is active or "present" only when the seeker is on stage). A male modern dancer performs a

Bageshree Vaze.

moody solo and the seeker re-enters, now dressed in a *salwar kamee* (the informal daily dress of many young women in India). The two dancers engage in a dance dialogue, deliberately incorporating "unrehearsed" devices, stopping at unexpected moments to simply stand and stare – either to "learn" a new dance movement or to suggest resistance towards the dancing of the other. The dancers present a performed studio session, re-enacting the creative process on stage. The feigned unpolished nature of the duet breaks the "performative" nature of the second scene and contrasts with the carefully plotted dance exercises from the first scene. By the climax of the encounter, the dancers are engaged in a power struggle, each trying to assert control over the other through dance technique. The seeker is shocked to confirm with the goddess that she has once again found herself dominated by a male figure, and she departs in frustration.

In the third scene the seeker dances with a male hip-hop dancer. She is now dressed in jeans and a black tank top, her hair is down and she hardly resembles the "typical" Indian classical dancer from the first scene. Nor does she use a great deal of Indian dance vocabulary in this scene. After "learning" a few sequences from the hip-hop dancer, which they perform together, the seeker attempts to teach the hip-hop dancer her own movements, which he ignores. The dancers interact on a physical level that is never seen in classical Indian dance performances: when she tries to break away from his movement sequence, she is picked up and flipped over by the hip-hop dancer. Ultimately, prompted by yet another failed creative interaction, the seeker engages in an indulgent dream sequence in which she and the goddess merge on the platform and all three men come to worship her. At this point, the goddess comes down from the pedestal to confront the seeker. The dancer and her alter-ego face each other downstage centre, only metres away from the audience: a girl in jeans and a black tank top and a woman in a silk sari, adorned in full classical ornamentation, and they talk.

443

Visions and Revisions

There is virtually no spoken narrative tradition in Indian classical dance. The narrative in dance choreographies that depict mythologies or stories is always communicated through poetry sung by the musicians. If an artist chooses to enlighten the audience with a presentation of the story beforehand, it is done as performance and within the performed role of the dancer, using stylized spoken language and accompanied by appropriate hand gestures and facial expressions. Thus for an experienced audience, this scene in which the dancers speak lines on par with a teenager's phone conversation with her mother, in North American accents and colloquial language, is startling. If the rebel seeker was slowly shedding her Indian classical dance persona (as indicated through costume changes), at this moment of staged dialogue the "performance" identity of both the rebel, in her jeans and tank top, and the goddess in full classical dress, is torn away completely.

As *The Rebel Goddess* concludes, the dancer is told to find her own path, neither to conform to the male power structure of her training, nor the expectations of her social settings, nor her own fantasized ideal of the goddess. There is a reprisal of the various dance duets with the guru, modern dancer and hip-hop dancer and then the seeker spins off into a "victorious" solo in classical Indian dance vocabulary (Kathak style dance). In reality, the victory is less clear cut. The first half of the programme is a traditional demonstration of classical repertoire: *The Rebel Goddess* is presented after the intermission, inadvertently leaving purists the opportunity to leave after the first half. The lengthy and extensive programme notes, not only about the piece itself but the personal motivating factors behind its conception, indicate an uneasiness with the presentation of such material, a need to clarify and explain the motives and the experimental content to the audience. Vaze concedes that, unlike the character in her drama who is ultimately validated by reinventing herself in her own image, Indian classical dancers in Toronto base their reputations on their classical repertoire as witnessed by critical, knowledgeable audiences. That is, they are validated by the very idealized persona of classical dance that Vaze's seeker was rebelling against.

It is, therefore, unclear if Vaze's project has really succeeded in providing a more realistic subtext for classical dance. She has, however, created an alternate text, based on her own "true" performance self and not the dignified, spiritual, remote Dancer created by a lifetime of cumulative training. She relies on various dance styles and vocabularies, a sporadically confused medley of North Indian, South Indian and jazz musical traditions and dissonant costuming to break the codes of the classical framework and express her individual artistic voice. Can this work, then, be considered classical? Can the artist as the seeker in the finale gain both the blessings of the guru and the goddess, attaining a balance between classical training and the personal inspiration? Vaze believes this is possible: "We go there [toward experimentation] because we can, because we have proven we excel in the traditional and are willing to take the risk of going further. Maybe it is not the right direction and maybe it will fail, but to simply repeat what we have been taught is to risk puppeting what was once a creative form."

The idea of using narrative and performed identity to broaden the scope of Indian classical dance is an exciting step and perhaps one that can only be taken in the particular conditions a city like Toronto offers: a flourishing Indian dance community at a geographically comforting arm's length from the dancers' gurus. The combination creates a space that literally allows the dancers freedom to take artistic responsibility, not only for the classical dance forms for which they have been given custody but also for new growth and development from an individual perspective. So long as the two responsibilities are not confused, these projects seem to have the support of the Toronto dance community and audiences. And, although not yet fully developed to its potential, projects such as *The Rebel Goddess* open the door for new experimental work that will, through the contemporary vision of the classical artist, stand or fail on its own merit.

References

Dandekar, Sarala. 1998. "Dance Carved in Stone: An Investigation of the Contemporary Presentation of Odissi Dance." Master's thesis, York University.

Hastrup, Kirstin. 1998. "Theatre as a Site of Passage: Some Reflections on the Magic of Acting". In F. Hughes-Freeland, ed. *Ritual, Performance, Media*. London: Routledge.

Marglin, Fredrique A. 1985. *Wives of the God King: The Ritual of the Devadasis of Puri*. New Delhi: Oxford University Press.

Schechner, Richard. 1985. *Between Theatre and Anthropology*. Philadelphia: The University of Pennsylvania Press.

Sparshott, Francis. 1995. *A Measured Pace: Toward a Philosophical Understanding of the Arts of Dance*. Toronto: University of Toronto Press.

Vaze, Bageshree. 1999. *The Rebel Goddess* Programme.

Wulff, Helena. 1998. "Perspectives toward Ballet Performance: Exploring, Repairing and Maintaining Frames." In F. Hughes-Freeland, ed. *Ritual, Performance, Media*. London: Routledge.

Contributors

Carol Anderson is a choreographer, teacher and writer. A founding member and former Artistic Director of Dancemakers, she now teaches in the Department of Dance at York University. She has published two biographies, *Judy Jarvis, Dance Artist* (1993) and *Rachel Browne: Dancing toward the Light* (1999), as well as a collection of writings by Canadian dancers, *This Passion: for the love of dance* (1998), and two volumes of commentary on the Canada Dance Festival, *Chasing the Tale of Contemporary Dance* (1999 and 2002).

Rosemary Jeanes Antze danced with the National Ballet of Canada and acted with La Mama ETC, New York before completing a master's degree in dance at York University. She has taught dance technique, history and anthropology at York University, the University of Waterloo and Ryerson University. Her scholarly interests include the dance and culture of India, oral tradition and women's stories. She has published a number of articles and book chapters. She also teaches yoga in Toronto and across Canada.

Carol Bishop has a background in both journalism and dance history. Her principal area of interest is early modern western theatre dance. As a specialist in cultural journalism, she has contributed articles to both general interest and academic publications. She has taught dance history at both Ryerson University and York University.

Anna Blewchamp, Associate Professor at York University, was the recipient of the Chalmers Award for Choreography and the Judy Jarvis Dance Foundation Award. She has choreographed, performed and taught internationally. She reconstructed Gweneth Lloyd's lost ballet *The Wise Virgins* in 1992 as part of her master's thesis in dance at York. She has published several articles on Canadian dance.

Amy Bowring is a graduate of York University's Fine Arts Cultural Studies Programme and has an M.A. in journalism from the University of Western Ontario. She is the Research Co-ordinator for Dance Collection Danse. She frequently lectures on Canadian dance and has published articles in the *International Dictionary of Modern Dance, Canadian Dance Studies* and *The Dance Current*. In 2000 she founded the web-based Society for Canadian Dance Studies.

Jody Bruner has master's degrees in dance and English from York University. She is the founder of Jody Bruner Business Communications, a company that provides training in writing and communication skills. She has presented papers at conferences of the Association for Canadian Theatre Research, the Society of Dance History Scholars and the International Association for Semiotic Studies. Her essay "Redeeming *Giselle*: Making a Case for the Ballet We Love to Hate" won the Gertrude Lippincott Prize for 1997.

Susan Cash, a graduate of the York University Department of Dance, is also a Certified Movement Analyst. She teaches in the Department of Dance at York University. Her choreography has been performed across Canada and internationally.

Clifford Collier, a former dancer with the Volkoff Canadian Ballet, danced and taught throughout Eastern Canada. He also choreographed numerous musicals. After earning a B.F.A. in dance from York University in 1975, he specialized in library and archival work. With Pierre Guilmette, he published *Dance Resources in Canadian Libraries* (1982) for the National Library of Canada.

Katherine Cornell is a writer, teacher and archivist who has a master's degree in dance from York University. She co-authored *Toronto Dance Theatre, 1968-1998: Stages in a Journey* (1999). She has presented papers at dance history conferences in Lisbon and Montreal and for the Association for Canadian Theatre Research conference in Sherbrooke, Quebec, where she won the 1999 Robert Lawrence Prize.

Sarala Dandekar received her master's degree in dance from York University. Trained in Indian classical dance, she has performed in India, the United States and Canada. She now teaches Odissi dance and yoga in various studios in Los Angeles, where she also works as a picture editor in independent film and documentary television.

Jennifer Fisher, Assistant Professor at the University of California at Irvine, has a master's degree in dance from York University and a Ph.D. from the University of California at Riverside. Her book *Nutcracker Nation: How an Old World Ballet Became a Christmas Tradition in the New World* was published in 2003. She has also written for *Maclean's*, *Dance Connection*, *Dance Research Journal* and the *Los Angeles Times*.

Norma Sue Fisher-Stitt, Associate Professor at York University, received her master's degree in dance from York University and her Ed.D. from Temple University. A graduate of the National Ballet School, she danced with the National Ballet of Canada for four years. Her research has focused on the potential of computer-assisted instruction in dance education. She is currently writing a book on the National Ballet School.

Anne Flynn, Professor at the University of Calgary, is a dancer, teacher and writer. She co-founded *Dance Connection* magazine, and she is co-editor with Lisa Doolittle of *Dancing Bodies Living Histories: New Writings about Dance and Culture* (2000).

Kathleen Fraser, who received her master's degree in dance from York University, specializes in the study of world dance and multiculturalism. She has taught at both the University of Toronto and York University. She is completing a book on female professional dancer-singers of Egypt between 1760 and 1870.

Pierre Lapointe, former dancer with Les Ballets Théâtre de Montréal and Les Ballets de Québec, studied classical ballet with Tatiana Lipkovska and Séda Zaré and jazz with Cynthia Hendrickson. A dance teacher for almost forty years in Sherbrooke and the Eastern Townships of Quebec, he earned a master's degree in dance from the Université du Québec à Montréal in 1998.

Allana Lindgren has a master's degree in dance from York University and is completing her Ph.D. in drama studies at the University of Toronto. She studied at the Royal Winnipeg Ballet School and also trained in baroque dance. She has presented papers in conferences of the Association for Canadian Theatre Research, the Society of Dance History Scholars and the Festival of Original Theatre. Her first book, *From Automatism to Modern Dance: Françoise Sullivan with Franziska Boas in New York*, was published in 2003.

Francis Mason has written dance articles and criticism throughout his career as cultural affairs officer at the U.S. embassies in Belgrade and London, and as assistant director of the Pierpont Morgan Library in New York. He co-authored with George Balanchine *Balanchine's Complete Stories of the Great Ballets* (1954). He has served for many years as Editor of *Ballet Review* and published *I Remember Balanchine: Recollections of the Ballet Master by Those Who Knew Them* (1991).

Kathryn Noxon is a graduate of York University's dance programme. A specialist in public relations and communications, she currently works with the Canadian Bar Association-Ontario and is the Programme Director for Volunteer Lawyers Service and the Project Manager for the Joint Action Committee on Equity and Diversity.

Selma Odom, Professor at York University, teaches dance history and writing. She has an M.A. in drama from Tufts University and a Ph.D. in dance studies from the University of Surrey. Her articles and reviews have appeared in many publications since the 1960s. Her research focuses on dance, music and education in the nineteenth and twentieth centuries. Current projects include *Musicians Who Move: People and Practice in Dalcroze Eurhythmics*, a book based on extensive fieldwork and historical research.

Pat Richards was one of the most esteemed dance artists in Nova Scotia and a faculty member at Dalhousie University until her death in 1998. Trained at the Laban Centre in England, she became active in Halifax as a dancer, teacher, choreographer and arts advocate. She sat on the boards of several national dance organizations and was honoured as Nova Scotia's Outstanding Cultural Educator. She also received the Dance in Canada Service Award and the DANS Award, the highest dance award in Nova Scotia.

Rhonda Ryman, Associate Professor at the University of Waterloo, has a master's degree from York University. She teaches dance notation, reconstruction and principles of dance technique. A prolific writer, she has published articles internationally. She is the author of several books including *Dictionary of Classical Ballet Terminology* (1995), and *Dictionary of Classical Ballet Terms: Cecchetti* (1998).

Holly Small, Professor at York University, is a graduate of York University's dance programme and received her master's degree from UCLA. Both a choreographer and performer, she has created work across Canada and internationally. She is the recipient of several choreographic awards.

Cheryl Smith completed a doctorate in history at the University of Toronto with a dissertation entitled "Stepping Out: Canada's Early Ballet Companies 1939-63." Her writings have appeared in a variety of publications. She currently teaches at the University of Waterloo.

Grant Strate was Resident Choreographer and Assistant to the Artistic Director at the National Ballet of Canada before founding Canada's first university dance programme at York University in 1970. From 1980 to 1989, he was the Director of the Centre for the Arts at Simon Fraser University. He has taught and choreographed around the world. He is the recipient of several honours and awards including the Jean Chalmers Award for Creativity in Dance, the Order of Canada, the Governor General's Performing Arts Award and an honourary doctorate from Simon Fraser University.

Françoise Sullivan has led a distinguished career as dancer, choreographer and visual artist. One of the earliest modern dancers in Quebec, she was part of the Automatist movement and a signatory of the *Refus Global* in 1948. She is recipient of the Prix du Québec Paul-Émile Borduas, the Order of Canada, the Order of Québec and honorary degrees from York University and the Université du Québec à Montréal. She teaches painting at Concordia University.

Iro Valaskakis Tembeck, Professor at the Université du Québec à Montréal, is a choreographer, dance historian and critic, who received her Ph.D. from Université de Montréal. She has published several books on dance in Quebec including *Dancing in Montreal: Seeds of a Choreographic History* (1994) and *La danse comme paysage* (2001).

Anton Wagner has a Ph.D. in drama studies from the University of Toronto. He was a Research Fellow at York University, where he served as the director of research and managing editor for the *World Encyclopedia of Contemporary Theatre*. He has edited several books on Canadian drama and theatre. He currently produces and directs television documentaries.

Mary Jane Warner, Professor at York University, teaches courses in Canadian dance history, reconstruction, education and movement analysis. She has an M.A. in dance and Ph.D. in theatre from Ohio State University. She is the author of *Laban Notation Scores: An International Bibliography* and *Toronto Dance Teachers, 1825-1925* (1995). She has written extensively on nineteenth and early twentieth century Canadian dance. She is co-author of the CD-ROM *Shadow on the Prairie: An Interactive Multimedia Dance History Tutorial* (1996).

Janet Wason received her master's degree in dance from York University. She is a Library Assistant in the Reference and Collection Development Department at the University of Waterloo, where she also has taught dance history, dance criticism and a course on women and theatre dance.

Leland Windreich is a dance writer who worked as a librarian at the Vancouver Public Library until his retirement in 1986. He has published extensively on ballet history including many articles and three books, *June Roper: Ballet Starmaker* (1999), *Dance Encounters: Leland Windreich Writing on Dance* (1998) and *Dancing for de Basil: Letters to her Parents from Rosemary Deveson, 1938-1940* (1996). He served for many years as an editor for both *Vandance* and *Dance International*.

Illustration Credits

Throughout this anthology, the images of many photographers give faces to dancers' stories and bring their movements to life. Too often, we do not know the names of those whose lenses captured key moments of a fleeting past. The editors are grateful to all of them and wish to thank those we can acknowledge specifically: Charles Aylett (page 349), Robert Etcheverry (page 385), Michael Kobayashi (page 318), Gerry Kopelow (page 323), Edouard Lock (page 383), David Morris (page 413), Maurice Perron (pages 15 and 19), Michael Slobodian (page 292) and Cylla von Tiedemann (pages 358, 366, 375, 390, 392, 395, 399, 402, 437 and 443).

Dance Collection Danse is the source of illustrations from the following portfolios:

15 Dancers	La La La Human Steps
15 Dance Laboratorium	Pierre Lapointe
Lawrence and Miriam Adams Postcard Collection	Gweneth Lloyd
	Jean Macpherson
Maud Allan	Terrill Maguire
Pete (Eugenie) Beatty	Judith Marcuse
Anna Blewchamp	Marial Mosher
Rachel Browne	O Vertigo
Canadian Dance News Photo Collection	Ellora Patnaik
Dance in Canada Photo Collection	Lois Smith
Marguerite Eagles	Françoise Sullivan
École supérieure de danse du Québec	Nesta Toumine
ENCORE! ENCORE!	Toronto Dance Theatre
Marion Errington	Iro Valaskakis Tembeck
Kathleen Fraser	Bageshree Vaze
Evelyn Geary	Boris Volkoff
Saida Gerrard	Janet Wason
Harbourfront Centre Photo Collection	Mary Williamson
Vera Keiss	Leland Windreich

Additional sources:

The Banff Centre Archives (page 278)

Harvard Theatre Collection (page 34)

Metropolitan Toronto Reference Library (pages 63, 68, 69 and 70)

National Film Board of Canada (pages 242, 248 and 250)

York University Library: Herman Arthur Voaden fonds (pages 117, 118, 123, 124, 125 and 127)

Dance Collection Danse and the editors would welcome information about errors and omissions so that they may be corrected in later printings.